Vital Records
of
RFORD
and
IERMONT

New Hampshire

1887-2004

Richard P. Roberts

HERITAGE BOOKS
2006

HERITAGE BOOKS
AN IMPRINT OF HERITAGE BOOKS, INC.

Books, CDs, and more   Worldwide

For our listing of thousands of titles see our website
at
www.HeritageBooks.com

Published 2006 by
HERITAGE BOOKS, INC.
Publishing Division
65 East Main Street
Westminster, Maryland 21157-5026

Copyright ' 2006 Richard P. Roberts

All rights reserved. No part of this book may be reproduced or transmitted in any form or by any means, electronic or mechanical, including photocopying, recording or by any information storage and retrieval system without written permission from the author, except for the inclusion of brief quotations in a review.

International Standard Book Number: 978-0-7884-3372-5

Other books by the author:

Alton, New Hampshire Vital Records, 1890-1997

Barnstead, New Hampshire Vital Records, 1887-2000

Barrington, New Hampshire Vital Records

Dover, New Hampshire Death Records, 1887-1937

Gilmanton, New Hampshire Vital Records, 1887-2001

Marriage Records of Dover, New Hampshire, 1835-1909

Marriage Records of Dover, New Hampshire, 1910-1937

Milton, New Hampshire Vital Records, 1888-1999

Moultonborough, New Hampshire Vital Records

New Castle, New Hampshire Vital Records, 1891-1997

New Hampshire Name Changes, 1768-1923

New Hampshire Name Changes, 1923-1947

Ossipee, New Hampshire Vital Records, 1887-2001

Rochester, New Hampshire Death Records, 1887-1951

Vital Records of Durham, New Hampshire, 1887-2002

Vital Records of Effingham and Freedom, New Hampshire, 1888-2001

Vital Records of Farmington, New Hampshire, 1887-1938

Vital Records of New Durham and Middleton, New Hampshire, 1887-1998

Vital Records of North Berwick, Maine, 1892-2002

Vital Records of Tamworth and Albany, New Hampshire, 1887-2003

Vital Records of Wakefield, New Hampshire, 1887-1998

Wolfeboro, New Hampshire Vital Records, 1887-1999

TABLE OF CONTENTS

Introduction 1

Orford Births 5

Orford Marriages 111

Orford Deaths 259

Piermont Births 379

Piermont Marriages 443

Piermont Deaths 551

INTRODUCTION

Early vital records of many New Hampshire towns can be located either through the State's Vital Records Department or on microfilms made available through LDS Family History Centers. Some, however, have been lost or are inaccessible for various reasons. A valuable, but labor intensive, source of information for events occurring in 1887 and thereafter is the vital statistics which are provided in a section of the Annual Town Reports of many New Hampshire towns. Many of these town reports have been collected at the New Hampshire State Library in Concord, as well as more local repositories.

The amount of information published in these Annual Town Reports varies tremendously over time. Early records are far more detailed and comprehensive. Recent records are rather cursory, but issues of confidentiality and sensitivity to the privacy of those residents still living offsets the lack of information of genealogical value.

While the information provided is often very helpful, one must remember that it is not fool-proof or universally accurate, nor is it the primary source or the actual vital record itself. The fact that much of the data is self-reported suggests that it is reliable. However, errors in transcription, spelling (particularly with respect to French-Canadian and European families), and printing often are obvious. In addition, there may be, for example, two children listed as the third child of a particular couple, or the mother's maiden name, age or place of birth differs or is inconsistent from one entry to another. It is also important to note that a birth, marriage or death may have been reported in another town although the subject resided in Lyme or Dorchester, or the entry may not have been made in the first place.

Despite these shortcomings, the information contained in the Annual Town Reports can be a valuable tool for the genealogist. Marriage and death records from the late 1800's often identify parents who were married nearly a century before. Finally, those families that have remained in Orford, Piermont or adjacent towns for several generations can be traced and connected to the present.

Births - To the extent the information is available, the entries in the list of births are given as follows: child's name; date of birth; place of birth (where provided); the number of children in the family; father's name, place of birth, age and occupation; and the mother's maiden name, age and place of birth. As noted above, the amount of information in earlier records is substantially greater than in more recent years.

At times, the given names of many children are missing from the early reports. In this case, the sex of the child is given and they are listed chronologically at the beginning of the surname heading. On occasion, the child's name can be determined from marriage or death records, as well as secondary sources. These names are shown in brackets where available.

Marriages - To the extent the information is available, the entries in the list of marriages follow this format: groom's name; groom's residence; bride's name; brides residence; date of marriage; place of marriage (where provided); H, signifying husband's information, and W, signifying wife's information, each in the following order - age, occupation, number of the marriage (if other than first), father's name, father's place of birth, father's occupation, mother's name, mother's place of birth, and mother's occupation. The name of the official conducting the marriage has been omitted but is generally provided in the original document. A separate listing of brides in alphabetical order follows this section in order to allow for cross-referencing.

Deaths - To the extent available, the entries in the list of deaths contain the following information: name of decedent; place of death; date of death; age at death; cause of death; marital status; birthplace; father's name; father's place of birth; mother's name; and mother's place of birth. Most of the entries listing a cause of death are self-explanatory.

ORFORD
BIRTHS

ACKERMAN,
daughter, b. 12/31/1902 in Orford; fifth; William J. Ackerman (teamster, 3-, St. Albans, VT) and Esther Emery (St. Albans, VT)
daughter, b. 12/7/1905 in Orford; first; Joseph C. Ackerman (farmer, 23, Alexandria) and Alice M. Merrill (22, Thetford, VT)

ADAMS,
son, b. 1/15/1898 in Orford; second; Guy C. Adams (laborer, 29, Johnson, VT) and Mary M. Ladeau (29, Hyde Park, VT)
stillborn daughter, b. 9/24/1958 in Hanover; fourth; Harold R. Adams (carpenter, Fairlee, VT) and Edna J. Bradley (Ansen, ME)
Ann Marie, b. 3/1/1951 in Lebanon; first; Harold R. Adams (carpenter, Fairlee, VT) and Edna Bradley (Anson, ME)
Connie Lee, b. 6/23/1955 in Lebanon; third; Harold R. Adams (carpenter, Fairlee, VT) and Edna J. Bradley (Anson, ME)
Lois May, b. 6/9/1952 in Lebanon; second; Harold R. Adams (carpenter, Fairlee, VT) and Edna J. Bradley (Anson, ME)

ALDRICH,
Jason Edgar, b. 10/5/1973 in Hanover; Billy E. Aldrich (24, Lebanon) and Linda Rae Brown (21, Colorado Springs, CO)

ALLEN,
son, b. 12/26/1897; third; Aaron P. Allen (laborer, 28, Poten, Canada) and Inez Folsom (26, Newport, VT)
Bertram Frederick, b. 11/28/1923; second; Bertram F. Allen (miller, Providence, RI) and Anna Breckett (W. Danville, VT)
John Herbert, II, b. 12/11/1983; John Allen and Aurora Garrett
Mary Anna, b. 4/6/1921 in St. Johnsbury, VT; first; Bertram F. Allen (miller, Providence, RI) and Anna Brickett (W. Danville, VT)

ALONSO,
Patricia Irene, b. 2/21/1962 in Hanover; third; Roberto E. Alonso (lawyer & ed., Havana, Cuba) and Edith Marion Thurau (Merkstein, Germany)
Vanessa Regina, b. 2/21/1962 in Hanover; second; Roberto E. Alonso (lawyer & ed., Havana, Cuba) and Edith Marion Thurau (Merkstein, Germany)

AMADON,
daughter, b. 10/3/1924; second; Wilman S. Amadon (laborer, Newark, VT) and Sylvia A. Murray (Westmore, VT)

AMBROSE,
Sheila Margaret, b. 1/30/1945 in Haverhill; second; David T. Ambrose (defense worker, Lexington, KY) and Marion Mae Flagg (Fairlee, VT); residences – Cincinnati, OH and Orford
Terrance Michael, b. 12/19/1943 in Haverhill; first; David T. Ambrose (US Marines, Lexington, KY) and Marion Mae Flagg (Fairlee, VT)

ANDREWS,
June Flora, b. 6/26/1935 in Orford; ninth; Clarence H. Andrews (farmer, Sutton) and Esther Hildreth (Haverhill)

ARCHER,
daughter, b. 1/18/1890 in Orford; sixth; Josiah H. Archer (laborer, 35, Orford) and Mary Hannaford (35, Fairlee, VT)
daughter, b. 9/23/1891 in Orford; seventh; Josiah H. Archer (laborer, 36, Orford) and Mary R. Hannaford (36, Fairlee, VT)
stillborn daughter, b. 1/8/1894 in Orford; first; Alanson A. Archer (laborer, 39, Orford) and Lizzie Morand (22, Somerville, MA)
son, b. 3/12/1896; second; Alanson Archer (laborer, Orford) and Lizzie Maroien (26, Cambridge, MA)
daughter, b. 10/1/1897; third; Alanson J. Archer (laborer, 46, Orford) and Lizzie Marrin (25, E. Cambridge, MA)
Eva Elvia, b. 4/22/1888; fifth; Josiah H. Archer (laborer, 33, Orford) and Mary R. Hannaford (33, Fairlee, VT)

ARMSTRONG,
David R., Jr., b. 5/29/1942 in Hanover; second; David R. Armstrong (machinist, Brooklyn, NY) and Hilda E. Doyle (New York City, NY)

ARNESEN-TRUNZO,
Melissa Denison, b. 6/22/1982; Thomas Trunzo and Deborah Arnesen

ARNOLD,
stillborn daughter, b. 1/1/1931 in Orford; third; Elwin R. Arnold (farmer, Haverhill) and Gertrude P. Owens (Littleton); residence – Piermont

ATKINS,
Richard Dana, b. 2/19/1920 in Hanover; third; Charles F. Atkins (minister, Yonkers, NY) and Irene E. Fenn (W. Winfield, NY)

ATWOOD,
Ryan Patrick, b. 2/27/1980 in Hanover; Caleb Atwood and Joyce Atwood

BACON,
Jarid Wright, b. 3/24/1975 in Hanover; Robert J. Bacon (25, PA) and Sally A. Wright (25, MO)

BAILEY,
Flora S., b. 12/31/1887 in Orford; sixth; Alpha N. Bailey (mechanic, 33, Andover, MA) and Mary N. Bailey (34, Orford)
Fredwick Archie, b. 7/6/1910; first; Archibald Bailey (laborer, 19, Vershire, VT) and Lena M. Wyman (18, Barton, VT)
Lucy Nellie, b. 6/12/1909; first; Charles C. Bailey (laborer, 24, Newbury, VT) and Ella B. Philbrick (19, Brownington, VT)
Norma Kay, b. 12/2/1939 in Orford; seventh; Karl Bailey (laborer, Barnet, VT) and Shirley Call (Canada)

BAKER,
son, b. 3/13/1888; first; Henry G. Baker (farmer, 27, Orford) and Inez A. Baker Smith (17, Orford)
daughter, b. 4/23/1889 in Orford; second; Henry Baker (farmer, 28, Orford) and Inez A. Smith (18, Orford)
son, b. 3/14/1891 in Orford; third; Henry G. Baker (farmer, 30, Orford) and Inez A. Smith (20, Orford)
son, b. 8/6/1898 in Orford; sixth; Henry G. Baker (blacksmith, 39, Orford) and Inez A. Smith (28, Orford)
son, b. 8/19/1907; first; Emile Houle (weaver) and Martha Baker (18); residence – Lowell, MA
Bradley Horace, b. 4/8/1902 in Orford; eighth; Henry G. Baker (blacksmith, 42, Orford) and Inez A. Smith (Orford)

David Hector Maclean, b. 10/26/1962 in Hanover; first; William H. Baker (mech. eng., Boston, MA) and Katharine F. Camp (Chicago, IL)
Dorothy Frances, b. 3/4/1918 in Orford; second; George H. Baker (farmer, Orford) and Alice M. Franklin (Orford)
Harry Frank, b. 9/20/1896; fifth; Henry G. Baker (balcksmith, 37, Orford) and Inez A. Smith (26, Orford)
Iona Inez, b. 6/28/1900 in Orford; seventh; Henry G. Baker (blacksmith, 40, Orford) and Inez A. Smith (29, Orford)
Joan S., b. 12/27/1937 in Hanover; second; Maurice S. Baker (laborer, Orford) and Hattie M. Streeter (Piermont)
Lula Belle, b. 6/22/1906 in Orford; tenth; Henry G. Baker (blacksmith, 46, Orford) and Inez A. Smith (36, Orford)
Marjorie Louise, b. 8/15/1926; first; Fred A. Baker (farmer, Orford) and Marjorie L. Spencer (Plymouth)
Maurice Sidney, b. 1/29/1904 in Orford; ninth; Henry G. Baker (blacksmith, 44, Orford) and Inez A. Smith (33, Orford)
Minnie F., b. 5/21/1893 in Orford; fourth; Henry G. Baker (laborer, 32, Orford) and Inez A. Smith (22, Orford)
Pauline Inez, b. 3/21/1928 in Orford; second; Fred Alvin Baker (farmer, Orford) and Lillian M. Spencer (Plymouth)
Ralph Edward, b. 1/9/1928 in Woodsville; first; Bradley Baker (laborer, Orford) and Clara B. Webster (Piermont)
Ronald Roy, b. 1/24/1936 in Hanover; first; Maurice S. Baker (laborer, Orford) and Hattie M. Streeter (Piermont)
Rosie Iola, b. 1/24/1910; eleventh; Henry G. Baker (blacksmith, 50, Orford) and Inez A. Smith (39, Orford)
Stewart Sidney, b. 11/26/1927 in Orford; first; Maurice Baker (laborer, Orford) and Hazel Downing (Topsham, VT)
Thomas Camp, b. 5/21/1965 in Hanover; William H. Baker (auto. dealer, Boston, MA) and Katherine F. Camp (Chicago, IL)
Virginia May, b. 9/13/1932 in Plymouth; third; Fred Baker (farmer, Orford) and Lillian Spencer (Plymouth)
William Henry, Jr., b. 9/5/1966 in Hanover; William H. Baker (auto dealer, Boston, MA) and Katherine Florence Camp (Chicago, IL)

BALL,
James Edward, b. 10/14/1970 in Haverhill; Edward J. Ball (23) and Norma L. Clark (22)

Katherine Leighton, b. 8/6/1999 in Lebanon; Perry Ball and Jeanne Ball
Matthew Steven, b. 10/3/2002 in Lebanon; Steven Ball and Connie Dyke

BARNES,
child, b. 6/8/1887 in Orford; second; Walter R. Barnes (physician, 32, Chelsea, VT) and Olive Vance (32, Albany, VT)
Lila May, b. 1/4/1974 in Hanover; Benjamin B. Stone (27, Cortland, NY) and Joyce E. Barnes (31, Hartford, CT)

BARONE,
Amico Jordan, b. 5/21/1984; Sydney Lonstreth Wright Lea and Margaret Robin Barone
Catherine Margaret, b. --/--/1989

BARRETT,
Malcolm, b. 4/21/1933 in Orford; third; Augustus J. Barrett (caretaker, Salem, MA) and Caroline Spooner (Franconia); residence - Franconia
William John, b. 7/18/1982; Gary Barrett and Karen Barrett

BARTLETT,
daughter, b. 7/12/1902 in Orford; third; William C. Bartlett (farmer) and Rena E. Drew (Holderness)

BARTON,
Taylor Allen, b. 12/1/2001 in Lebanon; Kyle Barton and Sarah Hook

BEAL,
Gertrude, b. 3/2/1893 in Orford; second; Frank J. Beal (mechanic, 31, Orford) and Elizabeth L. Avery (25, Orford)
Ruth Carver, b. 3/15/1892 in Orford; first; Frank J. Beal (mechanic, 30, Orford) and Elizabeth L. Avery (24, Orford)

BEAN,
child, b. 6/15/1887 in Orford; third; Charles L. Bean (farmer, 33, Sandwich) and Carrie E. Bean (24, Lyme)
son, b. 5/14/1889 in Orford; fourth; Charles L. Bean (farmer, 35, Sandwich) and Carrie E. Gardner (26, Lyme)

son, b. 11/28/1890 in Orford; fifth; Charles L. Bean (farmer, 36,
Sandwich) and Carrie E. Gardner (28, Lyme)
daughter, b. 3/5/1894 in Orford; second; Oliver L. Bean (farmer, 35,
Sandwich) and Elizabeth Ballam (25, Dorset, England)
son, b. 7/21/1896; third; Oliver L. Bean (farming, 37, Sandwich) and
Elizabeth Ballou (26, Dorset, England)
daughter, b. 10/24/1898 in Orford; fourth; Oliver L. Bean (farmer, 39,
Sandwich) and Elizabeth Ballam (28, Dorset, England)
daughter, b. 2/24/1901 in Orford; fifth; Oliver L. Bean (farmer, 42,
Sandwich) and Elizabeth Ballom (31, Dorset, England)
son, b. 10/16/1907; second; Joseph S. Bean (laborer, 25, Sharon,
VT) and Mabel M. Davis (21, Munsonville, PQ)
daughter, b. 2/11/1918 in Orford; sixth; Joseph S. Bean (laborer,
Sharon, VT) and Mabel Davis (Munsonville, PQ)
son, b. 11/27/1918 in Orford; seventh; Philip L. Bean (farmer,
Orford) and Blanche H. Burnham (Dorchester)
son, b. 7/17/1919 in Orford; seventh; Joseph S. Bean (none,
Sharon, VT) and Mabel Davis (Masonville, PQ); residence –
Concord
son, b. 8/10/1919 in Orford; sixth; Edwin G. Bean (farmer, Orford)
and Alice Marsh (Orford)
daughter, b. 11/4/1921 in Orford; eighth; Philip L. Bean (farmer,
Orford) and Blanche Burnham (Dorchester)
daughter, b. 4/7/1923; first; Ralph C. Bean (laborer, Orford) and
Florence Billington (Newbury, VT)
son, b. 10/2/1923; ninth; Joseph S. Bean (laborer, Sharon, VT) and
Mabel Davis (Masonville, PQ)
daughter, b. 1/10/1949 in Orford; stillborn; second; Fay Elson Bean
(laborer, Orford) and Arletta L. Smith (Middlesex, VT)
son, b. 12/27/1951 in Hanover; sixth; Philip L. Bean (farmer, Orford)
and Ida M. Prebor (Westford, VT)
Bale Nathaniel, b. 5/24/1916 in Orford; stillborn; sixth; Philip L. Bean
(farmer, 30, Orford) and Blanche H. Burnham (32, Dorchester)
Berkley Frank, b. 4/18/1924; tenth; Philip L. Bean (farmer, Orford)
and Blanch H. Burnham (Dorchester)
Bernard Charles, b. 4/18/1924; ninth; Philip L. Bean (farmer, Orford)
and Blanch H. Burnham (Dorchester)
Bertran Philip Lee, b. 2/25/1912 in Orford; third; Philip L. Bean
(farmer, 26, Orford) and Blanche H. Burnham (28, Dorchester)
Brianna Marie, b. 2/24/2000 in Lebanon; Alan Bean and Cheryl
Taylor-Bean

Carlie Mildred, b. 11/9/1908; third; Joseph S. Bean (farmer, 26, Sharon, VT) and Mabel M. Davis (22, Mansonville, PQ)
Carol Ann, b. 11/14/1961 in Hanover; first; Maurice Fay Bean (farmer, Dorchester) and Ann Marie Castiglione (Garwood, NJ)
Carrie J., b. 8/14/1907; first; Philip L. Bean (farmer, 22, Orford) and Blanche Burnham (24, Dorchester)
Charlotte Louise, b. 10/23/1940 in Hanover; third; Richard Heath Bean (laborer, Orford) and Beatrice Huntington (Corinth, VT)
Earl Richard, b. 11/15/1936 in Hanover; second; Richard H. Bean (laborer, Orford) and Beatrice Huntington (Corinth, VT)
Edith Evelyn, b. 7/26/1914 in Orford; first; Dana J. Bean (farmer, 23, Orford) and Nellie M. Wright (20, Piermont)
Fay Clarence, b. 8/19/1910; third; Joseph S. Bean (farmer, 26, Sharon, VT) and Mabel M. Davis (24, Mansonville, PQ)
Francis Youngman, b. 5/24/1916 in Orford; fifth; Philip L. Bean (farmer, 30, Orford) and Blanche H. Burnham (32, Dorchester)
George Lee, b. 2/23/1912 in Orford; third; Edwin G. Bean (farmer, 24, Orford) and Alice M. Marsh (21, Orford)
Gertrude Jeanette, b. 6/18/1946 in Hanover; third; Philip L. Bean (farmer, Orford) and Ida M. Prebor (Westford, VT)
Harold Edwin, b. 1/28/1911; second; Edwin G. Bean (farmer, Orford) and Alice M. Marsh (Orford)
Howard Ralph, b. 4/1/1926; second; Ralph C. Bean (laborer, Orford) and Florence H. Billingham (Newbury, VT)
Joseph Smith, b. 11/21/1916 in Orford; fifth; Joseph S. Bean (laborer, 34, Sharon) and Mabel M. Davis (30, Masonville, PQ)
Joyce Marie, b. 6/24/1947 in Haverhill; first; Fay E. Bean (farmer, Orford) and Arletta L. Smith (Middlesex, VT)
Malcolm Burnham, b. 6/25/1914 in Orford; fourth; Philip L. Bean (farmer, 28, Orford) and Blanche H. Burnham (31, Dorchester)
May E., b. 11/28/1891 in Orford; first; Oliver Lee Bean (farmer, 32, Candia) and Elizabeth Bolem (21, Weymouth, England)
Nera May, b. 7/16/1909; first; Edwin G. Bean (farmer, 22, Orford) and Alice M. Marsh (18, Orford)
Norman C., b. 12/25/1917 in Orford; fifth; Edwin G. Bean (farmer, Orford) and Alice M. Marsh (Orford)
Patricia Marie, b. 8/26/1964 in Hanover; Maurice F. Bean (farmer, Dorchester) and Anne M. Castiglione (Garwood, NJ)
Pauline Sandra, b. 2/25/1945 in Hanover; third; Philip Lee Bean (farmer, Orford) and Ida Mildred Prebor (Westford, VT)

Philip Lee, Jr., b. 10/7/1926; eleventh; Philip L. Bean (farmer, Orford) and Blanche H. Burnham (Dorchester)
Phillis Arlie, b. 11/13/1909; second; Philip L. Bean (farmer, 24, Orford) and Blanche H. Burnham (26, Dorchester)
Ray Charles, b. 1/26/1916 in Orford; second; Dana J. Bean (farmer, 25, Orford) and Nellie M. Wright (21, Piermont)
Roger Bertram, b. 7/20/1941 in Hanover; third; Bertram P. Bean (laborer, Orford) and Agnes A. Guilmette (St. Johnsbury, VT)
Ruth Alice, b. 8/28/1916 in Orford; fourth; Edwin G. Bean (farmer, 29, Orford) and Alice M. Marsh (25, Orford)
Wallace Berkley, b. 3/2/1904 in Orford; sixth; Charles L. Bean (farmer, 51, Sandwich) and Carrie E. Gardner (41, Lyme)
Warren Lee, b. 9/4/1947 in Haverhill; fifth; Philip L. Bean (farmer, Orford) and Ida M. Prebor (Westford, VT)

BEANE,
Charles Alexander, Jr., b. 11/1/1994 in Lebanon; Charles Alexander Beane, Sr. and Sara Lee Rice Beane

BEAUPRE,
Kenneth David, b. 12/8/2000 in Lebanon; Peter Beaupre and Malissa Beaupre
Samantha Helen, b. 3/21/2003 in Lebanon; Peter Beaupre and Malissa Daisey

BEDELL,
Frank Lincoln, b. 2/18/1944 in Hanover; first; Frank F. Bedell (US Army, Coxsackie, NY) and Frances P. Harvey (Changsha, China); residence – NY City and Orford
Irving S., b. 3/11/1904 in Orford; third; Harry G. Bedell (farmer, 42, Lyman) and Nellie E. Stinson (30, Haverhill)

BELVERE,
son, b. 3/24/1892 in Orford; fifth; Henry Belvere (lumberman, 35, Holland, VT) and Lizzie Nutbrown (30, St. Sylvester, Canada)

BENJAMIN,
Linda Ann, b. 5/3/1953 in Hanover; first; Dawson J. Benjamin (US Marine Corps, Norwich, VT) and Shirley H. Joslyn (Island Falls, ME)

BENNETT,
son, b. 1/15/1888; second; Justin S. Bennett (laborer, 43, Whitehall, NY) and Mary Sullivan (28, Northfield, VT)

BIGELOW,
daughter, b. 2/23/1891 in Orford; sixth; James H. Bigelow (laborer, 37, Gilmanton) and Ella M. Hicks (31, Haverhill)
daughter, b. 4/20/1894 in Orford; seventh; James H. Bigelow (laborer, 40, Gilmanton) and Ella M. Hicks (34, Haverhill)
Clinton Arthur, b. 9/17/1933 in Orford; third; Kenneth Bigelow (laborer, Laconia) and Gladys Elliott (Littleton); residence - Littleton

BLACK,
Susan Marie, b. 12/25/1957 in Haverhill; fifth; Robert Charles Black (carpenter, Littleton) and Dorothy J. Maxwell (Littleton)

BLAKE,
Bethany Jean, b. 4/24/1956 in Orford; fifth; Everett Leroy Blake (shovel op., Plymouth) and Flora M. Sanborn (Orford)
David Nathan, b. 6/3/1960 in Lebanon; first; Nathan L. Blake (student, Orford) and Nettie A. Pierson (Hanover)
Janice Eileen, b. 11/26/1959; Everett L. Blake and Flora M. Sanborn
Kathleen Louise, b. 1/4/1946 in Orford; third; Everett L. Blake (farmer, Plymouth) and Flora M. Sanborn (Orford)
Lucille Diane, b. 11/4/1943 in Orford; second; Everett L. Blake (machine oper., Plymouth) and Flora M. Sanborn (Orford); residence – Springfield, VT
Michael Everett, b. 3/23/1949 in Orford; fourth; Everett L. Blake (p. shovel op., Plymouth) and Flora M. Sanborn (Orford)
Nathan Leroy, b. 9/8/1941 in Orford; first; Everett L. Blake (laborer, Plymouth) and Flora M. Sanborn (Orford)

BLANCHARD,
Dora Ellen, b. 10/20/1916 in Orford; fifth; Raymond Blanchard (laborer, 34, Piermont) and Mabel Cushing (28, Newport, VT)
Edith Emma, b. 6/15/1910; second; Raymond Blanchard (laborer, 27, Piermont) and Mabelle Cushing (21, Newport, VT)
Eliza Emma, b. 6/4/1911; third; Raymond Blanchard (laborer, Piermont) and Mabel E. Cushing (Newport, VT)

BLATZ,
Jeremiah Allen, b. 9/2/1974 in Hanover; Joseph H. Blatz (36, Beech Grove, IN) and Charlotte S. Vinge (35, Syracuse, NY)

BLODGETT,
Clarence Lee, b. 1/4/1915 in Hanover; first; Clarence L. Blodgett (farmer, 39, Orford) and Jean MacLeod (28, Megantic, PQ)
James Roger, b. 6/15/1941 in Orford; first; Jerald Blodgett (mechanic, Bethel, VT) and Katie Grace Powers (Lowell, VT)

BOARDMAN,
Fay Ann, b. 7/29/1950 in Lebanon; fourth; Arthur C. Boardman (lumberman, Quebec) and Bertha M. Boardman (Haverhill)

BOCKUS,
Bonita Belle, b. 10/19/1946 in Orford; Walter D. Bockus (US Army, Wethersfield, CT) and Marion H. Nutter (Barnet, VT)

BONETT,
Frank E., b. 8/19/1894 in Orford; first; Silas N. Bonett (laborer, 39, Concord, VT) and Emma Hubbard (28, St. Johnsbury, VT)

BOUTWELL,
Madeline Fay, b. 8/30/1932 in Orford; ninth; Ray Boutwell (laborer, Stockbridge, VT) and Goldie Flint (Barnard, VT)

BRABAUT,
stillborn son, b. 3/8/1898 in Orford; first; Alex. Brabaut (carpenter, 22, Lowell, MA) and Olesene Chaindanait (28, Canada)

BRACKETT,
Anthony Truman, b. 11/30/1969 in Hanover; Truman H. Brackett (36, Boston, MA) and Kristin Sanborn (33, Hartford, CT)

BRITCH,
Allisen Marie, b. 9/27/1997 in Lebanon; Cecil Jay Britch and Lisa Marie Goodrich Britch
Logyn Marie, b. 2/10/2000 in Lebanon; Cecil Britch and Lisa Britch

BROCK,
daughter, b. 10/29/1888; second; Charles E. Brock (farmer, 37, Orford) and Mary E. Wyman (28, Beverly, MA)
stillborn son, b. 1/26/1894 in Orford; third; Charles E. Brock (farmer, 43, Orford) and Mary E. Wyman (34, Beverly, MA)
John Booth, b. 2/6/1948 in Hanover; second; Frederick W. Brock (farmer, Montpelier, VT) and Katherine R. Booth (Barre, VT)

BRODISH,
Linda Marie, b. 10/13/1943 in Hanover; first; John Brodish (US Army, Tampa, FL) and Bernice B. Bean (Newbury, VT)

BROOKS,
Bertha May, b. 5/8/1897; third; Rance R. Brooks (laborer, 47, Vershire, VT) and Elfie F. Adams (30, Windham, VT)
Robb Michael, b. 11/7/1988; Keith Brooks and Carol Brooks
Theresa Christine, b. 6/7/1991 in Hanover; Keith Brooks and Carol Brooks

BROWN,
child, b. 11/30/1887 in Orford; third; George R. Brown (farm laborer, 28, Concord) and Lucy J. Columbia (24, Canaan)
son, b. 3/12/1901 in Orford; second; Fred Walter Brown (laborer, 35, Warren) and Grace Degroosh (24, W. Fairlee, VT)
daughter, b. 2/9/1902 in Orford; third; Fred W. Brown (laborer, 46, Warren) and Grace DeGoosh (W. Fairlee, VT)
stillborn son, b. 3/30/1904 in Orford; fourth; Fred W. Brown (farmer, Warren) and Grace DeGoosh (22, W. Fairlee, VT)
Diane Kay, b. 1/6/1953 in Hanover; second; Richard E. Brown (mechanic, Lebanon) and Ruth Grace Ladd (Haverhill)
Diane Leah, b. 7/8/1943 in Hanover; third; Fred W. Brown, Jr. (shipping foreman, W. Fairlee, VT) and Josephine K. Downes (Casleton, VT)
Maureen Evelyn, b. 7/11/1942 in Orford; second; Fred Walter Brown (laborer, W. Fairlee, VT) and Josephine C. Downes (Casleton, VT)

BRUCKNER,
John Theodore, b. 8/16/1956 in Hanover; second; Karl Theodore Bruckner (legal editor, New York, NY) and Suzanne Berry (New York, NY)

BUNTEN,
John Forrest, b. 10/3/1958 in Haverhill; sixth; Forrest K. Bunten (farmer, Concord) and Evelyn A. Stephenson (Queen's Vil., NY)

BURNHAM,
Richard Amon, b. 3/13/1916 in Orford; first; Amos B. Burnham (laborer, 20, Dorchester) and Vernie M. Pease (19, Franconia)

BURRILL,
Minnie Ada, b. 1/8/1898 in Orford; third; James O. Burrill (laborer, 30, Lee, ME) and Della R. Leighton (20, Springfield, ME)

BURROUGHS,
David Filmore, b. 7/25/1928 in Orford; first; Robert O. Burroughs (farmer, Newbury, VT) and Amey B. Downing (W. Thornton); residence – Newbury, VT

BURWELL,
Oonagh Parlin, b. 5/20/2004 in Lebanon; Christopher Burwell and Tabatha Burwell

BUTMAN,
daughter, b. 7/28/1890 in Orford; fifth; George E. Butman (laborer, 35, Canaan) and Estelle G. Clough (33, Wentworth)
son, b. 1/30/1905 in Orford; second; Charles H. Butman (farmer, 46, Canaan) and Inez Brown (33, Barnstead, Canada)
Cynthia Ann, b. 6/7/1930 in Hanover; first; Warren Butman (weaver, Orford) and Doris F. Record (St. Johns, NB)
Grace Arlene, b. 9/17/1916 in Orford; second; Oscar F. Butman (carpenter, 24, Canaan) and Nellie Beaton (21, NS)
Herbert Charles, b. 9/5/1942 in Orford; second; Richard C. Butman (carpenter, Orford) and Marion Streeter (Orford)
Leola, b. 8/11/1913 in Orford; fourth; Lurlyn C. Butman (farmer, 31, Orford) and Hattie C. Bailey (31, Orford)
Paul Alpha, b. 8/5/1909; first; Lurlyn C. Butman (farmer, 27, Orford) and Hattie C. Bailey (27, Orford)
Pearl Alma, b. 3/14/1912 in Orford; third; Luelyn C. Butnam (farmer, 30, Orford) and Hattie C. Bailey (29, Orford)
Richard C., b. 12/30/1911; third; Charles H. Butman (farmer, Canaan) and Inez R. Brown (Barnstead, PQ)

Rodney, b. 1/4/1911; second; Lurlyn C. Butman (farmer, Orford) and Hattie C. Bailey (Orford)

BYERS,
William Albert, b. 6/2/1929 in Orford; first; Albert Charles Byers (lumberman, Denver, CO) and Ruth W. Ingerson (Providence, RI); residence – Rumney

BYRD,
Cecily Jany, b. 1/13/2000 in Orford; Harry Byrd and Nancy Byrd

CADY,
child, b. 3/3/1887 in Orford; third; Parker Cady (photographer, Warren, VT) and Amelia Niles Cady (Woodstock)

CAMPOPIANO,
Ella Mia, b. 12/15/2001 in Lebanon; Jason Campopiano and Amy Campopiano

CANTERBURY,
Samuel David, b. 12/16/2004 in Lebanon; David Shawn Canterbury and Andrea Violet Chase

CARDELL,
son, b. 3/4/1896; first; Louis E. Cardell (train dispatch, 25) and Carrie E. Hall 25, Orford); residence – Lowell, MA

CARL[E],
son, b. 5/14/1933 in Haverhill; ninth; Vernon Carl (laborer, Woodstock, NY) and Mae Bryer (Lancaster)
Audrey Minnie, b. 9/20/1924; fourth; Vernon Carle (laborer, Woodstock) and May Bryer (Lancaster)
Bernice Mae, b. 9/17/1930 in Hanover; eighth; Vernon C. Carle (farmer, NY) and Mae Bryer (Lancaster)
Wilson Joseph, b. 2/14/1921 in Orford; fourth; Vernon C. Carl (farmer, Lake Hill, NY) and Margaret M. Briar (Lancaster)

CARLTON,
David Merritt, b. 7/19/1958 in Hanover; first; Charles M. Carlton (grad. student, Poultney, VT) and Mary MacDonald (New York, NY)

CARR,
child, b. 5/7/1887 in Orford; sixth; Robert O. Carr (merchant, 35, Orford) and Mary E. Martin (36, Chelmsford, MA)
child, b. 11/16/1887 in Orford; second; George W. Carr (livery, 24, Plainfield) and Effie E. Dodge (24, New Boston)
son, b. 12/16/1889 in Orford; fourth; George W. Carr (stable keeper, 29, Plainfield) and Effie Dodge (26, New Boston)
daughter, b. 7/26/1892 in Orford; first; J. Frank Carr (merchant, 29, Meriden) and Lydia W. Carr (24, Orford)
daughter, b. 12/19/1895 in Orford; first; Clarence B. Carr (liveryman, 35, Plainfield) and Hittie R. Lang (33, Bath)
Janet, b. 5/5/1921 in Orford; second; Truman H. Carr (farmer, Andover) and Marion F. Foote (Orford)
John, b. 5/5/1921 in Orford; third; Truman H. Carr (farmer, Andover) and Marion F. Foote (Orford)
Persis, b. 6/11/1915 in Hanover; first; Trye H. Carr (farmer, 25, Orford) and Marion F. Foote (20, Orford)
Robert William, b. 5/28/1904 in Orford; first; Henry H. Carr (merchant, 24, Hanover) and Erma L. Harris (21, Whitney Point, NY)

CARTER,
Gerald Charles, b. 12/27/1942 in Hanover; third; Berkley L. Carter (weaver, Bramby, Canada) and Beatrice May Pierce (Pike)
Kyle Lawrence, b. 4/6/2004 in Lebanon; Seth Carter and Kelly Carter

CELESTINO,
Jacques Pardee, b. 11/30/1996 in Orford; Leon Angelo Celestino and Alice Rodgers Celestino
Nicholas John, b. 4/22/1994 in Orford; Leon Angelo Celestino and Alice Rodgers Celestino

CHAFFEE,
Clinton E., b. 4/21/1972 in Lebanon; George E. Chaffee (25, CT) and Victoria L. Fish (19, NH)

CHAMBERL[A]IN,
son, b. 10/19/1889 in Orford; second; C. S. Chamberlain (farmer, 34, Orford) and Cora Belle Nichols (24, Wentworth)

daughter, b. 8/14/1891 in Orford; third; Charles S. Chamberlain
(farmer, 36, Orford) and Cora Belle Nichols (26, Wentworth)
daughter, b. 8/4/1893 in Orford; fourth; C. S. Chamberlain (farmer,
38, Orford) and Cora B. Nichols (28, Wentworth)
daughter, b. 5/14/1898 in Orford; fifth; Charles S. Chamberlain
(farmer, 43, Orford) and Cora Belle Nichols (33, Wentworth)
Cecelia L., b. 1/4/1906 in Orford; seventh; Charles S. Chamberlin
(farmer, 51, Orford) and Cora B. Nichols (40, Wentworth)
Maude, b. 11/26/1902 in Orford; sixth; Charles S. Chamberlin
(farmer, 47, Orford) and Cora B. Nichols (Wentworth)

CHANDLER,
Eleanor Faye, b. 6/1/1948 in Haverhill; second; William J. Chandler
(truck driver, Utica, NY) and Marcelene K. Day (Littleton)

CHAPIN,
Beth Alice, b. 5/7/1956 in Hanover; fourth; Orrin Keyes Chapin
(electrician, Lyme) and Marjorie E. Ackerman (Hanover)
Donna Gail, b. 4/4/1964 in Lebanon; Gayle O. Chapin (carpenter,
Woodsville) and Sandra A. Martin (Richford, VT)
Jacob Orrin, b. 5/21/1997 in Lebanon; Jayme Owen Chapin and
Alicia May Mock Chapin
Jayme Owen, b. 10/16/1967 in Haverhill; Gayle O. Chapin
(carpenter, Woodsville) and Sandra A. Martin (Richford, VT)
Kippy Ann, b. 5/24/1962 in Lebanon; second; Gayle O. Chapin
(elec.-carpenter, Woodsville) and Sandra Ann Martin (Richford,
VT)
Linda Lois, b. 5/4/1951 in Hanover; third; Orrin K. Chapin
(electrician, Lyme) and Marjorie E. Ackerman (Hanover)
Patrick Owen, b. 6/21/1992 in Lebanon; Jayme Chapin and Alicia
Chapin
Terryl Esther, b. 5/19/1943 in Hanover; second; Orrin K. Chapin
(yardsman, Lyme) and Marjorie Ackerman (Hanover)

CHAPMAN,
child, b. 8/25/1887 in Orford; fourth; Perley A. Chapman (farmer, 40,
Tewksbury, MA) and Mary Willis (28, Warren)
son, b. 2/1/1890 in Orford; fifth; Perley A. Chapman (laborer, 43,
Tewksbury, MA) and Mary E. Willis (30, Warren)
son, b. 4/9/1892 in Orford; sixth; Perley A. Chapman (laborer, 45,
Tewksbury, MA) and Mary E. Willis (32, Warren)

daughter, b. 12/31/1894 in Orford; seventh; Perley A. Chapman
(laborer, 47, Tewksbury, MA) and Mary E. Willis (35, Warren)
daughter, b. 10/11/1905 in Orford; first; Fred G. Chapman (laborer,
25, Bedford, PQ) and Rose M. Dextrader (18, E. Bolton, PQ)
Jessie Helen, b. 5/31/1899 in Orford; ninth; Perley A. Chapman
(laborer, 52, Tewksbury, MA) and Mary E. Willis (39, Orford)
Martha J., b. 3/3/1902 in Orford; tenth; Perley A. Chapman (laborer,
55, Chicopee, MA) and Mary E. Willis (Warren)

CHASE,
daughter, b. 2/16/1906 in Orford; third; Warren S. Chase (laborer,
28, Orford) and Edith Simpson (20, Orford)
son, b. 3/16/1902 in Orford; first; Warren L. Chase (engineer, 22,
Orford) and Edith M. Simpson (Orford)
Andrea Violet, b. 10/6/1980 in Haverhill; Timothy Chase and Mary
Chase
Bernard B., b. 8/13/1893 in Orford; third; Ezra C. Chase (physician,
35, Piermont) and Margaret E. Brooks (32, Barnet, VT)
Cornelia Ann, b. 6/1/1936 in Haverhill; first; Maurice A. Chase
(carpenter, Orford) and Irene Mack (Orford)
Deborah Marie, b. 2/4/1984; Timothy Chase and Mary Chase
Edythe Evelyn, b. 10/4/1926; first; H. Dewey Chase (mechanic,
Wentworth) and Marion Batchelder (Newburyport, MA)
Kathryn Inez, b. 5/20/1982; Timothy Chase and Mary Chase
Maurice Allen, b. 8/7/1909; fourth; Warren S. Chase (carpenter, 31,
Orford) and Edith M. Simpson (23, Orford)
Muriel Lee, b. 9/23/1946 in Lebanon; third; Ralph E. Chase (truck
driver, Plymouth) and Jeanne Washburn (Hanover)
Rufus, b. 5/4/1903 in Orford; second; Warren L. Chase (engineer,
23, Orford) and Edith M. Simpson (19, Orford)
Shirley Jane, b. 10/21/1942 in Haverhill; first; Stanley R. Chase
(farmer, Orford) and Eleanor Avis Perry (Haverhill)
Stanley Richard, b. 8/31/1914 in Orford; fifth; Warren S. Chase
(carpenter, 34, Orford) and Edith M. Simpson (29, Orford)
Timothy Ross, b. 6/9/1952 in Haverhill; second; Stanley R. Chase
(farmer, Orford) and Eleanor A. Perry (Haverhill)

CHESLEY,
stillborn son, b. 8/30/1942 in Hanover; third; Harold M. Chesley
(laborer, Lyme) and Frances S. Ashley (Rumney)

Marilyn Frances, b. 5/23/1941 in Plymouth; second; Harold M. Chesley (farmer, Lyme) and Frances S. Ashley (Rumney)
Robert Harold, b. 9/3/1939 in Orford; first; Harold M. Chesley (farmer, Lyme) and Francese S. Ashley (Rumney)

CHOPLIN,
Eric Duncan, b. 6/24/1950 in Lebanon; first; Harry D. Choplin (chef, Hot Springs, WV) and Madeline E. Cummings (Woodsville)

CHURCHILL,
Shirley May, b. 5/29/1936 in Orford; first; Arthur B. Churchill (laborer) and Shirley M. Rich (Chazey, NY)

CLARK,
daughter, b. 3/10/1890 in Orford; first; George C. Clark (farmer, 23, Orford) and Gertie M. Keyes (20, Thetford, VT)
daughter, b. 7/7/1892 in Orford; second; George C. Clark (farmer, 25, Orford) and Gertie Keyes (23, Thetford, VT)
Calvin Robert, b. 3/26/1939 in Orford; first; George Clark (laborer, Meredith) and Harriet Spooner (Franconia)
George Lawrence, b. 9/15/1901 in Orford; fourth; George C. Clark (farmer, 34, Orford) and Gertrude Keyes (32, Thetford, VT)
James Keith, II, b. 3/14/1958 in Hanover; fourth; William G. Clark (farmer, Ridgewood, NJ) and Martha H. Balkcom (Macon, GA)
Jesse Keyes, b. 2/15/1908; fifth; George C. Clark (farmer, 40, Orford) and Gertrude M. Keyes (38, Thetford, VT)
Judson E., b. 1/25/1902 in Orford; first; Leander D. H. Clark (carpenter, 51, Vershire, VT) and Martha L. Bean (Piermont)
June Howard, b. 7/2/1950 in Hanover; second; William G. Clark (farmer, Ridgewood, NJ) and Msrtha C. Balchom (Macon, GA)
Martha Karen Ray, b. 6/13/1953 in Lebanon; third; William G. Clark (farmer, Ridgewood, NJ) and Martha H. Balkcom (Macon, GA)
William D., b. 8/1/1895 in Orford; third; George C. Clark (farming, 28, Orford) and Gertie M. Keyes (25, E. Thetford, VT)

CLIFFORD,
Cattlin Gayle, b. 12/30/1991 in Lebanon; Charles Clifford and Sheri Clifford
Charles Henry, b. --/--/1989
Charles Henry, IV, b. 2/9/1964 in Hanover; Charles H. Clifford (printer, Quincy, MA) and Joan M. Tyler (Woodsville)

Kate Tyler, b. 10/20/1970 in Lebanon; Charles H. Clifford, Jr. (34, Quincy, MA) and Joan M. Tyler (28, Woodsville)

CLOGSTON,
infant, b. 11/12/1959; Winston C. Clogston and Diana C. Marsh
Larry Gene, b. 6/18/1957 in Haverhill; fourth; Walter C. Clogston (laborer, Bradford, VT) and Betty Jean Godfrey (Fairlee, VT)

CLOUGH,
child, b. 12/9/1887 in Orford; seventh; Josiah D. Clough (farmer, 48, Washington, VT) and Ada Norris (37, Washington, VT)

COBURN,
David E., b. 7/8/1896; first; David Coburn (farmer, 22, Orford) and Mary E. Mann (20, Orford)

COCHRAN,
daughter, b. 7/29/1890 in Orford; first; Leroy Cochran (laborer, 21, Piermont) and Jennie M. Harris (21, Haverhill)

COFFIN,
Kevin Edson, b. 10/5/1964 in Haverhill; Ray E. Coffin (repairman, Brattleboro, VT) and Glenna L. Hildreth (Warren)
Linda Jean, b. 4/24/1956 in Haverhill; first; Ray E. Coffin, Jr. (garage man, Brattleboro, VT) and Glenna L. Hildreth (Warren)

COLE,
Jeanette Helen, b. 12/15/1927 in Orford; second; George Cole (carpenter, E. Haven, VT) and Margaret Partridge (Haverhill); residence – Norwich, VT

CONANT,
Louis Cowles, b. 9/14/1902 in Orford; first; William R. Conant (merchant, 46, Orford) and Anna L. Cowles (Norfolk, CT)

CONNELL,
Marian G., b. 9/27/1903 in Orford; first; Harry W. Connell (painter, 26, Barre, MA) and Addie B. Gage (20, Orford); residence – Barre, MA

COOK,
Ellen Catherine, b. 5/18/1996 in Lebanon; Brian Richard Cook and Kathryn Lynn Cartier Cook

COOLIDGE,
daughter, b. 11/28/1889 in Orford; third; John W. Coolidge (farmer, 49, Benton) and Emma L. Whitman (23, Orford)
Grace Stella, b. 4/16/1887 in Orford; second; John W. Coolidge (farmer, Benton) and Emma L. Whitman (Orford)

COPP,
Esther May, b. 12/28/1915 in Orford; second; Clarence E. Copp (farmer, 31, Warren) and Bessie M. Elliott (25, Haverhill)
Ruby Mable, b. 9/2/1918 in Orford; third; Clarence Copp (farmer, Warren) and Bessie M. Elliott (Haverhill)

COULBURN,
son, b. 6/21/1925; fifth; Clyde H. Coulburn (laborer, Dorchester) and Florence White (Lancaster)

COVEY,
Darlene Marie, b. 3/16/1952 in Haverhill; first; Donald R. Covey (laborer, W. Fairlee, VT) and Dorothy I. Marsh (Orford)

CREEDEN,
Kelly Elizabeth, b. 5/2/1984; Carl Creeden and Christine Creeden

CROSBY,
stillborn son, b. 1/30/1907; first; Willard Crosby (laborer, 20, Wentworth) and Bertha Pease (19, Haverhill); residence – Wentworth
Ray, b. 4/27/1908; third; Willard Crosby (laborer, 21, Wentworth) and Bertha Pease (20, Pike); residence – Wentworth
Ruby Mabel, b. 4/27/1908; second; Willard Crosby (laborer, 21, Wentworth) and Bertha Pease (20, Pike); residence – Wentworth

CROSS,
son, b. 8/19/1894 in Orford; second; Joseph D. Cross (farmer, 35, Buford, PQ) and Stella M. Whitman (25, Orford)

son, b. 5/22/1897; first; Horace H. Cross (farmer, 22, Benton) and
    Ada E. Libbey (19, Warren)
Lillian Ida, b. 12/30/1909; third; Joseph D. Cross (laborer, 51,
    Barford, PQ) and Agnes Merrill (37, Rumney)
Mildred, b. 2/8/1905 in Orford; fourth; J. Dwight Cross (laborer, 46,
    Barford, Canada) and Agnes Merrill (32, Rumney)
Ruth Agnes, b. 6/25/1902 in Orford; third; Joseph D. Cross (farmer,
    43, Barford, PQ) and Agnes Merrill (W. Rumney)

CROWE,
daughter, b. 2/15/1900 in Orford; first; John W. Crowe (farmer, 24,
    Franklin Ctr., PQ) and Olive S. Stetson (29, Orford)
Faith Jozlynn, b. 4/30/2004 in Lebanon; Ty Crowe and Ashley Merrill

CSERR,
Trillium Fitzgerald, b. 12/20/1999 in Lebanon; Robert Anthony Savell
    and Ruth Cserr

CUMMINGS,
Barbara Ann, b. 12/13/1945 in Orford; fifth; Leon O. Cummings (farm
    laborer, Thetford, VT) and Millie Y. French (Piermont)
Betty Lou, b. 7/17/1940 in Haverhill; fifth; Clyde Asa Cummings
    (laborer, Thetford Ctr., VT) and Rosie Ellen Tallman (Orford)
Clyde Asa, Jr., b. 2/19/1934 in Haverhill; third; Clyde A. Cummings
    (laborer, Thetford, VT) and Rose Tallman (Orford)
Everett Forest, b. 6/3/1911; eighth; James C. Cummings (farmer,
    Thetford, VT) and Lucy M. Allen (Lancaster)
James Asa, b. 2/25/1967 in Haverhill; Clyde A. Cummings (equip.
    oper., Haverhill) and Jane F. Andrews (Orford)
Judith Ann, b. 2/1/1948 in Haverhill; eighth; Clyde A. Cummings
    (laborer, Thetford Ctr., VT) and Rosie E. Tallman (Orford)
Norma Jane, b. 12/28/1943 in Lyme; sixth; Clyde A. Cummings
    (truck driver, Thetford Ctr., VT) and Rosie Ellen Tallman
    (Orford)
Richard Frank, b. 11/4/1935 in Haverhill; fourth; Clyde Cummings
    (truck driver, Thetford Ctr., VT) and Rosie Tallman (Orford)
Rosie Mary, b. 6/19/1931 in Woodsville; first; Clyde Asa Cummings
    (truck driver, Thetford, VT) and Rosie E. Tallman (Orford)
Sonia May, b. 5/17/1940 in Orford; first; Vernon Cummings (laborer,
    Orford) and Elane Hannaford (Norwich, VT)

Wallace John, b. 7/9/1945 in Lyme; seventh; Clyde A. Cummings (truck driver, Thetford Ctr., VT) and Rosie Ellen Tallman (Orford)

CUNNINGHAM,
Bessie Ida, b. 10/4/1935 in Orford; fourth; James D. Cunningham (painter, Fairlee, VT) and Ida Kidney (Monroe)
Franklin James, b. 1/30/1927 in Orford; second; James Cunningham (laborer, Fairlee, VT) and Ida Kidney (Monroe)
Richard Elberton, b. 12/5/1930 in Orford; third; James Cunningham (painter, Fairlee, VT) and Ida May Kidney (Monroe)

CURRIER,
son, b. 7/12/1905 in Orford; first; Samuel R. Currier (sectionhand, 38, Point Levis, PQ) and Anne M. Streeter (22, Monroe)
stillborn daughter, b. 10/22/1909; second; Alfred Currier (laborer, 28, Orford) and Maggie Rollins (19, Orford)
daughter, b. 6/8/1934 in Orford; fifth; Jessie W. Currier (farmer, Wentworth) and Victoria Downing (Orford)
Albert Weygandt, b. 9/30/1944 in Hanover; fifth; Jesse W. Currier (farmer, Wentworth) and Victoria E. Downing (Orford)
Alfred Joseph, b. 9/18/1928 in Orford; fifth; Jesse W. Currier (farmer, Wentworth) and Victoria Downing (Orford)
Ellen Alice, b. 8/5/1946 in Hanover; sixth; Jesse W. Currier (farmer, Wentworth) and Victoria E. Downing (Orford)
John Downing, b. 7/11/1925; second; Jesse W. Currier (farmer, Wentworth) and Victoria Downing (Orford)
Kevin Logan, b. 3/2/1975 in Hanover; Frank J. Currier, Jr. (24, NH) and Karen E. Logan (24, NH)
Norman Jesse, b. 2/20/1924; first; Jesse W. Currier (lumberman, Wentworth) and Victoria Downing (Orford)
Wesley Lorenzo, b. 7/5/1930 in Orford; sixth; Jesse Weston Currier (farmer, Wentworth) and Victoria E. Downing (Orford)
William Henry, b. 9/28/1907; second; Samuel L. Currier (laborer, 40, Point Levi, PQ) and Anne B. Streeter (24, Monroe); residence - Woodsville

CUSHING,
Clyde Oscar, b. 7/19/1919 in Orford; first; Harry Cushing (farmer, McIndoes, VT) and Pauline Gould (Lancaster)

CUSHMAN,
child, b. 1/3/1887 in Orford; second; Ernest W. Cushman (farmer, Lisbon) and Minnie E. Worthley (Bradford, VT)
Elizabeth, b. 12/1/1916 in Orford; first; Charles L. Cushman (farmer, 35, Orford) and Elizabeth McGeehin (30, Baltimore, MD)
Florence L., b. 8/6/1895 in Orford; third; E. W. Cushman (farrming, 44, Lisbon) and Min. E. Worthly (37, Bradford)

CUTTING,
child, b. 1/23/1887 in Orford; third; Samuel Q. Cutting (farmer, Orford) and Julia E. Gardner (Lyme)
daughter, b. 10/13/1888; fourth; Samuel Q. Cutting (farmer, 37, Orford) and Julia E. Gardner (28, Lyme)
son, b. 9/19/1892 in Orford; fifth; Samuel Q. Cutting (farmer, 40, Orford) and Julia E. Gardner (32, Lyme)
son, b. 6/11/1897; seventh; Samuel Q. Cutting (farmer, 45, Orford) and Julia E. Gardner (37, Lyme)
Adna J., b. 8/21/1895; sixth; S. L. Cutting (farming, 43, Orford) and Julia E. Gardner (35, Lyme)

DAIGE,
Roland Melvin, b. 11/10/1932 in Orford; second; Wilfred O. Daige (laborer, Bakersfield, VT) and Evelyn L. Chase (Wentworth)

DAISEY,
Aaron, b. 1/17/1980 in Haverhill; Joseph Daisey and Helen Daisey
Allen Lee, b. 10/8/1952 in Plymouth; fourth; Royden H. Daisey (laborer, DE) and Myrtle F. Chase (NH)
Amos Frederick, b. 12/14/1970 in Lebanon; Joseph E. Daisey (24, Wilmington, DE) and Helen M. Wilson (22, Bay Shore, LI, NY)
Daniel Scott, b. 5/9/1969 in Lebanon; Joseph E. Daisey (23, Wilmington, DE) and Helen M. Wilson (20, Long Island, NY)
Devin Scott, b. 8/14/2003 in Lebanon; Daniel Scott Daisey and Tonya Jean Sargent
Harry Royden, b. 3/30/1965 in Haverhill; Royden W. Daisey (laborer, Wilmington, DE) and Sheila M. Corliss (Littleton)
Lauren Catherine, b. 9/21/1996 in Haverhill; Amos Frederick Daisey and Holly Christine Lemay Daisey
Lisa Marie, b. 6/24/1966 in Haverhill; Royden W. Daisey (log roller, Wilmington, DE) and Sheila Mae Corliss (Littleton)

Melissa Jean, b. 7/18/1976 in Lebanon; Joseph E. Daisey (30, DE) and Helen M. Wilson (27, NY)
Richard Eugene, b. 10/23/1955 in Plymouth; fourth; Royden H. Daisey (chef, Millsboro, DE) and Myrtle F. Chase (Wentworth)

DANDREO,
Walter Edmund, b. 2/25/1911; second; Frank Dandreo (barber, Italy) and Elsie Smith (Orford)

DANFORTH,
Stephanie Anna, b. 6/13/1975 in Lebanon; William H. Danforth, Jr. (24, VT) and Gene D. Rolfe (24, VT)

DAVIS,
daughter, b. 3/1/1888; fifth; William Edwin Davis (laborer, 28, Moreton, England) and Annie E. L. Davis (25, Oxhill, England)
son, b. 7/7/1889 in Orford; sixth; William E. Davis (laborer, 29, England) and Annie E. Lines (26, England)
son, b. 1/9/1892 in Orford; first; Prescott W. Davis (laborer, 31, Orford) and Lillian Dyke (26, Tunbridge, VT)
son, b. 4/28/1892 in Orford; seventh; William E. Davis (laborer, 32, England) and Annie E. Lines (28, Oxhill, England)
daughter, b. 4/24/1898 in Orford; fifth; Alymer E. Davis (laborer, 39, Bolton, PQ) and Ida L. Clough (34, Lyman)
Brent Gerald, b. 5/1/1965 in Orford; Donald F. Davis (laborer, Enfield) and Ruth D. Fillian (Wentworth)
Brian Alphonse, b. 5/1/1965 in Orford; Donald F. Davis (laborer, Enfield) and Ruth D. Fillian (Wentworth)
Denise Marie, b. 2/19/1960 in Haverhill; third; Donald F. Davis (truck driver, Enfield) and Ruth D. Fillian (Wentworth)
Frank K., b. 7/30/1893 in Orford; second; Prescott W. Davis (farmer, 33, Orford) and Lillian S. Dike (27, Tunbridge, VT)
Margot Rose, b. 2/2/2001 in Lebanon; Robert Davis and Teresa Lust
Rebecca Dawn, b. 8/24/1963 in Lebanon; Donald F. Davis (laborer, Enfield) and Ruth D. Fillian (Wentworth)
Stacey Dee, b. 10/28/1967 in Haverhill; Donald F. Davis (sawyer, Enfield) and Ruth D. Fillian (Wentworth)
Tammy Lea, b. 5/13/1969 in Hanover; Donald F. Davis (42, Enfield) and Ruth D. Fillian (36, Wentworth)
Valerie Jean, b. 8/19/1956 in Lebanon; first; Donald Francis Davis (laborer, Enfield) and Ruth Delvina Fillian (Wentworth)

DAY,
Caleb Richard, b. 12/27/1999 in Lebanon; Robert Day and Sara Day
Cora Suzanne, b. 10/27/2002 in Lebanon; Robb Day and Sara Day
Dakota Paul, b. 2/10/1996 in Lebanon; Dusti Ann Day
Daniel Arthur, II, b. 8/30/1974 in Lebanon; Daniel A. Day (27, Hanover) and Deann K. Sanborn (19, Woodsville)

DAYTON,
Daniel F., b. 6/26/1919 in Hanover; first; James Henry Dayton (farmer, Somerville, MA) and Bessie Brock (Orford)

DEBLOIS,
Laura Eileen, b. 9/29/1973 in Lebanon; Alton G. Deblois (34, E. Ryegate, VT) and Shirley Jane Chase (30, Woodsville)
Michael Alton, b. 3/9/1966 in haverhill; Alton G. Deblois (cook, E. Ryegate, VT) and Shirley Jane Chase (Woodsville)
Richard Guy, b. 5/27/1969 in Haverhill; Alton G. Deblois (30, Orford) and Shirley H. Chase (27, Haverhill)

DELANEY,
Sean Patrick, b. 1/7/1991 in Hanover; Patrick Delaney and Anne Delaney

DENNIS,
daughter, b. 3/6/1893 in Orford; second; Fred A. Dennis (farmer, 33, Stratford) and Vina Bass (21, Stratford)
son, 10/15/1895 in Orford; third; Fred A. Dennis (farming, 33, Stratford) and Viena E. Bass (24, Stratford)
daughter, b. 2/25/1900 in Orford; first; Dwight J. Dennis (farmer, 29, Orford) and Lillian V. McCoy (17, Newport, VT)
stillborn son, b. 12/25/1901 in Orford; third; Myron A. Dennis (farmer, 39, Strafford) and Agnes L. Warren (35, Lyme)
son, b. 3/7/1906 in Orford; first; Newell A. Dennis (laborer, 24, Orford) and Lottie B. Roberts (14, Lyme)
Arthur Albert, b. 11/4/1951 in Hanover; first; Ralph E. Dennis (farmer, Hanover) and Ramona J. Wing (Orford)
Carl Walter, b. 11/2/1952 in Hanover; second; Ralph E. Dennis (farmer, Hanover) and Ramona J. Wing (Orford)
Craig M., b. 9/20/1972 in Lebanon; Russell J. Dennis (18, Hanover) and Mary Jane Seace (17, Hanover)

Edith Louise, b. 3/29/1909; third; Newell A. Dennis (farmer, 27, Orford) and Lottie B. Roberts (17, Lyme)
Elizabeth, b. 9/29/1907; second; Newell A. Dennis (laborer, 26, Orford) and Lottie B. Roberts (16, Lyme)
Evelyn M., b. 3/12/1922; first; Walter B. Dennis (farmer, Piermont) and Mary T. Rugg (Fairlee, VT)
Gerald F., b. 5/4/1938 in N. Springfield, VT; second; Dorman D. Dennis (farmer, Newbury, VT) and Ethel Fuller (Newbury, VT)
Lena Olive, b. 8/30/1913 in Orford; fourth; Newell A. Dennis (farmer, 32, Orford) and Lottie B. Roberts (22, Lyme)
Ralph, b. 5/17/1926; second; Walter Dennis (farmer, Piermont) and Thersa Rugg (Fairlee, VT)
Richard Gordon, b. 5/16/1923; second; Ernest C. Dennis (farmer, Orford) and Mildred F. Leach (Fairlee, VT)
Russell James, b. 7/21/1954 in Hanover; third; Ralph Edward Dennis (farmer, Hanover) and Ramona Jane Wing (Orford)
Wallis Ernest, b. 9/26/1920 in Hanover; first; Ernest C. Dennis (farmer, Orford) and Florence M. Leach (Fairlee, VT)

DERICK,
son, b. 6/14/1921 in Orford; ninth; George Derick (farmer, N. Troy, VT) and Lula Goodwin (Piermont)

DICKINSON,
child, b. 3/29/1887 in Orford; second; Wilbur Dickinson (laborer, Fairlee, VT) and Minnie Chase (Washington, VT)

DIMICK,
Nathaniel Joseph, b. 8/30/1998 in Lebanon; Gary Michael Dimick and Gail Temperley Dimick

DODGE,
Emily Elizabeth, b. 10/21/1981 in Hanover; Allen Dodge and Karen Dodge

DOMENK,
Rachel Loyola, b. 7/3/1932 in Orford; second; Paul Domenk (machinist, Kenosha, WI) and Lucretia Spiller (Providence, RI); residence – Kenosha, WI

DOMINQUE,
Stephanie Marie, b. 1/5/1980 in Hanover; James Dominque and Karen Dominque

DONALDSON,
daughter, b. 4/2/1891 in Orford; first; George B. Donaldson (laborer, 34, Peacham, VT) and Mary F. Whitman (19, Orford)
son, b. 10/24/1892 in Orford; second; George B. Donaldson (laborer, 27, Peacham, VT) and Mary F. Whitman (21, Orford)
Beatrice C., b. 2/10/1902 in Orford; third; George B. Donaldson (laborer, 34, Peacham, VT) and Mary H. Whitman (Orford)
Guy Barton, b. 3/26/1905 in Orford; fourth; George B. Donaldson (laborer, 38, Peacham, VT) and Mary H. Whitman (36, Orford)
Jennifer Lea, b. 10/26/1983; Thomas Donaldson and Sue Donaldson
Mark Freeman, b. 5/3/1909; sixth; Samuel H. Donaldson (laborer, 45, Peacham, VT) and Mary H. Whitman (37, Orford)
Maurice Arthur, b. 12/24/1906 in Orford; fifth; George B. Donaldson (laborer, 38, Peacham, VT) and Mary H. Whitman (34, Orford)

DONNELLY,
Christopher Jay, b. 2/26/1973 in Lebanon; William J. Donnelly (25, Hanover) and Kathryn L. Bacon (22, Thetford, VT)
Leslie Jay, b. 7/2/1911; first; Jay Will Donnelly (farmer) and Della A. Pease (Wentworth)
Lloyd Jon, b. 3/31/1944 in Hanover; first; Leslie J. Donnelly (US Army, Orford) and Hazel A. Sanborn (Orford)
Robert Joseph, Jr., b. 2/27/1945 in Hanover; first; Robert J. Donnelly (US Army, Lisbon) and Nellie M. Cummings (Thetford, VT)
Susan Marie, b. 7/27/1970 in Lebanon; William J. Donnelly (22, Hanover) and Kathryn L. Bacon (20, E. Thetford, VT)

DORF,
Shanti Sunshine, b. 2/8/1974 in Lebanon; William C. Dorf (23, Brooklyn, NY) and Janet E. Thompson (23, Long Island, NY)

DORION-RIPPE,
Ozyen Moss, b. 3/28/2004 in Orford; Daniel Rippe and Marie Dorion

DOW,
daughter, b. 1/17/1918 in Orford; sixth; Bert J. Dow (farmer, Canterbury) and Ethel Downing (Orford)
Bessie Mabel, b. 11/3/1916 in Orford; fifth; Bert Dow (farmer, 29, Canterbury) and Ethel E. Downing (24, Orford)
Dorothy A., b. 2/23/1919 in Orford; seventh; Bert J. Dow (farmer, NB) and Ethel E. Downing (Orford)
Douglas, b. --/--/1948 in Haverhill; fifth; Eustas D. Dow (clerk, London, England) and Marion M. Flagg (Fairlee, VT)
Willie Burt, b. 10/16/1912 in Orford; second; Bert Dow (farmer, 25, Canterbury, NB) and Ethel E. Downing (20, Orford)

DOWNING,
son, b. 4/19/1888; second; Willey E. Downing (farmer, 29, Wentworth) and Lura M. D. Poor (21, Orford)
daughter, b. 8/16/1892 in Orford; fifth; Willie E. Downing (farmer, 34, Wentworth) and Lina M. Poor (26, Orford)
son, b. 1/29/1896; sixth; William Eugene Downing (farming, 38, Wentworth) and Luna M. Poor (29, Orford)
daughter, b. 2/15/1898 in Orford; seventh; Willie E. Downing (farmer, 39, Wentworth) and Laura M. Poor (31, Orford)
daughter, b. 5/31/1907; eighth; William E. Downing (farmer, 49, Wentworth) and Luna M. Poor (40, Orford)
Angelia Luna Maria, b. 3/14/1905 in Orford; first; Dell Downing (18, Orford)
Virginia Eva, b. 1/26/1909; first; Ethel F. Downing (16, Orford)

DRABICK,
Tyler Wayne, b. 10/15/1982; Mark Drabick and Susan Drabick

DUBOIS,
Andrew James, b. 6/26/2003 in Lebanon; Marc DuBois and Moira DuBois

DUPREY,
Adrienne Michelle, b. 1/19/1967 in Hanover; Neil C. Duprey (teacher, Bellows Falls, VT) and Cheryl JoAnn Zink (Wheeling, WV)

DUVAL,
Jean, b. 7/28/1944 in Goffstown; first; Joseph E. Duval (US Army, Newton U. Falls, MA) and Katherine B. Small (Goffstown)
Nicole Morgan, b. 10/9/1980 in Lebanon; Raymond Duval and Kathy Duval

DYKE,
Adam Joseph, b. 1/19/1971 in Lebanon; Robert L. Dike (20, St. Cloud, MN) and Nancy L. Small (21, Lyme)
Adrian Joseph, b. 3/3/1998 in Haverhill; Adam Joseph Dyke and Donna A. Dempsey Dyke
Barbara Ann, b. 9/3/1949 in Orford; third; George C. Dyke (lumberman, Newbury, VT) and Beulah B. Bockus (Wethersfield, CT)
Brenda Eileen, b. 11/21/1948 in Orford; third; Benjamin F. Dyke, Jr. (lumberman, Newbury, VT) and Dorothy A. Dow (Orford)
Calvin Ronald, b. 5/21/1940 in Orford; first; Benjamin F. Dyke, Jr. (laborer, Newbury, VT) and Dorothy Alice Dow (Orford)
Connie Lee, b. 5/12/1965 in Lebanon; George C. Dyke (foreman, Newbury, VT) and Beulah B. Bockus (Wethersfield, CT)
Cynthia Wilkins, b. 8/10/1981 in Hanover; James Dyke and Barbara Dyke
Daniel Robert, b. 9/14/1962 in Lebanon; seventh; Robert F. Dyke (driller, Newbury, VT) and Doloris M. Urbanski (Rice, MN)
Francesca Carol, b. 7/2/1999 in Lebanon; Craig Dyke and Amy Dyke
James Robert, b. 11/30/1946 in Hanover; second; Robert F. Dyke (truck driver, Newbury, VT) and Doloris M. Urbanski (Rice, MN)
Jason Roger, b. 5/19/1973 in Lebanon; Alan F. Dyke (28, Bristol) and Joy Jean Wilson (26, Long Island, NY)
Jeffrey N., b. 7/23/1972 in Haverhill; Eugene L. Dyke (24, Foley, MN) and Christine E. Bunten (20, Concord)
Jennifer Marie, b. 6/21/1971 in Lebanon; Alan F. Dyke (26, Bristol) and Joy Jean Wilson (25, Bay Shore, LI, NY)
Kathy Mae, b. 7/23/1954 in Orford; fifth; George Carl Dyke (bulldozer op., Newbury, VT) and Beulah Belle Bockus (Wethersfield, CT)
Laurie Anne, b. 6/27/1963 in Plymouth; Alan F. Dyke (construction, Bristol) and Joan J. Randall (Plymouth)
Lee Mathew, b. 6/4/1967 in Haverhill; Robert F. Dyke (powderman, Newbury, VT) and Doloris M. Urbanski (Rice, MN)

Marcus John, b. 7/10/1996 in Haverhill; Adam Joseph Dyke and Donna Althea Dempsey Dyke

Michael Lewis, b. 1/14/1957 in Orfordville; sixth; George Carl Dyke (op. engineer, Newbury, VT) and Beulah Belle Bockus (Wethersfield, CT)

Nathaniel James, b. 8/7/1995 in Lebanon; Daniel Robert Dyke and Cara Jean Shepard Dyke

Norine Alice, b. 10/1/1951 in Orford; fourth; Benjamin F. Dyke, Jr. (lumberman, Newbury, VT) and Dorothy A. Dow (Orford)

Patrick Michael, b. 11/4/1981 in Lebanon; Michael Dyke and Mary Dyke

Sandra Lee, b. 6/13/1943 in Orford; second; Benjamin Dyke, Jr. (laborer, Newbury, VT) and Dorothy Dow (Orford)

Sharon, b. 4/1/1946 in Hanover; second; George C. Dyke (trucker, Newbury, VT) and Beulah B. Bockus (Wethersfield, CT)

Stefany Lauran, b. 11/23/1977 in Hanover; James R. Dyke (30, NH) and Barbara C. Wilkins (24, MA)

Terry Edward, b. 12/12/1952 in Orford; fourth; George C. Dyke (lumberman, Newbury, VT) and Beulah B. Bockus (Wethersfield, CT)

Therese Marie, b. 4/15/2000 in Lebanon; Adam Dyke and Donna Dyke

EATON,
Isabel Iris, b. 6/30/1997 in Lebanon; Gregory Kent Eaton and Suzanne Norris Rozgonyi Eaton

ECONOMY,
Evelyn Long, b. 3/4/1991 in Hanover; George Economy and Linda Economy

ELLIOTT,
stillborn son, b. 1/9/1933 in Orford; fourth; Stanley Elliott (laborer, Lyme) and Lula B. Baker (Orford)

Allen Conrad, b. 3/29/1929 in Orfordville; fourth; Stanley Carr Elliott (chauffeur, Lyme) and Lula Bell Baker (Orford)

Harry Frank, b. 4/26/1925; first; Stanley Elliott (chauffeur, Lyme) and Lula B. Baker (Orford); residence – Fairlee, VT

Irma Clorice, b. 6/15/1926; second; Ashton W. Elliott (herdsman, Haverhill) and Helena B. Foote (Portsmouth)

EMERSON,
daughter, b. 7/21/1918 in Orford; first; Harold Emerson (in army, Fairbury, NE) and Evelyn Carr (Andover)
Samuel Louis, b. 9/6/1996 in Lebanon; Melvin Paul Emerson and Amy Lou Messer Emerson

EMERY,
Esma Alice, b. 4/19/1917 in Orford; second; Fay S. Emery (farmer, Piermont) and Gladys Chesley (Lyme); residence – Piermont
Frank Maurice, b. 7/10/1909; first; Frank S. Emery (farmer, 28, Piermont) and Mary J. Horton (23, Orford)
Mariam, b. 10/6/1891 in Orford; third; Perkins C. Emery (laborer, 42, Washington, VT) and Mariam M. M----- (33, Eaton, PQ)

ESTES,
Tammy Jean, b. 8/27/1971 in Lebanon; Stephen L. Estes (25, E. Thetford, VT) and Geraldine Johnson (21, Lebanon)

ESTREN,
Gregory, b. 8/26/1978 in Hanover; Robert K. Estren (24, NY) and Geralyn Koblis (23, NJ)

EVANS,
son, b. 9/28/1897; second; William H. Evans (laborer, 35, Chateaugay, NY) and Myra B. Gilbert (29, Lyme)
Lexaphina Angleis, b. 4/19/2004 in Lebanon; James Evans and Lindsey Evans

FABRIZIO,
Evan Francis, b. 8/20/1992 in Lebanon; Mark Fabrizio and Gayle Fabrizio

FADDEN,
Thomas Raymond, b. 12/16/1988; Richard Fadden and Denise Fadden

FAIRCLOTH,
Deborah Jean, b. 8/17/1948 in Hanover; third; Obediah H. Faircloth (farmer, Valdosta, GA) and Elizabeth A. Land (Brooklyn, NY)

FILLIAN,
son, b. 9/17/1917 in Orford; first; Alphonse Fillian (farmer, Manchester) and Jessie Wood (Piermont)
daughter, b. 2/19/1920 in Orford; third; Alphonse Fillian (farmer, Manchester) and Jessie A. Wood (Piermont)
daughter, b. 7/5/1921 in Orford; fourth; Alphonce Fillian (farmer, Manchester) and Jesse Woods (Piermont)
daughter, b. 8/17/1928 in Orford; ninth; Alphonse J. Fillian (lumberman, Manchester) and Jessie A. Woods (Piermont)
Annette L., b. 10/6/1938 in Orford; thirteenth; Alphonse Fillian (woodsman, Manchester) and Jennie A. Woods (Piermont)
David Albert, b. 8/11/1927 in Orford; sixth; Alphonse Fillian (jobber, Manchester) and Jessie Woods (Piermont)
Deborah Lee, b. 6/26/1954 in Lebanon; second; William R. Fillian (laborer, Wentworth) and Edna Mae Canfield (Powers) (Hanover)
Delores Delvina, b. 11/17/1950 in Orford; second; David A. Fillian (farmer, Orford) and Hattie N. Shortt (Warren)
Dustin Fay, b. 2/16/1985; Randy Fillian and Patricia Fillian
Holly Elizabeth, b. 3/11/1978 in Hanover; Gary Lee Fillian (22, DE) and Cynthia Labombard (17, NH)
Richard Francis, b. 8/20/1918 in Orford; second; Alphonse J. Fillian (farmer, Manchester) and Jessie A. Wood (Piermont)
Robert Stanley, b. 6/24/1953 in Lebanon; fourth; Richard F. Fillian (mechanic, Orfordville) and Sara D. Holland (Rehoboth Beach, DE)
Robert William, b. 6/18/1952 in Lebanon; first; William R. Fillian (US Army, Wentworth) and Edna M. Canfield (Hanover)
Steven Douglas, b. 9/4/1956 in Haverhill; fifth; Richard F. Fellian (mach. operator, Orford) and Sara Dutton Holland (Rehoboth Beach, DE)

FINNEY,
daughter, b. 3/11/1901 in Orford; second; Frank Finney (farmer, 31, Orford) and Ida L. Barnes (30, Schoghticoke, NY)
son, b. 10/23/1902 in Orford; third; Frank G. Finney (farmer, 33, Orford) and Ida L. Barnes (Schaghticoke, NY)
daughter, b. 7/4/1921 in Orford; first; George H. Finney (laborer, Orford) and Doris Chamberlain (Orford)
George Henry, b. 11/15/1898 in Orford; first; Frank G. Finney (farmer, 29, Orford) and Ida L. Barnes (27, Schaghitcoke, NY)

George W., b. 12/16/1922; second; George H. Finney (laborer, Orford) and Doris Chamberlain (Orford)

FISH,
Victoria Lee, b. 6/10/1952 in Hanover; first; William L. Fish (lumberman, Randolph, VT) and Rachel A. Fillian (Wentworth)

FISHER,
Theophilus Ira, b. 5/20/1933 in Orford; fifth; Ezra G. Fisher (laborer, Lunenburg, VT) and Margaret Bischoff (Staten Island, NY)

FLETCHER,
Michael William, b. 6/5/1961 in Hanover; second; William H. Fletcher (pressman, Long Island, NY) and Irene Diane Stranis (Long Island, NY)

FLINT,
Clarence Thomas, b. 3/5/2003 in Lebanon; Clarence Flint and Shiloh Olisky
Jeanette Lucille, b. 8/3/1936 in Haverhill; first; Clinton Flint (laborer, Granville, VT) and Lena Lacoursere (Munson, MA)

FOOTE,
child, b. 12/19/1887 in Orford; first; George E. Foote (farmer, 27, Warren) and Sarah E. Foote (21, Warren)
daughter, b. 7/16/1894 in Orford; second; Harry B. Foote (farmer, 21, Warren) and Clarabel Felch (22, Cannon City, CO)
daughter, b. 7/28/1896; third; Harry B. Foote (farming, 23, Warren) and Claribel Felch (24, Canyon City, CO)
daughter, b. 5/5/1918 in Orford; first; Mildred Foote (Orford)
stillborn daughter, b. 1/1/1933 in Hanover; third; Edward Foote (farmer, Orford) and Rose Baker (Orford)
Bertram Harry, b. 2/27/1930 in Orford; first; Edward Foote (farmer, Orford) and Rose Baker (Orford)
Evelyn Marie, b. 12/27/1903 in Orford; seventh; Harry B. Foote (farmer, 31, Warren) and Claribel Felch (31, Canon City, CO)
Frances Ella, b. 4/7/1915 in Orford; fifth; Bert L. Foote (farmer, 40, Warren) and Julia Whitcher (39, Warren)
Harry H., b. 3/2/1905 in Orford; eighth; Harry B. Foote (farmer, 33, Warren) and Claribel Felch (33, Canon City, CO)

James H., b. 3/8/1893 in Orford; first; Harry B. Foote (farmer, 20, Warren) and Claribel Felch (21, Canyon City, CO)
Lewis Sidney, b. 7/30/1917 in Orford; twelfth; Harry B. Foote (farmer, Warren) and Claribel Felch (Can. City, CO)

FORD,
daughter, b. 7/22/1892 in Orford; sixth; Aaron D. Ford (farmer, 39, Corinth, VT) and Dora Howland (29, Easton)

FOX,
Benjamin Amos, b. 6/3/1966 in Hanover; Hugh R. Fox (local editor, Newark, NJ) and Linda Edna Schriever (Bay Shore, NY)
Caroline Rist, b. 12/2/1967 in Lebanon; Hugh R. Fox (lawyer, Newark, NJ) and Linda E. Schriever (Bayshore, NY)

FRANK,
Susan Lane, b. 10/15/1948 in Hanover; first; Lawrence B. Frank (mechanic, New York, NY) and Alma J. Treworgy (Roslyn Hts., NY)

FRANKE,
Erik Alexander, b. 8/3/1986; John Franke and Kimberly Franke

FRANKLIN,
Harry Emerson, b. 5/8/1909; first; Arthur L. Franklin (farmer, 26, Orford) and Marion H. Clark (19, Orford)
Lewis Ernest, b. 7/24/1937 in Hanover; first; Harry E. Franklin (farmer, Orford) and Ruby E. Pierson (E. Topsham, VT)
Priscilla Jeanne, b. 7/17/1943 in Hanover; second; Harry E. Franklin (farmer, Orford) and Ruby E. Pierson (Topsham, VT)
Ruth Elsie, b. 5/11/1910; second; Arthur L. Franklin (farmer, 27, Orford) and Marion H. Clark (20, Orford)
Walter Allen, b. 8/30/1945 in Hanover; third; Harry E. Franklin (farmer, Orford) and Ruby Ellen Pierson (Topsham, VT)

FREEMAN,
Everett, b. 4/11/1911; second; Charles Freeman (millman, Rumney) and Ora M. Smith (Sanbornton); residence – Warren

FRENCH,
child, b. 12/9/1887 in Orford; seventh; Josiah D. Clough (farmer, 35, Brunswick, VT) and Eliza Jane Gage (33, Orford)
son, b. 6/14/1888; third; Willie H. French (laborer, 33, Whitefield) and Alice M. Drown (33, Haverhill)
daughter, b. 7/14/1890 in Orford; third; Dexter S. French (farmer, 51, Corinth, VT) and Hattie P. Terrill (28, Clifton, PQ)
son, b. 9/15/1892 in Orford; fifth; George M. French (farmer, 41, Brunswick, VT) and Eliza J. Gage (38, Orford)
daughter, b. 10/31/1893 in Orford; sixth; Willie H. French (laborer, 38, Whitefield) and Alice M. Drown (38, Haverhill)
daughter, b. 1/29/1894 in Orford; first; Walter H. French (farmer, 31, Orford) and Francese Knight (23, Hartland, VT)
daughter, b. 4/8/1897; second; Walter H. French (farmer, 34, Orford) and Francese Knight (26, Hartland, VT)
daughter, b. 7/29/1900 in Orford; seventh; Willie H. French (farmer, 45, Orford) and Alice M. Drown (46, Haverhill)
James Edward, b. 10/23/1942 in Orford; second; Edward W. French (farm hand, Piermont) and Grace Bell Dean (Orford); residence – Piermont
Kathleen Hazel, b. 8/16/1934 in Orford; eighth; Fred G. French (farmer, Orford) and Elizabeth Wilson (Boston, MA)
Marion Evelyn, b. 12/18/1947 in Hanover; fifth; Lawrence W. French (woodsman, Haverhill) and Evelyn Kenniston (Kittery, ME)
Walter H., b. 4/22/1904 in Orford; third; Walter H. French (farmer, 41, Orford) and Frances Knight (33, Hartland)

FRIZZELL,
daughter, b. 3/16/1910; third; Charles H. Frizzell (harness maker, 62, Newbury, VT) and Ora Copp (30, Haverhill)

FULTON,
Christopher Bryant, b. 8/8/1991 in Lebanon; Thomas Fulton and Catherine Fulton
Erik Holm, b. 10/17/1987; Thomas Fulton and Catherine Fulton

FUMAGALI,
Flavio Pietro, b. 8/30/1935 in Hanover; first; Frank Fumagali (artist, Venice, Italy) and Filomena Sabatino (New York, NY)

GAGE,
daughter, b. 3/21/1892 in Orford; first; Everett L. Gage (laborer, 26, Orford) and Nellie F. Pebbles (19, Lyme)
daughter, b. 3/10/1903 in Orford; seventh; Everett L. Gage (farmer, 37, Orford) and Nellie F. Pebbles (29, Lyme)
Ada Alberta, b. 6/1/1896; third; Everett L. Gage (laborer, 30, Orford) and Nellie F. Pebbles (23, Lyme)
Clyde Harold, b. 6/25/1899 in Orford; fifth; Everett L. Gage (farmer, 32, Orford) and Nellie F. Pebbles (26, Lyme)
Eda May, b. 7/27/1897; fourth; Everett L. Gage (farmer, 31, Orford) and Nellie F. Pebbles (25, Lyme)
Myrtle Frasilla, b. 6/8/1901 in Orford; sixth; Everett L. Gage (farmer, 35, Orford) and Nellie F. Pebbles (28, Lyme)
Phillip E., b. 5/17/1894 in Orford; second; Everett L. Gage (farmer, 28, Orford) and Nellie F. Pebbles (21, Orford)

GAGNE,
Lois Madeline, b. 11/6/1930 in Orford; fourth; Frank C. Gagne (laborer, Whitefield) and Sahmer Z. Osgood (Ashland)

GALLUP,
Carol Jean, b. 2/28/1947 in Lebanon; second; Harley G. Gallup (carpenter, Plainfield, VT) and Ella C. Johnson (Minneapolis, MN)
Noreen Elizabeth, b. 12/1/1945 in Lebanon; second; Harley Gallup (carpenter, Plainfield, VT) and Ella Johnson (Minneapolis, MN)

GARDNER,
son, b. 8/20/1890 in Orford; first; Frank H. Gardner (laborer, 25, Lyme) and Martha A. Smith (19, Lyme)
stillborn son, b. 8/1/1894 in Orford; second; Frank H. Gardner (laborer, 29, Lyme) and Martha A. Smith (23, Lyme)
son, b. 9/17/1898 in Orford; fourth; Frank H. Gardner (blacksmith, 33, Lyme) and Martha A. Smith (27, Lyme)
daughter, b. 7/8/1902 in Orford; fifth; Frank H. Gardner (blacksmith, 37, Lyme) and Martha A. Smith (Lyme)
son, b. 1/17/1906 in Orford; seventh; Frank H. Gardner (blacksmith, 40, Lyme) and Martha A. Smith (35, Lyme)
Adolph Edmund, b. 5/13/1936 in Hanover; third; Harold H. Gardner (farmer, Orford) and Phyllis E. Scruton (Woodsville)

Doris E., b. 2/13/1904 in Orford; third; Ned F. Gardner (farmer, 29, Orford) and Hattie L. Cunningham (26, Orford)
Gail Gordon, b. 6/24/1916 in Orford; sixth; Ned F. Gardner (farmer, 41, Orford) and Hattie L. Cunningham (38, Orford)
Glenn Forest, b. 2/16/1902 in Orford; second; Ned F. Gardner (farmer, 26, Orford) and Hattie L. Cunningham (Orford)
Harlow Milton, b. 7/19/1904 in Orford; sixth; Frank H. Gardner (blacksmith, 39, Lyme) and Martha A. Smith (33, Lyme)
Harold Hillman, b. 8/13/1913 in Orford; fifth; Ned F. Gardner (farmer, 38, Orford) and Hattie I. Cunningham (35, Orford)
Roland Carl, b. 2/8/1935 in Hanover; second; Harold H. Gardner (laborer, Orford) and Phyllis E. Scruton (Woodsville)
Roland H., b. 12/7/1895 in Orford; third; F. H. Gardner (laborer, 30, Lyme) and Martha A. Smith (24, Lyme)
Wayne Nolan, b. 5/30/1937 in Hanover; fourth; Harold H. Gardner (farmer, Orford) and Phyllis Scruton (Woodsville)

GASPER,
George Arthur, b. 12/28/1926; first; Andrew J. Gasper (laborer, Orford) and Christina Morey (Orford)
Richard Donald, b. 2/16/1936 in Hanover; fourth; Andrew J. Gasper (mechanic, Goffstown) and Christina Morey (Orford)

GENDRON,
Christopher Rene, b. 9/6/1998 in Lebanon; Kurt Alan Gendron and Tanya D. Sytgles Gendron
Kenneth Rene, b. 9/11/1962 in Hanover; first; Wilfred E. Gendron (carpenter, Bradford, VT) and Shirley Ann Ladeau (Fairlee, VT)
Kurt Alan, b. 1965 in Hanover; Wilfred E. Gendron (mtce. man, Bradford, VT) and Shirley A. Ladeau (Fairlee, VT)
Lisa Arlene, b. 10/23/1967 in Lebanon; Wilfred E. Gendron (service man, Bradford, VT) and Shirley A. LaDeau (Fairlee, VT)
Stephanie Anne, b. 4/28/1994 in Haverhill; Kurt Alan Gendron and Tanya Dora Stygles Gendron

GEORGE,
Herbert Weston, b. 5/7/1911; second; James M. George (asst. supt. of county farm, Manchester) and Helen E. Snow (Charlestown); residence - Grasmere

GERMANA,
Montanna Rae, b. 12/14/1997 in Lebanon; Kirk James Germana and Amy Louise Pierson Germana

GIESING,
Emma Ann, b. 1/6/1987; Timothy Giesing and Karen Giesing
Mary, b. 8/12/1985; Timothy Giesing and Karen Giesing

GILBERT,
daughter, b. 3/11/1890 in Orford; third; John Gilbert (harnessmaker, 35, Chazy, NY) and Lydia Jane Grant (37, Vershire, VT)
daughter, b. 8/28/1904 in Orford; first; Leon E. Gilbert (conductor, 18, Orford) and Della A. Fay (18, Newton, MA); residence – Newton, MA
daughter, b. 8/4/1909; third; Leon Gilbert (salesman, 23, Orford) and Ella Fay (22, Newton, MA); residence – Enfield
Gordon Harry, b. 3/25/1926; first; Harry E. Gilbert (laborer, Lyme) and Flora E. Cassady (Kingsley Falls, PQ)
Jameson Michael, b. 1/13/2004 in Lebanon; Michael Gilbert and Ellen Gilbert
Lucille Mary, b. 6/16/1928 in Orford; tenth; Harry E. Gilbert (laborer, Lyme) and Flora E. Cassidy (Canada)
Theresa Vivian, b. 1/1/1930 in Orford; third; Harry E. Gilbert (laborer, Lyme) and Flora Cassidy (PQ)

GILLIS,
Andrew Robert, b. 2/6/1913 in Orford; first; William Gillis (farmer, 24, Scotland) and Annie C. Riddex (29, Scotland)

GILMAN,
son, b. 5/21/1891 in Orford; third; Joseph H. Gilman (farmer, 31, Campton) and Gertie A. Simpson (29, Orford)
son, b. 9/24/1892 in Orford; second; William H. Gilman (laborer, 35, Campton) and Clara B. Veasey (32, Bradford, VT)
Joyce Arlene, b. 9/24/1941 in Rockingham, VT; second; Sewell W. Gilman (teacher, Alstead) and Pauline F. Seaman (Nashua)
Martha S., b. 3/29/1905 in Orford; second; James H. Gilman (laborer, 55, Lyndon) and Alice G. Bushaw (30, Barnston, Canada)

GIROUX,
Marie Eleanor, b. 5/14/1935 in Haverhill; third; Arthur Giroux (farmer, Boston, MA) and Pearl Butman (Orford) (1936)
Robert Charles, b. 12/24/1932 in Orford; second; Arthur J. Giroux (laborer, E. Boston, MA) and Pearl A. Butman (Orford)

GLOVER,
Earl Archer, b. 6/26/1927 in Orford; second; Allen Earl Glover (laborer, New York, NY) and Annie M. Archer (Orford)

GODFREY,
daughter, b. 8/23/1897; sixth; Edward J. Godfrey (laborer, 37, Waterbury, VT) and Mary Farrell (28, Shipton, PQ)
Kevin Albert, b. 10/16/1961 in Haverhill; second; Albert P. Godfrey (laborer, Hanover) and Annette Louise Fillian (Orford)

GODSOE,
Robert Daniel, b. 2/10/1985; Thomas Godsoe and Lauren Godsoe

GONYER,
Mary Jane, b. 8/21/1947 in Hanover; first; Stanley D. Fish (laborer, Randolph) and Barbara F. Gonyer (Lancaster)

GONZALEZ,
Braydan Michael, b. 7/10/2001 in Lebanon; Michael Gonzalez and Holly Gonzalez

GOODWIN,
stillborn son, b. 4/11/1903 in Orford; third; Sherman Goodwin (clergyman, 34, Derry) and Ruth Russell (29, St. John, NB)
Charles Winslow, b. 9/22/1900 in Orford; first; Sherman Goodwin (clergyman, 33, Derry) and Ruth A. Russell (27, St. Johns, NB)
Everett Walter, b. 11/7/1910; first; Harry L. Goodwin (farmer, 20, Warren) and Bertha G. Gale (20, MA)
Henry Bussell, b. 1/11/1902 in Orford; second; Sherman Goodwin (minister, 34, Deary) and Ruth A. Russell (St. Johns, NB)

GOULD,
daughter, b. 4/29/1898 in Orford; first; Frank W. Gould (butter maker, 34, Hanover) and Lucy A. Ross (38, Hanover)

Brett Maynard, b. 9/21/1965 in Haverhill; Edward G. Gould (merchant, Jefferson) and Frances M. Huckins (Hanover)
Clayton Edward, b. 7/24/1970 in Haverhill; Edward G. Gould, Jr. (19, Lebanon) and Shirley M. Pushee (19)
Collin Edward, b. 5/24/1999 in Lebanon; Clayton Gould and Laurie Gould
Edward George, Jr., b. 2/6/1951 in Lebanon; first; Edward G. Gould (caretaker, Jefferson) and Frances M. Huckins (Hanover)
James Michael, b. 3/5/1949 in Haverhill; second; Walter F. Gould (farmer, Yonkers, NY) and Dorothy E. Winning (Eatontown, NJ)
Karyn Leigh, b. 4/21/1950 in Haverhill; third; Walter F. Gould (farming, Yonkers, NY) and Dorothy E. Winning (Eatontown, NJ)
Kayla Jean, b. 5/28/1997 in Lebanon; Clayton Edward Gould and Laurie Jean Denis Gould
Nathan George, b. 6/21/19876 in Woodsville; Edward G. Gould (25, NH) and Shirley M. Pushee (25, NH)
Peter, b. 12/5/1974 in Hanover; Clarence F. Gould (27, Whitefield) and Patricia A. Hosmer (22, Strafford, VT)
Richard Jay, b. 4/6/1944 in Haverhill; first; Walter F. Gould (farmer, Yonkers, NY) and Dorothy E. Winning (Eatontown, NJ)
Teresa Marie, b. 10/14/1957 in Lebanon; second; Edward George Gould, Sr. (painter, Jefferson) and Frances M. Huckins (Hanover)
Zachary Nathan, b. 10/18/2001 in Lebanon; Nathan Gould and Jessica Gould

GOUNDREY,
Melissa Rose, b. 4/16/1981 in St. Johnsbury, VT; Paul Goundrey and Althea Goundrey

GRADY,
Sean Michael, b. 7/30/1991 in Lebanon; Michael Grady and Janice Grady

GRANT,
Patricia Anne, b. 8/27/1954 in Lebanon; second; John Henry Grant (broker, Lyme) and Janet Piper (Lyme)

GRATTON,
Andrea Gail, b. 3/30/1948 in Lebanon; second; Fred L. Gratton (telephone man, Bethel, VT) and Jessie M. Lackey (W. Fairlee, VT)

GRAVES,
Lauren Elizabeth, b. 2/23/1980 in Hanover; Leonard Graves and Paula Graves

GRAY,
Daniel Alexander, b. 11/18/1993 in Lebanon; Todd Christopher Gray and Brenda Lea Giesing Gray
Jonathan K., b. 7/14/1972 in Haverhill; Bruce R. Gray (19, NH) and Linda P. Brown (22, Texas)
Mathew Scott, b. 9/27/1974 in Hanover; Richard C. Gray (26, Lebanon) and Norine A. Dyke (23, Orford)
Nicholas Ryan, b. 4/10/2003 in Lebanon; Scott Gray and Tammy Giesing
Paige Elaine, b. 5/31/1997 in Lebanon; Michael Shawn Gray and Laura Ingrid Taylor Gray
Savannah Olive, b. 8/30/2004 in Lebanon; Leonard Gray and Ericka Gray
Timothy Scott, b. 12/20/2001 in Lebanon; Scott Gray and Tammy Gray
Tristan Joshua, b. 5/28/1999 in Lebanon; Michael Gray and Laura Gray
Tyler Benjamin, b. 9/7/2001 in Lebanon; Benjamin Gray and Margaret Gray
Zackery Todd, b. 3/12/1998 in Lebanon; Todd Christopher Gray and Brenda L. Giesing Gray

GREEN,
Ann, b. 1/25/1940 in Orford; third; William E. Green (guide, hunter, Trenton, NJ) and Phyllis Boyer (Riverton, NJ)
Beatrice Anne, b. 12/1/1999 in Lebanon; David Green and Juliette Bianco
Clayton Mark, b. 6/3/1961 in Lebanon; third; William E. Green III (linotype op., Orford) and Donna Lee Morris (Massillon, OH)
David Matthew, b. 1/26/1965 in Lebanon; William E. Green III (lino. op., Orford) and Donna L. Morris (Massillon, OH)

Elisabeth Fisk, b. 8/23/1944 in Hanover; first; William E. Green, Jr. (US Army, Trenton, NJ) and Rebecca M. Munn (Lyme)
Jesse Scott, b. 6/7/1968 in Haverhill; W. Peter Green (laborer, 33, Orford) and Kathryn G. Fitzgerald (26, Hanover)
John Peter, b. 7/21/1963 in Lebanon; William Peter Green (carpenter, Orford) and Kathryn G. Fitzgerald (Hanover)
Maxwell Augustus, b. 5/30/1998 in Lebanon; David Lynn Green and Juliette Marie Bianco
Pamela, b. 1/15/1955 in Lebanon; first; Peter Green (laborer, Orford) and Barbara A. Whitcher (Warren)
Theresa Gale, b. 7/2/1961 in Lebanon; first; Peter Green (printer, Orford) and Kathryn G. Fitzgerald (Hanover)
Thomas Daniel, b. 4/6/1963 in Lebanon; William E. Green (linotype operator, Orford) and Donna L. Morris (Massillon, OH)
William E., 3rd, b. 1/28/1937 in Orford; second; William E. Green, Jr. (sportsman, Trenton, NJ) and Phyllis Boyer (Riverton, NJ)
William Peter, b. 5/13/1935 in Orford; first; William Edgar Green, Jr. (Trenton, NJ) and Phyllis Boyer (Riverton, NJ)

GREENL[E]Y,
daughter, b. 5/21/1890 in Orford; third; S. E. Greenly (farmer, 32, MN) and Lavina E. Rugg (23, Orford)
daughter, b. 1/8/1894 in Orford; fourth; Samuel E. Greenley (farmer, 35, St. Paul, MN) and Lavina L. Rugg (27, Orford)
son, b. 6/20/1897; fifth; Samuel E. Greenley (farmer, 39) and Lavina L. Rugg (30, Orford)
son, b. 2/4/1900 in Orford; sixth; Samuel E. Greenley (farmer, 42) and Lavina L. Rugg (33, Orford)
Chester George, b. 3/30/1904 in Orford; seventh; Samuel E. Greenley (farmer, 46) and Lavina L. Rugg (37, Orford)
Helen Theresa, b. 9/9/1913 in Orford; first; Vernon M. Greenly (farmer, 26, Orford) and Isabel Wilson (22, Deering)
Mabel J., b. 1/14/1907; eighth; Samuel E. Greenly (farmer, 48) and Lavina L. Rugg (40, Orford)

GRIFFITHS,
Joseph Morgan, b. 7/14/1960 in Lebanon; first; Griffith M. Griffiths (farmer, Llanbor, Wales) and Sarah Ditton (Galway, Ireland)

GROSS,
Miranda Lee, b. 6/6/1984; Brice Gross and Ellen Gross

Trevor Brice, b. 7/8/1985; Brice Gross and Ellen Gross

GUILMETTE,
David Edward, b. 2/20/1941 in Hanover; first; Edward D. Guilmette (salesman, Rochester, VT) and Erma E. Ford (Rochester, VT)

GUND,
John P., b. 7/3/1972 in Hanover; Henry Gund, III (40, Minneapolis, MN) and Marilyn J. Hantia (35, Hutchinson, KS)

GUNN,
Frances Bennett, b. 2/12/1984; Robert Gunn and Anne Gunn

HACKETT,
child, b. 10/20/1887 in Orford; first; David Hackett (farmer, 31, Haverhill) and Edna A. Marsh (17, W. Fairlee, VT)
son, b. 8/20/1889 in Orford; second; David D. Hackett (laborer, 32, Haverhill) and Edna A. Marsh (19, Fairlee, VT)
son, b. 9/22/1891 in Orford; third; David E. Hackett (laborer, 33, Haverhill) and Anna A. Marsh (21, W. Fairlee, VT)

HADLOCK,
Katie Ann, b. 5/3/1986; Roger Hadlock and Deborah Hadlock

HALL,
son, b. 7/21/1906 in Orford; third; Fred P. Hall (farmer, 39, Landaff) and Mary L. Chandler (35, Orford)
son, b. 3/29/1912 in Orford; fourth; Fred P. Hall (farmer, 45, Landaff) and Mary L. Chandler (40, Orford)
Ada J., b. 10/30/1902 in Orford; seventh; William B. Hall (farmer, 47, Manchester) and Ada J. Kibbee (Tunbridge, VT)
Gertrude L., b. 6/10/1905 in Orford; eighth; William B. Hall (farmer, 49, Manchester) and Adra J. Kibbee (39, Tunbridge, VT)
Graeme Edward, b. 4/22/1979 in Lebanon; David Hall and Meriel Hall
J. Harold, b. 9/30/1897; first; Fred P. Hall (farmer, 30, Landaff) and Mary L. Chandler (26, Orford)
Kenneth Learned, Jr., b. 5/30/1943 in Hanover; third; Kenneth L. Hall (farm manager, Alexandria) and Rosalie M. Fisher (Thornton)

Lucy Viola, b. 3/15/1908; ninth; William B. Hall (farmer, 52, Manchester) and Adra J. Kibbee (42, Tunbridge, VT)
Richard Kinsley, b. 10/1/1927 in Hanover; first; Henry K. Hall (farmer, Lyme) and Alice M. Robinson (Haverhill)
William B., Jr., b. 10/22/1900 in Orford; sixth; William B. Hall (farmer, 44, Manchester) and Ada Kibbee (35, Tunbridge, VT)

HAMILTON,
Leslie Jean, b. 2/28/1964 in Hanover; Richard C. Hamilton (school principal, Boston, MA) and Jean C. Paige (Quincy, MA)

HAMMOND,
daughter, b. 3/24/1891 in Orford; first; Eugene C. Hammond (laborer, 23, Lyme) and Olive S. Stetson (20, Orford)

HANNAFORD,
Hazen A., b. 5/31/1887 in Orford; second; Henry A. Hannaford (farmer, 29, Fairlee, VT) and Eva M. Rhodes (23, Orford)

HANSON,
Raechel Ann, b. 9/9/1990 in Hanover; Jonathan Hanson and Jeannie Hanson
Elizabeth, b. 10/11/1994 in Lebanon; Jonathan Garner Hanson and Jeannie Kathleen Reilly Hanson

HARRINGTON,
stillborn daughter, b. 8/4/1890 in Orford; fourth; Charles S. Harrington (compositor, 35, Roxbury, MA) and Clara H. Dayton (33, Orford); residence – Cambridgeport, MA
Joanne Lynn, b. 10/8/1962 in Haverhill; first; Cedrick E. Harrington (linotype op., Middlebury, VT) and Priscilla J. Franklin (Hanover)
Marcus Edward, b. 11/9/1965 in Haverhill; Cedrick E. Harrington (lino. op., Middlebury, VT) and Priscilla J. Franklin (Hanover)
Thomas Arthur, b. 6/30/1971 in Haverhill; Cedrick E. Harrington (29, Middlebury, VT) and Priscilla J. Franklin (27, Hanover)

HARRIS,
Kathryn Anne, b. 12/27/1984; Mark Harris and Joan Harris
Kyra Ann, b. 8/10/1982; Mark Harris and Joan Harris
Louis Allen, b. 9/11/1987; Mark Harris and Joan Harris

Marjorie Cornelia, b. 6/14/1908; first; Willard R. Harris (teacher, 27, Piermont) and Maude E. McPherson (23, Jordan River, NS)
Willard Robert, b. 3/22/1911; second; Willard R. Harris (teacher, Piermont) and Maude E. McPherson (Jordon River, NS)

HART,
Joshua James, b. 7/15/1975 in Hanover; James W. Hart (28, Canaan) and Darlene E. Ricker (20, Flint, MI)
Taunia L., b. 9/17/1972 in Haverhill; James W. Hart (25, Hanover) and Darlene E. Ricker (18, Flint, MI)

HATCH,
stillborn son, b. 7/28/1903 in Orford; first; Bert E. Hatch (barber, 23, Haverhill) and Addie M. Crown (24, Canada)

HEATH,
daughter, b. 4/16/1892 in Orford; seventh; Alvah B. Heath (farmer, 32, Reading, VT) and Mary Howland (32, Landaff)

HEBB,
Anna Pierce, b. 7/26/2004 in Lebanon; Timothy Hebb and Tina Hebb
Emily Lyn, b. 7/18/2001 in Lebanon; Jeff Hebb and Jessica Jorgensen
Jeffrey A., b. 5/17/1972 in Hanover; Allan F. Hebb (25, Bradford, VT) and Jane E. Pierce (23, Hanover)
Jennifer Jane, b. 12/3/1975 in Hanover; Allan F. Hebb (29, Bradford, VT) and Jane E. Pierce (27, Hanover)
Timothy Michael, b. 8/10/1979 in Hanover; Allan Hebb and Jane Hebb

HELTKAMP,
Robert Earl, b. 5/29/1934 in Woodsville; third; Donald N. Heltkamp (mechanic, Brooklyn, NY) and Marion Renfrew (Littleton)

HENDERSON,
William, b. 6/30/1987; Brian Henderson and Phyllis Henderson

HENDRICK,
Dylan Alexander, b. 5/16/2004 in Lebanon; Richard Hendrick and Delia Hendrick

HERBERT,
James Melvin, b. 6/20/1939 in Burlington, VT; first; James M. Herbert (forestry, Bolton, VT) and Clara Jane Dyke (Morrisville, VT)

HEWES,
Dorothy Lucille, b. 7/10/1929 in Orford; sixth; Fred Hewes (farmer, Lyme) and Ida Angell (Providence, RI)

HIBBARD,
Aaron Bruce, b. 11/1/1992 in Lebanon; Lawrence Hibbard and Karen Hibbard
Clarence D., b. 1/30/1895 in Orford; second; George A. Hibbard (farming, 35, Piermont) and Emma A. Whitham (22, Concord)
Ernest Earl, b. 9/28/1896; third; George A. Hibbard (farming, 36, Piermont) and Emma A. Whitman (23, Concord)
John, b. 5/13/1909; fourth; George A. Hibbard (farmer, 49, Piermont) and Emma A. Witham (37, Concord)
Neil Powers, b. 11/5/1933 in Orford; second; Carl Hibbard (laborer, Concord) and Bessie Ricker (Vershire, VT)
Sylvia Joyce, b. 6/14/1931 in Orford; first; Carl Hibbard (caretaker, Concord, VT) and Bessie Ricker (Vershire, VT)
Tanner Lee, b. 10/28/1994 in Lebanon; Lawrence Lloyd Hibbard and Karen Lee Landgraf Hibbard

HIGGINS,
Charles Lloyd, b. 12/18/1982; Frank Higgins and Theresa Higgins
Paul Robert, b. 7/17/1984; Francis Higgins and Theresa Higgins

HILL,
son, b. 11/21/1889 in Orford; third; Sylvester W. Hill (farmer, 48, Orford) and Nellie B. Chesley (41, Orford)
Ethel A., b. 5/17/1907; third; George T. Hill (laborer, 27, Piermont) and Flora L. Davis (23, McIndoes, VT)
Kevin Maurice, b. 7/10/1973 in Hanover; Richard H. Hill (27, Hanover) and Kathy Louise King (22, Hanover)
Naomi Lynn, b. 9/3/1992 in Lebanon; Gary Hill and Mary Hill

HOEHL,
Michael James, b. 6/6/1984; William Hoehl and Patricia Hoehl

HOLDEN,
Ashley Marie, b. 10/6/1993 in Lebanon; Stanley Frederick Holden, Jr. and Marie Lynn Taylor Holden

HOOD,
Harold Morris, b. 5/26/1943 in Haverhill; fourth; Harold R. Hood (farmer, Topsham, VT) and Wilhelmina Sawyer (Piermont)

HOOK,
Brian James, b. 7/20/1988; James Hook and Brenda Hook
Bruce Dale, b. 10/23/1955 in Haverhill; sixth; Lester E. Hook (manuscript clerk, Stamford, CT) and Marian A. Lanefski (Stamford, CT)
David William, b. 6/9/1990 in Hanover; James Hook and Brenda Hook
James Lester, b. 8/26/1953 in Haverhill; fourth; Lester E. Hook (machinist, Stamford, CT) and Marian Lanefski (Stamford, CT)
Jennifer Ann, b. 9/25/1985; James Hook and Brenda Hook
Martha Anne, b. 7/21/1957 in Haverhill; sixth; Lester Ellis Hook (maint. worker, Stamford, CT) and Marian A. Lanefski (Stamford, CT)
Ruth Marian, b. 4/1/1951 in Haverhill; second; Lester E. Hook (milk carrier, Stamford, CT) and Marian A. Lanefski (Stamford, CT)
Sarah Elizabeth, b. 10/27/1983; James Hook and Brenda Hook
Stephen Ellis, b. 10/23/1955 in Haverhill; fifth; Lester E. Hook (manuscript clerk, Stamford, CT) and Marian A. Lanefski (Stamford, CT)
Susan Louise, b. 4/1/1951 in Haverhill; third; Lester E. Hook (milk carrier, Stamford, CT) and Marian A. Lanefski (Stamford, CT)

HORTON,
child, b. 2/23/1887 in Orford; eighth; William H. Horton (farmer, Barnard, VT) and Mary J. Chesley (Barford, Canada)
Bernie M., b. 11/25/1895 in Orford; fourth; Walter S. Horton (farming, 51, Barnard, VT) and Mary M. Stone (37, Orford)
Byron Walter, b. 7/3/1914 in Orford; fourth; Walter A. Horton (clerk, 28, Orford) and Bessie A. Kenyon (25, Orford)
Claude Albert, b. 3/31/1918 in Orford; sixth; Walter A. Horton (farmer, Orford) and Bessie A. Kenyon (Orford)
Clyde Elbert, b. 3/31/1918 in Orford; fifth; Walter A. Horton (farmer, Orford) and Bessie A. Kenyon (Orford)

Floyd Kenyon, b. 3/22/1908; first; Walter A. Horton (farmer, 21, Orford) and Bessie A. Kenyon (19, Orford)
Jesse Carl, b. 10/27/1909; second; Walter A. Horton (farmer, 23, Orford) and Bessie A. Kenyon (20, Orford)
VeNeil Maude, b. 7/17/1911; third; Walter A. Horton (carpenter, Orford) and Bessie A. Kenyon (Orford)

HOWARD,
child, b. 10/31/1887 in Orford; fifth; Richardson Howard (farmer, 44, Lyme) and Julia Cutting (37, Canada)
Zadok C., b. 2/12/1893 in Orford; sixth; Rich. A. Howard (laborer, 48, Orford) and Julia A. Cutting (41, Canada)

HUBBARD,
Florence E., b. 4/1/1907; second; Willie E. Hubbard (laborer, 24, McIndoe, VT) and Ida B. Hall (20, Orford)
Leroy Melvin, b. 4/30/1908; third; Willie E. Hubbard (laborer, 25, Victory, VT) and Ida B. Hall (21, Orford)

HUCKINS,
Barbara Alice, b. 5/12/1937 in Hanover; sixth; George C. Huckins (laborer, Orford) and Hazel M. Williams (Hardwick, VT)
Clayton Maynard, b. 3/17/1932 in Hanover; fourth; George C. Huckins (laborer, Orford) and Hazel M. Williams (Hardwick, VT)
Frances Mary, b. 11/18/1928 in Hanover; second; George C. Huckins (mechanic, Orford) and Hazel M. Williams (Hardwick, VT)
G. Clifton, b. 1/28/1902 in Orford; second; George M. Huckins (farmer, 39, Wentworth) and Ella S. Lamprey (Orford)
George Roger, b. 6/8/1927 in Hanover; first; George C. Huckins (mill hand, Orford) and Hazel M. Williams (Hardwick, VT)
Gladys M., b. 11/9/1895 in Orford; first; George M. Huckins (carpenter, 32, Wentworth) and Ella S. Lamprey (28, Orford)
Helen Anne, b. 5/27/1934 in Hanover; fifth; G. Clifton Huckins (laborer, Orford) and Hazel M. Williams (Hardwick, VT)
Shirley Evelyn, b. 7/21/1930 in Hanover; third; George C. Huckins (laborer, Orford) and Hazel Williams (Hardwick, VT)

HUNTINGTON,
stillborn son, b. 7/30/1957 in Hanover; third; Sumner Huntington (st. hy. dep., Orford) and Bernice Bertha Bean (Newbury, VT)

Cynthia Ann, b. 8/1/1954 in Hanover; second; Sumner Huntington (laborer, Orford) and Bernice Bertha Bean (Newbury, VT)
Eric Scott, b. 3/25/1960 in Plymouth; first; Harold L. Huntington (mechanic, Barre, VT) and Mary J. Fields (Etna)
Ila Lucy, b. 12/2/1926; third; Guy Huntington (mechanic, Corinth, VT) and Mildred Cummings (Thetford, VT)
Jeffrey Lawrence, b. 3/7/1965 in Hanover; Harold L. Huntington (mechanic, Barre, VT) and Mary J. Fields (Etna)
Sumner Dana, b. 11/25/1924; second; Guy Huntington (mechanic, Corinth, VT) and Mildred Cummings (Thetford, VT)
Sumner Dana, Jr., b. 7/9/1946 in Hanover; first; Sumner Huntington (mail messenger, Orford) and Bernice B. Bean (Newbury, VT)

JACKSON,
Helen Margaret, b. 9/18/1912 in Orford; fourth; Charles S. Jackson (farmer, 38, Dudsville, PQ) and Elizabeth Hearn (30, Cookshire, PQ)
Howard Charles, b. 12/20/1908; second; Charles S. Jackson (farmer, 35, PQ) and Elizabeth Hearn (26, Cookshire, PQ)
Raymond Joseph, b. 8/15/1914 in Orford; fifth; Charles S. Jackson (farmer, 40, Dudswell, PQ) and Elizabeth Hearn (32, Cookshire, PQ)
Stuart A., b. 6/2/1907; first; Charles Jackson (blacksmith, 35, Dudsville, PQ) and Elizabeth A. Hearn (25, Hookshin, PQ)
William Herbert, b. 12/1/1910; third; Charles S. Jackson (farmer, 37, Dudsville, PQ) and Elizabeth Hearn (28, Cookshire, PQ)

JASPER,
son, b. 5/6/1930 in Hanover; second; Andrew J. Jasper (laborer, Goffstown) and Christia A. Morey (Orford)

JENKINS,
Leslie Forrest, b. 8/9/1946 in Orford; Leslie F. Jenkins (truck driver, Farmington, ME) and Barbara D. Ritchie (Gardiner, ME); residence – Farmington, ME

JENKS,
William Delbert L., b. 9/4/1927 in Orford; first; Delbert Jenks (laborer) and Josephine Learned (Orford)

JEWETT,
Jeffrey Matthew, b. 7/19/1974 in Hanover; Peter M. Jewett (32, Bath, ME) and Susan A. Pratt (27, Montpelier, VT)
Jonathan M., b. 8/14/1972 in Hanover; Peter M. Jewett (30, Bath, ME) and Susan A. Pratt (25, Montpelier, VT)
Julia Marie, b. 12/12/1969 in Hanover; Peter M. Jewett (27, Bath, ME) and Susan Ann Pratt (22, Montpelier, VT)

JOHNSON,
child, b. 1/15/1887 in Orford; third; Oscar D. Johnson (hotel keeper, Norwich, VT) and Mary E. Babcock (Thetford, VT)
son, b. 12/16/1892 in Orford; second; Scott S. Johnson (farmer, 32, Stratford) and Maria C. Shurburn (27, Orford)
Bernie, b. 8/15/1895 in Orford; third; Scott S. Johnson (farming, 35, Stratford) and M. C. Shurburn (30, Orford)
Cortlyn Virginia, b. 4/24/1985; Mark Johnson and Nance Johnson
Craig Arby, b. 7/12/1954 in Hanover; second; Arby N. Johnson, Jr. (dairy farmer, Woodsville) and Lois Fay Webler (Washington, DC)
Geraldine, b. 1/3/1950 in Lebanon; second; Robert L. Johnson (const. eng., S. Deerfield) and Lurlyn E. Dyke (S. Newbury, VT)
Gregory Louis, b. 10/17/1959; Robert L. Johnson and Lurline E. Dyke
Paula Elizabeth, b. 3/5/1952 in Lebanon; third; Arvid H. Johnson (contractor, Minneapolis) and Mary E. Strickland (Gouldsboro, NC)

JOHNSTON,
Elissa Grace, b. 1/27/1999 in Lebanon; Neil Johnston and Denise Johnston

JONES,
Brian Forrest, b. 8/10/1958 in Hanover; first; Robert C. Jones (teach. & inn, Wilkes-Barre, PA) and Esther M. Stephenson (Philadelphia, PA)

KAROL,
Fitzhugh Baylies, b. 5/31/1982; John Karol and Portia Karol

KASFIR,
Elizabetta, b. 1/14/1975 in Hanover; Nelson M. Kasfir (35, OH) and Sidney C. Littlefield (35, NH)

KELLEHER,
Kristen Elizabeth, b. 8/1/1978 in Hanover; James J. Kelleher (26, MA) and Barbara L. Hickey (25, MA)

KELLEY,
Fisher James, b. 11/1/2000 in Lebanon; Michael Kelley and Sperry Wilson Kelley
Harvey Wood, b. 7/12/1998 in Lebanon; Michael James Kelley and Sperry W. Wilson-Kelley

KENDALL,
Max, b. 4/10/1904 in Orford; first; Max Kendall and Mabel M. Davis (18, Munsonville, PQ); residence – Fairlee

KENDELL,
Lee James, b. 1/14/1980 in Lebanon; James Kendell and Nancy Kendell

KENNESON,
Robert Lee, b. 8/6/1953 in Haverhill; fourth; Walter E. Kenneson (laborer, Lowell, MA) and Pearl L. Moses (Hanover)
Sandra Lee, b. 6/1/1952 in Haverhill; second; Walter E. Kenneson (laborer, Lowell, MA) and Pearl L. Moses (Hanover)

KENYON,
Bessie A., b. 9/6/1889 in Orford; second; Carlos M. Kenyon (farmer, 38, Plainfield) and Abbie M. Terrell (23, Canaan)
Calvin, b. 3/18/1915 in Orford; second; stillborn; Walter C. Kenyon (merchant, 28, Orford) and Alice M. Ramsey (31, Wentworth)
Jesse R., b. 9/6/1889 in Orford; third; Carlos M. Kenyon (farmer, 38, Plainfield) and Abbie M. Terrell (23, Canaan)
Mumford Walter, b. 9/18/1920 in Orford; fourth; Walter C. Kenyon (merchant, Orford) and Alice Ramsey (Wentworth)
Priscilla, b. 1/27/1918 in Orford; third; Walter C. Kenyon (merchant, Orford) and Alice Ramsey (Wentworth)
Ruth Abbie, b. 1/2/1923; fifth; Walter C. Kenyon (merchant, Orford) and Alice M. Ramsey (Wentworth)

KIBBEE,
Eugene Edmund, b. 12/14/1908; fourth; Edmund M. Kibbee (farmer, 28, Orford) and Rose Burnon (24, Norwich, VT)

KIDDER,
Fred Albion, Jr., b. 10/28/1970 in Haverhill; Fred A. Kidder, Sr. (22, Lebanon) and Pamela J. Sanborn (16, Woodsville)

KILGORE,
Kendall James, b. 9/18/1943 in Hanover; fourth; Roland H. Kilgore (logger, Smithfield, ME) and Eleanor L. Downer (Lunenburg, VT)

KIMBALL,
daughter, b. 6/19/1894 in Orford; second; Charles H. Kimball (farmer, 34, Wentworth) and Carrie M. Webb (27, Lyme)
Forest Sidney, b. 12/16/1916 in Orford; first; Philimon Kimball (carpenter, 22, Westmore, VT) and Mary Smith (19, Orford)
Philemon, Jr., b. 1/14/1918 in Orford; second; Philemon Kimball (carpenter, Westmore, VT) and Mary C. Smith (Orford)

KISSICK,
Caroline Williams, b. 10/13/1993 in Lebanon; William Lee Kissick, Jr. and Catherine Hale McGrath

KLING,
Ernst Madsen, b. 8/24/1982; Peter Kling and Susan Kling
Kristen Augusta, b. 10/28/1984; Peter Kling and Susan Kling

KNAPP,
Allen, b. 8/26/1987; Dale Knapp and Grita Knapp
Avery John, b. --/--/1989
Brian Ray, b. 2/16/1983; Dale Knapp and Grita Knapp
Erik James, b. 12/7/1997 in Lebanon; David Kevin Knapp and Marcia Lynn Anderson Knapp
Judy Ann, b. 10/23/1975 in Lebanon; Dale H. Knapp (24, NH) and Jean M. Pushee (22, NH)

KNOX,
Peter Gaillard, III, b. 7/29/1998 in Lebanon; Peter Gaillard Knox, Jr. and Cindy A. Wells Knox

KORPELA,
stillborn daughter, b. 9/9/1956 in Hanover; first; Allen Edwin Korpela (law editor, VT) and Janet Winn (Rochester)

KOSNIK,
Ian Sullivan, b. 9/17/1997 in Lebanon; Christopher Paul Kosnik and Lindsay Elaine Hance Kosnik

LABERGE,
son, b. 12/10/1902 in Orford; first; Joseph Laberge (laborer, 2-, Montreal, Canada) and Ardell Lamontagne (Piermont)

LACKEY,
Jennifer Leigh, b. 9/15/1969 in Haverhill; Leroy H. Lackey (18, Cambridge, MA) and Paula E. Johnson (17, Lebanon)

LADD,
son, b. 6/3/1888; John H. Ladd (farmer, 25, Wentworth) and Laura B. Pike (19, Haverhill)
son, b. 10/2/1891 in Orford; first; John H. Ladd (farmer, 29, Meredith) and Laura E. Pike (23, Haverhill)
daughter, b.9/24/1894 in Orford; third; Horace F. Ladd (farmer, 26, Waterford, VT) and Carlie M. Poor (25, Danville, VT)
daughter, b. 6/3/1898 in Orford; fourth; Horace F. Ladd (farming, 30, Waterford, VT) and Carlye M. Poor (29, Danville, VT)
daughter, b. 2/8/1900 in Orford; fifth; Horace F. Ladd (laborer, 32, Danville, VT) and Carlie M. Poor (30, Waterford, VT)
Avis Amonetta, b. 4/22/1930 in Warren; first; Oscar Ladd (laborer, Pike) and Lindsie Mae Perry (Haverhill)
John Edward, b. 7/8/1918 in Orford; first; Charles P. Ladd (laborer, Haverhill) and Florence B. Abbott (New York, NY)
Maud Evelyn, b. 3/5/1914 in Orford; first; Burns H. Ladd (laborer, 22, Orford) and Edna F. Marsh (20, Orford)

LADEAU,
Albert Charles, b. 6/29/1909; second; Albert C. Ladeau (laborer, 22, Orford) and Abbey Cushman (18, Barnet, VT)
Ethel Florence, b. 10/3/1910; third; Albert C. Ladeau (laborer, 24, Orford) and Abbie P. Cushman (20, McIndoes Falls, VT)

LAFOE,
Gladys Rosie, b. 9/4/1910; seventh; John E. Lafoe (laborer, 43, Hartford, CT) and Rosie L. Morrison (32, Lemington, VT)

LAMERE,
daughter, b. 7/25/1898 in Orford; second; Alec. Lamere (laborer, 35, Three Rivers, PQ) and Ella E. Thompson (18, Derry)

LAMORE,
daughter, b. 1/27/1897; first; Alec Lamore (laborer, 34, Three Rivers, PQ) and Ella E. Thompson (17, Derry)

LAMOTT,
Dean Elwyn, b. 5/21/1919 in Orford; second; Elwin A. LaMott (butcher, Lyme) and Lela M. Willis (Orford)
Paul Irving, b. 6/20/1917 in Orford; first; Elwyn A. LaMott (miller, Lyme) and Lela M. Willis (Orford)

LAMPHERE,
Sierra Jade, b. 3/22/1999 in Lebanon; John Lamphere and Lisa Gagne

LANDGRAF[F],
Gregory Wayne, b. 7/3/1962 in Lebanon; third; Bruce T. Landgraf (tool, die mak., Harvey, IL) and Janet Lee Willis (Orford)
Karen Lee, b. 7/6/1958 in Lebanon; second; Bruce T. Landgraf (laborer, Harvey, IL) and Janet L. Willis (Orford)
Megan Ann, b. 12/20/1997 in Lebanon; Michael Bruce Landgraf and Kathleen Joan Murray Landgraf
Michael Bruce, b. 4/14/1956 in Lebanon; first; Bruce Ted Landgraf (factory worker, Harvey, IL) and Janet Lee Willis (Orford)
Ryan Michael, b. 12/20/1997 in Lebanon; Michael Bruce Landgraf and Kathleen Joan Murray Landgraf
Sarah Elizabeth, b. 3/23/1995 in Lebanon; Michael Bruce Landgraff and Kathleen Joan Murray Landgraf

LANDS,
Lawrence E., b. 9/13/1907; first; Leon R. Lands (farmer, 24, Fairfax, VT) and Mary R. L. Still (22, Claremont)

LANGE,
Christine Rose, b. 11/13/1966 in Barre, VT; John C. Lange (manager, Hartford, CT) and Jonilee Pierson (Woodsville)

LAVIGNE,
Georgia Baker, b. 2/6/1915 in Orford; fourth; Ezra Lavigne (laborer, 42, Bradford, VT) and Rosa Thebodeau (34, Danville, Canada)

LAWSON,
Corey Payson, b. 11/17/1979 in Lebanon; Terry Lawson and Cynthia Lawson

LEA,
Syndey Portia Barone, b. 12/18/1991 in Lebanon; Sydney Lea and Robin Lea

LEARNED,
son, b. 8/12/1906 in Orford; fifth; William E. Learned (farmer, 38, Wentworth) and Ida M. Bailey (27, Wakefield, MA)
Alpha B., b. 5/11/1917 in Orford; ninth; William E. Learned (farmer, Wentworth) and Ida May Bailey (Wakefield, MA)
Charles W., b. 10/25/1896; first; Jonas E. Learned (farming, 29, Orford) and Louise Laflame (17, Haverhill)
Chastina M., b. 7/1/1903 in Orford; third; William E. Learned (farmer, 30, Wentworth) and Ida M. Bailey (23, Andover, MA)
Clara Roxianna, b. 10/5/1900 in Orford; first; William E. Learned (laborer, 27, Wentworth) and Ida May Bailey (23, Wakefield, MA)
Florence Gertrude, b. 7/31/1915 in Orford; eighth; William E. Learned (farmer, 42, Wentworth) and Ida M. Bailey (36, Wakefield, MA)
George Ernest, b. 8/4/1908; sixth; William E. Learned (farmer, 32, Wentworth) and Ida M. Bailey (29, Wakefield, MA)
Hattie Flora, b. 2/8/1905 in Orford; fourth; William E. Learned (farmer, 31, Wentworth) and Ida M. Bailey (26, Wakefield, MA)
James William, b. 11/16/1901 in Orford; second; William E. Larned (farmer, 28, Wentworth) and Ida M. Bailey (23, Andover, MA)
Josie Delma, b. 5/12/1899 in Orford; second; Jonas G. Learned (farmer, 32, Orford) and Louise Laflam (20, Haverhill)
Vera Grace, b. 4/2/1910; seventh; William E. Learned (farmer, 36, Wentworth) and Ida M. Bailey (31, Wakefield, MA)

LEBARON,
Michael Dashnau, b. 6/17/1981 in Hanover; Barry LeBaron and Carol LeBaron

LEBERGE,
daughter, b. 3/28/1904 in Orford; second; Joseph Leberge (laborer, 27, Canada) and Ardell Lamontagne (20, Piermont)

LEE,
daughter, b. 7/14/1900 in Orford; first; Henry Lee (laborer, 36, Manchester) and Julia A. Thompson (16, Chicopee, MA)

LENO,
Beatrice Louise, b. 6/18/1917 in Orford; second; George Leno (farm laborer, Middlebury, VT) and Louise Hutchins (Ticonderoga, NY)

Burnice Luceal, b. 6/18/1917 in Orford; third; George Leno (farm laborer, Middlebury, VT) and Louise Hutchins (Ticonderoga, NY)

LESLIE,
Guy S., b. 12/14/1902 in Orford; first; Charles P. Leslie (painter, 3-, Orford) and Laura L. Spencer (Haverhill, MA)

LEWIS,
Kullen Marshall, b. 4/19/2003 in Lebanon; Eric Lewis and Krys Lewis

LIBBEY,
Menta Bell, b. 4/25/1887 in Orford; second; Horatio K. Libbey (farmer, Warren) and Rebecca J. Huckins (Warren)

LINDSAY,
Ernest A., b. 3/23/1887 in Orford; second; Thomas S. Lindsay (tinman, Adams, MA) and Maggie E. Harris (Ft. Edwards, NY)

LISTER,
Declan Gordon, b. 8/12/2003 in Lebanon; Jeff Lister and Jennifer Dyke

Grace Marie, b. 10/25/2001 in Lebanon; Jeff Lister and Jennifer Lister

LITCHFIELD,
Deborah Blanchard, b. 4/8/1955 in Hanover; ninth; Wilson G.
  Litchfield (farm mgr., Oak Bluffs, MA) and Arlene A. Blanchard
  (Farmington, ME)

LOCKE,
Addison Margaret, b. 12/1/2002 in Lebanon; Andrew Locke and
  Heather Scholl

LOUGEE,
Jessie May, b. 8/5/1909; first; Lydia M. Lougee (16, Piermont)

LUCE,
son, b. 9/9/1901 in Orford; Leslie F. Luce (farmer, 34, Tunbridge,
  VT) and Rose Hubbard (23, Canada)
Alice, b. 10/3/1895 in Orford; first; Leslie F. Luce (laborer, 28,
  Tunbridge, VT) and Rose E. Hubbard (19, PQ)
Perley Guy, b. 7/24/1903 in Orford; fifth; Leslie F. Luce (laborer, 35,
  Tunbridge, VT) and Rose E. Hubbard (27, PQ)

LYNES,
Madeline Rose, b. 8/10/1928 in Hanover; first; Harold Lynes (farmer,
  E. Hardwick, VT) and Veva Davis (Littleton)

MACE,
Brittany Elizabeth, b. 12/5/1985; John Mace and Jody Ann Mace
Gavin Ian, b. 6/17/1982; John Mace and Jodyann Mace

MACK,
son, b. 8/2/1912 in Orford; fifth; Fred Mack (farmer, 37, Piermont)
  and Mabel A. Ramsey (25, Orford)
son, b. 9/28/1922; ninth; Fred Mack (farmer, Piermont) and Mabel
  Ramsey (Orford)
son, b. 8/4/1924; tenth; Fred Mack (farmer, Piermont) and Mabel
  Ramsey (Orford)
Adelbert Wayne, b. 7/19/1916 in Orford; seventh; Fred Mack
  (farmer, 40, Piermont) and Mabel A. Ramsey (29, Orford)
Alfretta, b. 5/31/1904 in Orford; first; Fred Mack (farmer, 28,
  Piermont) and Mabel A. Ramsey (17, Orford)
Alice M., b. 6/29/1907; second; Fred Mack (farmer, 31, Piermont)
  and Mabel A. Ramsey (20, Orford)

Brian Lewis, b. 2/2/1957 in Hanover; second; Ralph Roger Mack (caretaker, Orford) and Helen E. McKenzie (Quincy, MA)
Evelyn Grace, b. 11/7/1914 in Orford; sixth; Fred Mack (farmer, 38, Piermont) and Mabel A. Ramsey (27, Orford)
Irene Althea, b. 12/27/1910; fourth; Fred Mack (farmer, 35, Haverhill) and Mabel A. Ramsey (24, Orford)
Ralph Roger, b. 7/9/1919 in Orford; eighth; Fred Mack (farmer, Piermont) and Mabel Ramsey (Orford)
Walter Ruel, b. 5/11/1909; third; Fred Mack (farmer, 33, Haverhill) and Mabel A. Ramsey (22, Orford)

MACQUEEN,
Maren Day, b. 11/5/2004 in Lebanon; Jeffery MacQueen and Tammy Louise Bruno

MADIGAN,
Michael Charles, b. 7/28/1978 in Haverhill; Michael C. Madigan (26, CT) and Bonnie L. Pike (25, NH)

MAGOON,
son, b. 10/1/1890 in Orford; third; Loren Magoon (laborer, 27, Corinth, VT) and Gertie D. Hackett (21, Boston, MA)
Alice, b. 1/25/1889 in Orford; second; Loren Magoon (laborer, 25, Corinth, VT) and Gertie G. Avery (19, Boston, MA)
Pauline Evelyn, b. 11/7/1944 in Haverhill; Earl E. Magoon (farmer, Corinth, VT) and Dorothy L. Eastman (St. Johnsbury, VT)

MARDEN,
Addie Martha, b. 12/27/1902 in Orford; first; George B. Marden (telegrapher, 2-, Jefferson) and Bessie E. Austin (Orford); residence – Jefferson

MARSH,
son, b. 1/29/1888; sixth; George W. Marsh (farmer, 45, W. Topsham, VT) and Mary E. Dickinson (38, W. Fairlee, VT)
daughter, b. 12/16/1890 in Orford; first; David C. Marsh (laborer, 23, W. Fairlee, VT) and Delia F. Smith (18, Corinth, VT)
son, b. 7/23/1892 in Orford; second; David C. Marsh (farmer, 24, W. Fairlee) and Delia F. Smith (19, Corinth, VT)
son, b. 2/15/1896; fourth; David C. Marsh (laborer, 29, W. Fairlee) and Delia F. Smith (24, Corinth, VT)

son, b. 6/19/1897; fifth; David C. Marsh (laborer, 30, W. Fairlee, VT) and Delia F. Smith (25, Corinth, VT)
son, b. 10/19/1898 in Orford; sixth; David C. Marsh (laborer, 31, Fairlee, VT) and Delia F. Smith (26, Corinth, VT)
son, b. 8/20/1901 in Orford; eighth; David C. Marsh (laborer, 34, W. Fairlee, VT) and Delia F. Smith (29, Corinth, VT)
son, b. 5/14/1923; second; Frank D. Marsh (farmer, Orford) and Ina W. Strue (Lyme)
stillborn daughter, b. 8/29/1945 in Orford; seventh; Ralph Marsh (chopper, Orford) and Gladys Cutler (Grafton)
daughter, b. 2/19/1952 in Orford; tenth; Ralph E. Marsh (laborer, Orford) and Gladys A. Cutler (Grafton)
Alan Trent, b. 8/24/1968 in Haverhill; Raymond L. Marsh (laborer, 28, Orford) and Betty J. Russin (26, Haverhill)
Albert Fred, b. 5/22/1927 in Orford; fourth; Frank D. Marsh (laborer, Orford) and Ina M. Strue (Lyme)
Beatrice Anna, b. 8/29/1937 in Orford; fifth; Walter Marsh (laborer, Orford) and Gladys Elliott (Littleton)
Bertram Elmer, b. 8/1/1929 in Orford; fifth; Frank D. Marsh (laborer, Orford) and Ida Millicent Strue (Lyme)
Bessie Edith, b. 9/27/1931 in Orford; fourth; Arthur L. Marsh (laborer, Orford) and Irene R. Goddard (St. Johnsbury, VT)
Beverly Jane, b. 5/3/1939 in Orford; fourth; Roy Clifton Marsh (laborer, Orford) and Grace Iola Cutler (Vershire, VT)
Beverly Jean, b. 2/25/1954 in Haverhill; second; Clinton Arthur Marsh (laborer, Orford) and Martha Lillian Tarr (Fitzwilliam)
Calvin Henry, b. 10/26/1929 in Orford; second; Arthur L. Marsh (laborer, Orford) and Irene R. Goddard (St. Johnsbury, VT)
Carl Henry, b. 3/16/1943 in Haverhill; seventh; Walter H. Marsh (lumberman, Orford) and Gladys Amy Elliott (Littleton)
Christine Mae, b. 8/27/1930 in Orford; third; Arthur Marsh (farmer, Orford) and Irene Goddard (St. Johnsbury, VT)
Clara Fern, b. 4/10/1981 in Haverhill; Scott Marsh and Deborah Marsh
Clifton Roy, b. 2/19/1934 in Orford; first; Roy Clifton Marsh (laborer, Orford) and Grace Iola Cutler (Vershire, VT)
Clyde Bert, b. 6/9/1906 in Orford; tenth; David C. Marsh (farmer, 39, W. Fairlee, VT) and Delia F. Smith (34, Corinth, VT)
Daniel Lee, b. 1/28/1955 in Orford; tenth; Ralph E. Marsh (laborer, Orford) and Gladys A. Cutler (Grafton)

Deborah Ann, b. 8/26/1961 in Lebanon; first; Henry Glenn Marsh (laborer, Orford) and Wanita Gail Marsh (Hanover)
Della F., b. 5/3/1904 in Orford; ninth; David C. Marsh (farmer, 37, W. Fairlee) and Delia F. Smith (32, Corinth)
Diana Carol, b. 8/8/1943 in Orford; seventh; Leon C. Marsh (laborer, Orford) and Irene M. Elliott (Littleton)
Dorothy Irene, b. 11/12/1935 in Orford; fifth; Leon Marsh (farmer, Orford) and Irene Elliott (Littleton)
Earle Elmer, b. 3/4/1935 in Haverhill; seventh; Arthur Marsh (laborer, Orford) and Irene Goddard (St. Johnsbury, VT)
Edna I., b. 10/11/1893 in Orford; third; David C. Marsh (laborer, 26, W. Fairlee) and Delia F. Smith (21, Corinth, VT)
Edward Arthur, b. 4/9/1947 in Woodsville; second; Ernest E. Marsh (farmer, Enfield) and Erma May Tarr (Marlboro)
Ellen Doris, b. 3/10/1905 in Orford; first; Elwin D. Marsh (laborer, 22, W. Fairlee, VT) and Florea A. Bailey (17, Orford)
Elsie Marian, b. 7/31/1925; third; Frank D. Marsh (farmer, Orford) and Ina M. Strue (Lyme)
Elwin E., b. 10/2/1938 in Orford; fourth; Ralph E. Marsh (laborer, Orford) and Gladys A. Cutler (Grafton)
Ernest Eugene, b. 9/10/1928 in Enfield; first; Walter H. Marsh (farmer, Orford) and Reta Goddard (Orleans, VT)
Ernest Eugene, Jr., b. 4/9/1947 in Woodsville; first; Ernest E. Marsh (farmer, Enfield) and Erma May Tarr (Marlboro)
Evelyn Vernie, b. 5/8/1915 in Orford; fourteenth; David C. Marsh (farmer, W. Fairlee, VT) and Delia F. Smith (Corinth, VT)
Floyde Kenneth, b. 7/15/1943 in Orford; sixth; Ralph E. Marsh (laborer, Orford) and Gladys A. Cutler (Grafton)
Fred Allen, b. 8/22/1935 in Orford; first; Glenn Marsh (farmer, Orford) and Verna Hibbard (Lyme)
Fred Clayton, b. 1/12/1928 in Orford; first; Fred C. Marsh (farmer, Orford) and Dorothy M. Merrill (Deerfield)
Garold James, b. 1/12/1941 in Orford; fifth; Roy Clifton Marsh (laborer, Orford) and Grace Iola Cutler (Vershire, VT)
George Elmer, b. 5/21/1940 in Haverhill; sixth; Walter H. Marsh (laborer, Orford) and Gladys Amy Elliott (Littleton)
Glenn, b. 10/5/1913 in Orford; thirteenth; David C. Marsh (farmer, 45, W. Fairlee, VT) and Delia F. Smith (41, Corinth, VT)
Grace Ina, b. 5/5/1933 in Orford; seventh; Frank D. Marsh (laborer, Orford) and Ina Stores (Lyme)
Hannah Maria, b. 9/23/1983; Scott Marsh and Deborah Marsh

Henry Glen, b. 5/28/1940 in Orford; third; Glen George Marsh
    (farmer, Orford) and Verna M. Hibbard (Orford)
Irving Walter, b. 12/2/1934 in Orford; fourth; Walter Marsh (laborer,
    Orford) and Gladys Elliott (Littleton)
Janet Maude, b. 1/2/1943 in Orford; Glenn G. Marsh (laborer,
    Orford) and Verna M. Hibbard (Lyme)
Joanne Linda, b. 3/1/1955 in Haverhill; third; Clinton A. Marsh
    (laborer, Orfordville) and Martha L. Tarr (Fitzwilliam)
Joyce Ann, b. 11/14/1937 in Orford; second; Glenn Marsh (farmer,
    Orford) and Verna Hibbard (Lyme)
Juanita Ann, b. 12/20/1940 in Orford; fifth; Ralph Ernest Marsh
    (laborer, Orford) and Gladys A. Cutler (Grafton)
Kathryn Ann, b. 12/23/1961 in Lebanon; first; Fred Allan Marsh
    (laborer, Orford) and Louise Myrtie Davis (Lyme)
Leon Charles, Jr., b. 9/27/1931 in Orford; first; Leon C. Marsh
    (laborer, Orford) and Irene M. Elliott (Littleton)
Leslie Herbert, b. 12/10/1945 in Haverhill; eighth; Walter H. Marsh
    (woodsman, Orford) and Gladys Amy Elliott (Littleton)
Lewis Arthur, b. 5/5/1928 in Orford; first; Arthur L. Marsh (farm hand,
    Orford) and Irene R. Goddard (St. Johnsbury, VT)
Lillian Eva, b. 11/8/1909; eleventh; David C. Marsh (farmer, 41, W.
    Fairlee, VT) and Delia F. Smith (37, Corinth, VT)
Lucile Lois, b. 1/18/1939 in Orford; second; Clyde Marsh (laborer,
    Orford) and Edith Stevens (Williamstown, VT)
Mark Clayton, b. 8/12/1955 in Lebanon; first; Leon C. Marsh, Jr.
    (laborer, Orford) and Helen A. Huckins (Hanover)
Mary Jane, b. 6/12/1948 in Orford; ninth; Ralph E. Marsh (laborer,
    Orford) and Gladys Cutler (Grafton)
Meagan Elizabeth, b. 5/22/1990 in Lebanon; Mark Marsh and Esther
    Marsh
Nicholas Lee, b. 1/29/1996 in Lebanon; Alan Trent Marsh and
    Sherry Ellen Wurtz Marsh
Paul Clyde, b. 9/23/1936 in Haverhill; first; Clyde B. Marsh (farmer,
    Orford) and Edith Stevens (Williamstown, VT)
Phyllis Jean, b. 1/5/1936 in Haverhill; eighth; Frank D. Marsh
    (laborer, Orford) and Ina Strew (Lyme)
Ray E., b. 8/26/1938 in Haverhill; ninth; Frank D. Marsh (farmer,
    Orford) and Ina Strue (Lyme)
Raymond Lee, b. 2/22/1940 in Orford; sixth; Leon Charles Marsh
    (laborer, Orford) and Irene Mabel Elliott (Littleton)

Richard Jean, b. 7/18/1940 in Orford; third; Clyde Bert Marsh (laborer, Orford) and Edythe Stevens (Williamstown, VT)
Robert Eugene, b. 9/10/1935 in Orford; second; Roy C. Marsh (laborer, Orford) and Grace Cutter (Vershire, VT)
Roycie, b. 1/15/1912 in Orford; twelfth; David Marsh (farmer, 43, W. Fairlee, VT) and Delia F. Smith (39, Corinth, VT)
Russell LeRoy, b. 10/5/1937 in Orford; third; Roy C. Marsh (laborer, Orford) and Grace I. Cutler (Vershire, VT)
Ryan Alan, b. 2/4/1995 in Lebanon; Alan Trent Marsh and Sherry Ellen Wurtz Marsh
Sandra Lea, b. 2/2/1977 in Hanover; Gloyd K. Marsh (33, NH) and Muriel E. Taylor (27, VT)
Sean Michael, b. 10/5/1991 in Lebanon; Alan Marsh and Sherry Marsh
Teresa Lee, b. 5/25/1964 in Haverhill; Raymond L. Marsh (veneer mill laborer, Orford) and Betty J. Russin (Woodsville)
Wallace Herbert, b. 1/4/1933 in Orford; fifth; Arthur Marsh (laborer, Orford) and Irene Goddard (St. Johnsbury, VT)
Wanda Marie, b. 4/14/1950 in Orford; eighth; Ralph E. Marsh (caretaker, Orford) and Gladys A. Cutler (Grafton)
William David, b. 12/1/1933 in Orford; fourth; Leon C. Marsh (laborer, Orford) and Irene E. Heath (Littleton)

MASON,
son, b. 1/14/1890 in Orford; seventh; Frank C. Mason (laborer, 31, Vineland, NJ) and Cora E. Pebbles (27, Tuftonboro)
Julia Alexis, b. 5/14/1999 in Lebanon; Patrick Mason and Amye Parker
Patrick Charles, b. 11/6/2000 in Lebanon; Shawn Mason and Amyre Mason

MAUGHAN,
Douglas Lloyd, b. 4/10/1954 in Lebanon; second; John H. Maughan (minister, Dodgeville, WI) and Doris Eleanor Tullis (Evansville, WI)
John Kenneth, b. 8/23/1952 in Lebanon; first; John H. Maughan (clergyman, Dodgeville, WI) and Doris E. Tullis (Evansville, WI)

MAYETTE,
daughter, b. 2/14/1896; sixth; Edward Mayette (laborer, 38, Canada) and Selestine Loche (36)

son, b. 2/14/1896; seventh; Edward Mayette (laborer, 38, Canada) and Selestine Loche (36)

son, b. 5/22/1898 in Orford; eighth; Edward Mayette (laborer, 40, Canada) and Selestine Locke (38, Canada)

McCLELLAN,
Owen Chandler, b. 11/20/1951 in Lebanon; first; Paul G. McClellan (clerk, Hanover) and Thelma J. Shaw (Lyme)

McCORMACK,
Margaret Ellen, b. 1/18/1995 in Lebanon; Bradley Steven McCormack and Elizabeth Anne Shaughnessy McCormack

McCRILLIS,
daughter, b. 6/11/1888; seventh; Aaron McCrillis (farmer, 50, Corinth, VT) and Julia Hackett (37, Haverhill)

McCUE,
Richard Edward, b. 10/2/1933 in Hanover; second; John J. McCue (machinist, Miller's Falls, MA) and Marjorie Stuart (N. Brookfield, MA)

McDONALD,
Abbey Lyn, b. 1/15/2004 in Lebanon; D. Jeremy McDonald and Bethany Hill

McEWAN,
Sheila Irene, b. 1/9/1937 in Haverhill; third; George L. McEwan (oil plant mgr., Lyme Ctr.) and Marcia A. Simmons (Piermont)

McGEE,
Lois L., b. 4/21/1938 in Orford; second; Kenneth McGee (laborer, Dorchester) and Frances Foote (Orford)

McGOFF,
Casey Brittany, b. 4/11/1990 in Haverhill; James McGoff and Deborah McGoff

Jamie Lynn Ashley, b. 11/6/1982; James McGoff and Deborah McGoff

Johnathan James, b. 4/28/1980 in Haverhill; James McGoff and Deborah McGoff

McINTIRE,
Ruth Bernice, b. 9/12/1914 in Orford; second; Vernon L. McIntire (fireman, 29, Jefferson) and Edna G. Pease (21, Wentworth)

McKEAGE,
Natalie J., b. 10/11/1917 in Orford; third; Raymond McKeage (farmer, Pittsburg) and Junie Gould (Colebrook)

McKEE,
Christopher Glenn, b. 7/7/1984; Henry McKee and Linda McKee
Henry Arthur, b. 7/27/1957 in Haverhill; first; William Burt McKee (Air Force, Plymouth) and Joyce Ann Marsh (Orford)
MaryAnn Louise, b. 9/6/1982; Henry McKee and Linda McKee

McKINNON,
Kyle John, b. 7/1/1997 in Lebanon; David Louis McKinnon and Donna Marie Olivere McKinnon

McLEOD,
Shirley Mae, b. 12/16/1948 in Orford; fourth; Nelson McLeod (laborer) and Blanche Rennon (Orleans, VT); residence – Vershire, VT

McMAHON,
Griffin Porter, b. 7/28/1997 in Lebanon; William Post McMahon and Sabina Leigh Miller McMahon
William Quinn, b. 10/27/1990 in Hanover; William McMahon and Sabina McMahon

McNUTT,
Jenna Kathleen, b. 12/12/1991 in Lebanon; Blair McNutt and Jennifer McNutt
Marissa Shannon, b. --/--/1989

McPHERSON,
Kate Bell, b. 3/27/1895 in Orford; second; J. H. McPherson (farming, 42, Brookfield, NS) and Cornelia Holden (35, NS)

McQUARRIE,
daughter, b. 4/22/1898 in Orford; third; William S. McQuarrie (laborer, 29, NB) and Emma E. Knights (20, S. Paris, ME)

John M., b. 6/29/1899 in Orford; sixth; William S. McQuarrie (laborer, 30, Albert Co., NB) and Emma Etta Knight (22, S. Paris, ME)

MELAHN,
Regina Ann, b. 7/15/1990 in Lebanon; David Melahn and Jayne Melahn

MELENDY,
Scott Robert, b. 1/16/1980 in Hanover; Jon Melendy and Gloria Melendy

MELLIN,
Jonathan Bates, b. 12/23/1963 in Haverhill; Donald B. Mellin (Stamford, CT) and Ruth E. Anderson (Charleroi, PA)

MERRILL,
Alice M., b. 9/12/1888; fourth; Elijah N. Merrill (laborer, 44, Hebron) and Isa. W. Greenough (32, Salem, MA)
Arlene May, b. 7/2/1935 in Hanover; fourth; Hiram P. Merrill (mechanic, Woodstock, VT) and Ruth A. Wyman (Chester, VT)
Kassie Lee, b. 8/6/1988; Robert Merrill and Donna Merrill

MESSER,
Amy Lou, b. 4/18/1967 in Lebanon; Paul B. Messer, Sr. (fireman, Arlington, MA) and Betty Lou Cummings (Haverhill)
Bethany Danielle, b. 4/12/1984; Paul Messer, Jr. and Ellen Messer
Christine Gay, b. 10/8/1961 in Lebanon; third; Paul B. Messier (clerk, Arlington, MA) and Betty Lou Cummings (Woodsville)
Wendee Leigh, b. 10/28/1964 in Lebanon; Paul B. Messer (custodian, Arlington, MA) and Betty L. Cummings (Haverhill)

MILES,
Donna Marie, b. 7/19/1948 in Orford; third; Adams T. Mles (lumber worker, Springfield, MA) and Theresa V. Deya (Brattleboro, VT)

MILLER,
Elaina Katharine, b. 4/4/1988; John Miller and Bethany Miller
Elizabeth Blake, b. 7/11/1991 in Lebanon; John Miller and Bethany Miller
Gwendlyn Elaine, b. 8/4/1933 in Hanover; seventh; Glenn E. Miller (farmer, N. Haverhill) and Maud A. Clifford (N. Haverhill)

MIRALDI,
Michael, b. 8/13/1987; Leonard Miraldi and Laura Miraldi

MISURACA,
James Christian Disco, b. 11/5/1988; James Misuraca and Annmarie Misuraca

MITCHELL,
Marin Blair, b. --/--/1989

MOATS,
Jared William, b. 4/18/1976 in Lebanon; David R. Moats (28, UT) and Kathleen A. Clarke (26, CT)

MOREY,
son, b. 12/25/1894 in Orford; first; Eddie S. Morey (farmer, 24, Thetford, VT) and Esther McIntyre (23, Inverness, Canada)
daughter, b. 4/4/1896; second; Eddie S. Morey (farmer, 28, Thetford, VT) and Esther McIntire (26, Inverness, Canada)
daughter, b. 4/9/1897; fourth; Charles H. Morey (laborer, 28, Nashua) and Lizzie M. Warner (27, Orford)
son, b. 1/4/1898 in Orford; fourth; Irving W. Morey (laborer, 35, Thetford, VT) and Annie McIntire (31, Inverness, Canada)
daughter, b. 2/22/1898 in Orford; fourth; Charles H. Morey (carpenter, 29, Nashua) and Lizzie M. Warner (28, Orford)
son, b. 11/1/1901 in Orford; fifth; Eddie S. Morey (farmer, 32, Thetford, VT) and Esther McIntyre (31, Inverness, PQ)
daughter, b. 3/6/1902 in Orford; fifth; David W. Morey (laborer, 39, Thetford, VT) and Annie McIntyre (Inverness, Canada)
son, b. 10/11/1903 in Orford; sixth; Eddie S. Morey (farmer, 34, Thetford, VT) and Esther McIntyre (33, Inverness, Canada)
daughter, b. 1/30/1905 in Orford; seventh; Eddie S. Morey (farmer, 34, Thetford, VT) and Esther McIntyre (33, Inverness, Canada)
daughter, b. 9/29/1908; ninth; Eddie S. Morey (farmer, 40, Thetford, VT) and Esther McIntyre (39, Inverness, Canada)
George Dewey, b. 2/9/1899 in Orford; fourth; Eddie S. Morey (farming, 29, Thetford, VT) and Esther McIntire (28, Inverness, Canada)
Ruth, b. 4/10/1906 in Orford; eighth; Eddie S. Morey (farmer, 35, Thetford, VT) and Esther McIntyre (35, Inverness, PQ)

Scott Allen, b. 9/15/1980 in Haverhill; Gerald Morey and Joanne Morey

MORRISON,
Samuel R., b. 1/11/1893 in Orford; first; Harry E. Morrison (farmer, 24, Orford) and Nellie J. Danforth (29, Pittsburg)

MORSE,
daughter, b. 3/3/1907; second; George O. Morse (laborer, 29, Jay, VT) and Lura A. Hatch (19, Jericho, VT)

MOSES,
Pearl Louise, b. 4/13/1929 in Hanover; first; Perley Moses (woodsman, Tunbridge, VT) and Eva May Morey (Bradford, VT)
Ruth Etta, b. 8/29/1935 in Haverhill; fourth; Perley Moses (laborer, Tunbridge, VT) and Eva Morey (Bradford, VT)

MOUSLEY,
son, b. 4/16/1892 in Orford; fifth; George W. Mousley (farmer, 31, Orford) and Julia E. Dyke (28, Lyme)
son, b. 11/11/1895 in Orford; sixth; G. W. Mousley (farming, 33, Lyme) and Julia L. Dike (31, Lyme)
daughter, b. 6/1/1897; sixth; George W. Mousley (farmer, 37, Lyme) and Julia E. Dyke (33, Lyme)
son, b. 8/4/1899 in Orford; seventh; George W. Mousley (farming, 37, Lyme) and Julia Dyke (35, Lyme)
son, b. 10/3/1906 in Orford; tenth; George W. Mousley (lumberman, 44, Lyme) and Julia E. Dyke (42, Lyme)
Walter O., b. 4/6/1904 in Orford; second; Oliver C. Mousley (laborer, 28, Orford) and Lela S. Sweet (22, Lyme)

MUNN,
Madeline Ruth, b. 5/28/1923; first; Reginald G. Munn (plumber, W. Fairlee, VT) and Lurlene Blodgett (Orford)
Ramona, b. 2/20/1903 in Orford; fifth; Charles H. Munn (liveryman, 33, Canterbury) and Kathleen Ordway (29, Stanton, MN)
Rowena Maud, b. 5/24/1900 in Orford; fourth; Charles H. Munn (liveryman, 26, Canterbury) and Katherine Ordway (21, Stanton, MN)

NAGLE,
Conor Barnes, b. 11/24/1995 in Lebanon; Warren Charles Nagle, Jr. and Joyce Anne Mechling Nagle

NARO,
Christopher Robert, b. 9/22/1981 in Hanover; Timothy Naro and Debra Naro

NAYLOR,
Riley Cole, b. 4/14/2002 in Lebanon; Scott Naylor and Jaimie Naylor

NEFF,
Robert Edward, b. 12/23/1932 in Orford; second; Leon Neff (laborer, Nashua) and Carlie Bean (Orford)

NELSON,
Winnifred Nellie, b. 3/15/1910; first; Frank F. Nelson (painter, 29, Acton, MA) and Stella Kirby (29, Lowell, MA); residence – Lowell, MA

NICHLESON,
Samuel Arthur, b. 4/2/1923; third; Dan. H. Nichleson (laborer, NS) and Florence Grand (Richmond, PQ)

NICHOLS,
Alvin Dana, b. 8/11/1952 in Haverhill; fifth; Dana A. Nichols (truck driver, E. Concord, VT) and Elizabeth I. Pike (Wells, ME)

NICHOLSON,
Ida M., b. 2/15/1895 in Orford; third; Angus Nicholson (farming, 39, Cape Breton) and Susan N. Coates (28, Newbury, VT)
Malcom S., b. 2/21/1888; first; Angus Nicholson (farmer, 35, Sidney Co., CB) and Susie M. Catis (22, Newbury, VT)
Sarah A., b. 5/21/1890 in Orford; first; Angus Nicholson (farmer, 36, NS) and Susie M. Coates (24, Newbury, VT)

NICKERSON,
Florence May, b. 3/28/1929 in Orford; seventh; Hugh Nickerson (laborer, NS) and Florence Grande (Richmond, PQ)
Margaret Elizabeth, b. 9/9/1930 in Orford; eighth; Hugh Nickerson (laborer, NS) and Florence Grande (Richmond, PQ)

NILES,
Vietta May, b. 5/29/1899 in Orford; first; George F. Niles (farmer, 43, Enfield) and Nellie E. Smith (25, Lyme)

NOLAN,
Randy George, b. 5/17/1965 in Hanover; Lee Nolan (mkt. & sales, Greensboro, NC) and Joan A. Smith (Fairlee, VT)

NORRIS,
son, b. 7/2/1890 in Orford; fourth; Elisha F. Norris (farmer, 34, Corinth, VT) and Emma D. French (29, Brunswick, VT)
daughter, b. 9/21/1892 in Orford; fifth; Elisha F. Norris (farmer, 36, Corinth, VT) and Emma D. French (31, Brunswick, VT)

NOYES,
Amanda Joan, b. 8/19/1987; Howard Noyes and Laurie Noyes
Elisabeth Joan, b. 11/9/2001 in Lebanon; David Noyes and Cheryl Noyes
Henry Maurice, b. 2/16/1968 in Haverhill; Howard R. Noyes (29, Piermont) and Joan Baker (31, Hanover)
Jennifer Anne Marie, b. 5/11/1991 in Lebanon; Stacy Noyes and Laurie Noyes
Penny Lee, b. 12/14/1971 in Haverhill; Howard R. Noyes (32, Piermont) and Joan S. Baker (33, Orford)
Scott David, b. 11/16/1973 in Lebanon; Howard R. Noyes (34, Piermont) and Joan Baker (35, Orford)
Stacey Allen, b. 12/15/1967 in Haverhill; Howard Roger Noyes (laborer, Piermont) and Joan S. Baker (Hanover)

NUTTER,
Elmer Edgar, b. 6/7/1966 in Lebanon; Theodore L. Nutter (laborer, Orford) and Sally Ann Fay (Lyme)
John Arthur, b. 5/17/1944 in Haverhill; Kenneth L. Nutter (US Army, Woodsville) and Evelyn R. Johnson (Wells River, VT)
Leighia Di-Ann, b. 3/15/1979 in Lebanon; John Nutter and Darlene Nutter
Loretta Claire, b. 2/12/1976 in Lebanon; John A. Nutter (31, NH) and Darlene Gladys Bluto (23, CT)
Pamona Lee, b. 10/11/1946 in Orford; Kenneth L. Nutter (laborer, Haverhill) and Evelyn R. Johnson (Wells River, VT)

Theodore Lawrence, b. 9/21/1942 in Orford; Kenneth L. Nutter (laborer, Woodsville) and Evelyn Johnson (Wells River, VT)
Vicky Ann, b. 7/6/1958 in Haverhill; first; Raymond G. Nutter, Jr. (store work, St. Johnsbury, VT) and Muriel K. Ash (Sheffield, VT)

O'BRIEN,
Daniel Anderson, b. 7/25/1986; John O'Brien and Debora O'Brien
Megan Tullar, b. 4/14/1980 in Hanover; John O'Brien and Deborah O'Brien
Michael John, b. 1/8/1982; John O'Brien and Deborah O'Brien

OLAFSON,
Kayla Ann, b. 8/8/2001 in Lebanon; Troy Olafson and Lisa Olafson

OLSON,
Eric Reuel, b. 9/29/1973 in Hanover; Francis L. Olson (31, Los Angeles, CA) and Ann A. Wilkerson (30, Bronxville, NY)

OSHEYACK,
Eli Ben-Israel, b. 5/7/1985; Gary Osheyack and Deborah Osheyack

PAGE,
stillborn son, b. 2/9/1897; fifth; Charles W. Page (laborer, 31, Orford) and Emma J. Dyke (31, Lyme)
daughter, b. 12/30/1898 in Orford; sixth; Charles W. Page (laborer, 32, Orford) and Emma J. Dyke (32, Lyme)
Leon, b. 5/14/1895 in Orford; fourth; Charles W. Page (laborer, 29, Orford) and Emma J. Dike (29, Lyme)
Leon G. F., b. 4/20/1893 in Orford; first; George F. Page (farmer, 28, Orford) and Addie M. Baker (33, Orford)

PALIFKA,
Robert Michael, b. 6/1/1970 in Lebanon; Robert M. Palifka (27, Hartford, CT) and Lucille G. Blake (26, Orford)
Sarah L., b. 11/14/1972 in Lebanon; Robert G. Palifka (30, Hartford, CT) and Lucille D. Blake (29, Orford)

PALMER,
Kathrine Della, b. 5/10/1969 in Lebanon; Arthur F. Palmer (33, NH) and Arlene D. Thompson (33, NH)

PAPIRMEISTER,
Sara Marissa, b. 3/13/1992 in Lebanon; Charles Papirmeister and Janet Papirmeister

PARKER,
Andrew Charlie, b. 7/10/1958 in Hanover; fourth; Charlie A. Parker (laborer, Newport, VT) and Freda L. Marsh (Wentworth)
Archie Ray, b. 9/2/1954 in Hanover; second; Charlie A. Parker (woodsman, Newport Ctr., VT) and Freda Iola Marsh (Warren)
Kenneth Russell, b. 5/17/1957 in Lebanon; third; Charles Andrew Parker (lumberman, Newport, VT) and Freda Iola Marsh (Warren)
Lori Elaine, b. 8/9/1977 in Hanover; Ralph E. Parker (21, NH) and Joanne Winn (20, RI)
Ralph Eugene, b. 4/6/1956 in Hanover; second; Charlie A. Parker (lumberman, Newport, VT) and Freda Iola Marsh (Wentworth)

PATCH,
son, b. 5/27/1888; fifth; William H. Patch (laborer, 35, Orford) and Ella M. Patch White (30, Orford)
daughter, b. 11/22/1889 in Orford; sixth; William H. Patch (laborer, 36, Orford) and Ella M. White (31, Orford)

PATTEN,
stillborn son, b. 4/5/1941 in Orford; fourth; John W. Patten (foreman, Hampden, ME) and Elizabeth M. Butters (Hartland, ME); residence – Bangor, ME

PATTON,
Mallory Louise Edith Reed, b. 10/4/1992 in Lebanon; Thomas Patton and Sally Patton

PAYER,
Charles A., b. 8/19/1904 in Orford; second; Charles E. Payer (farmer, 32, St. Leon, PQ) and Lara A. Alexander (30, Moncton, NB)

PEASE,
son, b. 9/15/1889 in Orford; second; Chase M. Pease (farmer, 31, Ellsworth) and Julia A. Pease (26, Orford)

daughter, b. 1/8/1895 in Orford; fourth; Francis R. Pease (laborer, 31, Ellsworth) and Mabel B. Sherburn (26, Orford)

daughter, b. 10/11/1898 in Orford; third; Chase M. Pease (farmer, 41, Ellsworth) and Julia M. Learned (35, Orford)

son, b. 10/10/1900 in Orford; second; Henry M. Pease (farmer, 48, Ellsworth) and Abbie M. Gale (37, Sandwich)

son, b. 5/17/1906 in Orford; seventh; Francis R. Pease (farmer, 43, Ellsworth) and Mabel C. Sherburn (38, Orford)

son, b. 7/28/1922; first; Clarence H. Perry (farmer, Orford) and Addie A. Bedell (Morrisville, VT)

daughter, b. 5/11/1924; second; Clarence H. Pease (farmer, Orford) and Addie Bedell (Morrisville, VT)

Arthur Samuel, b. 10/5/1946 in Haverhill; fifth; Glenn F. Pease (farmer, Orford) and Theda L. Howard (Wentworth)

Carol Marie, b. 3/15/1956 in Hanover; third; Gerald Edwin Pease (farmer, Plymouth) and Doris E. Quackenbush (Feeding Hills, MA)

Dale, b. 6/15/1936 in Plymouth; second; Doris H. Pease (at home, Orford)

Doris Hattie, b. 4/26/1902 in Orford; sixth; Francis R. Pease (farmer, 38, Ellsworth) and Mabel C. Sherburn (Orford)

Ethel Louise, b. 3/12/1906 in Orford; first; John C. Pease (farmer, 27, Wentworth) and Florence M. Edgerly (22, Lynn, MA)

Francis George, b. 1/3/1933 in Orford; third; Glenn Pease (farmer, Orford) and Theda Howard (Wentworth)

Gene Alan, b. 7/15/1954 in Hanover; second; Gerald Edwin Pease (farmer, Plymouth) and Doris E. Quackenbush (Feeding Hills, MA)

Gerald Edward, b. 11/1/1931 in Plymouth; second; Glenn Pease (carpenter, Orford) and Theda Howard (Wentworth)

Glenn Arthur, b. 11/15/1968 in Lancaster; Arthur S. Pease (teacher, 22, Haverhill) and Judith A. Cummings (20, Haverhill)

Harrison Gerald, b. 1/19/1953 in Hanover; first; Gerald E. Pease (farmer, Plymouth) and Doris E. Quackenbush (Feeding Hills, MA)

Helen Elizabeth, b. 3/14/1914 in Orford; third; Chester W. Pease (farmer, 28, Orford) and Stella A. Merrill (25, Wentworth)

Howard A., b. 3/6/1893 in Orford; first; Henry H. Pease (farmer, 40, Ellsworth) and Abbie M. Galt (30, Sandwich)

Howard Glenn, b. 5/8/1929 in Plymouth; first; Glenn Pease (farmer, Orford) and Theda L. Howard (Wentworth)

Irene Flora, b. 2/18/1935 in Orford; fourth; Glenn Pease (farmer, Orford) and Theda Howard (Wentworth)

Janet Lee, b. 7/2/1957 in Hanover; fourth; Gerald Edwin Pease (farmer, Plymouth) and Doris E. Quackenbush (Feeding Hills, MA)

Jeremy Scott, b. 2/9/1977 in Hanover; Gene A. Pease (22, NH) and Bonnie L. Guest (21, NY)

Sheryl Lynn, b. 9/25/1964 in Hanover; Gerald E. Pease (farmer, Plymouth) and Doriss E. Quackenbush (Feeding Hills, MA)

PEIRCE,
Leonard Woods, b. 6/10/1925; George A. Peirce (farmer, Frankfort, ME) and Clara M. Baker (Covington, KY)

PERCEY,
Wallace D., b. 10/28/1901 in Orford; first; Dan F. Percey (farmer, 23, Newport, VT) and Minnie B. Stetson (23, Orford)

PERKINS,
son, b. 6/20/1930 in Orford; sixth; Walter R. Perkins (laborer, Meredith) and Etta M. French (Meredith)

May Louise, b. 9/8/1912 in Orford; first; Ralph C. Perkins (farmer, 23, Hardwick, VT) and Maude L. Barnet (18, Walden, VT)

PERRY,
son, b. 4/20/1948 in Orford; second; Leighton A. Perry (millhand, N. Haverhill) and Lucille M. Gilbert (Orford)

Amanda Susan, b. 8/21/1975 in Lebanon; Tomas L. Perry (23, Hanover) and Janice L. Pundsack (26, St. Cloud, MN)

Anthony Wayne, b. 8/2/1943 in Haverhill; first; Leighton A. Perry (mill hand, Haverhill) and Lucille M. Gilbert (Orford)

David William, b. 11/27/1954 in Orfordville; Walter Harold Perry (mill worker, Saranac Lake, NY) and Beatrice B. Fillian (Wentworth)

Jesse Tomas, b. 9/22/1981 in Hanover; Tomas Perry and Janice Perry

Lisa Lucille, b. 4/26/1963 in Hanover; Leighton A. Perry (explosive engineer, Haverhill) and Lucille M. Gilbert (Orford)

Pamela Ann, b. 11/9/1952 in Orford; third; Walter H. Perry (laborer, Saranac, NY) and Beatrice B. Fillian (Wentworth)

Ranson Wayne, b. 10/6/1963 in Hanover; Anthony W. Perry (laborer, Woodsville) and Carol A. Chesley (Rochester)

Todd Leighton, b. 9/28/1964 in Hanover; Leighton A. Perry (const. foreman, Haverhill) and Lucille M. Gilbert (Orford)
Tomas Lindsey, b. 9/16/1951 in Hanover; third; Leighton A. Perry (lumberman, N. Haverhill) and Lucille M. Gilbert (Orford)
Tyler Ranson, b. 9/24/1990 in Hanover; Ranson Perry and Sheila Perry

PHILBRICK,
Ethel Irene, b. 10/20/1910; fifth; Willie J. Philbrick (laborer, 42, Brownington, VT) and Nellie E. J. Wilkie (37, Brownington, VT)

PICKERING,
Terry Lee, b. 11/15/1962 in Lebanon; second; Russell E. Pickering (teacher, Bellows Falls, VT) and Phyllis Ann Adams (Windsor, VT)

PIERCE,
son, b. 12/3/1891 in Orford; third; Frank J. Pierce (farmer, 39, Orford) and Alma Sulham (37, Hyde Park, VT)
daughter, b. 11/10/1897; fourth; Frank J. Pierce (blacksmith, 46, Orford) and Alma Sulham (44, Hyde Park, VT)
son, b. 8/4/1946 in Hanover; first; Chester A. Pierce (bus driver, Haverhill) and Dorothy M. Pike (Lyme)
Carolyn, b. 8/31/1917 in Hanover; first; Clarence W. Pierce (civil engineer, Fairlee, VT) and Ruth Carr (Andover)
Charles Rexford, b. 10/24/1954 in Hanover; third; Chester Arthur Pierce (bus operator, Pike) and Dorothy Mae Pike (Lyme Ctr.)
Christopher James, b. 2/4/2004 in Lebanon; Charles Pierce and Sharon Brooks
Jane Elizabeth, b. 7/27/1948 in Hanover; second; Chester A. Pierce (bus driver, Pike) and Dorothy Mae Pike (Lyme Ctr.)
Megan Lynn, b. 3/18/1983; Charles Pierce and Ruth Pierce

PIERSON,
Amy Louise, b. 8/28/1968 in Haverhill; Edward W. Pierson (laborer, 22, Hanover) and Shirley J. Jones (20, Morrisville, VT)
Carol Ellen, b. 10/3/1942 in Hanover; second; William L. Pierson (farm hand, Topsham, VT) and Dorothy F. Baker (Orford)
Edward Wallace, b. 9/9/1946 in Hanover; second; Wallace H. Pierson (laborer, Topsham, VT) and Evelyn N. Weeks (Fairlee, VT)

Lori Ann, b. 7/3/1971 in Haverhill; Edward W. Pierson (25, Hanover) and Shirley J. Jones (23, Morrisville, VT)
Nettie Alice, b. 4/30/1940 in Hanover; first; William L. Pierson (farmer, Topsham, VT) and Dorothy F. Baker (Orford)
Richard Allen, b. 3/15/1954 in Haverhill; fourth; Wallace H. Pierson (laborer, st. h., Topsham, VT) and Evelyn Nellie Weeks (Fairlee, VT)
Sheila Mae, b. 5/14/1948 in Lyme; third; Wallace H. Pierson (road laborer, Topsham, VT) and Evelyn N. Weeks (Fairlee, VT)
William Henry, b. 4/26/1947 in Hanover; third; William L. Pierson (farmer, Topsham, VT) and Dorothy F. Baker (Orford)
William Todd, b. 8/20/1969 in Haverhill; William H. Pierson (22, Hanover) and Charlotte G. Batchelder (20, Woodsville)

PIKE,
son, b. 6/11/1948 in Lyme; third; Horace E. Pike (laborer, Lyme) and Maxine Heath (Littleton)
son, b. 6/11/1948 in Lyme; stillborn; third; Horace E. Pike (laborer, Lyme) and Maxine Heath (Littleton)
Christine Sue, b. 4/21/1971 in Haverhill; Weymouth H. Pike, Jr. (19, Haverhill) and Susan M. Taylor (18, St. Johnsbury, VT)
Constance Louise, b. 7/11/1949 in Lebanon; fourth; Horace E. Pike (laborer, Lyme) and Maxine L. Heath (Littleton)
Devin Christopher, b. 7/29/2001 in Lebanon; Matthew Pike and Kelly Pike
Gary Chester, b. 7/4/1948 in Orford; third; Allie C. Pike (laborer, Lyme) and Marjorie Heath (Littleton)
Gloria Jean, b. 11/30/1950 in Lebanon; first; Weymouth H. Pike (laborer, Lyme) and Helen M. Marsh (Wentworth)
James Robert, b. 8/15/1980 in Haverhill; Weymouth Pike, Jr. and Susan Pike
Jennifer Mae, b. 10/22/1975 in Haverhill; Weymouth H. Pike, Jr. (23, Hanover) and Susan M. Taylor (23, St. Johnsbury, VT)
Lynn Ann, b. 2/26/1956 in Hanover; fourth; Allie Chester Pike (laborer, Lyme) and Marjorie May Heath (Littleton)
Shannon Elizabeth, b. 11/27/1997 in Lebanon; Matthew Edward Pike and Kelley Lynn Williams Pike

PIPER,
son, b. 1/11/1891 in Orford; sixth; Charles E. Piper (laborer, 33, Fairlee, VT) and Sabra Ann Emery (36, Stratford)

Miranda Mae Ann, b. 11/6/1995 in Lebanon; James Mason Piper and Tammy Jean Estes Piper

Percy R., b. 7/23/1889 in Orford; fifth; Charles E. Piper (laborer, 33, Lyme) and Sabra Ann Robins (36, Stratford, VT)

Samantha Elizabeth, b. 9/14/1999 in Lebanon; James Piper and Tammy Piper

PITMAN,
Timothy Judson, b. 1/31/1975 in Hanover; Richard W. Pitman (23, NH) and Mary E. Sobaski (23, CT)

PLAMONDON,
Katie Rebecca, b. 9/11/1983; Bruce Plamondon and Sally Plamondon

POLLETTA,
Matthew Paul, b. 12/28/1975 in Hanover; Thomas C. Polletta (29, Natick, MA) and Martha Mary Murphy (29, Salem, MA)

POOR,
Carrie Marie, b. 6/30/1998 in Lebanon; Maurice Harry Poor and Wanda G. Avery Poor

Crystal Lee Ann, b. 11/29/1999 in Lebanon; Maurice Harry Poor and Wanda Gratia Avery Poor

POPE,
Carl Richard, b. 3/31/1937 in Hanover; second; Henry J. Pope (salesman, Montreal, Canada) and Alice L. ----- (Derry)

POWERS,
Edna May, b. 9/19/1932 in Hanover; second; Aaron Powers (laborer, Whitefield) and Dorothy Kenney (CT) (1933)

PRATT,
Bruce E., b. 4/29/1894 in Orford; second; Ezra Bruce Pratt (28) and Mary L. Brooks (33, Orford)

PRESTON,
Vivian May, b. 6/10/1931 in Orford; first; Grace May Preston (Etna)

PROPER,
Dora E., b. 9/23/1906 in Orford; eleventh; Alonzo Proper (laborer, 36, Highgate, VT) and Emma J. Gardner (42, Newbury, VT)

PRUTER,
Karl James, b. 8/4/1948 in Lebanon; fourth; Hugo R. Pruter (minister, Poughkeepsie, NY) and Nancy L. Taylor (Chicago, IL)

PUSHEE,
Adrienne Michelle, b. 3/20/1981 in Hanover; Donald Pushee and Loretta Pushee
Amy Thelma, b. 9/12/1939 in Orford; second; Clarence L. Pushee (carpentry, Lyme) and Evelyn T. Tattersall (Lyme)
Clarence L., Jr., b. 2/26/1938 in Orford; first; Clarence L. Pushee (laborer, Lyme) and Evelyn Tattersall (Lyme)
Eugene Scott, b. 9/9/1970 in Haverhill; Clarence L. Pushee (Lyme) and Hazel B. Davis (31, Orford)
Joshua Dale Alan, b. 10/31/1994 in Lebanon; Dale Frank Pushee and Melissa Jean Buskey Pushee
Kristen Elizabeth, b. 4/19/1984; David Pushee and Michelle Pushee
Paula Ann, b. 1/1/1969 in Haverhill; Paul R. Pushee (24, Hanover) and Louella B. Whiting (17, Concord)
Sylvester Albert, b. 2/19/1941 in Orford; third; Clarence L. Pushee (laborer, Lyme) and Evelyn T. Tattersall (Lyme)

PUTNAM,
Hannah Cary, b. 1/15/1982; Craig Putnam and Sarah Putnam
Harlan Dean, b. 10/27/1939 in Orford; fourth; Ora Putnam (laborer, Bradford, VT) and Alberta Perry (Haverhill)
Sharon May, b. 2/4/1948 in Orford; fourth; Ora Putnam (laborer, Bradford, VT) and Alberta Perry (Haverhill)

QUACKENBUSH,
Gary Frederick, b. 3/28/1954 in Hanover; second; William C. Quackenbush (farmer, Springfield, MA) and June Mae Bryer (Fairlee, VT)
Russell Allen, b. 10/18/1951 in Hanover; first; William C. Quackenbush (carpenter, MA) and June M. Bryer (Fairlee, VT)
Seth Ladd, b. 12/31/1979 in Hanover; Gary Quackenbush and Lori Quackenbush

QUIMBY,
Linda Chandler, b. 6/1/1952 in St. Johnsbury, VT; fourth; Frank M. Quimby (laborer, Enfield) and Marceline K. Day (Littleton)

RAMSEY,
child, b. 1/30/1887 in Orford; fourth; James R. Ramsey (farmer, Piermont) and Nettie E. Sherburn (Orford)
Ruth Margaret, b. 2/10/1904 in Orford; third; Uric A. Ramsey (laborer, 39, Piermont) and Ruth E. Tallman (38, Orford)

RANDALL,
son, b. 3/18/1892 in Orford; third; Barnard Randall (farmer, 38, Ellsworth) and Rosa Simpson (30, Orford)
Vincent G., b. 12/3/1964 in Haverhill; Gary W. Randall (pressman, Plymouth) and Linda L. Hannett (Plymouth)

RAY,
Ean McKinley, b. 9/16/2004 in Lebanon; Ryan Ray and Kelly Ray

RAYNES,
Tyler Anthony, b. 12/9/1988; Donald Raynes and Loretta Raynes

RECORD,
Beverly Anne, b. 4/25/1933 in Hanover; first; William Record (laborer, Bucksport, ME) and Lurline Dyke (Newbury, VT)

REED,
Allen Gregory, b. 8/11/1947 in Hanover; first; Donald R. Reed (farmer, Stamford, CT) and Edna E. Gregory (Hanover)
Barbara Porter, b. 7/15/1950 in Hanover; second; Donald R. Reed (farmer, Stamford, CT) and Edna E. Gregory (Hanover)
Beverly Jean, b. 4/23/1936 in Hanover; second; Nelson F. Reed (farmer, Wilder, VT) and Ada I. Eastman (W. Newbury, VT)
Donna Lucille, b. 10/13/1959; Donald R. Reed and Edna E. Gregory
Jill Marie, b. 9/18/1955 in Hanover; third; Donald R. Reed (farmer, Stamford, CT) and Edna E. Gregory (Hanover)

RHO[A]DES,
daughter, b. 6/8/1890 in Orford; fourth; Wilbur Rhodes (laborer, 25) and Emma Simpson (26, Orford)

daughter, b. 5/28/1892 in Orford; fifth; Wilbur Rhodes (laborer, 27, Topsham, VT) and Emma L. Simpson (27, Orford)

Flossie Dell, b. 3/29/1904 in Orford; seventh; Wilbur Rhodes (laborer, 39, Waits River) and Emma L. Simpson (41, Orford)

John F. B., b. 2/26/1889 in Orford; third; Wilbur Rhodes (farmer, 24, Washington, VT) and Emma Rhodes (24, Orford)

Lettie Irene, b. 5/7/1898 in Orford; sixth; Wilber Rhodes (laborer, 33, Topsham, VT) and Emma L. Simpson (33, Orford)

Mildred May, b. 8/8/1906 in Orford; eighth; Wilbur F. Rhoades (laborer, 42, Waits River, VT) and Emma L. Simpson (42, Orford)

RICH,

Blair Robert, b. 11/9/1963 in Hanover; David A. Rich (laborer, Hanover) and Jacqueline Johnson (Hanover)

Clayton Robert, b. 9/19/1996 in New London; Daniel Jonathan Rich and Andrea Elizabeth Pickering Rich

Deena Marie, b. 8/25/1968 in Hanover; David A. Rich (laborer, 26, Hanover) and Jacqueline Johnson (23, Hanover)

Jelena Christine, b. 9/11/1995 in Orford; Michael Steven Rich and Sheena Marie Giesing Rich

Marissa Giesing, b. 9/11/1995 in Orford; Michael Steven Rich and Sheena Marie Giesing Rich

RICHARDSON,

George, b. 10/4/1953 in Lebanon; first; Frederick C. Richardson (teacher, Boston, MA) and Ingemarie Morgan (Waterbury, CT)

Grace, b. 8/18/1906 in Orford; second; Arthur J. Richardson (teamster, 42, Orford) and Hattie C. Gardner (39, Lyme)

Ina Clementine, b. 8/15/1898 in Orford; first; Arthur J. Richardson (teamster, 34, Orford) and Hattie C. Gardner (31, Lyme)

Margaret, b. 5/24/1955 in Lebanon; second; Frederick C. Richardson (teacher, Boston, MA) and Ingemarie C. Morgan (Waterbury, CT)

RICHMOND,

Helen Leas, b. 7/24/1958 in Hanover; first; Robert G. Richmond (foreign serv., Waltham, MA) and Helen S. Cothran (Baguio, PI)

Peter Herbert, b. 12/29/1937 in Orford; third; Gould S. Richmond (farmer, Byron, ME) and Hilda Lynch (NS)

Roberta, b. 6/18/1936 in Orford; second; Gould Richmond (farmer, Byron, ME) and Hilda Lynch (Annapolis, NS)

RICKER,
Angela Francis, b. 10/8/2004 in Orford; David Ricker and Melinda Ricker
Kevin Lawrence, b. 12/8/1960 in Hanover; fifth; Lawrence R. Ricker (const. work, Norwich, VT) and Beverly Record (Hanover)
Lucy, b. 5/23/1909; second; Eugene W. Ricker (laborer, 36, E. Haven, VT) and Louisa E. Towne (20, Kirby, VT)

ROBB,
Paul Robert, b. 12/8/1957 in Hanover; second; Robert C. Robb (minister, Windsor, ON) and Sandra Arlene Schultz (Clare, MI)

ROBERTS,
son, b. 1/15/1890 in Orford; fourth; Leonard M. Roberts (cooper, 56, Orford) and Emily Magoon (36, Stanstead, PQ)
Melanie Ann, b. 3/22/1982; Maurice Roberts and Martha Roberts
Meredith Allison, b. 3/12/1985; Maurice Roberts and Martha Roberts
Michael, b. 5/3/1979 in Hanover; Maurice Roberts and Martha Roberts
Morris Arthur, b. 3/2/1929 in Orford; second; Morris A. Roberts (clerk, Canada) and Clementine Richardson (Orford)

ROBIE,
Bryan Wyness, b. 3/21/1953 in Lebanon; third; Keith M. Robie (plant manager, Piermont) and Verna E. Tunker (Orange, VT)
Dwight Alan, b. 5/28/1949 in Lebanon; second; Keith M. Robie (foreman, Piermont) and Verna E. Tucker (Orange, VT)
Joan Elaine, b. 9/1/1960 in Lebanon; fifth; Keith M. Robie (plant super., Piermont) and Verna E. Tucker (Orange, VT)
Scott Edward, b. 5/7/1955 in Lebanon; fourth; Keith M. Robie (plant mgr., Piermont) and Verna E. Tucker (Orange, VT)

ROBINSHAW,
Robert Frederick, b. 8/7/1955 in Lebanon; first; Robert F. Robinshaw (US Marines, CT) and Shirley E. Nutter (Bradford, VT)

ROCKWELL,
Hanna Foster, b. 2/25/1996 in Lebanon; Adam Todd Rockwell and Toni Lee Gray Rockwell

ROLLINS,
child, b. 1/21/1887 in Orford; third; Fred E. Rollisn (farmer, Campton) and Emma A. Saunders (Hanover)
daughter, b. 6/1/1890 in Orford; fourth; Fred E. Rollins (laborer, 30, Campton) and Emma A. Sanders (21, Hanover)
daughter, b. 2/14/1900 in Orford; seventh; Fred E. Rollins (farmer, 40, Campton) and Emma Sanders (30, Hanover)
daughter, b. 10/20/1902 in Orford; ninth; Fred E. Rollins (farmer, 43, Campton) and Emma Launders (Hanover)
daughter, b. 8/2/1904 in Orford; third; Willis A. Rollins (laborer, 29, Orford) and Laura Durant (29, Topsham)
daughter, b. 10/23/1906 in Orford; tenth; Fred E. Rollins (farmer, 47, Campton) and Emma A. Saunders (37, Hanover)
son, b. 10/21/1916 in Orford; first; Ella M. Rollins (17, Wentworth)
Amy, b. 10/21/1898 in Orford; sixth; Fred E. Rollins (farmer, 39, Campton) and Emma A. Sanders (29, Hanover)
Eva D., b. 6/23/1889 in Orford; first; John O. Rollins (laborer, 27, Orford) and Jennie M. Tuttle (22, Topsham, VT)
Frank H., b. 6/23/1893 in Orford; second; Hiram B. Rollins (farmer, 29, Rumney) and Addie Hammond (20, Wentworth)
May A., b. 12/12/1905 in Orford; fourth; Willis A. Rollins (laborer, 30, Orford) and Laura Durant (30, Topsham, VT)
Minnie E., b. 7/28/1903 in Orford; second; Willis A. Rollins (laborer, 28, Orford) and Laura Durant (28, Topsham, VT)

RONDEAU,
Emily Irene, b. 8/12/1995 in Lebanon; David George Rondeau and Lois Jane Pushee Rondeau

ROSS,
stillborn son, b. 10/18/1895 in Orford; third; David P. Ross (farming, 33, Margurite, NS) and Jane Wilson (33, PQ)
stillborn child, b. 1/24/1897; fourth; David Ross (farmer, 32, Margurel, NS) and Jennie Wilson (32, Henrysburg, PQ)
daughter, b. 1/7/1898 in Orford; fifth; David P. Ross (farming, 35, Margaree, NS) and Jane Wilson (33, Henrysburg, PQ)

son, b. 1/10/1902 in Orford; fifth; David P. Ross (farmer, 39, Maryasel, NS) and Jennie Wilson (Hennysburg, PQ)
William Robert, III, b. 3/25/1992 in Lebanon; William Ross and Dorisann Ross

ROWE,
son, b. 3/24/1905 in Orford; fifth; Edward L. Rowe (merchant, 33, Corinth, VT) and Mary E. Ricker (35, Groton)
Edward L., b. 4/16/1907; sixth; Edward L. Rowe (postmaster, 36, Corinth, VT) and Mary L. Ricker (38, Groton, VT)

ROY,
Alannah Paige, b. 3/11/1995 in Lebanon; Anthony John Roy and Tammy Ann MacMillan Roy

RUFF,
Katelyn Joy, b. 5/5/1994 in Lebanon; Timothy Alan Tuff and Carol Sobetzer

RUSSELL,
son, b. 7/16/1890 in Orford; second; George H. Russell (farmer, 36, Orford) and Eliza A. French (36, Brunswick, VT)
daughter, b. 11/9/1899 in Orford; fifth; Fred Daniel Russell (laborer, 32, Turner, ME) and Eva Ellenwood (25, Hartford, PQ)
Catherine, b. 7/8/1919 in Hanover; second; Harry M. Russell (farmer, Orford) and Ida H. Robins (Atchinson, KS)
Fred, b. 4/29/1901 in Orford; sixth; Fred Russell (laborer, 33, Turner, ME) and Eva Ellenwood (26, Haniford, PQ)
Loraine Elizabeth, b. 1/9/1914 in Orford; first; Harry M. Russell (farmer, 32, Orford) and Ida H. Robinson (34, Atchinson, KS)

RUTLEDGE,
son, b. 10/13/1892 in Orford; third; Charles W. Rutledge (farmer, 36, NS) and Mary A. Wilson (32, Greensboro, VT)
son, b. 2/4/1918 in Orford; second; Harold C. Rutledge (laborer, Orford) and Myrtie B. Kimball (Orford)
Clarence R., b. 6/6/1896; fourth; Charles W. Rutledge (farming, 40, Amherst, NS) and Mary A. Wilson (36, Greensboro, VT)
Kimball Charles, b. 6/6/1915 in Orford; first; Harold C. Rutledge (farmer, 22, Orford) and Mertie B. Kimball (20, Orford)

RYAN,
Caitlyn Elizabeth, b. 10/23/2003 in Lebanon; Lewis Ryan and Heather Ryan

SALADINO,
daughter, b. 3/6/1920 in Orford; tenth; Joseph Saladino (farmer, Italy) and Bridged Connella (Italy)
Beatrice Leona, b. 8/5/1912 in Orford; eighth; Joseph Saladino (farmer, 32, Italy) and Camelia Brigida (32, Italy)
Margaret Josephine, b. 9/9/1910; seventh; Joseph Saladino (farmer, 36, Italy) and Brigida Cormella (30, Italy)

SANBORN,
son, b. 8/23/1894 in Orford; second; Asa O. Sanborn (farmer, 35, Hanover) and Hattie E. Stone (33, Orford)
daughter, b. 12/11/1921 in Orford; fifth; Harry J. Sanborn (farmer, Rumney) and Lula R. Blake (Plymouth)
stillborn daughter, b. 10/17/1928 in Orford; seventh; Harry J. Sanborn (farmer, Rumney) and Lulu B. Blake (Plymouth)
stillborn son, b. 5/24/1931 in Orford; eighth; Harry J. Sanborn (farmer, Rumney) and Lulu R. Blake (Plymouth)
Asa R., b. 3/19/1889 in Orford; first; Asa O. Sanborn (laborer, 30, Hanover) and Hattie E. Stone (28, Orford)
Bernard Malcolm, b. 7/6/1924; sixth; Harry J. Sanborn (farmer, Rumney) and Lula Blake (Plymouth)
Cindy Ann, b. 17/1973 in Lebanon; Franklin A. Sanborn (40, Orford) and Kathleen L. Blake (27, Orford)
Corinne Ida, b. 2/13/1936 in Orford; third; Robert Sanborn (laborer, Bath) and Evelyn Blake (Plymouth)
David M., b. 4/27/1938 in Orford; fourth; Robert Sanborn (farmer, Bath) and Evelyn Blake (Plymouth)
Dawn Marie, b. 5/30/1968 in Hanover; David M. Sanborn (laborer, 30, Orford) and Janice M. Hosmer (20, Stratford, VT)
Deann Kae, b. 7/2/1955 in Haverhill; second; Neil H. Sanborn (laborer, Orford) and Theresa M. Hudson (Lowell, MA)
Donna Jean, b. 5/20/1934 in Orford; second; Robert B. Sanborn (farmer, Bath) and Evelyn R. Blake (Plymouth)
Franklin Arthur, b. 11/9/1932 in Orford; second; Joseph H. Sanborn (farmer, Plymouth) and Ruth Franklin (Orford)
Harry Joseph, b. 7/30/1929 in Orford; first; Joseph H. Sanborn (farmer, Plymouth) and Ruth E. Franklin (Orford)

Hattie May, b. 3/19/1898 in Orford; third; Asa O. Sanborn
(lumberman, 39, Hanover) and Hattie E. Stone (37, Orford)
Hazel Abby, b. 7/22/1911; second; Fred J. Sanborn (veterinary sur.,
Bradford, VT) and Carrie A. Bacon (Arlington, MA)
James Arthur, b. 7/11/1936 in Orford; first; Richard Sanborn
(laborer, Lisbon) and Cora Blake (Plymouth)
Jane Lou, b. 11/17/1942 in Hanover; sixth; Robert B. Sanborn
(farmer, Beth) and Evelyn Ruth Blake (Plymouth)
Lonny Ferrin, b. 10/7/1968 in Lebanon; Franklin A. Sanborn (laborer,
35, Orford) and Kathleen L. Blake (22, Orford)
Mark Frederick, b. 7/19/1955 in Hanover; ninth; Robert B. Sanborn
(mill hand, Bath) and Evelyn R. Blake (Plymouth)
Melissa Dawn, b. 4/29/1957 in Haverhill; third; Neil Heath Sanborn
(laborer, Orford) and Theresa Mary Hudson (Lowell, MA)
Neil, b. 5/7/1937 in Orford; first; Joseph H. Sanborn (farmer,
Plymouth) and Helen E. Baker (Hanover)
Pamela Joan, b. 5/16/1954 in Haverhill; first; Neil Heath Sanborn
(carpenter, Orford) and Theresa Mary Hudson (Lowell, MA)
Paula Elizabeth, b. 11/8/1949 in Orford; first; Bernard M. Sanborn
(farmer, Orford) and Bernice L. Finney (Orford)
Rebecca Rae, b. 10/7/1948 in Orford; seventh; Robert B. Sanborn
(lumberman, Bath) and Evelyn R. Blake (Plymouth)
Robert B., b. 8/27/1932 in Orford; first; Robert B. Sanborn (farmer,
Lisbon) and Evelyn R. Blake (Plymouth)
Roxanne Blake, b. 11/20/1950 in Orford; eighth; Robert N. Sanborn
(mill hand, Bath) and Evelyn R. Blake (Plymouth)
Stephen Arthur, b. 6/26/1965 in Lebanon; Franklin A. Sanborn
(carpenter, Orford) and Kathleen L. Blake (Orford)
Susan Evelyn, b. 9/10/1940 in Orford; fifth; Robert Sanborn (farmer,
Bath) and Evelyn Blake (Plymouth)

SAUNDERS,
Albert Jessie, b. 7/3/1899 in Orford; second; Harry G. Saunders
(farmer, 33, Orford) and Nettie L. Mack (18, Piermont)
Alice G., b. 5/6/1907; sixth; Harry G. Saunders (farmer, 41, Orford)
and Nettie L. Mack (26, Piermont)
Charles Frank, b. 8/24/1901 in Orford; third; Harry G. Saunders
(farmer, 35, Orford) and Nettie L. Mack (20, Piermont)
Della N., b. 5/24/1897; first; Harry G. Saunders (farmer, 31, Orford)
and Nettie L. Mack (16, Piermont)

Grace Lizzie, b. 8/29/1903 in Orford; fourth; Harry G. Saunders
(farmer, 37, Orford) and Nettie L. Mack (22, Piermont)
Ralph Frank, b. 3/28/1905 in Orford; fifth; Harry G. Saunders
(farmer, 38, Orford) and Nettie L. Mack (23, Piermont)

SAVAGE,
child, b. 8/3/1887 in Orford; second; Thomas Savage (farmer, 31,
Orford) and Ida R. Savage (25, Piermont)
child, b. 9/21/1887 in Orford; first; John H. Savage (farmer, 26,
Benton) and Sallie P. Savage (18, Haverhill)
son, b. 11/23/1888; second; John H. Savage (farmer, 27, Benton)
and Sallie P. Carter (19, Haverhill)
son, b. 9/10/1889 in Orford; third; Thomas T. Savage (farmer, 33,
Orford) and Ida R. Mack (27, Piermont)
daughter, b. 2/27/1890 in Orford; third; John H. Savage (farmer, 28,
Benton) and Sally Carter (21, Haverhill)
daughter, b. 6/4/1891 in Orford; fourth; Thomas T. Savage (farmer,
34, Orford) and Ida A. Mack (29, Piermont)
son, b. 11/21/1892 in Orford; fourth; John H. Savage (farmer, 31,
Benton) and Sadie P. Carter (23, Haverhill)
daughter, b. 4/16/1898 in Orford; fifth; Thomas T. Savage (farmer,
42, Orford) and Ida R. Mack (34, Piermont)
son, b. 2/16/1900 in Orford; sixth; Thomas T. Savage (farmer, 43,
Orford) and Ida R. Mack (37, Piermont)

SAVERY,
Joseph Brian, b. 10/10/1984; Brian Savery and Wendy Savery
Matthew Ryan, b. 6/18/1990 in Lebanon; Brian Savery and Wendy
Savery

SCHAUER,
Barbara Ellen, b. 10/4/1952 in Haverhill; seventh; Leverne H.
Schauer (lumberman, Arnot, PA) and Lillian Margeson (N.
Reading, MA)

SCHOFIELD,
Edgar Lester, b. 11/24/1925; eighth; Ernest H. Schofield (laborer,
Everett, MA) and Gladys G. Johnstone (NS)
Ernest Henry, b. 11/18/1923; seventh; Ernest H. Schofield (laborer,
Everett, MA) and Gladys Johnson (Kentville, NS)

Harold Dexter, b. 11/5/1931 in Orford; eleventh; Ernest H. Schofield (laborer, Everett, MA) and Gladys G. Johnston (Kentsville, NS)
Levina Burnece, b. 7/22/1929 in Orfordville; tenth; Ernest H. Schofield (laborer, Everett, MA) and Gladys Johnston (Kentville, NS)
Lois Marjorie, b. 5/5/1928 in Orford; ninth; Ernest H. Schofield (laborer, Everett, MA) and Gladys G. Johnston (NS)
Verjinia Lillian, b. 12/20/1921 in Orford; sixth; Ernest H. Schofield (laborer, Everett, MA) and Gladys Johnson (Canfield, NS)

SCHORSCH,
child, b. 3/5/1987; Michael Schorsch and Elaine Schorsch
Aaron, b. 3/21/1983; Michael Schorsch and Elaine Himadi

SCHWARZ,
April Lynn, b. 8/26/1985; Thomas Schwarz and April Schwarz
Clinton George, b. 2/21/1964 in Hanover; George J. Schwarz (farmer, New York, NY) and Juanita A. Marsh (Orford)
Emily Jean, b. 7/25/1999 in Plymouth; Randy Schwarz and Adrienne Schwarz
Karen Marie, b. 6/6/1960 in Hanover; first; George J. Schwarz (farmer, New York, NY) and Juanita A. Marsh (Orford)
Lora Lee, b. 2/4/1963 in Hanover; George J. Schwarz (farmer, NY) and Juanita A. Marsh (Orford)
Mackenzie Maria, b. 6/13/1997 in Lebanon; Clinton George Schwarz and Robin Elaine Dugdale Schwarz
Randy, b. 7/3/1978 in Hanover; George Schwarz (39, NY) and Juanita Marsh (37, NH)
Thomas Ralph, b. 5/2/1961 in Hanover; second; George John Schwarz (farmer, Queen City, NY) and Juanita Ann Marsh (Orford)

SCOTT,
daughter, b. 6/16/1908; third; Athol P. Scott (lumberman, 34, Windham) and Edith M. Heald (28, Lowell, MA)

SEELEY,
Georgia, b. 8/8/1898 in Orford; fourth; Reuben Seeley (laborer, 29, NS) and Clersilda Blair (28, PQ)

SHARPS,
son, b. 2/18/1920 in Orford; second; Joseph Sharps (gardener, Cheshire, England) and Agnes Lane (Ham Surrey, England)
daughter, b. 1/29/1923; third; Joseph Sharpe (gardener, Cheshire, England) and Agnes M. Lane (Ham Surry, England)
Joseph Avery, b. 5/2/1926; fifth; Joseph Sharps (gardner, Merton, England) and Agnes M. Lane (Ham Surry, England)

SHAW,
Joy Elizabeth, b. 1/30/1949 in Orford; third; Norman E. Shaw, Jr. (laborer, Lyndonville, VT) and Eileen G. Cournoyer (W. Warwick, RI); residence – Fairlee, VT

SHEPARD,
Bernard Louis, b. 7/31/1937 in Orford; tenth; Frank Shepard (lumberman, NY) and Rose M. Bombard (NY)

SHERRY,
Alma E., b. 9/6/1922; fourth; Nicholas J. Sherry (plumber, Summit, NJ) and Marguerite A. Smith (Orford)

SHIPMAN,
Jared Wheeler, b. 2/24/1976 in Lebanon; Frederick W. Shipman (31, NJ) and Gail W. Thorndike (27, CT)

SHONTELL,
Susan Kay, b. 11/4/1971 in Haverhill; Fred E. Shontell (40, NH) and Ida M. Weeks (39, NH)

SIEMONS,
Tanner Robert, b. 6/15/2001 in Lebanon; Gary Siemons and Raquel Siemons

SILVER,
daughter, b. 3/13/1904 in Orford; first; Charles A. Silver (laborer, 22, Jefferson) and L. Blanche Dimick (19, Lyme)

SIMONS,
son, b. 4/23/1894 in Orford; first; Selar G. Simons (farmer, 35, Orford) and Eva May Hatch (23, W. Fairlee, VT)

SIMPSON,
child, b. 9/25/1887 in Orford; first; Willie E. Simpson (farmer, 29, Orford) and Minnie J. Savage (22, Benton)
son, b. 8/20/1890 in Orford; second; Herman Simpson (laborer, 31, Orford) and Ella M. Hackett (23, Orford)
John B., b. 9/8/1893 in Orford; third; H. L. Simpson (farmer, 34, Orford) and Ella M. Hackett (24, Orford)

SLEASMAN,
Caitlin Ann, b. 11/1/1986; Perry Sleasman and Brenda Sleasman

SLEEPER,
Erica Leslie, b. 3/14/1982; Eric Sleeper and Barbara Sleeper

SMITH,
child, b. 8/11/1887 in Orford; tenth; Alphonso Smith (farmer, 38, Manchester) and Clarinda Worthen (38, Wentworth)
daughter, b. 8/2/1890 in Orford; eleventh; Alphonso Smith (farmer, 41, Manchester) and Clarinda Worthen (41, Wentworth)
daughter, b. 6/3/1895 in Orford; first; Charles B. Smith (laborer, 20, Corinth, VT) and Cora A. Flanders (18, W. Fairlee, VT)
daughter, b. 2/21/1896; first; Clarence S. Smith (laborer, 27, Orford) and Sarah A. Archer (18, Orford)
daughter, b. 9/7/1897; second; Clarence S. Smith (laborer, 28, Lyme) and Sarah A. Archer (20, Orford)
stillborn daughter, b. 6/3/1898 in Orford; first; Carl C. Smith (laborer, 23, Windsor, VT) and Mary E. Mann (22, Orford)
son, b. 1/3/1901 in Orford; fourth; Clarence S. Smith (laborer, 31, Lyme) and Sarah A. Archer (23, Orford)
Abigail Rose, b. 5/11/1982; David Smith and Martha Smith
Amy Midori, b. 6/24/1970 in Hanover; Charles E. Smith (30, Orford) and Hideko Nagahama (31, Okinawa, Japan)
Brenda Margaret, b. 10/2/1947 in Haverhill first; Guy W. Smith (auto worker, Orford) and Virginia R. Roberts (Fairlee, VT)
Caddy Rose, b. 5/14/1896; second; Charles D. Smith (laborer, 21, Corinth, VT) and Rose Ann Flanders (19, W. Fairlee, VT)
Carrol Alphonso, b. 2/4/1899 in Orford; first; Carroll B. Smith (laborer, 22, Orford) and Mary Watson (23, Ireland)
Charles Christopher, b. 3/5/1966 in Hanover; Jean E. Smith (assoc. prof., Washington, DC) and Christine Johanna Zinsel (Berlin, Germany)

Charles Edward, b. 8/20/1939 in Orford; fifth; Allen Ivan Smith (laborer, Calais, ME) and Siltonia Bell Shonis (Duxbury, VT)
Clyde R., b. 3/11/1896; first; Arthur E. Smith (laborer, 27, Barnard, VT) and Alice M. Turner (19, Thetford, VT)
David Robert, b. 4/16/1952 in Haverhill; second; Guy W. Smith (repair man, Orford) and Virginia R. Roberts (Fairlee, VT)
Dennis Scott, b. 5/6/1966 in Hanover; Stanley R. Smith (floor boss, Lyme) and Rosie Mary Cummings (Woodsville)
Gene Wallace, b. 4/20/1939 in Orford; sixth; Hazen Lewis Smith (int. decorator, Quechee, VT) and Lizzie Belle King (E. Montpelier, VT)
Glenda Ellen, b. 12/15/1955 in Hanover; second; Stanley R. Smith, Jr. (trucker, Lyme) and Rosie Mary Cummings (Woodsville)
Glenn Eric, b. 6/16/1930 in Orford; second; Hazel Lewis Smith (laborer, Quechee, VT) and Lizzie Belle King (Montpelier, VT)
Guy Willis, b. 12/22/1923; first; Guy G. Smith (chauffeur, Fairlee, VT) and Laura M. Willis (Orford); residence – Fairlee, VT
Hazen Louis, Jr., b. 12/29/1937 in Orford; fourth; Hazen L. Smith (painter, Quechee, VT) and Lizzie King (E. Montpelier, VT)
Jedediah Eugene, b. 6/21/1979 in Lebanon; David Smith and Martha Smith
Jera Bushrod, b. 1/2/1905 in Orford; fifth; Carl C. Smith (laborer, 29, Windsor, VT) and Mary E. Mann (29, Orford)
Karen Lee, b. 11/15/1957 in Hanover; third; Stanley R. Smith (laborer, Lyme) and Rosie M. Cummings (Woodsville)
Kim Zeno, b. 2/10/1969 in Hanover; Charles E. Smith (29, Orford) and Hideka Nagahama (30, Okinawa)
Laurence Walter, b. 8/21/1925; first; Joel C. Smith (laborer, Orford) and Elizabeth Howe (Cornish Flat)
Leonard, b. 9/9/1937 in Orford; fourth; Joel C. Smith (farmer, Orford) and Elizabeth J. Howe (Cornish Flats)
Lillian May, b. 7/6/1899 in Orford; third; Clarence S. Smith (laborer, 30, Lyme) and Sarah A. Archer (22, Orford)
Lizzie, b. 11/3/1888; second; Eugene C. Smith (mason, 35, Orford) and Rosa Preston Smith (30, Monkton, MA)
Lloyd Everett, b. 8/9/1937 in Orford; third; Allen I. Smith (laborer, Calais, ME) and Siltonia Shonio (Duxbury, VT)
Melissa Ann, b. 5/10/1976 in Woodsville; Stanley R. Smith, Jr. (22, NH) and Faye A. Pike (20, NH)
Michelle Marie, b. 1/2/1964 in Hanover; Stanley R. Smith (floor boss, Lyme) and Rose Mary Cummings (Woodsville)

Naomi Bell, b. 9/24/1966 in Haverhill; Charles E. Smith (constr., Orford) and Hideke N. Nagahama (Okinawa)
Nicole Lynn, b. 3/11/1974 in Haverhill; Stanley R. Smith, Jr. (20, Hanover) and Faye A. Pike (18, Hanover)
Paul Arthur, b. 11/2/1953 in Haverhill; third; Guy W. Smith (auto body repair, Orford) and Virginia R. Roberts (Fairlee, VT)
Virginia Jane, b. 3/12/1936 in Orford; fourth; Hazen Smith (painter, Quechee, VT) and Lizzie King (E. Montpelier, VT)

SNOW,
Karen Joan, b. 9/4/1946 in Haverhill; first; Bernard D. Snow (cab driver, W. Fairlee, VT) and Pauline M. Adams (Dover)
Vergen R., b. 7/27/1893 in Orford; third; Herbert W. Snow (farmer, 35, Malone, NY) and Abbie E. Griffin (34, Marlow)

SOUTHWICK,
son, b. 5/23/1897; third; Fred E. Southwick (carpenter, 32, Concord) and Emma V. Ford (20, Orford)

SOUTHWORTH,
Jennifer Lynn, b. 10/5/1974 in Haverhill; David R. Southworth (25, Topeka, KS) and Christine M. Stearns (20, Lebanon)

SPAULDING,
Emily Ann, b. 2/17/1995 in Lebanon; Gary Conrey Spaulding and Paula Rae Balch Spaulding
Kristen Barbara, b. 9/18/1987; Gary Spaulding and Paula Spaulding
Stephanie Elizabeth, b. 12/7/1990 in Hanover; Gary Spaulding and Paula Spaulding

SPENCER,
son, b. 7/1/1920 in Orford; fifth; James E. Spencer (farmer, Wolfeville, NS) and Georgia P. Archer (Orford)
Edward Clinton, b. 3/18/1951 in Lebanon; first; Hugh E. Spencer (B & M RR, Piermont) and Evelyn B. Stetson (Piermont)
Fred Patridge, b. 5/27/1920 in Orford; third; Elmer Spencer (farmer, Stratford) and Tina Patridge (Haverhill)
Georgia May, b. 7/17/1924; sixth; James Spencer (farmer, Wolfville, NS) and Georgia Archer (Orford)
Hazel Velma, b. 6/7/1911; first; James E. Spencer (painter, Wolfville, NS) and Georgia P. Archer (Orford)

Hugh Edward, b. 6/15/1916 in Orford; third; James E. Spencer
 (painter, 34, Wolfville, NS) and Georgie P. Archer (24, Orford)
James Clinton, b. 7/4/1913 in Orford; second; James E. Spencer
 (painter, 29, Wolfeville, NS) and Georgia Archer (22, Orford)

SPOTTSWOOD,
James Andrew, b. 11/9/1974 in Hanover; Stephen A. Spottswood
 (28, Gainesville, FL) and Marion G. Thomson (26, Long Island,
 NY)

STANTON,
son, b. 12/19/1895 in Orford; third; John S. Stanton (laborer, 35, NJ)
 and Alice M. Gilbert (24, Burlington, VT)
Harry E., b. 2/8/1893 in Orford; second; John S. Stanton (laborer,
 32, Jersey City, NJ) and Alice M. Meserve (20, Burlington, VT)
Sadie Ellen, b. 6/18/1890 in Orford; first; John S. Stanton (farmer,
 29, Jersey City) and Alice May Meserve (17, Burlington, VT)

STEARNS,
infant, b. 2/25/1963 in Hanover; Eli R. Stearns (laborer, Etna) and
 Ramona H. Ladeau (Fairlee, VT)
Christine Marie, b. 5/4/1954 in Lebanon; first; Eli Robert Stearns
 (laborer, Etna) and Ramona Hilda Ladeau (Fairlee, VT)
Rhonda Lee, b. 7/3/1961 in Hanover; first; Reginald E. Stearns
 (truck driver, Lyme) and Pauline Dora LaDeau (Fairlee, VT)
Wayne Eli, b. 11/14/1960 in Hanover; third; Eli R. Stearns (truck
 driver, Etna) and Ramona H. LaDeau (Fairlee, VT)

STEINACHER,
Rudolph Rhea, b. 9/15/1946 in Hanover; first; Rudolph Steinacher
 (exp. & imp., Switzerland) and Patricia Ryan (Muskogee, OK)

STETSON,
child, b. 8/23/1904 in Orford; first; Louis O. Stetson (meat cutter, 26,
 Orford) and Bessie M. Drury (20, Worcester, MA); residence –
 Piermont
stillborn son, b. 5/21/1921 in Hanover; fourth; Harry W. Stetson
 (physician, Lyme) and Alice L. Greaves (Mapleville, RI)
Calvin Alden, b. 1/2/1914 in Orford; third; Harry W. Stetson
 (physician, 30, Lyme) and Alice L. Greaves (27, Mapleville, RI)

Charles Greaves, b. 1/21/1909; first; Harry W. Stetson (physician, 25, Lyme) and Alice L. Greaves (22, Mapleville, RI)
Ella M., b. 8/1/1895 in Orford; first; Charles W. Stetson (laborer, 21, Orford) and Nellie M. Brown (19, Andover)
Gardner King, b. 7/1/1925; first; Claude H. Stetson (mechanic, Wenchester) and Doris E. Gardner (Orford); residence – Newport
Larry Wesley, b. 1/20/1943 in Haverhill; Wesley F. Stetson (laborer, Piermont) and Edna Arline Lamay (Newbury, VT)
Myrtle Nell, b. 9/18/1905 in Orford; fourth; Will A. Stetson (laborer, 31, Thetford, VT) and Emma A. Brown (27, Andover)
Parker Francs, b. 6/27/1912 in Orford; second; Harry W. Stetson (physician, 28, Lyme) and Alice L. Greaves (26, Mapleville, RI)

STEVENS,
Dana, b. 4/11/1890 in Orford; third; Alvah M. Stevens (farmer, 30, Orford) and Angie H. Lamprey (26, Orford)
Faith G., b. 4/6/1893 in Orford; fourth; Alvah M. Stevens (farmer, 32, Orford) and Angie N. Lamprey (29, Orford)
Frances Arlene, b. 5/3/1950 in Lebanon; third; Fred H. Stevens (auto mechanic, E. Charlestown, VT) and Dorothy C. Hilt (Lewiston, ME)
Irene May, b. 6/25/1921 in Hanover; first; Maurice H. Stevens (farmer, Orford) and Ardelle C. Lynes (Hardwick, VT)
Isabelle Lufkin, b. 6/30/1930 in Hanover; second; Frank A. Stevens (lumber dealer, Orford) and Evelyn Lufkin (Thetford, VT); residence – Lyme
Leon O., b. 10/16/1889 in Orford; first; Orin E. Stetson (blacksmith, 23, Lyme) and Abbie J. Corliss (27, Orford)
Louis Maurice, b. 4/19/1923; second; Maurice H. Stevens (farmer, Orford) and Ardella C. Lynes (Hardwick, VT)
Margarite Eunice, b. 9/19/1926; fourth; Morris Stevens (laborer, Orford) and Adel Lynes (Hardwich, VT)
Morris Henry, b. 3/7/1900 in Orford; fifth; Alvah M. Stevens (farmer, 39, Orford) and Angie N. Lamprey (36, Orford)
Royce Neil, b. 12/25/1931 in Orford; seventh; Maurice H. Stevens (laborer, Orford) and Ardell C. Lynes (Hardwick, VT)
Wallace Alvah, b. 12/21/1928 in Hanover; first; Frank A. Stevens (lumber dealer, Orford) and Evelyn K. Lufkin (Thetford, VT)

STEWART,
Thelma Marion, b. 4/18/1929 in Orford; first; Edward Stewart (laborer, Concord, VT) and Ellen Patridge (Haverhill)

STILL,
daughter, b. 8/16/1904 in Orford; third; Eugene L. Still (farmer, 44, Orange) and Clara R. Clogston (42, Burke, VT)

STIMSON,
Jacob Joshua, b. 11/21/1998 in Lebanon; Andrew Philip Stimson and Maritza G. Godfrey-Stimson

STOCKWELL,
son, b. 10/31/1897; fourth; Charles E. Stockwell (laborer, 38, Stanbridge, PQ) and Emma J. Morse (24, Brome, PQ)

STONE,
Dorothy, b. 1/4/1906 in Orford; first; Edward P. Stone (farmer, 35, Burke, NY) and Grace M. Daniels (29, Boston, MA)
Marie Elizabeth, b. 7/17/1931 in Orford; fourth; Ernest Joseph Stone (truck driver, Hartford, VT) and Elizabeth M. Carter (Norwich, VT); residence – Hartford, VT

STOUT,
Lillian, b. 5/21/1999 in Lebanon; Arthur Stout and Barbara Stout
Taylor Mae, b. 3/16/1997 in Lebanon; Arthur Elkins Stout and Barbara B. Sargent Stout

STREETER,
Bruce Earl, b. 4/10/1965 in Lebanon; Carl M. Streeter (logger, Hanover) and Lucy E. Grimes (Eden, VT)
Carl Moody, b. 5/14/1928 in Hanover; fourth; Ray N. Streeter (farmer, Sugar Hill) and Stella Cushing (McIndoes Falls, VT)
Dennis Roy, b. 3/2/1960 in Lebanon; third; Carl M. Streeter (logger, Hanover) and Lucy E. Grimes (Eden, VT)
Ellen Marie, b. 2/11/1959; Carl M. Streeter and Lucy E. Grimes
Isabell Rachael, b. 8/28/1945 in Haverhill; second; Ralph R. Streeter (trucking, Wentworth) and Ethel F. Ladeau (Orford)
Lucas Trussell, b. 2/8/2001 in Lebanon; Bruce Streeter and Audrey Streeter

Marion M., b. 3/29/1912 in Orford; second; Roy N. Streeter (farmer, 25, Lisbon) and Stella M. Cushing (20, McIndoes, VT)
Roland Carl, b. 6/15/1908; first; Carl M. Streeter (laborer, 23, Lisbon) and Rosa M. Allen (17, Canada)
Travis Carl, b. 10/22/1993 in Lebanon; Bruce Earl Streeter and Audrey Ann Trussell Streeter
Winifred Alice, b. 9/27/1930 in Orford; first; Marion Streeter (Orford)

SUNBURY,
Helen Elizabeth, b. 1/10/1931 in Woodsville; stillborn; first; Arthur Sunbury (farmer, Waterford, VT) and Bernice Howe (W. Hopkinton)

SUPER,
Kaitlin Lee, b. 7/11/1985; Kenneth Super and Patrice Super
Lauren Anna, b. 2/23/1982; Kenneth Super and Patrice Super

SURPRENANT,
Samuel Parker, b. 3/31/2001 in Lebanon; Timothy Surprenant and Kirsten Surprenant

SWAN,
Charles Henry, b. 4/20/1928 in Hanover; first; Harold Wesley Swan (storekeeper, Haverhill) and Ruth Elizabeth Munn (W. Fairlee, VT)
Elizabeth Ann, b. 1/4/1936 in Hanover; fifth; Herbert R. Swan (undertaker, Haverhill) and Marion K. Sheridan (Whitefield)
Ellen Katherine, b. 8/19/1929 in Hanover; first; Herbert R. Swan (merchant, Haverhill) and Marion Sheridan (Whitefield)
George Thomas, b. 6/6/1931 in Hanover; second; Herbert R. Swan (merchant, Haverhill) and Marion Sheridan (Whitefield)
Henry Bailey, b. 3/7/1934 in Hanover; fourth; Herbert R. Swan (undertaker, Haverhill) and Marion K. Sheridan (Whitefield)
Robert Sheridan, b. 7/15/1932 in Hanover; third; Herbert R. Swan (merchant, Haverhill) and Marion Sheridan (Whitefield)
Russell Ordway, b. 2/11/1933 in Hanover; second; Harold W. Swan (road agent, Haverhill) and Ruth Munn (W. Fairlee, VT)

SWASEY,
Bradley Isaac, b. 11/25/2001 in Lebanon; Bradley Swasey and Helen Curry

SWETT,
son, b. 7/7/1904 in Orford; third; Curtis S. Swett (laborer, 28, Lyme) and Carrie O. Valley (21, Norwich)

TALLMAN,
son, b. 7/13/1924; ninth; Forest P. Tallman (laborer, Orford) and Jennie B. Rhodes (Orford)
Ada Elliot, b. 11/23/1908; second; Forest P. Tallman (laborer, 31, Orford) and Jennie B. Rhoades (22, Orford)
Bertha May, b. 12/5/1918 in Orford; seventh; Forest P. Tallman (laborer, Orford) and Jennie Rhodes (Orford)
Frank D., b. 9/13/1916 in Orford; sixth; Forest Tallman (laborer, 39, Orford) and Jennie B. Rhodes (30, Orford)
George Almon, b. 9/3/1914 in Orford; fourth; Forest P. Tallman (laborer, 34, Orford) and Jennie B. Rhodes (28, Orford)
Jerry William, b. 6/9/1912 in Orford; fourth; Forest P. Tallman (farmer, 35, Orford) and Jennie B. Rhoades (25, Orford)
Josephine S., b. 8/27/1938 in Haverhill; first; Merlyn Blake (auto dealer, Bradford, VT) and Lillian Tallman (Orford); residence – Bradford, VT and Orford
Lillian Margret, b. 10/11/1921 in Orford; eighth; Forest P. Tallman (farmer, Orford) and Jennie B. Rhodes (Orford)
Rosie Ellen, b. 10/6/1910; third; Forest P. Tallman (farmer, 33, Orford) and Jennie B. Rhoades (24, Orford)
Ruth Marion, b. 12/10/1926; tenth; Forest P. Tallman (laborer, Orford) and Jennie B. Rhoades (Orford)
Sidney J., b. 2/28/1907; first; Forest P. Tallman (laborer, 29, Orford) and Jennie B. Rhodes (20, Orford)

TARBOX,
stillborn son, b. 6/9/1892 in Orford; third; William A. Tarbox (farmer, 29, Piermont) and Costora Fuller (25, Northfield, MN)
child, b. 5/18/1894 in Orford; third; William A. Tarbox (farmer, 32, Piermont) and Castora Fuller (28, Northfield, MN); residence – Piermont
Lucy F., b. 6/9/1892 in Orford; second; William A. Tarbox (farmer, 29, Piermont) and Costora Fuller (25, Northfield, MN)

TARLETON,
Ian Slidell, b. 5/14/1984; Brian Tarleton and Alice Tarleton
Malcolm Edward, b. 11/18/1986; Brian Tarleton and Alice Tarleton

TARR,
Florence Marie, b. 10/13/1936 in Orford; fifth; Bert D. Tarr (lumberman, Litchfield, ME) and Dorothy Houston (Plymouth)
Marilyn Aubrey, b. 10/31/1937 in Orford; sixth; Bert Tarr (lumberman, Litchfield, ME) and Dorothy Houston (Plymouth)

TATHAM,
James Donald, b. 3/26/1955 in Hanover; first; Donald A. Tatham (logger, Wentworth) and Virginia J. Perry (N. Haverhill)
Lindsay Abigail, b. 6/30/1991 in Hanover; James Tatham and Jamie Tatham

TATTERSALL,
Mary Mae, b. 3/7/1930 in Hanover; first; Ernest Tattersall (farmer, Lyme) and Evelyn Cox (Concord)

TAYLOR,
daughter, b. 2/4/1893 in Orford; first; Charles E. Taylor (laborer, 20, Newport, VT) and Mabel E. Haley (21, Waterloo, IA)
Abigail Leighann Marie, b. 4/13/2004 in Lebanon; Timothy Taylor and Jennifer Taylor
Bruce F., Jr., b. 1/24/1972 in Haverhill; Bruce F. Taylor, Sr. (24, St. Johnsbury, VT) and Gloria Jean Pike (21, Lebanon)
Clifton Ray, b. 9/13/1976 in Woodsville; Larry Allen Taylor (22, VT) and Susan L. Hook (25, NH)
Hunter Alan, b. 12/6/2002 in Lebanon; Timothy Taylor and Jennifer Findley
Jaime Lynn, b. 10/20/1982; Harold Taylor and Theresa Taylor
Jason Lee, b. 3/12/1984; Dennis Taylor and Dawn Taylor
Julie Anne, b. 7/19/1979 in Haverhill; Larry Taylor and Susan Taylor
Kylie Ruth, b. 8/27/2004 in Lebanon; Rodney Taylor and Jennifer Hebb
Laura Ingrid, b. 3/31/1975 in Haverhill; Larry A. Taylor (20, St. Johnsbury, VT) and Susan L. Hook (23, Woodsville)
Margaret Ann, b. 8/23/1969 in Haverhill; Bruce F. Taylor (22, St. Johnsbury, VT) and Gloria J. Pike (18, Lebanon)
Matthew James, b. 7/6/1975 in Haverhill; Harold J. Taylor (24, St. Johnsbury, VT) and Theresa M. McGoff (17, Lunenburg, VT)
Olive Dorothy, b. 8/20/1909; first; George D. Taylor (clerk, 22, Nelson) and Menta L. Woodard (24, Woodstock)

Rodney Lee, b. 12/11/1970 in Haverhill; Ronald L. Taylor (22, Barnet, VT) and Mary Jane Marsh (22, Orford)
Susanna Lee, b. 9/20/1985; Robin Taylor and Lisa Taylor
Timothy James, b. 12/14/1977 in Haverhill; Bruce F. Taylor (30, VT) and Gloria J. Pike (27, NH)
Vronyka Ryly, b. 7/12/2004 in Lebanon; Elmer Taylor and Penny Taylor
Wayne Timothy, b. 5/20/1987; Dennis Taylor and Dawn Taylor

THOMAS,
Robert Thayer, b. 4/21/1928 in Hanover; first; Henry A. Thomas (salesman, Foxcroft, ME) and Clara Jane Thayer (Brooklyn, NY)

THOMPSON,
stillborn son, b. 3/25/1891 in Orford; third; Warner W. Thompson (laborer, 34, Goshen) and Christina Collins (34, Chicopee, MA)
son, b. 5/24/1892 in Orford; fifth; Warner W. Thompson (farmer, 31, Manchester) and Christina Collins (32, Chicopee, MA)
daughter, b. 10/11/1905 in Orford; second; Warner W. Thompson (farmer, 37, Goshen) and Virginia M. George (19, Barnet, VT)
Robert William, b. 7/1/1950 in Haverhill; second; Roland E. Thompson (plumber, Andover, MA) and Florence I. Smith (Wentworth)
Wallace E., b. 5/22/1909; first; Warner W. Thompson, Jr. (laborer, 17, Orford) and Charlotte Donaldson (18, Orford)
William R., b. 7/16/1903 in Orford; first; Warner W. Thompson (farmer, 46, Goshen) and Virginia George (16, E. Barnet, VT)

THOMSON,
Christine Delia, b. 2/8/1977 in Hanover; Robb R. Thomson (24, NY) and Andrea C. Flagg (24, ME)
Cynthia Gale, b. 1/10/1971 in Lebanon; David L. Thomson (27, Brooklyn, NY) and Brenda E. Dyke (22, Orford)
Dean Kelly, b. 8/9/1968 in Lebanon; David Thomson (auto mech., 25, Brooklyn, NY) and Brenda E. Dyke (19)
Jaden Noel, b. 9/17/2003 in Lebanon; Stacey F. Thomson and Christine White
Kelly Charlotte, b. 9/17/1984; Robb Thomson and Andrea Thomson
Kimberly Lauren, b. 4/8/1981 in Hanover; Robb Thomson and Andrea Thomson

Moriah Booth, b. 5/27/1974 in Hanover; Peter M. Thomson (32, Brooklyn, NY) and Glyneta O. Bonsey (30, Portsmouth)
Rebecca Ann, b. 11/10/1974 in Lebanon; David L. Thomson (31, Brooklyn, NY) and Brenda E. Dyke (25, Orford)
Simon Peter, b. 10/27/1980 in Hanover; Peter Thomson and Glyneta Thomson
Stacey, b. 5/3/1977 in Hanover; Thomas N. Thomson (31, NY) and Sheila M. Sweet (29, NH)
William Meldrim, b. 8/22/1970 in Hanover; Peter M. Thomson (28, Brooklyn, NY) and Glyneta O. Bonsey (26, Portsmouth)

THURSTON,
Ellen Marie, b. 12/24/1958 in Hanover; first; Justin L. Thurston (woodsman, Lyme) and Laura L. Paton (Williamstown, VT)

TILDEN,
Adele Grace, b. 7/8/2003 in Lebanon; Jeff Tilden and Jennifer Tilden
Samuel Baxter, b. 5/12/1999 in Lebanon; Jeffrey Tilden and Jennifer Tilden

TILLOTSON,
Wendell Earl, b. 12/24/1946 in Hanover; first; Wendell E. Tillotson (manager, Waits River, VT) and Ila L. Huntington (Orford)

TINGLEY,
Paul William, b. 4/4/1965 in Hanover; William J. Tingley (minister, Derby, CT) and Dee Peterson (Carrington, ND)
Susan Dee, b. 8/20/1963 in Hanover; William J. Tingley (minister, Derby, CT) and Dee Petersen (N. Carrington, ND)

TRASK,
Allen Stanton, b. 9/8/1930 in Orford; second; Frank Trask (laborer, NS) and Natalie A. Perry (Haverhill)
Edwin Clark, b. 6/26/1932 in Orford; third; Frank E. Trask (laborer, NS) and Natalie A. Perry (Haverhill)
Leland Willard, b. 12/8/1928 in Orford; first; Frank Trask (laborer, NS) and Alberta E. Perry (Haverhill)

TRAVER,
Jon Terry, b. 9/18/1940 in Hanover; second; Paul Carleton Traver (teacher, Hooksett) and Doris Mary Gates (Coxsackie, NY)

Thais G., b. 2/21/1938 in Hanover; first; Paul C. Traver (teacher, Hooksett) and Doris M. Gates (Coxsackie, NY)

TRUSSELL,
Marion Emma, b. 7/21/1898 in Orford; first; George F. Trussell (mechanic, 25, Orford) and Grace H. Tilton (21, Bristol)
child, b. 11/7/1906 in Orford; third; George F. Trussell (mechanic, 33, Orford) and Grace H. Tilton (29, Bristol)

TSAKIRIS,
Christian Derek, b. 9/6/1998 in Lebanon; Derek Todd Tsakiris and Laura A. Seymour Tsakiris
Gabriella Catherine, b. 9/27/2002 in Lebanon; Derek Tsakiris and Laura Tsakiris
Jacob Moses, b. 8/11/2000 in Lebanon; Derek Tsakiris and Laura Tsakiris

TULLAR,
Emily Louise, b. 9/10/1982; Rendell Tullar and Karen Tullar
George Lincoln, b. 12/1/1985; George Tullar and Sherre Tullar
George Lincoln, Jr., b. 8/10/1956 in Lebanon; fourth; George Lincoln Tullar (farmer, Corinth, VT) and Barbara W. Anderson (Hanover)
Molly Gomo, b. 4/14/1987; Rendell Tullar and Karen Tullar
Nancy Virginia, b. 3/31/1967 in Lebanon; George L. Tullar (farmer, Corinth, VT) and Barbara W. Anderson (Hanover)
Nathan Charles, b. 5/25/1980 in Hanover; Rendell Tullar and Karen Tullar
Sophie Garland, b. 11/12/2004 in Lebanon; Nathan Tullar and Carole Ann Cahill
Steven Lawrence, b. 10/5/1958 in Lebanon; fifth; George L. Tuller (farmer, Corinth, VT) and Barbara W. Anderson (Hanover)

TURNER,
daughter, b. 11/26/1891 in Orford; fourth; Henry Turner (laborer, 33, Derby, VT) and Rosa A. Dolloff (30, Newark, VT)

TURPIN,
Katherine Anne, b. 7/16/1977 in Hanover; Edward H. Turpin (28, VA) and Susan V. Talley (32, NY)

TWISS,
Milton Alden, b. 11/30/1909; first; Alden S. Twiss (bookkeeper, 24, Craftsbury, VT) and Martha I. Archer (20, Orford); residence – Hartford, VT

TYLER,
John Bonnett, b. 1/31/1952 in Hanover; third; Donald L. Tyler (rest. owner, NH) and Marion C. Bonnett (Fairlee, VT)

UNDERHILL,
son, b. 1/8/1897; second; Leon H. Underhill (farmer, 28, Piermont) and Jennie A. Norris (25, Corinth, VT)

URIE,
Harold T. H., b. 10/29/1896; first; Edward L. Urie (station agent, 22, Greensboro, VT) and Mary A. Archer (17, Orford); residence – St. Johnsbury, VT

VASIL,
Matthew Ryan, b. 3/21/1983; Thomas Vasil and Marilyn Vasil
Thomas Michael, b. 5/5/1981 in Hanover; Thomas Vasil and Marilyn Vasil

VILLAR,
Charles Edward, b. 5/27/1985; Paul Villar and Margaret Villar
Chelsea Mary, b. 4/1/1984; Paul Villar and Peggy Villar

VIRGE,
Leon, b. 7/19/1908; sixth; Willie A. Virge (laborer, 35, Northfield, VT) and Emma Ingerson (35, Jefferson)
Leona, b. 7/19/1908; fifth; Willie A. Virge (laborer, 35, Northfield, VT) and Emma Ingerson (35, Jefferson)

WASHBURN,
son, b. 11/20/1888; third; Frank E. Washburn (farmer, 41, Granville, VT) and Emma F. Lovejoy (31, Orford)
son, b. 5/26/1891 in Orford; fourth; Frank E. Washburn (farmer, 43, Granville, VT) and Emma F. Lovejoy (34, Orford)
stillborn daughter, b. 7/23/1921 in Hanover; third; Harvey L. Washburn (farmer, Orford) and Bernice M. Horton (Orford)

Charles A., b. 10/25/1893 in Orford; fifth; Frank E. Washburn
(farmer, 46, Granville, VT) and Emma F. Lovejoy (36, Orford)
Harvey Horton, b. 6/2/1937 in Hanover; sixth; Harvey L. Washburn
(farmer, Orford) and Bernice M. Horton (Orford)
Jeanne, b. 4/7/1923; fourth; Harvey L. Washburn (farmer, Orford)
and Bernice Horton (Orford)
Joice, b. 11/27/1925; fifth; Harvey L. Washburn (farmer, Orford) and
Bernice M. Horton (Orford)
Laura, b. 8/17/1920 in Hanover; first; Harvey Washburn (farmer,
Orford) and Bernice Horton (Orford)
Lucille, b. 7/23/1921 in Hanover; second; Harvey L. Washburn
(farmer, Orford) and Bernice M. Horton (Orford)
Neil Bradley, b. 5/28/1956 in Haverhill; first; Harvey H. Washburn
(laborer, Hanover) and Marlene S. Whitcher (Laconia)
Nicholas Franklin, b. 9/14/1988; Neil Washburn and Joanne
Washburn
Sharon Marie, b. 11/25/1964 in Plymouth; H. Horton Washburn
(truck driver, Hanover) and Marlene S. Whitcher (Laconia)

WATERBURY,
Charles Allan, b. 5/31/1960 in Lebanon; first; Allan G. Waterbury
(laborer, Norwalk, CT) and Shirley J. Weeks (Orfordville)
Lisa Marie, b. 8/1/1966 in Lebanon; Allan G. Waterbury (laborer,
Norwalk, CT) and Shirley Jean Weeks (Orford)
Stephen Michael, b. 10/22/1962 in Lebanon; second; Allan G.
Waterbury (laborer, Norwalk, CT) and Shirley Jean Weeks
(Orford)

WATERMAN,
daughter, b. 6/3/1892 in Orford; first; Clarence Waterman (laborer,
23, Bath) and Addie Hammond (19, Wentworth); residence –
Bath
Katherine Dawn, b. 3/26/2004 in Lebanon; Keith Waterman and
Emily Waterman
Zilla E., b. 5/17/1893 in Orford; first; A. A. Waterman (farmer, 23,
Thetford, VT) and Minnie M. Movery (19, Vershire, VT)

WEBB,
Betty Lucille, b. 7/4/1930 in Orford; first; Charles Daniel Webb
(laborer, Lyme) and Nera May Bean (Orford)

WEBSTER,
son, b. 7/29/1900 in Orford; second; Freeman H. Webster (farmer, 26, Haverhill) and Mabel A. Mann (22, Orford)

WEEKS,
Ann Marie, b. 5/20/1955 in Haverhill; third; Forrest W. Weeks (truck driver, Orford) and Muriel E. McDonald (Groton, VT)
Donald Karl, b. 11/12/1906 in Orford; first; George E. Weeks (mechanic, 26, Orford) and Ruth Evans (21, Piermont)
Florence Ella, b. 4/6/1916 in Orford; fourth; Alvin B. Weeks (farmer, 29, Nottingham) and Florence Hardy (26, Manchester); residence – Concord
Ida Marion, b. 7/29/1911; first; George F. Weeks (farmer, Manchester) and Bessie A. Davis (Lyman)
John Forrest, b. 4/13/1954 in Haverhill; second; Forrest Wm. Weeks (truck driver, Orford) and Muriel E. McDonald (Groton, VT)
Kenneth Lawrence, b. 1/10/1966 in Haverhill; David M. Weeks (laborer, Warren) and Ramona Lee Nutter (Orford)
Lean Joy, b. 8/28/1960 in Haverhill; third; Wayne A. Weeks (trucking, Orford) and Louella J. Godville (Warren)
Linda Jean, b. 10/16/1948 in Hanover; first; Forrest W. Weeks (truck driver, Orford) and Muriel E. McDonald (Groton, VT)
Loretta Jean, b. 1/31/1957 in Haverhill; first; Wayne Alvin Weeks (truck driver, Orford) and Louella Jean Godville (Warren)
Rose May, b. 11/8/1927 in Orford; eighth; Alvin B. Weeks (farmer, Deerfield) and Florence Hardy (Manchester)
Russell Leland, b. 12/3/1970 in Haverhill; David M. Weeks (26, Warren) and Ramona L. Nutter (24, Orford)
Shirley J., b. 4/20/1938 in Orford; second; Charles A. Weeks (laborer, Fairlee, VT) and Lillian Marsh (Orford)
Wayne Alvin, b. 11/28/1936 in Orford; first; Charles A. Weeks (laborer, Fairlee, VT) and Lillian Marsh (Orford)
Wayne Alvin, b. 10/10/1958 in Haverhill; second; Wayne A. Weeks (trucking, Orford) and Louella J. Godville (Warren)

WEIBEL,
Catherine E., b. 12/19/1917 in Orford; first; John G. Weibel (tel. lineman, Dracut, MA) and Elanor C. Davis (Orford)
George Franklin, b. 11/6/1913 in Orford; first; John G. Weibel (farmer, 26, Dracut, MA) and May M. Bryer (17, Lancaster)

WELCH,
Richard Alvin, b. 7/31/1951 in Haverhill; fourth; Walter E. Welch (laborer, Groton, VT) and Alberta L. Shepard (Hartford, VT)
Terri Lynn, b. 7/19/1971 in Hanover; Jack P. Welch (29, Lebanon) and Mary L. Gallup (28, Woodsville)

WEST,
daughter, b. 11/19/1889 in Orford; second; Edwin B. West (farmer, 34, Orford) and Margie L. Ames (24, Wentworth)

WESTGATE,
stillborn son, b. 9/22/1889 in Orford; first; Randal Westgate (farmer, 28, Cornish) and Kate Tarbox (24, Piermont)

WHEELER,
Dian Lee, b. 11/25/1950 in Haverhill; third; Elmer W. Wheeler (mechanic, Bath) and Beulah M. Stanley (E. Burke, VT)
Helen, b. 8/12/1895 in Orford; fifth; Horace Wheeler (farming, 40, Haverhill) and C. D. Winchester (27, Haverhill)
James Allen, b. 9/14/1939 in Orford; fourth; Burt O. Wheeler (laborer, Newbury, VT) and Blanche E. Adams (Bradford, VT)

WHITCHER,
Ivan B., b. 5/23/1917 in Orford; second; Howard E. Whitcher (creamery man, Wentworth) and Florence Gray (Dorchester)

WHITCOMB,
son, b. 4/23/1888; first; Dexter K. Whitcomb (butcher, 33, Orford) and Grace W. Whitcomb (26, N. Adams, MA)

WHITE,
daughter, b. 4/18/1896; first; Etta M. White (21, Waterloo, Canada)
Jeffrey David, b. 12/30/1984; Paul White and Marianne White
Myrtie E., b. 2/11/1899 in Orford; fourth; Theodore H. White (carpenter, 32, Portsmouth) and Ada L. Hibbard (32, Lancaster)

WHITEHILL,
Brandon Frank, b. 3/20/1995 in Lebanon; Norman Frank Whitehill, Jr. and Cindy Anne Sanborn-Whitehill
Jenna Jade, b. 6/16/1997 in Lebanon; Norman Frank Whitehill, Jr. and Cindy Anne Sanborn-Whitehill

WHITTAKER,
Bonnie Lou, b. 8/26/1963 in Hanover; Benjamin B. Whittaker (contractor, Enfield) and Nancy R. Davis (Brockton, MA)
Peter Mark, b. 5/11/1961 in Hanover; second; Benjamin Whittaker (carpenter, Enfield) and Nancy Ruth Davis (Brockton, MA)

WHITTEMORE,
son, b. 12/4/1901 in Orford; first; Luther L. Whittemore (clerk, 27, Plymouth) and Caroline W. Washburn (30, Lyme)

WILCOX,
John, b. 9/6/1957 in Haverhill; fourth; Richard William Wilcox (truck driver, Hartford, CT) and Antoinette Normandin (Port Chester, NY)

WILDER,
son, b. 8/15/1893 in Orford; first; Edwin E. Wilder (farmer, 34, Williamstown, VT) and Lillie J. Bickford (34, Orford); residence – ME

WILLARD,
George Frederick, b. 5/30/1906 in Orford; third; Fred A. Willard (poultry fancier, 22, Brooklyn, NY) and Eva M. Perkins (24, Orange, VT)
John Barker, b. 1/7/1913 in Orford; second; George R. Willard (farmer, 26, Brooklyn, NY) and Alice L. Dennis (20, Bradford, VT)
Lawrence Fay, b. 5/31/1911; first; George R. Willard (farmer, Brooklyn, NY) and Alice L. Dennis (Bradford, VT)
Marguerette F., b. 7/2/1905 in Orford; second; Fred A. Willard (laborer, 22, Brooklyn, NY) and Eva M. Perkins (22, Orange)

WILLEY,
Donna Rose, b. 1/16/1970 in Haverhill; Wilson M. Willey (33, Hanover) and Beverly A. Pebbles (33, Concord)
Duane Marshall, b. 1/19/1963 in Haverhill; Wilson M. Willey (lumber mill, Hanover) and Janet M. Marsh (Orford)
Wendy Marie, b. 1/3/1961 in Haverhill; first; Wilson M. Willey, Jr. (laborer, Hanover) and Janet Maude Marsh (Orford)
Wilson Marshall, b. 8/11/1936 in Hanover; fourth; Wilson M. Willey (laborer, Bradford, VT) and Rose I. Baker (Orford)

WILLIS,
daughter, b. 8/12/1897; first; Eugene F. Willis (farmer, 28, Lyme) and Nellie A. Flanders (27, Warren)
daughter, b. 3/27/1902 in Orford; second; Eugene F. Willis (carpenter, 32, Warren) and Nellie A. Flanders (Warren)
Carol Lynn, b. 2/24/1969 in Haverhill; Russell E. Willis (32, Orford) and Norma J. Baker (24, Laconia)
Christine Anne, b. 2/9/1965 in Lebanon; Russell E. Willis (carpenter, Orford) and Norma J. Baker (Laconia)
Clarence Daniel, b. 2/25/1908; third; Eugene F. Willis (carpenter, 38, Warren) and Nellie A. Flanders (38, Warren)
Cynthia Jean, b. 4/11/1962 in Hanover; second; Russell E. Willis (carpenter, Orford) and Norma Jean Baker (Laconia)
Janet Lee, b. 1/30/1933 in Orford; first; Clarence Willis (farmer, Orford) and Ruth M. Ibede (New Britain, CT)
Russell Eugene, b. 7/19/1936 in Orford; second; Clarence D. Willis (laborer, Orford) and Ruth M. Ibelle (New York, NY)

WILMOT,
Travis Merle, b. 10/12/1990 in Lebanon; Tony Wilmot and Cammie Wilmot

WILSON,
Harold, b. 11/4/1895 in Orford; second; Edward Wilson (farming, 35, Haringford) and Florence Spurr (30, NS)
Susan Gladys, b. 7/25/1899 in Orford; third; Edward Wilson (farming, 38, Hemingford, PQ) and Frances Spurr (33, Annapolis, NS)
William Alfred, b. 11/21/1964 in Lebanon; Alfred E. Wilson (farmer, Bayshore, NY) and Alma H. Brown (Brooklyn, NY)
Willow Amla, b. 5/17/2004 in Lebanon; William Wilson and Shannon Wilson

WINAGLE,
Jack Peterson, b. 1/19/1999 in Lebanon; Jeffrey Winagle and Amy Winagle

WINCHESTER,
Ava Isabelle, b. 11/5/2004 in Lebanon; Edward Winchester and Allison Winchester

WING,
daughter, b. 3/29/1900 in Orford; second; Milton L. Wing (farmer, 26, Chateaugay, NY) and Nina H. Courtney (21, Rochester, VT)
Lorraine Ann, b. 4/4/1932 in Orford; fourth; Albert Wing (farmer, Lyme) and Esther Small (Cornish)
Malcolm Duane, b. 3/5/1928 in Orford; second; Albert Earl Wing (farmer, Lyme) and Esther Martha Small (Cornish)
Maude, b. 9/4/1902 in Orford; third; Milton L. Wing (farmer, 29, Chateaugay, NY) and Nina H. Courtney (Rochester, NY)
Ramonda Jane, b. 10/28/1929 in Orford; third; Albert Earl Wing (farmer, Lyme) and Esther Martha Small (Cornish)

WOODARD,
son, b. 4/18/1907; third; Byron Woodard (farmer, 34, Enosburg, VT) and Belle Coburn (34, E. Berkshire, VT)

WOODWARD,
son, b. 7/14/1901 in Orford; second; Byron W. Woodward (farmer, 29, Enosburg, VT) and Belle Coburn (30, Berkshire, VT)
Cody Scott, b. 6/17/1997 in Lebanon; Scott Edward Woodward and Theresa Marie King Woodward
Emerson Byron, b. 6/6/1927 in Hanover; third; Norman C. Woodward (farmer, Orford) and Grace Lear (Sunapee)
Jennifer Lynn, b. 2/22/1995 in Lebanon; Scott Eugene Woodward and Theresa Marie King Woodward
Lucy, b. 11/11/1920 in Hanover; first; Norman C. Woodward (farmer, Orford) and Grace E. Lear (Sunapee)
Norman B., b. 3/28/1922; second; Norman S. Woodward (farmer, Orford) and Grace E. Lear (Sunapee)
Norman Coburn, b. 7/24/1898 in Orford; first; Byron N. Woodward (farmer, 26, Enosburgh, VT) and Belle Coburn (27, Berkshire, VT)
Scott Eugene, b. 9/18/1969 in Haverhill; Wendell L. Woodward (25, Lebanon) and Linda L. Estes (21, Hanover)

WRIGHT,
son, b. 4/18/1898 in Orford; second; Clarence K. Wright (farmer, 38, Orford) and Cora A. Carpenter (33, Fairlee, VT)
daughter, b. 1/22/1900 in Orford; third; Clarence K. Wright (farmer, 40, Orford) and Cora A. Carpenter (35, Fairlee, VT)

Charles, b. 6/17/1920 in Orford; third; Charles Wright (farmer, Piermont) and Mildred Durick (Piermont); residence – Piermont
Clarence, b. 10/31/1902 in Orford; fourth; Clarence K. Wright (farmer, 42, Orford) and Cora A. Carpenter (Fairlee, VT)
Nellie Julia, b. 6/14/1905 in Orford; second; John A. Wright (farmer, 24, Colebrook) and Maude A. Belford (19, Lyme); residence – Columbia
Parker E., b. 7/3/1894 in Orford; first; Clarence R. Wright (farmer, 34, Orford) and Eva A. Carpenter (29, Fairlee, VT)
Ralph E., b. 4/1/1903 in Orford; first; John A. Wright (farmer, 22, Colebrook) and Maud A. Bedford (17, Lyme)
Violet Minnie, b. 1/13/1912 in Orford; third; John A. Wright (farmer, 31, Colebrook) and Maude A. Belford (26, Lyme)

YONAITIS,
Edward Lawrence, b. 10/4/1984; Lawrence Yonaitis and Patricia Yonaitis

YOUMANS,
Charles L., 3rd, b. 12/30/1947 in Hanover; first; Charles L. Youmans, Jr. (student, Yonkers, NY) and Phyllis A. Klosti (New Orleans, LA)

YOUNG,
son, b. 6/18/1952 in Hanover; second; Leon F. Young (laborer, Orford) and Winifred A. Butman (Orford)
son, b. 2/13/1953 in Hanover; third; Leon F. Young (laborer, Orford) and Winifred A. Streeter (Orfordville)
Debora Louise, b. 2/19/1951 in Hanover; first; Leon F. Young, Jr. (US Army, Cpl., Orford) and Winifred A. Streeter (Orford)
Gail Marie, b. 9/2/1955 in Hanover; fifth; Leon F. Young (bulldozer opr., Orford) and Winifred A. Streeter (Orfordville)
James Richard, b. 2/5/1954 in Hanover; fourth; Leon Francis Young (truck driver, Orford) and Winifred A. Streeter (Orfordville)

ORFORD MARRIAGES

ABBOTT,
Fred W. of Orford m. Julia E. **Perkins** of Lyme 10/9/1890 in Piermont; H – 24, postmaster, b. W. Fairlee, VT, s/o J. F. Abbott (Bradford, VT, farmer); W – 26, domestic, b. Lyme, d/o J. N. Perkins (Lyme)

ADAMS,
John P., Jr. of Montpelier, VT m. Eda **Chioti** of Montpelier, VT 6/1/1933 in Orford; H – 26, clerk, b. Montpelier, VT, s/o John P. Adams (Montpelier, VT, farmer) and Laura Ropes (Waterbury, VT, housewife); W – 26, nurse, b. Modena, Italy, d/o Gaetano Chioti (Modena, Italy, stone cutter) and Adel Olivari (Modena, Italy, housewife)
Jon H. of Orford m. Trudy A. **Grant** of Bradford, VT 12/9/1978 in Piermont; H – b. NH, s/o Harry Adams and Margaret Douse; W – b. NH, d/o Wendell Grant and Marie Gauthier
Raymond H. of Orford m. Alice E. **Alger** of Fairlee, VT 1/21/1946 in Fairlee, VT; H – 25, service man, b. Haverhill, s/o Ralph Adams (Fairlee, VT, laborer) and Lois Partridge (Haverhill, housewife); W – 24, at home, b. E. Ryegate, VT, d/o Joseph Alger (Hartford, VT, station agt.) and Laura Rowe (Peacham, VT, housewife)

ALEXANDER,
George W. of Orford m. Mrs. Lavina **Warner** of Orford 1/7/1888 in Orford; H – 28, laborer, b. Plainfield, s/o Dennis B. Alexander (Plainfield, laborer) and Amanda Rogers (Lowell, MA, domestic); W – 55, domestic, 3rd, b. Woburn, MA, d/o Joseph W. Holden (laborer) and Sarah Crocker (Stoneham, MA)

ALLEN,
Burton S. of Orford m. Agnes L. **Pratt** of Orford 6/20/1896 in Wentworth; H – 28, farmer, b. Greensboro, VT, s/o Wyman H. Allen (farmer) and Jennie Hazelton (domestic); W – 25, domestic, 2nd, divorced, b. Orford, d/o Charles W. Clifford (farmer) and ----- Cross (domestic)
Douglas of CT m. Mellissa **Perrin** of CT 9/29/1990
John m. Aurora **Garrett** 7/2/1988
Josiah of Barre, VT m. Marion E. **Jones** of Barre, VT 12/7/1924 in Orford; H – 23, clerk, b. Uniontown, PA, s/o Aatt Allen (Dunbar, PA, merchant) and Effie Barre (Uniontown, PA, housewife); W

– 20, bookkeeper, b. Barre, VT, d/o Albert S. Jones (London, England, manufacturer) and Mary Stevenson (Scotland, manufacturer)

ANDERLE,
Nicholas m. Teresa **Snyder** 6/18/1988

ANDERSON,
William Arthur of Bradford, VT m. Dorothy E. **Woodward** of Orford 6/18/1975 in Ludlow, ME; H – 73, b. Ayrshire, Scotland, s/o William Anderson and Mary Plummer; W – 67, b. Bradford, VT, d/o Fredrick Sanborn and Lilla DeMar

ANDREWS,
Clarence H., III of Orford m. Lucille Eva **Ball** of Warren 10/11/1970 in Orford; H – 26, b. Milford, CT, s/o Clarence H. Andrews, II and Thelma Ryer; W – 23, d/o Herman G. Ball and Celia May Jones

Donald R. of Orford m. Dorothy M. **Barney** of Lebanon 10/22/1966 in Lebanon; H – 44, b. Haverhill, s/o Clarence H. Andrews, Sr. and Esther Hildreth; W – 45, b. Hanover, d/o John B. Bushee and Celia Callan

ANSELL,
Ray Harry of Orford m. Lula W. **Emerson** of Fairlee, VT 7/4/1927 in Fairlee, VT; H – 29, contractor, b. Manchester, s/o Everett Ansell and Margaret Gallagher (Ireland); W – 39, 2nd, b. Whitefield, d/o John H. Wilkins (England) and Lydia F. Quimby (Whitefield)

ANWAY,
Dennis Joseph of Orford m. Alejandra Graciela **Valverde** of Hanover 8/2/1977 in Hanover; H – 35, b. OH, s/o Glenwood Anway and Rita Geis; W – 26, b. Costa Rica, s/o Jose Luis Oriz and Ligia Brealey

ASHLEY,
Herbert A. of Dorchester m. Phylis A. **Bean** of Orford 12/14/1931 in Rumney; H – 31, RFD carrier, b. Dorchester, s/o Herbert H. Ashley (PQ, farmer) and Annie G. Pollard (PQ, housewife); W –

22, stenographer, b. Orford, d/o Phillip L. Bean (Orford, farmer) and Blanch H. Burnham (Dorchester, housewife)

ATKINS,
Charles F. of Orford m. Alice A. **Malcolm** of Milford, CT 4/11/1936 in Orford; H – 55, minister, 2nd, divorced, b. Yonkers, NY, s/o Charles Atkins (Nottingham, England, deceased) and Martha Field (Paterson, NJ, deceased); W – 52, student, 2nd, widow, b. Oakham, MA, d/o Jesse Allen (Oakham, MA, deceased) and Elizabeth Sumner (Gilead, CT, deceased)

ATWOOD,
Caleb of Orford m. Joyce **Cornetta** of Orford 5/6/1979

AUSTIN,
Chauncy G. of Orford m. Ada A. **Smith** of Lyme 12/9/1902 in Orford; H – 23, farmer, b. Fairfax, VT, s/o Albert J. Austin (Fairfax, VT, farmer) and Addie M. Baker (Orford, housewife); W – 23, domestic, b. Lyme, d/o Benjamin Smith (Wentworth, farmer) and Angeline Brown (Lyme, housewife)
Richard Lee of Concord m. Diane **Ricker** of Orford 8/28/1967 in Concord; H – 21, b. Bridgeport, CT, s/o King Austin and Doris Bernadette; W – 18, b. Hanover, d/o Lawrence Ricker and Beverly Record
Wayne S. of Ipswich, MA m. Shirley J. **Taylor** of Ipswich, MA 9/11/1976 in Orford; H – 34, b. MA, s/o Francis J. Austin and Edwina Alexander; W – 40, b. MA, d/o George E. Dupuis and Ella Tucker

AVERY,
Charles A. of Orford m. Julia G. **Caldon** of Campton 11/3/1889 in Campton; H – 29, farmer, b. Thornton, s/o Mary J. Willey (Ellsworth, domestic); W – 21, teacher, b. Campton, d/o Hattie E. Durgin (Campton, domestic)

BACON,
William P. m. Cheryl A. **Broughan** --/--/1989

BADGER,
Ernest W. of E. Montpelier, VT m. Florence **Hildreth** of Auburndale, MA 8/12/1932 in Piermont; H – 24, farmer, b. Williamstown, VT,

s/o Charles A. Badger (Orford, farmer) and Jennie Abbott (Cabot, VT, housewife); W – 21, teacher, b. Amesbury, MA, d/o Edward W. Hildreth (Lowell, MA, buffer) and Jennie Taylor (Glasgow, Scotland, housewife)

BAHLKOW,
Gary D. of Orford m. Kathleen Louise **Nogel** of Orford 10/3/1981

BAKER,
Bradley H. of Orford m. Clara B. **Webster** of Piermont 11/6/1926 in Orford; H – 24, laborer, b. Orford, s/o Henry G. Baker (Orford, blacksmith) and Inez Smith (Orford, housewife); W – 17, domestic, b. Piermont, d/o Walter Webster (Piermont, laborer) and Lizzie Howland (Piermont, housewife)

G. H. of Orford m. Alice M. **Franklin** of Orford 5/18/1915 in Piermont; H – 27, laborer, b. Orford, s/o Henry G. Baker (Orford, blacksmith) and Inez Smith (Orford, housewife); W – 35, domestic, b. Orford, d/o Lewis Franklin (Orford, farmer) and Rebecca Cushman (Lisbon, housewife)

Henry G. of Orford m. Inez **Smith** of Orford 6/13/1887 in Orford; H – 26, farmer, b. Orford, s/o Charles Baker (Orford, carpenter) and Susan Homer (Johnson, VT, domestic); W – 17, domestic, b. Orford, d/o Alphonso Smith (Orford, laborer) and Clara Worthen (Orford, domestic)

Maurice S. of Orford m. Hattie M. **Streeter** of Orford 5/8/1934 in Orford; H – 30, laborer, 2nd, b. Orford, s/o Henry G. Baker (Orford, wheelwright) and Inez Smith (Orford, housewife); W – 25, clerk, b. Piermont, d/o Ray N. Streeter (Sugar Hill, farmer) and Stella Cushing (McIndoes Falls, VT, housewife)

Ronald of Orford m. Janet **Pike** of Lyme 12/8/1969 in Enfield; H – 33, b. NH, s/o Maurice Baker and Hattie Streeter; W - 31, b. MA, d/o Leo Bradley and Florence Mayo

William Henry of Orford m. Katherine F. **Camp** of Lyme 3/19/1960 in Hanover; H – 29, engineer, b. Boston, MA, s/o Harold Woods Baker (Boston, MA) and Phoebe Little (Boston, MA); W – 24, nurse, b. Chicago, IL, d/o Edwin T. Camp (Newport, VT) and Katherine Sheldon (Trenton, NJ)

William Henry, III of Orford m. Sarita Marie **Dobbins** of Bradford, VT 9/25/1993

BALL,
Albert Leslie of Warren m. Jeanette Priscilla **Woodward** of Orford 7/27/1963 in Warren; H – 21, b. Warren, s/o Leslie A. Ball and Doris Mary Ledger; W – 18, b. Lebanon, d/o Norman C. Woodward and Grace Elmira Lear

Allan Max of Glencliff m. Carol Ann **Pierson** of Orford 1/7/1963 in Glencliff; H – 24, b. Woodsville, s/o Reginald H. Ball and Charlotte Griffin; W – 20, b. Manchester, d/o Wallace H. Pierson and Evelyn Weeks

Steven Albert of Orford m. Connie Lee **Dyke** of Orford 7/18/2001 in Orford

BARBER,
Joseph William, Jr. of Lebanon m. Josephine Shirley **Canfield** of Orford 11/22/1962 in Orford; H – 34, auctioneer, 2nd, b. ME, s/o Joseph W. Barber, Sr. and Elizabeth Levitt (Gardner, ME); W – 24, cashier, b. Woodsville, d/o Ernest J. Canfield (Jeffersonville, VT) and Ada Tallman (Orford)

BASSETT,
Frank Wright of Windsor, VT m. Grace P. **Whitman** of Windsor, VT 1/18/1941 in Orford; H – 42, molder, 2nd, b. Barre, VT, s/o Clinton M. Bassett (Barre, VT, stone cutter) and Inez Drown (Cady's Falls, VT, housewife); W – 43, secretary, b. Franklin, VT, d/o Silas R. Whitman (Abbots Corner, Canada, retired) and Luna Pearson (Franklin, VT, housewife)

BEAL,
Frank J. of Orford m. Elizabeth **Avery** of Orford 7/8/1891 in Orford; H – 30, mechanic, b. Orford, s/o Royal Beal (mechanic) and ---- - Johnson (Newbury, VT); W – 23, teacher, b. Orford, d/o Joshua K. Avery (carpenter) and Emeline Thompson (Claremont)

BEAN,
Bertram of Orford m. Lillian **Guilmette** of Orford 8/17/1946 in Bradford, VT; H – 34, farmer, 2nd, b. Orford, s/o Philip L. Bean (Orford, farmer) and Blanche A. Burnham (Dorchester, housewife); W – 36, housework, b. Lunenburg, VT, d/o Philip Guilmette (Canada) and Charlotte Hartshorn (Lunenburg, VT)

Carroll J. of Orford m. Lutheria M. **Heath** of Orford 3/15/1911 in Orford; H – 31, farmer, b. Orford, s/o Richard D. Bean (Piermont, farmer) and Eliza A. Bickford (Bradford, VT, housewife); W – 22, teacher, b. Barnet, VT, d/o Everett K. Heath (Newbury, VT, farmer) and Selina George (Monroe, housewife)

Charles m. Tammy **Dickey** 4/12/1986

Dana J. of Orford m. Nellie M. **Wright** of Piermont 4/161/1913 in Piermont; H – 22, farmer, b. Orford, s/o Charles L. Bean (Sandwich, farmer) and Carrie E. Gardner (Lyme, housewife); W – 19, domestic, b. Piermont, d/o Xymenius Wright (Warren, farmer) and Emma Harris (Warren, housewife)

Donald Fay of Orford m. Ruth Alfretta **Day** of Lyme Ctr. 12/22/1945 in Orford; H – 26, mechanic, b. Orford, s/o Edwin G. Bean (Orford, farmer) and Alice Marsh (Orford, housewife); W – 27, domestic, b. Lyme Ctr., d/o William W. Day (Bradford, VT, retired) and Mary E. Webster (Lyme, housewife)

Edwin G. of Orford m. Alice M. **Marsh** of Orford 8/27/1908 in Lyme; H – 21, farmer, b. Orford, s/o Charles L. Bean (Sandwich, farmer) and Carrie E. Gardner (Lyme, housewife); W – 17, domestic, b. Orford, d/o David C. Marsh (W. Fairlee, VT, farmer) and Delia F. Smith (Corinth, VT, housewife)

Fay C. of Orford m. Bessie A. **Burnham** of Orford 5/4/1912 in Hanover; H – 23, farmer, 2nd, widower, b. Orford, s/o Charles L. Bean (Sandwich, farmer) and Carrie E. Gardner (Lyme, housewife); W – 22, domestic, b. Dorchester, d/o Frank Y. Burnham (Concord, farmer) and Josephine E. Coburn (Wentworth, housewife)

Fay Elson of Orford m. Arletta L. **Smith** of Orford 9/8/1945 in Lyme; H – 21, laborer, b. Orford, s/o Joseph Bean (Sharon, VT, deceased) and Mabel Davis (Quebec, Canada, retired); W – 16, at home, b. Middlesex, VT, d/o Allen Smith (Calais, ME, laborer) and Sitonia Shonio (Duxbury, VT, housewife)

Frank L. of Orford m. Elizabeth M. **Siegfried** of New York 8/8/1920 in N. Woodstock; H – 36, farmer, b. Orford, s/o Charles L. Bean (Sandwich, farmer) and Carrie Gardner (Lyme, housewife); W – 34, at home, 2nd, widow, b. Lyme, d/o George H. Clifford (Hanover, laborer) and Mary A. Symonds (Cambridge, MA, housekeeper)

Harold E. of Orford m. Anita V. **Huse** of Bradford, VT 7/8/1936 in Lyme; H – 25, mechanic, b. Orford, s/o Edwin G. Bean (Orford, farmer) and Alice Marsh (Orford, housewife); W – 20, domestic, b. Bradford, VT, d/o Carl E. Huse (E. Corinth, VT, farmer) and Marion Flower (Hartland, VT, housewife)

John Edward of Bradford, VT m. Pamela Ann **Perry** of Orford 8/1/1970 in Orford; H – 19, b. Hanover, s/o Richard H. Bean and Beatrice Huntington; W – 18, b. Orford, d/o Walter H. Perry and Beatrice Fillian

Joseph S. of Orford m. Blanche H. **Rogers** of Fairlee, VT 6/16/1939 in Fairlee, VT; H – 22, laborer, b. Orford, s/o Joseph S. Bean (Sharon, VT) and Mabel M. Davis (Masonville, PQ); W – 19, b. Fairlee, VT, d/o Clarence M. Rogers (W. Fairlee, VT) and Beryl Lufkin (Bradford, VT)

Maurice Fay of Orford m. Anne Marie **Castiglione** of Staten Island, NY 11/6/1960 in Orfordville; H – 45, farmer, b. Dorchester, s/o Fay C. Bean (Orford) and Bessie A. Burnham (Dorchester); W – 31, at home, b. Garwood, NJ, d/o Dominic Castiglione (Italy) and Clementine Falzone (NY)

Norman C. of Orford m. Dorothy L. **Lewis** of Lisbon 2/17/1939 in Lyme; H – 21, laborer, b. Orford, s/o Edwin G. Bean (Orford, farmer) and Alice Marsh (Orford, housewife); W – 24, domestic, b. W. Barrington, RI, d/o Loren Ray Lewis (Cortland, NY, tourists) and Mabel Alton (Pawtucket, RI, housewife)

Oliver L. of Orford m. Elizabeth **Ballam** of Lyme 9/23/1889 in Lyme; H – 31, farmer, b. Sandwich, s/o Jonathan G. Bean (Sandwich, farmer) and Sarah J. Brickett (Auburn); W – 19, domestic, b. England, d/o George Ballam (Blanfield, England, farmer)

Philip L. of Orford m. Blanche H. **Burnham** of Orford 9/19/1906 in W. Fairlee, VT; H – 21, farmer, b. Orford, s/o Charles L. Bean (Sandwich, farmer) and Carrie E. Gardner (Lyme, housewife); W – 23, domestic, b. Dorchester, d/o Frank Y. Burnham (Concord, farmer) and Josephine E. Coburn (Wentworth, housewife)

Ralph Carl of Orford m. Florence **Billingham** of Fairlee, VT 9/22/1922 in Fairlee, VT; H – 21, laborer, b. Orford, s/o Moses Bean (Sandwich, farmer) and Esther Randall (Wentworth, housewife); W – 17, b. Newbury, VT, d/o James Billingham (England) and Julia V. Perrin (Island Pond, VT)

Wallace B. of Orford m. Josie M. **Fadden** of Piermont 6/19/1929 in Piermont; H – 25, chauffeur, b. Orford, s/o Charles L. Bean (Sandwich, farmer) and Carrie E. Gardner (Lyme, housewife);

W – 24, teacher, b. Thornton, d/o Dana Fadden (Thornton, farmer) and Esther Downing (Thornton, housewife)

Warren Lee of Orford m. Kathryn Ann **Larocque** of N. Thetford, VT 7/2/1965 in Lyme; H – 18, b. Hanover, s/o Philip Lee Bean and Ida Prebor; W – 17, b. Haverhill, d/o Raymond A. Larocque and Louise G. Adams

BEAUPRE,
Peter E. of Piermont m. Malissa J. **Daisey** of Orford 7/4/1997

BELYEA,
Jay I. of Orford m. Judith A. **Pushee** of Orford 8/15/1998

Philip Roy of Warren m. Lauren Elizabeth **Cook** of Orford 9/4/1971 in Orford; H – 22, b. Woodsville, s/o Roland M. Belyea and Lydia E. Derosia; W – 20, b. Woodsville, d/o Foster G. Cook, Jr. and Jean A. Smith

Roy R. of Plymouth m. Eileen L. **Robie** of Orford --/28/1972 in Piermont; H – 25, b. Plymouth, s/o Ronald Belyea and Esther Anderson; W – 25, b. Lebanon, d/o Keith Robie and Verna Tucker

BENJAMIN,
Robert L. of Bradford, VT m. Patricia A. **Perry** of Orford 12/31/1959 in Bradford, VT; H – 20, mechanic, b. Bradford, VT, s/o Lawrence J. Benjamin (Cabot, VT) and Catherine Blake (W. Fairlee, VT); W – 16, student, b. Windsor, VT, d/o Walter Perry (Saranac, NY) and Beatrice Fillian (Wentworth)

BERGGREN,
Karl Erik of Orford m. Mary Evelyn **Hoss** of Orford 10/10/1973 in Orford; H – 37, b. Stockholm, Sweden, s/o John A. Berggren and Karen E. Gran; W – 30, b. Lenoir City, TN, d/o Omer Goodwin and Lorene Rodgers

BIERS,
Richard P. of Orford m. Jeanette A. **Colburn** of W. Rumney 11/14/1934 in Plymouth; H – 22, chauffeur, b. Jannersville, NY, s/o Albert P. Biers (Saugerties, NY, farmer) and Lizzie Carle (Woodstock, NY, housewife); W – 19, at home, b. S. Weymouth, d/o Clyde H. Colburn (Dorchester, laborer) and Florence E. White (Lancaster, housewife)

BILLINGS,
Charles, Jr. of Boulder, CO m. Karen M. **MacDonald** of Boulder, CO 5/26/1996

BISCHOFF,
David F. m. Lynn M. **Parker** --/--/1989

BLAIR,
Elsworth J. m. May Arvilla **Marcott** 10/20/1956 in Orford; H – 72, laborer, 2nd, b. Barnet, VT, s/o Joseph W. Blair (Barnet, VT) and Minnie Whitcher (Peacham, VT); W – 44, housework, 2nd, b. Claremont, d/o Arthur E. Temple (Windsor, VT) and Flora Seaver (Claremont)

BLAKE,
Everett Leroy of Orford m. Flora M. **Sanborn** of Orford 9/3/1940 in Porter, ME; H – 23, laborer, b. Plymouth, s/o Harry Blake (Plymouth, laborer) and Elizabeth Hamilton (Frederickton, NB, deceased); W – 18, domestic, b. Orford, d/o Harry Sanborn (Rumney, farmer) and Lula Blake (Plymouth, housewife)

Fay E. of Orford m. Lucy O. **Bayley** of Bradford, VT 12/27/1900 in Washington, VT; H – 20, laborer, b. Corinth, VT, s/o Charles F. Blake (Corinth, VT) and Josie Southwick (Washington, VT); W – 18, domestic, b. Bradford, VT, d/o Ned Bayley (merchant)

Michael E. of Orford m. Susan Marie **Dionne** of Swanzey Center 10/19/1973 in Jackson; H – 24, b. Orford, s/o Everett L. Blake and Flora Sanborn; W – 20, b. Keene, d/o Hector Dionne and Elsie Scott

Nathan LeRoy of Orford m. Nettie Alice **Pierson** of Orford 1/23/1960 in Orford; H – 19, student, b. Orford, s/o Everett L. Blake (Plymouth) and Flora M. Sanborn (Orford); W – 18, clerical wk., b. Hanover, d/o William L. Pierson (Topsham, VT) and Dorothy F. Baker (Orford)

BLANCHARD,
Jesse of Lebanon m. Margaret Ellen **Orem** of Lebanon 8/25/2001 in Orford

BLODGETT,
Robert Weston m. Theresa Mary **Sanborn** 7/27/1958 in W. Rumney; H – 24, truck driver, b. Wentworth, s/o George M. Blodgett (Wentworth) and Minnie Belle Hunt (Lancaster); W – 20, house work, 2nd, b. Lowell, MA, d/o Ferman W. Hudson (NS) and Lillian Margarson (N. Reading, MA)

BOARDMAN,
Clyde W. of Orford m. Audrey M. **Carle** of Orford 12/26/1944 in Haverhill; H – 19, US Navy, b. Barre, VT, s/o Joseph W. Boardman (laborer) and Eva Cowdrie; W – 20, at home, b. Orford, d/o Vernon C. Carle (N. Woodstock, NY, laborer) and Maggie May Bryer (Lancaster, housewife)

George R. of St. Johnsbury, VT m. Benita J. **Miller** of Orford 12/28/1946 in St. Johnsbury, VT; H – 24, sectionman, b. Wolcott, VT, s/o Ermine P. Boardman (Wolcott, VT) and Myrtle Davis (Wolcott, VT); W – 16, b. E. Barre, VT, d/o Joseph Miller (Sutton, PQ) and Marjorie Hunt (Knowlton, PQ)

BONNETT,
Robert Wilcox of Orford m. Isabelle Joyce **Smith** of Hanover 8/28/1950 in Hanover; H – 26, assayer, b. NH, s/o Frank E. Bonnett (Orford) and Rose C. Wilcox (VT); W – 19, secretary, b. VT, d/o Winslow Smith (VT) and Gladys I. Burnham (VT)

BOONE,
Philip Gordon of Orford m. Emily Anna **Bridges** of Philadelphia, PA 8/9/2003 in Orford

BORNE,
Albert of Barre, VT m. Aurora C. **Aja** of Barre, VT 5/10/1952 in Orford; H – 23, stock man, b. Belfast, Ireland, s/o Alfred Borne (Berkinhead, England) and Florence McGranaghan (Belfast, Ireland); W – 30, inspector, b. Websterville, VT, d/o Higinil Aja (Santander, Spain) and Theresa Malanda (Santander, Spain)

BOWEN,
Clarence S. of Orford m. Jennie E. **Gammell** of Haverhill 10/11/1890 in Orford; H – 26, farmer, 2nd, b. Corinth, VT, s/o Guy Bowen (Corinth, VT, farmer); W – 19, domestic, b. Barnet, VT, d/o Emerson Hammell (Canada, farmer)

BOWKER,
James F. of Lyme m. Carole A. **Lavoie** of Orford 9/13/1946 in Lebanon; H – 31, truck driver, b. Lunenburg, VT, s/o Edward F. Bowler (Lunenburg, VT, manufacturing) and Mattie M. Vance (Lunenburg, VT, housewife); W – 36, teacher, b. E. Haverhill, d/o Henry Lavoie (Benton, farmer) and Nellie Dearborn (E. Haverhill, housewife)

BOWMAN,
Philip B. of Orford m. Wilma **Stevens** of Orford 1/23/1981

BOYNTON,
Arthur m. Carol **Damiani** 3/20/1987

BRADY,
David of Enfield m. Connie **Adams** of Orford 9/11/1982

BRALEY,
David of Orford m. Nancy **Lary** of Orford 8/28/1982

BRESNAHAN,
Brian D. of Lyndonville, VT m. Janice Heather **Parkington** of Orford 5/27/1973 in Orford; H – 25, b. Lyndonville, VT, s/o Donald Bresnahan and Joan Goff; W – 20, b. Norwalk, CT, d/o Tom Parkington and Dorothy Crofts

BROCK,
Charles E. of Orford m. Mary B. **Hurst** of Manchester 11/4/1896 in Orford; H – 45, farmer, 2nd, b. Orford, s/o Asahel Brock (Barrington, farmer) and Almina Savage (Deerfield, MA, domestic); W – 33, domestic, 2nd, divorced, b. NS, d/o Michael Cadwell (farmer) and Elizabeth ----- (domestic)

BROWN,
Charles Jerry of White River Jct., VT m. Marion Evelyn **Joslyn** of Hartford, VT 8/25/1973 in Orford; H – 49, b. Orford, s/o Wesley Brown and Myrtle Goss; W – 41, b. Hanover, d/o Walter H. French and Abbie Greenwood
Gary of Orford m. Terri **Daniels** of Orford 9/5/1992
Herbert N. of Brookline, MA m. Elizabeth **Leavitt** of Boston, MA --/-- /1972 in Orford; H – 28, b. Arlington, VA, s/o Herbert Brown and

Ada Alpaugh; W – 28, b. St. Louis, MO, d/o John C. Leavitt and Mary E. Hochbaum

Lester Rupert of Winchester m. Eda May **Chase** of Orford 9/9/1901 in Orford; H – 27, physician, b. Vershire, VT, s/o Asa A. Brown (Wentworth) and Viola B. Philbrick (Sanborntown); W – 18, domestic, b. Piermont, d/o Ezra C. Chase (Piermont, physician) and Margaret E. Brooks (McIndoes Falls, housewife)

Raymond H. of Franklin m. Leona **Cookman** of Orford 8/24/1930 in E. Andover; H – 27, truck driver, b. Haverhill, MA, s/o Henry G. Brown (Haverhill, MA, farmer) and Harriet O. Fitzgerald (Biddeford, ME, housewife); W – 25, domestic, 2nd, widow, b. Orford, d/o Edward Morey (Union Village, VT, farmer) and Esther McIntyre (Plattsburgh, NY, laborer)

Robert Burdett m. Jeanette **Moss** 6/9/1957 in Orford; H – 39, dealer, 3rd, b. Enosburg Falls, VT, s/o Rollin E. Brown (Bakersfield, VT) and Bertha C. Morway (Enosburg, VT); W – 36, secretary, 2nd, b. Detroit, MI, d/o Clarence J. Patterson (Detroit, MI) and Elizabeth Von Junga (Detroit, MI)

Roy H. of Orford m. Sarah J. **Montgomery** of Orford 6/23/1952 in Piermont; H – 58, laborer, 2nd, b. Concord, VT, s/o Ithima I. Brown (Morrisville, VT) and Caroline Spring (Craftsbury, VT); W – 60, domestic, 2nd, b. Bethlehem, d/o George Place (Whitefield) and Elnora Fisher (Craftsbury, VT)

BURBANK,
Edmund A. of Orford m. Flora A. **Brooks** of Orford 8/31/1890 in Haverhill; H – 25, laborer, b. Canada, s/o William Burbank (Canada, farmer); W – 25, domestic, b. Thetford, VT, d/o Daniel Brooks (Thetford, VT, mechanic)

BURKE,
James A. of Orford m. Jane S. **Bender** of Orford 5/30/1998

BURNHAM,
A. B. of Rumney m. Vernie M. **Pease** of Orford 8/28/1915 in Wentworth; H – 19, farmer, b. Dorchester, s/o F. Y. Burnham (Concord, farmer) and Alta M. Brown (Wentworth, housewife); W – 19, domestic, b. Franconia, d/o Francis R. Pease (Ellsworth, farmer) and M. C. Sherburne (Orford, housewife)

Eugene Reginald of Hartford, VT m. Linnie Esther **Ray** of Hartford, VT 2/6/1971 in Orford; H – 20, b. Lebanon, s/o Reginald E.

Burnham and Dorothy Douglas; W – 20, b. Plymouth, VT, d/o Leslie R. Ray and Verna M. Pretty

BURRELL,
Donald H. of Orford m. Dana M. **Schwartz** of W. Lebanon 5/16/1998

BUSH,
Douglas m. Kim **Chapman** 10/8/1986

BUTMAN,
Charles H. of Orford m. Inez **Brown** of Orford 5/11/1898 in Orford; H – 38, laborer, 2nd, widower, b. Canaan, s/o Frank Butman (Post Mills, VT, farmer) and Susan T. Colby (Canaan, housewife); W – 26, dressmaker, b. Canada

Herbert Charles of Orford m. Carol Janice **Campbell** of Lyme 10/20/1962 in Lyme; H – 20, machine op., b. Orford, s/o Richard C. Butman (Orford) and Marion Streeter (Orford); W – 15, waitress, b. Lebanon, d/o Zane E. Campbell (Thetford, VT) and Delores Piper (Chicago, IL)

Herbert Charles of Orford m. Suzanne **Pushee** of Lyme 1/22/1965 in Orford; H – 22, 2nd, b. Orford, s/o Richard C. Butman and Marion M. Streeter; W – 18, b. Hanover, d/o Roger C. Pushee and Isabelle Uline

Lewis F. of Orford m. Effie M. **Simpson** of Haverhill 10/29/1906 in Haverhill; H – 21, creamery man, b. Orford, s/o Charles H. Butman (Canaan, farmer) and Alma Clough (Wentworth, housewife); W – 19, telephone op., b. Orford, d/o Eugene W. Simpson (Orford, carpenter) and Minnie Savage (Orford, housewife)

Lurlyn C. of Orford m. Hattie C. **Bailey** of Orford 4/25/1903 in Orford; H – 21, laborer, b. Orford, s/o Charles H. Butman (Canaan, farmer) and Alma Clough (Wentworth, housewife); W – 21, domestic, b. Orford, d/o Alpha N. Bailey (Andover, MA, mechanic) and Mary Niles (Orford, housewife)

Richard C. of Orford m. Marion M. **Streeter** of Orford 11/12/1933 in Orford; H – 21, laborer, b. Orford, s/o Charles H. Butman (Canaan, retired) and Inez R. Brown (Barnston, PQ, housewife); W – 21, domestic, b. Orford, d/o Ray N. Streeter (Sugar Hill, farmer) and Stella Cushing (McIndoes Falls, VT, housewife)

Warren F. of Orford m. Doris F. **Record** of Orford 2/1/1930 in Plymouth; H – 24, weaver, b. Orford, s/o Charles H. Butman (Canaan, laborer) and Inez Brown (Stanstead, Canada, housewife); W – 23, at home, b. St. Johns, NB, d/o William R. Record (Upham, NB, farmer) and Mary Sullivan (Salt Springs, NB, housewife)

BYERS,
Albert C. of Rumney m. Ruth W. **Ingerson** of Orford 6/4/1928 in Lebanon; H – 39, lumberman, b. Demer City, CO, s/o Israel Byers (St. Johns, NB, RR man) and Celia Patchel (St. Johns, NB, housewife); W – 21, at home, b. Providence, RI, d/o William Ingerson (lumberman) and Flora Dupie (Providence, RI, housewife)

William A. of Orford m. Nancy **Boyce** of Hill 10/13/1950 in Franklin; H – 21, lumberman, b. Orford, s/o Albert C. Byers (Denver, CO) and Ruth I. Ingerson (E. Greenwich, MA); W – 20, office work, b. Concord, d/o Lanson Boyce (Contoocook) and Marion Smith (Waltham, MA)

CADY,
Thomas J. of Fairlee, VT m. Lee Marie **Harwood** of Fairlee, VT 8/17/1974 in Orford; H – 21, b. Springfield, VT, s/o Clarence H. Cady and Rosilda E. Caron; W – 20, b. Shirley, MA, d/o Raymond J. Harwood and Florence Lindsey

CANFIELD,
Ernest John of Lebanon m. Ada Ellis **Tallman** of Orford 9/28/1930 in Orford; H – 21, laborer, b. Lebanon, s/o George Canfield (Plattsburgh, NY, laborer) and Margaret Drowns (Bridgewater, ME, housewife); W – 21, domestic, b. Orford, d/o Forrest P. Tallman (Orford, laborer) and Jennie B. Rhodes (Orford)

CANTERBURY,
David Shawn of Warren m. Andrea Violet **Chase** of Orford 4/14/2004 in Orford

CAPLAN,
David of Lawrence, MA m. Dorothy **Brown** of Lawrence, MA 8/19/1929 in Portsmouth; H – 33, mgr. of busses, 2nd, divorced, b. Haverhill, MA, s/o Louis Caplan (Rega, Russia, retired) and

Lena Rubenstein (Rega, Russia, housewife); W – 21, at home, b. Lawrence, MA, d/o Moses Brown (Commonitz, Russia, retired) and Rosalie Elfond (Commonitz, Russia, at home)

CARL,
Albert J. of Orford m. Grace **Hill** of Brown Sta., NY 11/17/1921 in Orford; H – 26, laborer, b. Shady, NY, s/o Alfonzo H. Carl (Saugaties, NY, laborer) and Minnie Law (Troy, NY, housekeeper); W – 32, housekeeper, b. Brown Sta., NY, d/o Maurice Hill (Ireland, laborer) and Louise Springs (Marbleton, NY, housekeeper)
Vernon of Orford m. Margaret M. **Weibel** of Orford 5/13/1916 in Orford; H – 22, laborer, b. Mink Hollow, NY, s/o Alphonso Carl (Saugerties, NY, laborer) and Minnie Law (Troy, NY, housewife); W – 20, housewife, 2nd, divorced, b. Lancaster, d/o Wilmer Bryer (Laconia, blacksmith) and Lucy Allen (Lancaster, housewife)

CARLE,
Ronald m. Beverly Jane **Smith** 5/21/1955 in Orford; H – 22, clerk, b. Woodsville, s/o Vernon Carle (Poughkeepsie, NY) and May Bryer (Lancaster); W – 20, domestic, b. Hanover, d/o Roland Smith (Whitefield) and Bernadeen Tobin (Hanover)

CARLTON,
Charles Merritt m. Mary **MacDonald** 8/31/1957 in Hanover; H – 28, stud. teacher, b. Poultney, VT, s/o Clarence R. Carlton (Poultney, VT) and Margaret L. Pennell (Farmington, ME); W – 21, at home, b. New York City, NY, d/o Clarence Epstean (New York City) and Catherine A. MacDonald (Lansing, MI)

CARPENTER,
George Richard of Orford m. Ramona **Harrington** of Thetford, VT 10/20/1977 in Hanover; H – 42, b. VT, s/o George Carpenter, Sr. and Florence Magoon; W – 46, b. VT, d/o Earle Harrington and Gail Leavitt
Seth Maxwell of Pittsburgh, PA m. Christy Lynn **Sparks** of Pittsburgh, PA 9/4/1993

CARR,
Clarence H. of Orford m. Hittie R. **Lang** of Orford 10/27/1890 in Orford; H – 30, livery stable, b. Plainfield, s/o Philip M. Carr (Meriden, wheelwright); W – 28, teacher, b. Bath, d/o David R. Lang (Bath, lawyer)

Edward of Orford m. Florence **McIndoe** of Fairlee, VT 8/23/1919 in Orford; H – 26, farmer, b. Carroll, s/o David Carr (Danville, PQ, farmer) and Rose White (Northfield, VT, housewife); W – 21, domestic, b. Fairlee, VT, d/o David McIndoe (Newbury, VT, farmer) and Ada Kelley (Bradford, VT, housewife)

Francis Winthrop of W. Burke, VT m. Carol Anne **Knight** of W. Burke, VT 4/27/1968 in Orford; H – 36, b. VT, s/o Frank B. Carr and Martha Shaw; W – 26, b. VT, d/o Edelbert G. Wheelock and Jeanette Greenwood

Henry H. of Orford m. Erma L. **Harris** of Orford 9/9/1903 in Orford; H – 24, clerk, b. Hanover, s/o Robert O. Carr (Orford, merchant) and Mary E. Martin (N. Chelmsford, MA, housewife); W – 20, domestic, b. Whitney Pt., NY, d/o Elmer D. Harris (Truxton, NY, traveling salesman) and Mary J. Geer (Lebanon, NY, housewife)

J. Frank of Orford m. Lydia W. **Carr** of Orford 10/17/1889 in W. Lebanon; H – 24, jeweler, b. Meriden, s/o Philip M. Carr (Meriden, wheelwright) and Persis D. Huntoon (Meriden); W – 21, domestic, b. Orford, d/o Hazen E. Carr (Orford, farmer) and Martha J. Eaton (Wentworth)

Lewis P., Jr. of Orford m. Sadie R. **Muchmore** of Piermont 10/29/1889 in Piermont; H – 21, clerk, b. Meriden, s/o Lewis P. Carr (Orford, machinist) and Martha E. Howes (NY); W – 17, teacher, b. Piermont, d/o Henry S. Muchmore (Concord, farmer) and Sarah M. Chase (Warren)

CARTER,
Joseph Carroll m. Ruby Lila **Northhouse** 12/3/1957 in Orford; H – 70, retired, 4th, b. Dunbarton, s/o Joseph Theodore Carter (Island Pond, VT) and Julia Azora Farnham (Hyde Park, VT); W – 64, housekeeper, 4th, b. E. Hampton, CT, d/o Charles Nelson Darling (S. Roverdale, CT) and Cora Lavira Bennett (Webster, MA)

Lawrence Buddy of Orford m. Catherine Anne **Ross** of Orford 10/29/1999

CARVER,
Douglas W. of Plainfield m. Susan Carter **Hall** of Orford 2/12/1966 in Lyme; H – 23, b. Lebanon, s/o Frederick E. Carver and Jessie M. Graham; W – 26, b. MA, d/o Marshall G. Hall and Emily A. White

CASSANI,
John of Barre, VT m. Linda **Ceuci** of Barre, VT 6/16/1934 in Orford; H – 36, draftsman, b. Montpelier, VT, s/o Louis Cassani (Arciste, Italy, carver) and Mary Tomoli (Baveno, Italy, housewife); W – 33, stenographer, b. Barre, VT, d/o Anae'eto Ceuci (San Donato, Italy, granite mfgr.) and Carmello Colette (San Donato, Italy, housewife)

CASSONE,
Peter of NY m. Catherine **Pugh** of NY 3/10/1990

CELESTINO,
Leon Angelo of Orford m. Alice **Rodgers** of Orford 6/26/1993

CHANDLER,
Henry J. of Ladora, IA m. Ethel M. **Bean** of Orford 2/18/1902 in Orford; H – 37, farmer, b. Piermont, s/o James Chandler (Piermont, farmer) and Liveria K. Bickford (Piermont, housewife); W – 23, teacher, b. Orford, d/o Richard Bean (Piermont, farmer) and Eliza Bickford (Bradford, VT, housewife)

CHAPIN,
Gaylo O. of Orford m. Sandra Ann **Martin** of S. Corinth, BT 6/20/1959
Jayme Owen m. Alicia May **Mock** --/--/1989

CHAPLIN,
Harry Duncan of Pike m. Madeline E. **Cummings** of Orford 6/15/1950 in Newbury, VT; H – 25, cook, b. Hot Springs, VA, s/o John C. Chaplin (Hot Springs, VA) and Irma Arrington (Bradford, VA); W – 18, at home, b. Woodsville, d/o Clyde Cummings (Thetford, VT) and Rosie Tallman (Orford)

CHAPMAN,
Paul of NY m. Melinda **Snider** of NY 11/27/1982

CHASE,
Daniel R. of Orford m. Clara P. **Wood** of Lebanon 7/10/1905 in Burlington; H – 26, physician, b. Piermont, s/o Ezra C. Chase (Piermont, physician) and Margaret E. Brooks (McIndoes, VT, housewife); W – 26, mill operative, b. Lebanon, d/o George H. Wood (Lebanon, farmer) and Georgia Dudley (Hanover, housewife)

George F. of Orford m. Mary P. **Bosence** of Campton 7/13/1921 in Warren; H – 18, ball stitcher, b. Orford, s/o John W. Chase (Orford, blacksmith) and Alma Day (Haverhill, housekeeper); W – 18, machine oper., b. St. Johns, NB, d/o James P. Bosence (Cornwall, England, band sawyer) and Emma Golden (St. Johns, NB, housewife)

John K. of Nashua m. Esther **Morey** of Orford 6/29/1897 in Orford; H – 47, farmer, 2nd, b. Piermont, s/o Moody Chase (farmer) and Almira Kendrick; W – 45, domestic, 2nd, d/o Samuel Rowe and Eliza Morrow

John W. of Orford m. Alma **McDuffee** of Haverhill 7/28/1902 in Orford; H – 26, blacksmith, b. Orford, s/o John B. Chase (Orford, blacksmith) and Ann Flanders (Warren, housewife); W – 26, domestic, 2nd, divorced, b. Haverhill, d/o Charles Day (Haverhill, mason) and Esther Hartwell (Piermont, housewife)

Morris A. of Orford m. Irene A. **Mack** of Orford 6/13/1934 in Lisbon; H – 24, carpenter, b. Orford, s/o Warren S. Chase (Orford, carpenter) and Edith Simpson (Pike, housewife); W – 23, domestic, b. Orford, d/o Fred Mack (Piermont, farmer) and Mabel Ramsey (Orford, housewife)

Penrose W. of Orford m. Geneva Agnes **Copp** of Fairlee, VT 4/24/1943 in Fairlee, VT; H – 21, US soldier, b. Campton, s/o George Chase (Orford) and Mary Bosence (NB); W – 18, domestic, b. Fairlee, VT, d/o Clarence E. Copp (Warren) and Bessie M. Elliott (Haverhill)

Ralph Eugene of Plymouth m. Jeanne **Washburn** of Orford 7/20/1941 in Plymouth; H – 20, mechanic, b. Plymouth, s/o Rufus E. Chase (Orford, laborer) and Lillian Batchelder (Plymouth, housewife); W – 18, housework, b. Hanover, d/o Harvey L. Washburn (Orford, farmer) and Bernice Horton (Orford, housewife)

Robin A. of Lyme m. Karen Sue **Wynkoop** of Lyme 6/14/1977 in Lyme; H – 22, b. CA, s/o Dana Chase and Allethaire; W – 27, b. OH, d/o Philip Wynkoop

Rufus E. of Orford m. Maywood E. **Chase** of Orford 5/24/1942 in Wentworth; H – 39, farmer, 3rd, b. Orford, s/o Warren S. Chase (Orford, farmer) and Edith Mae Simpson (Orford, housewife); W – 37, domestic, 2nd, b. Roxbury, VT, d/o Walter Edson (Bethel, VT, farmer) and Myrtle C. Mann (Tunbridge, BVT, housewife)
Stanley R. of Orford m. Eleanor A. **Perry** of Orford 11/14/1937 in N. Haverhill; H – 23, merchant, b. Orford, s/o Warren S. Chase (Orford, farmer) and Edith Simpson (Orford, housewife); W – 23, at home, b. Ctr. Haverhill, d/o Charles A. Perry (Whitefield, clerk) and Inez Lindsey (Orford, housewife)
Timothy R. of Orford m. Mary E. **Mountfort** of Wentworth 7/16/1977 in Rumney; H – 25, b. NH, s/o Stanley Chase and Eleanor Perry; W – 19, b. RI, d/o Rev. G. Richard Mountfort, Jr. and Violet Gladys Overlock

CLAFLIN,
Edwin Loomis m. Lucy Betsy Elizabeth **Dike** 10/5/1957 in Woodsville; H – 69, retired, 2nd, b. Lyme, s/o Preston Claflin (Lyme) and Addie Loomis (Colebrook); W – 71, retired, 3rdm b. VT, d/o Freeman A. Dike (VT) and Julia F. Brown (VT)
Franklin George of Bradford, VT m. Diana Carol **Marsh** of Orford 8/24/1962 in Orford; H – 22, mechanic, b. Corinth, VT, s/o Fred Herbert Claflin (Corinth, VT) and Vera Claire Monroe (Corinth, VT); W – 19, at home, 2nd, b. Orford, d/o Leon C. Marsh, Sr. (Orford) and Irene M. Elliott (Littleton)
Herbert of Corinth, VT m. Emma **Avery** of Corinth, VT 1/27/1887 in Orford; H – 28, farmer, b. Topsham, VT, s/o William Claflin (Corinth, VT, farmer) and Irena Fletch (Topsham, VT, domestic); W – 18, domestic, b. Vershire, VT, d/o Charles Avery (Corinth, VT, printer) and Belle Magoon (Corinth, VT, domestic)
Richard of Bradford, VT m. Sharon **Pushee** of Bradford 3/3/1983
William H. S. of Corinth, VT m. Eda **Dow** of Stratford, VT 6/1/1889 in Orford; H – 26, farmer, b. Corinth, VT, s/o William Claflin (Corinth, VT, farmer) and Irena Claflin (Topsham, VT); W – 18, domestic, b. Stratford, VT, d/o George H. Dow (Stratford, VT, farmer) and Ida Dow (Tunbridge, VT)
Willis B. of Orford m. Julia E. **McCrillis** of Orford 10/24/1893 in Orford; H – 38, farmer, b. Topsham, VT, s/o William N. S. Claflin (Marshfield, VT, farmer) and Irene Felch (Topsham, VT, domestic); W – 42, domestic, 2nd, divorced, b. Haverhill, d/o

Kelley Hackett (Bath, farmer) and Sarah Hutton (England, domestic)

CLARK,
Charlie W. of Lyme m. Ruth A. **Bean** of Orford 9/3/1934 in Lyme; H – 29, farmer, b. Thetford, VT, s/o Gilman A. Clark (Thetford, VT, farmer) and Harriet R. Houston (Strafford, VT, housewife); W – 18, at home, b. Orford, d/o Edwin F. Bean (Orford, farmer) and Alice M. Marsh (Orford, housewife)
Douglas E. m. Irene L. **Pease** --/--/1989
George C. of Orford m. Gertrude M. **Keys** of Lyme 1/15/1889 in Orford; H – 21, farmer, b. Orford, s/o Daniel C. Clark (Orford, farmer) and Sarah Richardson (Hartland, VT); W – 19, domestic, b. Thetford, VT, d/o ----- Keyes (Stratford, VT, merchant) and ----- Keyes (Lyme)
George L. of Hanover m. Harriet P. **Spooner** of Orford 7/16/1938 in N. Haverhill; H – 22, farmer, b. Meredith, s/o William D. Clark (Meredith, laborer) and Nora Lafoe (Belmont, housewife); W – 18, housework, b. Franconia, d/o Henry E. Spooner (Franconia, deceased) and Tillie E. Partridge (Haverhill, housewife)
Leander D. H. of Orford m. Martha L. **Bean** of Orford 4/26/1899 in Orford; H – 48, carpenter, b. Vershire, VT, s/o Daniel E. Clark (Berwick, ME) and Lucy P. Brown (Berwick, ME); W – 24, teacher, b. Piermont, d/o Richard D. Bean (Berwick, ME) and Eliza A. Bickford (Berwick, ME)
William G., Sr. of Orford m. Caryl Hicks **Smith** of Norwich, VT 11/22/1973 in Hanover; H – 55, b. Ridgewood, NJ, s/o Ray Clark and Ethel Kunzman; W – 45, b. Flushing, NY, d/o Orton Hicks and Lois Paddock

CLEMENTS,
Scott Allen of Bradford, VT m. Dorisann **Dyke** of Orford 11/6/1971 in Orford; H – 19, b. Norwich, VT, s/o Allen G. Clements and Ruth Brainerd; W – 18, b. St. Cloud, MN, d/o Robert F. Dyke and Deloris Urbanski
Scott Allen of Orford m. Kathryn **Green** of Orford 6/11/1977 in Orford; H – 25, b. NH, s/o Allen Clements and Ruth Brainerd; W – 35, b. NH, d/o William Fitzgerald and Marion Simonds

CLEVELAND,
Dennis Allen of Terre Haute, IN m. Catherine **Hall** of Orford 6/29/1969 in Orford; H – 22, b. IN, s/o Harold L. Cleveland and Lillian Ederer; W – 22, b. MD, d/o Harvey P. Hall and Barbara Poole

CLIFFORD,
Charles Henry, Jr. of Orford m. Joan Margaret **Tyler** of Orford 7/14/1960 in Orford; H – 24, printer, b. Quincy, MA, s/o Charles H. Clifford, Sr. (E. Milton, MA) and Hazel Butson (Woodsville); W – 17, secretary, b. Woodsville, d/o Donald L. Tyler, Sr. (N. Haverhill) and Marion C. Bonnett (Fairlee, VT)

Lewis H. of Orford m. Cena I. **Hadlock** of Piermont 7/20/1896 in Orford; H – 20, farmer, b. Wentworth, s/o Charles W. Clifford (Haverhill, farmer) and Mary J. Cross (Sutton, PQ, housewife); W – 18, domestic, b. Jay, VT, d/o S. P. Hadlock (Piermont, farmer) and Luella A. Day (Greensboro, VT, housewife)

Louis H. of Orford m. Lottie L. **Rollins** of Piermont 12/24/1908 in Wentworth; H – 32, laborer, 3rd, widower, b. Wentworth, s/o Charles W. Clifford (Haverhill, farmer) and Mary Cross (Sutton, PQ, housewife); W – 16, domestic, b. Orford, d/o Hiram B. Rollins (Rumney, farmer) and Addie J. Patch (Carroll, housewife)

CLOGSTON,
Willie of Lyme m. Ada **Patch** of Lyme 8/28/1902 in Orford; H – 22, farmer, b. Lyme, s/o William Clogston (Lyme, farmer) and Hattie Columbia (Dorchester, housewife); W – 17, domestic, b. Orford, d/o William Patch (Orford, laborer) and Ella White (Orford, housewife)

CLOUGH,
George L. of Orford m. Emma E. **Goodwin** of Warren 7/4/1887 in Wentworth; H – 22, farmer, b. Piermont, s/o Horace Clough (Washington, VT, farmer) and Anna Sargent (Hooksett, domestic); W – 20, domestic, b. Warren, d/o John Goodwin (Warren, farmer) and Hannah Sherwill (Orange, VT, domestic)

George L. of Orford m. Etta I. **Bartlett** of Laconia 6/22/1902 in Wentworth; H – 37, carpenter, 2nd, divorced, b. Horace Clough (Washington, VT, farmer) and Ann G. Sargent (Bow, housewife); W – 21, domestic, b. Laconia, d/o Stephen Bartlett (laborer) and Alma E. Borroughs (Troy, VT, housewife) John, III of Orford m. Debra **Edmands** of Fairlee, VT 4/14/1979

COBB,
Leon E. of Lyndon, VT m. Maybelle P. **Brooks** of Lyndon, VT 10/17/1931 in Orford; H – 42, salesman, 2nd, divorced, b. Stowe, VT, s/o Enos Bert Cobb (Stowe, VT, farmer) and Florence Emower (Gardner, MA, housewife); W – 25, billing clerk, b. Sheffield, VT, d/o Carlyle L. Brooks (Sheffield, VT, farmer) and Grace M. Jenness (Sheffield, VT, housewife)

COCHRAN,
Charles W. of Piermont m. Nellie E. **Lawrence** of Orford 10/11/1887 in Orford; H – 23, farmer, b. Piermont, s/o Charles Cochran (Washington, VT, farmer) and Sophie Cochran (Wentworth); W – 21, domestic, b. Washington, VT, d/o Chase Lawrence (Fairlee, VT, farmer) and Martha Lawrence (Orange, VT, domestic)

CODY,
Kenneth of Orford m. Jamie **Burton** of Orford 9/27/1980

COFFIN,
Ray Edison, Jr. of Orford m. Annie May **Sharon** of Lincoln 5/29/1965 in Lincoln; H – 28, 2nd, b. Brattleboro, VT, s/o Ray E. Coffin and Lillian E. Bleary; W – 21, 2nd, b. Lincoln, d/o Edward Wiggett and Erma Wright

COLLOPY,
Joseph W. of Dunstable, MA m. Danielle A. **Nantel** of Hudson 9/2/2001 in Orford

COLOMBE,
Herman A. of Barre, VT m. May L. **Wheeler** of Barre, VT 9/22/1932 in Orford; H – 21, cook, b. Barre, VT, s/o John Colombe (Champlain, NY, lumper) and Mabel Mayo (Chezy, NY, waitress); W – 18, governess, b. Bethel, VT, d/o Alvin Wheeler (Ellenburg, NY, laborer) and Lillian Dana (Lowell, VT, housewife)

CONBOY,
George Edwin m. Helena Miranda **Greenleaf** 6/15/1957 in
 Peterborough; H – 61, textile work, b. W. Swanzey, s/o John
 Conboy (Ireland) and Josephine Eurkery (Somerville, MA); W –
 57, housework, b. W. Swanzey, d/o Charles Greenleaf (W.
 Swanzey) and Grace Bourne (Winchester)

CONNOR,
Paul Rich of Lexington, MA m. Carol Jean **Gallup** of Orford
 9/11/1971 in Orford; H – 28, b. Cambridge, MA, s/o Thomas
 Connor and Cecelia Samuel; W – 24, b. Lebanon, d/o Harley G.
 Gallup and Ella Johnson

COOK,
Foster George, Jr. of Hanover m. Jean Althea **Smith** of Orford
 11/16/1949 in Lebanon; H – 20, student, b. NY, s/o Foster G.
 Cook (VT) and Mercades Salas (Porto Rico); W – 18, secretary,
 b. Fairlee, VT, d/o George Smith, Jr. (Fairlee, VT) and Leona
 M. Strout (Alton, ME)
Timothy Robert of Orford m. Karen **McDonough** of Orford 10/9/1971
 in Hanover; H – 25, b. Bryn Mawr, PA, s/o Thomas N. Cook
 and Monica Batchelor; W – 22, b. Philadelphia, PA, d/o Donald
 McDonough and Mary T. Ingolia

COPP,
Franklin Lloyd of Fairlee, VT m. Joy Audrie **Miller** of Orford
 6/10/1951 in Bradford, VT; H – 23, b. Fairlee, VT, s/o Clarence
 Copp (Warren) and Bessie Elliott (Haverhill); W – 19, at home,
 b. E. Barre, VT, d/o Joseph G. Miller (Sutton, PQ) and Marjorie
 Hunt (Knowlton, PQ)

CORLISS,
Benjamin C. of Orford m. Helen F. **Gilbert** of Orford 1/29/1902 in
 Orford; H – 29, blacksmith, b. Orford, s/o John S. Corliss
 (Orford, farmer) and Olive E. Cheney (Stowe, VT, housewife);
 W – 21, domestic, b. Brownington, VT, d/o Carlos D. Gilbert
 (Brownington, VT) and Helen S. Barnes (Chelsea, VT)

CORPIERI,
Ernest F. of Fairlee, VT m. Evelyn Grace **Mack** of Orford 2/2/1936 in
 Fairlee, VT; H – 23, clerk, b. Bradford, VT, s/o Ernest Corpieri

(Italy, merchant) and Lottie Ford (Bradford, VT, deceased); W – 21, at home, b. Orford, d/o Fred Mack (Piermont, farmer) and Mabel Ramsey (Orford, housewife)
Stuart Carleton of Orford m. Donna Lynne **Baker** of Orford 8/12/2000 in Orford

CORPORON,
David m. Deborah **Hodgson** 6/7/1986

COUHIG,
Frank of Newbury, VT m. Etta **White** of Orford 10/1/1898 in Orford; H – 24, farmer, b. Bathurst, NB, s/o John Couhig (Bathurst, NB, farmer) and Mary A. Ryan (Cambleton, housewife); W – 23, domestic, b. Waterloo, PQ, d/o David White (farmer) and Patience Boardman (housewife)

COVEY,
Richard E., Jr. of Bradford, VT m. Marilyn J. **Bunten** of Orford 3/9/1974 in Orford; H – 19, b. Barre, VT, s/o Richard E. Covey, Sr. and Lois O'Donnell; W – 19, b. Concord, d/o Forrest K. Bunten and Evelyn Stephenson

CROSS,
George H. of Claremont m. Florence M. **Dennis** of Orford 5/16/1942 in Lyme; H – 44, carpenter, 2nd, b. Claremont, s/o Lucius P. Cross (Unity, retired) and Mary Ann Burns (N. Charlestown, housewife); W – 42, housekeeper, 2nd, b. Fairlee, VT, d/o William F. Leach (New London, farmer) and Florence E. Paine (Fairlee, VT, housewife)
Joseph Dwight of Orford m. Agnes **Whitcher** of Orford 12/17/1901 in Orford; H – 43, laborer, 3rd, widower, b. Barford, PQ, s/o Joseph Cross (Stanstead, PQ, farmer) and Lovina Edwards (Athens, VT, housewife); W – 29, domestic, 2nd, widow, b. W. Rumney, d/o Blaisdell H. Merrill (Plymouth, farmer) and Sarah H. Woodman (Lowell, MA, housewife)

CROWE,
Ty Jayson of Orford m. Ashley Lynn **Merrill** of Orford 9/4/2004 in Orford

CUMMINGS,
Clyde A. of Orford m. Rosie Ellen **Tallman** of Orford 7/12/1930 in Vershire, VT; H – 21, truck driver, b. Thetford, VT, s/o Asa Cummings (Thetford, VT, laborer) and Nellie M. Randall (Wentworth); W – 19, domestic, b. Orford, d/o Forrest Tallman (Orford, laborer) and Jennie B. Rhodes (Orford)
Clyde Asa, Jr. m. June Flora **Andrews** 5/4/1955 in Piermont; H – 21, US Air Force, b. Woodsville, s/o Clyde A. Cummings (Thetford Ctr., VT) and Rosie E. Tallman (Orford); W – 19, tel. operator, b. Orford, d/o Clarence H. Andrews (Sutton) and Esther Hildreth (Haverhill)
Vernon D. of Orford m. Marjorie **Hannaford** of Bradford, VT 11/7/1939 in Bradford, VT; H – 19, farming, b. Fairlee, VT, s/o Henry J. Cummings (Thetford, VT) and Lena Vezina (Sherbrooke, Canada); W – b. Norwich, VT, d/o Hazen A. Hannaford (Orford) and Eva A. Rhodes (Orford)
Wallace John of Orford m. Valerie **Williams** of Hartford, VT 12/11/1970 in Brattleboro, VT; H – 25, b. Lyme, s/o Clyde A. Cummings, Sr. and Rose Tallman; W – 20, b. VT, d/o Allen H. Williams and Barbara M. Leary

CUNNINGHAM,
George H. of Orford m. Alice G. **Sanborn** of Orford 10/8/1892 in Piermont; H – 38, farmer, 2nd, b. Orford, s/o John Cunningham (farmer) and Jane B. Smith; W – 26, domestic, b. Hanover, d/o John Sanborn (Bradford, VT, farmer) and Martha Fitch (Enfield)
George H. of Orford m. Mary N. **Bailey** of Orford 1/9/1909 in Orford; H – 54, laborer, 3rd, b. Orford, s/o John Cunningham (Groton, VT, farmer) and Betsey Smith (Dalton, housewife); W – 54, housewife, 2nd, b. Orford, d/o Benjamin F. Niles (Orford, farmer) and Mary Newell (Orford, housewife)

CURRIER,
Alfred T. of Orford m. Maggie M. **Rollins** of Orford 4/9/1905 in Wentworth; H – 24, laborer, b. Orford, s/o Towle Currier (Lowell, MA, farmer) and Rose Hoyt (Corrino, ME, housewife); W – 15, domestic, b. Orford, d/o Fred E. Rollins (Campton, farmer) and Emma A. Saunder (Hanover, housewife)
George E. of Orford m. Anna Mae **Carrier** of Fairlee, VT 11/28/1923 in Meredith; H – 44, laborer, b. Vershire, VT, s/o Lewis Currier (Canada, laborer) and Lucia Straw (Vershire, VT, housewife);

W – 37, domestic, 2nd, b. Monroe, d/o Wilfred H. Streeter (PQ, laborer) and Amanda Raymond (Cov. Falls, VT, housewife)

Jessie W. of Orford m. Victoria E. **Downing** of Orford 5/16/1923 in Haverhill; H – 26, farmer, b. Wentworth, s/o John Currier (Wentworth, farmer) and Alice Sharp (S. Boston, MA, housewife); W – 16, domestic, b. Orford, d/o Willie E. Downing (Wentworth) and Luna Poor (Orford, housewife)

Norman J. of Orford m. Alice E. **Keneson** of Wentworth 5/15/1948 in Plymouth; H – 24, farm mgr., b. Orford, s/o Jesse W. Currier (Wentworth, farmer) and Victoria Downing (Orford, housewife); W – 19, factory wkr., b. Wentworth, d/o Charles D. Keneson (Wentworth, farmer) and Gladys H. Howard (Wentworth, housewife)

CURTIS,

Harry O. of W. Lebanon m. Beverly P. **Peck** of W. Lebanon 7/18/1969 in Orford; H – 35, b. NH, s/o Harry M. Curtis and Alma Sill; W – 39, b. VT, d/o Leonard Anair and Grace Astbury

DAISEY,

Allen L. of Orford m. Linda L. **Fitzbag** of Orford 8/31/1974 in Orford; H – 22, b. Plymouth, s/o Royden H. Daisey and Myrtle Chase; W – 22, b. Derry, d/o John H. Fitzbag and Violet L. Dephresney

Amos Frederick of Orford m. Holly Cristine **Lemay** of Orford 8/14/1993

Daniel Scott of Orford m. Tonya Jean **Sargent** of Orford 9/20/2003 in Orford

Joseph Ernest of Orford m. Helen Marie **Wilson** of Orford 5/25/1968 in Orford; H – 22, b. DE, s/o Harry Royden Daisey and Myrtle Chase; W – 19, b. NY, d/o Alfred E. Wilson and Alma Brown

Richard Eugene of Orford m. Donna Jean **Tirrell** of Durham 2/21/1976 in Durham; H – s/o Royden H. Daisey and Myrtle Chase; W – 22, b. NH, d/o Theron L. Terrill and Alma Brown

Royden of Orford m. Gloria **Taylor** of Orford 5/5/1990

Royden H. of Orford m. Myrtle F. **Chase** of Orford 9/25/1943 in Orford; H – 31, caretaker, 2nd, b. Millboro, DE, s/o Joseph E. Daisey (Bethlehem, MD, farmer) and Della May Dickerson (Laurel, DE, housewife); W – 19, domestic, b. Wentworth, d/o Leon Edward Chase (Wentworth, farmer) and Maywood E. Edison (Roxbury, VT, housewife)

Royden Wayne of Orford m. Sheilah Mae **Corliss** of Orford 9/26/1964 in Orford; H – 20, b. Wilmington, DE, s/o Royden H. Daisey and Myrtle Florence Chase; W – 18, b. Littleton, d/o Bernard Corliss and Guelda Brownell

DALTON,
Paul of Orford m. Madison **Fitzpatrick** of Enfield 3/14/1992

DANIELSON,
Charles of Orford m. Jane **McLaughlin** of Orford 8/7/1982

DAUGHERTY,
Michael of VT m. Rebecca **Bellows** of Orford 8/18/1990

DAVIS,
Brent of Orford m. Diane **Hutchins** of Plymouth 6/1/1990
Brian m. Elizabeth **Dunnells** 12/7/1985 in Orford
Chester C. of Winthrop, MA m. Daisy D. **Smith** of Orford 4/24/1911 in Orford; H – 23, tradesman, b. Calais, ME, s/o George A. Davis (Calais, ME, sea captain) and Emma J. Davis (Mi.town, NB, housewife); W – 28, clerk, b. Bethel, VT, d/o John R. Smith (Orford, merchant) and Mary J. Perkins (Barnard, VT, housewife)
Donald Francis m. Ruth Delvina **Fillian** 2/11/1956 in N. Thetford, VT; H – 28, lumbering, b. Enfield, s/o Gerald W. Davis (N. Groton) and Hattie Davis (Derby Line, VT); W – 22, at home, b. Wentworth, d/o Alphonse Fillian (Manchester) and Jessie A. Woods (Piermont)
Floyd Ellis of Orford m. Myrtle E. **Cummings** of Orford 12/23/1944 in Orford; H – 40, radio repair man, b. Orford, s/o Aylmer E. Davis (Mansonville, PQ) and Ida L. Clough (Lisbon); W – 34, cook, b. Thetford, VT, d/o Asa Cummings (Thetford, VT, chef) and Nellie Randall (Wentworth)
Hiram W. of Orford m. Julia C. **Mousley** of Lyme 2/2/1887 in Orford; H – 30, shoemaker, 2nd, widower, b. E. Corinth, VT, s/o Thomas W. Davis (Albany, VT, shoemaker) and Harriet E. Reed (Fairlee, VT, domestic); W – 46, domestic, 2nd, widow, b. Orford, d/o Thomas Quint (Orford, laborer) and Jane Archer (Orford, domestic)
John P. of Orford m. S. Josephine **Lovejoy** of Orford 12/23/1891 in Orford; H – 42, farmer, b. Orford, s/o John T. Davis (farmer)

and Lavina Whitcomb (Lyme); W – 45, domestic, b. Orford, d/o
Clark Lovejoy (farmer) and ----- Brown (Orford)

Perry Adelbert of Lyme m. Gladys M. **Sanborn** of Orford 1/--/1919 in
Lyme; H – 22, farming, b. Thetford, VT, s/o William E. Davis
(England, engineer) and Annie E. Lines (England, housewife);
W – 20, at home, b. Plymouth, d/o Joseph Sanborn (Rumney,
farming) and Flora M. Hutchins (housewife)

Prescott W. of Orford m. Lillian L. **Dike** of Lyme 10/8/1891 in White
River Jct., VT; H – 31, farmer, b. Orford, s/o John T. Davis
(farmer) and Lavina Whitcomb (Lyme); W – 26, domestic, 2nd,
b. Tunbridge, VT, d/o Harry Dyke (shoemaker)

DAY,

Daniel A. of Hanover m. Deann K. **Sanborn** of Orford 6/29/1974 in
Orford; H – 27, b. Hanover, s/o Jerald F. Day and Madeline A.
Durkee; W – 19, b. Woodsville, d/o Neil H. Sanborn and
Theresa M. Hudson

DAYTON,

James H. of Orford m. Bessie L. **Brock** of Orford 5/2/1917 in Orford;
H – 40, farmer, b. Somerville, MA, s/o Henry E. Dayton (Orford)
and Lillian M. Browne (Portland, ME); W – 28, domestic, b.
Orford, d/o Charles E. Brock (Orford) and Mary E. Wyman
(Beverly, MA)

DEARBORN,

Thomas G. of Chelsea, VT m. Ida G. **Savage** of Chelsea, VT
11/17/1905 in Orford; H – 33, hotel clerk, 2nd, b. Chelsea, VT,
s/o H. W. Dearborn (Chelsea, VT, furniture dealer) and Olivia S.
Godfrey (Chelsea, VT, housewife); W – 33, hotel cook, 3rd, b.
Royalton, VT, d/o Christopher George (Tunbridge, VT, farmer)
and Helen Chandler (Chittenden, VT, housewife)

DEBLOIS,

Alton Guy of Orford m. Shirley Jane **Chase** of Orford 6/9/1962 in
Wentworth; H – 23, US Navy, b. E. Ryegate, VT, s/o Melvin G.
Deblois (Lowell, VT) and Beatrice L. Irwin (St. Johnsbury, VT);
W – 19, at home, b. Woodsville, d/o Stanley R. Chase (Orford)
and Eleanor A. Perry (Haverhill)

Richard Guy of Orford m. Helen Colette **Eppig** of Burlington, VT
6/4/1994

DeCOLFMACKER,
Robert John of Dover m. Stacy Lynn **Vielleux** of Dover 7/5/2003 in Orford

DELAURIER,
Gregory of Somerville, MA m. Jeannette M. **Frey** of Somerville, MA 8/17/1996

DENNIS,
Albert B. of Orford m. Maude A. **Piper** of Lyme 3/3/1903 in Orford; H – 20, laborer, b. Stratford, s/o Fred A. Dennis (Stratford, farmer) and Mary Gamsby (Colebrook, housewife); W – 18, domestic, b. Lyme, d/o Walter G. Piper (Lyme, lumber dealer) and Hattie Estey (Lyme, housewife)

Byron H. of Orford m. Eva M. **Spencer** of Piermont 7/25/1892 in Haverhill; H – 23, farmer, b. Orford, s/o Emore Dennis (Strafford, farmer) and Olive Cross (Troy, VT); W – 19, domestic, b. Piermont, d/o Nehemiah Spencer (Piermont, mason) and Helen Dennis

Carl W. of Lebanon m. Mary E. **Gilman** of Lebanon 1/24/1981

Ernest C. of Orford m. Florence M. **Leach** of Fairlee, VT 11/14/1917 in Woodsville; H – 21, farmer, b. Orford, s/o Fred A. Dennis (Whitefield) and Veina Bass (Stratford); W – 18, domestic, b. Fairlee, VT, d/o William F. Leach (Claremont) and Florence E. Paine (Fairlee, VT)

George W. of Orford m. Carrie F. **Church** of Vershire, VT 8/13/1887 in Piermont; H – 25, farmer; W – 19, domestic

Leroy E. of Orford m. Effie A. **Gage** of Orford 1/1/1910 in Lyme; H – 22, farmer, b. Strafford, s/o Dewer Dennis (Strafford, farmer) and Sarah A. Curtis (Strafford, housewife); W – 17, domestic, b. Orford, d/o Everett L. Gage (Orford, farmer) and Nellie F. Pebbles (Lyme, housewife)

Newell A. of Orford m. Lottie B. **Roberts** of Lyme 12/11/1905 in Orford; H – 24, laborer, b. Orford, s/o Emore Dennis (Strafford, VT, farmer) and Olive Cross (Troy, VT, housewife); W – 14, domestic, b. Lyme, d/o Thomas W. Roberts (Lyme, laborer) and Louise Strue (Lyme, housewife)

Ralph Edward of Orford m. Ramona Jane **Wing** of Lyme 11/3/1950 in Manchester; H – 24, farmer, b. Hanover, s/o Walter B. Dennis (Piermont) and Theresa Rugg (Fairlee, VT); W – 21, at home, b. Orford, d/o Albert Wing (Lyme) and Esther Small (Cornish)

Wallace E. of Orford m. Evelyn **Clark** of Orford 7/22/1946 in Orford; H – 25, student, b. Hanover, s/o Ernest C. Dennis (Orford, farmer) and Florence M. Leach (Fairlee, VT, housewife); W – 19, at home, b. Fairlee, VT, d/o Charles A. Clark (Calais, ME, salesman) and Ida M. Nash (Calais, ME, housewife)

DERRICK,
George E. of Orford m. Lulu M. **Goodwin** of Orford 2/18/1896 in Orford; H – 23, farming, b. Waterloo, LC, s/o Campbell Derrick (Sherbrook, LC, farmer) and Patience Wood (Waterloo, LC, domestic); W – 18, domestic, b. Piermont, d/o John Goodwin (Hanover, farmer) and Melissa Goodwin (Sherbrook, LC, domestic)

DERVIN,
Daniel Arthur of Tarrytown, NY m. Katherine Ramsey **Chaplin** of Orford 6/27/1964 in Hanover; H – 29, b. Omaha, NE, s/o Arthur T. Dervin and Mamie Hudson; W – 30, b. Baltimore, MD, d/o Henry D. Chaplin and Anne Ramsey

DESRUISSEAUX,
R. L. of Manchester m. Lorna **McEwan** of Orford 5/8/1948 in Manchester; H – 22, shoe worker, b. Manchester, s/o L. J. Desruisseaux (Canada, mill worker) and Lydia E. Croteau (Canada, mill worker); W – 21, at home, b. Lyme, d/o Harry A. McEwan (Canada, carpenter) and Alice E. Clark (Plainfield, housewife)

DEWITT,
William of Bradford, VT m. Patricia **Jones** of Bradford, VT 12/8/1979

DIBBERN,
William of Barre, VT m. Patricia E. **Cummings** of Wells River, VT 6/9/1978 in Orford; H – b. MA, s/o Henry Dibbern and Ruth MacLean; W – b. MA, d/o Lee A. Gilbault and Mavis I. White

DICKEY,
Joshua of Portsmouth m. Katherine **Berwick** of Orford 6/29/2002 in Bradford, VT

DIMICK,
Gary Michael of Orford m. Gail **Temperley** of Orford 3/20/1993

DOMINGUE,
James H. of Lebanon m. Karen M. **Schwarz** of Lebanon 10/21/1978 in Orford; H – b. NH, s/o Morris A. Domingue and Florence Gagne; W – b. NH, d/o George Schwarz and Juanita Marsh

DONALDSON,
George B. of Orford m. Mary H. **Whitman** of Orford 9/13/1890 in Lebanon; H – 24, farmer, b. Peacham, VT, s/o Mark Donaldson (Canada, farmer); W – 18, domestic, b. Orford, d/o Caleb F. Whitman (Orford, farmer)

Samuel H. of Orford m. Mary H. **Donaldson** ofOrford 10/9/1908 in Lyme; H – 45, laborer, b. Peacham, VT, s/o Mark Donaldson (Stanstead Plain, Canada, laborer) and Charlotte LaLeau (Peacham, VT, housewife); W – 36, housewife, 2nd, widow, b. Orford, d/o Caleb F. Whitman (Orford, farmer) and Mary W. Norris (Wentworth, housewife)

DONELLY,
Robert C. of Stonington, CT m. Lillian **Schauer** of Orford 8/12/1966 in Orford; H – 47, b. Kingston, RI, s/o Robert J. Donelly and Bertha P. Larkin; W – 45, b. N. Reading, MA, d/o Frederick Margeson and Everlena Orborn

DONNELLY,
Leslie Jay of Orford m. Hazel Abbie **Sanborn** of Orford 6/24/1938 in Orford; H – 26, salesman, b. Orford, s/o Jay W. Donnelly (farmer) and Della A. Pease (Bradford, VT, housewife); W – 26, teacher, b. Orford, d/o Fred J. Sanborn (Bradford, VT, veterinary) and Carrie A. Bacon (Arlington, MA, housewife)

Robert J. of Orford m. Nellie M. **Cummings** of Orford 1/30/1944 in Orford; H – 28, US Army, b. Lisbon, s/o Jay W. Donnelly (McIndoes, VT, nurseryman) and Della A. Pease (Easton, housewife); W – 18, at home, b. Thetford, VT, d/o Asa Cummings (Thetford, VT, laborer) and Nellie Randall (Wentworth)

DORMAN,
Thomas E. of Sharon, VT m. Jill M. **Forbush** of Sharon, VT 6/14/1997

DOW,
Bert of Wentworth m. Ethel **Downing** of Orford 11/18/1909 in Orford; H – 23, laborer, b. Canterbury, NB, s/o David Dow (Canterbury, NB, farmer) and Annie Cummings (Houlton, ME, housewife); W – 17, domestic, b. Orford, d/o Willie E. Downing (Wentworth, farmer) and Luna M. Poor (Orford, housewife)

Earl Chester of Rumney m. Ruth Ingerson **Byers** of Orford 10/25/1969 in Orford; H – 62, b. NH, s/o David Dow and Annie Cummings; W – 62, b. RI, d/o Willie B. Ingerson and Flora M. Zubee

DOWNING,
George E. of Orford m. Elizabeth T. **Young** of Belfast, ME 3/31/1923 in Orford; H – 34, farmer, b. Orford, s/o Willie E. Downing (Wentworth, farmer) and Luna Poor (Orford, housewife); W – 26, nurse, 2nd, b. Ft. Lawrence, NS, d/o Henry DeBlois (H. Co., NS, farmer) and Olive Pemberton (H. Co., NS, housewife)

Richard Lee, Jr. of Wentworth m. Janet Mary **Dyke** of Orford 5/2/1964 in Orford; H – 23, b. Plymouth, s/o Richard L. Downing and Elsie Krahenbuhl; W – 19, b. St. Cloud, MN, d/o Robert F. Dyke and Dolores Urbanski

Roland E. of Orford m. Hazel E. **Boynton** of Meredith 6/19/1920 in Meredith; H – 24, farmer, b. Orford, s/o Willie E. Downing (Wentworth, farmer) and Luna Poor (Orford, housewife); W – 22, stenographer, b. Meredith, d/o Mead Boynton (Meredith, farmer) and Alice Lawrence (Laconia, housewife)

DREESBACH,
Philip P. of Montclair, NJ m. Muriel F. **Jennings** of New York, NY 9/3/1927 in Orford; H – 28, sales engineer, b. Chicago, IL, s/o Philip Dreesbach (Beardstown, IL, broker) and Mary Hellman (Chicago, IL, housewife); W – 25, at home, b. Brooklyn, NY, d/o John E. Jennings (Brooklyn, NY, engineer) and Florence Booth (Hartford, CT, housewife)

DREW,
Richard Henry of Lyme m. Delores Delvina **Fillian** of Orford 8/22/1970 in Orford; H – 25, b. Lyme, s/o Leslie Drew and Irene Blake; W – 20, b. Orford, d/o David Fillian and Hattie Shortt

DUNBAR,
Christopher White of E. Thetford, VT m. Brandy Lynn **Goodrich** of Orford 11/20/2004 in Orford

DURGIN,
Peter of Fairlee m. Claire **DiPrisco** of Orford 7/31/1982

DURKEE,
James C. of Orford m. Susan A. **Tuttle** of Orford 3/31/1996

DUVAL,
Raymond of Orford m. Kathy **Wain** of Orford 12/25/1980

DWYER,
Nelson S. of Orford m. Mary E. Hall **Tanssell** of Orford 9/12/1900 in White River Jct., VT; H – 27, laborer, b. Greensboro, VT, s/o William Dwyer (Salem, VT, farmer) and Ana McKay (Canada); W – 18, domestic, b. Lebanon, d/o Benjamin F. Tanssell (Orford) and Emma A. Russell (Orford)

DYER,
Leslie Allen of Sharon, VT m. Margaret Ann **Cameron** of Hartford, VT 2/6/1971 in Orford; H – 20, b. Lebanon, s/o James E. Dyer and Joyce Hazen; W – 19, b. Lebanon, d/o Leslie Ray (foster) and Verna M. Pretty (foster)

Lyman T. of Orford m. Isabel W. **Doan** of Orford 11/27/1948 in Hanover; H – retired, 2nd, widower, b. New York, NY, s/o Henry L. Dyer (Boston, MA, retired) and Mary Jones (New York, NY, housewife); W – housewife, 2nd, widow, b. Winchester, MA, d/o John T. Wilson (Boston, MA, lawyer) and Pl'ant'ne Cushman (Orford, housewife)

DYKE,
Alan of Orford m. Joan J. **Randall** of Wentworth 9/9/1961 in Wentworth; H – 16, b. Bristol, s/o George C. Dyke (Newbury, VT) and Beulah B. Bockus (Wethersfield, CT); W – 17,

waitress, b. Plymouth, d/o William F. Randall (Wentworth) and
Juanita Downing (Wentworth)
Alan Frederick of Orford m. Joy Jean **Wilson** of Orford 7/11/1970 in
Orford; H – 25, b. Bristol, s/o George C. Dyke and Beulah
Bockus; W – 23, b. Bay Shore, LI, NY, d/o Alfred E. Wilson and
Alma H. Brown
Benjamin F., Jr. of Orford m. Dorothy Alice **Dow** of Wentworth
12/30/1939 in Plymouth; H – 20, woodsman, b. Newbury, VT,
s/o Benjamin F. Dyke (Pompanoosuc, VT, woodsman) and
Ethel Jessaman (Newbury, VT, housewife); W – 20, at home, b.
Orford, d/o Cuthbert J. Dow (Canterbury, NB, woodsman) and
Ethel E. Downing (Orford, housewife)
Calvin Ronald of Orford m. Jane M. **Borger** of Waltham, MA
11/10/1962 in Orford; H – 22, machine op., b. Orford, s/o
Benjamin F. Dyke, Jr. (Newbury, VT) and Dorothy Dow
(Orford); W – 21, clerical wk., b. Queens, NY, d/o Francis
Borger (NY) and Elizabeth J. Winkel (Jamaica, LI)
Daniel of Orford m. Cara **McGinnis** of Orford 7/4/1990
Eugene Leo of Orford m. Christine Evelyn **Bunten** of Orford
11/15/1970 in Orford; H – 22, b. St. Cloud, MN, s/o Robert F.
Dyke and Delores Urbanski; W – 18, b. Concord, d/o Forrest
Bunten and Evelyn Stephens
Eugene Leo of Orford m. Elinor Elaine **Hays** of Orford 2/18/1978 in
Orford; H – b. MN, s/o Robert Dyke and Delores Urbanski; W –
b. PA, d/o Edward Gardiner and Jeanette Burgess
George Carl of Orford m. Beulah B. **Bockus** of Bristol 11/16/1943 in
Fairlee, VT; H – 21, truck operator, b. Newbury, VT, s/o
Benjamin F. Dyke (Norwich, VT) and Ethel Jessman (Newbury,
VT); W – 17, housemaid, b. Wethersfield, CT, d/o Harry Bockus
(Hartford, CT) and Jessie Deming (Wethersfield, CT)
James Robert of Orford m. Barbara Claire **Wilkins** of Reading, MA
7/12/1975 in Orford; H – 29, b. St. Cloud, MN, s/o Robert F.
Dyke and Doloris Urbanski; W – 22, b. Boston, MA, d/o Howard
P. Wilkins and Florence Cooke
Michael of Orford m. Mary **Pushee** of Orford 5/17/1980
Robert Leon of Orford m. Nancy Carol **Small** of Lyme 10/17/1969 in
Orford; H – 19, b. MN, s/o Robert F. Dyke and Dolores M.
Urbanski; W – 19, b. NH, d/o Harry A. Small and Daisey B.
Melendy
Terry m. Elizabeth **Holloway** 9/26/1987
Tracy of Orford m. Lori **Haywood** of Orford 6/4/1983

EDGAR,
William B. of Summit, NJ m. Patricia S. **Hammond** of New York, NY 11/28/1952 in Orford; H – 20, US Navy, b. San Francisco, CA, s/o Malcolm S. Edgar (Philadelphia, PA) and Frances G. Belknap (Newport, RI); W – 22, secretary, b. New Haven, CT, d/o John W. Hammond (Cambridge, MA) and Adelaide Meara (New York, NY)

EDWARDS,
Jason m. Susan **Keller** 8/25/1984 in Orford

ELLIOTT,
Ashton W. of Fairlee, VT m. Helen B. **Foote** of Orford 11/3/1920 in Warren; H – 26, farmer, b. Haverhill, s/o Sam Elliott (Haverhill, farmer) and Eugenia Davis (Haverhill, housewife); W – 20, domestic, b. Plymouth, d/o Harry B. Foote (Warren, farmer) and Clarabell Felch (Canyon City, CO, housewife)
Martin Edward of Orford m. Evelyn Vera **Bean** of Fairlee, VT 2/1/1950 in Franklin; H – 22, payroll acct., b. Littleton, s/o Warren Elliott (Craftsbury, VT) and Nellie Steere; W – 26, dental asst., 2nd, b. Claremont, d/o Almond Leach (Easton) and Hattie Alger
Stanley C. of Orford m. Lula B. **Baker** of Orford 11/15/1924 in Lyme; H – 22, laborer, b. Lyme, s/o Harry A. Elliott (Lyme, laborer) and Susan Carr (Orange, VT, housewife); W – 18, domestic, b. Orford, d/o Henry G. Baker (Orford, blacksmith) and Inez Smith (Orford, housewife)

ELLIS,
Keith D. of Lakewood, CO m. Clara Fern **Marsh** of Orford 8/10/2002 in Bradford, VT
Robert Paul of Orford m. Michele Ann **LaBelle** of Orford 6/19/1976 in Orford; H – 26, b. IL, s/o Robert Paul Ellis III and Dorothy Lane; W – 24, b. IN, d/o Richard Joseph LaBelle and Dorothy Helen Haney

EMERSON,
Harold B. of Orford m. Evelyn **Carr** of Orford 9/10/1918 in Lyme Ctr.; H – 29, soldier, b. Fairbury, NE, s/o W. L. Emerson (Piermont, merchant) and Mary L. Beals (Gloucester, MA, housewife); W –

20, clerk, b. Andover, d/o George W. Carr (Plainfield, liveryman) and Effie E. Dodge (N. Boston, housewife)

EMERY,
Nathan N. of Orford m. Dani J. **Cate** of Bath 8/7/1999

EMLIN,
Robert Peabody of Orford m. Julia Ellen **Seeley** of Lyme 7/3/1971 in Hanover; H – 24, b. Philadelphia, PA, s/o Robert L. Emlin and Cora Weld Peabody; W – 24, b. New York City, NY, d/o Lewis E. Seeley and Helen Quinn

ESSELSTRYN,
Erik Canfield of Claversack, NY m. Susan **Pomeroy** of Scarsdale, NY 4/17/1965 in Orford; H – 27, b. New York, NY, s/o Caldwell B. Esselstryn and Harriet Erikson; W – 24, b. New York, NY, d/o Richard B. Pomeroy and Charlotte Harriman

ESTES,
Rodney Scott of Orford m. Tamara Marie **Roy** of Orford 5/15/1993
Russell Gene of Lyme m. Noreen Elizabeth **Gallup** of Orford 6/6/1964 in Orford; H – 20, b. Hanover, s/o Leonard Estes and Evelyn Powers; W – 18, b. Lebanon, d/o Harley G. Gallup and Ella Johnson
Stephen Lee of W. Lebanon m. Geraldine **Johnson** of Orford 6/6/1969 in Orford; H – 23, s/o Clyde Estes, Sr. and Jane Harthorn; W – 19, b. NH, d/o Robert L. Johnson and Lurline E. Dyke

EVANICH,
David Paul of Hanover m. Martha Huntington **Gluek** of Orford 12/18/1976 in Hanover; H – 24, b. WA, s/o Frank Joseph Evanich and Elizabeth Ellen Miller; W – 23, b. MI, d/o Alvin Charles Gluek and Ellen Rider

EVANS,
Brian Timothy of Lebanon m. Stacey Lyn **Severance** of Lebanon 6/1/2002 in Orford
Leighton John m. Kathleen Louise **Frost** 8/11/1956 in Orford; H – 23, dairy plant, 2nd, b. S. Ryegate, VT, s/o John H. Evans (Topsham, VT) and Theresa I. Brown (S. Ryegate, VT); W – 18,

at home, b. Groton, VT, d/o Allie Frost (Groton, VT) and Ruby M. Page (Woodsville)

FADDEN,
Edward of Piermont m. Lois Henrietta **Bean** of Orford 2/28/1942 in Haverhill; H – 27, farmer, b. W. Thornton, s/o Dana Fadden (W. Thornton, farmer) and Esther Downing (W. Thornton, housewife); W – 18, domestic, b. Orford, d/o Ralph C. Bean (Orford, farmer) and Florence Billingham (Newbury, VT, housewife)
Richard m. Denise **Fournier** 12/31/1987

FAHEY,
Clifford E. of Orford m. Amy J. **Shepard** of Orford 9/25/2004 in Orford

FARNHAM,
Bruce Stanley m. Sondra Eve **Clifford** 10/27/1957 in Orford; H – 22, mechanic, b. Woodsville, s/o Stanley E. Farnham (Orange, VT) and Alice Sanborn (Corinth, VT); W – 19, at home, b. Woodsville, d/o Charles H. Clifford (E. Milton, MA) and Hazel Butson (Woodsville)

FEIGL,
Mark of Norwich, VT m. Mary **Brunette** of Norwich, VT 8/22/1992

FIELDS,
John E. of Orford m. Melissa A. **Smith** of Bradford, VT 3/31/1998

FILLIAN,
David A. of Orford m. Hattie N. **Shortt** of Warren 8/31/1947 in Warren; H – 20, laborer, b. Orford, s/o Alphonse J. Fellian (sic) (Manchester, laborer) and Jennie Woods (Piermont, housewife); W – 18, domestic, b. Warren, d/o George A. Shortt (Walpole, farmer) and Nellie M. Wright (Piermont, housewife)
Gary I. of Orford m. Josephine R. **Whiting** of Penacook 9/7/1974 in Orford; H – 19, b. Lewes, DE, s/o William R. Fillian and Edna Canfield; W – 16, b. NH, d/o George L. Whiting and Georgette A. Place
Gary Lee of Orford m. Cynthia Louise **LaBombard** of Orford 10/22/1977 in Orford; H – 22, b. DE, s/o William Fillian and

Edna Canfield; W – 17, b. NH, d/o William LaBombard and April Roberts
Randy of Orford m. Patricia **Bean** of Orford 6/6/1983
William R. of Orford m. Edna Mae [-------] 4/14/1952 in Warren; H – 21, US Army, b. Wentworth, s/o Alphonse J. Fillian (Manchester) and Jessie Woods (Piermont); W – 19, at home, b. Hanover, d/o Aaron Powers (Whitefield) and Dorothy Kenney (CT)

FINNEY,
Frank G. of Orford m. Ida L. **Barnes** of Springfield, MA 10/20/1897 in White River Jct., VT; H – 28, farmer, b. Orford, s/o Henry J. Finney and Mary Emerton; W – 26, domestic, b. NY
Frank Garth m. Donna Jean **Sanborn** 10/8/1955 in Orford; H – 21, US Army, b. CT, s/o George H. Finney (Orford) and Doris Chamberlain (Orford); W – 21, IBM employee, b. Orford, d/o Robert B. Sanborn (Bath) and Evelyn Blake (Plymouth)
George Henry of Orford m. Doris **Chamberlain** of Orford 8/18/1920 in Orford; H – 21, laborer, b. Orford, s/o Frank G. Finney (Orford, farmer) and Ida Barnes (Schaghthticoke, NY, housewife); W – 22, teacher, b. Orford, d/o C. S. Chamberlain (Orford, farmer) and Cora B. Nickols (Wentworth, housewife)
George W. of E. Hartford, CT m. Margaret F. **Harvey** of Brooklyn, NY 7/20/1947 in Orford; H – 24, dock builder, b. Orford, s/o George H. Finney (Orford, const. supt.) and Doris Chamberlain (Orford, housewife); W – 26, clerk, b. China, d/o Edwin Deeks Harvey (Wyvenhoe, England, minister, deceased) and Florinda Lincoln (Oakham, MA, housewife)
Ralph Gary m. Corinne Ida **Sanborn** 1/1/1957 in Orford; H – 22, ap. carpenter, b. Hartford, CT, s/o George H. Finney (Orford) and Doris Chamberlain (Orford); W – 20, at home, b. Orford, d/o Robert B. Sanborn (Bath) and Evelyn Blake (Plymouth)

FISH,
Robert G. of Orford m. Beatrice C. **Sunn** of Lebanon 2/7/1948 in Lebanon; H – 22, wood chopper, b. Randolph Ctr., VT, s/o Charles H. Fish (Randolph, VT, laborer) and Alice Martin (Rochester, VT, housewife); W – 19, at home, b. Lebanon, d/o Genge N. Sunn (Moretown, VT, truck driver) and Helen M. Kimball (Enfield Ctr., housewife)

William Lewis of Orford m. Rachel Alicia **Fillian** of Orford 12/29/1951 in Warren; H – 20, laborer, b. Randolph, VT, s/o Charles Harold Fish and Alice E. Martin (Rochester, VT); W – 16, at home, b. Wentworth, d/o Alphonse J. Fillian (Manchester) and Jessie Woods (Piermont)

FLANDERS,
Harry H. of Warren m. Mabel E. **Chapman** of 5/22/1899 in Warren; H – 24, farmer, b. Warren, s/o Sylvester Flanders (Warren) and Sarah Willey (Warren); W – 19, b. Orford, d/o Perley Chapman (Tewksbury, MA) and Marry Etta Willis (Warren)

FLINT,
Alan S. of Randolph, VT m. Joyce **Washburn** of Orford 6/15/1946 in Orford; H – 24, photographer, b. Randolph, VT, s/o Harold Flint (Randolph, VT, mechanic) and Anne McDougall (Lewis, NY, housewife); W – 20, beautician, b. Hanover, d/o Harvey L. Washburn (Orford, farmer) and Bernice M. Horton (Orford, housewife)
Clarence Thomas of Orford m. Shiloh Marie **Olisky** of Orford 8/24/2002 in Orford
Ralph of Pittsfield, VT m. Helen H. **Fifield** of Pittsfield, VT 11/7/1936 in Orford; H – 29, laborer, b. Braintree, VT, s/o Myron Flint (Randolph, VT, laborer) and Mary Scott (Granville, VT, housewife); W – 30, domestic, 2nd, divorced, b. Rochester, VT, d/o Will Hossington (Rochester, VT, farmer) and Etta Pond (Bethel, VT, housewife)

FLYNN,
Malachy G. of Orford m. Shannon M. **Ziehm** of Orford 10/11/1997

FOOTE,
Edward Burtram of Orford m. Rose Iola **Baker** of Orford 1/29/1928 in Piermont; H – 20, laborer, b. Orford, s/o Harry B. Foote (Warren, farmer) and Claribel Felch (Canon City, CO, housewife); W – 18, domestic, b. Orford, d/o Henry G. Baker (Orford, blacksmith) and Inez Smith (Orford, housewife)
Harry B. of Orford m. Clara B. **Felch** of Piermont 5/3/1892 in Piermont; H – 19, farmer, b. Warren, s/o James E. Foote (Warren, farmer) and Juidth A. Huckins (Warren); W – 20,

domestic, b. Denver, CO, d/o Henry H. Felch (Piermont, mechanic) and Kate Bradbury (Haverhill)

Parker E. of Orford m. Elizabeth **Boudrean** of Ipswich, MA 8/30/1919 in Orford; H – 21, chauffeur, b. Orford, s/o Harry B. Foote (Warren, farmer) and Claribel Felch (Cannon Co., CO, housewife); W – 20, mill ins., b. Meteghan Sta., NS, d/o James Boudrean (Halifax, teamster) and Monique Deveau (Meteghan Sta., NS)

FOSTER,
Arthur B. of Quincy, MA m. Nellie V. **Barnes** of Orford 6/16/1910 in Orford; H – 26, carpenter, b. Quincy, MA, s/o Charles C. Foster (Roxbury, MA, carpenter) and Sarah E. Brown (Quincy, MA, housewife); W – 26, instr. music, b. Lyme, d/o Walter R. Barnes (Chelsea, physician) and Olive E. Vance (Albany, housewife)

FOX,
Cylon A. of Plymouth m. Mildred **Derick** of Orford 7/18/1922 in Orford; H – 24, hotel clerk, b. Woodstock, s/o George Fox (Plymouth, laborer) and Jennie Bigelow (Wells River, teacher); W – 19, domestic, b. Piermont, d/o George Derick (Wells River, teacher) and Lula Goodwin (Piermont, housewife)

FRANKLIN,
Arthur L. of Orford m. Marion H. **Clark** of Orford 7/1/1908 in Orford; H – 25, farmer, b. Orford, s/o Lewis Franklin (Orford, farmer) and Rebecca Cushman (Lisbon, housewife); W – 18, domestic, b. Orford, d/o George C. Clark (Orford, farmer) and Gertrude M. Keyes (Thetford, VT, housewife)

Arthur L. of Orford m. Marion **Chamberlain** of Orford 11/9/1921 in Orford; H – 39, farmer, 2nd, divorced, b. Orford, s/o Lewis Franklin (Orford, farmer) and Rebecca Cushman (Lisbon, housewife); W – 30, nurse, b. Orford, d/o C. S. Chamberlain (Orford, farmer) and Cora B. Nichols (Wentworth, housewife)

Harry E. of Orford m. Ruby Ellen **Pierson** of Orford 10/12/1936 in Orford; H – 27, farmer, b. Orford, s/o Arthur L. Franklin (Orford, farmer) and Marion Clark (Orford, nurse); W – 26, at home, b. Topsham, VT, d/o Ernest Pierson (Topsham, VT, farmer) and Nettie Wright (Topsham, VT, deceased)

Harry Emerson of Orford m. Clara Belle **Baker** of Orford 1/5/1971 in Piermont; H – 61, b. Orford, s/o Arthur L. Franklin and Marion

Clark; W – 62, b. Piermont, d/o Walter C. Webster and Lizzie Howland

Walter Allen of Orford m. Judy Mae **Pike** of Orford 6/6/1975 in Orford; H – 30, b. Hanover, s/o Harry E. Franklin and Ruby Pierson; W – 19, b. Wentworth, d/o Weymouth H. Pike, Sr. and Helen Marsh

FRENCH,

Harold C. of W. Lebanon m. Mabel Elizabeth **Lee** of W. Lebanon 9/20/1967 in Orford; H – 66, b. Honolulu, HI, s/o Samuel P. French and Florence Kelsey; W – 60, b. Arlington, MA, d/o John W. Cook and Lillian Saben

Walter D. of Orford m. Edna Agnes **Orr** of Boston, MA 8/23/1949 in Lebanon; H – 22, cook, b. Manchester, s/o Fred G. French (Orford, laborer) and Elizabeth A. Wilson (W. Somerville, MA, housewife); W – 20, waitress, b. Boston, MA, d/o Robert B. Orr (Lowell, MA, ret. engineer) and Clara M. Eckberg (Boston, MA, housewife)

FULLINGTON,

Ronald Bruce of Hanover m. Sandra Lee **Dyke** of Orford 8/3/1963 in Orford; H – 20, b. Hanover, s/o Haslett D. Fullington and Ruth Hadlock; W – 20, b. Orford, d/o Benjamin F. Dyke, Jr. and Dorothy A. Dow

GAGE,

Everett L. of Orford m. Nellie **Pebbles** of Orford 4/19/1890 in Lyme; H – 25, farmer, b. Orford, s/o Luther S. Gage (Orford, farmer); W – 17, domestic, b. Lyme, d/o William S. Pebbles (Orford, farmer)

GAINES,

James of Brooklyn, NY m. Pamela **Butler** of Brooklyn, NY 7/7/1983

GAITLEY,

Michael John of Albany, NY m. Judith Mary **Burns** of Rensselaer, NY 8/18/1962 in Orford; H – 22, manager, b. Albany, NY, s/o John E. Gaitley and Laura E. Russell (Albany, NY); W – 21, teacher, b. Albany, NY, d/o Marshall F. Burns and Virginia Hackel

GALLUP,
William H. of Orford m. Sandra Jean **Lackey** of Hanover 9/8/1973 in Hanover; H – 19, b. Lyme, s/o Harley G. Gallup and Ella C. Johnson; W – 20, b. Hanover, d/o Douglas R. Lackey and Eleanor J. Pruneau

GARDNER,
Frank H. of Orford m. Martha J. **Smith** of Lyme 11/6/1889 in Wentworth; H – 24, laborer, b. Lyme, s/o James K. Gardner (Lyme, farmer) and Emeline F. Breck (Orford); W – 18, domestic, b. Lyme, d/o Benjamin Smith (Lyme, farmer) and Angeline Worthen (Orford)

Frank H. of Orford m. Alberta E. **Hubbell** of Orford 6/29/1921 in Woodsville; H – 55, blacksmith, 2nd, widower, b. Lyme, s/o James R. Gardner (Lyme, farmer) and Emeline Breck (Warren, housewife); W – 55, housekeeper, 2nd, widow, b. Wolcott, VT, d/o Andrew Olstead (Elmore, VT, farmer) and Lavina Merritt (Elmore, VT, housewife)

Harold H. of Orford m. Phyllis E. **Scruton** of Bradford, VT 11/21/1932 in Newport; H – 19, laborer, b. Orford, s/o Ned F. Gardner (Orford, laborer) and Hattie Cunningham (Orford, housewife); W – 16, at home, b. Woodsville, d/o Walter S. Scruton (Topsham, VT, engineer) and Iva Humphrey (Piermont, veneer worker)

V. F. of Orford m. Hattie **Cunningham** of Orford 11/10/1897 in Newport; H – 22, farmer, b. Orford, s/o James R. Gardner (farmer) and Emeline F. Brick; W – 20, domestic, b. Orford, d/o George Cunningham (laborer) and Analine Mitchell (housewife)

GARONE,
Gregory of VT m. Kathleen **Plante** of Orford 8/25/1990

GARRETT,
Eugene Earl, Jr. m. Ethel Jane **McKee** 6/21/1958 in Orfordville; H – 26, laborer, b. Sharon, s/o Eugene E. Garrett (Wadbury, GA) and Laura M. Cummings (Keene); W – 18, at home, b. W. Rumney, d/o Kenneth W. McKee (Dorchester) and Frances E. Foote (Warren)

Floyd Alfred m. June Althea **Marsh** 12/6/1952 in Fairlee, VT; H – 25, truck driver, b. Winchendon, MA, s/o Eugene Garrett (Woodbury, GA) and Lauramay Cummings (Keene); W – 16, at

home, b. Wentworth, d/o Ralph Marsh (Orford) and Gladys
    Cutler (Grafton)
James Dalton of Orford m. Carline Rae **Tibbitts** of Orford 5/10/1975
    in Orford; H – 21, b. Lebanon, s/o Floyd A. Garrett and June A.
    Marsh; W – 19, b. Brooklyn, NY, d/o Robert E. Jackson and
    Joyce Paquin
Leonard S. of Orford m. Bonny M. **Goewey** of Claremont 11/4/1972
    in Orford; H – 19, b. Windsor, VT, s/o Floyd A. Garrett and June
    A. Marsh; W – 24, b. Claremont, d/o Carl B. Stoughton and
    Blanche E. Frohock
Walter Wilfred of Warren m. Dorothy Ann **Taylor** of Orford 2/22/1969
    in Orford; H – 31, b. NH, s/o Eugene E. Garrett and Laura
    Cummings; W – 24, b. VT, d/o Elmer L. Taylor and Phyllis
    Royston

GASPARRO,
Christopher of Cedar Rapids, IA m. Jenny L. **Randolph** of Cedar
    Rapids, IA 10/17/1998

GASPER,
Andrew J. of Orford m. Christina A. **Morey** of Orford 7/3/1926 in
    Fairlee, VT; H – 42, steam engineer, b. Goffstown, s/o John
    Gasper (England) and Mary Gardner (Canada); W – 17, b.
    Orford, d/o Eddie S. Morey (Norwich, VT, farmer) and Esther
    McIntire (Canada, housewife)
George Arthur of Orford m. Ruth Alice **Bryer** of Orford 12/15/1964 in
    Piermont; H – 37, b. Woodsville, s/o Andrew J. Gasper and
    Christine Morey; W – 53, b. Fairlee, VT, d/o Henry G.
    Cummings and Alice Bacon

GENDRON,
Bernard m. Michelle **May** 5/10/1986
Kurt of Orford m. Tanya **Stygles** of Orford 8/24/1991
Wilfred E. of W. Fairlee, VT m. Shirley Anne **Ladeau** of Orford
    7/3/1959

GERMANA,
Erik J. of Orford m. Amy L. **Heath** of Orford 9/12/1997

GIBSON,
Terry L. of Madison, OH m. Sarah **Hall** of Orford --/27/1972 in Orford; H – 24, b. Painesville, OH, s/o Theren J. Gibson and Ida M. Smith; W – 23, b. Tacoma, MD, d/o Harvey P. Hall and Barbara H. Poole

GILBERT,
Harry E. of Orford m. Fannie E. **Welch** of Lyme 9/27/1909 in Lyme; H – 30, laborer, b. Lyme, s/o John A. Gilbert (Lyme, farmer) and Elizabeth Post (Ogdensburg, NY, housewife); W – 16, domestic, b. Topsham, VT, d/o George H. Welch (Groton, VT, laborer) and Nettie Lawrence

Harry E. of Orford m. Flora E. **Nutter** of Orford 11/14/1925 in Lyme; H – 50, laborer, 2nd, b. Lyme, s/o John Gilbert (Lyme, laborer) and Elizabeth Post (NY, housewife); W – 34, housework, 2nd, b. Canada, d/o Leon L. Casady (Canada, laborer) and Mary J. Preast (Canada, housewife)

GIROUX,
Arthur Joseph of Orford m. Pearl Alma **Butman** of Orford 3/29/1930 in Lyme; H – 30, laborer, b. E. Boston, MA, s/o Joseph I. Giroux (Canada, farmer) and Catherine Hoppell (E. Boston, MA, housewife); W – 18, at home, b. Orford, d/o Lurlyn C. Butman (Orford, farmer) and Hattie Bailey (Orford, housewife)

GLOVER,
Alan Earle of Hartland, VT m. Anna M. **Archer** of Orford 4/11/1925 in Orford; H – 31, farmer, 2nd, b. Littleton, s/o James A. Glover (Littleton, farmer) and Julia DeBerri (Littleton, housewife); W – 28, domestic, b. Orford, d/o Alanson Archer (Orford, laborer) and Elizabeth Moran (Boston, housewife)

GODFREY,
Kevin m. Monica **Valdes** 6/22/1985 in Orford

Roy B. of Lyme m. Della Edyth **Marsh** of Orford 11/1/1923 in Lyme; H – 30, farmer, b. W. Fairlee, VT, s/o William Godfrey (W. Fairlee, VT, farmer) and Ada Dennison (Washington, VT, housewife); W – 19, domestic, b. Orford, d/o David C. Marsh (W. Fairlee, VT, farmer) and Delia Smith (Corinth, VT, housewife)

GOMO,
Richard Kendall of Norwich, VT m. Genevieve Marie **Andrews** of White River Jct., VT 9/10/1950 in Orford; H – 23, chef, b. Strafford, VT, s/o Elmer C. Gomo (Northfield, VT) and Lillian Kendall (Strafford, VT); W – 21, tel. operator, b. N. Haverhill, d/o Clarence H. Andrews (Sutton) and Esther L. Hildreth (N. Haverhill)

GONYER,
Clyde W. of Lunenburg, VT m. Margaret **LaMontagne** of Orford 6/20/1981

GOODRICH,
Brian W. of Orford m. Becky A. **Benjamin** of Orford 8/24/1996
Howard C. of Thetford, VT m. Vivian C. **Fuller** of Weston, VT 12/2/1933 in Orford; H – 28, mechanic, b. Rutland, VT, s/o Thomas Goodrich (Ellensburg, NY, farmer) and Melindy Realou (Ellensburg, NY, housewife); W – 25, domestic, b. Weston, VT, d/o Alonzo Fuller (Weston, VT, farmer) and Caroline Wilder (MI, housewife)

GOODWIN,
Harry L. of Orford m. Bertha G. **Gale** of Orford 12/21/1908 in Wentworth; H – 18, farmer, b. Warren, s/o Walter H. Goodwin (Warren, farmer) and Georgia S. Pease (housewife); W – 18, domestic, b. Boston, MA, d/o ----- Brown

GOULD,
Clayton Edward of Orford m. Laurie Jean **Denis** of Orford 8/6/1994
Edward G. of Orford m. Frances M. **Huckins** of Orford 6/11/1947 in Plymouth; H – 20, laborer, b. Jefferson, s/o Everett E. Gould (Waterville, ME, laborer, deceased) and Mildred Elliott (Littleton, housewife); W – 18, student, b. Hanover, d/o George C. Huckins (Orford, board sawyer) and Hazel M. Williams (Hardwick, VT, housewife)
Edward G., Sr. of Orford m. Adell B. **Page** of Orford 1/6/1973 in Orford; H – 45, b. Jefferson, s/o Everett Gould and Mildred Elliott; W – 44, b. Woodsville, d/o Livermore Bailey and Corrie Ramsdell
Edward George, Jr. of Orford m. Shirley Marie **Pushee** of Lyme 1/31/1970 in Orford; H – 19, b. Lebanon, s/o Edward G. Gould,

Sr. and Frances M. Huckins; W – 19, b. Hanover, d/o Donald L. Pushee and Mabel O'Donnell

Nathan G. of Orford m. Jessica A. **Hugg** of Orford 10/3/1998

GRADY,
Michael A. m. Janice E. **Blake** --/--/1989

GRANT,
Alanson W. of Lyme m. Evelyn V. **Marsh** of Orford 5/31/1935 in Lyme; H – 24, laborer, b. Lyme, s/o Fred W. Grant (Lyme, farmer) and Viola E. Ware (Thetford, VT, housewife); W – 20, at home, b. Orford, d/o David Marsh (W. Fairlee, VT, farmer) and Delia Smith (Topsham, VT, housewife)

John Henry m. Janet Piper **Evans** 4/10/1954 in Hollis; H – 45, insurance, 2nd, b. Lyme, s/o George Pelton Grant (Lyme) and Ethel M. Pushee (Lyme); W – 34, at home, 2nd, b. Lyme, d/o Frank Alden Piper (Lyme) and Vivian French (Orford)

GRAVES,
Leonard Phillip of Cleveland, OH m. Paula Elizabeth **Sanborn** of Orford 8/28/1971 in Orford; H – 21, b. OH, s/o William Graves and Jeannette Lyons; W – 21, b. Orford, d/o Bernard M. Sanborn and Bernice Finney

GRAY,
Bruce of Orford m. Pauline E. **Gray** of Orford 12/17/1977 in Piermont; H – 25, b. NH, s/o Harley E. Gray and Joyce Greer; W – 31, b. NH, d/o Leonard Estes and Evelyn Powers

Dale Edward of Lyme m. Barbara Ann **Dyke** of Orford 1/9/1971 in Orford; H – 20, b. Lebanon, s/o Richard H. Gray and Olive A. Thompson; W – 21, b. Orford, d/o George C. Dyke and Beulah B. Bockus

Edmund of Orford m. Karen **Newton** of Fairlee, VT 10/2/2002 in Fairlee, VT

Harley, Jr. of Lyme Ctr. m. Joyce Elaine **Greer** of Orford 6/30/1950 in Lyme; H – 18, laborer, b. Lyme Ctr., s/o Harley Gray (Lyme) and Hattie Pike (Lyme); W – 17, at home, b. Bradford, VT, d/o Nelson R. Greer (Littleton) and Dorothy E. A. Sanborn (Bradford, VT)

Leonard Richard of Orford m. Ericka Jean **Fullington** of Orford 9/16/2000 in Hanover

Lester E. of Orford m. Nellie M. **Chesley** of Lyme 5/21/1925 in Orford; H – 39, laborer, b. Orford, s/o Hiram Gray (Canada, laborer) and Sarah Simpson (Rumney, housewife); W – 32, domestic, b. Lyme, d/o Frank Chesley (W. Fairlee, VT, farmer) and Louise Morey (W. Fairlee, VT, housewife)

Lester E. of Orford m. Alice C. **King** of Lyme 11/2/1930 in Lyme; H – 44, laborer, 2nd, widower, b. Orford, s/o Hiram Gray (Canada, laborer) and Sarah Simpson (Orford, housewife); W – 39, housewife, 2nd, widow, b. W. Fairlee, VT, d/o Frank Chesley (W. Fairlee, VT, farmer) and Louise Morey (W. Fairlee, VT, housewife)

Lester Elmer of Orford m. Marjorie W. **George** of Lyme 8/14/1945 in Orford; H – 59, caretaker, 3rd, divorced, b. Orford, s/o Hiram Gray (carpenter) and Sarah Simpson (Orford, housewife); W – 48, cook, 2nd, divorced, b. E. Brookfield, VT, d/o Harley Wheatley (St. Johnsbury, VT, farmer) and Altie Banks (Corinth, VT, housewife)

Matthew Scott of Orford m. Nicole Lynn **Smith** of Orford 9/3/2000 in Orford

Richard C. of Lyme m. Norine A. **Dyke** of Orford 9/16/1967 in Hanover; H – 19, b. Lebanon, s/o Richard H. Gray and Olive Thompson; W – 15, b. Orford, d/o Benjamin F. Dyke, Jr. and Dorothy Alice Dow

Scott Matthew of Orford m. Tammy Christine **Giesing** of Orford 7/3/1993

Steve of Rowley, MA m. Jennifer **Stebbins** of Rowley, MA 2/14/2004 in Orford

Todd of Orford m. Brenda **Giesing** of Orford 9/1/1990

William A. of Piermont m. Roberta K. **Pike** of Piermont 10/28/2000 in Piermont

GREEN,

Peter m. Barbara Ann **Whitcher** 9/27/1954 in Warren; H – 19, elephant trainer, b. Orford, s/o William Edgar Green, Jr. (Trenton, NJ) and Phyllis Boyer (Riverton, NJ); W – 18, at home, b. Warren, d/o Maurice A. Whitcher (Warren) and Helen Marion Ball (Landaff)

William Edgar, III m. Donna Lee **Morris** 8/1/1958 in Orford; H – 21, self emp., b. Orford, s/o William E. Green (Trenton, NJ) and Phylis Boyer (Riverton, NJ); W – 23, waitress, b. Massilon, OH, d/o Samuel T. Morris (OH) and Helen Kaylor (OH)

William Peter of Orford m. Kathryn Gale **Fitzgerald** of Thetford, VT 12/13/1959

GREENLY,
V. Merrill of Orford m. Isabelle M. **Wilson** of Henniker 6/12/1912 in Nashua; H – 24, farmer, b. Orford, s/o Samuel E. Greenly (St. Paul, MN, farmer) and Lavina Rugg (Orford, housewife); W – 21, domestic, b. Deering, d/o Alvah Wilson (Lowell, MA, farmer) and Lizzie Gilmore (Deering, housewife)

GREER,
Arthur A. of Orford m. Elaine R. **Paige** of Orford 11/29/1952 in Orford; H – 14, student, b. Middleboro, MA, s/o Nelson R. Greer (Bethlehem) and Dorothy E. Sanborn (Bradford, VT); W – 17, at home, b. St. Johnsbury, VT, d/o Clinton K. Paige (Groton, VT) and Katie W. Abbott (McIndoes, VT)
Nelson Raymond m. Eleanor Dix **Messer** 12/25/1953 in Keene; H – truck driver, 2nd, b. NH, s/o William T. Greer (NB) and Ida Howard (Littleton); W – artist, 2nd, b. VT, d/o Ernest A. Dix (Brattleboro, VT) and Sarah Louise Putnam (Springfield, VT)

GRIMES,
Ronald G. of Brandon, VT m. Ruth Ella **McKee** of Orford 8/22/1959

GULICK,
Kenneth of Ely, VT m. Chris **LaMontagne** of Orford 10/20/1979

GUNETTE,
Homer of Orford m. Marcell **Boutheliiere** of Lincoln 9/3/1935 in Plymouth; H – 36, laborer, b. Dorchester, Canada, s/o Alfred Gunette (St. Odilon, Canada, farmer) and Delia LaMere (Canada, housewife); W – 45, housewife, 2nd, b. Poquetville, Canada, d/o Philippe Boutheliiere (NB, farmer) and Celeste Godin (NB, housewife)

GUYER,
John W. of Orford m. Julia L. **Guyer** of Orford 6/26/1948 in Piermont; H – 53, farmer, 2nd, divorced, b. Lunenburg, VT, s/o Alfred Guyer (Magog, Canada, taxi man) and Mary E. Gadley (Waterford, VT, housewife); W – 51, housewife, 2nd, divorced, b.

Orford, d/o Alexander LeMire (Three Rivers, Canada, farmer) and Ella Thompson (Derry, housewife)

John W. of Orford m. Gladys E. **Chabot** of Orford 11/9/1968 in Orford; H – 73, b. VT, s/o Alfred Guyer and Mary Gadner; W – 66, b. NH, d/o Henry Lee and Clementine Thompson

HALE,
David of Hermosa Beach, CA m. Ingrid **Miller** of Hermosa Beach, CA 9/6/1992

HALL,
Francis H. of Montpelier, VT m. Clara E. **Nickols** of Orford 12/24/1887 in Orford; H – 33, laborer, b. Northfield, s/o Randall Hall (farmer) and Mary Sheoman (Moretown, VT, farmer); W – 34, domestic, 2nd, widow, b. Orford, d/o John Phelps (farmer) and ----- Hancock (Orford)

Frank P. of Orford m. Susie M. **Abbott** of Deerfield 11/9/1892 in Candia; H – 25, farmer, b. Orford, s/o John Hall (Candia, farmer) and Susan P. Brown; W – 18, domestic, b. Suncook, d/o James Abbott (Suncook, laborer) and Susan Conner (Candia)

Fred P. of Orford m. Mary L. **Chandler** of Orford 3/15/1892 in Orford; H – 25, farmer, b. Landaff, s/o Henry K. Hall (Landaff, farmer) and Maria Wells; W – 20, domestic, b. Orford, d/o Anson L. Chandler (Warren, carpenter) and Emily J. Williams (Orford)

Henry K. of Orford m. Alice **Robinson** of Haverhill 5/31/1927 in Orford; H – 24, farmer, b. Lyme, s/o Fred P. Hall (Landaff, farmer) and Mary L. Chandler (Orford, housewife); W – 17, housekeeping, b. Haverhill, d/o Kenneth Robinson (Lyme, farmer) and Maude Hobbs (Haverhill, housewife)

Julio Enrriguez of Grafton m. Traci Ann **Costa** of Orford 8/26/1995

HAMEL,
Stephen of Orford m. Deanne **French** of Orford 7/18/1992

HAMMOND,
William A. of Roanoke, VA m. Dorothy G. **Fillian** of Orford 9/11/1938 in Rumney; H – 24, chauffeur, b. Roanoke, VA, s/o William and Nancy; W – 18, domestic, b. Orford, d/o Alphonse Fillian

(Manchester, laborer) and Jennie A. Woods (Piermont, housewife)

HANCOCK,
William P. of Portland, ME m. Lindsay **Huntington** of Portland, ME 9/16/1979 in Orford; H – b. PA, s/o William P. Hancock and Patricia Clay; W – b. NY, d/o James K. Huntington and Barbara Bearstow

HANNAFORD,
Hazen A. of Orford m. Frances M. **Kimball** of Fairlee, VT 10/21/1910 in Fairlee, VT; H – 26, laborer, b. Orford, s/o Henry A. Hannaford (Fairlee, VT, teamster) and Eva A. Rhoades (Orford, housewife); W – 31, housewife, 2nd, b. Samuel Cunningham (Bradford, VT, laborer) and Jane Freeman (Fairlee, VT, housewife)

HANSON,
Gregory Joseph of Orford m. Joyce Marie **Fillip** of Orford 7/15/1995

HARDING,
Glen Paul of Orford m. Colleen Elizabeth **LaValley** of Orford 6/25/1994

HARNSBERGER,
Jeffrey of W. Lebanon m. Donna **Schuck** of Orford 6/25/1992

HARRIMAN,
William Bert of Lyme m. Dora Daisy **Taylor** of Orford 10/31/1936 in Bellows Falls, VT; H – 32, truck driver, 2nd, divorced, b. Haverhill, s/o Henry D. Harriman (Littleton) and Alice Cox (Holderness); W – 38, 2nd, divorced, b. Thetford, VT, d/o Fred J. Taylor (Thetford, VT) and Daisy C. Wilder

HARRINGTON,
Cedrick Emanuel of Orford m. Priscilla Jeanne **Franklin** of Orford 9/18/1961 in Orford; H – 19, pressman apprentice, b. Middlebury, VT, s/o Edson E. Harrington (Ripton, VT) and Jennie Columbe (Bristol, VT); W – 18, at home, b. Hanover, d/o Harry E. Franklin (Orford) and Ruby Ellen Pierson (Topsham)

Deane Edward of White River Jct., VT m. Nancy Alma **Teeter** of White River Jct., VT 1/2/1964 in Orford; H – 28, b. Randolph, VT, s/o Edward Harrington and Elizabeth Gifford; W – 18, b. Union Village, VT, d/o Walter Teeter and Alma Powers
Marcus of Orford m. Elisa **Verb** of NY 7/21/1990

HARRIS,
Mark Steven of Orford m. Joan Marie **Carvalho** of Orford 9/26/1981
Willard R. of Orford m. Maude **McPherson** of Orford 6/1/1904 in Orford; H – 23, farmer, b. Piermont, s/o Ruben Harris (Manchester) and Lucretia Peebles (Orford, housewife); W – 19, domestic, b. Jordan River, d/o Jason H. McPherson (Brookfield, NS, farmer) and Cornelia Holden (Jordan River, housewife)

HART,
James W. of E. Thetford, VT m. Darlene E. **Ricker** of Orford --/26/1972 in Orford; H – 25, b. Hanover, s/o Lawrence F. Hart and Esther M. Young; W – 18, b. Flint, MI, d/o Lawrence R. Ricker and Beverly Record
Lawrence G. of Lyme Ctr. m. Susan Evelyn **Sanborn** of Orford 6/27/1959

HARTLEY,
Gerald of Elgin AFB m. Kayne **Chapman** of Elgin AFB 8/8/1983

HASLAM,
Edward m. Ann **Cougle** 9/25/1988

HATCH,
Bert E. of Orford m. Addie M. **Crowe** of Orford 7/15/1901 in Orford; H – 21, barber, b. Haverhill, s/o James E. Hatch (jeweler); W – 22, domestic, b. Canada

HATFIELD,
Cameran A. of Cumberlin, ME m. Charlotte **Pomeroy** of Orford 6/27/1959

HAZEN,
Irving A. of White River Jct., VT m. Mary M. **Carr** of Orford 9/9/1896 in Orford; H – 28, teacher, b. Hartford, VT, s/o Noah B. Hazen

(Hartford, VT, real estate agent) and Alice S. Dutton (Hartford, VT, housewife); W – 22, teacher, b. Meriden, d/o Robert O. Carr (Orford, merchant) and Mary E. Martin (Chelmsford, MA, housewife)

HEATH,
Jeffrey Earl of Orford m. Amy Louise **Pierson** of Orford 3/26/1994

HEBB,
Allan Ford of Orford m. Jane Elizabeth **Pierce** of Orford 9/14/1968 in Orford; H – 22, b. VT, s/o Guy A. Hebb and Marjorie Aldrich; W – 20, b. NH, d/o Chester A. Pierce and Dorothy Pike
Jeffrey Allan of Orford m. Jessica Lyn **Jorgensen** of Orford 9/27/2003 in Orford
Timothy Michael of Orford m. Tina Alicia **Swezey** of Orford 7/27/2003 in Newbury, VT

HEINSIMER,
James of Hartford, VT m. Rita **Pink** of Hartford, VT 6/23/1979

HENDERSON,
Paul W. of Merrimack m. Alice **Schneiderheinz** of Merrimack 8/29/1933 in Merrimack; H – 21, cow tester, b. Merrimack, s/o Norris Henderson (Merrimack, farmer) and Elizabeth Sanborn (Epping, housewife); W – 26, musician, b. Manchester, d/o Emile Schneiderheinz (Manchester) and Marguerite Limmeres (Germany, housewife)

HENDRICK,
Richard M. of Orford m. Delia **Cimpean** of Orford 10/22/1997

HIBBARD,
Carl W. of Orford m. Bessie M. **Ricker** of W. Fairlee, VT 9/6/1927 in Orford; H – 24, laborer, b. Concord, VT, s/o Earl M. Hibbard (Lancaster, laborer) and Josie G. Powers (Lunenburg, VT, housewife); W – 21, domestic, b. Vershire, VT, d/o Wesley Ricker (Burke, VT, farmer) and Abbie Hammer (Vershire, VT, housewife)
Lawrence of Orford m. Karen **Landgraf** of Orford 9/15/1990

HIGDON,
Kenneth Guy of Plainfield, CT m. Heidi Jean **Miller** of Orford 7/26/2003 in Orford

HIGGINS,
Frank H. of Orford m. Gertrude Lillian **Abbott** of Norwich 4/16/1977 in Norwich, VT; H – 44, b. CT, s/o Francis C. Higgins and Marry-anna Fodi; W – 48, b. NY, d/o William Carl Olsen and Margaret Carroll
Scott Timothy of Wallingford, CT m. Heather Ann **Alger** of Wallingford, CT 10/9/1993

HILD,
David m. Susan **Miller** 8/24/1985 in Orford

HILL,
Jeffrey Alan of Topsham, VT m. Kristina Ann **Hayes** of Topsham, VT 6/21/2003 in Orford
John A. of Orford m. Inez S. **Baker** of Orford 8/10/1935 in Canaan; H – 54, laborer, 2nd, b. Sherbrooke, Canada, s/o John Hill (Terry Town, Ireland, carpenter) and Bridget Pigeon (Fardown, Ireland, housewife); W – 65, housewife, 2nd, b. Orford, d/o Alfonso Smith (Lyme, farmer) and Clarenda Worthen (Orford, housewife)

HILLBORN,
Ernest C. of Valley City, ND m. Grace E. **Washburn** of Orford 8/5/1908 in Orford; H – 31, nurseryman, b. Ripon, WI, s/o Edward C. Hillborn (Uxbridge, ON, woodturner) and Celia Pond (Senaca, NY, housewife); W – 27, teacher, b. Frank E. Washburn (Granville, VT, farmer) and Emma F. Lovejoy (Orford, housewife)

HINES,
(Capt.) Stanley of NS m. Ethel F. **Washburn** of Quincy, MA 7/3/1922 in Orford; H – 59, retired, 2nd, b. NS, s/o Benjamin Hines (NS, mariner) and Catherine V. Murphy (NS, housewife); W – 43, nurse, b. Boston, d/o George W. Washburn (Pomfret, VT, manager) and Francena Mann (Orford, housewife)

HNADELSMAN,
Paul of Orford m. Margaret **Hogg** of Orford 7/5/1980

HODGSON,
John Helmes of E. Orange, NJ m. Alice **Doan** of Winchester, MA 7/20/1929 in Orford; H – 21, broker, b. Brooklyn, NY, s/o Walter C. Hodgson (Brooklyn, NY, merchant) and Florence Purcell (Brooklyn, NY, housewife); W – 19, at home, b. Meadville, PA, d/o Frank C. Doan (Nelsonville, OH, minister) and Isabel Wilson (Winchester, MA, at home)

HOEHL,
William of Orford m. Patricia **Noyes** of Orford 5/6/1979

HOISINGTON,
Douglas of New London, CT m. Nicole **Leger** of New London, CT 7/25/1992

HOLDEN,
Stanley Frederick, Jr. of Orford m. Marie Lynn **Taylor** of Orford 7/2/1993

HOLMAN,
Paul R. of Leominster m. Isabel **Doan** of Winchester 8/4/1926 in Orford; H – 22, manufacturer, b. Leominster, MA, s/o William E. Holman (Leominster, MA, manufacturer) and Alice Rockwell (Leominster, MA, housewife); W – 21, student, b. Meadville, PA, d/o Frank C. Doan (Nelsonville, OH, minister) and Isabel Wilson (Winchester, MA, housewife)

HOLT,
Arthur Ray of Orford m. Helen L. **Smith** of Fairlee, VT 9/21/1923 in Lyme; H – 21, laborer, b. N. Woodstock, VT, s/o George S. Holt (Whitefield, farmer) and Emily Ellsworth (Wentworth, housewife); W – 21, domestic, b. Fairlee, VT, d/o George E. Smith (Bath, farmer) and Lilla Welton (Bradford, VT, housewife)

HOOD,
Horace of Groton, VT m. Laura A. **Usher** of Groton, VT 6/7/1891 in Orford; H – 46, farmer, b. Topsham, VT, s/o Enos Hood

(farmer) and -----; W – 45, domestic, 2nd, b. Corinth, VT, d/o Isaac Williams (farmer) and -----

Raymond W. of Orford m. Norma J. **Willis** of Orford 8/24/1974 in Orford; H – 40, b. Newbury, VT, s/o Harley J. Hood and Margaret Mitchell; W – 30, b. Laconia, d/o Herman Baker and Georgia Gale

HOOK,
Bruce m. Betty Jane **Russin** --/--/1988
Stephen of Orford m. Teresa **Gould** of Orford 7/12/1980

HORTON,
Walter A. of Orford m. Bessie A. **Kenyon** of Orford 10/1/1907 in Orford; H – 21, clerk, b. Orford, d/o Walter S. Horton (Barnard, VT, farmer) and Mary S. Stone (Orford, housewife); W – 18, domestic, b. Orford, d/o Carlos M. Kenyon (Plainfield, farmer) and Abbie Tyrrell (Canaan, housewife)

Walter A. of Orford m. Ethel M. **Grant** of Lyme 9/14/1937 in Lyme; H – 51, carpenter, 2nd, widower, b. Orford, s/o Walter S. Horton (E. Barnard, VT, farmer) and Mary Stone (Orford, housewife); W – 46, matron, 2nd, widow, b. Lyme, d/o Clarence S. Pushee (Lyme, farmer) and Fannie C. Post (Lyme, housewife)

HOWARD,
Alan m. Martha **Owen** 7/4/1987

HUBBARD,
William Edward m. Mildred **Johnson** 7/25/1955 in Warren; H – 72, carpenter, 2nd, b. Canaan, VT, s/o Charles Hubbard (Old Town, ME) and Emma Stewart; W – 58, housework, 2nd, b. W. Fairlee, VT, d/o Wells Silloway (Bradford, VT) and Lilla Moore (Danville, VT)

HUCKINS,
George C. of Orford m. Hazel M. **Williams** of Jericho, VT 6/21/1926 in N. Haverhill; H – 24, laborer, b. Orford, s/o George M. Huckins (Wentworth, farmer) and Ella S. Lamprey (Orford, housewife); W – 24, teacher, b. Hardwick, VT, d/o Joseph Williams (Concord, granite cutter) and Maude Zottman (Burlington, VT, housewife)

George M. of Orford m. Ella S. **Lamprey** of Orford 3/3/1890 in Orford; H – 26, carpenter, b. Wentworth, s/o Joseph Cross (Wentworth, laborer); W – 22, teacher, b. Orford, d/o George W. Lamprey (Orford, carpenter)

HULL,
Preston Howard of Enosburg Falls, VT m. Ann Marie **Adams** of Orford 9/1/1973 in Orford; H – 26, b. Enosburg, VT, s/o Lynford Hull and Ruth Preston; W – 22, b. Lebanon, d/o Harold R. Adams and Edna Bradley

HUMPHREY,
Wilbert of Orford m. Margaret F. **Courtney** of Orford 10/11/1932 in Plymouth; H – 34, farmer, b. Canada, s/o William Humphrey (Albert Mines, Canada, farmer) and Elizabeth Cahoon (Albert Mines, Canada, housewife); W – 45, housekeeper, 2nd, b. London, England, d/o Arthur W. Bowdger (London, England, bartender) and Mary A. Dutchborn (London, England, housewife)

HUNT,
Lee F. of Anderson, IN m. Martha J. **Carr** of Orford 1/1/1908 in Orford; H – 30, physician, b. Alexandria, IN, s/o John W. Hunt (IN, physician) and Etta T. Brickley (IN, housewife); W – 25, housewife, b. Orford, d/o Robert O. Carr (Orford, merchant) and Mary E. Martin (Chelmsford, MA, housewife)

Reginald R. of Monroe m. Mabel M. **Dyke** of Orford 10/14/1922 in N. Haverhill; H – 19, papermaker, b. Monroe, s/o Henry O. Hunt (Monroe, machinist) and Flora Ingerson (Littleton, housewife); W – 20, housemaid, b. Lyme, d/o Fred Dyke (Lyme, farmer) and Emma Tattersall (Lyme, housewife)

HUNTINGTON,
Arthur F. of New Rochelle, NY m. Dorothy A. **Schmedes** of New Rochelle, NY 7/18/1963 in Orford; H – 56, b. New Rochelle, NY, s/o James A. Huntington and Caroline Pine; W – 53, b. New York, NY, d/o James A. Atwater and Virginia Sage

C. W. of Barre, VT m. Bertha M. **Griffin** of Orford 12/24/1895 in Orford; H – 24, manufacturer, b. Barre, VT, s/o W. D. Huntington (Washington, VT, laborer); W – 23, domestic, b. Keene, d/o Allen S. Griffin (Marlow, farmer)

Guy S. of Corinth m. Mildred **Cummings** of Orford 9/3/1922 in Orford; H – 18, farming, b. Corinth, VT, s/o Dana Huntington (Washington, VT, farmer) and Ila Marston (Corinth, VT, housewife); W – 17, domestic, b. Thetford, VT, d/o James Cummings (Thetford, VT, farmer) and Lucy Allen (Lancaster, housewife)

Guy Sylvester of Orford m. Katherine Clark **Griggs** of Bradford, VT 11/1/1969 in Springfield, VT; H – 66, b. VT, s/o Dana Huntington and Ila Masten; W – 51, b. VT, d/o Ernest W. Clark and Jennie Whitehill

Harold L. m. Mary Jane **Fields** 1/10/1958 in Hanover; H – 30, mechanic, b. Barre, VT, s/o Harold K. Huntington (Washington, VT) and Laura LeLime (E. Barre, VT); W – 19, at home, b. Etna, d/o John Fields (Canaan) and Meda Roberts (Lyme)

Harold Lawrence m. Irene Flora **Pease** 11/5/1955 in Hanover; H – 28, mechanic, 2nd, b. Barre, VT, s/o Harold K. Huntington (Washington, VT) and Laura LaLime (E. Barre, VT); W – 20, secretary, b. Orford, d/o Glenn F. Pease (Orford) and Theda L. Howard (Wentworth)

Sumner of Orford m. Bernice B. **Bean** of Orford 9/6/1945 in Haverhill; H – 20, mail carrier, b. Orford, s/o Guy S. Huntington (Corinth, VT, mechanic) and Mildred Cummings (Thetford, VT, housewife); W – 23, US Service WAC, b. Orford, d/o Joseph Bean (Sharon, VT, deceased) and Mabel Davis (Quebec, Canada, retired)

HUNTLEY,

Douglas Harold m. Irene May **Davis** 6/28/1953 in Fairlee, VT; H – 18, cook, b. Barre, VT, s/o Merton C. Huntley (Waterbury, VT) and Elsie Chandler (E. Barre, VT); W – 20, office worker, b. Lyme, d/o Gerald W. Davis (N. Groton) and Hattie K. Davis (Canada)

HUTCHINS,

Gerald F. of Wentworth m. Beatrice A. **Hadley** of Orford 9/19/1934 in Orford; H – 23, farmer, b. Wentworth, s/o Lester C. Hutchins (Rumney, farmer) and Katie Foster (Rumney, housewife); W – 24, nurse, b. Boston, MA, d/o Edwin C. Hadley (Hartland, VT, farmer) and Mattie C. Woods (Bath, housewife)

INGELL,
Fred Elbert of Orford m. Ray **Sherwood** of Orford 1/26/1919 in Orford; H – 33, laborer, b. Springfield; W – 35, domestic, b. NY, d/o Myron B. Sherwood (NY, farming) and Sarah Stoutt (NJ)

INGERSON,
Benjamin H. of Orford m. Annie D. **Hinckley** of Montreal, Canada 3/19/1909 in Orford; H – 36, laborer, 2nd, b. Lyman, s/o Hiram Ingerson (Lyman, farmer) and Luella Briggs (Lyman, housewife); W – 34, dressmaker, 2nd, b. Bangor, ME, d/o Julia ----- (housewife)

IRLE,
Stephen m. Kathy **Dyke** 8/26/1984 in Fairlee, VT

JACKSON,
Jeffrey m. Beverly **Lewis** 8/5/1987
Stuart A. of New York, NY m. Janet **Story** of Riverton, NJ 3/14/1959

JENKINS,
James D. of Pittsburgh, PA m. Roberta **Richmond** of Orford 8/29/1959
Leslie Forrest of W. Springfield, MA m. Edith **Bingham** of W. Springfield, MA 4/14/1962 in Orford; H – 44, laborer, b. Farmington, ME, s/o Joseph Jenkins (Byron, ME) and Lillian Ware (Union, ME); W – 38, bus girl, b. W. Springfield, MA, d/o James Bingham (Belfast, Ireland) and Edith Hoy (Belfast, Ireland)

JOHNSON,
Robert L. of Concord m. Lurline E. **Record** of Orford 3/18/1939 in Orford; H – 25, truck driver, b. S. Deerfield, s/o Nils Johnson (Sweden, carpenter) and Caroline Johnson (Sweden, housewife); W – 21, maid, 2nd, divorced, b. S. Newbury, VT, d/o Benjamin F. Dyke (Pompanoosuc, VT, mill man) and Ethel Jesseman (Newbury, VT, housewife)

JOHNSTON,
Archibald F. m. Tamara **Zaldastani** --/--/1989
Eric Toson of Virginia Beach, VA m. Mary Jean **LeClair** of Virginia Beach, VA 6/24/1995

JONES,
Alden Emery of Hanover m. Sarah Joanne **Buker** of Hanover 8/28/2004 in Lyme

KANGAS,
William of Belmont m. Joanne **Cressey** of Orford 9/5/1992

KAROL,
John J., Jr. of Orford m. Portia **Fitzhugh** of Orford 6/21/1980

KEATS,
John m. Carolyn **Cummings** 7/2/1988

KELLEY,
Ralph N. of Plymouth m. Myrtle M. **Dennis** of Orford 5/28/1921 in Laconia; H – 25, order clerk, b. Campton, s/o John A. Kelley (Plymouth, teamster) and Alice M. Fadden (Thornton, housekeeper); W – 18, machine oper., b. Haverhill, d/o Byron H. Dennis (Piermont, farmer) and Cora Spencer (Stratford, housewife)

KENNEDY,
Kenneth H. of Orford m. Alma Pearl **Giroux** of Orford 10/25/1943 in White River Jct., VT; H – 27, Army, 2nd, b. Easton, ME, s/o Jesse J. Kennedy (Canada) and Eva Anne St. Pierre (Canada); W – 31, home, 2nd, b. Orford, d/o Lurlyn Butman (Orford) and Hattie Bailey (Orford)

KENYON,
Walter C. of Orford m. Alice M. **Blodgett** of Orford 5/14/1912 in Orford; H – 25, merchant, b. Orford, s/o Carlos M. Kenyon (Plainfield, farmer) and Abbie M. Tyrrell (Canaan, housewife); W – 28, domestic, 2nd, divorced, b. Wentworth, d/o James R. Ramsey (Piermont, farmer) and Annette Sherburn (Orford, housewife)

KESEK,
David of Orford m. Barbie **Nickles** of Orford 12/31/1989

KIDDER,
Fred Albion of Bradford, VT m. Pamela Joan **Sanborn** of Orford 6/20/1970 in Orford; H – 23, b. Lebanon, s/o Keith A. Kidder and Nora Thurston; W – 16, b. Woodsville, d/o Neil Sanborn and Theresa Hudson
Fred Albion, II of Orford m. Rachel Lee **Bettis** of Orford 12/24/2004 in Orford

KING,
Dana m. Linda **Bryant** 4/12/1986

KLING,
P. Chase of Gilford m. Susan Page **Butler** of Orford 7/29/1978 in Orford; H – b. NH, s/o Peter Madsen Kling and Cynthia Ann Guild; W – b. NY, d/o John R. Butler and Cynthia Hodgson

KLOEBLEN,
William m. Barbara **Meier** 8/25/1984 in Orford

KNAPP,
David of Orford m. Marcia **Anderson** of Orford 10/16/1982

KNOWLTON,
Spencer of ME m. Hilary **Harwood** of ME 8/30/1980

KOPF,
William Howard of Woodstock, VT m. Margaret Ann **Taylor** of Orford 6/23/2001 in Orford

KOSNIK,
Christopher of Harrisonburg, VA m. Lindsay **Hance** of Orford 8/15/1992

KULICK,
Paul E. of Fairlee, VT m. Sally **Young** of Roselle, NJ 8/29/1948 in Orford; H – 26, asphalt dist., b. Norwalk, CT, s/o John Kulick (Czechoslovakia, cattle dealer) and V. Neklovich (Czechoslovakia, housewife); W – 18, student, b. Roselle, NJ, d/o Edward H. Young (Bovina Ctr., NY, Boy Scout Ex.) and Marie Frick (Hudson, NY, housewife)

KURIE,
Robert of Orford m. Karen **Burnett** of Orford 5/27/1979

LABELLE,
John m. Donna **Bomhower** 10/31/1987

LABOUNTY,
Francis F. of Hanover m. Irene M. **Adams** of Orford 8/22/1936 in Hanover; H – 23, mail carrier, b. Albany, VT, s/o Joseph LaBounty (Enosburg Falls, VT, farmer) and Sadie Dion (Enosburg, VT, deceased); W – 18, domestic, b. Haverhill, d/o Ralph Adams (Fairlee, VT, carpenter) and Lois Patridge (Haverhill, housewife)
Joseph of Orford m. Carrie A. **Sanborn** of Orford 9/23/1940 in Hanover; H – 65, laborer, 2nd, widower, b. Sheldon, VT, s/o Joseph Labounty (Canada, farmer) and Sophronis Labounty (Canada, housewife); W – 58, housewife, 2nd, divorced, b. Arlington, MA, d/o Major Bacon (S. Boston, MA, mason) and Abbie Rosella Wood (Strafford, VT, housewife)

LACKEY,
Douglas Richard of Orford m. Eleanor Janet **Pruneau** of Lyme 6/30/1951 in Lyme; H – 19, milk tester, b. Fairlee, VT, s/o Louis L. Lackey (W. Fairlee, VT) and Elizabeth M. Bard (W. Fairlee, VT); W – 19, secretary, b. New Britain, CT, d/o Ernest J. Pruneau (New Britain, CT) and Gerda Rasmussen (Copenhagen, Denmark)

LADD,
Burns H. of Orford m. Edna F. **Marsh** of Orford 11/9/1912 in Wentworth; H – 21, laborer, b. Orford, s/o John H. Ladd (Meredith, farmer) and Laura B. Pike (Haverhill, housewife); W – 19, domestic, b. Orford, d/o David C. Marsh (W. Fairlee, VT, farmer) and Delia F. Smith (Corinth, VT, housewife)
Charles P. of Orford m. Florence B. **Abbott** of Orford 9/1/1917 in Orford; H – 22, farm laborer, b. Haverhill, s/o John H. Ladd (Meredith) and Laura B. Pike (Haverhill); W – 23, domestic, b. New York City, d/o William Abbott and Christine Lundburg
John H. of Orford m. Laura B. **Pike** of Haverhill 6/27/1887 in E. Haverhill; H – 25, laborer, b. Meredith, s/o John Ladd (Meredith, laborer) and Hannah Prescott (Meredith, domestic); W – 18,

domestic, b. Haverhill, d/o Burnes Pike (Haverhill, laborer) and ---- French (Haverhill, domestic)

Oscar C. of Orford m. Lindsie Mae **Perry** of Orford 7/31/1929 in Ctr. Haverhill; H – 29, laborer, b. Pike, s/o John H. Ladd (laborer) and Laura B. Pike (Pike, housewife); W – 17, at home, b. Ctr. Haverhill, d/o Charles A. Perry (Whitefield, laborer) and Inez Lindsey (Benton, housewife)

LADEAU,

Charles W. of Orford m. Florence **Herbert** of Orford 8/12/1911 in Orford; H – 55, farmer, 2nd, b. Colchester, VT, s/o Francis Ladeau (Canada, farmer) and Eliza Ladeau (Canada, housewife); W – 63, housewife, 2nd, b. Ross Point, VT, d/o Peter Pecore (Canada, farmer) and Julia Richard (Canada, housewife)

Kenneth J. of Orford m. Arlene **Trussell** of Orford 7/23/1966 in Topsham, VT; H – 60, b. Hartford, VT, s/o James LaDeau and Dora C. Smith; W – 51, b. Fairlee, VT, d/o George F. Trussell and Grace H. Hilton

Levi J. of Orford m. Dora C. **Smith** of Orford 10/27/1904 in Piermont; H – 26, barber, b. Hyde Park, VT, s/o Frank Ladeau (farmer) and Pauline Jacobs (housewife); W – 18, teacher, b. Orford, d/o Alphonso Smith (Lyme, farmer) and Clarinda Worthen (Lyme, housewife)

LAMERE,

Aleck of Orford m. Ella E. **Thompson** of Orford 4/13/1896 in Piermont; H – 33, farmer, b. Canada, s/o Nelson Lamere (Canada, farmer); W – 16, domestic, b. Derry, d/o W. W. Thompson (Goshen, farmer) and Laura Burt (Whitingville, MA, domestic)

LAMONTAGNE,

Gilbert Edgar of Orford m. Margaret Josephine **McGoff** of Orford 9/28/1960 in Orford; H – 41, mechanic, b. Concord, VT, s/o Joseph LaMontagne (Sherbrook, PQ) and Lavina Guyer (St. Johnsbury, VT); W – 24, domestic, 2nd, b. Lunenburg, VT, d/o Eugene LaMotte (Canada) and Emily Rainville

LAMPHERE,

George of Bethesda, MD m. Jean **Smoke** of Orford 8/24/1991

LANDER,
Richard Edward of Yonkers, NY m. Gloria E. **LaPoint** of E. Corinth, VT 9/27/1963 in Orford; H – 22, b. Yonkers, NY, s/o Clifford H. Lander and Violet M. Pratt; W – 25, b. E. Corinth, VT, d/o George LaPoint and Ardella Matthews

LANDGRAF,
Bruce Ted m. Janet Lee **Willis** 5/27/1955 in Orford; H – 22, shoe super, b. Harvey, IL, s/o Myron J. Landgraf (Chicago, IL) and Pearl B. Anderson (Blue Island, IL); W – 22, lab. tech., b. Orford, d/o Clarence D. Willis (Orford) and Ruth M. Ibelle (New Britain, CT)
Gregory Wayne of Orford m. Natalia **Erastova** of Orford 7/2/2004 in Orford

LANDS,
Leon of Cambridge, VT m. Mary **Still** of Orford 6/30/1906 in Orford; H – 23, farmer, b. Fairfax, VT, s/o John Leland (KS, farmer) and Bertha Wright (Fairfax, VT, housewife); W – 21, domestic, b. Claremont, d/o Benjamin W. Still (Hancock, farmer) and Mary E. Bragg (W. Fairlee, VT, housewife)

LANG,
Paul of Orford m. Mary L. **Emerson** of Orford 7/2/1901 in Orford; H – 41, attorney, b. Bath, s/o David R. Lang (Bath, attorney) and Josophine R. Smith (Bath, housewife); W – 40, domestic, 2nd, divorced, b. Gloucester, d/o George T. Beals (Gloucester) and Mary E. Head (Gloucester)

LANGLEY,
Shawn R. of Hartford, VT m. Christine S. **Pike** of Hartford, VT 9/21/1997

LANGMAID,
George B. of Orford m. Annie H. **Smith** of Manchester 6/4/1913 in Lyme; H – 42, gen. agt., 2nd, widower, b. Brockton, MA, s/o Charles Langmaid (Brockton, MA, shoemaker) and Rosy Morrison (Weymouth, MA, housewife); W – 36, domestic, b. N. Scituate, MA, d/o Fred M. Smith (Manchester) and Minnie Gaines (Malone, NY)

LARSON,
Brian Pierce of Denver, CO m. Karen Ann **Casey** of Denver, CO 9/4/1993

LASELLE,
Oscar D. of Orford m. Mary M. **Corliss** of Grantham 9/11/1895 in Plainfield; H – 27, mechanic, b. Keene, s/o Edward Laselle (NY, farmer); W – 20, domestic, b. Grantham, d/o John Corliss (Ashland)

LAWSON,
Terry George of Lyme m. Cynthia Lynn **Godfrey** of Orford 9/10/1977 in Orford; H – 22, b. NH, s/o George Lawson and Joanne Brady; W – 18, b. NH, d/o Albert Godfrey and Annette Fillian

LEA,
Sydney of Orford m. Robin **Barone** of Orford 7/9/1983

LEARNED,
Charles W. of Orford m. Annie R. **Bedell** of Orford 5/13/1943 in Orford; H – 46, farmer, b. Orford, s/o Jonas G. Learned (Orford, farmer) and Louisa Laflam (Piermont, housewife); W – 46, domestic, 2nd, b. Beebe, VT, d/o Ed. Colby (Stratford, VT, carpenter) and Florence Kennison (retired)

Jonas G. of Orford m. Louisa **Laflame** of Wentworth 3/25/1895 in Plymouth; H – 28, farmer, b. Orford, s/o George E. Learned (Orford, farmer); W – 17, domestic, b. Piermont, d/o Thomas Laflame (farmer)

Jonas G. of Orford m. Arabelle H. **Clark** of Piermont 10/30/1912 in Haverhill; H – 45, farmer, 2nd, widower, b. Orford, s/o George E. Learned (Orford, farmer) and Chastina Hartwell (Haverhill, housewife); W – 51, teacher, 2nd, widow, b. Haverhill, d/o Josiah Hardy (Haverhill, section man) and Ann Bailey (Alexandria, dressmaker)

William E. of Orford m. Ida M. **Bailey** of Orford 6/1/1900 in Orford; H – 26, laborer, b. Wentworth, s/o George E. Learned (Reading, VT, farmer) and Christina Hartwell (Piermont); W – 22, domestic, b. Wakefield, MA, d/o Alpha N. Bailey (Andover, MA, blacksmith) and Mary E. Niles (Orford)

LEBARGE,
Joe of Orford m. Ardell **Lemontague** of Piermont 11/22/1901 in Piermont; H – 25, laborer, b. Montreal, Canada, s/o Paul Labarge (farmer) and Mary Tarble (housewife); W – 16, domestic, b. Piermont, d/o Jeddio Lamontagne (Quebec, farmer) and Lucy Kimball (housewife)

LEE,
Jeff of VT m. Julie **Snizek** of VT 6/30/1990

LEIGH,
Henry of Orford m. Julia A. **Thompson** of Orford 11/20/1898 in Piermont; H – 35, laborer, b. Manchester, s/o John Leigh (cheesemaker) and Mary ----- (housewife); W – 15, domestic, d/o Warner W. Thompson (farmer) and Christina Collins (housewife)

LESTER,
Paul of Orford m. Fay **Cicotte** of Orford 12/20/1980

LIGHTNER,
G. Cass of Washington, DC m. Cornelia P. **Griggs** of Thetford Ctr., VT 7/10/1943 in Orford; H – 56, engineer, 2nd, b. Detroit, MI, s/o Edwin L. Lightner (Danville, NY, retired) and Jane Cass (Seevickley, PA, retired); W – 38, clerk, 2nd, b. Detroit, MI, d/o Ellery D. Preston (Detroit, MI, retired) and Florence Lathrop (Jackson, MI, retired)

LISTER,
Jeffrey G. of Orford m. Jennifer M. **Dyke** of Orford 9/21/1996

LOCKWOOD,
Brocton Dewey of Carbondale, IL m. Katharine **Gratz** of Scarsdale, NY 7/11/1964 in Orford; H – 20, b. HI, s/o Randolph S. D. Lockwood and Bonnie Mae Allen; W – 21, b. New York, NY, d/o Louis Paul Gratz and Jean C. Young

LOISELLE,
Lance Christopher of Essex Jct., VT m. Jennifer Mae **Pike** of Essex Jct., VT 8/21/1999

LOOK,
Scott W. of Orford m. Nettie A. **Pierce** of Putney, VT 9/27/1905 in Westmoreland; H – 24, farmer, b. Haverhill, s/o Isaac Look (laborer) and Elizabeth Drown (Haverhill, MA, housewife); W – 42, dressmaker, b. Wardsboro, VT, d/o Clark Pierce (Putney, VT, farmer) and Isadore Watson (Wardsboro, VT, housewife)

LOUANIS,
Edwin J. of Orford m. Edith M. **Simons** of Orford 9/30/1924 in Lyme; H – 38, farming, b. Sherbrooke, Canada, s/o Joseph Louanis (Canada, farming) and Mary Trombly (Montreal, housewife); W – 34, domestic, b. Orford, d/o John Cooledge (Benton, farming) and Emma Whitman (Orford, housewife)

LUCE,
Leslie F. of Orford m. Rosa **Hubbard** of Orford 4/11/1894 in Piermont; H – 26, farmer, b. Chelsea, VT, s/o Jarvis Luce (Strafford, VT, farmer) and Mary Clark (Sharon, VT, domestic); W – 18, domestic, b. Bath, d/o Charles Hubbard (carpenter) and Mary Hubbard (carpenter)

LUDWIG,
Dan m. Georgette **Wolf** 11/11/1988

LUSCO,
Leon David of W. Fairlee, VT m. Delia Hart **Towle** of W. Fairlee, VT 7/2/1945 in Orford; H – 23, farmer, b. W. Fairlee, VT, s/o Leon Lusco (Charlotte, VT, farmer) and Angie Hodge (Canada, housewife); W – 25, at home, b. Cavendish, VT, d/o Charles A. Hodge (Claremont, deceased) and Annie S. Hart (Claremont, housewife)

LYNCH,
Randy Harold m. Stacy Lee **Wadsworth** --/--/1989

LYNES,
Frank Edward m. Nettie E. **Waterhouse** 8/4/1953 in Craftsbury, VT; H – 80, retired, 2nd, b. Highgate, VT, s/o Franklin L. Lynes and Elizabeth McIntosh; W – 71, housewife, 2nd, b. Glover, VT, d/o James Calderwood (Scotland) and Caroline Spring (Glover, VT)

Frank Robert of Orford m. Christine E. **Nystrom** of Orford 2/10/1952 in Orford; H – 20, farmer, b. Hanover, s/o Harold F. Lynes (Hardwick, VT) and Vena Belle Dow (Littleton); W – 20, at home, b. Waltham, MA, d/o Carl E. Nystrom (Sweden) and Lillian E. Swanson (Boston, MA)

LYONS,
Gerald J. of Orford m. Ann M. **Smith** of Orford 7/27/2002 in W. Stewartstown

MACCAMPBELL,
Donald of Cambridge, MA m. Kathleen **Rickenbaugh** of Cambridge, MA 7/1/1937 in Orford; H – 27, literary agent, b. Philadelphia, PA, s/o David MacCampbell (Louisville, KY, ins. agent) and Louise Ketcham (Washington, DC, housewife); W – 23, secretary, b. Pittsburgh, PA, d/o Calvin Rickenbaugh (Tarentum, PA, physician) and Kathleen Gooding (Dover, DE, deceased)

MACE,
John A. of Orford m. JodyAnn **Ricker** of Orford 10/28/1978 in Orford; H – b. NY, s/o Leigh Mace and Leona Baker; W – b. NH, d/o Lawrence Ricker and Beverly Record

MACK,
Brian Lewis of Orford m. Lori Ann **Wilmott** of Lyme 10/1/1977 in Orfordville; H – 20, b. NH, s/o Ralph Roger Mack and Helen McKensie; W – 18, b. NH, d/o Archie Frank Wilmott and Dorothy Brady

Delbert Wayne of Orford m. Patricia Southworth **Hammond** of Orford 6/6/1964 in Orford; H – 47, b. Orford, s/o Fred Mack and Mabel A. Ramsey; W – 33, b. New Haven, CT, d/o John W. Hammond and Adelaide Meara

Fred of Orford m. Mabel A. **Ramsey** of Orford 2/3/1903 in Orford; H – 26, farmer, b. Piermont, s/o Ruel Mack (Orford, farmer) and Elizabeth Holmes (Haverhill, housewife); W – 17, domestic, b. Orford, d/o James Ramsey (Piermont, farmer) and Annette Sherburn (Orford, housewife)

Quentin Philip of Orford m. Joyce Ann **Nutter** of Orford 6/8/1963 in Orford; H – 20, b. Windsor, VT, s/o Ralph R. Mack and Helen

McKenzie; W – 21, b. Barre, VT, d/o Kenneth L. Nutter and
   Evelyn R. Johnson
Ralph Roger of Orford m. Helen E. **McKenzie** of Orford 12/11/1941
   in Windsor, VT; H – 22, mill man, b. Orford, s/o Fred Mack
   (Piermont, farmer) and Mabel A. Ramsey (housewife); W – 18,
   at home, b. Quincy, MA, d/o Lewis S. McKenzie (Quincy, MA)
   and Annie E. Copley (Lawrence, MA, housewife)

MACQUEEN,
Jeffrey James of Orford m. Tammy Louise **Bruno** of Orford
   10/14/2000 in Newbury, VT

MADIGAN,
Michael C. of Orono, ME m. Bonnie L. **Pike** of Orford --/--/1972 in
   Bradford, VT; H – 20, b. CT, s/o John E. Madigan and
   Georgianna Boivin; W – 19, b. Hanover, d/o Weymouth H. Pike
   and Helen M. Marsh

MALLAS,
George Peter of New Rochelle, NY m. Eileen May **Dorcey** of New
   Rochelle, NY 6/26/1993

MALLETT,
Richard B. of Orford m. Karen M. **Bixby** of Orford 3/23/2002 in
   Orford

MALLOY,
Mark of Wallingford, CT m. Melissa **Howard** of N. Thetford, VT
   5/4/1991

MANSON,
Mark m. Kathy **Chiasson** 9/21/1984 in Orford

MARDEN,
George B. of Jefferson m. Bessie E. **Austin** of Orford 2/15/1902 in
   Orford; H – 21, telegraph op., b. Whitefield, s/o Elijah F. Marden
   (Jefferson, farmer) and Martha E. Hutchins (Whitefield,
   housewife); W – 17, domestic, b. Orford, d/o Albert Austin
   (Fairfax, VT, farmer) and Addie M. Baker (Orford, housewife)

MARSH,
Alan T. m. Sherry E. **Wurtz** --/--/1989
Arthur L. of Orford m. Irene **Goddard** of Enfield 7/18/1926 in Wentworth; H – 27, laborer, b. Orford, s/o David C. Marsh (W. Fairlee, VT, farmer) and Delia Smith (E. Corinth, VT, housewife); W – 16, domestic, b. St. Johnsbury, VT, d/o Thomas Goddard (Hartford, Canada, farmer) and Mae Palmer (Holland, VT, housewife)
Clyde D. of Orford m. Edith F. **Stevens** of Orford 9/24/1932 in Lyme; H – 26, laborer, b. Orford, s/o David C. Marsh (W. Fairlee, VT, farmer) and Delia Smith (E. Corinth, VT, housewife); W – 18, at home, b. Williamstown, VT, d/o William Stevens (Williamstown, VT, laborer) and Ethel Colby (Beebe Plain, VT, housewife)
David C. of Orford m. Delia F. **Smith** of Corinth, VT 12/25/1889 in Orford; H – 21, laborer, b. W. Fairlee, VT, s/o G. W. Marsh (Topsham, VT, farmer) and Mary A. Dickinson (W. Fairlee, VT); W – 18, domestic, b. Corinth, VT, d/o Joseph Smith (Corinth, VT, farmer) and Irene Felch (Corinth, VT)
Elwin D. of Orford m. Flora A. **Bailey** 2/8/1904 in Orford; H – 21, laborer, b. W. Fairlee, s/o George D. Marsh (Topsham, VT, farmer) and Mary Dickerson (W. Fairlee, VT, housewife); W – 16, domestic, b. Orford, d/o Alpha N. Bailey (Andover, MA, mechanic) and Mary Niles (Orford, housewife)
Elwin Ralph of Orford m. Janet Eva **Marsh** of Lyme 6/26/1964 in Lyme; H – 25, b. Orford, s/o Ralph E. Marsh and Gladys Cutler; W – 26, b. Hanover, d/o John C. Balch and Marion L. Giarue
Ernest E. of Orford m. Erma M. **Tarr** of Orford 6/22/1946 in Bradford, VT; H – 18, soldier, b. Enfield, s/o Walter Marsh (Orford, laborer) and Rita Goddard (Orleans, VT, deceased); W – 16, at home, b. Marlborough, d/o Bert Tarr (ME) and Dorothy Houston (Ashland)
Floyd Kenneth of Orford m. Muriel Elaine **Taylor** of Orford 10/2/1970 in Orford; H – 27, b. Orford, s/o Ralph E. Marsh and Gladys Cutler; W – 21, b. Barnet, VT, d/o Elmer Taylor and Phyllis Royston
Frank D. of Orford m. Ina M. **Strue** of Lyme 3/4/1920 in Orford; H – 24, laborer, 2nd, divorced, b. Orford, s/o David C. Marsh (W. Fairlee, VT, farmer) and Delia Smith (Corinth, VT); W – 21, domestic, b. Lyme, d/o William Strue (Lyme) and Cora Avery (Lyme, domestic)

Frank E. of Orford m. Adelle **Barnett** of Walden, VT 7/16/1917 in Hartford, VT; H – 21, farm laborer, b. Orford, s/o David C. Marsh (W. Fairlee, VT) and Delia Smith (Corinth, VT); W – 17, domestic, b. Walden, VT, d/o Calvin Barnett (Cabot, VT) and Malina Lamosa (Cabot, VT)

Fred A. of Orford m. Nancy L. **Hudson** of Orford --/8/1972 in Piermont; H – 37, b. Orford, s/o Glenn G. Marsh and Verna M. Hibbard; W – 18, b. Woodsville, d/o Edward J. Hudson and Etta May Pike

Fred Allen m. Louise Myrtle **Davis** 8/25/1956 in Orfordville; H – 20, laborer, b. Orford, s/o Glenn Marsh (Orford) and Verna Hibbard (Lyme); W – 22, bookkeeper, b. Lyme, d/o Gerald W. Davis (Groton) and Hattie Davis (Beebe Jct., Canada)

Fred C. of Orford m. Beulah C. **Cutting** of Piermont 5/13/1916 in Haverhill; H – 23, laborer, b. Orford, s/o David E. Marsh (W. Fairlee, VT, farmer) and Delia F. Smith (Corinth, VT, housewife); W – 16, domestic, b. Orford, d/o fred D. Cutting (Warren, farmer) and Sadie Flanders (Warren, housewife)

Fred C. of Orford m. Dorothy M. **Merrill** of Deerfield 2/26/1924 in Orford; H – 31, laborer, 2nd, b. Orford, s/o David C. Marsh (W. Fairlee, VT, farmer) and Delia Smith (Waits River, VT); W – 23, housework, b. Deerfield, d/o Herbert Merrill and Mary M. Donald (Candia, cooking)

George C. of Orford m. Mary E. **Bailey** of Orford 9/30/1903 in Lebanon; H – 23, engineer, b. W. Fairlee, VT, s/o George W. Marsh (W. Topsham, VT, farmer) and Mary Dickinson (W. Fairlee, VT, housewife); W – 20, domestic, b. Springfield, VT, d/o Joseph Bailey (Springfield, farmer) and Nellie Gilman (Grafton, housewife)

George W. of Orford m. Mabell L. **Whittier** of Haverhill, MA 5/17/1902 in Orford; H – 59, farmer, 2nd, widower, b. Topsham, VT, s/o Moody Marsh (Topsham, VT, farmer) and Annie Philbrick (Corinth, VT, housewife); W – 16, domestic, b. Ossipee, d/o Andrew J. Whittier (Cotton Valley, safe maker) and Ada L. Brown (Boston, MA)

Glenn G. of Orford m. Verna M. **Hibbard** of Orford 6/26/1935 in Lyme; H – 21, farmer, b. Orford, s/o David C. Marsh (W. Fairlee, VT, farmer) and Delia Smith (Topsham, VT, housewife); W – 19, domestic, b. Lyme, d/o Clarence Hibbard (Orford, creamery man) and Maude Curtis (Piermont, housewife)

Henry G. of Orford m. Wanita **Balch** of Orford 12/24/1960 in Orford; H – 20, maintenance laborer, b. Orford, s/o Glenn G. Marsh (Orford) and Verna M. Hibbard (Lyme); W – 18, domestic, b. Lyme, d/o Raymond Balch (Lyme) and Esther Smith (Post Mills, VT)

Leon C. of Orford m. Irene Elliott **Heath** of Littleton 3/10/1930 in Orford; H – 32, farmer, b. Orford, s/o David C. Marsh (W. Fairlee, VT, farmer) and Delia Smith (E. Corinth, VT, housewife); W – 22, nurse, 2nd, divorced, b. Littleton, d/o Will R. Elliott (Dalton, n. watchman) and Anne Howland (Franconia, housewife)

Leon C., Jr. of Orford m. Helen A. **Huckins** of Orford 12/24/1952 in Orford; H – 21, US Army, b. Orford, s/o Leon C. Marsh (Orford) and Irene M. Elliott (Littleton); W – 18, at home, b. Hanover, d/o George C. Huckins (Orford) and Hazel M. Williams (Barre, VT)

Mark m. Esther **Dobbins** 6/1/1985 in Orford

Ralph E. of Orford m. Gladys A. **Cutler** of Wentworth 4/30/1933 in Ashland; H – 30, laborer, b. Orford, s/o David C. Marsh (W. Fairlee, VT, farmer) and Delia Smith (Corinth, VT, housewife); W – 18, at home, b. Grafton, d/o Judson Cutler (Stowe, VT, laborer) and Myrtle C. Mann (Tunbridge, VT, housewife)

Raymond Lee of Orford m. Betty Jane **Russin** of Bradford, VT 12/15/1960 in Orford; H – 20, laborer, b. Orford, s/o Leon C. Marsh, Sr. (Orford) and Irene M. Elliott (Littleton); W – 18, waitress, b. Woodsville, d/o Hugh K. Russin (Jericho, VT) and Pauline Jennings (W. Fairlee, VT)

Roy C. of Orford m. Grace I. **Cutler** of Wentworth 7/11/1933 in Lyme; H – 21, truck driver, b. Orford, s/o David C. Marsh (W. Fairlee, VT, farmer) and Delia Smith (Corinth, VT, housewife); W – 16, at home, b. Vershire, VT, d/o Judson Cutler (Stowe, VT, laborer) and Myrtle C. Mann (Tunbridge, VT, housewife)

Walter of Orford m. Gladys **Bigelow** of Orford 8/7/1934 in Orford; H – 34, laborer, 2nd, b. Orford, s/o David C. Marsh (W. Fairlee, VT, farmer) and Delia Smith (Waits River, VT, housewife); W – 29, housekeeper, 2nd, b. Littleton, d/o William R. Elliott (Dalton, mechanic) and Anna B. Howland (Littleton, housewife)

Walter H. of Orford m. Retar **Manchester** of Enfield 6/4/1926 in Orford; H – 27, laborer, b. Orford, s/o David C. Marsh (W. Fairlee, VT, farmer) and Delia Smith (E. Corinth, VT, housewife); W – 23, domestic, 2nd, b. Enfield, d/o Thomas

Goddard (Hartford, Canada, farmer) and Mae Palmer (Holland, VT, housewife)

MARSHALL,
Harry C. of Orford m. Ruth T. **Crowell** of Manchester 3/1/1916 in Manchester; H – 34, farmer, b. Plymouth, s/o William H. Marshall (Buffalo, NY, farmer) and Lane Kenyon (Plainfield, housewife); W – 27, nurse, b. Norwich, CT, d/o Gideon Crowell (S. Yarmouth, MA) and Mary Crowell (S. Yarmouth, MA, housewife)
Stuart A. of Orford m. Dorothea J. **Bancroft** of Durham 4/1/1945 in Bradford, VT; H – 26, soldier, b. Franklin, s/o William H. Marshall (Orford, farmer) and Laura M. Crowell (Norwich, CT, housewife); W – 24, teacher, b. Brooklyn, NY, d/o George D. Bancroft (Brooklyn, NY, druggist) and Lillian Bownes (Brooklyn, NY, housewife)

MARTIN,
Harry F. of Bradford, VT m. Cary Jane **Pierson** of Orford 5/14/1938 in W. Newbury, VT; H – 26, farmer, 2nd, divorced, b. Bradford, VT, s/o Henry W. Martin (Bradford, VT) and Effie Hadlock (Newport, VT); W – 18, domestic, b. Topsham, VT, d/o Ernest Pierson (Topsham, VT, farmer) and Nettie Wright (Topsham, VT, deceased)
Peter of Orford m. Lucretia **Sterling** of Hanover 1/--/1980

MARTINDALE,
Philip Howard of Orford m. Katie Lyn **Flanders** of Orford 8/30/2003 in Orford

MATTOON,
Floyd S., Jr. of W. Fairlee, VT m. Diane W. **Salls** of Randolph, VT 12/16/1972 in Orford; H – 25, b. Hanover, s/o Floyd Mattoon, Sr. and Alice Towle; W – 25, b. NH, d/o Earle Winget and Lois Ingalls

MATYKA,
John m. Deborah **Stevens** 1/1/1988
John of Orford m. Maria L. **Moody** of Orford 7/2/2000 in Orford

McBAIN,
John of Orford m. Flora H. **MacLeod** of Orford 7/28/1915 in Orford; H – 44, farmer, 2nd, widower, b. Savoch, Scotland, s/o John McBain (Scotland, farmer) and Mary Edmond (Drake Myve, Ellon, Scotland, housewife); W – 19, domestic, b. S. Whitton, PQ, d/o Gordon McLean (Marsboro, PQ, laborer) and Mary MacLeod (S. Whitton, PQ, housewife)

McCARTHY,
James of Orford m. Gwendolyn **Shirley** of Orford 2/27/1982

McCLELLAN,
Paul Gifford of W. Lebanon m. Thelma Joy **Shaw** of Orford 11/7/1950 in Lyme; H – 21, warehouse worker, b. Hanover, s/o Genge T. McClelland (Lawrence, MA) and Ethel Frances Sawyer (Topsham, VT); W – 18, at home, b. Lyme, d/o Norman E. Shaw, Sr. (St. Johnsbury, VT) and Ara A. Wentworth (Lunenburg, VT)

McGOFF,
James of Orford m. Deborah **Kenyon** of Bradford, VT 2/14/1979

McGOVERN,
Robert of Northport, FL m. Jane **Polston** of Northport, FL 6/6/1992

McINTYRE,
Michael E. of Orford m. Maria S. **Durso** of Orford 8/14/1999

McKEE,
Henry m. Donna **Charbono** --/--/1989
Henry Arthur of Orford m. Linda Rose **Wilson** of Antrim 11/23/1977 in Deering; H – 20, b. NH, s/o William McKee and Joyce Marsh; W – 20, b. NH, d/o Wayne Wilson and Rose Marie Davy
Henry Arthur of Orford m. Heidi Leigh **Gardyne** of Orford 10/9/2004 in Orford
William Bert m. Joyce Ann **Marsh** 3/17/1956 in Orford; H – 18, laborer, b. Plymouth, s/o Kenneth W. McKee (Dorchester) and Frances E. Foote (Orford); W – 18, waitress, b. Orford, d/o Glenn G. Marsh (Orford) and Verna M. Hibbard (Lyme)

McLEOD,
James H. of Barre, VT m. Ivis E. **Chase** of Barre, VT 10/17/1933 in Orford; H – 22, plumber, b. Barre, VT, s/o James McLeod (Scotland, plumber) and Jessie Hay (Scotland, housewife); W – 19, at home, b. Barre, VT, d/o Frank L. Chase (Glover, VT, foreman) and Dora H. Murphy (Albany, VT, housewife)

Joseph W. of Plymouth m. Edna G. **McIntire** of Orford 11/24/1926 in Plymouth; H – 48, store manager, 2nd, b. Ashland, s/o William McLeod (Ashland, carpenter) and Mary L. Ellison (Holderness, housewife); W – 34, housewife, 2nd, b. Wentworth, d/o Francis R. Pease (Ellsworth, farmer) and Mabel C. Sherburn (Orford, housekeeper)

McMACKIN,
Carleton E. of Orford m. Evalyn **Gibson** of Bradford, VT 9/28/1967 in Lyme; H – 65, b. Boston, MA, s/o Thomas I. McMackin and Matilda Beller; W – 63, b. Newbury, VT, d/o Arthur D. Runnels and Bertha Gansby

McMAHON,
William m. Sabina **Miller** 8/29/1987

McPHERSON,
Jason of Orford m. Cynthia **Waterman** of Orford 11/7/1898 in Piermont; H – 43, farmer, 2nd, widower, b. NS, s/o B. B. McPherson (NS, farmer); W – 42, domestic, b. NS, d/o Filson Waterman

MERCHANT,
Donald Raymond m. Hazel Grace **Horne** 8/24/1957 in Orford; H – 31, teacher, b. Gloucester, MA, s/o Raymond P. Merchant (Gloucester, MA) and Frances Gochey (Derby, VT); W – 25, secretary, b. Long Beach, CA, d/o Tracey Leroy Horne (Franklin) and Irene Elizabeth Chartier (Hartford, CT)

MERCIER,
Ronald Wayne of Bradford, VT m. Sandra Ann **Bourque** of Orford 3/29/1975 in Montpelier, VT; H – 24, b. VT, s/o Robert E. Mercier and Beatrice H. Nourse; W – 22, b. NH, d/o Alfred E. Bourque and Marilyn DeRonount

MERRILL,
Allison Herbert of Orford m. Mildred Beatrice **Madsen** of Orford 3/10/1951 in Orford; H – 54, laborer, 3rd, b. Candia, s/o Herbert I. Merrill (Deerfield) and Mary S. MacDonald (Candia); W – 52, domestic, 4th, b. Littleton, d/o William R. Elliott (NH) and Anna Belle Howland (NH)

Myron S. of Plymouth m. Hattie S. **Learned** of Orford 8/14/1926 in Plymouth; H – 23, painter, b. Thornton, s/o F. G. Merrill (Thornton, mason) and Myrtle E. Fox (Sharon, VT, housewife); W – 21, housework, b. Orford, d/o William E. Learned (Orford, farmer) and Ida M. Bailey (Orford, housewife)

MERTENS,
Richard J. of Bridgeport, CT m. Marion V. **Stockman** of Bradford, VT 11/29/1941 in Orford; H – 32, machinist, b. Bridgeport, CT, s/o Frank A. Mertens (Bridgeport, CT, office work) and Jane B. McMunn (Patterson, NJ, housewife); W – 22, nurse, b. Lowell, VT, d/o Harold L. Stockman (Georgia, VT, laborer) and Hallie M. Colbeth (Lowell, VT, housewife)

MESSER,
Lowell of Orford m. Debra **Fontaine** of Fairlee 6/12/1982

Paul Bridgeman m. Betty Lou **Cummings** 12/24/1958 in Orford; H – 19, laborer, b. Arlington, MA, s/o William B. Messer; W – 18, at home, b. Woodsville, d/o Clyde A. Cummings (Thetford, VT) and Rosie Tallman (Orford)

MICHAUD,
Gerald G. m. Patricia H. **Mack** of Orford 2/1/1975 in Andover, NB; W – 44, b. New Haven, CT, d/o John W. Hammond and Adelaide Meara

MILES,
Elbridge C. of Orford m. Della M. **Austin** of Orford 5/21/1937 in Woodsville; H – 46, farmer, b. Irasburg, VT, s/o Charles T. Miles (Irasburg, VT, farmer) and Alice (Irasburg, VT, domestic); W – 40, domestic, b. Enosburg, VT, d/o Ransom Austin (VT, farmer) and Jean Hendricks (Concord, VT, domestic)

MILLER,
Caryl of Orford m. Judy **White** of Orford 8/8/1992

Caryl Wayne m. Margaret L. **Reeves** 11/28/1958 in Orford; H – 20, US Army, b. Woodsville, s/o Wayne C. Miller (Haverhill) and Martha E. True (Haverhill); W – 21, mach. oper., b. Mars Hill, ME, d/o Otto R. Reeves (Augusta, ME) and Rose Raymond (Winthrop, ME)

Fred H. of St. Johnsbury, VT m. Edna M. **Cushing** of St. Johnsbury, VT 9/29/1938 in Orford; H – 38, salesman, 2nd, divorced, b. Burlington, VT, s/o Fred F. Miller (Gary, VA, railway employee) and Susan H. O'Neal (Burlington, VT, ret. housewife); W – 27, stenographer, b. Derby, VT, d/o Timothy R. Cushing (Derby, VT, butcher) and Emma Labounty (Newport, VT, ret. housewife)

John T. of Lyme m. Bethany J. **Blake** of Orford 7/8/1981

MILLICAN,
John m. Wendy **Adams** 10/5/1985 in Orford

MILO,
Robert D. of Montpelier, VT m. Ruth **Preston** of Randolph, VT 1/28/1934 in Orford; H – 24, carpenter, b. Montpelier, VT, s/o William Milo, Sr. (Roxbury, VT, shoemaker) and Ellen Allen (Montpelier, VT, housewife); W – 23, domestic, 2nd, b. Burlington, VT, d/o Fred Preston (Strafford, VT, ins. agent) and Mary Udall (Wolcott, VT, housewife)

MISURACA,
James m. AnnMarie **[name not given]** 5/25/1985 in Etna

MITCHELL,
William George of Charlestown, MA m. Ann Morrison **Barry** of Charlestown, MA 8/14/1993

MONTGOMERY,
Richard of Indianapolis, IN m. Elizabeth A. **Button** of Los Angeles, CA 6/14/1935 in Orford; H – 21, reporter, b. Dorchester, MA, s/o Harry Montgomery (Boston, MA, advertiser) and Amie Chapman (Boston, MA, housewife); W – 20, student, b. Stonington, ME, d/o Max L. Button (E. Berkshire, VT, treasurer) and Mabel Boss (Stonington, ME, housewife)

MOREY,
Bradley Z. of Orford m. Alice E. **Fish** of Lebanon 9/21/1951 in Lebanon; H – 48, road agent, 2nd, b. Orford, s/o Edward Morey (VT) and Esther McIntyre (Inverness, PQ); W – 47, housewife, 2nd, b. Rochester, VT, d/o George Martin (VT) and Cora English (VT)

Bradley Zenas m. Clementine Ina **Roberts** 11/17/1953 in Woodsville; H – 51, road agent, 3rd, b. Orford, s/o Edward S. Morey (Thetford, VT) and Esther McIntyre (Inverness, Canada); W – 55, diner manager, 2nd, b. Orford, d/o Arthur J. Richardson (Orford) and Hattie Gardner (Orford)

Charles H. of Chelsea, VT m. Lizzie W. **Avery** of Orford 12/20/1891 in Orford; H – 23, farmer, b. Nashua, s/o Mills C. Morey (farmer) and ----- (Fairlee, VT); W – 22, domestic, b. Orford, d/o James Warner (shoemaker) and ----- Warner

Eddie S. of Orford m. Ester **McIntyre** of Bradford, VT 12/12/1893 in Piermont; H – 24, farmer, b. Thetford, VT, s/o Zenos Morey (Strafford, VT, farmer) and Eliza Newcomb (Thetford, VT, domestic); W – 22, domestic, b. PQ, d/o Daniel McIntyre (PQ, farmer) and Agnes McIntyre (PQ, domestic)

Erving W. of Orford m. Annie **McIntyre** of Canada, PQ 10/31/1888 in Orford; H – 27, laborer, 2nd, b. Thetford, VT, s/o Zenes Morey (Thetford, VT, farmer) and Elizabeth E. Morey (housewife); W – 23, domestic, b. Canada, d/o David McIntyre (Canada, farmer) and Agnes McIntyre (housewife)

Gerald of Orford m. Joanne **Pike** of Orford 6/14/1980

Scott Allen of Orford m. Meghan Nicole **Gauthier** of W. Chesterfield 5/25/2002 in Brattleboro, VT

MORIN,
Romeo Edward, Jr. m. Doris Helene **Davis** 8/23/1958 in Orford; H – 23, teacher, b. Littleton, s/o Romeo E. Morin (Lac Magantic, Canada) and Ellen Townsend (Lebanon); W – 22, teacher, b. Woodsville, d/o Gerald W. Davis (Groton) and Hattie K. Davis (Beebe Jct., Canada)

MORRISON,
Harry E. of Orford m. Nellie J. **Danforth** of Colebrook 3/26/1890 in Colebrook; H – 21, farmer, b. Orford, s/o Samuel R. Morrison (Fairlee, VT, farmer); W – 28, teacher, b. Pittsburg, d/o Roswell W. Danforth (Pittsburg, carriage maker)

Harry E. of Orford m. Frances **Buzzell** of Haverhill 11/25/1896 in Haverhill; H – 28, farmer, 2nd, b. Orford, s/o Samuel R. Morrison (Fairlee, VT, farmer) and Adelizea Merrill (Orford, housewife); W – 27, teacher, b. Vershire, VT, d/o John C. Bugbee (merchant) and Mary D. Darling (Stratford, VT, domestic)

S. R. of Orford m. Ellen M. **Clark** of Orford 10/6/1915 in Orford; H – 22, farmer, b. Orford, s/o H. E. Morrison (Orford, farmer) and Nellie J. Danforth (Pittsburg, housewife); W – 23, stenographer, b. Orford, d/o George C. Clark (Orford, farmer) and Gertrude M. Keyes (Thetford, VT, housewife)

MORSE,

Kenneth B. of Lisbon m. Lucy Ellen **Young** of Orford 6/1/1933 in Orford; H – 21, laborer, b. Boston, MA, s/o Clarence Morse (Kansas City, KS, farmer) and Marion Brisbois (Boston, MA, housewife); W – 17, housework, b. Winterport, ME, d/o Alton E. Young (Winterport, ME, mechanic) and Elizabeth Tennyson (Ft. Lawrence, NS, housewife)

MOSES,

Harry A. of Rumney m. Dell **Downing** of Orford 11/8/1906 in Wentworth; H – 24, farmer, b. Wentworth, s/o Andrew J. Moses (Groton, farmer) and Eda M. Huntress (Meredith, housewife); W – 20, domestic, b. Willie E. Downing (Wentworth, farmer) and Luna M. Poor (Orford, housewife)

Jonathan of Orford m. Hattie B. **Hawkins** of Orford 10/13/1948 in Orford; H – retired, 4th, widower, b. Tunbridge, VT, s/o Ora F. Moses (Barnard, VT, basket maker) and Margaret Barton (Montpelier, VT, housewife); W – housekeeper, 4th, widow, b. W. Fairlee, VT, d/o Henry Howland (Easton, farmer) and Mary Jane Norton (Stratford, VT, housewife)

Perley of Orford m. Eva May **Morey** of Orford 9/15/1928 in Piermont; H – 22, laborer, b. Tunbridge, VT, s/o Jonathan Moses (Tunbridge, VT, basket maker) and Emma Jerome (housewife); W – 31, domestic, b. Bradford, VT, d/o Eddie S. Morey (Thetford, VT, farmer) and Esther McIntire (Canada, housewife)

MOULTON,

Ernest K. of Springfield, MA m. Minnie W. **Cushman** of Orford 6/30/1925 in Orford; H – 48, laborer, 2nd, b. Corinth, VT, s/o George C. Moulton (Corinth, VT, farmer) and Jennie Bouroughs

(Corinth, VT, housewife); W – 64, housewife, 2nd, b. Bradford, VT, d/o B. L. Worthley (Bradford, VT, farmer) and Emily M. Coburn (W. Fairlee, housewife)

MOVELLE,
Paul A. of Orford m. Sarah D. **Kendall** of Orford 6/20/1981

MUNN,
Reginold G. of Fairlee, VT m. Lurleen **Blodgett** of Orford 5/12/1922 in Bradford, VT; H – 25, clerk, b. W. Fairlee, VT, s/o Charles H. Munn (W. Fairlee, VT) and Kathaleen Ordway (Minneapolis); W – 20, b. Orford, d/o Clarence Blodgett (Orford, farmer) and Alice Ramsey (Wentworth)

NAYLOR,
Scott B. of Orford m. Jaimie J. **Teller** of Orford 8/28/1999

NEFF,
Leon G. of Concord m. Carlie M. **Bean** of Orford 12/18/1924 in Concord; H – 24, mechanic, b. Nashua, s/o Edward W. Neff (Nashua, RR emp.) and Mary Dennis (Canada, housewife); W – 16, at home, b. Orford, d/o Joseph S. Bean (Sharon, VT, housewife) and Mabel Davis (Masonville, PQ, housewife)

NELSON,
Harry Leslie, Jr. of Malden, MA m. Alice G. **Ricker** of Orford 6/22/1963 in Orford; H – 40, b. W. Fairlee, VT, s/o Harry L. Nelson and Beatrice E. Russ; W – 20, b. Norwich, VT, d/o Ralph Sargent and Ruth Preston

NEWCOMB,
Asahel W. of Orford m. Inez **Woodbury** of Orford 10/10/1901 in Orford; H – 70, farmer, 2nd, widower, b. Orford, s/o Asabel Newcomb (Thetford, VT, farmer) and Laura Taylor (housewife); W – 39, domestic, b. Sheffield, England, d/o Lafayette Woodbury (Sheffield, England) and May King

NICKERSON,
Christopher of Orford m. Amy **Auger** of Orford 3/31/1979

NILES,
George F. of Orford m. Nellie E. **Smith** of Orford 4/3/1894 in Piermont; H – 38, farmer, 2nd, b. Orford, s/o Benjamin F. Niles (Orford, farmer) and Mary S. Newell (Orford, domestic); W – 20, teacher, b. Lyme, d/o Edgar Smith (Lyme, farmer) and Delia Worthen (Lyme, domestic)

NOLET,
Roger J. of Orford m. Rita F. **Lambert** of Lebanon 7/14/1951 in Lebanon; H – 21, lumberman, b. Tarrytown, NY, s/o Leo Paul Nolet (Canada) and Angeline Caouette (Canada); W – 24, nursing, b. Lebanon, d/o Donald Lambert (VT) and Alice Rameor (NH)

NOVICK,
Michael A. of Orford m. Regina **McCarthy** of Orford 8/22/1981

NOYES,
Howard, Jr. m. Laurie **Ellis** 6/7/1986
S. David of Orford m. Cheryl Ann **Stokes** of Orford 8/26/2000 in Orford
Stacy of VT m. Laurie **Fay** of VT 9/22/1990

NUNGESSER,
William Lynn, Jr. of Orford m. Susan Marshall **Taylor** of Hanover 9/24/1971 in Hanover; H – 24, b. Cleveland, OH, s/o William L. Nungesser, Sr. and Catherine E. Simons; W – 23, b. Hartsdale, NY, d/o George A. Taylor and Winifred -----

NUTTER,
Elmer of Orford m. Kimberly **Gray** of Orford 7/25/1992
John of Orford m. Linda **Rich** of Orford 9/25/1982
Kenneth L. of Orford m. Doris E. **Pease** of Orford 11/22/1972 in Orford; H – 53, b. Woodsville, s/o John Nutter and Flora Cassidy; W – 40, b. Feeding Hills, MA, d/o Frederick O. Quackenbush and Grace Hackett
Theodore of Orford m. Donna **Chapin** of Orford 7/17/1982
Theodore Lawrence of Orford m. Sally Ann **Fay** of Fairlee, VT 9/29/1962 in Orford; H – 20, laborer, b. Orford, s/o Kenneth L. Nutter (Woodsville) and Evelyn Johnson (Wells River, VT); W –

18, domestic, b. Lyme, d/o Elmer Fay (Grafton) and Mercy Adams (Fairlee, VT)

Theodore Lawrence of Orford m. Frances Emma **Becker** of Coventry, CT 11/14/1970 in Orford; H – 28, b. Orford, s/o Kenneth L. Nutter and Evelyn Johnson; W – 19, d/o Francis D. Pike and Emma Machia

NYSTROM,

Albert E. of Orford m. Helen F. **Terrill** of White River Jct., VT 2/10/1952 in Orford; H – 30, RR worker, b. Cambridge, MA, s/o Carl E. Nystrom (Sweden) and Lillian E. Swanson (Boston, MA); W – 31, laundry worker, 2nd, b. Norwich, VT, d/o William J. Crowley (Boston, MA) and Claire B. Hill (Wilder, VT)

Alden Edmund of Glencliff m. Karen Lee **Smith** of Orford 7/2/1977 in Orford; H – 20, b. NH, s/o Robert Nystrom, Sr. and Marcella Horton; W – 19, b. NH, d/o Stanley Smith, Sr. and Mary Cummings

O'BRIEN,

John of Thetford Ctr., VT m. Deborah **Tullar** of Orford 6/30/1979

O'KEEFE,

Stephen m. Susan **DeMarle** 12/31/1987

OLSEN,

Peter of Orford m. Shawn **Hamilton** of Orford 3/20/1992

ORDWAY,

Eugene m. Sandra **Smith** 6/29/1985 in Orford

OSMER,

Harry m. Bonnie **Lindquist** 8/15/1987

OSTEN,

Henry Van Dyne of New York, NY m. Lois Ann **Miller** of Miami Beach, FL 8/11/1952 in Orford; H – 26, lawyer, b. Brooklyn, NY, s/o George F. Osten (New York, NY) and Mabel Hendrickson (Brooklyn, NY); W – 23, at home, b. Cincinnati, OH, d/o Peter W. Miller (Cincinnati, OH) and Viola M. McCaffery (Cincinnati, OH)

PAGE,

Freeman G. of Orford m. Addie M. **Austin** of Orford 8/7/1891 in Orford; H – 28, farmer, b. Orford, s/o Thomas J. Page (farmer) and Jane Smith (Orford); W – 31, domestic, 2nd, b. Orford, d/o Charles ----- (carpenter) and ----- (VT)

PAIGE,

Asahel D. of New Salem, MA m. Eva Viola **Hall** of Orford 5/1/1906 in Orford; H – 27, lumber dealer, b. Athol, MA, s/o Alba D. Paige (New Salem, MA, lumber dealer) and Allie Haskell (Athol, MA, housewife); W – 31, clerk, b. Orford, d/o John Hall (Candia, farmer) and Susan Brown (Candia, housewife)

PALIFKA,

Robert George of Windsor, CT m. Lucille D. **Blake** of Orford 5/22/1965 in Orford; H – 22, b. Hartford, CT, s/o George H. Palifka and Helen Hajkowski; W – 21, b. Orford, d/o Everett L. Blake and Flora M. Sanborn

Robert M. of Orford m. Leah M. **Platenik** of Orford 9/29/2002 in Hartford, VT

PARKER,

Charles Andrew m. Freda Iola **Marsh** 7/2/1953 in Orford; H – 30, laborer, b. Newport Ctr., VT, s/o Walter J. Parker (Adj. Cliffs, Canada) and Carrie Kitterage (Newport Ctr., VT); W – 18, at home, b. Wentworth, d/o Ralph E. Marsh (Orford) and Gladys Cutler (Grafton)

Graham m. Penelope **Dobb** 12/31/1985 in Orford

I. Willis of Orford m. Lottie **Lyon** of Brookfield, VT 6/30/1900 in Orford; H – 25, farmer, b. Brookfield, VT, s/o William W. Parker (Brookfield, VT) and Fanny Grant (Brookfield, VT); W – 17, domestic, d/o Charles Lyon (Brookfield, VT) and Charlotte Powell (Brookfield, VT)

Ralph Eugene of Orford m. Ann Lee Shepard **Rutledge** of Orford 6/25/1994

PATCH,

George M. of Orford m. Mary L. **Humiston** of Pawtucket, RI 9/12/1906 in Orford; H – 40, carpenter, b. Orford, s/o Daniel Patch (Orford, farmer) and Lydia D. Phelps (Orford, housewife);

W – 22, mill operative, b. Powers Court, PQ, d/o Eunice Homiston (farmer) and Clara Crowe (housewife)

PATRICK,
Thomas W. of Hinesburg, VT m. Norma E. **Sisters** of Hinesburg, VT 8/30/1937 in Orford; H – 27, clerk, b. Hinesburg, VT, s/o Rufus Patrick (Hinesburg, VT, town clerk) and Josie Reed (Hinesburg, VT, housewife); W – 23, waitress, b. Huntington, VT, d/o Henry Sisters (Williston, VT, farmer) and Grace Shattuck (Huntington, VT, housewife)

PEARCE,
Dale of CA m. Patricia **Allen** of CA 9/25/1982

PEARSON,
David Axel of Orford m. Linda Lois **Chapin** of Orford 7/5/1969 in Orford; H – 21, b. NJ, s/o Axel P. Pearson and Irene E. Lindgren; W – 18, b. NH, d/o Orrin K. Chapin and Marjorie Ackerman

PEASE,
Arthur Samuel of Orford m. Judith Ann **Cummings** of Orford 4/20/1968 in Orford; H – 21, b. NH, s/o Glenn F. Pease and Theda Howard; W – 20, b. NH, d/o Clyde A. Cummings, Sr. and Rose Tallman

Chester W. of Orford m. Stella A. **Merrill** of Wentworth 5/9/1907 in Wentworth; H – 21, farmer, b. Orford, s/o Chase M. Pease (Ellsworth, farmer) and Julia A. Learned (Orford, housewife); W – 17, domestic, b. Rumney, d/o Charles H. Merrill (Newbury, blacksmith) and Amanda Davis (Wentworth, housewife)

Clarence H. of Orford m. Addie A. **Bedell** of Orford 6/28/1916 in Wentworth; H – 26, farmer, b. Orford, s/o Chase M. Pease (Ellsworth, farmer) and Julia A. Learned (Orford, housewife); W – 21, teacher, b. Morrisville, VT, d/o Fred C. Bedell (Morrisville, VT, painter) and Catherine E. Ledeau (Morrisville, VT, housewife)

Francis R. of Wentworth m. Mabel C. **Sherburn** of Orford 2/5/1887 in Piermont; H – 24, laborer, b. Ellsworth, s/o Samuel Peace (Ellsworth, farmer) and Sarah Randall (Ellsworth, domestic); W – 19, domestic, b. Orford, d/o Luther Sherburn (Loudon, farmer) and Charlotte Clifford (Wentworth, domestic)

Gene m. Diane **Ball** 8/29/1987

Gene Alan of Orford m. Bonnie Lee **Guest** of Orford 7/30/1976 in Orford; H – 22, b. NH, s/o Gerald Pease and Doris Quackenbush; W – 20, b. CT, d/o George A. Guest and Marygale Wilson

Gerald E. of Orford m. Rita A. **Carter** of Brentwood 12/16/1972 in Exeter; H – 41, b. Plymouth, s/o Glenn Pease and Theda L. Howard; W – 33, b. Exeter, d/o James L. O'Brien and Valerea Barbert

Gerald Edwin of Orford m. Doris Edith **Quackenbush** of Orford 11/4/1951 in Orford; H – 19, farmer, b. Plymouth, s/o Glenn F. Pease (Orford) and Theda Howard (Wentworth); W – 19, at home, b. Feeding Hills, MA, d/o Fred. Quackenbush (Northampton, MA) and Grace E. Hackett (Woonsocket, RI)

Glenn F. of Orford m. Theda L. **Howard** of Wentworth 9/30/1928 in Canterbury; H – 22, farmer, b. Orford, s/o Francis R. Pease (Ellsworth, farmer) and Mabel Sherburn (Orford, housekeeper); W – 22, domestic, b. Wentworth, d/o George Howard (Lancaster, farmer) and Flora Lowd (Plymouth, housewife)

Harrison of Lewisville, TX m. Kimberly **Austin** of Lewisville, TX 3/17/1999

Howard Glenn of Orford m. Barbara Mae **Robie** of Plymouth 9/6/1951 in Plymouth; H – 22, soldier, b. Plymouth, s/o Glenn F. Pease (Orford) and Theda Howard (Wentworth); W – 19, student, b. Cabot, VT, d/o Ernest S. Robie (Bristol) and Alice M. Matthews (Groton)

PELLETIER,

Thomas Louis of New London, CT m. Verna Jane **Smith** of Orford 9/15/1951 in New London, CT; H – 19, mason appr., b. New London, CT, s/o Louis Pelletier and Louise A. Enos; W – 19, at home, b. Wheelock, VT, d/o Thomas H. Smith and Etta B. Judd

PERKINS,

Ralph E. of Orford m. Maude **Barnett** of Walden, VT 11/4/1911 in Orford; H – 22, farmer, b. Hardwick, VT, s/o Edgar E. Perkins (Walden, VT, farmer) and Bertha Stone (Hardwick, VT, housewife); W – 18, domestic, b. Walden, VT, d/o Arch. Barnett (farmer) and Vina Morey (housewife)

PERO,
Elwin N. of Thetford, VT m. Alberta L. **Preston** of Orford 9/17/1946 in Thetford, VT; H – laborer, b. Thetford, VT, s/o Harry C. Pero (Norwich, VT) and Edith Godfrey (W. Fairlee, VT); W – housework, b. W. Fairlee, VT, d/o William H. Preston (Pawtucket, RI) and Mabel P. French (Thetford, VT)

PERRY,
Anthony Wayne of Orford m. Carol Ann **Chesley** of Lyme Ctr. 6/16/1963 in Glencliff; H – 19, b. Woodsville, s/o Leighton A. Perry and Lucille M. Gilbert; W – 17, b. Manchester, d/o Herman T. Chesley and Virginia Bowen

David William of Orford m. Kathryn Lee **Grimes** of Lyme 2/19/1977 in Lyme; H – 21, b. NH, s/o Walter Perry and Beatrice Fillian; W – 18, b. NH, d/o William E. Green III and Donna Lee Morris

Leighton A. of Orford m. Lucille V. **Gilbert** of Orford 8/21/1942 in Orford; H – 20, laborer, b. Haverhill, s/o Charles A. Perry (Whitefield, minister) and Inez Lindsey (Benton, housewife); W – 14, at home, b. Orford, d/o Harry Gilbert (Lyme, laborer) and Flora Cassidy (Canada, housewife)

Walter H. of Orford m. Beatrice B. **Fillian** of Orford 11/12/1942 in White River Jct., VT; H – 28, logging, b. Saranac, NY, s/o Charlie Perry (Saranac, NY) and Priscilla Facto (Saranac, NY); W – 19, housewife, b. Wentworth, d/o Alphonse Fillian (Manchester, farmer) and Jessie Woods (Orford, housewife)

PETERSEN,
Andrew of Orford m. Sharon **Downing** of Fairlee 6/18/1982

PHELAN,
Jack m. Marianne **Newman** 10/10/1988

PHILBRICK,
Alvin S. of Orford m. Emma J. **Moulton** of Orford 11/26/1919 in Manchester; H – 69, ret. farmer, 3rd, widower, b. Wentworth, s/o Samuel Philbrick (Sanbornton, farmer) and Mary S. Roberts (Sanbornton, housewife); W – 48, nurse, b. Thetford, VT, d/o Anson Moulton (Ellsworth, farmer) and Emeline Randall (Ellsworth, housewife)

Timothy J. of Orford m. Brenda J. **Rockwell** of Orford 8/1/1981

PHILLIPS,
Daniel of MI m. Bessie **Fagan** of MI 10/27/1980

PIACENTINI,
Robert George, Jr. of Haddam, CT m. Karen Elizabeth **Mack** of Haddam, CT 5/29/2004 in Orford

PICKNELL,
Forrest Otto m. Roseanna Diane **Coburn** --/--/1989

PIERCE,
Charles Rexford of Orford m. Sharon Jane **Brooks** of Orford 7/22/2000 in Orford
Chester A. of Orford m. Dorothy May **Pike** of Orford 4/13/1942 in Haverhill; H – 29, chauffeur, b. Pike, s/o Arthur R. Pierce (Pike, fireman) and May D. Patridge (Littleton, housewife); W – 26, domestic, b. Lyme, d/o Lon Charles Pike (Lyme, farmer) and Lucie E. Jewell (Baldin Mills, Canada, housewife)

PIERSON,
Amos F. of Orford m. Bernice N. **Emery** of Orford 4/18/1937 in Orford; H – 22, farmer, b. Topsham, VT, s/o Ernest Pierson (Topsham, VT, farmer) and Nettie E. Wright (Topsham, VT, housewife); W – 21, domestic, b. Piermont, d/o Fay S. Emery (Piermont, farmer) and Gladys Chesley (Lyme, housewife)
Edward Wallace of Orford m. Shirley Jean **Jones** of Orford 8/20/1965 in Orford; H – 18, b. Hanover, s/o Wallace H. Pierson and Evelyn N. Weeks; W – 17, b. Morrisville, VT, d/o Gordon Jones and Lucy E. Grimes
Richard Allen of Orford m. Lucinda Lee **Pushee** of Orford 9/24/1977 in Orford; H – 23, b. NH, s/o Wallace Henry Pierson and Evelyn Weeks; W – 18, b. NH, d/o Frank Albert Pushee and Marcia Lee Bedoe
Wallace H. of Orford m. Evelyn N. **Weeks** of Orford 4/5/1944 in Piermont; H – 35, US Army, b. Topsham, VT, s/o Ernest Pierson (Topsham, VT, farmer) and Nettie A. Wright (Topsham, VT); W – 22, at home, b. Fairlee, VT, d/o Alvin B. Weeks (Deerfield, merchant) and Florence Hardy (Manchester, housewife)
William L. of Orford m. Dorothy F. **Baker** of Orford 6/17/1938 in Piermont; H – 25, farmer, b. Topsham, VT, s/o Ernest Pierson

(Topsham, VT, farmer) and Nettie Wright (Topsham, VT, deceased); W – 20, domestic, b. Orford, d/o George H. Baker (Orford, farmer) and Alice M. Franklin (Orford, housewife)

PIKE,
Allie Chester of Lyme m. Marjorie M. **Heath** of Orford 11/29/1941 in Orford; H – 18, farmer, b. Lyme, s/o Earl H. Pike (Lyme, farmer) and Myrtie Coates (NB, housewife); W – 16, domestic, b. Littleton, d/o Max Heath (Littleton, laborer) and Irene Elliott (Littleton, housewife)
Horace E. of Lyme Ctr. m. Maxine **Pike** of Orford 10/16/1946 in Orford; H – 25, lumberman, 2nd, b. Lyme, s/o Earl H. Pike (Lyme Ctr., farmer) and Myrtle Costes (NB, housewife); W – 20, housewife, 2nd, b. Littleton, d/o Max B. Heath (painter) and Irene Elliott (Littleton, housewife)
Horace Earle of Orford m. Maxine L. **Heath** of Orford 11/2/1942 in Orford; H – 22, laborer, b. Lyme, s/o Earl Henry Pike (farmer) and Myrtle Coach (Canada, housewife); W – 16, at home, b. Littleton, d/o Max Heath (Lisbon, laborer) and Irene Elliott (Littleton, housewife)
Weymouth H., Jr. of Orford m. Susan M. **Taylor** of Orford 11/6/1972 in Fairlee, VT; H – 20, b. Hanover, s/o Weymouth H. Pike, Sr. and Helen Marsh; W – 20, b. Barnet, VT, d/o Elmer Taylor and Phyllis Roystan
Weymouth Henry of Orford m. Helen Mae **Marsh** of Orford 9/23/1950 in Lyme; H – 22, laborer, b. Lyme Ctr., s/o Earl H. Pike (Lyme Ctr.) and Myrtle H. Coates (Canada); W – 17, at home, b. Wentworth, d/o Ralph E. Marsh (Orford) and Gladys A. Cutler (Grafton)

PIPER,
James Mason of Lyme m. Tammy Jean **Estes** of Orford 7/16/1994
Scott m. Lisa **Farnham** 6/25/1988

PIZZICA,
Frank Joseph, Jr. of Nanuet, NY m. Linda Jane **Garrettson** of New York, NY 8/30/1969 in Orford; H – 23, b. NY, s/o Frank Pizzica, Sr. and Marie Colantuoni; W – 22, b. PA, d/o Charles Garrettson and Bettie Benner

PLANTE,
Albert of Orford m. Gertrude **Prescott** of Orford 12/30/1990

PLUMLEY,
George of Orford m. Minnie L. **Simonds** of Orford 10/25/1919 in Orford; H – 52, laborer, b. Saugerties, NY, s/o John Plumley (Saugerties, NY, laborer) and Phoebe Reynolds (Woodstock, NY, housewife); W – 50, housekeeper, 2nd, widow, b. Troy, NY, d/o Melvin Law (Troy, NY, laborer) and Christina Ryne (Lanesville, NY, housewife)

POCOCK,
Erle V. of Meredith m. Lucille N. **Holloway** of Orford 10/1/1972 in Meredith; H – 65, b. Canada, s/o George R. Pocock and Ethel Corliss; W – 63, b. NH, d/o Charles C. Bailey and Etta Philbrick

POTRY,
Arthur of Orford m. Beverly **Andrews** of Orford 9/7/1964 in Bradford, VT; H – 25, b. Nashua, s/o Alfred Potry and Yvonne Vallee; W – 22, b. Lebanon, d/o Clarence H. Andrews, Jr. and Thelma Ryra

PRESSON,
Joseph Anthony of New York City m. Nancy Jo **Bagnall** of New York City 9/4/1976 in Orford; H – 26, b. FL, s/o Hermon Winifred Presson and Ruby Adieliea; W – 22, b. CA, d/o Joseph Albert Bagnall and Phyllis Luck

PURDY,
George M. of Orford m. Lillian **DeLong** of Orford 7/29/1939 in Orford; H – 76, blacksmith, 2nd, b. Glenn's Falls, NY, s/o George Purdy (blacksmith) and Sarah Barber (housewife); W – 62, housework, 2nd, divorced, b. Troy, NY, d/o Warren A. DeLong (Saratoga Springs, NY, engineer) and Mary E. Lenger (Gloversville, NY, housewife)

PUSHEE,
Clarence Lee, Jr. m. Hazel Beth **Davis** 7/17/1955 in Orford; H – 17, painter, b. Orford, s/o Clarence L. Pushee (Lyme) and Evelyn T. Tattersall (Lyme); W – 16, at home, b. Lyme Ctr., d/o Gerald W. Davis (Groton) and Hattie K. Davis (Beebe Jct., Canada)

David of Orford m. Michelle **Smith** of Orford 7/31/1982
Donald m. Jane **Slayton** 7/5/1986
Donald Elmer of Orford m. Loretta Jean **Weeks** of Orford 10/2/1976 in Orford; H – 21, b. NH, s/o Donald E. Pushee and Mabel Claudia O'Donnell; W – 19, b. NH, d/o Wayne A. Weeks and Louella J. Godville
Paul Ralph of Orford m. Louella B. **Whiting** of Concord 2/10/1968 in Penacook; H – 23, b. NH, s/o Olyph D. Pushee and Doris Johnson; W – 16, b. NH, d/o George L. Whiting and Georgiette Place
William of Orford m. Kimberly **Dyke** of Orford 4/26/1982

QUACKENBUSH,
Gary F. of Orford m. Lori **Brown** of Orford 4/15/1978 in Hanover; H – b. NH, s/o William Quackenbush and June Bryer; W – b. NH, d/o Richard Brown and Ruth Ladd
Lyle m. Karen **Gladstone** 11/21/1987
Robert H. of Orford m. Elaine Ruth **Bryer** of Orford 10/30/1951 in Orford; H – 26, carpenter, b. Springfield, MA, s/o Fred. Quackenbush (Northampton, MA) and Grace E. Hackett (Woonsocket, RI); W – 21, at home, b. Fairlee, VT, d/o Allen J. Bryer (W. Burke, VT) and Ruth A. Cummings (Fairlee, VT)
William of Orford m. June **Bryer**of Orford 11/3/1950 in White River Jct., VT; H – 29, carpenter, 2nd, b. Springfield, MA, s/o F. C. Quackenbush (Northampton, MA) and Grace E. Hackett (Woonsocket, RI); W – 19, at home, b. Fairlee, VT, d/o Allen J. Bryer (VT) and Ruth Cummings (Fairlee, VT)

QUIMBY,
Clyde of Thetford, VT m. Carrie **Hill** of Thetford, VT 5/11/1908 in Orford; H – 24, painter, b. Dorchester, s/o John Quimby (Manchester, brick mason) and Frances Kenniston (Thetford, VT, housewife); W – 20, teacher, b. Chateaugay, NY, d/o Enoch Hill (Chateaugay, NY, carpenter) and Mina Young (Burke, NY, housewife)

RADFORD,
Ernest W. of Orford m. Mary E. **Rhodes** of Orford 6/1/1916 in Orford; H – 44, farmer, b. Wentworth, s/o James Radford (England, butcher) and Cynthia Eames (Wentworth, housewife); W – 26, domestic, b. Orford, d/o Wilbur Rhodes

(Waits River, VT, farmer) and Emma Simpson (Orford, housewife)

RANDALL,
Alfred of Orford m. Benita **Burnell** of Orford 8/9/1991

RATHBURN,
Daniel David of Orford m. Sylvia Carol **Picknell** of Orford 12/6/1968 in Orford; H – 22, b. VT, s/o Delbert Rathburn and Evelyn Mary Cilley; W – 24, b. NH, d/o Caroll Picknell and Katherine Johnson

RAY,
Rowell Randolph of Warren m. Marjorie Ruth **Davis** of Orford 7/23/1960 in Orford; H – 18, student, b. Laconia, s/o Floyd R. Ray (Dorchester, MA) and Doris Rowell (Meredith); W – 19, clerical wk., b. Lyme, d/o Gerald W. Davis (Groton) and Hattie K. Davis (Beebe Jct., Canada)

RECORD,
Leonard W. of W. Rumney m. Lurline E. **Dyke** of Orford 7/5/1932 in Rumney; H – 24, laborer, b. Bucksport, ME, s/o William H. Record (NB, farmer) and Mary T. Sullivan (NB, housewife); W – 18, at home, b. Norwich, VT, d/o Benjamin F. Dyke (Pompanoosuc, VT, lumberman) and Ethel L. Jesseman (housewife)

REED,
Allen Gregory of Orford m. Shirley Yvonne **Perkins** of Lyme 2/24/1967 in Lyme; H – 19, b. Hanover, s/o Donald R. Reed and Edna E. Gregory; W – 19, b. Lebanon, d/o Harry W. Perkins and Martha E. Hardy

Donald R. of Orford m. Edna Eva **Gregory** of Lyme 8/16/1946 in Piermont; H – 31, farmer, b. Stamford, CT, s/o Clarence C. Reed (Mt. Kisco, NY, farmer) and Elizabeth E. Allen (New York City, NY, housewife); W – 24, nurse, b. Hanover, d/o Frank T. Gregory (Grantham, farmer) and Sadie Porter (Canada, housewife)

Jesse Jonathan of Plymouth m. Kathryn Inez **Chase** of Orford 8/16/2003 in Wentworth

REICHERT,
Eric O. of Hanover m. O. Teresa **Valencia** of Hanover 6/30/1998

RENNIE,
James Edward of Hanover m. Ann Elizabeth **Borger** of Orford
10/27/1962 in Wentworth; H – 19, carpenter, b. Newark, NJ, s/o
Edward John Rennie (NH) and Edna M. Mase (NY); W – 20, at
home, b. NY, d/o Francis Borger (NY) and Elizabeth J. Winkel
(Jamaica, LI)

RHODES,
George W. of Orford m. Mabel E. **Chapman** of Orford 4/23/1916 in
Lyme; H – 31, farmer, b. Orford, s/o Wilbur Rhodes (Waits
River, VT, farmer) and Emma Simpson (Orford, housewife); W
– 36, nurse, 2nd, divorced, b. Orford, d/o Perley A. Chapman
(Tewksbury, MA, laborer) and Mary E. Willis (Warren,
housewife)

RICH,
Michael of Hanover m. Sheena **Giesing** of Orford 8/17/1991

RICHARDSON,
Arthur J. of Orford m. Hattie C. **Gardner** of Orford 4/3/1889 in
Orford; H – 25, farmer, b. Orford, s/o John Richardson (Lisbon,
farmer) and Clara P. Johnson (Bradford, VT); W – 21,
domestic, b. Lyme, d/o James R. Gardner (Lyme, farmer) and
Emeline Breck (Lyme)

RICHMOND,
Philip L. of Newport m. Chestina M. **Learned** of Orford 10/25/1924 in
Claremont; H – 26, shoemaker, b. Dorchester, MA, s/o Rog. S.
Richmond (Assonet, MA, engineer) and Emma J. Young (NH,
nurse); W – 21, nurse, b. Orford, d/o William E. Learned
(Wentworth, farmer) and Ida Bailey (Wakefield, MA, housewife)
Robert Gould m. Helen Sperry **Cothran** 6/22/1957 in Orford; H – 22,
student, b. Waltham, MA, s/o Gould S. Richmond (Byron, ME)
and Hilda Mae Lynch (Perotte, NS); W – 21, student, b.
Philippines, d/o Wade R. Cothran (Greenwood, SC) and Helen
Arinda Leas (Oakland, CA)

RICKER,
Keith Reginald of Orford m. Susan Lucille **Whitehill** of Lyme 9/25/1970 in Orford; H – 20, b. Hanover, s/o Lawrence R. Ricker and Beverly Record; W – 20, d/o Alton L. Whitehill and Pearl Sayers
Kevin of Orford m. Kelly **Barber** of Orford 5/18/1980
Kevin m. Suzanne **Bouley** 9/5/1987

RIGG,
Sidney J. of Chelsea, VT m. Viola M. **Leonard** of Chelsea, VT 12/6/1928 in Orford; H – 25, granite cutter, 2nd, widower, b. Chamberlain, SD, s/o Charles E. Rigg (Western Spring, IL, farmer) and Caroline Jewell (Lawrence, MA, housewife); W – 24, domestic, 2nd, divorced, b. Winooski, VT, d/o Henry Shortsleve (Keyesville, NY, farmer) and Daisy LaBrake (Keyesville, NY, housewife)

RIPPE,
Daniel F. of Orford m. Marie-Douce M. **Sorion** of Orford 3/1/2004 in Orford

ROBERTS,
Cyrus L. of Orford m. Annabell **Beaton** of Florence, NS 11/30/1916 in Canaan; H – 26, clerk, b. Orford, s/o Leomarch Roberts (Orford, farmer) and Emily Magoon (Washington, VT, housewife); W – 19, table girl, b. Sidney Mines, NS, d/o Philip Beaton (Florence, NS, engineer) and Jessie Patterson (Florence, NS, housewife)
Maurice A. of Manchester m. Ina C. **Richardson** of Orford 11/20/1924 in Hanover; H – 20, truck driver, b. Waterloo, Canada, s/o Medice Robert (Canada, carpenter) and Delia Grew (Canada, housewife); W – 26, domestic, b. Orford, d/o Arthur J. Richardson (Orford, teaming) and Hattie Gardner (Lyme, housewife)
Maurice A., Jr. of Orford m. Volisa Mae **Jewett** of Fairlee, VT 3/9/1951 in Lyndon, VT; H – 21, cook, b. Orford, s/o Maurice A. Roberts (S. Stukely, PQ) and Clementine Richardson (Orford); W – 19, tel. operator, b. Hanover, d/o Vernon W. Jewett (Wilder, VT) and Mildred Higgins (Mt. Vernon, MA)
Philip John of Orford m. Virginia Low **Thorndike** of Orford 12/31/1977 in Orford; H – 32, b. NH, s/o Philip John Roberts,

Sr. and Dorothy Drake; W – 32, b. MA, d/o Albert Thorndike and Jeanie Paine

Thomas W. of Bradford, VT m. Ella M. **Patch** of Orford 11/18/1893 in Orford; H – 36, farmer, 2nd, widower, b. Dorchester, s/o Thomas F. Roberts (Raymond, farmer) and Caroline Smith (Wentworth, domestic); W – 36, domestic, 2nd, widow, b. Orford, d/o Peter White (Canada, laborer) and Rebecca Pierce (Barnet, VT, domestic)

ROBIE,
Scott E. of Orford m. Carol L. **Colby** of Bradford, VT 6/22/1974 in Bradford, VT; H – 19, b. Lebanon, s/o Keith M. Robie and Verna Tucker; W – 19, b. Waterbury, CT, d/o John E. Colby, Sr. and Carolyn Benjamin

ROBINSHAW,
Robert Frederick m. Shirley Etta **Nutter** 2/4/1955 in Orford; H – 17, US Marines, b. New London, CT, s/o Robert Robinshaw and Minnie Pearl; W – 15, at home, b. Bradford, VT, d/o Kenneth L. Nutter (Woodsville) and Evelyn R. Johnson (Wells River, VT)

ROBINSON,
Dana of Orford m. Susan **Jarvis** of Orford 5/14/1983

George A. of Lebanon m. Ruth Mary **Sargent** of Lebanon 5/28/1966 in Orford; H – 53, b. N. Thetford, VT, s/o Arthur J. Robinson and Abbie Winnim; W – 43, b. Enfield, d/o William H. Preston and Mabel French

Robert Allen of Norwich, VT m. Donna Lee **Green** of Orford 1/1/1971 in Orford; H – 30, b. Windsor, VT, s/o Elmer W. Robinson and Rosaline Peoples; W – 35, b. Massillon, OH, d/o Samuel T. Morris and Helen Kaylor

Samuel A. of Bangor, ME m. Mildred M. **Cook** of Natick, MA 9/1/1948 in Orford; H – 25, student, b. Bangor, ME, s/o H. L. Robinson (Bangor, ME, doctor) and Lida B. Shofield (MA, housewife); W – 30, nurse, 2nd, divorced, b. Natick, MA, d/o Richard E. Doyle (Natick, MA, supervisor) and Helen Collins (Natick, MA, housewife)

ROGERS,
Benjamin Andrew of Orford m. Emily Elizabeth **Dodge** of Orford 8/21/2004 in Cornish

Lloyd Byron of W. Newbury m. Mila May **Egley** of Washington, VT
8/25/1923 in Orford; H – 21, farming, b. Newbury, VT, s/o Byron
Rogers (Newbury, VT, farmer) and Ella Williams (Corinth, VT,
housewife); W – 18, domestic, b. Chicago, IL, d/o John H.
Egley (Crescent City, IL, merchant) and Alma St. John
(Hartford, CT, housewife)

ROLLINS,
Hiram B. of Orford m. Addie A. **Hammond** of Bradford, VT
5/15/1893 in Piermont; H – 29, farmer, b. Rumney, s/o Moses
J. Rollins (Campton, carpenter) and Ester M. Brown (Rumney,
domestic); W – 20, domestic, b. Wentworth, d/o Byron
Hammond (Wentworth, laborer) and Lecta M. Smith (domestic)

ROSS,
William, Jr. of Fairlee, VT m. Dorisann **Dyke** of Orford 4/14/1979

ROWELL,
Francis Everett m. Lois Louise **McKee** 5/18/1954 in Vershire, VT; H
– 18, miner, b. Montpelier, VT, s/o Francis Charles Rowell
(Lyme) and Eleanor M. Dickinson (Vershire, VT); W – 16,
student, b. Orford, d/o Kenneth W. McKee (Dorchester) and
Frances E. Foote (Orford)

RUSH,
Herbert of Orford m. Mary L. **Willey** of Hanover 11/26/1923 in
Orford; H – 38, laborer, b. Orford, s/o John Rush; W – 22,
domestic, 2nd, b. Lemster, d/o Francis LaMay (laborer) and Ida
Bishop (Canada, housewife)

RUTLEDGE,
Hibbert T. of Orford m. C. Jennie **Wilson** of Greensboro, VT
2/24/1892 in Greensboro, VT; H – 28, farmer, b. NS, s/o
Thomas Rutledge (Stanley, NS, farmer) and Mary J. Stiles; W –
24, teacher, b. Greensboro, VT, d/o William Wilson (Scotland,
farmer)

SALMONS,
Larry, Jr. of Orford m. Kimberly M. **Ouimet** of Orford 12/7/1996

SANBORN,
Bernard Malcolm of Orford m. Bernice Louise **Williams** of Orford 3/18/1949 in Wentworth; H – 24, farmer, b. Orford, s/o Harry J. Sanborn (Rumney) and Lula Blake (Plymouth); W – 27, tel. operator, 2nd, b. Orford, d/o George H. Finney (Orford) and Doris Chamberlain (Orford)

David Moore of Orford m. Janice May **Hosmer** of Grantham 6/26/1965 in Grantham; H – 27, b. Orford, s/o Robert B. Sanborn, Sr. and Evelyn R. Blake; W – 17, b. Strafford, VT, d/o Ralph E. Hosmer and Mable M. Nelson

Ernest F. of Orford m. Beatrice L. **Hall** of Orford 9/24/1945 in Wentworth; H – 47, machinist, 2nd, widower, b. Norwich, VT, s/o Fred J. Sanborn (Bradford, VT, veterinary) and Carrie Bacon (Arlington, MA, housewife); W – 38, shoe worker, 2nd, divorced, b. Nashua, s/o Eugene Dugre (LaPoint du Lac, Canada, deceased) and Georgiana Houle (Canada, deceased)

Fred J. of Orford m. Carrie L. **Pike** of Lyme 11/22/1938 in Haverhill; H – 58, veterinary, 2nd, divorced, b. Bradford, VT, s/o Charles A. Sanborn (Rumney, farmer) and Abbie Chase (Bradford, VT, housewife); W – 41, domestic, b. Lyme, d/o Fred L. Pike (Lyme, laborer) and Anna B. Roberts (Lyme, housewife)

John of Orford m. Anna **Rowell** of Bradford, VT 11/23/1941 in Bradford, VT; H – 20, laborer, b. Hanover, s/o Fred J. Sanborn (Bradford, VT, veterinary) and Carrie Bacon (Arlington, MA, housewife); W – 20, waitress, b. Corinth, VT, d/o Fred Richardson (Corinth, VT) and Nellie M. Beede (Corinth, VT)

Joseph H. of Orford m. Ruth E. **Franklin** of Orford 6/6/1928 in Orford; H – 21, laborer, b. Plymouth, s/o Harry J. Sanborn (Plymouth, farmer) and Lula Blake (Plymouth, housewife); W – 18, domestic, b. Orford, d/o Arthur L. Franklin (Orford, farmer) and Marian Clark (Orford, nurse)

Joseph H. of Orford m. Helen E. **Baker** of Orford 10/31/1935 in Orford; H – 29, farmer, 2nd, b. Plymouth, s/o Harry J. Sanborn (Rumney, farmer) and Lulu Blake (Plymouth, housewife); W – 19, at home, b. Orford, d/o George H. Baker (Orford, farmer) and Alice Franklin (Orford, housewife)

Neil Heath m. Theresa May **Hudson** 10/22/1953 in Orford; H – 16, student, b. Orford, s/o Joseph H. Sanborn (Plymouth) and Helen E. Baker (Hanover); W – 15, student, b. Lowell, MA, d/o Furman W. Hudson (Yarmouth, NS) and Lillian Mangerson (N. Reading, MA)

Richard H. of Hanover m. Carolyn C. **Chapin** of Orford 6/21/1947 in Lyme; H – 19, laborer, b. Lebanon, s/o Otis Miller Sanborn (Dummer, janitor) and Grace E. Perkins (Gorham, housewife); W – 18, stenographer, b. Hanover, d/o Orrin S. Chapin (Claremont, MA, laborer) and Alice H. DeGoosh (Hartland, VT, housewife)

Robert Bayard, Jr. of Orford m. Sarah Naomi **Hart** of Lyme Ctr. 6/15/1961 in Lyme Ctr.; H – 28, electronic tech., b. Orford, s/o Robert B. Sanborn, Sr. (Bath) and Evelyn Blake (Plymouth); W – 22, nurse, b. Lebanon, d/o Earl William Hart (Hanover) and Dorothy Knickerbocker (Marion, MI)

Stephen Arthur of Orford m. Kimberly Tatro **Thurston** of Orford 9/18/1999

William G. of Bradford, VT m. Helen E. **Smith** of Bradford, VT 10/15/1932 in Orford; H – 21, farmer, b. Bradford, VT, s/o Fred Sanborn (Bradford, VT, farmer) and Lilla Demar (Franklin, housewife); W – 22, at home, b. Quechee, VT, d/o Lewis W. Smith (Orford, farmer) and Eva A. Archer (Orford, housewife)

SANDERS,

Frank E. of Orford m. H. H. **Hammond** of Stannard, VT 6/20/1894 in Meredith; H – 21, laborer, b. Orford, s/o Sylvester J. Saunders (Wentworth, farmer) and Nancy S. Eastman (Danbury, domestic); W – 19, domestic, b. W. Boylston, d/o Calvin Hammond (Canada, farmer) and Harriet Seymour (VT, domestic)

Harry G. of Orford m. Nettie L. **Mack** of Orford 4/7/1896 in Plymouth; H – 29, farmer, b. Orford, s/o Sylvester J. Sanders (Wentworth, farmer) and Nancy S. Eastman (Danbury, housewife); W – 15, domestic, b. Piermont, d/o Ruel F. Mack (Haverhill) and Elizabeth Holmes (Haverhill)

SANDERSON,

Robert Currier of Orford m. Susan Ann **Lauzetta** of Orford 5/3/1975 in Hanover; H – 29, b. Hanover, s/o Harold Sanderson and Jeanne Currier; W – 25, b. Brooklyn, NY, d/o John Lauzetta and Jane Warner

SARGENT,

Norman P. of Orford m. Grace J. **Kathan** of Walpole 6/16/1935 in Walpole; H – 23, teacher, b. Sunapee, s/o Willis H. Sargent

(Bradford) and Mattie B. Palmer (Warner, housekeeper); W – 20, teacher, b. Westmoreland, d/o Clark A. Kathan (Chester, VR, section man) and Emma L. Felch (Walpole, housewife)

SAWYER,
Albert H. of Beverly, MA m. Grace C. **Snow** of Orford 8/31/1908 in Orford; H – 25, machinist, b. Manchester, s/o Albert F. Sawyer (Alstead, carpenter) and Alice J. Putnam (Hooksett, housewife); W – 22, teacher, b. Orford, d/o Herbert W. Snow (Malone, NY, farmer) and Abbie S. Griffin (Marlow, housewife)
Amos B. of Bradford, VT m. Menta M. **Woodward** of Orford 5/22/1920 in Orford; H – 24, office clerk, b. Bradford, VT, s/o Amos B. Sawyer (Fairlee, VT, farmer) and Nancy Avery (Topsham, VT, dressmaker); W – 25, clerk, b. Lyme, d/o Herbert Woodward (Montgomery, VT, farmer) and Jennie Coburn (E. Burkshire, VT, housewife)

SCHARZENBERGER,
Joseph of St. Veit, Austria m. Caitlin **Watson** of Orford 10/31/1991

SCHAUER,
Paul Scott of Westerly, RI m. Denise **Alexander** of Orford 8/29/1969 in Hanover; H – 20, b. NH, s/o Laverne Schauer and Lillian Margeson; W – 19, b. WA, d/o Rod Alexander and Marilyn Maxey

SCHILLABER,
Charles Russell m. Lynn **McCann** 8/5/1956 in Orford; H – 26, student, b. Newport, MA, s/o John James Schillaber (Portsmouth) and Eleanor Smith (Tilton); W – 22, dietitian, b. New York, NY, d/o Fred F. McCann (ME) and Elita Virginia Allen (ME)

SCHORSCH,
Michael of Orford m. Elaine **Himadi** of Orford 8/28/1982

SCHROEDER,
Thomas Edward of Arcade, NY m. Hilary **Kligerman** of Orford 8/26/1968 in Hanover; H – 21, b. IN, s/o Louis Schroeder and Dorothy Roberts; W – 21, b. OH, d/o Merton M. Kligerman and Louise Minster

SCHWARZ,
Clinton of Orford m. Robin **Sawyer** of Orford 5/16/1992
George J. of Orford m. Juanita Ann **Marsh** of Orford 7/11/1959
Randy A. of Orford m. Adrienne S. **Albaugh** of Orford 1/9/1999
Randy Allen of Orford m. Prudence Louise **Bechard** of Orford 9/4/2004 in Orford
Robert of Orford m. Rosenna **Milner** of Orford 3/17/1979

SEACE,
James Chester of Hanover m. Pauline Sandra **Bean** of Orford 9/9/1963 in Wentworth; H – 24, b. Hanover, s/o Arthur F. Seace and Esther M. Pressy; W – 18, b. Hanover, d/o Philip L. Bean and Ida M. Prebor

SEMEN,
Peter Michael of E. Thetford, VT m. Jessica Leah **Cook** of E. Thetford, VT 10/23/2004 in Sugar Hill

SERGENT,
Ralph David of Orford m. Penny Lee **Noyes** of Orford 5/16/1993

SEWELL,
Micah Alexander of Raleigh, NC m. Bethany Laurel **Berwick** of Orford 5/22/2004 in Bradford, VT

SHAFER,
Bartron B., Jr. of Orford m. Esther V. **Applebee** of Haverhill 9/7/1963 in Orford; H – 22, b. Derry, s/o Bartron B. Shafer and Ida M. Prebor; W – 18, b. Woodsville, d/o Willis A. Applebee and Esther Watson

SHEARER,
Richard A. of Bradford, VT m. Juanita M. **Fuller** of Bradford, VT 5/25/1929 in Orford; H – 21, laborer, b. Boiling Springs, PA, s/o J. S. Shearer (Steelton, PA, florist) and Frances Steel (E. Corinth, VT, housewife); W – 18, assistant town clerk, b. Riverside, d/o Frank Fuller (S. Canaan, VT, machinist) and Lou Wright (Clarksburg, housewife)

SHELLEY,
Sidney C. of Haverhill m. Flora E. **Archer** of Orford 4/7/1895 in Haverhill; H – 21, farmer, b. Haverhill, s/o John C. Shelley (Haverhill, lawyer); W – 20, domestic, b. Orford, d/o Henry Stevens (Wentworth, farmer)

SHEPARD,
Ray of Orford m. Lorraine **Peck** of Bradford, VT 8/14/1948 in Newbury, VT; H – 21, farmer, b. Hanover, s/o Frank Shepard (Moria, NY, farmer) and Rose Bombard (Malone, NY, housewife); W – 18, b. Woodsville, d/o Merton Peck (Peacham, VT) and Alice Lund (Groton, VT)
Robinson of Havana, Cuba m. Myra E. **Foster** of Orford 3/30/1931 in Orford; H – 34, teacher, b. Bangor, ME, s/o John S. Shepard (Canaan, merchant) and Alice M. Robinson (Bangor, ME, housewife); W – 24, at home, b. Wentworth, d/o Walter N. Foster (Wentworth, farmer) and Leona C. Nichols (Orford, housewife)
Russell of Orford m. Kathleen Ethel **Shepard** of Fairlee, VT 5/28/1949 in Lyme; H – 37, laborer, 3rd, b. Brushton, NY, s/o Frank F. Shepard (Bombay, NY) and Rose Bombard (Brushton, NY); W – 33, housework, 3rd, b. Hanover, d/o Wilber George (Hanover) and Ethel Sanborn (Brattleboro, VT)
Russell F. of Orford m. Kathleen E. **George** of Fairlee, VT 6/25/1932 in Lebanon; H – 21, laborer, b. Brushton, NY, s/o Frank Shepard (Brushton, NY, farmer) and Rose Bombard (Bangor, NY, housewife); W – 18, at home, b. Norwich, VT, d/o Bert George (carpenter)

SHERRY,
Nicholas of Summit, NJ m. Margaret A. **Smith** of Orford 7/19/1916 in Orford; H – 22, machinist, b. Summit, NJ, s/o Timothy J. Sherry (VA, grocer) and Annie Mooney (VA, housewife); W – 20, domestic, b. Orford, d/o Clarence S. Smith (Lyme, farmer) and Sarah Archer (Orford, housewife)

SHONIO,
Gardner Warren of Orford m. Claribel Selena **Dunakin** of Hartford, CT 7/5/1951 in Lyme; H – 36, laundry worker, 2nd, b. Duxbury, VT, s/o Jesse Drury Shonio (Duxbury, VT) and Lillian A. Warren (Moretown, VT); W – 38, housework, 3rd, b. Hartford, CT, d/o

Wilbur E. Partridge (Wallingford, CT) and Grace Snow (Meriden, CT)

SIBOLE,
Gary Richard of Marlboro, MA m. Brenda Maureen **Casey** of Marlboro, MA 8/5/1995

SIEMONS,
Gary R. of Orford m. Raquel J. **Welch** of Orford 5/18/1996

SIMONDS,
C. G. of Orford m. Eva M. **Hatch** of W. Fairlee, VT 6/15/1892 in Corinth, VT; H – 23, farmer, b. Orford, s/o Royal W. Simons (Orford, farmer) and Lucina Eggleston (E. Burke, VT); W – 21, domestic, b. W. Fairlee, VT, d/o M. V. B. Hatch (Hardwick, VT, farmer) and Amelia Humphrey (W. Fairlee, VT)

SKINNER,
Harris F., Jr. of Orford m. Marjorie I. **Perry** of Haverhill 9/26/1942 in Haverhill; H – 20, airplane packer, b. Laramie Co., WY, s/o Harris F. Skinner (Lowell, VT, farmer) and Rose Brown (Bridgewater, housewife); W – 21, tele. operator, b. Warren, d/o George Dana Perry (Jefferson, telegraph op.) and Gladys T. Clifford (Malden, MA, housewife)

SLEEPER,
Eric C. of Fairlee, VT m. Barbara J. **Martin** of Orford 9/26/1981
Finlay P. of Haverhill m. Helen E. **Carr** of Orford 3/20/1916 in Orford; H – 32, grain dealer, b. Haverhill, s/o Francis S. Sleeper (Lowell, MA, grain dealer) and Jane F. Page (Haverhill, housewife); W – 20, domestic, b. Orford, d/o Clarence H. Carr (Plainfield, farmer) and Hittie R. Lang (Bath, housewife)

SMITH,
Arthur E. of Orford m. Alice M. **Turner** of Thetford, VT 11/28/1894 in Piermont; H – 25, laborer, b. Barnard, VT, s/o John R. Smith (Orford, farmer) and Mary J. Perkins (Barnard, VT, domestic); W – 18, domestic, b. Thetford, VT, d/o Allen O. Turner (Thetford, VT, drover) and Edna Gove (Thetford, VT, domestic)
Carl C. of Orford m. Mary E. **Mann** of Orford 4/8/1897 in Piermont; H – 22, laborer, b. Windsor, VT, s/o John R. Smith (laborer) and

Mary Perkins; W – 21, domestic, b. Orford, d/o Zerah C. Mann (laborer) and Jane Jicks

Carl Wilbur of Orford m. Florence May **Cutler** of Orford 2/14/1929 in Fairlee, VT; H – 23, laborer, b. Gilford, s/o Claude R. Smith (New Hampton) and Flora M. Wilkinson (Gilford); W – 18, b. Orford, d/o Judson Cutler (Waterbury, VT) and Myrtle C. Mann (Roxbury, VT)

Carrol B. of Orford m. May **Watson** of Boston, MA 7/17/1897 in Orford; H – 21, farmer, b. Orford, s/o Alphonso P. Smith and Clarinda Worthen; W – 22, domestic, b. Ireland

Clarence S. of Orford m. Sarah A. **Archer** of Orford 9/18/1895 in Lyme; H – 26, farmer, b. Lyme, s/o Alphonso Smith (Lyme, farmer); W – 18, domestic, b. Orford, d/o Josiah H. Archer (Orford, farmer)

David m. Brenda **Johnson** 7/26/1986

David Robert of Orford m. Martha May **Pike** of Lyme Ctr. 10/18/1975 in Orford; H – 30, b. Fairlee, VT, s/o Guy W. Smith and Virginia Roberts; W – 20, b. Norwalk, CT, d/o Lon J. Pike and Susan Waterbury

Dennis m. Michelle **Ayala** 7/18/1987

Eddie E. of Orford m. Augusta **Johnson** of Chicago, IL 8/31/1904 in Piermont; H – 26, liveryman, b. Stockbridge, s/o John R. Smith (Orford, farmer) and Mary J. Perkins (Barnard, VT, housewife); W – 25, domestic, b. Dennison, IA, d/o August Johnson (Sweden, mechanic) and Elizabeth Peterson (Sweden, housewife)

Hazen L. of Fairlee, VT m. Lizzie B. **King** of E. Corinth, VT 12/9/1929 in Orford; H – 21, laborer, b. Quechee, VT, s/o Lewis W. Smith (Orford, laborer) and Eva Archer (Orford, housewife); W – 20, at home, b. E. Montpelier, VT, d/o Leon A. King (Hyde Park, VT, laborer) and Marion E. Johnston (E. Montpelier, VT, housewife)

Ivan Lester m. Hazel Louise **Young** 6/30/1954 in Lyme; H – 23, laborer, b. Moretown, VT, s/o Allan Smith (Calais, ME) and Siltonia B. Shondo (Duxbury, VT); W – 21, at home, b. Hanover, d/o Leon F. Young (Hanover) and Louise M. Columbia (St. Albans, VT)

Joel C. of Orford m. Elizabeth J. **Howe** of Cornish Falt 2/1/1925 in Fairlee, VT; H – 24, laborer, b. Orford, s/o Clarence Smith (Lyme, laborer) and Sarah Archer (Orford, housewife); W – 18, domestic, b. Cornish, d/o Henry B. Howe (Plainfield) and Clara M. Darwin (MN)

Lewis W. of Orford m. Eva E. **Archer** of Orford 10/31/1906 in Orford; H – 22, farmer, b. Orford, s/o Alphonzo Smith (Manchester, farmer) and Clarinda Worthen (Wentworth, housewife); W – 18, domestic, b. Orford, d/o Josiah H. Archer (Orford, farmer) and Mary R. Hannaford (Fairlee, VT, housewife)

Robert H. of Orford m. Marylyn A. **Robinson** of Post Mills, VT 12/3/1952 in Orford; H – 20, US Air Force, b. Fairlee, VT, s/o George E. Smith (Fairlee, VT) and Leona Strout (Old Town, ME); W – 18, at home, b. Post Mills, VT, d/o Myron Robinson (Thetford, VT) and Mildred Ackerman (Orford)

Stanley R., Jr. of Orford m. Faye Ann **Pike** of Orford 8/17/1973 in Orford; H – 19, b. Hanover, s/o Stanley R. Smith, Sr. and R. Mary Cummings; W – 18, b. Hanover, d/o Weymouth H. Pike, Sr. and Helen Marsh

Stanley Richard of Hanover m. Rosie Mary **Cummings** of Orford 1/29/1949 in Wentworth; H – 21, carpenter, b. Lyme, s/o Benjamin R. Smith (Lyme) and Josephine M. Dennis (Lyme); W – 17, at home, b. Woodsville, d/o Clyde A. Cummings (Thetford, VT) and Rosie Tallman (Orford)

William Gunner of Wilder, VT m. AnnMarie **Cappiali** of Wilder, VT 9/30/1995

SNELLING,
Jeffrey m. Deborah **Raynes** 6/20/1986

SNOW,
Bernard D. of Orford m. Pauline M. **Adams** of Orford 3/23/1946 in Fairlee, VT; H – 25, mine driller, b. W. Fairlee, VT, s/o Ralph Snow (Burlington, VT) and Elizabeth Bard (W. Fairlee, VT); W – 17, waitress, b. Dover, d/o Ezra L. Adams (Fairlee, VT) and Mary E. Dolan (Charlestown, MA)

SOBETZER,
Jay of Plymouth m. Kathryn **Marsh** of Orford 5/7/1983

SOPER,
Taylor of Orford m. Vicki **Greenwood** of Lebanon 9/23/1991

SOUTHARD,
Charles G. of Haverhill m. Mary J. **Lang** of Orford 9/20/1893 in Orford; H – 27, merchant, b. Haverhill, s/o L. W. Southard (Walpole, farmer) and Hitta B. Kimball (Haverhill, teacher); W – 21, teacher, b. Orford, d/o David R. Lang (Bath, lawyer) and Josephine R. Smith (Bath, teacher)

SOUZA,
Thomas of Orford m. Donna **Willey** of Orford 11/1/1990

SPECTORSKY,
Auguste of Chicago, IL m. Elizabeth **Bullock** of New York, NY 9/22/1944 in Orford; H – 34, journalist, 2nd, b. Paris, France, s/o Isaac Spectorsky (Russia, educator) and Frances Herbert (Poland, camp director); W – 37, editor, 2nd, b. St. Joseph, MO, d/o Eugene H. Bullock (KS, retired) and Beulah Devorrs (MO, retired)

SPENCER,
Hugh E. of Orford m. Evelyn B. **Stetson** of Piermont 6/10/1947 in Claremont; H – 30, trackman, b. Orford, s/o James E. Spencer (Wolfville, NS, int. dec., deceased) and Georgia Archer (Orford, housewife, deceased); W – 19, mill worker, b. Piermont, d/o Clinton W. Stetson (Piermont, lumberman) and Edna Robie (Piermont, housewife)
James C. of Orford m. Flora M. **Aldrich** of Vershire, VT 10/13/1935 in Bradford, VT; H – painter, b. Orford, s/o James E. Spencer (NS, painter) and Georgia Archer (Orford, housewife); W – 17, domestic, b. Vershire, VT, d/o Delmore C. Aldrich (W. Fairlee, VT, farmer) and Emma Carr (Tunbridge, VT, housewife)
James C. of Orford m. Lois **Dickey** of Newbury, VT 1/14/1939 in Newbury, VT; H – 26, painter, 2nd, divorced, b. Orford, s/o James E. Spencer (NS) and Georgia Archer (Orford); W – 19, b. Bradford, VT, d/o Pearl Dickey (Bradford, VT) and Marion McAllister (Manchester)

SPOONER,
Henry E. of Orford m. Ruth A. **Baker** of Milford 8/11/1934 in Franconia; H – 21, laborer, b. Franconia, s/o Henry E. Spooner (Franconia, inn keeper) and Tillie Partridge (Haverhill, housewife); W – 24, teacher, b. Altoona, PA, d/o Newton C.

Baker (Altoona, PA, farmer) and Cora Fitts (Altoona, PA, housewife)

SPOTTSWOOD,
Stephen Alexander of Orford m. Marion Gale **Thomson** of Orford 5/30/1969 in Orford; H – 22, b. AL, s/o Gurran Spottswood and Marian Harrold; W – 21, b. NY, d/o Meldrim Thomson, Jr. and Gale Kelly

STANLEY,
Maurice of New Britain, CT m. Margaret **Sammond** of New York City 6/14/1919 in Orford; H – 32, manufacturer, b. Granby, CT, s/o Timothy Stanley (New Britain, CT, manufacturer) and Theresa Bartholomeu (Granby, CT); W – 30, teacher, b. Milwaukee, WI, d/o Charles E. Sammon (Brooklyn, NY, manufacturer) and Jean Stowell (Milwaukee, WI)

STEARLY,
Gary m. Louise **Grasmere** 10/6/1984 in New London

STEARNS,
Frank A. of Lyme m. Evalyn K. **Lufkin** of Orford 9/1/1926 in Orford; H – 40, farmer, b. Orford, s/o Alvah M. Stevens (Orford, lumberman) and Angie N. Lamprey (Rumford, ME, farmer); W – 32, teaching, b. Thetford, VT, d/o Edgar C. Lufkin (Rumford, ME, farmer) and Genevieve Wilmot (Thetford, VT, housewife)
Reginald E. of Plainfield m. Pauline Dora **LaDeau** of Orford 7/2/1960 in Orford; H – 19, truck driver, b. Lyme, s/o Fred O. Stearns (Plainfield) and Doris L. Hazelton (Bristol); W – 21, stitcher, b. Fairlee, VT, d/o Kenneth J. LaDeau (Warren) and Merle A. Trussell (Fairlee, VT)

STEELE,
Robert of Williamstown, MA m. Jennifer **Brackett** of Orford 7/15/1978 in Orford; H – b. VT, s/o Robert Steele and Eileen Walker; W – b. NH, d/o Truman Brackett and Kristin Sanborn

STEFANAZZI,
Eugene of Barre, VT m. Elsie Ella **Nutter** of Orford 1/1/1934 in Williamstown, VT; H – 29, granite mfgr., b. Vologna, Italy, s/o Carlo Stefanazzi (Italy) and Antonia Marcini (Italy); W – 24,

domestic, b. Barnet, VT, d/o John Nutter (Barnet, VT, farmer) and Flora Cassidy (Kings Falls, Canada, housewife)

STETSON,

Otis W. of Lyme m. Lydia D. **Stevens** of Orford 11/18/1896 in Orford; H – 60, farmer, 3rd, b. Enfield, s/o Amos Stetson (farmer) and Sabrina Wheeler (housewife); W – 63, domestic, 3rd, b. Orford, d/o Dolf Phelps (farmer)

Willie A. of Lyme m. Mary L. **Pratt** of Orford 3/3/1894 in Lyme; H – 20, farmer, b. Lyme, s/o Otis W. Stetson (Lyme, farmer) and Maria L. Elliott (Thetford, VT, domestic); W – 24, domestic, 2nd, b. Orford, d/o David Brooks (Orford, laborer) and Ellen Smith (Orford, domestic)

STEVENS,

Dana E. of Orford m. Frances **Hall** of Orford 6/28/1916 in Orford; H – 26, civ. eng., b. Orford, s/o Alvah M. Stevens (Orford, farmer) and Angie Lamprey (Orford, housewife); W – 22, dressmaker, b. Boston, MA, d/o Francis H. Hall (Northfield, VT, laborer) and Clara E. Phelps (Orford, housewife)

STILL,

Charles E. of Orford m. Maggie M. **Shay** of Orford 5/12/1904 in Lyme; H – 24, farmer, b. Manchester, s/o Benjamin W. Still (Hancock, farmer) and Mary E. Bragg (W. Fairlee, VT, housewife); W – 26, domestic, b. Manchester, d/o ----- Shay

Grover C. of Lyme m. Bessie E. **Judd** of Thetford, VT 12/6/1908 in Lyme; H – 23, carpenter, b. Claremont, s/o Benjamin W. Still (Hancock, farmer) and Marietta C. Bragg (W. Fairlee, VT, housewife); W – 18, teacher, b. Thetford, VT, d/o John Judd (Thetford, VT, farmer) and Frances Powell (Thetford, VT, housewife)

STIMSON,

Andrew P. of Orford m. Maritza G. **Godfrey** of Orford 7/21/1998

STRAIDEL,

Laurence Brian of Gaithersburg, MD m. Charlotte Alexis **Flower** of Gaithersburg, MD 9/27/2003 in Orford

STREETER,
Bruce of Orford m. Audrey **Trussell** of Orford 9/14/1991
Carl Moody of Orford m. Lucy Emma **Jones** of Orford 7/19/1951 in
 Orford; H – 23, farmer, b. Hanover, s/o Ray N. Streeter (Lisbon)
 and Stella Cushing (McIndoes, VT); W – 20, domestic, 2nd, b.
 Eden, VT, d/o Chester Grimes (N. Hyde Park, VT) and Glenna
 French (Canada)
Dennis of Orford m. Wendy **Milligan** of Orford 7/17/1999
Peter F. of Fairlee, VT m. Sarah A. **Smith** of Orford 7/17/1926 in
 Fairlee, VT; H – 47, section man, b. Munroe, s/o Wilfred H.
 Streeter (Canada) and Amanda Raymond (Derby Line, VT); W
 – 48, domestic, 2nd, b. Orford, d/o Josiah H. Archer (Orford,
 sexton) and Mary Hannaford (Fairlee, VT, housewife)
Ralph Ray of Orford m. Ethel F. **Ladeau** of Wells River, VT
 3/24/1940 in Orford; H – 21, laborer, b. Wentworth, s/o Mary
 Robbins (Melrose, MA, domestic); W – 20, domestic, b. Orford,
 d/o Albert Charles Ladeau (Orford, lumberman) and Abbie P.
 Cushing (McIndoes Falls, VT, housewife)
Ray N. of Orford m. Stella **Cushing** of Orford 11/5/1908 in Orford; H
 – 21, laborer, b. Lisbon, s/o Rollin Streeter (Lisbon, laborer) and
 Hattie Decker (Berlin, housewife); W – 18, domestic, b.
 McIndoes, VT, d/o George Cushing (McIndoes, VT, laborer)
 and Dora ----- (housewife)

STRONG,
Charles of Orford m. Milly **Ingersoll** of Carroll 1/27/1893 in Orford; H
 – 32, farmer, b. Orford, s/o Ephraim B. Strong (Orford, farmer)
 and Amanda Page (Wentworth, domestic); W – 20, domestic, b.
 Carroll, d/o John Ingersoll (farmer) and Almira Sherwood
 (Littleton, domestic)

STYGLES,
Michael of Piermont m. Lean **Weeks** of Orford 12/13/1980

SUPER,
Kenneth of Orford m. Patrice **Sullivan** of Orford 9/27/1980
Kenneth G. of Orford m. Elene A. **Ainalovan** of Orford 6/25/1999

SUTTON,
Mark of Orford m. Cindy **Sweat** of Orford 6/29/1991

SWALLOW,
John of Orford m. Mary E. **Chapman** of Orford 4/26/1911 in Bradford, VT; H – 71, gardener, 2nd, widower, b. Highgate, VT, s/o Peter Swallow (W. Chelmsford, MA, farmer) and Sarah Boyington (Canada, housewife); W – 51, housewife, 2nd, divorced, b. Warren, d/o Daniel S. Willis (Mansfield, MA, farmer) and Marinda D. Hazelton (Orford, housewife)

SWAN,
Charles Henry of Orford m. Elizabeth Alice **Bailey** of Orford 3/25/1951 in Orford; H – 22, US Army, b. Hanover, s/o Harold W. Swan (Haverhill) and Ruth E. Munn (W. Fairlee, VT); W – 21, at home, b. Fairlee, VT, d/o Lawrence F. Bailey (Lyme) and Kittie Mae Hatch (Alton, ME)

Harold W. of Orford m. Ruth E. **Munn** of Fairlee, VT 6/22/1927 in Fairlee, VT; H – 32, merchant, b. Haverhill, s/o Charles M. Swan (Suncook) and Kate Thomas (Haverhill); W – 29, b. W. Fairlee, VT, d/o Charles H. Munn (Canterbury) and Kathleen M. Ordway (Stanton, MN)

SWEET,
Kristofer Bryan of Orford m. Jenny Lynn **Rodewald** of Orford 9/2/2000 in Orford

SZYMANSKI,
James of PA m. Rose **O'Hanlon** of PA 10/27/1990

TALLMAN,
Forest P. of Orford m. Jennie B. **Rhoades** of Orford 4/12/1906 in Orford; H – 28, farmer, b. Orford, s/o James H. Tallman (Orford, farmer) and Elizabeth Smith (Manchester, housewife); W – 19, domestic, b. Orford, d/o Wilbur Rhoades (Waits River, VT, laborer) and Emma Simpson (Orford, housewife)

John C. of Orford m. Verna L. **Smith** of Lyme 3/7/1948 in Orford; H – 24, garage att., b. Orford, s/o Forrest P. Tallman (Orford, laborer, deceased) and Jennie Rhodes (Orford, housewife, deceased); W – 18, at home, b. Lyme, d/o Benjamin Smith (Lyme, mill hand) and Josephine Dennis (Lyme, housewife)

Sidney J. of Orford m. Mabel E. **Dunbar** of Corinth, VT 7/30/1932 in Orford; H – 25, laborer, b. Orford, s/o Forest Tallman (Orford, farmer) and Jennie Rhodes (Orford, housewife); W – 20, housekeeper, b. Lyme, d/o Robert A. Dunbar (Potton, Canada, laborer) and Edith M. Simpson (Bradford, VT, housewife)

Sidney J. of Orford m. Evelyn M. **Ellsworth** of Vershire, VT 6/20/1938 in Piermont; H – 31, farmer, 2nd, divorced, b. Orford, s/o Forrest P. Tallman (Orford, farmer) and Jennie B. Rhodes (Orford, deceased); W – 18, domestic, b. Hanover, d/o Merton Ellsworth (Underhill, VT, farmer) and Helen F. Chamberlain (W. Fairlee, VT, housewife)

TATHAM,
Donald A. of Orford m. Gretchen E. **Edington** of Wentworth 7/13/1996
James m. Carol **Luhman** 9/22/1984 in Orford
James of Orford m. Jamie **Raymond** of Orford 1/20/1991

TAYLOR,
Bruce F., Jr. of Orford m. Lisa A. **Mayotte** of Guilford, VT 5/17/1997
Bruce Frederick of Orford m. Gloria Jean **Pike** of Orford 3/14/1969 in Orford; H – 21, b. VT, s/o Elmer L. Taylor and Phyllis Royston; W – 18, b. NH, d/o Weymouth Pike and Helen Marsh
Harold James of Orford m. Theresa Marie **McGoff** of Orford 5/10/1975 in Orford; H – 24, b. St. Johnsbury, VT, s/o Elmer L. Taylor and Phyllis L. Royston; W – 18, b. Lunenburg, VT, d/o James McGoff and Margaret Lamotte
Larry A. of Orford m. Susan L. **Hook** of Orford --/22/1972 in Orford; H – 18, b. St. Johnsbury, VT, s/o Elmer L. Taylor and Phyllis Royston; W – 21, b. Woodsville, d/o Lester E. Hook and Marian Lanefski
Matthew J. of Orford m. Lori K. **Leete** of Wells River, VT 8/23/2003 in W. Newbury, VT
Rodney I. of Orford m. Donna L. **Merrill** of Orford 7/5/1997
Ronald Leslie of Orford m. Mary Jane **Marsh** of Orford 10/2/1970 in Orford; H – 22, b. Barnet, VT, s/o Elmer L. Taylor and Phyllis Royston; W – 22, b. Orford, d/o Ralph E. Marsh and Gladys Cutler
Timothy James of Orford m. Jennifer May **Findley** of Orford 9/30/2000 in Orford

TENNEY,
Howard A. of Alexandria m. Marion H. **Nutter** of Orford 10/6/1932; H – 21, truck driver, b. Alexandria, s/o Herbert W. Tenney

(Danbury, farmer) and Jennie E. Heath (Grafton, housewife); W
– 19, housekeeper, b. Orford, d/o John D. Nutter (Barnet, VT,
farmer) and Flora A. Cassidy (King's Falls, Canada, housewife)
Stephen C. of Newport m. Suzette **Wyman** of Orford 9/12/1981

THAYER,
Gilbert M. of Brooklyn, NY m. Emma B. **Nichols** of Orford 9/24/1902
in Orford; H – 25, clerk, b. Brooklyn, NY, s/o Joseph Thayer
(Concord, MA, clerk) and Jane H. Brown (Maramiac, NY,
housewife); W – 21, domestic, b. Boston, MA, d/o Milo F.
Nichols (MA, clerk) and Clara E. Phelps (Orford, housewife)

THEN,
Oscar Anthony of Dominican Rep. m. Elaine Margaret **Shumway** of
Orford 10/3/1970 in Orford; H – 29, b. Dominican Rep., s/o
Manuel Then and Emma Oller; W – 26, d/o Carroll R. Shumway
and Katherine Duprey

THOMAS,
Martin C. of Barre, VT m. Aimee M. **Thomas** of Barre, VT
11/28/1940 in Orford; H – 40, mechanic, b. Enosburg, VT, s/o
Marcus Thomas (Enosburg, VT, farmer) and Nettie Lagroe
(Montgomery, VT, deceased); W – 43, domestic, b. Roxbury,
VT, d/o Roy Fuller (Brookfield, VT, farmer) and Etta Blanchard
(Brookfield, VT, housewife)

THOMPSON,
Joseph A. of Orford m. Grace M. **Archer** of Orford 11/5/1917 in
Orford; H – 26, laborer, b. Canada, s/o Joseph G. Thompson
(Canada) and Annie M. Devey (Canada); W – 26, domestic, b.
Colebrook, d/o Charles Archer (Orford) and Olive Barnett
(Colebrook)
Warner W., Jr. of Orford m. Charlotte M. **Donaldson** of Orford
12/12/1908 in Orford; H – 18, laborer, b. Orford, s/o Warner W.
Thompson (Goshen, farmer) and Christina Collins (Chicopee,
MA, housewife); W – 18, domestic, b. Orford, d/o George B.
Donaldson (Peacham, VT, laborer) and Mary H. Whitman
(Orford, housewife)
Wayne Joseph of Lyme m. Ruth Marian **Hook** of Orford 6/4/1971 in
Orford; H – 22, b. Hanover, s/o Charles A. Thompson and Ruby

Watson; W – 20, b. Haverhill, d/o Lester E. Hook and Marian Lanefski

THOMSON,

David L. of Orford m. Brenda Eileen **Dyke** of Orford 12/3/1966 in Orford; H – 23, b. Brooklyn, NY, s/o Meldrim Thomson, Jr. and Gale Kelley; W – 18, b. Orford, d/o Benjamin F. Dyke, Jr. and Dorothy Dow

Rob Roy of Orford m. Andrea Christine **Flagg** of Wolfeboro 7/26/1975 in Wolfeboro; H – 25, b. Pt. Jefferson, NY, s/o Meldrim Thomson, Jr. and Gale Kelley; W – 25, b. Calais, ME, d/o Calvin Flagg and Verna Boynton

Thomas N. of Orford m. Sheila M. **Sweet** of E. Corinth, VT 9/10/1966 in E. Corinth, VT; H – b. Pt. Jefferson, NY, s/o Meldrim Thomson, Jr. and Gale Kelley; W – 18, b. Woodsville, d/o Wilfred Sweet and Dorothy Perdue

TILLOTSON,

Wendell E. of Bradford, VT m. Ida L. **Huntington** of Orford 2/4/1945 in Orford; H – 20, farm laborer, b. Topsham, VT, s/o Martin L. Tillotson (Groton, VT, farmer) and Ella Mae Hood (Topsham, VT, housewife); W – 18, student, b. Orford, d/o Guy S. Huntington (Corinth, VT, mail carrier) and Mildred Cummings (Thetford, VT, housewife)

Wendell Earle of Groton, VT m. Julia Elizabeth **Thayer** of Groton, VT 8/20/1970 in Orford; H – 36, b. Topsham, VT, s/o Martin Tillotson and Ella Hood; W – 42, d/o Jules Langlois and Mary Louise Dechaine

TITUS,

Calvin Augustus, Jr. m. Cornelia Ann **Chase** 3/24/1956 in Orford; H – 19, air line mech., b. Salem, MA, s/o Calvin Augustus Titus, Sr. (Boston, MA) and Genevieve MacDougall (Glace Bay, Canada); W – 19, domestic, b. Woodsville, d/o Maurice A. Chase (Orford) and Irene Mack (Orford)

TREVITHICK,

Earl M. of Post Mills, VT m. Doris **Brailey** of Ely, VT 10/10/1935 in Orford; H – 22, mechanic, b. Vershire, VT, s/o John Trevithick (Butter, MT, mechanic) and Nina McClure (Nashville, TN, housewife); W – 30, at home, 2nd, b. N. Thetford, VT, d/o Henry

Hartsor (N. Thetford, VT, farmer) and Edna Hill (Chatagay, NY, housewife)

TREWORGY,
James A. of Washington, DC m. Hewan K. **Tomlinson** of Washington, DC 8/29/1998

TROMBLEY,
Albert J. of Barre, VT m. Lillian M. **Tallman** of Orford 10/16/1939 in Barre, VT; H – 22, truck driver, b. Bakersfield, VT, s/o Joseph Trombly (St. Albans, VT) and Mary Grover (St. Albans, VT); W – 18, housework, b. Orford, d/o Forrest P. Tallman (Orford, farmer) and Jennie Rhodes (Orford, housewife)
Scott D. of Orford m. Kelly J. **Baade** of Fairlee, VT 7/20/1996

TRUNZO,
Thomas, Jr. of Orford m. Deborah **Arnesen** of Orford 2/6/1982

TULLAR,
Nathan Charles of Orford m. Carole Ann **Cahill** of Orford 6/28/2003 in Bradford, VT
Rendell Carl of Orford m. Karen Louise **Phelps** of Strafford, VT 5/21/1977 in Thetford, VT; H – 23, b. NH, s/o George Tullar and Barbara Anderson; W – 23, b. NH, d/o Elmer Gomo and Gertrude Jordan
Steven m. Cathy **Lahmann** 5/27/1984 in Orford

TUTTLE,
William of Rockville, CT m. Susan **Magoon** of Long Island, NY 12/12/1969 in Vernon, CT; H – 29, b. Corinth, VT, s/o Allen E. Tuttle and Alfreda J. Sweet; W – 23, b. Orford, d/o George A. Wilson and Mildred Andreason

TWISS,
Alden S. of Hartford, VT m. Martha I. **Archer** of Orford 6/16/1909 in Orford; H – 24, clerk, b. Craftsbury, VT, s/o Frank P. Twiss (Marshfield, VT, farmer) and Jennie M. Tillotson (Craftsbury, VT, dressmaker); W – 19, telephone operator, b. Orford, d/o Josiah H. Archer (Orford, farmer) and Mary R. Hannaford (Fairlee, VT, housewife)

ULRICH,
Phillip m. Christine **Messer** 11/14/1987

ULZ,
Andrew of Orford m. Cheryl **Honney** of Orford 9/6/1992

UNDERHILL,
Berton D. of Piermont m. Mabelle R. **Carle** of Orford 10/22/1935 in W. Newbury, VT; H – 23, farmer, b. Piermont, s/o Leon H. Underhill (Piermont, farmer) and Jennie A. Norris (Corinth, VT, housewife); W – 17, at home, b. Malden, NY, d/o Vernon Carle (Woodstock, NY, laborer) and Mae Bryer (Lancaster, housewife)

VASIL,
Thomas of Orford m. Marilyn E. **Kowal** of Orford 7/12/1980

VEGHTE,
Lewis of Washington, DC m. Barbara Ruth **Hess** of Cedar Rapids, IA 12/27/1964 in Orford; H – 37, b. Schoharie, NY, s/o Lewis Veghte, Sr. and Alice Louise Mead; W – 22, b. Cedar Rapids, IA, d/o Russell I. Hess and Ruth Alice Hendricks

VENNING,
James of Jefferson, MA m. Lise **Miller** of Northboro, MA 9/9/1983

VICTOR,
Edward W. of Brooklyn, NY m. Kate **Phelps** of Brooklyn, NY 10/21/1896 in Orford; H – 45, physician, 2nd, b. Newtown, LI, s/o Theodore Victor (merchant) and Emily A. Fowler (housewife); W – 39,. nurse, b. Orford, d/o John H. Phelps (farmer) and Charlotte Hancock (housewife)

VILLAR,
Paul of Orford m. Peg **Demers** of Orford 6/25/1983

VINCENT,
William m. Patricia **Sears** --/--/1989

VON DETTE,
Archie F. of Orford m. Josephine **Vezina** of Orford 10/25/1947 in Piermont; H – 58, steel worker, 2nd, widower, b. Brandon, VT, s/o Adolpheus Von Dette (Canada, marble worker, deceased) and Louise Rabideau (Plattsburg, NY, housewife, deceased); W – 43, housework, b. Lennoxville, Canada, d/o Leon Vezina (Quebec, farmer) and Mary Parker (Canada, housewife)

WAGSTAFF,
Eric Mark of Orford m. Rebecca **Thomson** of Orford 7/24/1999

WALLACE,
John m. Suellen **Clegg** 6/9/1985 in Plainfield

WARD,
John Lawrence, Jr. of AK m. Sarah Leigh **French** of Anchorage, AK 10/8/1994

WASHBURN,
Frank E. of Orford m. Antoinette **Drew** of Orford 3/29/1926 in Orford; H – 78, farmer, 2nd, b. Granville, VT, s/o George Washburn (Pomfret, VT, farmer) and Lucy Hewett (Pomfret, VT, housewife); W – 78, domestic, 2nd, b. NS, d/o B. B. McPherson (NS, farmer) and Catherine Wheelock (Lunenburg, NS, housewife)
H. Horton of Orford m. Geraldine J. **Estes** of Orford 12/29/1976 in Orford; H – 39, b. NH, s/o Harvey L. Washburn and Bernice H. Horton; W – 26, b. NH, d/o Robert L. Johnson and Lurline E. Dyke
Harvey Horton m. Marlene S. **Whitcher** 11/24/1955 in N. Haverhill; H – 18, farming, b. Hanover, s/o Harvey L. Washburn (Orford) and Bernice Horton (Orford); W – 18, at home, b. Laconia, d/o Maurice A. Whitcher (Warren) and Helen M. Ball (Landaff)
Harvey I. of Orford m. Bernice M. **Horton** of Orford 6/3/1919 in Orford; H – 27, farmer, b. Orford, s/o Frank E. Washburn (Pomfret, VT, farmer) and Emma Lovejoy (Orford, housewife); W – 23, stenographer, b. Orford, d/o Walter S. Horton (Barnard, VT, farmer) and Mary Stone (Orford, housewife)
Neil of Orford m. Joanne **Harrington** of Orford 12/31/1982

WATERBURY,
Allan Gilbert m. Shirley Jean **Weeks** 8/13/1956 in N. Haverhill; H – 22, US Army, b. Norwalk, CT, s/o Leon E. Waterbury (Norwalk, CT) and Elizabeth Litchfield (Brooklyn, NY); W – 18, at home, b. Orford, d/o Charles A. Weeks (Fairlee, VT) and Lillian Marsh (Orford)

WATERS,
Joel of Orford m. Charlotte **Mathieu** of Orford 6/27/1992

WATSON,
Leonard W. of Hudson, MA m. Isabelle L. **Lufkin** of Orford 7/23/1924 in Orford; H – 31, merchant, b. Sutton, s/o Harvey Watson (Sutton, painter) and Emma Wheeler (Sutton, matron); W – 29, teacher, b. Thetford, VT, d/o Egar C. Lufkin (Rumford, ME, farmer) and Genevieve Wilmot (Thetford, VT, housewife)

WEBBER,
Parker G. of Orford m. Lillian **DeLong** of Orford 4/3/1937 in Orford; H – 56, carpenter, 2nd, divorced, b. N. Shapleigh, ME, s/o Parker G. Webber (N. Shapleigh, ME, retired) and Mary Merrow (Milton Mills); W – 57, housework, 3rd, divorced, b. Troy, NY, d/o William DeLong (Saratoga Springs, NY, engineer) and Mary E. Lerger (Gloversville, NY, housewife)

WEBSTER,
Freeman H. of Piermont m. Mabel **Mann** of Orford 6/20/1898 in Piermont; H – 24, laborer, b. Haverhill, s/o Charles Webster (Boscawen, farmer) and Belle Knapp (Haverhill, housewife); W – 20, domestic, b. Orford, d/o Zerah Mann (farmer) and Jane Hicks (housewife)
Herbert E. of Lyme Ctr. m. Emily A. **Stevens** of Lebanon 7/6/1969 in Orford; H – 68, b. VT, s/o John H. Webster and Abbie Coates; W – 74, b. VT, d/o Orton Mousley and Hattie Fales

WEEKS,
Alvin B. of Orford m. Florence W. **Hardy** of Orford 11/6/1906 in Orford; H – 20, farmer, b. Nottingham, s/o George A. Weeks (machinist) and Angeline L. Turner (Highlandsville, MA, housewife); W – 17, domestic, b. Manchester, d/o Charles H.

Hardy (Clarksville, farmer) and Annie R. Turner (Norwich, VT, housewife)

Charles A. of Orford m. Lillian Eva **Marsh** of Orford 11/22/1930 in Lyme; H – 22, laborer, b. Fairlee, VT, s/o Alvin B. Weeks (Nottingham, farmer) and Florence Hardy (Manchester, housewife); W – 21, at home, b. Orford, d/o David C. Marsh (W. Fairlee, VT, farmer) and Delia Smith (Corinth, VT, housewife)

David Merrill of Orford m. Ramona Lee **Nutter** of Orford 7/31/1965 in Orford; H – 21, b. Warren, s/o Henry E. Weeks and Jessie M. Spencer; W – 18, b. Orford, d/o Kenneth L. Nutter and Evelyn Johnson

George W. of Orford m. Gladys P. **Dow** of Orford 6/20/1934 in Lyme; H – 23, farmer, b. Bradford, VT, s/o Alvin B. Weeks (Nottingham, patrolman) and Florence Hardy (Manchester, housewife); W – 28, at home, b. Whitefield, d/o Robert Dow (Lisbon, retired) and Edna Richie (Whitefield, housewife)

Robert m. Lisa **Waterbury** 8/22/1987

Wayne Alvin m. Louella Jean **Godville** 7/1/1955 in Orford; H – 18, st. highway dept., b. Orford, s/o Charles A. Weeks (Fairlee, VT) and Lillian E. Marsh (Orford); W – 18, at home, b. Warren, d/o James Godville (Lithuania) and Edna Short (Warren)

WEIBEL,

John G. of Orford m. Margaret May **Bryer** of Orford 6/22/1913 in Piermont; H – 25, laborer, b. Lowell, MA, s/o Casper Weibel (Germany, laborer) and Catherine Wehinger (Germany, housewife); W – 17, domestic, b. Lancaster, d/o Clarence W. Bryer (Laconia, blacksmith) and Lucy M. Allen (Lancaster, housewife)

WEINHEIMER,

Sidney of Orford m. Anne **Harvis** of Orford 9/1/1978 in Orford; H – b. PA, s/o Ralph Weinheiimer and Martha Volleeiller; W – b. NY, d/o Alexander Schwartzman and Simona Cann

WEISBURGER,

Donald of Orford m. Robin **Phillips** of Orford 6/23/1991

WELCH,

Jack P. of Enfield m. Mary Lynn **Gallup** of Orford 10/15/1966 in Enfield; H – 24, b. Lebanon, s/o John P. Welch and Rose E.

Beaupre; W – 23, b. Woodsville, d/o Harley G. Gallup and Ella C. Johnson

WHEELER,
James m. Deena **Rich** 3/28/1987

WHITAKER,
Donald of New York, NY m. Marie **Benzemann** of New York, NY 7/13/1991

WHITCOMB,
Edward E. of Newport, VT m. Mayme A. **Dennis** of Orford 12/3/1892 in Orford; H – 22, telegrapher, b. Norwich, VT, s/o Joseph Whitcomb (Stratford, VT, farmer) and Mary M. Hopkins (Tunbridge, VT); W – 17, domestic, b. Orford, d/o Emore Dennis (Stratford, farmer) and Olive Cross (Troy, VT)

WHITE,
Burton A. of New Britain, CT m. Eva B. **Weldon** of New Britain, CT 9/8/1917 in Orford; H – 37, furniture salesman, 2nd, widower, b. N. Bangor, NY, s/o Joseph H. White (PQ) and Abigail Mott (N. Bangor, NY); W – 41, housekeeper, b. New Britain, CT, d/o Oliver H. Weldon (New Britain, CT) and Hannah Gilbert (Warren, MA)

Fred S. of Haverhill m. Amelia **Rowden** of Haverhill 10/5/1901 in Swiftwater; H – 28, carpenter, b. NS, s/o John S. White (NS, farmer) and Mary Smith (NS, housewife); W – 18, domestic, b. Canada, d/o George Rowden (Canada, railroading) and Rachel Neugent (Haverhill, housewife)

Milton L. of W. Fairlee, VT m. Barbara Alice **Huckins** of Orford 7/4/1959

Paul m. Marianne **Bermingham** 5/26/1984 in Orford

WHITING,
Tex of Penacook m. Ann Marie **Weeks** of Orford 7/16/1973 in Penacook; H – 18, b. NH, s/o George Whiting and Georgette A. Place; W – 18, b. Haverhill, d/o Forrest W. Weeks and Muriel McDonald

WHITTAKER,
Benjamin, Jr. of W. Danville, VT m. Nancy Ruth **Davis** of Orford 6/20/1959

WHITTEMORE,
Luther L. of Orford m. Carrie W. **Washburn** of Lyme 9/14/1898 in Lyme; H – 24, clerk, b. Plymouth, s/o Peter Whittemore (farmer) and Elizabeth Woodworth (housewife); W – 27, domestic, b. Lyme, d/o Allen G. Washburn (farmer)

WILBUR,
Chandler A. of Orford m. Emily **Lamphere** of Orford 6/20/1896 in Orford; H – 47, mechanic, 2nd, b. Surry, VT, s/o Chandler Wilbur (mechanic) and Maria C. Dean (housewife); W – 41, housekeeper, 2nd, b. Canada, d/o Joseph Straw and Margaret Colby

WILCOX,
Harry P. of Orford m. Eliza H. **Gaskill** of Orford 10/22/1921 in Orford; H – 45, farmer, 2nd, widower, b. Orford, s/o David Wilcox (Orford, farmer) and Ada Mitchell (Piermont, housewife); W – 38, housekeeper, 2nd, divorced, b. Orford, d/o Walter S. Horton (Barnet, VT, farmer) and Mary S. Stone (Orford, retired)

WILLARD,
Leonard W. of Orford m. Jennie E. **Buck** of Haverhill 6/21/1913 in Haverhill; H – 55, clerk, 2nd, widower, b. Brooklyn, NY, s/o John S. Willard (Orford, merchant) and Mary Wilcox Willard (Orford, housewife); W – 38, teacher, b. Haverhill, d/o Lyman Buck (Waterford, VT, farmer) and Lucia W. Buck (Newbury, VT, housewife)

Ritchie P. of Strafford, VT m. Gladys S. **Titus** of Strafford, VT 8/25/1935 in Orford; H – 31, clerk, b. Bellows Falls, VT, s/o Fred. A. Willard (Brooklyn, NY, carpenter) and Eva M. Perkins (Orange, housekeeper); W – 26, teacher, b. Strafford, VT, d/o John N. Titus (Vershire, VT, farmer) and Louella Button (Tunbridge, VT, housewife)

WILLEY,
Duane m. Kathie **Wadleigh** 6/6/1988

Wilson M. of Orford m. Rose Baker **Foote** of Orford 7/29/1935 in Canaan; H – 22, laborer, b. Bradford, VT, s/o Harry Willey (Topsham, VT, mail carrier) and Amie Morrill (W. Fairlee, VT, housewife); W – 25, at home, 2nd, b. Orford, d/o Henry G. Baker and Inez Smith (Orford, housewife)

Wilson Marshall, Jr. of Orford m. Janet Maude **Marsh** of Orford 7/9/1960 in Orford; H – 23, laborer, b. Hanover, s/o Wilson M. Willey, Sr. (Bradford, VT) and Rose I. Baker (Orford); W – 17, at home, b. Orford, d/o Glenn G. Marsh (Orford) and Verna M. Hibbard (Lyme)

Wilson Marshall, Jr. of Orford m. Beverly Ann **Donovan** of Concord 4/12/1969 in Loudon; H – 33, b. NH, s/o Wilson M. Willey, Sr. and Rose Baker; W – 33, b. NH, d/o Burdette V. Pebbles and Yvonne M. Audette

WILLIAMS,

Ezra N. of Vershire, VT m. Thelma A. **Moody** of Vershire, VT 10/29/1919 in Orford; H – 22, farmer, 2nd, divorced, b. Orange, VT, s/o Asa A. Williams (Orange, VT, farmer) and Lizzie Tillotson (Orange, VT, housewife); W – 18, housekeeper, 2nd, widow, b. Vershire, VT, d/o Dexter Moody (Vershire, VT, farmer) and Jennie Rowell (Vershire, VT, housewife)

Jason C. of Salisbury, MD m. Danielle T. **LaBruna** of Salisbury, MD 8/9/1997

Norman E. of Lisbon m. Marcelene K. **Day** of Orford 11/21/1945 in Lisbon; H – 19, US Army, b. Lisbon, s/o Neal Williams (Lisbon, mill hand) and Ethel Dexter (Yonkers, NY, housewife); W – 17, at home, b. John Day (NS, woodsman) and Lillian Guilmette (Lunenburg, VT, housewife)

Roy m. Wendee **Messer** 5/28/1988

Warren of Orford m. Anne **Mason** of Piermont 11/1/1979

WILLIS,

Clarence of Orford m. Marcia **McEwan** of Lyme 10/20/1979

Russell of FL m. Jane **Graves** of FL 9/11/1982

WILLSON,

Todd Alan of Orford m. Amy L. **Pierson** of Orford 9/7/2002 in Orford

WILSON,
Alfred B. of Wilmette, IL m. Ella P. **Morse** of Orford 10/17/1910 in Orford; H – 49, cashier, b. Chicago, IL, s/o John B. Wilson (Goole, England, contractor) and Ann Raper (Snaith, England, housewife); W – 34, housewife, 2nd, b. Concord, d/o Fred J. French (Meriden, farmer) and Ella Carr (Orford, housewife)

Carl of Orford m. Claudia **Colon** of Orford 12/12/1978 in Orford; H – b. CT, s/o Leonard Wilson and Carrie Sherman; W – b. CT, d/o David Hawks and E. Shirley Machie

Dale Alan of Hinsdale m. Jennifer-Lynn **McDonald** of Hinsdale 8/8/1993

John W. of Orford m. Marilla H. **Boody** of Northwood 10/23/1909 in Farmington; H – 65, agent, 2nd, b. Lawrencetown, NS, s/o Joseph Wilson (NS, farmer) and Mary Langly (NS, domestic); W – 57, domestic, 2nd, b. Northwood, d/o David Hoyt (Northwood) and Mary D. Foss (Northwood, domestic)

William A. of Orford m. Shannon L. **Kendall** of Orford 9/6/1997

WINCHESTER,
Claude W. of Orford m. Elsina M. **Leach** of Haverhill 1/5/1952 in N. Haverhill; H – 21, logging, b. ME, s/o Guy W. Winchester (ME) and Helen Burrows (Saco, ME); W – 19, b. VT, d/o Lloyd E. Leach (Saco, ME) and Bessie L. Shute (NH)

WITT,
Warren Ruggles of Leominster, MA m. Edith Ella **Thomas** of Bradford, VT 7/1/1929 in Orford; H – 20, banker, b. N. Brookfield, MA, s/o Charles Warren Witt (Brookfield, MA, mail carrier) and Carrie L. Wyman (Weymouth, MA, housewife); W – 22, saleslady, b. Foxcroft, ME, d/o Fredrick B. Thomas (St. Johns, NB, retired) and Mary L. Scott (Glasville, NY, housewife)

WOOD,
Charles of Orford m. Patience **White** of Orford 10/24/1894 in Orford; H – 41, farmer, b. Sherbrooke, s/o Hazen Wood (Sherbrooke, laborer); W – 38, domestic, 2nd, b. Swanton, PQ, d/o Joseph Boardman (Waterloo, PQ, laborer) and Eliza Porter (domestic)

WOODES,
Ronald L. of Orford m. Linda J. **Perry** of Orford 1/2/1999

WOODWARD,
Elton C. of Orford m. Charlotte F. **Wood** of Bradford, VT 10/31/1940 in Thetford, VT; H – 36, clerk, b. Lyme, s/o Herbert E. Woodward (Richford, VT, farmer) and Jennie Colburn (Berkshire, VT, housewife); W – 33, housewife, 2nd, divorced, b. Danielson, CT, d/o Washington Bullard (Providence, RI) and Annie Jacobs (Danielson, CT)

Elton Carmi m. Dorothy Elizabeth Abbie **Greer** 11/14/1953 in Orford; H – 49, gardner, 2nd, b. Lyme, s/o Herbert E. Woodward (Montgomery, VT) and Jennie L. Colburn (Berkshire, VT); W – 45, teacher, 2nd, b. Bradford, VT, d/o Fred H. Sanborn (Bradford, VT) and Lilla Demar (Franklin)

Norman B. of Orford m. Patricia **Couillard** of Bradford, VT 8/26/1946 in Lyme; H – 24, mechanic, b. Hanover, s/o Norman Woodward (Orford, farmer) and Grace E. Lear (Sunapee, housewife); W – 20, glass blower, b. Bradford, VT, d/o Joseph A. D. Couillard (Canada, blacksmith) and Mary Ouellette (Canada, housewife)

Norman C. of Orford m. Grace Elmira **Lear** of Orford 10/1/1919 in Orford; H – 21, farmer, b. Orford, s/o Byron Woodward (Enosburg, VT, farmer) and Belle Coburn (E. Berkshire, VT, housewife); W – 21, governess, b. Sunapee, d/o Roy P. Lear (Sunapee, mechanic) and Mabel M. Johnson (Lebanon, housewife)

Ronald m. Linda **Hastings** 3/3/1984 in Plainfield

Ronald Lee of Orfordville m. Ellen Marie **Streeter** of Orfordville 2/18/1977 in Orford; H – 22, b. NH, s/o Emerson Woodward and Ruth Gray; W – 18, b. NH, d/o Carl Streeter and Lucy Grimes

Scott Eugene of Orford m. Theresa Marie **King** of Orford 10/2/1993

Wendell L. of Orford m. Linda Lee **Estes** of Lyme 2/12/1966 in Lyme; H – 22, b. Lebanon, s/o Norman C. Woodward and Grace E. Lear; W – 18, b. Hanover, d/o Leonard Estes and Evelyn D. Powers

WORTHMAN,
Paul of New York, NY m. Linda **Gratz** of Orford 7/11/1965 in Orford; H – 24, b. New York, NY, s/o Herman J. Worthman and Lola Blaustein; W – 24, b. New York, NY, d/o Louis P. Gratz and Jean Young

WRIE,
Edward L. of Greensboro m. Mary A. **Archer** of Orford 11/21/1895 in Orford; H – 21, RR man, b. Greensboro, s/o Thomas Wrie (Scotland, farmer); W – 17, domestic, b. Orford, d/o Josiah H. Archer (Orford, farmer)

WRIGHT,
John A. of Orford m. Maud A. **Belford** of Orford 10/19/1901 in Orford; H – 20, laborer, b. Colebrook, s/o John Wright (Boston, MA, farmer) and Melvina Osgood (Milford, housewife); W – 15, domestic, b. Lyme, d/o George H. Belford (farmer) and Emma Woods (Littleton, housewife)
Leon P. of Fairlee, VT m. Ruth C. **Cunningham** of Orford 3/25/1942 in Fairlee, VT; H – 22, laborer, b. Haverhill, s/o Harry E. Wright (Piermont) and Edith C. Ranno (Haverhill); W – 16, at home, b. Fairlee, VT, d/o James Cunningham (Fairlee, VT) and Ida Kidney (Monroe)
Storer E. of Columbia m. Ethel M. **Jordan** of Colebrook 1/2/1902 in Orford; H – 20, laborer, b. Columbia, s/o John Wright (Boston, MA, farmer) and Melvina Osgood (Milford, housewife); W – 17, domestic, b. Colebrook, d/o Edwin Jordan (Bangor, ME) and Lucy Hall (Canaan, VT)

WURTZ,
John of Bradford, VT m. Sandra **Fay** of Bradford, VT 10/5/1991

YOUNG,
Albert C. of Montpelier, VT m. Blanche A. **Straw** of Waitsfield, VT 10/9/1932 in Orford; H – 29, farmer, 2nd, b. E. Montpelier, VT, s/o Claude Young (Worcester, VT, mechanic) and Mabel Cutler (E. Montpelier, VT, housewife); W – 28, at home, b. Marshfield, VT, d/o Clarence C. Straw (Hereford, PQ, farmer) and Edith L. Damon (Dixville, PQ, housewife)
Leon F., Jr. of Lyme m. Winifred A. **Streeter** of Orford 1/25/1951 in Bradford, VT; H – 21, soldier, b. Orford, s/o Leon F. Young (Chateaugay, NY) and Louise M. Columbia (St. Albans, VT); W – 20, b. Orford, d/o Richard Butman (Orford) and Marion Streeter (Orford)
Mowry Wayne of Ely, VT m. Jacqueline M. **Landgraf** of Orford 12/27/1951 in Orford; H – 22, farmer, b., S. Kingston, RI, s/o Ernest Young (W. Greenwich, RI) and Mabel Wood (Coventry,

RI); W – 22, stenographer, b. Harvey, IL, d/o Myron J. Landgraf (Chicago, IL) and Pearl B. Anderson (Chicago, IL)

Abbott, Florence B. – Ladd, Charles P.
Abbott, Gertrude Lillian – Higgins, Frank H.
Abbott, Susie M. – Hall, Frank P.
Adams, Ann Marie – Hull, Preston Howard
Adams, Connie – Brady, David
Adams, Irene M. – LaBounty, Francis F.
Adams, Pauline M. – Snow, Bernard D.
Adams, Wendy – Millican, John
Ainalovan, Elene A. – Super, Kenneth G.
Aja, Aurora C. – Borne, Albert
Albaugh, Adrienne S. – Schwarz, Randy A.
Aldrich, Flora M. – Spencer, James C.
Alexander, Denise – Schauer, Paul Scott
Alger, Alice E. – Adams, Raymond H.
Alger, Heather Ann – Higgins, Scott Timothy
Allen, Patricia – Pearce, Dale
Anderson, Marcia – Knapp, David
Andrews, Beverly – Potry, Arthur
Andrews, Genevieve Marie – Gomo, Richard Kendall
Andrews, June Flora – Cummings, Clyde Asa, Jr.
Applebee, Esther V. – Shafer, Bartron B., Jr.
Archer, Anna M. – Glover, Alan Earle
Archer, Eva E. – Smith, Lewis W.
Archer, Flora R. – Shelley, Sidney C.
Archer, Grace M. – Thompson, Joseph A.
Archer, Martha I. – Twiss, Alden S.
Archer, Mary A. – Wrie, Edward L.
Archer, Sarah A. – Smith, Clarence S.
Arnesen, Deborah – Trunzo, Thomas, Jr.
Auger, Amy – Nickerson, Christopher
Austin, Addie M. – Page, Freeman G.
Austin, Bessie E. – Marden, George B.
Austin, Delia M. – Miles, Elbridge C.
Austin, Kimberly – Pease, Harrison
Avery, Elizabeth – Beal, Frank J.
Avery, Emma – Claflin, Herbert
Avery, Lizzie W. – Morey, Charles H.
Ayala, Michelle – Smith, Dennis

Baade, Kelly J. – Trombley, Scott D.
Bagnall, Nancy Jo – Presson, Joseph Anthony

Bailey, Elizabeth Alice – Swan, Charles Henry
Bailey, Flora A. – Marsh, Elwin D.
Bailey, Hattie C. – Butman, Lurlyn C.
Bailey, Ida M. – Learned, William E.
Bailey, Mary E. – Marsh, George C.
Bailey, Mary N. (Niles) – Cunningham, George H.
Baker, Clara Belle (Webster) – Franklin, Harry Emerson
Baker, Donna Lynne – Corpieri, Stuart Carleton
Baker, Dorothy F. – Pierson, William L.
Baker, Helen E. – Sanborn, Joseph H.
Baker, Inez S. (Smith) – Hill, John A.
Baker, Lula B. – Elliott, Stanley C.
Baker, Rose Iola – Foote, Edward Bertram
Baker, Ruth A. – Spooner, Henry E.
Balch, Wanita – Marsh, Henry G.
Ball, Diane – Pease, Gene
Ball, Lucille Eva – Andrews, Clarence H., III
Ballam, Elizabeth – Bean, Oliver L.
Bancroft, Dorothea J. – Marshall, Stuart A.
Barber, Kelly – Ricker, Kevin
Barnes, Ida L. – Finney, Frank G.
Barnes, Nellie V. – Foster, Arthur B.
Barnett, Adelle – Marsh, Frank E.
Barnett, Maude – Perkins, Ralph E.
Barney, Dorothy M. (Bushee) – Andrews, Donald R.
Barone, Robin – Lea, Sydney
Barry, Ann Morrison – Mitchell, William George
Bartlett, Etta I. – Clough, George L.
Bayley, Lucy O. – Blake, Fay E.
Bean, Bernice B. – Huntington, Sumner
Bean, Carlie M. – Neff, Leon G.
Bean, Ethel M. – Chandler, Henry J.
Bean, Evelyn Vera (Leach) – Elliott, Martin Edward
Bean, Lois Henrietta – Fadden, Edward
Bean, Martha L. – Clark, Leander D. H.
Bean, Patricia – Fillian, Randy
Bean, Pauline Sandra – Seace, James Chester
Bean, Phylis A. – Ashley, Herbert A.
Bean, Ruth A. – Clark, Charlie W.
Beaton, Annabell – Roberts, Cyrus L.
Bechard, Prudence Louise - Schwarz, Randy Allen

Becker, Frances Emma – Nutter, Theodore Lawrence
Bedell, Annie A. – Pease, Clarence H.
Bedell, Annie R. (Colby) – Learned, Charles W.
Belford, Maud A. – Wright, John A.
Bellows, Rebecca – Daugherty, Michael
Bender, Jane S. – Burke, James A.
Benjamin, Becky A. – Goodrich, Brian W.
Benzemann, Marie – Whitaker, Donald
Bermingham, Marianne – White, Paul
Berwick, Bethany Laurel - Sewell, Micah Alexander
Berwick, Katherine – Dickey, Joshua
Bettis, Rachel Lee - Kidder, Fred Albion, II
Bigelow, Gladys (Elliott) – Marsh, Walter
Billingham, Florence – Bean, Ralph Carl
Bingham, Edith – Jenkins, Leslie Forrest
Bixby, Karen M. – Mallett, Richard B.
Blake, Bethany J. – Miller, John T.
Blake, Janice E. – Grady, Michael A.
Blake, Lucille D. – Palifka, Robert George
Blodgett, Alice M. (Ramsey) – Kenyon, Walter C.
Blodgett, Lurleen – Munn, Reginold C.
Bockus, Beulah B. – Dyke, George Carl
Bomhower, Donna – LaBelle, John
Boody, Marilla H. (Hoyt) – Wilson, John W.
Borger, Ann Elizabeth – Rennie, James Edward
Borger, Jane M. – Dyke, Calvin Ronald
Bosence, Mary P. – Chase, George F.
Boudrean, Elizabeth – Foote, Parker E.
Bouley, Suzanne – Ricker, Kevin
Bourque, Sandra Ann – Mercier, Ronald Wayne
Bouthelliere, Marcell – Gunette, Homer
Boyce, Nancy – Byers, William A.
Boynton, Hazel E. – Downing, Roland E.
Brackett, Jennifer – Steele, Robert
Brailey, Doris (Hartsor) – Trevithick, Earl M.
Bridges, Emily Anna – Boone, Philip Gordon
Brock, Bessie L. – Dayton, James H.
Brooks, Flora A. – Burbank, Edmund A.
Brooks, Maybelle P. – Cobb, Leon E.
Brooks, Sharon Jane – Pierce, Charles Rexford
Broughan, Cheryl A. – Bacon, William P.

Brown, Dorothy – Caplan, David
Brown, Inez – Butman, Charles H.
Brown, Lori – Quackenbush, Gary F.
Brunette, Mary – Feigl, Mark
Bruno, Tammy Louise – MacQueen, Jeffrey James
Bryant, Linda – King, Dana
Bryer, Elaine Ruth – Quackenbush, Robert H.
Bryer, June – Quackenbush, William
Bryer, Margaret May – Weibel, John G.
Bryer, Ruth Alice (Cummings) – Gasper, George Arthur
Buck, Jennie E. – Willard, Leonard W.
Buker, Sarah Joanne - Jones, Alden Emery
Bullock, Elizabeth – Spectorsky, Auguste
Bunten, Christine Evelyn – Dyke, Eugene Leo
Bunten, Marilyn J. – Covey, Richard E., Jr.
Burnell, Benita – Randall, Alfred
Burnett, Karen – Kurie, Robert
Burnham, Bessie A. – Bean, Fay C.
Burnham, Blanche H/ - Bean, Philip L.
Burns, Judith Mary – Gaitley, Michael John
Burton, Jamie – Cody, Kenneth
Butler, Pamela – Gaines, James
Butler, Susan Page – Kling, P. Chase
Butman, Pearl Alma – Giroux, Arthur Joseph
Button, Elizabeth A. – Montgomery, Richard
Buzzell, Frances – Morrison, Harry E.
Byers, Ruth (Ingerson) - Dow, Earl Chester

Cahill, Carole Ann – Tullar, Nathan Charles
Caldon, Julia G. – Avery, Charles A.
Cameron, Margaret Ann – Dyer, Leslie Allen
Camp, Katherine F. – Baker, William Henry
Campbell, Carol Janice – Butman, Herbert Charles
Canfield, Josephine Shirley – Barber, Joseph William, Jr.
Cappiali, AnnMarie – Smith, William Gunner
Carle, Audrey M. – Boardman, Clyde W.
Carle, Mabelle R. – Underhill, Berton D.
Carr, Evelyn – Emerson, Harold B.
Carr, Helen E. – Sleeper, Finlay P.
Carr, Lydia W. – Carr, J. Frank
Carr, Martha J. – Hunt, Lee F.

Carr, Mary M. – Hazen, Irving A.
Carrier, Anna Mae (Streeter) – Currier, George E.
Carter, Rita A. (O'Brien) – Pease, Gerald E.
Carvalho, Joan Marie – Harris, Mark Steven
Casey, Brenda Maureen – Sibole, Gary Richard
Casey, Karen Ann – Larson, Brian Pierce
Castiglione, Anne Marie – Bean, Maurice Fay
Cate, Dani J. – Emery, Nathan N.
Ceuci, Linda – Cassani, John
Chabot, Gladys E. (Lee) – Guyer, John W.
Chamberlain, Doris – Finney, George Henry
Chamberlain, Marion – Franklin, Arthur L.
Chandler, Mary L. – Hall, Fred P.
Chapin, Carolyn C. – Sanborn, Richard H.
Chapin, Donna – Nutter, Theodore
Chapin, Linda Lois – Pearson, David Axel
Chaplin, Katherine Ramsey – Dervin, Daniel Arthur
Chapman, Kayne – Hartley, Gerald
Chapman, Kim – Bush, Douglas
Chapman, Mabel E. – Flanders, Harry H.
Chapman, Mabel E. – Rhodes, George W.
Chapman, Mary E. (Willis) – Swallow, John
Charbono, Donna – McKee, Henry
Chase, Andrea Violet – Canterbury, David Shawn
Chase, Cornelia Ann – Titus, Calvin Augustus, Jr.
Chase, Eda May – Brown, Lester Rupert
Chase, Ivis E. – McLeod, James H.
Chase, Kathryn Inez – Reed, Jesse Jonathan
Chase, Maywood E. (Edson) – Chase, Rufus E.
Chase, Myrtie F. – Daisey, Roydon H.
Chase, Shirley Jane – Deblois, Alton Guy
Chesley, Carol Ann – Perry, Anthony Wayne
Chesley, Nellie M. – Gray, Lester E.
Chiasson, Kathy – Manson, Mark
Chioti, Eda – Adams, John P., Jr.
Church, Carrie F. – Dennis, George W.
Cicotte, Fay – Lester, Paul
Cimpean, Delia – Hendrick, Richard M.
Clark, Arabelle H. (Hardy) – Learned, Jonas G.
Clark, Ellen M. – Morrison, S. R.
Clark, Evelyn – Dennis, Wallace E.

Clark, Marion H. – Franklin, Arthur L.
Clegg, Suellen – Edwards, Jason
Clifford, Sondra Eve – Farnham, Bruce Stanley
Coburn, Rosenna Diane – Picknell, Forrest Otto
Colburn, Jeanette A. – Biers, Richard P.
Colby, Carol L. – Robie, Scott E.
Colon, Claudia (Hawks) – Wilson, Carl
Cook, Jessica Leah - Semen, Peter Michael
Cook, Lauren Elizabeth – Belyea, Philip Roy
Cook, Mildred M. (Doyle) – Robinson, Samuel A.
Cookman, Leona (Morey) – Brown, Raymond H.
Copp, Geneva Agnes – Chase, Penrose W.
Corliss, Mary M. – Laselle, Oscar D.
Corliss, Sheilah Mae – Daisey, Royden Wayne
Cornetta, Joyce – Atwood, Caleb
Costa, Traci Ann – Hall, Julio Enrriguez
Cothran, Helen Sperry – Richmond, Robert Gould
Cougle, Ann – Haslam, Edward
Couillard, Patricia – Woodward, Norman B.
Courtney, Margaret F. (Bowdger) – Humphrey, Wilbert
Creasey, Joanne – Kangas, William
Crowe, Addie M. – Hatch, Bert E.
Crowell, Ruth T. – Marshall, Harry C.
Cummings, Betty Lou – Messer, Paul Bridgeman
Cummings, Carolyn – Keats, John
Cummings, Judith Ann – Pease, Arthur Samuel
Cummings, Madeline E. – Chaplin, Harry Duncan
Cummings, Mildred – Huntington, Guy S.
Cummings, Myrtle E. – Davis, Floyd Ellis
Cummings, Nellie M. – Donnelly, Robert J.
Cummings, Patricia E. (Gilbault) – Dibbern, William
Cummings, Rosie Mary – Smith, Stanley Richard
Cunningham, Hattie – Gardner, V. F.
Cunningham, Ruth C. – Wright, Leon P.
Cushing, Edna M. – Miller, Fred H.
Cushing, Stella – Streeter, Ray N.
Cushman, Minnie W. (Worthley) – Moulton, Ernest K.
Cutler, Florence May – Smith, Carl Wilbur
Cutler, Gladys A. – Marsh, Ralph E.
Cutler, Grace I. – Marsh, Roy C.
Cutting, Beulah C. – Marsh, Fred C.

Daisey, Malissa J. – Beaupre, Peter E.
Damiani, Carol – Boynton, Arthur
Danforth, Nellie J. – Morrison, Harry E.
Daniels, Terri – Brown, Gary
Davis, Doris Helene – Morin, Romeo Edward, Jr.
Davis, Hazel Beth – Pushee, Clarence Leslie, Jr.
Davis, Irene May – Huntley, Douglas Harold
Davis, Louise Myrtie – Marsh, Fred Allen
Davis, Marjorie Ruth – Ray, Rowell Randolph
Davis, Nancy Ruth – Whittaker, Benjamin, Jr.
Day, Marcelene K. – Williams, Norman E.
Day, Ruth Alfretta – Bean, Donald Fay
DeLong, Lillian – Webber, Parker G.
DeLong, Lillian – Purdy, George M.
DeMarle, Susan – O'Keefe, Stephen
Demers, Peg – Villar, Paul
Denis, Laurie Jean – Gould, Clayton Edward
Dennis, Florence M. (Leach) – Cross, George H.
Dennis, Mayme A. – Whitcomb, Edward E.
Dennis, Myrtie M. – Kelley, Ralph N.
Derick, Mildred – Fox, Cylon A.
Dickey, Lois – Spencer, James C.
Dickey, Tammy – Bean, Charles
Dike, Lillian L. – Davis, Prescott W.
Dike, Lucy Betsy Elizabeth – Claflin, Edwin Loomis
Dionne, Susan Marie – Blake, Michael E.
DiPrisco, Claire – Durgin, Peter
Doan, Alice – Hodgson, John Helmes
Doan, Isabel – Holman, Paul R.
Doan, Isabel W. (Wilson) – Dyer, Lyman T.
Dobbins, Esther – Marsh, Mark
Dobbins, Sarita Marie – Baker, William Henry, III
Dodge, Emily Elizabeth - Rogers, Benjamin Andrew
Donaldson, Charlotte M. – Thompson, Warner W., Jr.
Donaldson, Mary H. (Whitman) – Donaldson, Samuel H.
Donovan, Beverly Ann (Pebbles) – Willey, Wilson Marshall, Jr.
Doob, Penelope – Parker, Graham
Dorcey, Eileen May - Mallas, George Peter
Dow, Dorothy Alice – Dyke, Benjamin F., Jr.
Dow, Eda – Claflin, William H. S.
Dow, Gladys P. – Weeks, George W.

Downing, Dell – Moses, Harry A.
Downing, Ethel – Dow, Bert
Downing, Sharon – Petersen, Andrew
Downing, Victoria E. – Currier, Jessie W.
Drew, Antoinette (McPherson) – Washburn, Frank E.
Dunakin, Claribel Selena (Partridge) – Shonio, Gardner Warren
Dunbar, Mabel E. – Tallman, Sidney J.
Dunnells, Elizabeth – Davis, Brian
Durso, Maria S. – McIntyre, Michael E.
Dyke, Barbara Ann – Gray, Dale Edward
Dyke, Brenda Eileen – Thomson, David L.
Dyke, Connie Lee – Ball, Steven Albert
Dyke, Dorisann – Clements, Scott Allen
Dyke, Dorisann – Ross, William, Jr.
Dyke, Janet Mary – Downing, Richard Lee, Jr.
Dyke, Jennifer M. – Lister, Jeffrey G.
Dyke, Kathy – Irle, Stephen
Dyke, Kimberly – Pushee, William
Dyke, Lurline E. – Record, Leonard W.
Dyke, Mabel M. – Hunt, Reginald R.
Dyke, Norine A. – Gray, Richard C.
Dyke, Sandra Lee – Fullington, Ronald Bruce

Edington, Gretchen E. – Tatham, Donald A.
Edmands, Debra – Clough, John, III
Egley, Mila May – Rogers, Lloyd Byron
Ellis, Laurie – Noyes, Howard, Jr.
Ellsworth, Evelyn M. – Tallman, Sidney J.
Emerson, Lula W. (Wilkins) – Ansell, Ray Harry
Emerson, Mary L. (Beals) – Lang, Paul
Emery, Bernice N. – Pierson, Amos F.
Eppig, Helen Colette – Deblois, Richard Guy
Erastova, Natalia - Landgraf, Gregory Wayne
Estes, Geraldine J. (Johnson) – Washburn, H. Horton
Estes, Linda Lee – Woodward, Wendell L.
Estes, Tammy Jean – Piper, James Mason
Evans, Janet (Piper) – Grant, John Henry

Fadden, Josie M. – Bean, Wallace B.
Fagan, Bessie – Phillips, Daniel
Farnham, Lisa – Piper, Scott

Fay, Laurie – Noyes, Stacy
Fay, Sally Ann – Nutter, Theodore Lawrence
Fay, Sandra – Wurtz, John
Felch, Clara B. – Foote, Harry B.
Fields, Mary Jane – Huntington, Harold L.
Fifield, Helen H. (Hossington) – Flint, Ralph
Fillian, Beatrice B. – Perry, Walter H.
Fillian, Delores Delvina – Drew, Richard Henry
Fillian, Dorothy G. – Hammond, William A.
Fillian, Rachel Alicia – Fish, William Lewis
Fillian, Ruth Delvina – Davis, Donald Francis
Fillip, Joyce Marie – Hanson, Gregory Joseph
Findlay, Jennifer May – Taylor, Timothy James
Fish, Alice E. (Martin) – Morey, Bradley Z.
Fitzbag, Linda L. – Daisey, Allen L.
Fitzgerald, Kathryn Gale – Green, William Peter
Fitzhugh, Portia – Karol, John J., Jr.
Fitzpatrick, Madison – Dalton, Paul
Flagg, Andrea Christine – Thomson, Rob Roy
Flanders, Katie Lyn – Martindale, Philip Howard
Flower, Charlotte Alexis – Straidel, Laurence Brian
Fontaine, Debra – Messer, Lowell
Foote, Helen B. – Elliott, Ashton W.
Foote, Rose (Baker) – Willey, Wilson M.
Forbush, Jill M. – Dorman, Thomas E.
Foster, Myra E. – Shepard, Robinson
Fournier, Denise – Fadden, Richard
Franklin, Alice M. – Baker, G. H.
Franklin, Priscilla Jeanne – Harrington, Cedrick Emanuel
Franklin, Ruth E. – Sanborn, Joseph H.
French, Deanne – Hamel, Stephen
French, Sarah Leigh – Ward, John Lawrence, Jr.
Frey, Jeannette M. – DeLaurier, Gregory
Frost, Kathleen Louise – Evans, Leighton John
Fuller, Juanita M. – Shearer, Richard A.
Fuller, Vivian C. – Goodrich, Howard C.
Fullington, Ericka Jean – Gray, Leonard Richard

Gage, Effie A. – Dennis, Leroy E.
Gale, Bertha G. – Goodwin, Harry L.
Gallup, Carol Jean – Connor, Paul Rich

Gallup, Mary Lynn – Welch, Jack P.
Gallup, Noreen Elizabeth – Estes, Russell Gene
Gammell, Jennie E. – Bowen, Clarence S.
Gardner, Hattie C. – Richardson, Arthur J.
Gardyne, Heidi Leigh - McKee, Henry Arthur
Garrett, Aurora – Allen, John
Garrettson, Linda Jane – Pizzica, Frank Joseph, Jr.
Gaskill,, Eliza H. (Horton) – Wilcox, Harry P.
Gauthier, Meghan Nicole – Morey, Scott Allen
George, Kathleen E. – Shepard, Russell F.
George, Marjorie W. (Wheatley) – Gray, Lester Elmer
Gibson, Evalyn (Runnels) – McMackin, Carleton E.
Giesing, Brenda – Gray, Todd
Giesing, Sheena – Rich, Michael
Giesing, Tammy Christine – Gray, Scott Matthew
Gilbert, Helen F. – Corliss, Benjamin C.
Gilbert, Lucille V. – Perry, Leighton A.
Gilman, Mary E. – Dennis, Carl W.
Giroux, Alma Pearl (Butman) – Kennedy, Kenneth H.
Gladstone, Karen – Quackenbush, Lyle
Gluek, Martha Huntington – Evanich, David Paul
Goddard, Irene – Marsh, Arthur L.
Godfrey, Cynthia Lynn – Lawson, Terry George
Godfrey, Maritza G. – Stimson, Andrew P.
Godville, Louella Jean – Weeks, Wayne Alvin
Goewey, Bonny M. (Stoughton) – Garrett, Leonard S.
Goodrich, Brandy Lynn - Dunbar, Christopher White
Goodwin, Emma E. – Clough, George L.
Goodwin, Lulu M. – Derrick, George E.
Gould, Teresa – Hook, Stephen
Grant, Ethel M. (Pushee) – Horton, Walter A.
Grant, Trudy A. – Adams, Jon H.
Grasmere, Louise – Stearly, Gary
Gratz, Katharine – Lockwood, Brocton Dewey
Gratz, Linda – Worthman, Paul
Graves, Jane – Willis, Russell
Gray, Kimberly – Nutter, Elmer
Gray, Pauline E. (Estes) – Gray, Bruce
Green, Donna Lee (Morris) – Robinson, Robert Allen
Green, Kathryn – Clements, Scott Allen
Green, Kathryn Lee – Perry, David William

Greenleaf, Helena Miranda – Conboy, George Edwin
Greenwood, Vicki – Soper, Taylor
Greer, Dorothy Elizabeth Abbie (Sanborn) – Woodward, Elton Carmi
Greer, Joyce Elaine – Gray, Harley, Jr.
Gregory, Edna Eva – Reed, Donald R.
Griffin, Bertha M. – Huntington, C. W.
Griggs, Cornelia P. (Preston) – Lightner, G. Cass
Griggs, Katherine (Clark) – Huntington, Guy Sylvester
Guest, Bonnie Leigh – Pease, Gene Alan
Guilmette, Lillian – Bean, Bertram
Guyer, Julia L. (LeMire) – Guyer, John W.

Hadley, Beatrice A. – Hutchins, Gerald F.
Hadlock, Cena I. – Clifford, Lewis H.
Hall, Beatrice L. (Dugre) – Sanborn, Ernest F.
Hall, Catherine – Cleveland, Dennis Allen
Hall, Eva Viola – Paige, Asahel D.
Hall, Frances – Stevens, Dana E.
Hall, Sarah – Gibson, Terry L.
Hall, Susan Carter – Carver, Douglas W.
Hamilton, Shawn – Olsen, Peter
Hammond, Addie A. – Rollins, Hiram B.
Hammond, H. H. – Sanders, Frank E.
Hammond, Patricia S. – Edgar, William B.
Hammond, Patricia Southworth – Mack, Delbert Wayne
Hance, Lindsay – Kosnik, Christopher
Hannaford, Marjorie – Cummings, Vernon D.
Hardy, Florence W. – Weeks, Alvin B.
Harrington, Joanne – Washburn, Neil
Harrington, Ramona – Carpenter, George Richard
Harris, Erma L. – Carr, Henry H.
Hart, Sarah Naomi – Sanborn, Robert Bayard, Jr.
Harvey, Margaret F. – Finney, George W.
Harvis, Anne (Schwartzman) – Weinheimer, Sidney
Harwood, Hilary – Knowlton, Spencer
Harwood, Lee Marie – Cady, Thomas J.
Hastings, Linda – Woodward, Ronald
Hatch, Eva M. – Simonds, C. G.
Hawkins, Hattie B. (Howland) – Moses, Jonathan
Hayes, Kristina Ann – Hill, Jeffrey Alan
Hays, Elinor Elaine (Gardiner) – Dyke, Eugene Leo

Haywood, Lori – Dyke, Tracy
Heath, Amy L. – Germana, Erik J.
Heath, Irene (Elliott) – Marsh, Leon C.
Heath, Lutheria M. – Bean, Carroll J.
Heath, Marjorie M. – Pike, Allie Chester
Heath, Maxine L. – Pike, Horace Earle
Herbert, Florence (Pecore) – Ladeau, Charles W.
Hess, Barbara Ruth – Veghte, Lewis, Jr.
Hibbard, Verna M. – Marsh, Glenn G.
Hildreth, Florence – Badger, Ernest W.
Hill, Carrie – Quimby, Clyde
Hill, Grace – Carl, Albert J.
Himadi, Elaine – Schorsch, Michael
Hinckley, Annie D. – Ingerson, Benjamin H.
Hodgson, Deborah – Corporon, David
Hogg, Margaret – Hnadelsman, Paul
Holloway, Elizabeth – Dyke, Terry
Holloway, Lucille N. (Bailey) – Pocock, Erle V.
Honney, Cheryl – Ulz, Andrew
Hook, Ruth Marian – Thompson, Wayne Joseph
Hook, Susan L. – Taylor, Larry A.
Horne, Hazel Grace – Merchant, Donald Raymond
Horton, Bernice M. – Washburn, Harvey L.
Hosmer, Janice May – Sanborn, David Moore
Hoss, Mary Evelyn (Goodwin) – Berggren, Karl Erik
Howard, Melissa – Malloy, Mark
Howard, Theda L. – Pease, Glenn F.
Howe, Elizabeth J. – Smith, Joel C.
Hubbard, Rosa – Luce, Leslie F.
Hubbell, Alberta E. (Olstead) – Gardner, Frank H.
Huckins, Barbara Alice – White, Milton L.
Huckins, Frances M. – Gould, Edward G.
Huckins, Helen A. – Marsh, Leon C., Jr.
Hudson, Nancy L. – Marsh, Fred A.
Hudson, Theresa May – Sanborn, Neil Heath
Hugg, Jessica A. – Gould, Nathan G.
Humiston, Mary L. – Patch, George M.
Huntington, Ida L. – Tillotson, Wendell E.
Huntington, Lindsay – Hancock, William P.
Hurst, Mary B. (Cadwell) – Brock, Charles E.
Huse, Anita V. – Bean, Harold E.

Hutchins, Diane – Davis, Brent

Ingersoll, Milly – Strong, Charles
Ingerson, Ruth W. – Byers, Albert C.

Jarvis, Susan – Robinson, Dana
Jennings, Muriel F. – Dreesbach, Philip P.
Jewett, Volisa Mae – Roberts, Maurice A., Jr.
Johnson, Augusta – Smith, Eddie E.
Johnson, Geraldine – Estes, Stephen Lee
Johnson, Mildred (Silloway) – Hubbard, William Edward
Johnston, Brenda – Smith, David
Jones, Lucy Emma (Grimes) – Streeter, Carl Moody
Jones, Marion E. – Allen, Josiah
Jones, Patricia – DeWitt, William
Jones, Shirley Jean – Pierson, Edward Wallace
Jordan, Ethel M. – Wright, Storer E.
Jorgensen, Jessica Lyn – Hebb, Jeffrey Allan
Joslyn, Marion Elaine – Brown, Charles Jerry
Judd, Bessie E. – Still, Grover C.

Kathan, Grace J. – Sargent, Norman P.
Keller, Susan – Edwards, Jason
Kendall, Sarah D. – Movelle, Paul A.
Kendall, Shannon L. – Wilson, William A.
Keneson, Alice E. – Currier, Norman J.
Kenyon, Bessie A. – Horton, Walter A.
Kenyon, Deborah – McGoff, James
Keys, Gertrude M. – Clark, George C.
Kimball, Frances M. (Cunningham) – Hannaford, Hazen A.
King, Alice C. (Chesley) – Gray, Lester E.
King, Lizzie B. – Smith, Hazen L.
King, Theresa Marie – Woodward, Scott Eugene
Kligerman, Hilary – Schroeder, Thomas Edward
Knight, Carol Anne (Wheelock) – Carr, Francis Winthrop
Kowal, Marilyn E. – Vasil, Thomas

LaBelle, Michele Ann – Ellis, Robert Paul
LaBombard, Cynthia Louise – Fillian, Gary Lee
LaBruna, Danielle T. – Williams, Jason C.
Lackey, Sandra Jean – Gallup, William H.

Ladeau, Ethel F. – Streeter, Ralph Ray
LaDeau, Pauline Dora – Stearns, Reginald E.
Ladeau, Shirley Anne – Gendron, Wilfred E.
Laflame, Louisa – Learned, Jonas G.
Lahmann, Cathy – Tullar, Steven
Lambert, Rita F. – Nolet, Roger J.
LaMontagne, Chris – Gulick, Kenneth
LaMontagne, Margaret – Gonyer, Clyde W.
Lamphere, Emily (Straw) – Wilbur, Chandler A.
Lamprey, Ella S. – Huckins, George M.
Landgraf, Jacqueline M. – Young, Mowry Wayne
Landgraf, Karen – Hibbard, Lawrence
Lang, Hittie R. – Carr, Clarence H.
Lang, Mary J. – Southard, Charles G.
LaPoint, Gloria E. – Lander, Richard Edward
Larocque, Kathryn Ann – Bean, Warren Lee
Lary, Nancy – Braley, David
Lauzetta, Susan Ann – Sanderson, Robert Currier
LaValley, Colleen Elizabeth – Harding, Glen Paul
Lavoie, Carole A. – Bowker, James F.
Lawrence, Nellie E. – Cochran, Charles W.
Leach, Elsina M. – Winchester, Claude W.
Leach, Florence M. – Dennis, Ernest C.
Lear, Grace Elmira – Woodward, Norman C.
Learned, Chestina M. – Richmond, Philip L.
Learned, Hattie F. – Merrill, Myron S.
Leavitt, Elizabeth – Brown, Herbert N.
LeClair, Mary Jean – Johnston, Eric Toson
Lee, Mabel Elizabeth (Cook) – French, Harold C.
Leete, Lori K. – Taylor, Matthew J.
Leger, Nicole – Hoisington, Douglas
Lemay, Holly Cristine – Daisey, Amos Frederick
Lemontague, Ardell – Lebarge, Joe
Leonard, Viola M. (Shortsleve) – Rigg, Sidney J.
Lewis, Beverly – Jackson, Jeffrey
Lewis, Dorothy L. – Bean, Norman C.
Lindquist, Bonnie – Osmer, Harry
Lovejoy, S. Josephine – Davis, John P.
Lufkin, Evalyn K. – Stearns, Frank A.
Lufkin, Isabelle L. – Watson, Leonard W.
Luhman, Carol – Tatham, James

Lyon, Lottie – Parker, I. Willis

MacDonald, Karen M. – Billings, Charles, Jr.
MacDonald, Mary – Carlton, Charles Merritt
Mack, Evelyn Grace – Corpieri, Ernest F.
Mack, Irene A. – Chase, Morris A.
Mack, Karen Elizabeth - Piacentini, Robert George, Jr.
Mack, Nettie L. – Sanders, Harry G.
Mack, Patricia H. (Hammond) – Michaud, Gerald G.
MacLeod, Flora G. – McBain, John
Madsen, Mildred Beatrice (Elliott) – Merrill, Allison Herbert
Magoon, Susan (Wilson) – Tuttle, William
Malcolm, Alice A. (Allen) – Atkins, Charles F.
Manchester, Retar (Goddard) – Marsh, Walter H.
Mann, Mabel – Webster, Freeman H.
Mann, Mary E. – Smith, Carl C.
Marcott, May Arvilla (Temple) – Blair, Elsworth J.
Marsh, Alice M. – Bean, Edwin G.
Marsh, Clara Fern – Ellis, Keith D.
Marsh, Della Edyth – Godfrey, Roy B.
Marsh, Diana Carol – Claflin, Franklin George
Marsh, Edna F. – Ladd, Burns H.
Marsh, Evelyn V. – Grant, Alanson W.
Marsh, Freda Iola – Parker, Charles Andrew
Marsh, Helen Mae – Pike, Weymouth Henry
Marsh, Janet Eva (Balch) – Marsh, Elwin Ralph
Marsh, Janet Maude – Willey, Wilson Marshall, Jr.
Marsh, Joyce Ann – McKee, William Bert
Marsh, Juanita Ann – Schwarz, George J.
Marsh, June Althea – Garrett, Floyd Alfred
Marsh, Kathryn – Sobetzer, Jay
Marsh, Lillian Eva – Weeks, Charles A.
Marsh, Mary Jane – Taylor, Ronald Leslie
Martin, Barbara J. – Sleeper, Eric C.
Martin, Sandra Ann – Chapin, Gaylo O.
Mason, Anne – Williams, Warren
Mathieu, Charlotte – Waters, Joel
May, Michelle – Gendron, Bernard
Mayotte, Lisa A. – Taylor, Bruce F., Jr.
McCann, Lynn – Schillaber, Charles Russell
McCarthy, Regina – Novick, Michael A.

McCrillis, Julia E. (Hackett) – Claflin, Willis B.
McDonald, Jennifer-Lynn – Wilson, Dale Alan
McDonough, Karen – Cook, Timothy Robert
McDuffee, Alma (Day) – Chase, John W.
McEwan, Lorna – Desruisseaux, R. L.
McEwan, Marcia – Willis, Clarence
McGinnis, Cara – Dyke, Daniel
McGoff, Margaret Josephine (LaMotte) – LaMontagne, Gilbert Edgar
McGoff, Theresa Marie – Taylor, Harold James
McIndoe, Florence – Carr, Edward
McIntire, Edna G. (Pease) – McLeod, Joseph W.
McIntyre, Annie – Morey, Erving W.
McIntyre, Ester – Morey, Eddie S.
McKee, Ethel Jane – Garrett, Eugene Earl, Jr.
McKee, Lois Louise – Rowell, Francis Everett
McKee, Ruth Ella – Grimes, Ronald G.
McKenzie, Helen E. – Mack, Ralph Roger
McLaughlin, Jane – Danielson, Charles
McPherson, Maude – Harris, Willard R.
Meier, Barbara – Kloeblen, William
Merrill, Ashley Lynn - Crowe, Ty Jayson
Merrill, Donna L. – Taylor, Rodney L.
Merrill, Dorothy M. – Marsh, Fred C.
Merrill, Stella A. – Pease, Chester W.
Messer, Christine – Ulrich, Phillip
Messer, Eleanor (Dix) – Greer, Nelson Raymond
Messer, Wendee – Williams, Roy
Miller, Benita J. – Boardman, George R.
Miller, Heidi Jean – Higdon, Kenneth Guy
Miller, Ingrid – Hale, David
Miller, Joy Audrie – Copp, Franklin Lloyd
Miller, Lise – Venning, James
Miller, Lois Ann – Osten, Henry Van Dyne
Miller, Sabina – McMahon, William
Miller, Susan – Hild, David
Milligan, Wendy – Streeter, Dennis
Milner, Rosenna – Schwarz, Robert
Mock, Alicia May – Chapin, Jayme Owen
Montgomery, Sarah J. (Place) – Brown, Roy H.
Moody, Maria L. – Matyka, John
Moody, Thelma A. – Williams, Ezra N.

Morey, Christina A. – Gasper, Andrew J.
Morey, Esther (Rowe) – Chase, John K.
Morey, Eva May – Moses, Perley
Morris, Donna Lee – Green, William Edgar, III
Morse, Ella P. (French) – Wilson, Alfred B.
Moss, Jeanette (Patterson) – Brown, Robert Burdett
Moulton, Emma J. – Philbrick, Alvin S.
Mountfort, Mary E. – Chase, Timothy R.
Mousley, Julia C. (Quint) – Davis, Hiram W.
Muchmore, Sadie R. – Carr, Lewis P., Jr.
Munn, Ruth E. – Swan, Harold W.

Nantel, Danielle A. – Collopy, Joseph W.
Newman, Marianne – Phelan, Jack
Newton, Karen – Gray, Edmund
Nichols, Emma B. – Thayer, Gilbert M.
Nickles, Barbie – Kesek, David
Nickols, Clara E. (Phelps) – Hall, Francis H.
Nogel, Kathleen Louise – Bahlkow, Gary D.
Northhouse, Ruby Lila (Darling) – Carter, Joseph Carroll
Noyes, Patricia – Hoehl, William
Noyes, Penny Lee – Sergent, Ralph David
Nutter, Elsie Etta – Stefanazzi, Eugene
Nutter, Flora E. (Casady) – Gilbert, Harry E.
Nutter, Joyce Ann – Mack, Quentin Philip
Nutter, Marion H. – Tenney, Howard A.
Nutter, Ramonda Lee – Weeks, David Merrill
Nutter, Shirley Etta – Robinshaw, Robert Frederick
Nystrom, Christine E. – Lynes, Frank Robert

O'Hanlon, Rose – Szymanski, James
Olisky, Shiloh Marie – Flint, Clarence Thomas
Orem, Margaret Ellen – Blanchard, Jesse
Orr, Edna Agnes – French, Walter D.
Ouimet, Kimberly M. – Salmons, Larry, Jr.
Owen, Martha – Howard, Alan

Page, Adell B. (Bailey) – Gould, Edward G., Sr.
Paige, Elaine R. – Greer, Arthur A.
Parker, Lynn M. – Bischoff, David F.
Parkington, Janice Heather – Bresnahan, Brian D.

Patch, Ada – Clogston, Willie
Patch, Ella M. (White) – Roberts, Thomas W.
Pease, Doris E. (Quackenbush) – Nutter, Kenneth L.
Pease, Irene Flora – Huntington, Harold Lawrence
Pease, Irene L. – Clark, Douglas E.
Pease, Vernie M. – Burnham, A. B.
Pebbles, Nellie – Gage, Everett L.
Peck, Beverly P. (Anair) – Curtis, Harry O.
Peck, Lorraine – Shepard, Ray
Perkins, Julia E. – Abbott, Fred W.
Perkins, Shirley Yvonne – Reed, Allen Gregory
Perrin, Mellissa – Allen, Douglas
Perry, Eleanor A. – Chase, Stanley R.
Perry, Linda J. – Woodes, Ronald L.
Perry, Lindsie Mae – Ladd, Oscar C.
Perry, Marjorie I. – Skinner, Harris F., Jr.
Perry, Pamela Ann – Bean, John Edward
Perry, Patricia A. – Benjamin, Robert L.
Phelps, Karen Louise (Gomo) – Tullar, Rendell Carl
Phelps, Kate – Victor, Edward W.
Philips, Robin – Weisburger, Donald
Picknell, Sylvia Carol – Rathbun, Daniel David
Pierce, Jane Elizabeth – Hebb, Allan Ford
Pierce, Nettie A. – Look, Scott W.
Pierson, Amy L. – Willson, Todd Alan
Pierson, Amy Louise – Heath, Jeffrey Earl
Pierson, Carol Ann – Ball, Allan Max
Pierson, Cary Jane – Martin, Harry F.
Pierson, Nettie Alice – Blake, Nathan LeRoy
Pierson, Ruby Ellen – Franklin, Harry E.
Pike, Bonnie L. – Madigan, Michael C.
Pike, Carrie L. – Sanborn, Fred J.
Pike, Christine S. – Langley, Shawn R.
Pike, Dorothy May – Pierce, Chester A.
Pike, Faye Ann – Smith, Stanley R., Jr.
Pike, Gloria Jean – Taylor, Bruce Frederick
Pike, Janet – Baker, Ronald
Pike, Jennifer Mae – Loiselle, Lance Christopher
Pike, Joanne – Morey, Gerald
Pike, Judy Mae – Franklin, Walter Allen
Pike, Laura B. – Ladd, John H.

Pike, Martha May – Smith, David Robert
Pike, Maxine (Heath) – Pike, Horace E.
Pike, Roberta K. – Gray, William A.
Pink, Rita – Heinsimer, James
Piper, Maude A. – Dennis, Albert B.
Plante, Kathleen – Garone, Gregory
Platenik, Leah A. – Palifka, Robert M.
Polston, Jane – McGovern, Robert
Pomeroy, Charlotte – Hatfield, Cameran A.
Pomeroy, Susan – Esselstryn, Erik Canfield
Pratt, Agnes L. (Cross) – Allen, Burton S.
Pratt, Mary L. (Brooks) – Stetson, Willie A.
Prescott, Gertrude – Plante, Albert
Preston, Alberta L. – Pero, Elwin N.
Preston, Ruth – Milo, Robert D.
Pruneau, Eleanor Janet – Lackey, Douglas Richard
Pugh, Catherine – Cassone, Peter
Pushee, Judith A. – Belyea, Jay L.
Pushee, Lucinda Lea – Pierson, Richard Allen
Pushee, Mary – Dyke, Michael
Pushee, Sharon – Claflin, Richard
Pushee, Shirley Marie – Gould, Edward George, Jr.
Pushee, Suzanne – Butman, Herbert Charles

Quackenbush, Doris Edith – Pease, Gerald Edwin

Ramsey, Mabel A. – Mack, Fred
Randall, Joan J. – Dyke, Alan
Randolph, Jenny L. – Gasparro, Christopher
Ray, Linnie Esther – Burnham, Eugene Reginald
Raymond, Jamie – Tatham, James
Raynes, Deborah – Snelling, Jeffrey
Record, Doris F. – Butman, Warren F.
Record, Lurline E. (Dyke) – Johnson, Robert L.
Reeves, Margaret L. – Miller, Caryl Wayne
Rhoades, Jennie B. – Tallman, Forest P.
Rhodes, Mary E. – Radford, Ernest W.
Rich, Deena – Wheeler, James
Rich, Linda – Nutter, John
Richardson, Ina C. – Roberts, Maurice A.
Richmond, Roberta – Jenkins, James D.

Rickenbaugh, Kathleen – MacCampbell, Donald
Ricker, Alice G. (Sargent) – Nelson, Harry Leslie, Jr.
Ricker, Bessie M. – Hibbard, Carl W.
Ricker, Darlene E. – Hart, James W.
Ricker, Diana – Austin, Richard Lee
Ricker, JodyAnn – Mace, John A.
Roberts, Clementine Ina (Richardson) – Morey, Bradley Zenas
Roberts, Lottie B. – Dennis, Newell A.
Robie, Barbara Mae – Pease, Howard Glenn
Robie, Eileen L. – Belyea, Roy R.
Robinson, Alice – Hall, Henry K.
Robinson, Marylyn A. – Smith, Robert A.
Rockwell, Brenda J. – Philbrick, Timothy J.
Rodewald, Jenny Lynn – Sweet, Kristofer Bryan
Rodgers, Alice – Celestino, Leon Angelo
Rogers, Blanche H. – Bean, Joseph S.
Rollins, Lottie L. – Clifford, Louis H.
Rollins, Maggie M. – Currier, Alfred T.
Ross, Catherine Anne – Carter, Lawrence Buddy
Rowden, Amelia – White, Fred S.
Rowell, Anna – Sanborn, John
Roy, Tamara Marie – Estes, Rodney Scott
Russin, Betty Jane – Marsh, Raymond Lee
Russin, Betty Jane – Hook, Bruce
Rutledge, Ann Lee Shepard – Parker, Ralph Eugene

Salls, Diane W. – Mattoon, Floyd S., Jr.
Sammond, Margaret – Stanley, Maurice
Sanborn, Alice G. – Cunningham, George H.
Sanborn, Carrie A. (Bacon) – Labounty, Joseph
Sanborn, Corinne Ida – Finney, Ralph Gary
Sanborn, Deann K. – Day, Daniel A.
Sanborn, Donna Jean – Finney, Frank Garth
Sanborn, Flora M. – Blake, Everett Leroy
Sanborn, Gladys M. – Davis, Perry Adelbert
Sanborn, Hazel Abbie – Donnelly, Leslie Jay
Sanborn, Pamela Joan – Kidder, Fred Albion
Sanborn, Paula Elizabeth – Graves, Leonard Phillip
Sanborn, Susan Evelyn – Hart, Lawrence G.
Sanborn, Theresa Mary (Hudson) – Blodgett, Robert Weston
Sargent, Ruth Mary (Preston) – Robinson, George A.

Sargent, Tonya Jean – Daisey, Daniel Scott
Savage, Ida G. (George) – Dearborn, Thomas G.
Sawyer, Robin – Schwarz, Clinton
Schauer, Lillian (Margeson) – Donelly, Robert C.
Schmedes, Dorothy A. (Atwater) – Huntington, Arthur F.
Schneiderheinz, Alice – Henderson, Paul W.
Schuck, Donna – Harnsberger, Jeffrey
Schwartz, Dana M. – Burrell, Donald H.
Schwarz, Karen M. – Domingue, James H.
Scruton, Phyllis E. – Gardner, Harold H.
Sears, Patricia – Vincent, William
Seeley, Julia Ellen – Emlin, Robert Peabody
Severance, Stacey Lyn – Evans, Brian Timothy
Sharon, Annie May (Wiggett) – Coffin, Ray Edison, Jr.
Shaw, Thelma Joy – McClellan, Paul Gifford
Shay, Maggie M. – Still, Charles E.
Shepard, Amy J. - Fahey, Clifford E.
Shepard, Kathleen Ethel (George) – Shepard, Russell
Sherburn, Mabel C. – Pease, Francis R.
Sherwood, Ray – Ingell, Fred Elbert
Shirley, Gwendolyn – McCarthy, James
Shortt, Hattie N. – Fillian, David A.
Shumway, Elaine Margaret – Then, Oscar Anthony
Siegfried, Elizabeth M. (Clifford) – Bean, Frank L.
Simonds, Minnie L. (Law) – Plumley, George
Simons, Edith M. – Louanis, Edwin J.
Simpson, Effie M. – Butman, Lewis F.
Sisters, Norma E. – Patrick, Thomas W.
Slayton, Jane – Pushee, Donald
Small, Nancy Carol – Dyke, Robert Leon
Smith, Ada A. – Austin, Chauncy G.
Smith, Ann M. – Lyons, Gerald J.
Smith, Annie H. – Langmaid, George B.
Smith, Arletta L. – Bean, Fay Elson
Smith, Beverly Jane – Carle, Ronald
Smith, Caryl Hicks (Hicks) – Clark, William G., Sr.
Smith, Daisy D. – Davis, Chester C.
Smith, Delia F. – Marsh, David C.
Smith, Dora C. – Ladeau, Levi J.
Smith, Helen E. – Sanborn, William G.
Smith, Helen L. – Holt, Arthur Ray

Smith, Inez – Baker, Henry G.
Smith, Isabel Joyce – Bonnett, Robert Wilcox
Smith, Jean Althea – Cook, Foster George, Jr.
Smith, Karen Lee – Nystrom, Alden Edmund
Smith, Margaret A. – Sherry, Nicholas
Smith, Martha J. – Gardner, Frank H.
Smith, Melissa A. – Fields, John E.
Smith, Michelle – Pushee, David
Smith, Nellie E. – Niles, George F.
Smith, Nicole Lynn – Gray, Matthew Scott
Smith, Sandra – Ordway, Eugene
Smith, Sarah A. (Archer) – Streeter, Peter F.
Smith, Verna Jane – Pelletier, Thomas Louis
Smith, Verna L. – Tallman, John C.
Smoke, Jean – Lamphere, George
Snider, Melinda – Chapman, Paul
Snizek, Julie – Lee, Jeff
Snow, Grace C. – Sawyer, Albert H.
Snyder, Teresa – Anderle, Nicholas
Sorion, Marie-Douce M. - Rippe, Daniel F.
Sparks, Christy Lynn – Carpenter, Seth Maxwell
Spencer, Eva M. – Dennis, Byron H.
Spooner, Harriet P. – Clark, George L.
Stebbins, Jennifer - Gray, Steve
Sterling, Lucretia – Martin, Peter
Stetson, Evelyn B. – Spencer, Hugh E.
Stevens, Deborah – Matyka, John
Stevens, Edith F. – Marsh, Clyde D.
Stevens, Emily A. (Mousley) – Webster, Herbert E.
Stevens, Lydia D. (Phelps) – Stetson, Otis W.
Stevens, Wilma – Bowman, Philip B.
Still, Mary – Lands, Leon
Stockman, Marion V. – Mertens, Richard J.
Stokes, Cheryl Ann – Noyes, S. David
Story, Janet – Jackson, Stuart A.
Straw, Blanche A. – Young, Albert C.
Streeter, Ellen Marie – Woodward, Ronald Lee
Streeter, Hattie M. – Baker, Maurice S.
Streeter, Marion M. – Butman, Richard C.
Streeter, Winifred A. – Young, Leon F., Jr.
Strue, Ina M. – Marsh, Frank D.

Stygles, Tanya – Gendron, Kurt
Sullivan, Patrice – Super, Kenneth
Sunn, Beatrice C. – Fish, Robert G.
Sweat, Cindy – Sutton, Mark
Sweet, Sheila M. – Thomson, Thomas N.
Swezey, Tina Alicia – Hebb, Timothy Michael

Tallman, Ada Ellis – Canfield, Ernest John
Tallman, Lillian M. – Trombley, Albert J.
Tallman, Rosie Ellen – Cummings, Clyde A.
Tanssell, Mary E. Hall – Dwyer, Nelson S.
Tarr, Erma M. – Marsh, Ernest E.
Taylor, Dora Daisy – Harriman, William Bert
Taylor, Dorothy Ann – Garrett, Walter Wilfred
Taylor, Gloria – Daisey, Royden
Taylor, Margaret Ann – Kopf, William Howard
Taylor, Marie Lynn – Holden, Stanley Frederick, Jr.
Taylor, Muriel Elaine – Marsh, Floyd Kenneth
Taylor, Shirley J. (Dupuis) – Austin, Wayne S.
Taylor, Susan M. – Pike, Weymouth H., Jr.
Taylor, Susan Marshall – Nungesser, William Lynn, Jr.
Teeter, Nancy Alma – Harrington, Deane Edward
Teller, Jaimie J. – Naylor, Scott B.
Temperley, Gail – Dimick, Gary Michael
Terrill, Helen F. (Crowley) – Nystrom, Albert E.
Thayer, Julia Elizabeth (Langlois) – Tillotson, Wendell Earle
Thomas, Aimee M. – Thomas, Martin C.
Thomas, Edith Ella – Witt, Warren Ruggles
Thompson, Ella E. – Lamere, Aleck
Thompson, Julia A. – Leigh, Henry
Thomson, Marion Gale – Spottswood, Stephen Alexander
Thomson, Rebecca – Wagstaff, Eric Mark
Thorndike, Virginia Low – Roberts, Philip John
Thurston, Kimberly Tatro – Sanborn, Stephen Arthur
Tibbitts, Carline Rae – Garrett, James Dalton
Tirrell, Donna Jean – Daisey, Richard Eugene
Titus, Gladys S. – Willard, Ritchie P.
Tomlinson, Hewan K. – Treworgy, James A.
Towle, Delia Hart – Lusco, Leon David
Trussell, Arlene – LaDeau, Kenneth J.
Trussell, Audrey – Streeter, Bruce

Tullar, Deborah – O'Brien, John
Turner, Alice M. – Smith, Arthur E.
Tuttle, Susan A. – Durkee, James G.
Tyler, Joan Margaret – Clifford, Charles Henry, Jr.

Usher, Laura A. – Hood, Horace

Valdes, Monica – Godfrey, Kevin
Valencia, O. Teresa – Reichert, Eric O.
Valverde, Alejandra Graciela – Anway, Dennis Joseph
Verb, Elisa – Harrington, Marcus
Vezina, Josephine – Von Dette, Archie F.
Vielleux, Stacy Lynn – DeColfmacker, Robert John

Wadleigh, Kathie – Willey, Duane
Wadsworth, Stacy Lee – Lynch, Randy Harold
Wain, Kathy – Duval, Raymond
Warner, Lavina (Holden) – Alexander, George W.
Washburn, Carrie W. – Whittemore, Luther L.
Washburn, Ethel F. – Hines, (Capt.) Stanley
Washburn, Grace E. – Hillborn, Ernest C.
Washburn, Jeanne – Chase, Ralph Eugene
Washburn, Joyce – Flint, Alan S.
Waterbury, Lisa – Weeks, Robert
Waterhouse, Nettie E. (Calderwood) – Lynes, Frank Edward
Waterman, Cynthia – McPherson, Jason
Watson, Caitlin – Scharzenberger, Joseph
Watson, May – Smith, Carrol B.
Webster, Clara B. – Baker, Bradley H.
Weeks, Ann Marie – Whiting, Tex
Weeks, Evelyn N. – Pierson, Wallace H.
Weeks, Lean – Stygles, Michael
Weeks, Loretta Jean – Pushee, Donald Elmer
Weeks, Shirley Jean – Waterbury, Allan Gilbert
Weibel, Margaret M. (Bryer) – Carl, Vernon
Welch, Fannie E. – Gilbert, Harry E.
Welch, Raquel J. – Siemons, Gary R.
Weldon, Eva B. – White, Burton A.
Wheeler, May L. – Colombe, Herman A.
Whitcher, Agnes (Merrill) – Cross, Joseph Dwight
Whitcher, Barbara Ann – Green, Peter

Whitcher, Marlene S. – Washburn, Harvey Horton
White, Etta – Couhig, Frank
White, Judy – Miller, Caryl
White, Patience (Boardman) – Wood, Charles
Whitehill, Susan Lucille – Ricker, Keith Reginald
Whiting, Josephine R. – Fillian, Gary L.
Whiting, Louella B. – Pushee, Paul Ralph
Whitman, Grace P. – Bassett, Frank Wright
Whitman, Mary H. – Donaldson, George B.
Whittier, Mabell L. – Marsh, George W.
Wilkins, Barbara Claire – Dyke, James Robert
Willey, Donna – Souza, Thomas
Willey, Mary L. (LaMay) – Rush, Herbert
Williams, Bernice Louise (Finney) – Sanborn, Bernard Malcolm
Williams, Hazel M. – Huckins, George C.
Williams, Valerie – Cummings, Wallace John
Willis, Janet Lee – Landgraf, Bruce Ted
Willis, Norma J. (Baker) – Hood, Raymond W.
Wilmott, Lori Ann – Mack, Brian Lewis
Wilson, C. Jennie – Rutledge, Hibbert T.
Wilson, Helen Marie – Daisey, Joseph Ernest
Wilson, Isabelle M. – Greenly, V. Merrill
Wilson, Joy Jean – Dyke, Alan Frederick
Wilson, Linda Rose – McKee, Henry Arthur
Wing, Ramona Jane – Dennis, Ralph Edward
Wolf, Georgette – Ludwig, Dan
Wood, Charlotte F. – Woodward, Elton C.
Wood, Clara P. – Chase, Daniel R.
Woodbury, Inez – Newcomb, Asahel W.
Woodward, Dorothy E. – Anderson, William Arthur
Woodward, Jeanette Priscilla – Ball, Albert Leslie
Woodward, Menta M. – Sawyer, Amos B.
Wright, Nellie M. – Bean, Dana J.
Wurtz, Sherry E. – Marsh, Alan T.
Wyman, Suzette – Tenney, Stephen C.
Wynkoop, Karen Sue – Chase, Robin A.

Young, Elizabeth T. (DeBlois) – Downing, George E.
Young, Hazel Louise – Smith, Ivan Lester
Young, Lucy Ellen – Morse, Kenneth B.
Young, Sally – Kulick, Paul E.

Zaldastani, Tamara – Johnston, Archibald F.
Ziehm, Shannon M. – Flynn, Malachy G.

[no surname given], Edna Mae – Fillian, William R.
[no surname given], AnnMarie – Misuraca, James

Orford Deaths

ABBOTT,
Eva Mae, d. 12/16/1931 at 47/7/28 in Orford; housewife; married; b. New Hampton; Samuel H. Tyrrell (Keene) and Ruth Westcott (Manchester)
Florence Estella, d. 7/10/1959 at 71 in Orford

ACKERSON,
Elmer C., d. 1/14/1970 at 99 in Orford; farmer; b. Halsey, NJ; Moses Ackerson and Sarah Hiles

ADAMS,
Albert, d. 8/2/1970 at 84 in Haverhill; laborer; b. Medway, MA; William Adams and Mary Ryan
Edna J., d. 1/10/2000 in Lebanon; John Bradley and Beatrice Goodwin
Harry, d. 6/6/1988
Margaret D., d. 12/1/1993 in Lebanon; Pleney Douse and Elizabeth -
Sarah Thompson, d. 9/28/1929 at 71 in Orford; retired; widow; b. NJ; Allen Thompson (NJ) and Suzanna L. Davis (NJ)

AIKEN,
Andrew, d. 1/1/1913 at 45/9/11 in Orford; chronic Brights disease; laborer; single; b. Wentworth; Hiram Aiken and Esther Smith

ALEXANDER,
Lavina, d. 7/1/1888 at 57 in Orford; domestic; married; b. Woburn, MA; Joseph Holden and Sarah Crocker (Stoneham, MA)
Rodney W., d. 8/17/1998 in Orford; Russell Alexander and Ruth Wilson

ALGER,
Arthur W., d. 5/14/1974 at 73 in Hanover; retired; b. Hanover; William T. Alger and Alma Caswell
Sanford, d. 5/26/1967 at 80 in Haverhill; retired; b. New Bedford, MA; Thomas Alger and Emma Tripp

ALLEN,
Bertram F., d. 1/4/1956 at 62/0/10 in Hanover; grain store mgr.; married; b. Providence, RI; James Allen and Mary Middleton
Bertram F., d. 11/13/2004 in Haverhill; Bertram F. Allen and Anna Brickett

Hattie M., d. 4/15/1905 at 53/9/18 in Orford; housewife; married; b.
  Gilmanton; David Hull and Eliza Wells
Lydia Elizabeth, d. 11/22/1896 at 72/3/13 in Hartford, VT;
  independent; married; b. Orford; Dyer T. Hinckley (Thetford,
  VT)

AMES,
George H., d. 5/2/1920 at 77/6/8 in Fitchburg
Pamelia, d. 1/6/1889 at 68/11/19 in Piermont; pneumonia;
  housewife; widow; b. Orford; John Homans and Peggy Ames

AMSDEN,
Susan B., d. 3/2/1919 at 82/7/18 in Enfield; retired; widow; b. Orford;
  David Johnson (Wentworth) and Ruth Brown (Orford)

ANDERSON,
Dorothy, d. 7/28/2003 in Lebanon; Frederick Sanborn and Lilla
  Demar
Mary, d. 4/15/1965 at 87 in Haverhill; housewife; b. Macon, GA;
  James Hollifield and Sarah Perry
William H., d. 7/30/1962 at 66/1/9 in Orford; dir. of athletics; married;
  b. E. Liberty, PA; Grant Anderson and Lenore Merkel

ANDREWS,
Clarence, Sr., d. 6/5/1977 at 88 in Hanover; farmer; b. NH; Fred C.
  Andrews and Orra Blodgett
Esther, d. 1/13/1990 in Woodsville; Samuel Hildreth and Emma
  Andrew

ANTHONY,
Lewis F., d. 7/8/1968 at 79 in Haverhill; office wk. retired; b. MA;
  Lewis Anthony and Mary Phillips

ARCHER,
daughter, d. 1/8/1894 at – in Orford; stillborn; b. Orford; Alanson A.
  Archer (Orford) and Lizzie Morand
daughter, d. 11/4/1900 at 0/0/12 in Orford; cholera infantum; b.
  Orford; Alanson J. Archer (Orford) and Lizzie J. Moroien
  (Cambridge, MA)

Addie Lizzie, d. 11/21/1900 at 0/0/29 in Orford; marasmus; b. Orford; Alanson J. Archer (Orford) and Lizzie J. Moroien (Cambridge, MA)

Alanson J., d. 12/18/1926 at 78/0/15 in Lisbon; retired farmer; b. Orford; James Archer (Orford) and Mary Hutchinson (Lyme)

Charles, d. 4/15/1898 at 74/8/11 in Orford; paralysis; farmer; widower; Amasa Archer

Charles H., d. 4/11/1920 at 57/1/7 in Orford; farmer; married; b. Orford; Charles Archer (Orford) and Emeline Archer (Orford)

Helen S., d. 12/11/1993 in Lebanon; William Scott and Lillian Kiley

Ida, d. 2/21/1991 in Hanover

Joseph G., d. 7/26/1936 at 40/4/10 in Orford; carpenter; married; b. Orford; Hanson J. Archer (Orford) and Elizabeth Morren (Cambridge, MA)

Josiah, d. 6/27/1889 at 82/11/15 in Orford; old age; farmer; widower; b. Orford; Josiah Archer (Haddam, CT) and Bridget Phelps (Haddam, CT)

Josiah H., d. 4/4/1938 at 83/11/28 in Fairlee, VT; farmer; widower; b. Orford; James M. Archer and Mary Hutchins

Lizzie E., d. 3/28/1905 at 33/3/11 in Orford; housewife; married; b. E. Cambridge, MA; Isaac Morrin (England) and Elizabeth Warren (England)

Mary Rebecca, d. 4/19/1928 at 73/4/10 in Orford; housewife; married; b. Fairlee, VT; Thomas Hannaford (Hebron, CT) and Rebecca Fish (Wentworth)

Olive, d. 6/5/1956 at 85/7/22 in Lyme; own home; widow; b. Colebrook; Truman Barnet and Harriet Philbro

ARNOLD,
daughter, d. 1/1/1931 at – in Orford; b. Orford; Elwin R. Arnold (Haverhill) and Gertrude P. Owens (Littleton)

ARRUDA,
Rachelle A., d. 1/6/1998 in Orford; Victor Drolet and Bernice Gauthier

AUBERT,
Georgianna, d. 9/20/1975 at 90 in Laconia; housewife; b. Canada

AUBUT,
Francis, d. 1/9/1976 at 80 in Orford; retired; b. Canada; Francis Aubut, Sr.

AVERY,
Bert, d. 1/9/1944 at 78/6/6 in N. Ashland; Joshua Avery (Orford) and Emma M. Thorndyke (Claremont)
Joshua K., d. 4/4/1892 at 76/5/24 in Orford; carpenter; married; b. Orford; Jesse Avery
Mary E., d. 3/27/1925 at 73/6/3 in Newport, VT; retired; widow; b. Orford; William Howard (Orford) and Sarah Howard (Sharon, VT)
Willard B., d. 10/8/1917 at 65/0/10 in Newport, VT; married; buried West Cem.

BACON,
Blanche Nina, d. 6/4/1961 at 79/2/17 in Orford; housewife; widow; b. Strafford, VT; Harvey C. Sweet and Minnie Jordan

BADGER,
Ardelle Catherine, d. 7/19/1957 at 52/1/21 in Claremont; housewife; married; b. Hardwick, VT; Frank Ed. Lynes and Mary A. Calderwood

BAILEY,
Alpha N., d. 7/26/1902 at 48/1/26 in Orford; injury to spinal cord; mechanic and carpenter; married; b. Andover, MA; John T. Bailey (Andover, MA) and Orrilla Norcross (Barre, VT)

BAIN,
Alexander R., d. 1/10/1969 at 64 in New York, NY

BAKER,
son, d. 8/20/1907 at 0/0/1 in Orford; inanition; b. Orford; Emile Houle and Martha Baker
Alice F., d. 11/14/1951 at 72 in Hanover; housewife; married; b. Orford; Lewis Franklin and Rebecca Cushman
Bert, d. 10/21/1954 at 85/7/19 in Haverhill; laborer; widower; b. Huntington, VT; Orin Baker and Flora Jewel
Bradley Horace, d. 1/9/1970 at 67 in Haverhill; carpenter; b. Orford; Henry G. Baker and Inez Smith

George Henry, d. 8/11/1954 at 66/4/28 in Orford; farmer; widower; b. Orford; Henry Giles Baker and Inez Amelia Smith

Harold W., d. 2/24/1948 at 66/4/28 in Orford; ret. surgeon; married; b. Boston, MA; William H. Baker (Medford, MA) and Charlotte B. ----- (Boston, MA)

Harry F., d. 10/15/1918 at 21/0/19 in NY; soldier; single; b. Orford; Henry G. Baker (Orford) and Inez A. Smith (Orford)

Hattie, d. 5/27/1985 in Hanover

Henry Gage, d. 3/9/1934 at 75/3/16 in Orford; wheelwright; married; b. Orford; Charles Baker (Orford) and Susan Horner (Johnson, VT)

Jennie Porter Mills, d. 10/28/1928 at 71/10/7 in Orford; none; widow; b. Boston, MA; John F. Mills (Grafton, VT) and Sarah R. Dudley

Leonard, d. 5/16/1934 at 49/6/13 in Orford; retired; single; b. Boston, MA; Frank W. Baker (Franklin, MA) and Jennie Mills (Boston, MA)

Louise Fish Davis, d. 1/30/1951 at 84 in Orford; housewife; widow; b. Dorchester; Daniel C. Davis and Lavisa Quimby

Maurice, d. 8/28/1959 at 55 in Orford

Pauline Inez, d. 4/9/1928 at 0/0/19 in Orford; b. Orford; Fred Baker (Orford) and Lillian Spencer (Plymouth)

Phoebe Little, d. 6/14/1962 at 72/8/28 in Orford; housewife; widow; b. Boston, MA; Thomas S. Little and Christie MacLean

Ralph Edward, d. 1/8/1929 at 0/11/29 in Orford; b. Haverhill; Bradley Baker (Orford) and Clara Webster (Piermont)

Ronald R., d. 9/15/2004 in Lyme; Maurice Baker and Hattie Streeter

BALCH,

John F., d. 1/17/1970 at 19 in Orford; student; b. Hanover; John F. Balch and Marion Gerue

BALL,

Emily Stetson, d. 3/8/1897 at 67/3/11 in Orford; domestic; single; William Stetson (Lyme) and Sarah M. Newell (Orford)

BALSINDE,

Francisca, d. 2/5/1966 at 78 in Haverhill; housewife; b. Cuba; Antonio Valdes Balsinda and Maria R. Arocha

BARNES,
Elijah B., d. 1/8/1888 at 77/5 in Orford; farmer; married; b. Washington, CT; Caleb Barnes and Jane Baldwin
Olive E., d. 1/16/1913 at 58/5 in Orford; cancer of stomach; housewife; married; b. Albany, VT; Stephen Vance and Maria Hall
Roger Walter, d. 1/18/1934 at 79/0/5 in Braintree, MA; physician; married

BARRETT,
D. Truman, d. 8/2/1991 in Hanover; Day Barrett and Carrie Brown

BARSS,
Mattie S., d. 7/11/1921 at 51/1/26 in Orford; domestic; married; b. St. Armond, Canada; Sherman Scofield (Canada) and Emily Beals (VT)

BASS,
Chester A., d. 7/25/1898 at 79/9/7 in Orford; Bright's disease; widower; Peter Bass (Braintree, MA) and Anna Hardy (Braintree, MA)
Emeline M., d. 5/14/1893 at 69/3/26 in Orford; disease heart; domestic; b. Randolph, VT; Augustus Hobart (Braintree, MA) and Hannah Thayer

BATCHELDER,
child, d. 8/12/1892 at – in Cambridge, MA; premature birth; Frank E. Batchelder and Alice H. Batchelder

BAXTER,
Ethel S., d. 4/17/1947 at 55/5/16 in Andover

BEAL,
Alfred Johnson, d. 12/30/1956 at 68/0/11 in Malden, MA; ret. violin maker; married; b. Malden, MA; Fenner Beal and Alfretta McLellan
Alfretta, d. 3/17/1948 at 79/7/17 in Malden, MA; retired; widow; b. Portpique, NS; Joseph S. McLellan (Portpique, NS)
Elizabeth L., d. 7/23/1944 at 76/10/27 in Bath, ME; retired; widow; b. Orford; Joshua Avery (Orford) and Emma M. Thorndyke (Claremont)

Fenner L., d. 1/2/1936 at 68/9/3 in Malden, MA; retired; married; b. Orford; Royal Beal (Lyme) and Josephine Johnson (Newbury, VT)

Frank J., d. 4/20/1923 at 62/5/9 in Cambridge, MA; garage man; married; b. Orford; Royal Beal (Lyme) and Josaphine Johnson (Newbury, VT)

Gertrude, d. 8/3/1894 at 1/5/1 in Orford; acute bronch.; b. Orford; Frank J. Beal (Orford) and Elizabeth L. Avery

Gustava, d. 3/18/1890 at 76/2/18 in Orford; congestion of brain; domestic; single; b. Orford; David R. Beal (Lyme) and Abigail Carver (Deerfield, MA)

Josephine J., d. 5/8/1919 at 90 in Plymouth; housewife; widow; b. Newbury, VT; Frank Johnson (Newbury, VT)

BEAN,

son, d. 10/19/1907 at 0/0/3 in Orford; inanition; b. Orford; Joseph S. Bean (Sharon, VT) and Mabel M. Davis (Munsonville)

daughter, d. 1/10/1949 at -- in Orford; b. Orford; Fay E. Bean and Arletta L. Smith

son, d. 12/27/1951 at 3 hrs. in Hanover; b. Hanover; Philip L. Bean and Ida M. Prebor

Agnes A. Guilmette, d. 1/26/1944 at 27/11/26 in Orford; housewife; married; b. Lunenburg, VT; Philip Guilmette (Canada) and Charlotte Hatshorn (Lunenburg, VT)

Anne M., d. 10/19/1999 in Lebanon; Domenic Castiglione and Clementine Falzone

Bernard C., d. 6/30/1946 at 22/2/3 in Dorchester; laborer; single; b. Orford; Philip L. Bean (Orford) and Blanche A. Burnham (Dorchester)

Bertram, d. 4/7/1984 in Lebanon

Bessie A., d. 1/17/1969 at 79 in Rumney; retired; b. Dorchester; Frank Y. Burnham and Josephine Coburn

Blanche B., d. 5/12/1934 at 50 in Hanover; housewife; married; b. Dorchester; Frank Burnham (Concord) and Josie Colburn (Wentworth)

Carrie, d. 3/14/1988

Carrie E., d. 9/21/1961 at 98/8/19 in Orford; ret. housewife; widow; b. Lyme; James Gardner and Emaline Brickett

Carroll J., d. 3/25/1956 at 76/4/5 in Waterbury, VT; retired; married; b. Orford; Richard D. Bean and Eliza A. Bickford

Charles L., d. 11/24/1931 at 77/8/14 in Orford; farmer; married; b. Sandwich; Jonathan G. Bean (Sandwich) and Sally H. Bricked (Auburn)

Clarence G., d. 1/13/1959 at 75 in Orford

Dana James, d. 12/8/1916 at 26/0/11 in Orford; pul. tuberculosis; farmer; married; b. Orford; C. L. Beane (Sandwich) and Carrie Gardner (Lyme)

Donald F., d. 12/16/1973 at 54 in Lyme; janitor; b. Orford; Edwin G. Bean and Alice Marsh

Edith E., d. 4/15/1915 at 0/8/20 in Orford; suppurating adenitis of throat; b. Orford; Dana J. Bean (Orford) and Nellie M. Wright (Piermont)

Edwin G., d. 6/6/1963 at 75 in Orford; farmer; b. Orford; Charles L. Bean and Carrie Gardner

Esther A., d. 3/23/1911 at 66/1/12 in Orford; la grippe; housewife; married; b. Ellsworth; James Randall (Sanbornton) and Eleanor Avery (Ellsworth)

Fay C., d. 8/31/1910 at 0/0/12 in Orford; b. Orford; Joseph S. Bean (Sharon, VT) and Mabel C. Davis (Mansonville, PQ)

Fay C., d. 6/3/1915 at 26/0/20 in Orford; myologenous leukemia; farmer; b. Orford; Charles L. Bean (Sandwich) and Carrie E. Gardner (Lyme)

Florence, d. 3/8/1990 in Hanover; James Billingham and Julia Perrin

Frank L., d. 9/15/1961 at 77/4/19 in Plymouth; painter; widower; b. Orford; Charles Bean and Carrie Gardner

George O., d. 2/10/1897 at 0/6/20 in Orford; b. Orford; Oliver L. Bean (Sandwich) and Elizabeth Ballam (England)

Howard, d. 5/1/1938 at 12/1 in Hanover; school; b. Orford; Ralph Bean (Orford) and Florence Billingham (Fairlee, VT)

Ida M., d. 5/10/1967 at 49 in W. Lebanon; housewife; b. Westford, VT; Paul Prebor and Augusta Koss

Jeffrey, d. 1/23/1988

Jonathan G, d. 8/26/1897 at 82/6/1 in Orford; farmer; married; b. Sandwich; Gilman Bean

Joseph S., d. 10/9/1924 at 41/6/2 in Orford; laborer; married; b. Sharon, VT; Lee C. Bean (VT) and Mary Claflin (VT)

Mabel M., d. 12/23/1947 at 61/9/16 in Orford; housekeeper; widow; b. Mansonville, PQ; Alymer Davis (Canada) and Ida Clough

Malcolm B., d. 8/6/1948 at 34/1/11 in Orford; beekeeper; single; b. Orford; Philip L. Bean (Orford) and Blanche Burnham (Dorchester)

Maurice, d. 8/1/1987
Moses G., d. 10/19/1914 at 63/7/2 in Orford; mitral endocarditis; farmer; widower; b. Sandwich; Johnathan G. Bean (Sandwich) and Sally H. Brickett (Auburn)
Nathaniel, d. 5/24/1916 at 0/0/0 in Orford; stillborn; b. Orford; Philip L. Bean (Orford) and B. H. Burnham (Dorchester)
Philip L., Jr., d. 6/30/1946 at 19/8/20 in Dorchester; laborer; single; b. Orford; Philip L. Bean (Orford) and Blanche A. Burnham (Dorchester)
Philip Lee, d. 4/4/1965 at 79 in Orford; farmer; b. Orford; Charles L. Bean and Carrie E. Gardner
Ralph C., d. 7/18/1973 at 72 in Springfield, MA; farmer; b. Orford; Moses Bean and Esther Randall
Richard, d. 5/31/1976 at 64 in Hanover; farmer; b. NH; Carroll Bean and Lutheria M. Heath
Richard, d. --/--/1989
Ruth, d. 3/26/2004 in Lebanon
Sally H., d. 2/23/1901 at 80/6/27 in Orford; valvular disease of heart; widow; b. Auburn; ----- Brickett
Vernie M., d. 6/27/1911 at 23/0/16 in Orford; pernicious vom. of pregnancy; housewife; married; b. Orford; Aaron McCrillis (Corinth, VT) and Julia E. Hackett (Haverhill)
Warren L., d. 9/7/1975 at 28 in Whitefield; pressman; b. Orford; Philip L. Bean and Ida Prebar

BEANE,
Arlene E., d. 12/30/2004 in Lebanon; John Barnes and Saddie Barnes

BEATTIE,
Kenneth, d. 7/7/1958 at 75/10/24 in Haverhill; laborer; widower; b. Danby, Canada; Thomas Beattie and Margaret Buckley

BECTON,
Frederick I., d. 12/28/1959 at 79 in Hanover
Janet M., d. 3/5/1964 at 82 in Orford; housewife; b. Baltimore, MD; Thomas McGechin and Ella Ross

BEDELL,
Andrew, d. 6/30/1985 in Haverhill

Arthur H., d. 11/12/1934 at 44/0/24 in Orford; section worker; married; b. Jefferson; John Thomas Bedell (Jefferson) and Mary Monroe (Lancaster)
Bertha I., d. 12/20/1981 in Haverhill; Cemuel Clegg and Mary Gallimore
Catherine Elizabeth, d. 9/15/1942 at 70/9/14 in Wentworth; ret. housewife; widow; b. Hyde Park, VT; Frank Ladeau and Pauline Jacobs
Frederick C., d. 12/6/1922 at 54 in Hanover; lumberman; married; b. Charles Bedell and Abbie Stewart
George P., d. 3/13/1961 at 65/11/4 in Barre, VT; retired farmer; married; b. Greensboro, VT; Andrew Bedell and Mary A. Hussey

BEEBE,
Alfreda Hanford, d. 2/7/1912 at 50/1/17 in Orford; apoplexy; married; b. Haverhill; Nelson A. Hanford and Lurinda French

BELFORD,
Emma J., d. 5/31/1930 at 76/2/8 in Claremont; housewife; married; b. Littleton; Louis Wood (Canada) and Mary L. Maynard (Canada)
George H., d. 4/25/1936 at 81/10/10 in Menden

BELIVEAU,
Adrienne, d. 1/4/1986

BENNETT,
Pearl, d. 5/5/1985 in Orford
Selah Barnard, d. 10/14/1968 at 70 in Haverhill; farmer; b. Montgomery, VT; Sherman Bennett and Isabel Carter

BERGDAHL,
Carl, d. 10/24/1958 at 73 in Haverhill; railroad worker; single; b. Sweden; John Bergdahl and Augusta -----

BERGERON,
Richard, d. 12/27/1990 in White River Jct., VT; Ludger Bergeron and Beatrice Hines

BICKFORD,
John, d. 5/5/1896 at 74/12 in Orford; farming; married; b. Piermont; Isaac Bickford (Northwood, VT) and Lucinda Coburn (Orford)

BISCHOFF,
Ralph F., d. 11/25/1997 in Orford; Rudolph Bischoff and Louise Burkhardt

BLAESI,
Wilhelmine, d. 6/26/1963 at 82 in Haverhill; housewife; b. Brooklyn, NY; Martin Horstman and Wilhelmine -----

BLAKE,
Albert, d. 5/11/1888 at 62/1/20 in Orford; farmer; married; b. Grantham; William Blake and Ruhama Pixley (Stratford, VT)
Flora S., d. 7/21/2004 in Orford; Harry Sanborn and Lulu Sanborn
John, d. 11/18/1888 at 78/11/14 in Orford; farmer; widower; b. Lisbon, ME; William Blake (Lisbon, ME) and ----- Davis

BLANCHARD,
Eliza E., d. 8/3/1911 at 0/2 in Orford; choked to death on bottle; b. Orford; Ray Blanchard (Piermont) and Mabel E. Cushing (Newport, VT)

BLISS,
Louis B., d. 5/20/1972 at – in Hartford, VT; laborer; b. Canada; Henry Bliss and Mae Cisco

BLODGETT,
C. L., Jr., d. 1/7/1915 at 0/0/3 in Hanover; suboccupital hem.; b. Hanover; C. L. Blodgett (Orford) and Jeane McLeod (Megantic, PQ)
Clarence L., d. 10/8/1935 at 60/2/21 in Orford; farmer; widower; b. Orford; Webster P. Blodgett (Plymouth) and Dilla Pebbles (Orford)
Della H., d. 6/19/1926 at 85/6/7 in Orford; housewife; b. Orford; John Pebbles (Salem, MA) and ----- Weed
Jeanne, d. 9/18/1922 at 36/6/1 in Orford; housewife; married; b. Megantic, Canada; John McLeod (Megantic, Canada) and Marie McLain (Scotland)

Webster P., d. 3/4/1911 at 77/6/26 in Orford; apoplexy; farmer; married; b. Plymouth; Asacel Blodgett (Groton) and Priscilla Webster (Plymouth)

BLOOD,
Amos J., d. 8/13/1895 at 83/10/1 in Orford; paral. dropsy; farmer
Edwin B., d. 1/26/1899 at 67/8/21 in Orford; paresis; carpenter; divorced; b. Orford; Asa Blood and Phebe Rugg
Fanny K., d. 8/30/1907 at 86/11/27 in Orford; valvular disease of the heart; housewife; widow; b. Lyme; David R. Beale (Lyme) and Abigail Carver (Deerfield)
George F., d. 11/11/1896 at 63/6/9 in Lawrence, MA
John Henry, d. 11/16/1900 at 63/6/7 in Orford; accidental; farmer; married; b. Orford; Amos J. Blood (Fairlee, VT) and Rebecca Cushman (Landaff)
Martha J., d. 7/21/1906 at 80/1/24 in Orford; housewife; married; b. Orford; Benjamin H. Niles (Newbury, VT) and Martha D. Savage (Orford)
Nancy Chase, d. 4/25/1889 at 86/1/12 in Orford; old age; housewife; widow
Rebecca W., d. 3/6/1893 at 79/7/24 in Orford; bronchitis; housewife; b. Landaff; Stephen Cushman (Coventry, CT) and Martha Coleman
Sylvester, d. 9/11/1906 at 86/3/14 in Orford; farmer; married; b. Orford; Samuel Blood (Chelmsford, MA) and Bethiah Cole

BOARDMAN,
Eliza, d. 3/28/1909 at 102/4 in Orford; widow; b. St. Charles, PQ; ----- Thomas and ----- Porter
George H., d. 2/7/1928 at 78/4/16 in Bristol
Harry, d. 5/8/1904 at 0/0/20 in Orford; b. Piermont; George Boardman (Canada) and Jennie Goodwin (Canada)
William E., d. 3/10/1967 at 67 in Orford; laborer; b. Quebec; Luke Boardman and Josie Page

BOHN,
Jacob Lloyd, d. 12/12/1982 in Orford; Henry Bohn and Percida Bordner

BONDREAU,
Minnie D., d. 5/9/1942 at 70/11 in Orford; housewife; widow; b. Arishaw, NS; ----- (Metegan Sta., NS)

BONNETT,
Frank E., d. 4/2/1962 at 67/7/2 in Hartford, VT; mail carrier; married; b. Orford; Silas Bonnett and Emma Hubbard

BOONE,
Paul D., d. 1/15/1999 in Lebanon; John Boone and Ruth Meyes

BOOTH,
Isabella Blann, d. 9/6/1958 at 72 in Piermont; retired; widow; b. Aberdeen, Scotland; Thomas Blann and Isabella Petrie
John, d. 11/2/1948 at 69/4/10 in Barre, VT; estimator; b. Scotland; George Booth (Scotland) and Barbara Copland (Scotland)

BOYCE,
Clinton, d. 9/10/1985 in Orford

BRADFORD,
Calvin F., d. 3/27/1906 at 75/0/8 in Orford; farmer; widower; b. Barnard, VT; Ebenezer Bradford (Barnard, VT) and Mary Davis (Barnard, VT)
Mary, d. 9/1/1915 at 76/8/7 in Orford; cerebral softening; housewife; widow; b. Plainfield; Parker Carr (Grantham) and Phebe M. Little (Springfield)

BRADISH,
William, d. 1/4/1982 in Orford; Robert Bradish and Emma -----

BRAYNARD,
Bertha, d. 10/26/1983 in Lebanon; Harvey Braynard and Sarah Emerson
Harvey T., d. 3/22/1938 at 77/5 in Orford; farmer; widower; b. Haverhill; Lysandser Braynard (Haverhill) and Rachael A. Foster (Wentworth)
Sarah M., d. 12/31/1924 at 60/5/8 in Orford; housewife; married; b. Piermont; Robert Emmerson (Piermont) and Beby Wilcox (Canada, PQ)

BRENNAN,
Addie P., d. 6/9/1922 at 76/10; in Orford; housekeeper; widow; b. Grafton, MA; Henry Powers (Washington, VT) and Florence Kelley (Portsmouth)

BREWSTER,
Catherine F., d. 9/15/1895 at 79/4/1 in Orford; old age; housekeeper; b. Corinth, VT; Benjamin F. Sleeper and Sarah Sleeper

BRIGGS,
Stanley H., d. 1/5/1963 at 62 in Asbury Park, NJ

BROCK,
Asahel, d. 10/31/189 at 85/0/25 in Orford; farmer; widower; b. Barrington
Bessie M., d. 10/14/1936 at 74/8/21 in Manchester; housekeeper; widow; b. Gaspereau, NS; Michael Coldwell (NS) and Elizabeth ----- (Yarmouth, NS)
Charles E., d. 6/11/1924 at 73/3/18 in Bedford; farmer; married; b. Orford; Asahel Brock (Orford) and Almira S. Savage (Orford)
Mary E., d. 1/26/1894 at 34/11/15 in Orford; veterine hem.; housewife; b. Beverly, MA; Matthew E. Wyman (Yarmouth, NS) and Mary E. Stanley

BRODISH,
Linda Marie, d. 10/15/1943 at 0/0/2 in Hanover; b. Hanover; John Brodish (Tampa, FL) and Bernice B. Bean (Newbury, VT)

BROPHY,
Ann, d. 6/8/1969 at 53 in Hanover; b. NY; John Brophy and Margaret Dodds

BROUGHAN,
Richard C., d. 12/19/1995 in Lebanon; Charles Broughan and Carol Allspaugh

BROWN,
son, d. 3/12/1901 at – in Orford; died soon after birth; b. Orford; Fred W. Brown (laborer) and Grace Degoost (W. Fairlee, VT)
son, d. 3/30/1904 at – in Orford; b. Orford; Fred W. Brown (Warren) and Grace DeGoosh (W. Fairlee, VT)

Herbert L., d. 5/16/1930 at 69/8/24 in Orford; retired; married; b. Petersham, MA; James Brown (MA) and Harriet Houghton (MA)

Mary A., d. 1/15/1911 at 52/9 I n Orford; acute capillary bronchitis; housewife; widow; b. Andover; Henry J. Finney (Orford) and Mary A. Emerton

Raymond H., d. 10/2/1959 at 57 in Orford

Rosa Ina, d. 8/6/1889 at 1/8/6 in Orford; cholera infantum; b. Orford; George R. Brown (VT) and Lucy Columbia (Canaan)

Sally Ann, d. 12/6/1962 at 2/4/16 in Hanover; b. Hanover; Richard E. Brown and Ruth Ladd

William, d. 3/21/1910 at 93/6/15 in Orford; farmer; widower; b. Orford; Samuel Brown (Orford) and Betsey Abbott

William B., d. 1/19/1968 at 90 in Orford; farmer; b. Hyde Park, VT; John Brown and Annie -----

BRYER,

Allen Joseph, d. 11/2/1961 at 61 in Fairlee, VT; laborer; married; b. W. Burke, VT; Wilbur Bryer and Lucy Mabel Allen

BUGBEE,

Harriet V., d. 6/23/1897 at 72/6/6 in Orford; housewife; widow; b. Morristown, VT; Joseph Stafford

BUNTEN,

Evelyn, d. 10/14/1991 in Orford; Claude Stephenson and Evelyn Deneauville

BURROUGHS,

infant, d. 12/3/1929 at – in Newbury, VT; Robert Burroughs

BUTMAN,

Charles H., d. 1/16/1933 at 74/2/11 in Orford; retired farmer; married; b. Canaan; Frank Butman (Canaan) and Susan Colby (Canaan)

George E., d. 10/15/1891 at 36/5/27 in Orford; laborer; married; b. Canaan; Frank Butman (Canaan) and Susan T. Colby

Hattie C., d. 12/7/1934 at 52/7/28 in Orford; housewife; married; b. Orford; Alpha Bailey (MA) and Mary Niles (Orford)

Inez B., d. 3/22/1960 at 88/8/12 in Orford; retired housewife; widow; b. Barnston, Canada; Haskel Brown and Nancy Rix

Leola, d. 10/3/1913 at 0/1/22 in Orford; whooping cough; b. Orford;
Lurlyn C. Butman (Orford) and Hattie C. Bailey (Orford)

Lurlyn C., d. 1/1/1960 at 78/2/16 in Hanover; retired; widower; b.
Orford; Charles Butman and Anna Clough

Marion S., d. 8/25/1994 in Lebanon; Ray Streeter and Stella
Cushing

Richard Colby, d. 9/14/2003 in Orford; Charles Butman and Inez
Brown

Rodney, d. 1/15/1911 at 0/0/12 in Orford; broncho pneumonia; b.
Orford; Lurlyn C. Butman (Orford) and Hattie C. Bailey (Orford)

BUTSON,
James N., d. 7/30/1916 at 51/1/28 in Hanover; cancer of ascending
colon; farmer; married; b. Topsham, VT; John Butson (Bristol,
England) and Sarah Norton (Bristol, England)

BUZZELL,
Mary Darling, d. 5/4/1900 at 55/3/2 in Orford; chronic bronchitis;
milliner; widow; b. Vershire, VT; Jesse Darling (Vershire, VT)
and Mehitable Heath (Vershire, VT)

BYERS,
Charles Albert, d. 7/28/1964 at 80 in Orford; lumber dealer; b.
Denver, CO; Israel Byers and Celia Patchel

CANFIELD,
Ernest John, d. 8/26/1977 at 66 in Hanover; ironworker; b. NH;
George Canfield and Marguerite Downing

CARBONE,
William Benedict, d. 8/18/1940 at 45/2/6 in Orford; clerk; widow; b.
Charlestown, MA; Pisquelle Carbone (Italy) and Marion
Cozanzi (Italy)

CARLSTROM,
Axel E., d. 7/5/1957 at 74/7/6 in Concord; watchmaker; married; b.
Sweden; Axel Carlstrom

CARPENTER,
Edwin D., d. 5/9/1908 at 67/2/17 in Orford; cerebral hemorrhage; farmer; b. Fairlee, VT; Ephraim Carpenter (Fairlee, VT) and Eliza A. Brown (Fairlee, VT)

CARR,
infant, d. 5/9/1887 at 0/0/1 in Orford; b. Orford; Robert O. Carr (Orford) and Mary Martin (Chelmsford, VT)

Bradley M., d. 5/17/1892 at 7/9/3 in Orford; fracture of skull; b. Orford; Robert O. Carr and Mary E. Martin

Charles Hiram, d. 6/17/1945 at 85/3/29 in Orford; real est. agent; married; b. Plainfield; Philip M. Carr (Plainfield) and Persis D. Huntoon (Orford)

Clarice Mabel, d. 5/30/1965 at 59 in Enfield; housewife; b. N. Strafford; Burton C. Jennings and Jennie Joslyn

Effie Evelyn, d. 9/21/1932 at 69/3/21 in Orford; housewife; married; b. New Boston; Solomon Dodge and Mary E. Christie

Erma H., d. 2/18/1949 at 64/9/19 in Orford; housewife; married; b. Whiting's Pt., NY; Elmer D. Harris and Mary Jane Geer

Frances I., d. 3/8/1975 at 80 in Hanover; postal worker; b. VT; Gilman Bacon and Frances E. Green

Fred P., d. 5/30/1968 at 91 in Hartford, VT; lawyer; Orford; John O. Carr and Mary Edwards

George Wallace, d. 2/7/1934 at 71/5/17 in Orford; caretaker; widower; b. Plainfield; Philip Carr (Plainfield) and Persis Huntoon (Gorham)

Gilman Reid, d. 8/30/1917 at 0/0/20 in W. Fairlee, VT; buried West Cem.

Henry H., d. 8/30/1966 at 86 in Haverhill; insurance agent; b. Hanover; Robert O. Carr and Mary Martin

Hittie R., d. 3/19/1960 at 98/1/11 in Haverhill; retired postmistress; widow; b. Bath; David R. Lang and Hittie Ricker

Jesse K., d. 11/2/1895 at 49/4/2 in Ft. Payne; frac. of brain; b. Orford; Jesse Carr

John Oscar, d. 8/1/1916 at 68/9/27 in Orford; cerebral inport; farmer; married; b. E. Plainfield; Parker Carr (Grantham) and P. M. Little

Marion Frances, d. 11/6/1955 at 61/3/20 in Saratoga Spr., NY; housewife; married; b. Orford; Harry B. Foote and Claribel Felch

Mary E., d. 12/1/1925 at 74/8/14 in Orford; housewife; married; b.
    Chelmsford; William Martin (Norwich) and Mary R. Hadley
Mary E., d. 3/27/1942 at 95/6/29 in Enfield; retired
Maud A., d. 9/3/1962 at 76/7/20 in Orford; housekeeping; widow; b.
    Lyme; George Belford and Emma J. Wood
Parker, d. 6/14/1888 at 81/11/8 in Orford; farmer; widower; b.
    Plainfield; Peter Carr (Cabot, VT) and Sarah Mitchell (Andover)
Reid D., d. 9/26/1967 at 72 in Hartford, VT; b. Andover; George Carr
    and Effie Dodge
Robert O., d. 11/16/1937 at 86/1/3 in Orford; merchant; widower; b.
    Orford; Phillip Carr (Plainfield) and Persis Huntoon (Unity)
Robert W., d. 6/2/1969 at 65 in Fairlee, VT; insurance; b. Orford;
    Henry H. Carr and Emma Harris
Ruby C., d. 12/10/1973 at 62 in St. Johnsbury, VT; nurse; b. Groton,
    VT; Ernest F. Clark and Minnie G. Adams
True H., d. 8/13/1963 at 73 in Hinsdale; b. Orford; George W. Carr
    and Effie Dodge

CARRON,
Mark D., d. 8/22/1926 at 69/0/29 in Boston, MA; retired

CARTER,
Beatrice M., d. 4/25/1972 at 62 in Los Alamos, NM; retired
    custodian; b. Pike; Arthur Pierce and May D. Patridge
Burnham, d. 7/4/1979 in Orford; Samuel Thompson Carter and
    Annie Burnham
Fannie, d. 7/6/1937 at 89/3/14 in Haverhill; housekeeper; widow; b.
    Montgomery Ctr., VT; Alonzo Watkins and Roiza Upham
Margaret, d. 11/25/1992 in Lebanon; Frank Pillatt and Ada Lutey

CARVER,
Alforato, d. 10/5/1930 at 91 in NY; housewife; widow
Herbert Newell, d. 3/14/1928 at 51/5/21 in Orford; farmer; single; b.
    MA; Fred L. Carver (ME) and Elfreda Dodge (ME)

CATHRALL,
Mabel, d. 4/10/1982 in Orford; Harry Ross McCubbin and Grace
    McCubbin

CELLEY,
Angela L., d. 1/31/1931 at 71 in Malden, MA; at home; widow; b. Vershire, VT; William Eastman (Vershire, VT) and Angela Gove (Strafford, VT)

CHAMBERLAIN,
Asahel D., d. 5/25/1907 at 78/10/20 in Orford; cerebral hemorrhage; retired; married; b. Thetford, VT; R. Chamberlin (Thetford, VT) and ----- Taylor

Charles S., d. 8/13/1925 at 70/9/9 in Orford; farmer; married; b. Orford; Ashel Chamberlain (Thetford, VT) and Ruby S. Baldwin (Orford)

Cora B., d. 10/8/1925 at 60/4/28 in Orford; domestic; widow; b. Wentworth; Samuel Nichols (Concord) and Angelia Smith (Lyme)

M. H., d. 4/5/1915 at 47/2/1 in Orford; chronic interstitial nephritis; domestic; single; b. Orford; A. D. Chamberlain (Thetford, VT) and R. S. Baldwin (Orford)

Ralph, d. 1/5/1964 at 74 in Plymouth; laborer; b. Orford; Charles S. Chamberlain and Corabelle Nichols

Ruby S., d. 3/12/1909 at 77/11/8 in Orford; housewife; widow; b. Orford; Isaac Daldwin and ----- Haselton

William E., d. 10/15/1920 at 61/4/11 in Orford; clerk; single; b. Orford; As'bel D. Chamberlain (Thetford, VT) and Ruby S. Baldwin (Orford)

CHANDLER,
Emily J., d. 3/20/1905 at 61/2/25 in Orford; housewife; married; b. Orford; Moses Williams (Orford) and Aluni Simons (Orford)

Stevens, d. 2/12/1892 at 89/9/5 in Orford; old age; farmer; married; b. Piermont; Seth Chandler

William, d. 6/28/1889 at 52/8/22 in Orford; marasmus; carpenter; married; b. Orford; Calvin Chandler

CHAPIN,
Alice D., d. 9/29/1976 at 86 in Hanover; b. VT; Elmer DeGoosh and Belle Keyes

Orrin K., d. 12/18/1977 at 61 in Hanover; electrician; b. NH; Orrin Chapin and Alice DeGoosh

Orrin S., d. 1/22/1973 at 79 in Haverhill; retired; b. Charlemont, MA; Elmer Chapin and Eliza Hurley

CHAPLIN,
Henry Dunster, d. 11/19/1965 at 71 in Orford; publisher; b. Dedham, MA; Heman Chaplin and Martha Crowell

CHAPMAN,
Evelyn H., d. 9/28/1922 at 25/7/14 in Concord; housework; single; b. Orford; Perley Chapman (Chicopee, MA) and Mary E. Willis (Warren)
Jessie Helen, d. 12/27/1899 at 0/6/27 in Orford; pneumonia; b. Orford; P. A. Chapman (Orford) and Mary Willis (Warren)
Martha J., d. 8/26/1902 at 0/5/23 in Orford; cholera infantum; b. Orford; Perley A. Chapman (Tewksbury, MA) and Mary E. Willis (Warren)
Maxwell F., d. 6/10/1969 at 77 in Franklin; laborer; b. Orford; Perley Chapman and Mary E. Willis
Perley Amasa, d. 10/8/1916 at 69/8/2 in Orford; chronic myocarditis; laborer; divorced; b. Tewksbury, MA; H. A. Balcom and M. Chapman
Roscoe F., d. 5/26/1958 at 68/3/25 in Haverhill; laborer; single; b. Orford; P. A. Chapman and Mary E. Willis

CHARTRAND,
Joseph L., d. 10/6/1974 at 59 in Orford; laborer; b. Fitchburg, MA; Joseph Chartrand and Josephine Valade

CHASE,
Alma A., d. 10/7/1955 at 80/0/18 in Hanover; widow; b. Haverhill; Charles Day and Esther Hartwell
Annie E., d. 5/17/1934 at 86/11 in Orford; housework; widow; b. Warren; Samuel Flanders (Boston, MA) and Annie Foote (Warren)
Charles L., d. 3/30/1949 at 74/7/22 in Orford; laborer; single; b. Wentworth; Simeon P. Chase and Sarah Cheasby
Edith, d. 12/2/1966 at 81 in Haverhill; ret. housewife; b. Orford; Gene Simpson and Minnie Savage
Eleanor A., d. 12/3/2000 in Plymouth; Charles A. Perry and Inez C. Lindsay
George, d. 1/6/1972 at 68 in Franconia; retired; b. Orford; John B. Chase and Alma A. Day
Irene M., d. 6/6/1979 in Hanover; Fred Mack and Mabel Ramsey

John B., d. 2/13/1907 at 78/4 in Orford; chronic endocarditis; blacksmith; married; b. Orford; ----- Chase and Nancy Savage

John W., d. 7/5/1911 at 34/11/29 in Orford; shock from ampu., gunshot; blacksmith; married; b. Orford; John B. Chase (Orford) and Ann Flanders (Warren)

Lavina, d. 3/7/1889 at 71/7/7 in Orford; disease of heart; widow; b. Plymouth; Bachelor Clement and Prudence Willoughby

Marian, d. 1/21/1974 at 67 in Hanover; housekeeper; b. Orford; Warren S. Chase and Edith Simpson

Maurice A., d. 11/15/1974 at 65 in Hanover; laborer; b. Orford; Warren S. Chase and Edith Simpson

Rufus Eugene, d. 1/8/1950 at 46 in Orford; laborer; married; b. Orford; Warren S. Chase and Edith Simpson

Stanley R., d. 1/22/1995 in Orford; Warren S. Chase and Edith Simpson

Warren S., d. 11/17/1949 at 71/1/26 in Orford; laborer; married; b. Orford; John B. Chase and Annie Flanders

CHENEY,

Abbie L., d. 10/1/1910 at 61/9/25 in Orford; housewife; married; b. Montgomery, VT; Alonzo G. Watkins (Mendon, VT) and Louisa Upham (Montgomery, VT)

CHESLEY,

Frank, d. 8/7/1935 at 77/2/15 in Lyme; farmer; widower; b. W. Fairlee, VT; John E. Chesley and Hannah Moody

John E., d. 8/16/1892 at 64/5 in Orford; pneumonia; farmer; married; b. Compton, PQ; John Chesley (Colchester) and Ruth Draper (Plymouth)

Louisa, d. 11/1/1933 at 75/1 in Lyme; housewife; married; b. W. Fairlee, VT; Benjamin Morey (Strafford, VT) and Nancy Rowell (NY)

Martha B., d. 4/29/1892 at 63/11/11 in Pittsburgh, PA; dropsy

CHURCHILL,

Charles Benjamin, d. 4/13/1928 at 80 in Brookline, MA; trader; b. Guilford, CT; Cyrus Churchill (New Briton, CT) and Clarissa Churchill (Guilford, CT)

Corrinne H., d. 1/8/1924 in Brookline, MA; received in Orford from MA cemetery 7/17/1925

Katherine, d. 8/31/1968 at 95 in Hartford, VT

CLAFLIN,

Emma Davis, d. 1/1/1941 at 79/0/11 in Manchester; housewife; widow; b. Brunswick, VT; Davis B. French and Charlotte Morey

Josie, d. 10/21/1942 at 64/6/14 in Haverhill; housewife; married; b. Lunenburg, VT; James Powers (Lunenburg, VT) and Louise Phillips (Dalton)

Julia, d. 10/27/1935 at 83/5/22 in Orford; retired; widow; b. Haverhill; David Hackett (Hardwick, VT) and Ann Hutton (England)

Willie B., d. 7/16/1928 at 72/4/19 in Orford; farmer; married; b. Topsham, VT; William Claflin (Marshfield, VT) and Irene Felch (Topsham, VT)

CLARK,

Adaline W., d. 4/4/1943 at 79/10/19 in Orford; housewife; married; b. Grafton; Henry S. Wheelock (Weymouth, MA) and Mary M. Littlefield (ME)

Burton L., d. 4/10/1957 at 84 in Bellows Falls, VT; retired; widower

Daniel C., d. 1/29/1909 at 74/9/4 in Orford; farmer; married; b. Orford; Jonathan Clark (Boscawen) and Hannah Cross (Orford)

Elizabeth S., d. 3/19/1967 at 65 in Angola, IN; housewife; ----- Stearns

Gertrude Keyes, d. 7/13/1942 at 72/9/23 in Putney, VT

Henrietta, d. 2/22/1934 at 91/10/22 in New Britain, CT; widow

Henry M., d. 7/21/1909 at 63/8/15 in Orford; retired; married; b. Campton; Joshua Clark (Sanbornton) and Syrina Palmer (Sanbornton)

Jennie E., d. 9/24/1938 at 87/11/26 in Orford; housewife; widow; b. Brandon, VT; Charles Geer (England) and Hannah Passone (England)

John B., d. 12/26/1924 at 41 in Orford; laborer; single; b. Manchester; William C. Clarke (Manchester) and Mary Tewksbury (Manchester)

Martha B., d. 10/30/1971 at 52 in Orford; housewife; b. Macon, GA; Marcus C. Balckum and Martha Howard

Mary A., d. 4/25/1964 at 98 in Randolph; b. Orford; Daniel C. Clark and Sarah M. Richardson

Ray, d. 9/28/1947 at 64/1/2 in Orford; bond broker; married; b. St. Louis, MO; Lincoln Ellis Clark (Tuscaloosa, AL) and Jetta Glennon (Ireland)

Sarah M., d. 7/29/1932 at 91/9/21 in Windsor, VT

CLAYTON,
Gladys, d. 7/31/1977 at 75 in Hanover; b. MS; John Legler and Henrietta Buddig
Harold E., d. 4/22/1967 at 67 in Hanover; mill owner; b. Lowell, MA; Harry E. Clayton and Hannah Demsnay

CLIFFORD,
Charles H., d. 1/26/2001 in Orford; Charles Clifford and Eva Johnson
Hazel Butson, d. 4/29/1993 in Orford; Charles A. Butson and Eva McVety

CLOGSTON,
baby, d. 11/12/1959 at 11 hrs. in Hanover
John H., d. 8/24/1904 at 81/3/18 in Orford; farmer; widower; Abner P. Clogston and Rachel Gould

CLOUGH,
Ada Norris, d. 4/3/1888 at 37/6/1 in Orford; housewife; married; b. Washington, VT; John A. Norris (Derry) and Susan Walker (Williamstown, VT)
Albert H., d. 5/13/1895 at 26/8/28 in Orford; consumption; grocer; b. Orford; Horace Clough and Anna G. Sargent
Dudley E., d. 11/11/1953 at 71 in Orford; farm labor; married; b. Bath; Solon Clough and Lizzie Weeks
Edith M., d. 6/27/1948 at 75/10/9 in Medford, MA; farmer; single; b. Orford; Josiah D. Clough (Washington, VT) and Ada M. Norris (Washington, VT)
Edna A., d. 11/25/1902 at 23/8/10 in Orford; chronic peritonitis; dressmaker; single; b. Orford; Josiah D. Clough (Washington, VT) and Ada M. Norris (Washington, VT)
Ethel Knight, d. 10/14/1918 at 31/8/15 in Orford; housewife; married; b. Franconia; C. M. Knight (Lincoln) and Minnie Clement (Warren)
Horace, d. 10/15/1929 at 92/10/10 in Concord; farmer; widower; b. Washington, VT; Fredrick Clough (Washington, VT) and ----- Sanborn (Washington, VT)
Josiah D., d. 2/13/1922 at 82/2/24 in Orford; farmer; widower; b. Washington, VT; Amini Clough and Cum't Sanborn

COBURN,
Annabelle G., d. 2/2/1923 at 65 in Lyme
David, d. 10/1/1898 at 2/2/23 in Orford; dysentery; b. Orford; Mary E. Mann (Orford)
David, d. 4/17/1925 at 82/9/5 in Fairlee, VT; widower
David E., d. 9/16/1948 at 75/1/22 in Hanover; farmer; married; b. E. Berkshire, VT; David Coburn (E. Berkshire, VT) and Lucy Smith (Berkshire, VT)
Lewis, d. 4/4/1964 at 87 in Lyme; farmer; b. Berkshire, VT; David Coburn and Lucy Smith
Minnie, d. 6/4/1974 at 92 in Haverhill; retired; b. Wentworth; George Rennels and Mary Taylor

COCHRAN,
Thomas S., d. 8/13/1926 at 58/6/3 in Woodsville; retired; b. New York, NY; Thomas S. Cochran (Scotland) and Agnes Stiochen (Scotland)

COLBURN,
son, d. 7/5/1925 at 0/0/15 in Orford; b. Orford; Clyde H. Colburn (Dorchester) and Florence White (Lancaster)
Alvah, d. 11/22/1934 at 28/1/14 in Hanover; farmer; single; b. Lyme; Lewis Coburn (Berkshire, VT) and Minnie Runnels (Wentworth)
Helen, d. 5/10/1932 at 27 in Hanover; teacher; single; Lewis Colburn and Eva Smith (Lyme)
Mary P., d. 7/20/1960 at 81 in Lyme; retired housewife; widow; b. Lyme; Albert Pushee and Sarah F. Jeffers

COLBY,
Celia, d. 11/22/1972 at 90 in Haverhill; retired; b. Stark; Flander Hartwell and Clarice Shaw

COLE,
William M., d. 12/15/1960 at 94/10/5 in New Britain, CT; retired; married; b. Boston, MA; Albert B. Cole and Mary E. Morse

CONANT,
Hamilton S., d. 3/19/1921 at 69/9/25 in Stoneham, MA; minister; married; b. Orford; Horace H. Conant (Craftsbury, VT) and Susan Stimson (Greensboro, VT)

Horace H., d. 5/28/1901 at 88/7/15 in Orford; old age; harness maker; widower; b. Craftsbury, VT; Newell Conant and Sally Pierce

Susan S., d. 5/18/1895 at 80/11/2 in Orford; dis. of liver; housekeeper; b. Greensboro; Seba Stimson and Phillapee Allen

William H., d. 2/24/1968 at 86 in White Plains, NY; b. White Plains, NY

William R., d. 2/25/1923 at 66 in Hanover; postmaster; married; b. Orford; Horace H. Conant (Canterbury, VT) and Susan Stimson (Gainsboro, VT)

CONKEY,
Robert, d. 8/24/1976 at 19 in Orford; b. MI; Albert R. Conkey and Ethel Walker

CONNELL,
Addie G., d. 10/10/1960 at 87/0/6 in Stewartstown; housewife; divorced; b. Orford; Luther S. Gage and Adeline Niles

CONVERSE,
Amy E., d. 2/27/1937 at 75/1/12 in Newport; retired; widow; b. Orford; Iremus H. Pingree (Thetford, VT) and Laura Curier (Thetford, VT)

Herbert B., d. 11/10/1921 at 66/3/7 in Claremont; farmer; married; b. Lyme; Benjamin Converse (Lyme) and Mary A. Brown (Rumney)

COOLIDGE,
Emma L., d. 3/29/1890 at 24/11/27 in Orford; quick consumption; domestic; single; b. Orford; Caleb F. Whitman (Orford) and Mary W. Norris (Wentworth)

Ralph A., d. 5/4/1928 at 41/9 in Plymouth; laborer; single; b. Orford; John W. Coolidge (Benton) and Emma Whitman (Orford)

COOPIG,
Marion Etta, d. 7/20/1923 at 46/8 in Glencliff; cook; married; b. Canada; Daniel White (Waterloo, PQ) and Paulina Boardman (Waterloo, PQ)

CORLISS,
Edward A., d. 10/1/1894 at 26/0/16 in Orford; consumption; farmer;
   b. Orford; John S. Corliss (Orford) and Olive E. Cheney
Helen G., d. 4/3/1944 at 71/2/9 in Los Angeles, CA; married; b.
   Orford; John Corliss (Orford) and Olive Cheney (Stowe, VT)
Helen G., d. 6/4/1971 at 91 in San Diego, CA; housewife; b.
   Brownington, VT; Carlos Gilbert and Helen F. Barnes
Helen M., d. 9/28/1907 at 74/5/23 in Orford; apoplexy; housewife;
   widow; b. Bradford, VT; Jonathan Martin and Martha Barnes
John M., d. 11/22/1887 at 57/6/7 in Orford; farmer; married; b.
   Orford; Elihu Corliss (Alexandria) and Harriet C. Dayton
   (Orford)
John Seymour, d. 5/20/1900 at 73/1/23 in Orford; heart disease;
   farmer; married; b. Orford; Alexander Corliss and Abigail Marsh
Lora, d. 3/1/1890 at 60/10 in Fairlee, VT; catarrhal bronchitis;
   housewife; widow; b. Norwich, VT
Mary E., d. 4/28/1894 at 17/0/2 in Orford; consumption; b. Orford;
   John S. Corliss (Orford) and Olive E. Cheney
Olive E., d. 12/24/1911 at 75/1/10 in Orford; chronic tuberculosis;
   housewife; widow; b. Stowe, VT; William Cheney and Olive E.
   Savage

COUTEMANCHE,
Ludivine, d. 11/29/1983 in Lebanon; Joseph Godin and Dianne
   Beaulieux

COVEY,
John Alexander, d. 5/31/1920 at 40/4/4 in Orford; farmer; married; b.
   E. Gr'st'd, England; George Covey (England) and Helen
   Newington (England)

CREIGHTON,
Dorothy, d. 7/28/1984 in Hanover

CROSBY,
son, d. 1/30/1907 at – in Orford; stillborn; b. Orford; Willard Crosby
   (Wentworth) and Bertha Pease (Haverhill)
Ray, d. 5/6/1908 at 0/0/10 in Orford; acute bronchitis; b. Orford;
   Willard Crosby (Wentworth) and Bertha Pease (Pike)

CROSS,
Eugene P., d. 2/26/1950 at 71 in Bradford, VT; carpenter (ret.); single; b. Orford; Joseph D. Cross and Annette Curtis

Joseph Dwight, d. 3/6/1911 at 52/4/17 in Orford; broncho pneumonia; farmer; married; b. Barford, PQ; Joseph Cross (Stanstead, PQ) and Lovina Edwards (Athens, VT)

Leon Dwight, d. 3/10/1901 at 6/6/19 in Orford; tubercular meningitis; b. Orford; James D. Cross (laborer, Warren) and Stella Mutman (Orford)

Stella M., d. 12/20/1900 at 31/5/7 in Orford; phthisis pulmonalis; housewife; married; b. Orford; Caleb F. Whitman (Lyme) and Mary Norris (Orford)

William J., d. 6/1/2003 in Lebanon; William Tiffany Cross and Anne Monaghan Cross

CROWE,
John, d. 9/7/1931 at 58/4/12 in Orford; farmer; divorced; b. Franklin Ctr., PQ; John Crowe (Ireland) and Lucy Wilson

Lucy, d. 12/28/1919 at 85/8/11 in Orford; none; widow; b. Canada

CROWELL,
Mary N., d. 8/9/1936 at 80/10/14 in Concord; widow; b. S. Yarmouth, MA; Nelson Crowell (S. Yarmouth, MA) and Mary Crowell (Yarmouth, MA)

CUMMINGS,
Clyde, d. 1/14/1978 at 68 in Haverhill; maintenance; married; b. Thetford, VT; Asa Cummings and Nellie Randall

Clyde A., d. 8/28/2004 in Piermont; Clyde A. Cummings and Rosie Tallmann

Henry J., d. 7/26/1938 at 62/4/16 in Orford; farmer; married; b. Thetford, VT; James C. Cummings and Elizabeth T. Webber (Newbury, VT)

James, d. 2/29/1944 at 63/10/14 in Hanover; farmer; married; b. Thetford, VT; James Cummings (Thetford, VT) and Elizabeth Webber (Newbury, VT)

Lucy M., d. 7/2/1946 at 69/9/11 in Orford; housewife; widow; b. Lancaster; Charles Allen (Lancaster) and Martha Jewell (Guildhall, VT)

Norman Jane, d. 5/11/1944 at 0/4/14 in Hanover; b. Lyme; Clyde A. Cummings (Thetford Ctr., VT) and Rosie Tallman (Orford)

Rosie E., d. 3/17/1969 at 58 in Orford; housewife; b. Orford; Forrest Tallman and Jennie B. Rhodes

CUNNINGHAM,
Alice G., d. 7/7/1905 at 39/3/23in Orford; housewife; married; b. Hanover; John Sanborn (Bradford) and Martha Fitch (Hanover)
Analine, d. 5/14/1891 at 35/2/20 in Orford; married; b. Brooklyn, NY; Samuel Mitchell (Albany, NY) and Catharine Gorman
George H., d. 6/11/1913 at 58/10/17 in Orford; arterio sclerosis; farmer; married; b. Orford; John Cunningham and Betsey L. Smith
James Daniel, d. 5/24/1940 at 64/1/2 in Orford; painter; married; b. Fairlee, VT; Samuel Cunningham (Bradford, VT) and Jane Freeman (Fairlee, VT)
Mary F., d. 12/3/1920 at 66/11/7 in Orford; domestic; widow; b. Orford; Benjamin F. Niles (Orford) and Mary Newell (Orford)
Samuel, d. 3/27/1928 at 78/2/27 in Haverhill; farmer; widower; b. Bradford, VT; Josiah Cunningham (Groton, VT) and Lydia Merrill (Bradford, VT)

CURRIER,
daughter, d. 10/22/1909 at – in Orford; b. Orford; Alfred Currier (Orford) and Maggie Rollins (Orford)
daughter, d. 6/9/1934 at 18 hrs. in Orford; b. Orford; Jesse W. Currier (Wentworth) and Victoria Downing (Orford)

CUSHING,
Clyde Oscar, d. 3/5/1920 at 0/6/15 in Lisbon; b. Orford; Harry J. Cushing (McIndoes, VT) and Alice Pauline Gould (Lancaster)

CUSHMAN,
Charles Lewis, d. 11/1/1/1965 at 84 in Orford; ret. farmer; b. Orford; Ernest Cushman and Minnie Worthley
Elizabeth, d. 12/5/1916 at 0/0/5 in Orford; prem. birth; b. Orford; C. L. Cushman (Orford) and Eliz. McGechin (Baltimore, MD)
Elizabeth M., d. 2/23/1949 at 63/0/26 in Haverhill; housewife; married; b. Baltimore, MD; Thomas H. McGechin and Ella Ross
Ernest W., d. 9/5/1922 at 71/7/29 in Orford; farmer; married; b. Lisbon; James Cushman (Lisbon) and Jane Clough (Lyman)
Frank E., d. 6/21/1922 at 75/1/7 in Orford; farmer; single; b. Lisbon; James Cushman (Lisbon) and Jane Clough (Lyman)

Hartwell C., d. 6/26/1901 at 92/11/10 in Orford; old age; R. merchant; widower; b. Landaff; Stephen Cushman and Martha Coleman

James G., d. 2/10/1894 at 75/10/10 in Orford; a fall; farmer; b. Lisbon; Luther Cushman (Coventry, CT) and Fanny Coleman

Jane, d. 2/2/1901 at 88/8/23 in Orford; old age; widow; b. Lyman; Abner Clough and Nancy Corey

John J., d. 1/5/1891 at 86/6/11 in Orford; farmer; widower; b. Landaff; Stephen Cushman (Lisbon) and Martha Colman

Mary A. E., d. 2/12/1890 at 74/9/16 in Orford; influenza; housewife; married; b. Taunton, MA; Hilliard Earl and Mary Ware

Mary E. Piper, d. 6/27/1892 at 49/11/22 in Orford; diabetes; domestic; married; b. Orford; Elijah P. Piper and Maria Fuller

Minnie Worthley, d. 10/11/1944 at 86 in Glensode, PA; housewife; widow; b. Bradford, VT; B. L. Worthley (Bradford, VT) and Emily M. Coburn (W. Fairlee, VT)

Nancy J., d. 1/24/1890 at 41/0/26 in Orford; phthisis pulmonalis; housewife; single; b. Lisbon; James Y. Cushman (Lisbon) and Janet Clough (Lyman)

Peleg E., d. 11/9/1893 at 51/6 in Orford; heart failure; farmer; b. Orford; H. C. Cushman (Landaff) and Mary Ann Earl

William A., d. 5/6/1909 at 72/7/26 in Orford; c. engineer; divorced; b. Fall River, MA; Hartwell C. Cushman (Landaff) and Mary A. Earl (Taunton, MA)

CUTTER,

Charles A., d. 7/9/1923 at 67 in Orford; farmer; widower; b. Cambridge, MA; Cyrus D. Cutter (Orford) and Mary S. Williams (Orford)

Roistine, d. 1/3/1915 at 66/10/28 in Orford; acute indigestion; housewife; b. Landaff; Luther Grant (Tolland, CT) and Huldah Hamilton (Windsor, CT)

CUTTING,

daughter, d. 10/18/1888 at 0/0/5 in Orford; b. Orford; Samuel Q. Cutting (Orford) and Julia E. Gardner (Lyme)

Fred G., d. 9/15/1953 at 66 in Worcester, MA; married; b. Orford; Samuel Cutting and Julia Gardner

Hollis A., d. 2/7/1898 at 78 in Orford; bronchial consumption; farmer; widower; b. VT; Iscah A. Cutting (Lyme) and Ellen ----- (Brookfield, VT)

Ina F., d. 3/5/1934 at 52 in Concord; teacher; single; b. Orford; Samuel Cutting (Orford) and Julia Gardner (Lyme)

Julia, d. 10/19/1935 at 76/7/2 in Auburn, MA; retired; widow; b. Lyme; James Gardner (Lyme) and Emeline Brick (Lyme)

Nancy Q., d. 1/1/1903 at 88/9/14 in Orford; capillary bronchitis; widow; housekeeper; b. Orford; Samuel Quint and Roxana Stebins

Samuel Q., d. 11/12/1920 at 69/4/23 in Worcester; farmer; married; b. Orford; Amaziah Cutting (Orford) and Nancy S. Quint (Orford)

DAISEY,

Lauren C., d. 10/27/1996 in Lebanon; Amos Daisey and Holly Lemay

Myrtle F., d. 10/29/2003 in Haverhill; Leon Chase and Maywood Edson

DALE,

Alfred H., d. 9/28/1958 at 86/4/1 in Haverhill; teamster; single; b. Rexton, NB; William Dale and Elizabeth Porter

Richard Andrew, d. 2/23/1965 at 82 in Concord; lumberman; b. NB; William Dale and Elizabeth Foster

DAME,

Harriett F., d. 4/2/1926 at 87/4/16 in Fremont, NE; housewife; widow; b. Lyman; Rinalco Moulton (Lyman) and ----- Kent (Rumney)

DANA,

Ada, d. 12/11/1929 at 58/8/20 in Boston, MA; none; single; b. Boston, MA; Thomas Dana (Springfield, VT) and Mary C. Baldwin (Putney, VT)

Mary Catherine, d. 9/1/1918 at 76/6/28 in Orford; none; widow; b. Putney, VT; Sewall Baldwin (Sudbury, MA) and Rebecca Hyde

William F., d. 8/5/1920 at 57/1/10 in Orford; judge; single; b. Somerville, MA; Thomas Dana (Springfield, VT) and Mary K. Baldwin (Putney, VT)

DANIELS,

George W., d. 1/7/1923 at 77/3/11 in Orford; retired; married; b. Canaan; Ozia H. Daniels (Plainfield) and Mary Richardson (Canaan)

Laura, d. 4/16/1998 in Lebanon; Clifford Main and Minnie Bragg

DAVIS,
son, d. 8/4/1889 at 0/0/28 in Orford; convulsions; b. Orford; William E. Davis (England) and Annie E. Lines (England)
Alymer E., d. 6/29/1918 at 59/8/17 in Orford; laborer; married; b. Bolton, PQ; Enoch Davis (Hyde Park, VT) and Medora White (Hyde Park, VT)
C. Howard, d. 5/27/1932 at 13/4/21 in Orford; single; b. Fairlee, VT; Carl A. Davis (Lyman) and Marion Howard (Northfield, MA)
Carl Aylmer, d. 2/6/1969 at 77 in Littleton; police officer; b. Lyman; Aylmer Davis and Ida Clough
Charles, d. 5/17/1953 at 75 in Hanover; retired; widower; b. N. Grafton; Daniel Davis and Lavica Quimby
Charles C., d. 11/8/1922 at 67/4 in Orford; laborer; single; b. Orford; John Davis (Holderness) and Lavinia Whitcomb (Lyme)
Floyd, d. 5/2/1983 in Orford; Aylmer Davis and Ida Clough
George C., d. 4/13/1918 at 80 in Orford; farmer; widower; b. Danville, VT; John Davis
Gerald, d. 8/28/1985 in Hanover
Hattie K., d. 1/9/2002 in Bradford, VT; Alvah Davis and Myrtie Woodard
Ida L., d. 12/5/1943 at 79/11 in Hanover; widow; b. Lyman; ----- Clough (Lisbon) and Louella Ingerson (Lyman)
John P., d. 11/8/1922 at 72/5 in Orford; laborer; widower; b. Orford; John Davis (Holderness) and Lavinia Whitcomb (Lyme)
John T., d. 4/17/1905 at 83/1/3 in Orford; farmer; married; b. Wentworth; ----- and Mehitable Phelps
Kendall M., d. 8/26/1906 at 59/6/4 in Orford; RR engineer; married; b. Orford; John T. Davis (Wentworth) and Lavina Whitcomb (Lyme)
Lavina W., d. 6/12/1912 at 86/9/26 in Lyme; senility; housewife; widow; b. Lyme; Jonathan Whitcomb (Randolph, MA) and Lydia Clark (Canaan)
Mary A. M., d. 4/7/1888 at 27/6/25 in Brooklyn, NY; housewife; widow; b. Brooklyn, NY; Samuel P. Mitchel (Orford) and Catharin Gorman (Albany, NY)
Myrtie E., d. 7/20/1970 at 60 in Hanover; housewife; b. VT; Asa Cummings and Nellie Randall

Nettie Ethel, d. 6/23/1888 at 0/3/22 in Orford; b. Orford; William Edwin Davis (Moreton, England) and Annie E. Davis (Oxhill, England)

Robert C., d. 10/7/2004 in Ware, MA; Welcome Davis and Sarah Jones

S. B. H., d. 12/18/1892 at 75/11 in Orford; housewife; widow; b. Chester

S. Josephine, d. 10/24/1902 at 56/6 in Orford; cancer; housewife; married; b. Orford; Clark Lovejoy and Sabrina Brown

DAY,

Alfreta T. S., d. 9/23/1894 at 32/2/2 in Orford; phthisis pulmonalis; housewife; John S. Simpson (Topsham, VT) and Caroline Bowen

Alice Electa Worcester, d. 11/29/1979 in Orford; Dean C. Worcester and Nannon Leas

Jasper G., d. 8/8/1916 at 65/4/23 in Bristol; arterio sclerosis; laborer; married; b. Haverhill; Jeremiah Day (Wentworth) and Elmira Teary

Philip S., d. 4/24/1963 at 78 in Montreal, Canada; b. VT; Jasper Day

DAYTON,

Bessie Brock, d. 2/3/1955 at 66/3/4 in Orford; housewife; married; b. Orford; Charles E. Brock and Mary Wyman

Edward J., d. 4/17/1912 at 66/2/23 in Orford; diabetis melitis; musician; single; b. Orford; Henry Dayton (Orford) and Julia A. Whitcomb (Johnstown, NY)

Eliza, d. 2/20/1892 at 81 in Orford; pneumonia; domestic; single; b. Orford

Henry, d. 4/6/1894 at 85/10/28 in Orford; old age; mechanic; b. Orford; James H. Dayton (Gastonburge) and Lucinda Morey

Henry E., d. 3/28/1921 at 77/0/13 in Yonkers, NY; hatter; married; b. Orford; Henry Dayton (Orford) and Julia Whitcomb

James Henry, d. 11/6/1957 at 80/8/28 in Canaan; retired; widower; b. Somerville, MA; Henry E. Dayton and Lillian Browne

Julia A., d. 1/13/1894 at 72 in Orford; old age; housewife; b. Orford; Rufus Whitcomb

Lillian M., d. 8/3/1937 at 81/10/10 in Orford; housekeeper; widow; b. Portland, ME; James Brown (Tonquay, England)

DEBLOIS,
Beatrice, d. 2/21/2000 in Hanover; Joseph Irwin and Lillian Laclair
Julia M., d. 12/22/1972 at 92 in Orford; housewife; b. Canada; Lewis Bilbeault and Isabelle Roger
Melvin, d. --/--/1989

DEFORD,
Barbara A., d. 10/2/1996 in Orford; John Spadora and Joan Leduc

DEMAREST,
Martha S., d. 2/26/1961 at 11/6/23 in Orford; b. Cooperstown, NY; William Demarest and Victoria Salvatore

DEMO,
Edward L., d. 5/8/1994 in Lebanon; Edward Demo and Mary C. Lapier

DENNIS,
daughter, d. 4/25/1893 at 0/1/22 in Orford; spina bifida; b. Orford; Fred A. Dennis (Strafford) and Vina Bass
son, d. 12/25/1901 at – in Orford; stillborn; b. Orford; Myron A. Dennis (farmer, Strafford) and Agnes L. Warren (Lyme)
Agnes W., d. 4/19/1911 at 44/7/4 in Orford; diabetes mellitus; housewife; married; b. Lyme; Ruel A. Warren (Lyme) and Fidelia Culling (Lyme)
Carrie C., d. 7/26/1923 at 54/8/26 in Lyme; housewife; married; b. Vershire, VT; George A. Church (Vershire, VT) and Sarah Aldrich (Corinth, VT)
Emore, d. 2/22/1909 at 67/9/23 in Orford; farmer; married; b. Stratford; Emore Dennis (Stratford) and Olive Cross (Troy, VT)
Evelyn Marie, d. 6/14/1947 at 25/3/2 in Orford; single; b. Hanover; Walter B. Dennis (Piermont) and Theresa Rugg (Fairlee, VT)
Frank A., d. 10/3/1909 at 52/3/5 in Orford; engineer; divorced; b. Stratford; William Dennis (Stratford) and Lucebia Curtis (Stratford)
Fred A., d. 5/16/1933 at 73 in Hanover; retired; married; b. Stratford; William Dennis
George Henry, d. 2/6/1959 at 54 in Zellwood, FL
George W., d. 3/5/1940 at 77/6 in Lyme; farmer; widower; b. Stratford; Emore Dennis (Stratford) and Mary Haynes (Warren)
Mary, d. 5/28/1990 in Bradford, VT; Edward Rugg and Eliza Bellville

Newell, d. 5/4/1919 at 37/10/9 in Benton; f. laborer; single; b. Orford; Emore Dennis (Stratford) and Olive Cross (Troy)
Viena Elvira, d. 12/28/1961 at 89 in St. Petersburg, FL; retired; widow; b. Stratford; ----- Bass
Walter B., d. 10/31/1972 at 77 in Bradford, VT; retired; b. Piermont; Byron Dennis and Eva Spencer
William, d. 11/21/1923 at 58 in Orford; filer; single; b. Stratford; William Dennis (Stratford) and Loosebia Curtis (Stratford)

DERRICK,
Eliza V., d. 8/4/1913 at 15/10/19 in Orford; acute dilitation of heart; single; b. Wentworth; George Derrick (N. Troy, VT) and Lulu Goodwin (Piermont)

DESMOND,
Juliette G., d. 3/19/2003 in Lebanon; Zotic Dansereau
Robert, d. 11/16/1980 in Orford; John R. Desmond and Carolyn B. Metcalf
William, d. 1/4/2003 in Orford; Robert Desmond and Juliette Dansereau

DEVER,
Vera Phylis, d. 3/26/1923 at 1/8/18 in Springfield, MA; Bertha Fuller

DICKERSON,
Clydia C., d. 8/28/1887 at 2/1/1 in Orford; b. Orford; W. Dickerson (Newbury, VT) and Minnie Chase (Washington, VT)

DICKINSON,
Charles Perkins, d. 11/29/1956 at 79/0/24 in Brattleboro, VT; clothier; widower; b. Bristol; Charles H. Dickinson and Ida M. Gordon
Esma, d. 7/2/1950 at 64 in Hanover; housewife; married; b. Northwood; Byron H. Marston and Lulu Barry

DILLON,
Edith B., d. 7/7/1981 in Hanover; Thomas Dillon and Edith Burgess

DIONNE,
Jeanette H., d. 7/6/2004 in St. Petersburg, FL

DONAHUE,
Harold F., d. 10/5/1943 at 42/6/4 in Hanover; caretaker; married; b. Barre, VT; Jeremiah Donahue and Laura Clark

DONALDSON,
George B., d. 7/22/1908 at 41/2/23 in Orford; typhoid fever; laborer; married; b. Peacham, VT; Marcus Donaldson (Stanstead Pn., Canada) and Charlotte LaLearn (Canada)

Jesse George, d. 3/14/1918 at 24/4/18 in Orford; in Navy; b. Orford; George B. Donaldson (Peacham, VT) and Mary E. Whitman (Orford)

DONNELLY,
Della A., d. 12/2/1968 at 79 in Attleboro, MA; housewife; b. Wentworth; Francis R. Pease and Mabel Sherburn

Jay W., d. 9/20/1953 at 68 in Orford; retired; married; b. Colebrook; William J. Donnelly and Edith Lampson

William J., d. 6/23/1926 at 64/0/8 in Orford; retired barber; b. Lemmington, VT; William Donnelly (Ireland) and Ellen Gilbert (Ireland)

DOOLEY,
William, d. 1/23/19166 at 84 in Haverhill; insurance; b. Boston, MA; Thomas H. Dooley and Rose Ann -----

DOTEN,
Edna, d. 5/13/1936 at 50/9/29 in Orford; housewife; married; b. S. Strafford, VT; Aaron McCrillis (Corinth, VT) and Julia Hackett (Haverhill)

DOW,
Mary Etta, d. 9/20/1934 at 75/1/4 in Orford; housewife; married; b. Warren; Daniel S. Willis (Foxboro, MA) and Marinda Hazelton (Orford)

Roland Earl, d. 4/6/1910 at 0/0/28 in Orford; b. Wentworth; Bert Dow (Canterbury, NB) and Ethel Downing (Orford)

DOWNING,
Elizabeth T., d. 6/28/1933 at 36 in Hanover; housewife; married; b. Ft. Lawrence, NS; Henry DeBlois (Hands Co., NS) and Olive Pemberton (Hands Co., NS)

George Elmon, d. 10/12/1941 at 53/5/23 in Hanover; farmer; widower; b. Orford; Willie E. Downing (Wentworth) and Luna M. Poor (Orford)

Lida, d. 10/22/1970 at 76 in Orford; homemaker; b. Houlton, ME; David Dow and Annie Horton

Luna, d. 3/24/1937 at 70/5/24 in Orford; housekeeper; widow; b. Orford; Stephen B. Poor (Vershire, VT) and Marion M. George (Strafford, VT)

Willie E., d. 12/3/1916 at 58/3/17 in Orford; pul. tuberculosis; farmer; married; b. Wentworth; J. L. Downing (Meredith) and M. J. Ellsworth (Wentworth)

DUNBAR,

Alice Mary, d. 6/14/1955 at 89/4/10 in Cambridge, MA; retired; single; b. Orford; ----- Dunbar and Laura Carr

Edith May, d. 5/14/1942 at 55/5/21 in Bradford, VT; married

Laura A., d. 10/27/1943 at 102/3 in Somerville, MA; widow; b. Orford; Jesse K. Carr and Mary S. Bean

DUNN,

Charlie, d. 1/28/1940 at 8 hrs. in Haverhill; b. Haverhill; Edward L. Dunn (Pasadena, CA) and Eva M. Deering (Guildhall, VT)

DYER,

Isabel W., d. 5/11/1968 at 92 in Haverhill; housewife; b. Winchester, MA; John T. Wilson and Pleasantine Cushman

DYKE,

Benjamin F., Jr., d. 3/1/1997 in Orford; Benjamin Dyke, Sr. and Ethel Jesseman

Benjamin F., Sr., d. 2/14/1971 at 79 in Haverhill; farmer; b. Pompanoosuc, VT; Volney Dyke and Elizabeth Nash

Dorothy, d. 4/17/1990 in Lebanon; Cuthbert Dow and Ethel Wright

Ethel, d. 11/21/1967 at 68 in Hanover; housewife; b. Newbury, VT; Irvin Jesseman and Elizabeth LaFrance

George, d. 11/6/1987

Lee Matthew, d. 2/21/1970 at 2 in Orford; b. Haverhill; Robert F. Dyke and Delores Urbanski

Nathaniel J., d. 12/26/1997 in Lebanon; Daniel Dyke and Cara Shepard

EAGLESON,
Marie A., d. 8/9/1972 at 92 in Haverhill; housewife; b. New York, NY; Henry W. Blumer and Marie A. Friesz
William H., d. 2/22/1981 in Hanover; William H. Eagleson and Marie Blumer

EASTMAN,
Angeline, d. 12/25/1891 at 77/5/21 in Orford; domestic; widow; b. Strafford, VT; Nathaniel Gove (Vershire, VT) and Mary Jones
Ann S., d. 7/1/1896 at 72/4/18 in Orford; housewife; widow; b. Orford; Benjamin F. Trussell (Hopkinton) and Sophia Derby (Orford)

EDGAR,
Roberta F., d. 5/21/1981 in Hanover; Steven Bzdewka and Florence Stachurski

EDGELL,
Annette, d. 6/8/1902 at 72/5/29 in Orford; cerebral hemorrhage; single; b. Orford; Moses Edgell and Sarah Mason

EDSON,
Samson Walter, d. 9/30/1951 at 73 in Orford; laborer; widower; b. Bethel, VT; Daniel N. Edson and Charlotte E. -----

ELLIOTT,
son, d. 1/9/1933 at – in Orford; b. Orford; Stanley Elliott (Lyme) and Lula B. Baker (Orford)
A. H., d. 10/14/1892 at 72/7/20 in Orford; marasmus; domestic; widow; b. Corinth, VT; Benjamin F. Sleeper (NH) and Sarah Sleeper (Corinth, VT)
Allen Conrad, d. 4/24/1929 at 0/0/26 in Lyme; b. Orford; Stanley Elliott (Lyme) and Lula Baker (Orford)
Ashton W., d. 8/25/1973 at 77 in Springfield, MA; farmer; b. Haverhill; Samuel Elliott
Helena B., d. 10/28/1926 at 26/2/5 in Lowell, MA; housewife; b. Portsmouth; Harry B. Foote (Warren) and Claribel Felch (Canon City, CO)
Lula B., d. 12/31/1934 at 28/6/3 in Hanover; housewife; married; b. Orford; Henry G. Baker (Orford) and Inez Smith (Orford)

ELLSWORTH,
Hannah W., d. 2/16/1919 at 70/8/8 in Orford; housekeeper; widow;
   b. Ellsworth; James Randall (Ellsworth) and Eleanor Avery
   (Ellsworth)

EMERSON,
Donald, d. 5/30/1978 at 35 in Orford; truck driver; b. Windsor, VT;
   Henry F. Emerson and Ruth Sheltry

EMERY,
Hattie M., d. 9/17/1892 at 0/11 in Orford; cholera infantum; b. Orford;
   Perkins C. Emery (Washington, VT) and Marion E. Moulton
   (Canada)
Sally B., d. 3/21/1892 at 80/1 in E. Thetford, VT; old age; housewife;
   married

EVANS,
Clifford H., d. 9/21/1938 ay 43 in Orford; mechanic; married; b.
   Madbury; Harry Evans (Madbury) and Bertha R. Swain
   (Barrington)
Elmira G., d. 2/24/1901 at 33/6/25 in Orford; tuberculosis; housewife;
   married; b. Lyme; John Gilbert (Barford, PQ) and Elizabeth
   Post
William H., d. 3/2/1904 at 40/2 in Orford; laborer; widower; b.
   Belmont, NY; Daniel S. Evans and Anna E. McAll

FARMER,
Edith, d. 10/21/2003 in Orford; George Sevasin and Esther Oates
Rudy C., d. 6/10/2003 in Fortunes Rock, ME

FAY,
Addison G., d. 2/8/1929 at 52/5/12 in Tampa, FL; retired; married; b.
   Kenia, OH; A. Orville Fay (Concord, MA) and Martha Adams
   (Concord, MA)
Addison Orville, d. 6/1/1928 at 29/4/14 in Lakeland, FL; fruit grower;
   divorced; b. Boston, MA; Addison Grant Fay (Zenim, OH) and
   Emily Wilson (Winchester, MA)
Edgar S., d. 10/15/1966 at 79 in Orford; railroad; b. Derry; Loren E.
   Fay and Rose -----

FIELD,
Simon C., d. 12/11/1915 at 95/5/26 in Orford; mitral stenosis; farmer; widower; b. Northfield, VT; Seth P. Field (Covington, CT) and Sarah Closson (Thetford, VT)

FIFIELD,
Clifford C., d. 2/17/1978 at 75 in Haverhill; b. NH; Tilton Fairfield and Emma Crane
Frances E. W., d. 3/29/1889 at 77/11/24 in Orford; cancer of rectum; housewife; widow; b. Orford; Jeduthan Wilcox
Thomas J., d. 11/28/1888 at 85/9 in Concord; tailor; married; b. Plainfield; Joseph Fifield (Plainfield) and Hannah Pettengill (Salisbury, MA)

FILLIAN,
son, d. 9/18/1917 at 0/0/1 in Orford; b. Orford; Alphonse Fillian (Manchester) and Jessie Wood (Piermont)
son, d. 8/17/1928 at – in Orford; b. Orford; Alphonse Fillian (Manchester) and Jessie A. Wood (Piermont)
David A., d. 1/4/1975 at 47 in Orford; laborer; b. Orford; Alphonse Fillian and Jessie Wood
Delvinia, d. 7/27/1932 at 12/5/8 in Plymouth; b. Orford; Alphonse Fillian (Manchester) and Jessie Woods (Piermont)
Edna, d. 3/9/1990 in Hanover; Ernest Canfield and Ada Tolman
Hattie N., d. 2/27/1973 at 43 in Hanover; housewife; b. Warren; George Shortt and Nellie Wright
Jessie, d. 6/29/1967 at 71 in Hanover; housewife; b. Piermont; Charles Wood and Patience Boardman

FINNEY,
Charles E., d. 1/10/1907 at 76/4 in Orford; asthenia; farmer; married; b. Orford; Benjamin Finney and Lucy Newell
Doris, d. 3/27/1983 in Orford; Charles Chamberlin and Cora Nichols
Elizabeth, d. 1/29/1919 at Sherbrooke, PQ; widow
Frank George, d. 7/18/1918 at 48/11/3 in Orford; farmer; married; b. Orford; Henry Finney (Orford) and Mary A. Emerton
Henry J., d. 8/26/1894 at 63/7/19 in Orford; diabetes; farmer; b. Orford; Benjamin Finney
Ida, d. 8/1/1942 at 74 in Hartford, CT; ret. housewife; widow; b. Schaghticoke, NY

Margaret F., d. 10/28/1961 at 40/8/19 in Canton, CT; housewife; married; b. Changsha, China; Edwin D. Harvey and Florinda Lincoln

FLAGG,
Hazel, d. 9/18/2004 in Woodsville; Henry Bulley and Alice Johnson

FLANDERS,
Anna, d. 4/8/1889 at 80/10/10 in Orford; old age
Rufus, d. 3/12/1948 at 88/1/10 in Orford; ret. laborer; widower; b. Warren; Emery Flanders (Warren)

FOOTE,
daughter, d. 1/1/1933 at – in Hanover; b. Hanover; Edward Foote (Orford) and Rose Baker (Orford)
Abagail E., d. 4/21/1909 at 83/1/18 in Orford; housewife; widow; b. Sanbornton; Josiah Swain and Jane Eaton
Charles Guy, d. 9/13/1956 at 80/0/7 in Orford; retired farmer; married; b. Warren; Charles G. Foote and Emma MacMurphy
Claribel, d. 6/18/1946 at 73 in Warren; b. Canon City, CO; Henry H. Felch (Piermont) and Kate Bradbury (Haverhill)
Evelyn Marie, d. 3/8/1920 at 16/2/11 in Orford; none; single; b. Orford; Harry B. Foote (Warren) and Clarabelle Felch (Cripple Creek, IO)
Harry B., d. 3/20/1951 at 84 in Springfield, MA; retired; widower; b. Warren; James E. Foote and Judith Huckins
James E., d. 5/5/1921 at 73/8/1 in Orford; farmer; married; b. Warren; Samuel E. Foote (Thetford, VT) and Abegail Swain (Warren)
Judith H., d. 10/20/1925 at 73/3/13 in Orford; retired; widow; b. Warren; Thomas P. Huckins (NH) and Lucretia Berry (Warren)
Mildred L., d. 3/12/1941 at 44/7/17 in Gardner, ME; housewife; married; b. Portsmouth; Harry B. Foote (Warren) and Claribel Felch (CO)
Parker Emery, d. 7/16/1957 at 59/3/19 in Liberty, NY; chauffeur; married; b. Portsmouth; Harry B. Foote and Claribel Felch
Ruth Pearl, d. 2/27/1920 at 1/9/22 in Orford; b. Orford; Mildred Foote (Orford)
Samuel E., d. 10/12/1895 at 72/7/30 in Piermont; dis. of heart; farmer; b. Warren; Elias Foote and Phebe Richardson

FORD,
Aaron D., d. 10/31/1931 at 71/1/9 in Haverhill; retired; married; b. Corinth, VT; Aaron B. Ford (Corinth, VT) and Sarah J. Wiser (Corinth, VT)
Mary Sartwell, d. 1/3/1888 at 81 in Orford; housewife; widow; Asa Sartwell

FOSTER,
Arthur B., d. 1/7/1933 at 47/3/27 in Braintree, MA; married

FOURNIER,
Alice B., d. 2/21/1976 at 82 in Woodsville; housewife; b. VT; William Bacon and Mary Ann Parker

FRANKLIN,
Arthur L., d. 2/25/1972 at 89 in Haverhill; farmer; b. Orford; Lewis Franklin and Rebecca Cushman
Benjamin, d. 2/13/1895 at 77/1/13 in Orford; consumption; farmer; b. Lyme; George Franklin and Electa Smith
Clara, d. 12/29/1984 in Orford
Edwin C., d. 2/25/1928 at 79/11/11 in Orford; farmer; single; b. Lyme; Benjamin Franklin (Lyme) and Martha Morris (W. Fairlee, VT)
Harry Emerson, d. 11/16/2003 in N. Haverhill; Arthur Franklin and Marion Clark
Lewis, d. 4/25/1926 at 71/2/28 in Orford; farmer; widower; b. Orford; Benjamin Franklin (Lyme) and Martha Morris (Thetford, VT)
Lewis Ernest, d. 4/10/1995 in Orford; Harry Franklin and Ruby Pierson
Marion C., d. 6/6/1926 at 34/9/22 in Hanover; housewife; b. Orford; Charles C. Chamberlin (Orford) and Cora B. Nichols (Wentworth)
Martha J., d. 8/18/1908 at 82/7/11 in Orford; apoplexy; housewife; widow; b. Thetford, VT; Augustus Morris (Stow, CT) and Susan Langley (W. Fairlee, VT)
Rebecca Palmer, d. 1/30/1939 at 85/0/29 in Orford; housewife; widow; b. Lisbon; James Y. Cushman (Lisbon) and Jane Clough (Lyman)
Ruby P., d. 9/30/1964 at 54 in Haverhill; housewife; b. Topsham, VT; Ernest Pierson and Nettie Wright
Walter, d. 4/14/1988

FRENCH,
daughter, d. 7/17/1890 at 0/0/3 in Orford; marasmus; b. Orford; Dexter S. French (farmer, Corinth, VT) and Hattie P. Terrill (Clifton, PQ)
Alice Lavina, d. 1/4/1900 at 6/2/4 in Orford; acute nephritis; b. Orford; Willie H. French (Landaff) and Alice W. Drown (Haverhill)
David B., d. 6/22/1890 at 78/5/25 in Orford; heart disease; farmer; married; b. Corinth, VT; Mark French (Corinth, VT) and Betsey Burpee (Corinth, VT)
Elias, d. 7/12/1933 at 95/4/17 in Orford; retired; single; b. Orford; Jesse French (Plainfield) and Anne Chamberlain (VT)
Esther L., d. 9/29/1901 at 4/0/5 in Wilder, VT; dysentery; b. Orford; Walter H. French (farmer)
Fred Z., d. 11/18/1933 at 83/3/18 in Orford; retired; married; b. Meriden; Jesse French (Plainfield) and Anne Chamberlain (VT)
Hattie M., d. 7/18/1964 at 85 in Detroit, MI; retired; Frederick French and Ella Carr
Henry, d. 8/28/1898 at 65/3/12 in Orford; paralysis; mechanic; widower; b. Plainfield; Jesse French (Plainfield) and Ann Chamberlain
Mary Ella, d. 11/4/1936 at 82/8/14 in Orford; retired; widow; b. Orford; Philip Carr (Plainfield) and Persis Huntoon (Goshen)
Norman C., d. 10/3/1994 in Lebanon; Fred G. French and Elizabeth Wilson
Walter H., d. 2/5/1933 at 70/1/15 in Lyme; sheriff; married; b. Orford; Henry French (Plainfield) and Emeline Kenyon (Plainfield)

FRIZZELL,
Ora, d. 3/16/1910 at 30 in Orford; housewife; married; b. Haverhill; George W. Copp

FULLER,
Henry A., d. 6/24/1915 at 73/4/1 in Orford; cerebral hemorrhage; farmer; Anson Fuller and Diana Clough

GAGE,
Luther S., d. 1/5/1890 at 67/2/24 in Orford; senile gangrene; widower; farmer; b. Orford; Eben Gage and Sally Stone

Rozilla B. Hall, d. 2/18/1888 at 69/6/23 in Orford; housewife; widow; b. Orford; Richard B. Hall (Orford) and Sarah H. Aiken (Wentworth)

GALE,
Charles M., d. 2/10/1908 at 57/9/20 in Orford; pneumonia; farmer; married; b. Warren; Jacob Gale (Alexandria) and Mary Heath (Canterbury)
Edna E., d. 7/20/1892 at 15/3/16 in Orford; acute tuberculosis; single; b. Warren; Charles M. Gale and Mary J. Kimball

GALLUP,
Charles H., d. 4/14/1956 at 70/9/10 in Woodsville; retired farmer; widower; b. Plainfield, VT; Hoyt Gallup and Lizzie Glidden
Harry M., d. 6/9/1961 at 73/1/8 in Haverhill; divorced; b. Plainfield, VT; Hoyt Gallup and Lizzie Glitton

GARDNER,
daughter, d. 11/30/1900 at 0/0/1 in Orford; patent foramen ovale; b. Orford; Ned F. Gardner (Orford) and Hat. L. Cunningham (Orford)
Edmond James, d. 3/16/1942 at 5/10/3 in Piermont; b. Orford; Harold H. Gardner (Orford) and Phyllis E. Scruton (Woodsville)
Emeline F., d. 5/18/1916 at 79/11/18 in Orford; epithelioma of right side of face; domestic; widow; b. Lyme; Nathan Breck and Hannah Chapin
Frank H., d. 7/5/1934 at 70 in Worcester, MA; blacksmith; widower; b. Lyme; James R. Gardner (Lyme) and Emeline Brick (Lyme)
Hattie, d. 5/20/1930 at 52/6/10 in Orford; housewife; married; b. Orford; John Coolidge and Adeline Mitchell (Orford)
James R., d. 7/8/1903 at 71/0/11 in Orford; suicide by drowning; farmer; married; b. Lyme; William Gardner and Rachel Gardner
Martha A., d. 4/13/1909 at 38/3/1 in Orford; housewife; widow; b. Lyme; Benjamin Smith (Wentworth) and Angeline B. Worthen (Orford)
Menta M., d. 1/19/1937 at 34/6/11 in Worcester, MA; nurse; single; b. Orford; Frank H. Gardner (Lyme) and Martha A. Smith (Lyme)
Ned Forrest, d. 6/7/1957 at 82/1/19 in Bradford, VT; laborer; b. Orford; James R. Gardner and Emeline Breck

GARRETT,
Floyd "Red", d. 2/14/2003 in White River Jct., VT; Eugene Earl Garrett and Laura Mae Cummings

GASPAR,
Andrew, d. 11/30/1947 at 57/4/2 in Concord; fireman; married; b. Goffstown

GASPER,
Ruth, d. 6/26/1987

GASSETT,
Harry E., d. 12/20/1960 at 77/3/13 in Orford; laborer; widower; b. Orford; George R. Gassett and Sara Jane Patch
Mary Jane, d. 2/1/1894 at 13/4/21 in Orford; spinal men.; b. Orford; George R. Gassett and Sarah Jane Patch

GEORGE,
Earl F., d. 12/12/1973 at 61 in Haverhill; disabled; b. NH; Wilber A. George and Ethel Sanborn

GIFFIN,
Eliza H., d. 3/27/1889 at 57/1/21 in Orford; Brights dis., kidneys; married; b. Gilsum; Solomon Mack (Gilsum) and Adeline Knights (Marlow)
John, d. 6/14/1907 at 77/8/9 in Orford; taxaemia; farmer; widower; b. Sutton; ----- Giffin (Marlow) and Elizabeth Sawyer (Alstead)

GILBERT,
Carlos D., d. 9/21/1905 at 63/5/28 in Orford; farmer; widower; b. Brownington, VT; Chester Gilbert (Brownington, VT) and Lucy Douglas (Chelsea, VT)
Flora, d. 4/8/1963 at 70 in Barre, VT; retired; b. Kingsley Falls, Canada; Leon L. Cassidy and Mary Jane Priest
George I., d. 8/15/1887 at 22/6/13 in Orford; laborer; single; b. Lyme; Israel H. Gilbert (Lyme) and Minerva J. Cutting (Lyme)
Harry Edwin, d. 9/23/1956 at 81/5/22 in Orford; retired; divorced; b. Lyme; John Gilbert and Lizzie Post

GILE,
William R., d. 8/18/1952 at 74 in Orford; retired; married; b. W. Hartford, VT; Henry Gile and Jeannie Larnard

GILMAN,
Angeline W., d. 8/11/1900 at 71/1 in Orford; apoplexy; housewife; widow; b. Rumney; Benjamin Brown

Arthur K., d. 2/27/1920 at 28/8/28 in Orford; painter; single; b. Poultney, VT; John Gilman and Mary Lisson (Hartford, NY)

Enoch, d. 12/18/1895 at 67/3/11 in Orford; dis. of liver; farmer; b. Thornton; Jeremiah Gilman and Mary Foss

GLOVER,
Annie, d. 9/28/1941 at 43/11/28 in Haverhill; housework; divorced; b. Orford; Alanson Archer (Orford) and Elizabeth Moran (Boston, MA)

James, d. 11/19/1933 at 65 in Hanover; painter; married; b. Littleton; Franklin R. Glover

GLUEK,
Alvin C., d. 5/19/2001 in Hanover; Alvin Gluek and Helen Carothers

GODFREY,
Albert, d. 3/12/1990 in Hanover; Floyd Godfrey and Marion Barker

Annette L., d. 11/19/2001 in Lebanon; Alphonso Fillian and Jessie Woods

Della, d. 10/29/1929 at 25 in Hanover; housewife; married; b. Orford; David Marsh (W. Fairlee, VT) and Delia F. Smith (Corinth, VT)

Roy B., d. 2/17/1975 at 81 in E. Thetford, VT; retired; b. W. Fairlee, VT; William L. Godfrey and Ada Dennison

GOODHUE,
Nettie S., d. 12/2/1944 at 68/2/10 in Concord; school teacher; divorced; b. Corinth, VT; Josiah P. Sargent (Candia) and Emelie Worthley

GOULD,
Frances H., d. 12/3/1971 at 43 in Haverhill; housewife; b. Hanover; George C. Huckins and Hazel M. Williams

GOULETTE,
Clara E., d. 1/12/1968 at 75 in Hanover; b. VT; Will Goulette and Mary Gardner

GOURLEY,
Emma S., d. 1/31/1948 at 78/8/12 in Franklin; housewife; widow; b. Hanover; Sylvester Saunders and Nancy S. Eastman (Danbury)

GOVE,
Emily H., d. 4/28/1906 at 62/10/17 in Orford; housewife; widow; b. Sandwich; Daniel Tappan (Sandwich) and Naomi Vitum (Sandwich)

GRANT,
Carlos Alonzo, d. 9/7/1898 at 41/5 in Orford; gun-shot wound; laborer; married

GRAY,
Leslie E., d. 11/1/1907 at 26/7/7 in Orford; diabetes mellitus; laborer; single; b. Orford; Hiram Gray and Sarah Simpson
Lester E., d. 2/24/1959 at 73 in Orford
Nellie, d. 7/7/1929 at 36/9/29 in Hanover; housewife; married; b. Hanover; Frank Chesley (W. Fairlee, VT) and Louise Morey (W. Fairlee, VT)
Sarah, d. 2/10/1939 at 81/4/16 in Haverhill; retired; widow; b. Rumney; John Simpson (Rumney) and Mary Brown (Rumney)

GREEN,
Harvey, d. 1/21/1906 at 60/1/14 in Orford; farmer; widower; b. Walpole
William Edgar, Jr., d. 4/22/1965 at 52 in Vero Beach, FL; anim. exhib.; b. Trenton, NJ; William Edgar Green and Annie Fisk
William Peter, d. 4/12/1975 at 39 in Orford; mason; b. Orford; William E. Green and Phyllis Boyer

GREENE,
John, Sr., d. --/--/1989
Marilla W., d. 7/25/1903 at 83/11/29 in Orford; acute bronchitis; housewife; widow; b. Mendon, VT; John Greggs (CT) and Charlotte Farnum (Walpole)

GREENL[E]Y,
Charles Jones, d. 1/2/1939 at 53/3/23 in Orford; farmer; single; b. Highmore, SD; Samuel E. Greenley (MN or Canada) and Lavina Rugg (Orford)
Clifton P., d. 10/6/1975 at 75 in Antrim; janitor; b. Orford; Samuel E. Greenley and Lavina Rugg
Della Harriet, d. 1/8/1958 at 67/7/17 in Orford; retired teacher; single; b. Orford; Samuel Greenly and Lavina Rugg
Larina, d. 8/27/1953 at 86 in Orford; home; widow; b. Orford; Merrill Rugg and Amanda Ellis
Samuel, d. 11/19/1944 at 86/8/15 in Hanover; retired; married; b. St. Paul, MN; Lazerby Greenly (England) and Louisa Stephens
Verna Maude, d. 4/4/1947 at 53/2/26 in Orford; teacher; single; b. Orford; Samuel E. Greenly (St. Paul, MN) and Lavina L. Rugg (Orford)
Warren Laurence, d. 12/14/1965 at 68 in Orford; farmer; b. Orford; Samuel E. Greenly and Lavina L. Rugg

GREENWOOD,
Harry W., d. 4/30/1975 at 64 in Hanover; laborer; b. VT; John Greenwood and Eva McGill

GREGGS,
Charlotte, d. 12/3/1887 at 92/7/10 in Orford; domestic; widow; b. Walpole; Roger Farnam (Lyme) and Precilla Hall

GRIGGS,
Marion Trussell, d. 10/13/1918 at 20/2/25 in Fairlee, VT; housewife; married; b. Orford; George F. Trussell (Orford) and Grace H. Tilton (Bristol)
Roger, d. 3/9/1943 at 0/1/9 in Springfield, VT
Roger C., d. 3/9/1933 at 0/1/9 in Springfield, VT
Shirley Anna, d. 10/11/1918 at 5 hrs. in Fairlee, VT; b. Fairlee, VT; R. H. Griggs and Marion Trussell

GRIMES,
Nathan, d. 2/17/1888 at 76/3/7 in Orford; farmer; married; b. Orford; Nathan Grimes (MA) and Mehepsa'h Lovejoy (Rindge)

GRINNELL,
Elizabeth Cole, d. 8/1/2003 in Greenwich, CT; William Morse Cole and Fanny Rolfe

GRUBB,
Francis A., d. 2/7/1936 at 67/10/18 in Orford; jeweler; married; b. Clon Inel, Ireland; Robert Grubb (Ireland) and Annie Parker (Ireland)

GUEST,
Jennie Huntington, d. 11/1/1940 at 83/2/20 in Orford; housewife; widow; b. Irvington, NY; James P. Huntington (New Rochelle, NY) and Mary E. Hudson (New Rochelle, NY)

GUND,
Henry, III, d. 10/26/1994 in Orford; Henry Gund II and Mary Burton

GUPTILL,
Leroy A., d. 2/25/1968 at 63 in Haverhill; counselor; b. ME; Albion Guptill and Leatitia Taylor
Marion A., d. 4/3/1978 at 66 in Orford; housewife; b. MA; Lester Abbott and Florence Brackett

GUYER,
John W., d. 7/15/1974 at 74 in Orford; retired; b. Lunenburg, VT; Alfred Guyer and Mary E. Gadley
Julia L., d. 5/2/1966 at 69 in Littleton; housewife; b. Orford; Alex Lemire and Ella Thompson

HACKETT,
son, d. 11/7/1888 at 0/8 in Orford; b. Vershire, VT; James Hackett (Orford) and Lizzie ----- (VT)
infant, d. 10/15/1891 at 0/0/23 in Orford; b. Orford; David Hackett (Fairlee, VT) and Anna A. Marsh
Albert, d. 3/24/1891 at 32 in Bradford, VT; farmer; married; Moses D. Hackett
Edna A., d. 7/12/1892 at 22 in Orford; inflammation of stomach; domestic; married; b. W. Fairlee, VT; George W. Marsh and Mary E. Dickerson
James A., d. 11/10/1934 at 70/7/15 in Bradford, VT; married

Sarah, d. 10/9/1893 at 65/3/4 in Orford; apoplexy; housewife; b. Topsham, VT; Enos Felch

HADLOCK,
Clayton, d. 3/25/1986

HALE,
Daniel T., d. 2/3/1893 at 59/10/19 in Orford; Addison's disease; lumberman; b. Orford; Aaron Hale (NH) and Mary Kent
Mary Kent, d. 12/5/1892 at 94/0/10 in Cambridge, MA; domestic; widow

HALL,
Bessie, d. 6/18/1981 in Orford; George Dennis and Carrie Church
Buhamah, d. 6/1/1888 at 78/5/25 in Woodstock; housewife; widow; b. Wentworth; Henry Sanders and Mary Haines (Orford)
Charles C., d. 7/21/1921 at 57/4/23 in Orford; grocery clerk; single; b. Easton; Henry K. Hall (Easton) and Maria Wells
Clara Ella, d. 6/2/1923 at 71/11/29 in Orford; retired; widow; b. Orford; John H. Phelps (Orford) and Charlotte Hancock (Orford)
Emily Alden, d. 7/22/1995 in Lebanon; Alden Perley White and Jessie Carter
Frank H., d. 11/28/1912 at 74/2/5 in Orford; cerebral hemorrhage; laborer; married; b. Lyme; Joel Hall and Joanna Furbush
Frank William, d. 10/22/1940 at 50/10/28 in Lyme; farmer; married; b. Easton; William R. Hall (Allistown) and Adria J. Kibble (Tunbridge, VT)
Fred P., d. 11/21/1927 at 60/8/26 in Hanover; farmer; married; b. Landaff; Henry K. Hall (Landaff) and Mariah Wells (Landaff)
Harry Gay, d. 4/29/1961 at 65/10 in Orford; welder; married; b. Montpelier, VT; Timothy Hall and Julia Wilkins
Harvey P., d. 6/19/1975 at 65 in Hanover; retired; b. Lebanon; William Hall and Gertrude Porter
Josephine, d. 3/11/1926 at 71/11/11 in Orford; housewife; widow; b. Orford
Marshall G., d. 10/8/1974 at 69 in Hanover; physician; b. Marblehead, MA; Herbert Hall and Eliza Goldwaithe
Perley, d. 6/19/1954 at 74/2/28 in Concord; laborer; married; b. NH; Henry K. Hall and Roystine Grant

Susan P., d. 7/5/1899 at 68/2/21 in Hanover; heart disease; housewife; married; b. Candia; William Brown (Candia) and Polly Smith (Candia)

William B., d. 7/15/1916 at 15/8/23 in Fairlee, VT; acc. drowning; single; b. Orford; William B. Hall (Manchester) and Adra J. Kibbee (Tunbridge, VT)

William B., d. 11/19/1927 at 71/8/4 in Concord; farmer; divorced; b. NH; John Hall (NH) and Susan Brown (Canada)

HAMLETT,
John L., d. 7/23/1889 at 50 in Orford; chronic bronchitis; farmer; single

HAMMOND,
Adelaide M., d. 9/19/1962 at 59/6/18 in Hanover; housewife; married; b. New York City, NU; Frank Meara and Alice Sykes

Carrie M., d. 11/29/1901 at 10/8/5 in Orford; hemorrhage of bowels; b. Orford; E. C. Hammond (laborer, Lyme) and Olive S. Stetson (Orford)

John W., d. 11/17/1962 at 78/3/10 in Orford; physician; widower; b. Cambridge, MA; I. W. Hammond and Clara Ellen Tweed

HANCOCK,
Mary B. S., d. 11/10/1892 at – in Buffalo, NY; asthenia; housewife; married; b. Barnet

HANNAFORD,
Eva, d. 2/2/1917 at 52/11/11 in Hanover; housewife; married; b. Orford; Asa S. Rhodes (Grafton, VT) and Eliza Lovejoy

Frances Maud, d. 12/31/1942 at 66/4/19 in Orford; housework; divorced; b. Fairlee, VT; Samuel Cunningham (Bradford, VT) and Jennie Freeman (Fairlee, VT)

Hazen A., d. 5/13/1976 at 88 in Boscawen; painter; b. NH; Henry Hannaford and Eva Rhodes

Henry A., d. 2/28/1936 at 78/3/27 in Orford; janitor; widower; b. Fairlee, VT; Thomas Hannaford (Hill) and Rebecca Fisk (Wentworth)

Richard, d. 5/27/1941 at 76/10/26 in Haverhill; carpenter; divorced; b. Orford; Thomas Hannaford (Sanbornton) and Rebecca Fisk (Nashua)

HARD,
Eva Winifred, d. 7/2/1965 at 80 in Lebanon; housewife; b. Lowell, MA; George Kirby and Annie Whiting

HARRINGTON,
Clara D., d. 8/4/1890 at 33/7/21 in Orford; uterine hemorrhage; married; Henry Dayton (Orford) and Julia Whitcomb (NY)
Edson, d. 11/17/1983 in Hanover; Edward Harrington and Elizabeth Race
Jennie, d. 6/28/1986

HARRIS,
Hannah B., d. 4/9/1890 at 90/7/10 in Orford; old age; housewife; widow; b. Derryfield; John Webster (Atkinson) and Anna Buswell (Bradford, MA)
Louis Allen, d. 9/13/1987
Lucretia H., d. 4/17/1900 at 60/11/10 in Orford; pernicious anemia; housewife; married; b. Orford; John Pebbles (Salem, MA) and Dilla H. Weed (Unity)
Marjorie Cornelia, d. 9/22/1909 at 1/3/8 in Orford; b. Orford; Willard R. Harris (Piermont) and Maude E. McPherson (Jordan River, NS)
Maude M., d. 1/14/1966 at 80 in Gardiner, ME; retired; b. Jordan, NS; Jason H. McPherson and Cornelia Holden
Reuben, d. 8/1/1913 at 82/0/8 in Orford; cerebral hemorrhage; farmer; widower; b. Manchester; Willard Harris (Bedford) and Hannah B. Webster (Derrfield)
Willard Robert, d. 5/1/1939 at 58/9/5 in Manchester; teacher; married; b. Piermont; s/o Reuben Harris (Manchester) and Lucretia Pebbles (Orford)

HARTLEY,
Edna M., d. 3/2/1977 at 84 in Hanover; homemaker; b. Wentworth; Francis Pease and Mabel Sherburne

HARTWELL,
Hannah B., d. 3/15/1897 at 73 in Orford; housewife; widow; b. Holland; Trustine Bickford
Isaac, d. 5/2/1888 at 62/1/20 in Orford; farmer; married; b. Grantham; Daniel Hartwell and Priscilla Joslyn

John H., d. 9/10/1923 at 77/7/8 in Orford; retired; widower; b. Piermont; Isaac Hartwell (Grantham) and Hannah Bickford (Canada)

Priscilla, d. 11/28/1879 at 76/7/5 in Stoneham, MA (1891)

HARVEY,

Edwin Deeks, d. 9/30/1947 at 67/3/4 in Orford; minister; married; b. Wyvenhoe, England; Edwin Harvey (Wyvenhoe, England) and Mary Page (Fringrinhoe, England)

HASELTON,

George L., d. 10/19/1889 at 15/9/17 in Orford; phthisis pulmonalis; single; b. Orford; John L. Haselton (Orford) and Lacinda R. Gardner (Lyme)

HATCH,

Benjamin, d. 4/11/1907 at 89/10/10 in Orford; cancer of omentum; carpenter; married; b. Hanover; Benjamin Hatch and Sally Woodbury

Claire S., d. 3/31/1972 at 87 in Hanover

Frank W., d. 2/20/1967 at 88 in Windsor, VT; b. Haverhill; James E. Hatch and Nancy Smith

Lois, d. 12/27/1933 at 38/7/12 in Orford; housewife; married; b. Haverhill; John Chapman and Clara Hartley

HAVEN,

Kenneth, d. 6/2/1999 in Orford; William Haven and Marjorie Davis

HAWKINS,

Lyman Alymer, d. 3/17/1940 at 66/1/28 in Fairlee, VT; farmer; single; b. Bolton Ctr., Canada; Fred Hawkins (Plattsburg, NY) and Rosetta Whitehead (Broom Woods, Canada)

HAZEN,

Adelbert C., d. 10/22/1970 at 72 in Hanover; retired; b. NY; Irving Hazen and Mary Carr

Irving A., d. 10/19/1926 at 58/1/26 in Queens, NY; teaching

Maria, d. 2/10/1935 at 35/6/16 in Utica, NY; housewife; married; b. Cooperstown, NY

Mary C., d. 6/4/1921 at 46/9/10 in Richmond Hill, NY; housewife; married; b. Meriden; Robert O. Carr (Orford) and Mary E. Martin (Chelmsford, MA)

HEATH,
Abner T., d. 12/6/1914 at 79/9/4 in Orford; intestinal obstruction; farmer; married; b. Newbury, VT; Amos K. Heath (Newbury, VT) and Lutheria Childs (Bath)
Everett K., d. 6/30/1916 at 76/1/26 in Orford; sudden death, cause unknown; S.M. on RR; b. Newbury, VT; Amos Heath and Lutheria Childs (Bath)
Lewis B., d. 8/3/1889 at 1/6/15 in Haverhill; dysentery; b. Piermont; Alba Byron Heath (Reading, VT) and Mary Howland (Landaff)

HEBB,
Guy A., d. 10/2/2004 in Orford; Garnet Hebb and Edna Hollard

HENDERSON,
Ethel Haideen, d. 7/20/1965 at 57 in Hanover; b. Brooklyn, NY; Anfred C. Henderson and Ethel Paffard
Ethel P., d. 3/6/1975 at 96 in Fairlee, VT; retired; b. Brooklyn, NY; Walter Passard and Henrietta Wright

HIBBARD,
Earl M., d. 11/15/1922 at 54/9/24 in Orford; laborer; divorced; b. Lancaster; Moses Hibbard (Piermont) and Elizabeth Bickford (Orford)
Elizabeth M., d. 11/30/1910 at 77/4/9 in Orford; housewife; widow; b. Orford; Isaac Bickford (Northfield) and Lucinda Coburn (Orford)
Emma A, d. 1/21/1955 at 82/9/1 in Orfordville; housewife; widow; b. Concord; John Witham and Dolly Stales
Maude, d. 6/9/1979 in Haverhill; George McFosty and Susie Harris

HILL,
Ernest, d. 4/16/1987
Inez Smith, d. 1/26/1956 at 87/1/17 in Haverhill; retired housewife; widow; b. Orfordville; Alphonse Smith and Clarinda Worthen
Richard H., d. 1/15/2003 in Lebanon; Maurice Hill and Goldie Hutchins
Shirley R., d. 5/21/1972 at 46 in Orford; housewife; b. New Bedford, MA; William Rose, Sr. and Alice Cormica

HINES,
Ethel, d. 12/9/1961 at 82 in Brookline, MA; retired nurse; widow; b. Newtonville, MA; George Washburn and A. Francina Mann

HODGSON,
Alice Doan, d. 12/18/1995 in Orford; Frank Carleton Doan and Isabel Wilson

John H., II, d. 1/4/1995 in Lebanon; Walter Hodgson and Florence Purcell

HOISINGTON,
Charles, d. 4/30/1987

HOLT,
Nellie F., d. 5/3/1941 at 67/8/14 in Newport; housewife; married; b. Orford; William Pebbles and Almena Tyler

HOOK,
Lester, d. 8/1/1979 in Boothbay Harbor, ME; Samuel Hook and Evelyn Faucett

HOOKER,
William George, d. 10/13/1932 at 75/4/19 in Orford; farmer; widower; b. England

HOPWOOD,
Leon Farley, d. 11/2/1954 at 39/11/2 in Orford; mechanic; married; b. Litchfield; James W. Hopwood and Ethel Farley

HORGAN,
Catherine C., d. 2/28/1998 in Lebanon; William Burns and Johanna Crofton

HORTON,
Allen, d. 12/7/1892 at 88/1/23 in Orford; farmer; widower; b. Rehoboth

Bessie K., d. 10/29/1936 at 47/3 in Los Angeles, CA; housewife; married; b. Orford; Carlos M. Kenyon (Plainfield) and Abbie Tyrell (Canaan)

Claude Albert, d. 4/3/1918 at 0/0/2 in Orford; b. Orford; Walter A. Horton (Orford) and Bessie A. Kenyon (Orford)

Clyde Elbert, d. 4/3/1918 at 0/0/2 in Orford; b. Orford; Walter A. Horton (Orford) and Bessie A. Kenyon (Orford)

Emma, d. 2/14/1984 in Hanover

Ethel M., d. 3/5/1969 at 77 in Bradford, VT; housewife; b. Lyme; Clarence Pushee and Fanny Post

Henry Arthur, d. 5/11/1957 at 68/5/11 in Orford; carpenter; married; b. Piermont; William Horton and Mary Chesley

Mary S., d. 7/23/1924 at 66/7/23 in Windsor, VT; retired; widow; b. Orford; Samuel Stone (Orford) and Martha J. Niles (Orford)

Maurice, d. 7/18/1978 at 76 in Haverhill; laborer; b. Goshen; Charles H. Horton and Frances Kempton

Walter S., d. 12/14/1919 at 75/2/29 in Orford; farmer; married; b. Barnard, VT; Allen Horton and Lucinda Smith

HOWARD,
John, d. 10/29/1891 at 75/6/21 in Orford; jeweler; b. Orford; William Howard (Chester) and Betsey Pierce

Minnie J., d. 12/28/1890 at 3/1/28 in Orford; capillary bronchitis; b. Orford; Anson R. Howard (Lyme) and Julia A. Cutting (Canada)

Thomas, d. 5/21/1896 at 74 in Orford; single; b. Orford

HOWE,
Clifford M., d. 1/4/1968 at 66 in Hartford, VT; farmer; b. Cornish; Henry Howe and Clara Dorwin

HOWLAND,
Amanda, d. 7/29/1891 at 40 in Orford; single; b. Landaff; Samuel Howland (Landaff) and Lucinda Bowles

Lucinda, d. 12/24/1898 at 81/2/6 in Orford; bled to death varicose veins

Samuel, d. 6/3/1889 at 74/5/25 in Orford; pneumonia; farmer; married; b. Lisbon; Stephen Howland (Lisbon) and Polly Parker (Lisbon)

HUBBARD,
Charles H., d. 8/25/1904 at 67/7/16 in Orford; farmer; married; b. Bangor, ME

Minnie K., d. 4/29/1966 at 69 in Haverhill; housewife; b. Somerville, MA; Frank R. Wilder and Mary King

William, d. 11/15/1963 at 81 in Orford; lumber sawyer; b. Monroe; Horace Hubbard and Emma Stewart

HUCKINS,
Clayton M., d. 3/12/1953 at 20/11/26 in Wang-jing-Myon, Korea; US Army; single; b. Hanover; George C. Huckins and Hazel M. Williams

Ella L., d. 8/26/1937 at 70/1/16 in Orford; ret. housewife; widow; b. Orford; George W. Lamprey (Orford) and Celinda Trussell (Orford)

G. Clifton, d. 12/8/1992 in Orford; George Huckins and Ella Lamprey

George M., d. 1/30/1933 at 69/6/26 in Orford; farmer; married; b. Wentworth; Joseph Cross (Wentworth) and Eliza Batchelder (Wentworth)

Gladys M., d. 5/24/1977 at 81 in Unity; school teacher; b. NH; George M. Huckins and Ella Lamprey

Hazel, d. 10/20/1982 in Franconia; Joseph Williams and Maude Zottman

Thomas P., d. 4/7/1889 at 76/8/27 in Orford; rheumatism heart; farmer; married; b. New Hampton; John Huckins (New Hampton) and Judith Perkins (New Hampton)

HUMMEL,
Roland, Jr., d. 7/9/2004 in Lebanon; Roland Hummel and Adelel Von Oslin

HUMPHREY,
Margaret J., d. 1/25/1935 at 52/2/23 in Orford; housewife; married; b. London, England; Arthur Bowdidge (London, England) and Mary Dutchburn

HUNTINGTON,
son, 7/30/1957 at 0/0/0 in Hanover; b. Hanover; S. D. Huntington and Bernice B. Bean

Eric C., d. 4/3/1998 in Enfield; Harold Huntington and Mary Jane Fields

Guy S., d. 5/20/1976 at 72 in Hanover; mail carrier; b. VT; Dana Huntington and Ila Masten

Harold, d. 3/5/1987

Irene Pease, d. 5/2/1956 at 21/2/14 in Orford; secretary; married; b. Orford; Glenn F. Pease and Theda Howard

James S., d. 8/27/1939 at 16/8/4 in Hanover; student; single; b. Claremont; Guy S. Huntington (Corinth, VT) and Mildred Cummings (Thetford, VT)

Laura L., d. 10/24/1966 at 71 in Haverhill; housewife; b. Barre, VT; George Lalime and Sara Geneau

Mildred C., d. 1/7/1968 at 63 in Haverhill; housewife; b. Thetford, VT; James Cummings and Lucy Allen

Nera Webb, d. 5/29/1994 in Lebanon; Edwin Bean and Alice Marsh

HUTCHINS,
Henry H., d. 4/19/1952 at 61/6/16 in Winchester, MA

Sadie Isabelle, d. 8/2/1977 at 83 in Lebanon; housewife; b. MA; William Horrell and Ella Maguire

HYLAND,
Lovinia H., d. 10/25/1973 at 56 in Burlington, VT; housewife; b. Lyme; Robert Dunbar and Edith Simpson

IBELLE,
Blanche May, d. 11/4/1959 at 78 in Hanover

Harold H., d. 2/12/1960 at 81/4/22 in Orford; salesman; widower; b. New Britain, CT; William Ibelle

INGERSON,
Flora Mary, d. 9/26/1956 at 81/9/30 in Orford; retired; widow; b. Ashburnham, MA; Peter Zubee and Ardelia Flint

Willie Burt, d. 8/9/1941 at 66/7/16 in Orford; farmer; married; b. Epping; Isaac Redding (NS) and Katie Burt (USA)

JACKSON,
John, d. 11/30/1948 at 82/11/10 in Orford; ret. chauffeur; married; b. England

JACQUES,
Charles, d. 12/14/1889 at 80/9/6 in Orford; disease of heart; single; b. Boston, MA; Samuel Jacques and Harriet Whittemore

JENKINS,
Annabelle, d. 2/21/1960 at 84/4/25 in Orford; retired housewife; widow; b. Taunton, MA; Edwin Brown and Henrietta Arnold

JENKS,
Delbert O., d. 1/2/1973 at 72 in Orford; laborer; b. Warren; William F. Jenks and Emma Smith

Elbridge, d. 1/28/1982 in Orford; Edward Jenks and Clara LaMotte
William D. L., d. 10/4/1927 at 0/1 in Fairlee, VT; b. Orford; Delbert Jenks and Josephine Learned

JEWELL,
Ida, d. 7/9/1935 at 52/10/26 in Hanover; housewife; married; b. Wentworth; Joseph Sanborn (Ellsworth) and Flora Hutchins (Rumney)

JOHNSON,
Anna J., d. 9/14/1943 at 62/7/18 in Orford; housewife; divorced; b. Byfield, MA; Hiram Pillsbury (Byfield, MA) and Emily Bailey (Newton)
David, d. 12/4/1893 at 81/8/5 in Orford; stomach disease; carpenter; b. Wentworth; Henry Johnson (Rumney) and Rebecca Brown
Donald B., d. 9/10/1994 in Orford; Paul Johnson and Madleine Schreiber
Edward, d. 8/3/1937 at 59/4/7 in Bradford, VT; lawyer; single; Edward P. Johnson and Jennie G. Farra
Emelyn, d. 2/1/1962 at 79 in Rahway, NJ; John Race
Lurline D., d. 7/5/1980 in Hanover; Benjamin Dyke and Ethel L. Jesseman
Orpha E., d. 5/19/1935 at 79/4/22 in Orford; single; b. Bradford, VT; Elliott Johnson (Bradford, VT) and Sarah Taylor (Bradford, VT)
Robert Louis, d. 7/9/1969 at 56 in Orford; operating engineer; b. S. Deerfield; Nils Johnson and Caroline -----
Ruth, d. 3/31/1906 at 90/11/9 in Orford; housewife; widow; b. Orford; Richard Brown (Orford) and Rebecca Robbins (Dunstable)
Samuel, d. 8/2/1957 at 76/3/12 in Hanover; watchmaker; single; b. Sweden; John Johnson and Emily -----
Sarah T., d. 2/23/1893 at 76/10 in Orford; ch. bronchitis; housewife; b. Hartland, VT; Alvan Taylor and Orpha Ransom

KEEFER,
Dorothea F., d. 1/28/2002 in Orford; Elmer Franklin and Hanna Cole

KELLER,
Grace, d. 1/6/1985 in Hanover
John A., d. 4/26/1976 at 67 in Hanover; printer; b. NY; John Keller, Sr. and Florence Veanable

KELLEY,
Mary I., d. 9/10/1981 in Hanover; Henry Downing and Agnes Patenaude

KEMP,
Mary A. H., d. 12/15/1893 at 80/11/19 in Orford; old age; domestic; b. Randolph, VT; Augustus Hobart and Hannah Thayer

KENNEDY,
Kenneth, d. 4/8/1978 at 61 in Concord; retired; b. Easton, ME; Jesse Kennedy and Eva St. Peter

KENNISON,
Pearl, d. 3/26/1972 at 42 in Hanover; housewife; b. Hanover; Perley Moses and Eva Morey

KENNISTON,
Walter E., d. 1/23/1968 at 64 in Piermont; laborer; William Kenniston

KENT,
Helen A., d. 9/12/1904 at 68/5/29 in Orford; single; b. Orford; Moses Kent and Mary S. -----

KENYON,
Abbie M., d. 6/30/1916 at 19/9/27 in Orford; acute dilitation of heart; housewife; married; b. Canaan; Samuel Tyrrell (Canaan) and Ruth Wescott (Manchester)
Betsey M., d. 1/3/1909 at 92/8/9 in Orford; housewife; widow; b. Plainfield; Nathaniel French (Plainfield)
Calvin, d. 3/18/1915 at – in Orford; stillborn; b. Orford; Walter C. Kenyon (Orford) and Alice M. Ramsey (Wentworth)
Carlos M., d. 2/15/1917 at 65/7/5 in Orford; farmer; married; b. Plainfield; Mumford H. Kenyon (Plainfield) and Betsy French (Plainfield)
Mumford H., d. 3/28/1898 at 85/11/29 in Orford; bronchial pneumonia; farmer; married; b. Plainfield; Mumford Kenyon and Betsey Cogswell
O. W., d. 2/19/1892 at 7/11/11 in Lebanon; disease of heart
Philo C., d. 6/24/1889 at 68/8/24 in Brattleboro, VT; asphyxia

KEYES,
Richard, d. 3/14/1939 at 80/11/26 in Hanover; farmer; single; b. St. Johns, NB; John Keyes (Scotland) and Margaret Scott (Scotland)

KILTON,
Judson L., d. 3/18/1896 at 21/7/14 in Orford; laborer; single; b. Grafton; Martin Kilton (Grafton) and Fannie A. Lindsay (Eaton, PQ)

KIMBALL,
Alvah, d. 4/19/1925 at 75/9/6 in Amherst; retired; married; b. Wentworth; Joseph Kimball (Wemtworth) and Julia Chase (Deerfield)
Carrie, d. 8/17/1944 at 78/7/6 in Concord; housewife; widow; b. Lyme; Otis Webb (Lyme) and Mary Clyne (Lyme)
Charles H., d. 3/14/1929 at 69/4/14 in Lebanon; farmer; married; b. Wentworth; Joseph Kimball (Wentworth) and Julia Chase (Deerfield)
Frederick S., d. 12/17/1916 at 0/0/12 in Orford; prem. birth; b. Orford; Phil. Kimball (Westmore, VT) and Mary Smith (Orford)
Harry J., d. 6/9/1928 at 41/3/11 in Lebanon; laborer; divorced; Charles H. Kimball (Wentworth) and Carrie Webb (Lyme)
Joseph, d. 3/11/1902 at 76/10/9 in Orford; pulmonary hemorrhage; farmer; widower; b. Wentworth; Joseph Kimball (Wentworth) and Sally Bailey
Lucina M., d. 3/23/1895 at 46/6/23 in Orford; pneumonia; housekeeper; b. Piermont; Moses Colby and Elizabeth E. Clement
Mary S., d. 5/15/1892 at 79/4/12 in Orford; paralysis; housewife; married; Thomas Roberts and Hannah Morgan
Paul R., d. 5/11/1965 at 43 in Piermont; teacher; b. Barton, VT; Philemon Kimball and Mary Smith
Philemon, d. 6/24/1962 at 67 in Barton, VT
Sally, d. 12/1/1907 at 81/4/3 in Orford; old age; domestic; single; b. Wentworth; Joseph Kimball (Wentworth) and Sally Bailey

KING,
Clyde, d. 11/15/1987
Faith, d. 12/20/1961 at 67/0/10 in Hanover; housewife; married; b. Crete, NE; A. D. Fruch and Mary Morse

KNIGHTS,
Maurice, d. 1/22/1991 in Hanover; Roy Knights and Della Wheeler

LABERGE,
Lucy L., d. 9/27/1905 at 1/6/29 in Orford; b. Orford; Joseph Laberge (Canada) and Ardelle Lamontagne (Piermont)

LABOUNTY,
Carrie Amelia, d. 3/4/1954 at 71/7/10 in Hanover; housewife; married; b. Arlington, MA; Major Bacon and Abbie Rosella Wood
Joseph, d. 11/13/1954 at 79/10/19 in Hanover; laborer; widower; b. Sheldon, VT; Joseph LaBounty and Sophronia LaBounty

LACASSE,
Charles J., d. 4/8/1979 in Hanover; George LaCasse and Zirella Racine

LACKEY,
Elizabeth, d. 12/21/1986
Norma Welch, d. 12/5/1993 in Lebanon; Lorrin Welch and Margaret

LADD,
son, d. 6/4/1888 at 0/0/1 in Orford; b. Orford; John H. Ladd (Meredith) and Laura B. Pike (Haverhill)
Burns Heath, d. 3/1/1943 at 51/4/27 in Hanover; laborer; married; b. Orford; John Ladd (Center Harbor) and Laura Pike (Pike)
Charles P., d. 9/20/1975 at 80 in Woodsville; retired; b. Pike; John H. Ladd and Laura B. Pike
Edward J., d. 5/6/1923 at 19/6/24 in Haverhill; John H. Ladd (Meredith) and ----- (Haverhill)
Florence A., d. 3/22/1948 at 53/11/1 in Orford; housewife; married; b. New York, NY; William Abbott (England) and Christine ----- (Sweden)
John H., d. 5/12/1913 at 50/8/26 in Orford; sarcoma; merchant; married; b. Meredith; John H. Ladd and Hannah Prescott
Laura B., d. 6/25/1917 at 48/8/6 in Haverhill; housewife; widow; b. Haverhill; Burns H. Pike (Haverhill) and Eliza French (Hanover)
Lindsie Mae, d. 5/3/1995 in Orford; Charles Perry and Inez Lindsie
Oscar C., d. 11/26/1994 in Bradford, VT; John H. Ladd and Laura Pike

LADEAU,
Albert C., d. 5/17/1975 at 88 in Springfield, VT
Charles, d. 4/14/1935 at 77/4/21 in Haverhill; widower; b. Rochester, VT; Francis Ladeau
Dora C., d. 3/12/1971 at 84 in Haverhill; housewife; b. Orford; Alphonso Smith and Clarinda Worthen
Florence, d. 10/17/1931 at 82/7 in Orford; housewife; married; b. St. Johns, PQ; Pierre Ditroimason (St. Johns, PQ) and Julie Richard (St. Johns, PQ)
James, d. 3/9/1962 at 84/9/13 in Orford; barber; married; b. Hyde Park, NJ; Frank Ladeau and Pauline Jacobs
Kenneth J., d. 4/14/1974 at 68 in Haverhill; laborer; b. Hartford, VT; James Ladeau and Dora C. Smith
M. Arlene T., d. 2/15/1999 in Lebanon; George Trussell and Grace Tilton

LAMERE,
Alexander, d. 6/29/1938 at 80 in Orford; farmer; widower; b. Three Rivers, PQ; Nelson LaMere (Canada)
Ella E., d. 2/2/1902 at 19 in Orford; pulmonary tuberculosis; housewife; married; b. Derry; Warner W. Thompson (Gorham) and Laura Burt (Whitinsville, MA)

LAMONTAGNE,
Gilbert E., d. 12/16/1975 at 56 in Hanover; junk dealer; b. Concord, VT; Joseph LaMontagne and Lavina Guyer

LAMPREY,
Celinda T., d. 8/12/1922 at 80/10/5 in Orford; housekeeper; widow; b. Orford; Benjamin Trussell (Boscawen) and Asenath England (Lyme)
Daniel, d. 2/24/1928 at 77/6/27 in Piermont; single; Daniel Lamprey and Mary M. Coffen
Elisha, d. 7/23/1892 at 87/10/16 in Orford; old age; farmer; married; b. Hampton; Samuel Lamprey (Hampton) and Anna Johnson (Hampton)
Frank, d. 3/8/1925 at 71 in Holnesburg, PA; b. Lyme; Daniel Lamprey and Mary M. Coffen
George W., d. 3/3/1911 at 74/9 in Orford; la grippe; carpenter; married; b. Orford; Samuel Lamprey (Hampton) and Eunice Dutton (Orford)

John J., d. 6/25/1946 at 80/8/13 in Orford; retired; single; b. Orford; George W. Lamprey (Orford) and Celinda Trussell (Orford)

John W., d. 8/19/1904 at 70/1/21 in Orford; farmer; married; b. Orford; Samuel Lamprey (Hampton) and Eunice Dutton (Orford)

Joseph D., d. 9/2/1905 at 30/3/29 in Orford; laborer; single; b. Orford; John W. Lamprey (Orford) and Mary Eastman (Vershire, VT)

Marinda, d. 8/27/1904 at 64/6/20 in Concord; domestic; single; b. Orford; Elisha Lamprey (Hampton) and Susan Fifield (Orford)

Samuel N., d. 9/16/1903 at 61/5/16 in Orford; softening of the brain; farmer; single; b. Orford; Elisha Lamprey (Hampton) and Susan Fifield (Orford)

Susan, d. 6/3/1894 at 86/10/4 in Orford; old age; housewife; b. Orford; Jeremiah Fifield (Hampton) and Mary Wise

LANDGRAF,
Bruce, d. 1/12/1992 in Orford; Myron Landgraf and Pearl Anderson

LANE,
Jean, d. 7/21/1984 in Hanover

Mary B., d. 9/30/1896 at 97/0/3 in Orford; housewife; widow; b. Topsham, VT; ----- Bailey

Myra S., d. 4/24/1900 at 58/9/24 in Orford; congestion of lungs; dressmaker; single

LANG,
Josephine, d. 5/21/1920 at 82/4/3 in Haverhill; widow

Mary L., d. 11/2/1933 at 72/8 in Orford; retired; widower; b. Gloucester, MA; George T. Beal (Gloucester, MA) and Mary E. Head (Gloucester, MA)

LAPRISE,
Wilhelmina, d. 5/21/1967 at 68 in Orford; housewife; b. Canada; Joseph Bouchard and Alphonsine LaFountain

LARNED,
Clara R., d. 9/20/1901 at 0/11/13 in Orford; cholera infantum; b. Orford; W. E. Larned (farmer, Wentworth) and Ida M. Bailey (Andover, MA)

LATHE,
Alzada, d. 10/28/1917 at 57/6/27 in Orford; housekeeper; single; b. Newport, VT; Robert R. Lathe (Newport, VT) and Martha L. Collins (Jay, VT)

LATTY,
John, d. 1/15/1952 at 78 in Orford; laborer; married; b. England; Thomas Latty and Carrie Young

LAVOIE,
Henry J., d. 2/24/1957 at 73/6/6 in Haverhill; farmer; married; b. Warren; Lewis Lavoie and Adelaide Corin
Nellie D., d. 1/3/1961 at 79/5/17 in Haverhill; housewife; widow; b. Haverhill; Henry Dearborn and Annie Currier

LAWRENCE,
Bessie I., d. 9/25/2004 in Woodsville; James Cunningham and Ida Kidney
Herbert T., d. 4/26/1995 in Lebanon; Harry T. Lawrence and Lena Edgett
Phyllis B., d. 3/20/1994 in Orford; Benjamin R. Boyer and Louise Groves

LEACH,
Almond, d. 9/2/1949 at 84/5/26 in Hanover; widower; b. Craftsbury, VT

LEAMERE,
Effa, d. 5/12/1912 at 13/9/17 in Hanover; typhoid fever; b. Orford; Alec Leamore (PQ) and Ella Thompson (Derry)

LEARNED,
Charles H., d. 3/8/1909 at 56/5/20 in Concord; farmer; single; b. Orford; James M. Learned (Weathersfield, VT) and Orilla Darracott (Windsor, VT)
Charles W., d. 11/25/1968 at 72 in Newport; farmer retired; b. Orford; Jonas G. Learned and Louise Laflam
Fred E., d. 3/14/1969 at 64 in Hartford, VT; b. Orford; William E. Learned and Ida M. Bailey

George E., d. 1/18/1906 at 74/6/18 in Orford; farmer; widower; b. Reading, VT; James M. Learned (Weathersfield, VT) and Orilla Darracott (Windsor, VT)

George Ernest, d. 7/6/1928 at 19/11/2 in Piermont; laborer; single; b. Orford; William E. Learned (Wentworth) and Ida M. Bailey (Lyme)

Ida Bailey, d. 3/23/1964 at 86 in Watertown, MA; retired housewife; b. Waitsfield, MA; Alpha Bailey and Mary Niles

James M., d. 8/14/1895 at 86/4/20 in Orford; old age; farmer; b. Wethersfield; David W. Learned and Martha Miller

Jonas, d. 3/27/1939 at 74/11 in Hanover; farmer; widower; b. Orford; George Learned (VT) and Chastina Hartwell (Piermont)

Josephine, d. 9/3/1938 at 39/3/21 in Orford; housework; single; b. Orford; Jonas G. Learned (Orford) and Louise LaFlame (Piermont)

LEMIRE,
Roger Joseph, d. 3/11/1947 at 26/5/1 in Orford; clerk; single; b. Manchester; Treffle Lemire (St. Monique, Canada) and Mary Roberge (Manchester)

LEONARD,
Lester Edwin, d. 1/14/1901 at 14/9 in Orford; la grippe; single; b. Barre, VT; Joseph W. Leonard (farmer, Barre, VT) and Lona E. Cutts (Barre, VT)

LESLIE,
John, d. 6/23/1903 at 69/2/20 in Orford; cirrhosis of liver; painter; married; b. Calais, ME; Charles Leslie (Scotland) and ----- Campbell (Scotland)

LEWIS,
Charles, d. 12/21/1888 at 39/11 in Orford; farmer; married

LINDGREN,
Annette Carlson, d. 7/9/1954 at 77/6/21 in Orford; housewife; widow; b. Sweden; Carl Nelson

Carl, d. 12/27/1953 at 74 in Orford; retired; married; b. Sweden; Carl A. Lindgren and Annie Anderson

LINDLEY,
Harold, d. 11/22/1992 in Orford; Frank Lindley and Hope Briggs

LINES,
Mehitable G., d. 3/19/1888 at 83/9/12 in Orford; housewife; widow; b. Orford

LINTHICUM,
John M., d. 1/17/1949 at 5/4/28 in Hanover; b. Ft. Jay, Governor's Isl., NY; John Linthicum and Viola Tupper

LITTLEFIELD,
Leroy Charles, d. 5/19/1954 at 62 in Orfordville; painter; single; b. Danbury

LIVETT,
Edwin, d. 5/9/1889 at 20 I n Haverhill; drowning; pauper; single; b. Lisbon

LOCKE,
Kenneth Bernard, d. 8/7/1979 in Hartford, VT; Horace Locke and Etta Little
Norman W., d. 2/22/1890 at 26/10 in Orford; diabetes mellitus; farmer; married; b. Janesville, WI; S. D. Locke (Richfield, NY) and Ellen J. Parker (NY)

LONG,
B. Wesley, d. 10/1/1959 at 65 in Hanover

LOUAN[N]IS,
Bernard, d. 6/8/1914 at 0/0/22 in Orford; acute gastro enteritis; b. Bradford, VT; Edwin Louannis (Canada) and Julia Bailey (W. Fairlee, VT)
Edwin, d. 8/21/1935 at 52/4/14 in Haverhill; farmer; married; b. Canada

LOVE,
Dorothy, d. 6/15/1987
Lawrence R., d. 8/9/1971 at 69 in Orford; telegrapher; b. St. Martin's, Canada; Robert Love and Loretta Davies

LOVEJOY,
Sabrina, d. 5/20/1888 at 72/3/8 in Orford; housewife; widow; b. Orford; Samuel Brown (Orford) and Betsey Abbott (Warren)

LOWELL,
Josiah F., d. 1/6/1929 at 90/9/21 in Piermont; retired farmer; widower; b. Piermont; Richard Lowell (England) and Mehitable Flanders (Piermont)

Martha McAlister, d. 6/1/1920 at 84/4/29 in Piermont; housewife; married; b. Piermont; Joseph McAlister (Plymouth) and Mary Muchmore (Orford)

LUCAS,
Ellen M., d. 5/28/1913 at 85/1/29 in Orford; acute bronchitis; widow; b. W. Fairlee, VT; Augustus Morris (Woodstock, CT) and Susan Langley (W. Fairlee, VT)

LUFKIN,
Edgar C., d. 1/20/1952 at 94 in Hanover; retired farmer; widower; b. Rumford, ME; Newell Lufkin and Lucy Kimball

Mary Genevieve, d. 11/18/1936 at 70/11/11 in Orford; retired; married; b. Thetford, VT; Joseph Wilmot (Thetford, VT) and Luceria A. Graham (Rumford, ME)

Wallace W., d. 9/16/1961 at 60/9/2 in Orford; farmer; single; b. Thetford, VT; Edgar Lufkin and Genevieve Wilmot

LYNDE,
Emma Jane, d. 5/29/1939 at 82/4/8 in Orford; nurse; widow; b. Haverhill; Stephen Perkins (Lisbon) and Achsah Glynn (Chester, VT)

LYNES,
Frank Edward, d. 8/17/1957 at 84/7/21 in Craftsbury, VT; retired; married; b. Highgate, VT; Franklin L. Lynes and Elizabeth McIntosh

Harold F., d. 8/15/1953 at 44 in Franklin; truck driver; married; b. Hardwick, VT; Frank E. Lynes and Mary A. Colderwood

Mary A., d. 5/13/1952 at 81 in Orford; housewife; married; b. Glover, VT; James -----

MACCHI,
John, d. 11/1/1995 in Orford; John Mario Macchi and Josephine Mazzuchelli

MACK,
son, d. 8/2/1912 at 0/0/1 in Orford; lack of vitality; b. Orford; Fred Mack (Piermont) and Mabel A. Ramsey (Orford)
Alfretta, d. 6/3/1904 at 0/0/2 in Orford; b. Orford; Fred Mack (Piermont) and Mabel A. Ramsey (Orford)
Barbara, d. 1/9/2000 in Lebanon; Lawrence Ward and Edna McCloughn
Ethel P., d. 2/7/2000 in Bradford, VT; Lon C. Pike and Lucy Jewell
Fred, d. 9/14/1938 at 62/6/29 in Orford; farmer; married; b. Piermont; Ruel F. Mack (Haverhill) and Grace Holmes (NH)
Helen M., d. 9/18/1997 in Haverhill; Lewis McKenzie and Annie -----
John, d. 6/5/1934 at 69/8/3 in Henniker; farmer; single; b. Piermont; Ruel Mack (Haverhill) and Elizabeth Holmes (Ryegate, VT)
Kenneth Reginald, d. 7/9/1944 in Central Italy; US Army; single; b. Orford; Fred Mack and Mabel Ramsey; buried in Orford 6/4/1949
Mabel Althea, d. 12/9/1944 at 57/10/9 in Orford; housewife; widow; b. Orford; James Ramsey (Piermont) and Nettie Sherburn (Orford)
Ollie G., d. 3/6/1954 at 75/10/7 in Orford; laborer; single; b. Piermont; Rouel Mack and Elizabeth Holmes
Ruel F,. d. 5/12/1906 at 78/9/27 in Orford; farmer; married; b. Haverhill; Joseph Mack (Haverhill) and ----- (Piermont)
Walter, d. 6/21/1985 in Orford
Walter Edwin, d. 10/11/1932 at 58/7/4 in Orford; farmer; single; b. Piermont; Ruel Mack (Piermont) and Grace E. Holmes (Haverhill)

MAGOON,
Alice, d. 10/17/1889 at 0/9 in Orford; heart disease; b. Orford; Loren Magoon (Washington, VT) and Gertie G. Avery (Boston, MA)

MAGUIRE,
Louise M., d. 11/16/1974 at 88 in Atlantic City, NJ

MAKINSON,
Lizzie, d. 8/5/1950 at 79 in Orford; retired; single; b. S. Windsor, CT; Peter L. Makinson and ----- Thresher

MANCHESTER,
Bertha C., d. 3/17/1975 at 82 in Hanover; teacher; b. Barnet, VT; Frank Manchester and Ida Stuart
Frank Ford, d. 3/14/1920 at 57/1/17 in Orford; farmer; married; b. Barnet, VT; Lemuel Manchester (Barnet, VT) and Caroline Davis (Canada)

MANN,
Alice S., d. 4/2/1947 at 77/10/13 in Bradford, VT; retired; widow; b. Scotland; Alexander Swanson (Scotland) and Ellen Snook (England)
Ann S., d. 3/12/1902 at 84/2/1 in Orford; capillary bronchitis; housewife; widow; b. Orford; Johnathan Sawyer (Orford) and Ruth Phelps (Orford)
Asaph, d. 11/11/1888 at 75/9/11 in Orford; farmer; married; b. Orford; Asaph Mann (Orford) and Mary Barham (Hebron, CT)
Charles A., d. 1/13/1940 at 81/9/5 in Orford; retired; married; b. Orford; Charles Asaah Mann (Orford) and Ann Savage (Orford)
John Thomas, d. 1/5/1918 at 62 in Orford; farm help; single; b. Orford; Aseph Mann (Orford) and Ann Sawyer (Orford)
Mary Mason, d. 1/19/1888 at 102/1/23 in Orford; housewife; widow; b. Lyme; Jonathan Mason (Woodstock, CT) and Deborah Mason (Woodstock, CT)
Zerah C., d. 4/17/1899 at 49 in Orford; peritonitis; laborer; divorced; b. Orford; Carlos Mann

MARSH,
stillborn daughter, d. 8/29/1945 at – in Orford; b. Orford; Ralph Marsh (Orford) and Gladys Cutler (Grafton)
daughter, d. 2/19/1952 at 10 min. in Orford; b. Orford; Ralph E. Marsh and Grace A. Cutler
Arthur L., d. 12/20/1960 at 62/1/29 in Laconia; retired; widower; b. Orford; David C. Marsh and Delia Smith
Bessie, d. 2/5/1936 at 4/4/9 in Haverhill; b. Orford; Arthur Marsh (Orford) and Irene Goddard (St. Johnsbury, VT)

Christine Mae, d. 12/4/1930 at 0/3/7 in Orford; b. Orford; Arthur Louis Marsh (Orford) and Irene Ruth Goddard (St. Johnsbury, VT)

David C., d. 5/10/1952 at 84 in Orford; retired farmer; married; b. W. Fairlee Ctr., VT; George Marsh and Mary Dixon

Delia, d. 12/30/1953 at 80 in Hanover; retired; widow; b. Corinth, VT; Joseph Smith and Irene Felch

Ernest, d. 8/7/1991 in Orford; Walter Marsh and Rita Goddard

Flora A., d. 9/3/1937 at 49/8/2 in Claremont; housekeeper; married; b. Orford; Alpha N. Bailey (Andover, MA) and Mary F. Niles (Enfield)

Frank D., d. 10/28/1953 at 57 in Hanover; roof and chimney sweep; married; b. Orford; David C. Marsh and Delia Smith

Fred, d. 2/9/1986

Fred C., d. 1/6/1948 at 55/5/14 in Hanover; farmer; married; b. Orford; David C. Marsh (W. Fairlee, VT) and Delia T. Smith (Corinth, VT)

Fred Clayton, d. 2/16/1928 at 0/1/4 in Orford; b. Orford; Fred C. Marsh (Orford) and Dorothy Merrill (Deerfield)

Gladys Althea, d. 4/5/1969 at 55 in Orford; housewife; b. Grafton; Justin Cutler and Myrtle Mann

Glenn G., d. 9/5/1968 at 54 in Orford; equip. operator; b. Orford; David Marsh and Delia Smith

Ina Strue, d. 12/25/1950 at 52 in Lebanon; housewife; married; b. Lyme; William Strue and Cora Lovejoy

Irene M., d. 1/31/1999 in N. Haverhill; William Elliott and Annabelle Howland

Irene Ruth, d. 3/27/1959 at 49 in Laconia

Leon, Sr., d. 4/6/1982 in Hanover; Davis Marsh and Delia Smith

Mary E., d. 1/2/1894 at 45/2/16 in Orford; pneumonia; housewife; b. W. Fairlee, VT; Elijah Dickerson and Mary Nelson

Moody, d. 10/18/1896 at 90/0/27 in Orford; farmer; widower; b. Topsham, VT; Isaac Marsh (Topsham, VT)

Ralph E., d. 1/3/1975 at 73 in Hanover; trucking; b. Orford; David Marsh and Delia Smith

Ray Edward, d. 12/27/1940 at 2/4/1 in Haverhill; b. Haverhill; Frank D. Marsh (Orford) and Ina Strue (Lyme)

Retar, d. 10/23/1931 at 28 in Strafford, VT; housewife; married; b. Enfield; Thomas Goddard (Hartford, Canada) and Mae Palmer (Holland, VT)

Vermon A., d. 1/12/1917 at 0/2/28 in Orford; b. Piermont; Fred C. Marsh (Orford) and Beulah Cutting (Piermont)

Wallace, d. 4/30/1933 at 0/3/26 in Orford; b. Orford; Arthur Marsh (Orford) and Irene Goddard (St. Johnsbury, VT)

Walter H., d. 11/12/1955 at 55/7/11 in Haverhill; laborer; married; b. Orford; David Marsh and Delia Smith

MARSHALL,

Harry C., d. 7/12/1921 at 39/8/22 in Fairlee, VT; milk dealer; married; b. Plymouth; William H. Marshall and Jennie L. Kenyon

Jane L., d. 7/2/1917 at 73/2/5 in Orford; housewife; married; b. Plainfield; Mumford H. Kenyon (Plainfield) and Betsy French (Plainfield)

Laura May, d. 12/5/1961 at 74/10/11 in Bradenton, FL; retired; widow; b. Norwich, CT; Gideon Crowell

Mary C., d. 12/3/1947 at 39/9/11 in Bradford, VT

Neil William, d. 4/4/1920 at 2/7/8 in Orford; b. Goffstown; William Hays Marshall (Orford) and Laura M. Crowell (Norwich, CT)

Ruth C., d. 5/2/1974 at 85 in Manchester; retired nurse; b. Norwich, CT; Gideon T. Crowell and Mary A. -----

William Hayes, d. 3/23/1957 at 81/6/16 in Haverhill; farmer; married; b. Orford; William Marshall and Jane Kenyon

William Henry, d. 8/25/1930 at 89/8/27 in Orford; retired farmer; widower; b. Buffalo, NY; Thomas Marshall

MARSTON,

Philobe S., d. 9/1/1888 at 66/3/12 in Orford; housewife; widow; b. Greensboro, VT; Sera Stimpson and ----- Allen

MARTIN,

Anna S., d. 11/14/1950 at 48 in Orford; housewife; married; b. Windsor, CT; James Stone and Fannie Wilson

Mary R., d. 1/7/1890 at 63/1 in Orford; disease of liver; widow; b. Shirley, MA; Peter Hadley (Marlboro, MA) and Elizabeth Green (Westford, MA)

MASON,

Burt Elmer, d. 10/14/1951 at 61 in Orford; blacksmith; divorced; b. Topsham, VT; Almon Mason and Mary Page

Charles Peter, d. 1/2/1993 in Lebanon; Charles P. Macak, Sr. and Betty J. Delany

Grace B., d. 10/21/1955 at 85/9/26 in Hanover; widow; b. Barnet, VT; John Morse and Nancy Sinclair

Margaret, d. 3/27/1936 at 40 in Hanover; at home; single; b. Barnet, VT; Thomas Mason (Vernon, VT) and Grace Moss (Waterford, VT)

Thomas, d. 3/2/1936 at 70 in Hanover; farmer; married; b. Vernon, VT; Thomas Mason (Ireland) and Jane Johnston (Scotland)

MASTERS,
Wesley Gordon, d. 10/16/2004 in W. Roxbury, MA; Weldon Irving Masters and Florence E. Foster

MAY,
Emily Wilson, d. --/--/1964 in Winter Haven, FL; ret. housewife; b. Winchester, MA; John T. Wilson and Pleasantine Cushman; interment – 10/4/1965

MAYETTE,
Alfred, d. 10/17/1898 at 0/4/24 in Orford; dysentery; b. Orford; Edward Mayette (Canada) and Selistine Mayette (Canada)

MAYO,
Nettie E., d. 1/8/1891 at 24/6/8 in Orford; domestic; married; b. Piermont; Charles Cochran (Wentworth) and Sophia A. Wallace

Susan, d. 4/21/1902 at 87/4/24 in Orford; old age; housewife; widow; b. Kirby, VT; ----- Rider (Scotland) and ----- White (Leominster, MA)

McCARTHY,
James B., d. 5/7/1994 in Orford; Charles J. McCarthy and Edna M. Burgoyne

McCRELLIS,
Mabel, d. 2/4/1899 at 18/11 in Orford

Willie E., d. 10/31/1899 at 17/3/12 in Orford; pulmonary phthisis; single; b. Corinth, VT; Aaron McCrillis and Julia Hackett

McCRILLIS,
Harlie E., d. 6/1/1917 at 42/9 in Lebanon; buried Dame Hill

McDONALD,
Annie, d. 5/4/1968 at 78 in Haverhill; housewife; b. NC; Rufus Haffines

McDONNELL,
Thelma C., d. 6/13/2001 in Orford; Harry Hutchins and Sadie -----
William P., d. 11/30/1965 at 52 in Haverhill; ins. broker; b. New York, NY; John McDonnell and Catherine Broderick

McEWAN,
Bertram, d. 7/19/1971 at 75 in Lyme; carpenter; b. Wolf Island, ON; John McEwan and Diantha Rattery

McGECHIN,
Mary Brown, d. 6/3/1931 at 76/8/24 in Orford; retired; widow; b. Baltimore, MD; William S. Brown (MD)

McINTIRE,
Mabel, d. 4/10/1935 at 0/0/2 in Plymouth; b. Plymouth; Roger McIntire (Orford) and Lois Homer (Campton)

McKEE,
Kenneth, d. 6/3/1982 in Haverhill; William McKee and Ethel Armstrong

McKENZIE,
Annie, d. 11/2/1974 at 76 in Hanover; retired; b. Lawrence, MA; John Copley and Annie -----
Lewis, d. 2/21/1973 at 72 in Hanover; retired; b. Quincy, MA; Stuart McKenzie and Eliza Hurley

McKIM,
David, d. 10/12/1917 at 64 in Seattle, WA; buried West Cem.

McMACKIN,
Edna W., d. 2/18/1967 at 69 in Hanover; housewife; b. Bundale, MS; Henry Wilkerson and Josephine Wyatt

McMANN,
Morris H., d. 6/8/1922 at 13/2/29 in Orford; b. Lyme; Henry McMann (Groveton) and Mabel Cutting (Lyme)

McMORROUGH,
Benford, d. 2/28/1974 at 51 in Acapulco, Mexico; Thomas McMorrough and Ruth -----

McPHERSON,
Beriah B., d. 1/11/1906 at 81/9 in Orford; farmer; widower; b. Brookfield, NS; Donald McPherson (Scotland) and Leticia Parker (Annapolis, NS)
Catharine W., d. 7/20/1904 at 80/8/22 in Orford; housewife; married; b. Lunenburg, NS; Calvin Wheelock (Annapolis Co., NS) and Mary Pennell (Annapolis Co., NS)
Cornelia, d. 3/18/1897 at 37/2/9 in Orford; housewife; married; b. Jordan River, NS; Thomas Holden (Jordan River, NS) and Mary Harlow (Sable River, NS)
Cynthia W., d. 3/26/1912 at 56/7/18 in Orford; acute indigestion; housewife; married; b. S. Brookfield, NS; Filson Waterman (Pleasant R., NS) and Susan Harlow (N. Brookfield, NS)
Jason H., d. 3/18/1931 at 73/2/9 in Orford; retired; married; b. Brookfield, NS; Beriah B. McPherson (Brookfield, NS) and Catherine Wheelock (Lunenburg, NS)

MEKOS,
Michael, d. 9/2/1984 in Hanover

MERRILL,
Alice M., d. 9/24/1888 at 0/0/12 in Orford; b. Orford; Elijah N. Merrill (Hebron) and Isa. W. Greenough (Salem, MA)
Allison, d. 7/1/1967 at 70 in Haverhill; laborer; b. Candia; Herbert Merril and Mary McDonald
Mildred, d. 7/22/1962 at 63/11/9 in Haverhill; housewife; married; b. Littleton; William Elliott and Anna -----
Robert, d. 3/25/1990 in Orford; Robert Merrill and Blanche Brown
Stephen, d. 1/22/1895 at 85/1 in Orford; cap. bronchitis; farmer

MERRIMAN,
Dorothy, d. 10/12/2000 in Lebanon; Fred Merriman and Winifred Packard
Gladys, d. 6/9/2001 in Woodsville; Fred Merriman and Winifred Parkard
Winifred E., d. 3/15/1981 in Orford; George W. Packard and Ella M. Pollard

MESANTEL,
Auboe, d. 1/20/1988

MESSIER,
Mylon I., d. 9/4/1960 at 75/11/19 in Orford; retired; married; b. Thetford, VT; Isaac H. Messier and Abbie Ricker

MILES,
Eliza K., d. 3/18/1897 at 76/5/4 in Orford; housewife; widow; b. Randolph, VT; Stephen Herrick (Randolph, VT) and Eliza King (Tunbridge, VT)
Henry, d. 8/6/1944 at 71 in DC

MILLER,
Martha, d. 1/2/2004 in Hanover; Henry True and Inez Briggs
Wayne C., d. 5/11/1980 in Hanover; Charles Miller and Ian Mason

MILLS,
Edward, d. 6/17/1976 at 29 in Orford; student; b. NH; Edward Mills and Louise Campbell

MINARD,
Edith A., d. 10/22/1966 at 96 in Orford; housewife; b. Norwich, VT; Orimel Newcomb and Jennie Wells

MOFFAT,
Alexander, d. 12/5/1990 in Bradford, VT; Alexander Moffat and Sally Decamp

MOODY,
Mary E. R., d. 3/10/1912 at 75/11/10 in Orford; Addison's disease; housewife; widow; b. Wentworth; Isaac Fisk and Mary Brown (Nashua)
Violet M., d. 5/22/1964 at 51 in Lebanon; housewife; b. Orford; John A. Wright and Maud A. Belford

MOORE,
Alexander A., d. 4/13/1974 at 83 in Orford; supervisor; b. Scotland; John F. Moore and Margaret Moffat
Amelia J., d. 12/3/1914 at 70 in Orford; chronic endocarditis; widow

MOREY,
Annie V., d. 2/15/1934 at 69/8/14 in Warren; housewife; widow; b. Inverness, Canada
Clementine, d. 1/2/1987
David R., d. 5/23/1896 at 57/11/16 in Orford; farming; married; b. Strafford, VT; Roswell Morey (Strafford, VT) and Louisa Robinson (W. Fairlee, VT)
Edward, d. 6/24/1948 at 78/11/9 in Orford; farmer; married; b. Thetford, VT; Zenas Mann (Strafford, VT) and Eliza Newcomb (Thetford, VT)
Edward H., d. 2/1/1891 at 64/1/3 in Orford; farmer; married; b. Orford; Moody Morey (Lyme) and Rhoda Whitman
Elizabeth, d. 12/18/1904 at 68/0/4 in Orford; housewife; married; b. Thetford, VT; Simeon Newcomb (Thetford, VT)
Esther, d. 9/17/1951 at 82 in Orford; housewife; widow; b. Inverness, PQ; Daniel McIntyre and Agnes -----
George D., d. 5/11/1971 at 72 in Hartford, VT; laborer; b. Orford; Edward Morey and Esther McIntyre
Hazen, d. 5/15/1984 in Hanover
Irvin W., d. 3/16/1903 at 42/6/12 in Orford; obstruction of bowels; laborer; married; b. Thetford, VT; Zenas Morey (Strafford, VT) and Elizabeth Newcomb (Thetford, VT)
Lillian M., d. 9/16/1948 at 53/6/15 in Orford; housewife; married; b. Fairlee, VT; Sherman Rogers (MA) and Minnie Morris
Ray, d. 6/25/1901 at 10/10/2 in Orford; acute albuminum; b. Bradford, VT; Irving W. Morey (laborer, Union Village, VT) and Annie McIntire (Canada)
Ruth, d. 12/2/1906 at 0/7/22 in Orford; b. Orford; Eddie S. Morey (Thetford, VT) and Esther McIntyre (Inverness, PQ)
Sarah A., d. 1/5/1897 at 45 in Orford; housewife; widow; b. W. Fairlee, VT; Hiram Russell and Susan Clement
Susan B., d. 7/11/1907 at 74/3/28 in Orford; uremia; housewife; widow; b. Hyde Park, VT; ----- Horner (Hyde Park, VT)
Violette J., d. 3/19/1898 at 0/0/25 in Orford; marasmus; b. Orford; Charles H. Morey (Nashua) and Lizzie M. Warner (Orford)
Zenas, d. 7/20/1913 at 82/11/20 in Orford; acute enentis; farmer; widower; Roswell Morey (Strafford, VT) and Louisa Robinson (W. Fairlee, VT)

MORGAN,
Annie V., d. 5/5/1944 at 78/8/5 in Andover, MA; housewife; married;
    b. Lawrence, MA; Richard Whitley (Lancashire, England) and
    Margaret Haigh (England)

MORRILL,
Benjamin, d. 3/20/1889 at 77/6/14 in Orford; paralysis; merchant;
    married; b. Danville, VT; Samuel Morrill and Sally Pillsbury
Harriet M., d. 4/27/1895 at 73/6/19 in Orford; amenia; housekeeper;
    b. Landaff; Jonathan Simons and Nancy J. Gordon

MORRIS,
George R., d. 4/7/1905 at 77/0/11 in Orford; carpenter; single; b.
    Schenectady, NY; Royal Morris and Lucinda Dayton (Orford)

MORRISON,
Adeliza M., d. 5/29/1900 at 65/2/10 in Orford; valvular disease of
    heart; housewife; married; b. Orford; Stephen Merrill (Orford)
    and Adeline Tole (Piermont)
Frances Buzzell, d. 8/25/1954 at 85/8/3 in Senatobia, MS;
    housewife; widow; b. Vershire, VT; John C. Buzzell and Mary A.
    Darling
Harry E., d. 8/4/1923 at 55/3 in Haverhill; farmer; married; b. Orford;
    Samuel R. Morrison (Fairlee, VT) and Adliza Merrill (Orford)
L. A., d. 2/15/1895 at 20/6 in Boston; pneumonia; b. Orford; Samuel
    R. Morrison (farmer) and Adeliza M. Merrill
Nellie J., d. 3/11/1895 at 33/1/16 in Orford; tuberculosis;
    housekeeper; b. Pittsburg; R. M. Danforth and Lucy A. Barnes
Samuel R., d. 4/11/1905 at 71/6/5 in Orford; lumber dealer; widower;
    b. Fairlee, VT; Dan W. Morrison (Fairlee, VT) and Viersher
    Gage (Orford)

MORSE,
Grace Marsh, d. 11/27/1952 at 19 in Loudon; waitress; divorced; b.
    Orford; Frank D. Marsh and Ida Strue
Hattie B. Hawkins, d. 11/28/1950 at 76 in Orford; housewife;
    married; b. W. Fairlee, VT; Henry Howland and Mary Norton
Linda, d. 2/22/1953 at 1/3/8 in Canaan; b. Lebanon; Harold Morse
    and Grace Marsh

MOSES,
Eva, d. 9/1/1986
Jonathan, d. 9/20/1954 at 77/10/14 in Haverhill; retired; widower; b. Tunbridge, VT; Ora F. Moses and Margaret Barton
Ralph William, d. 1/24/1971 at 58 in Orford; carpenter; b. NH; George Moses and Anna Gale

MOULTON,
Lucy Ellen, d. 11/10/1921 at 70/8 in Orford; domestic; married; b. Calis; John King

MOUSLEY,
son, d. 11/11/1895 at 0/0/1 in Orford; convulsions; b. Orford; George W. Mousley (farmer) and Julia S. Dike
daughter, d. 9/14/1897 at 0/3/13 in Orford; b. Orford; George W. Mousley (Lyme) and Julia K. Dyke (Lyme)
Catherine J., d. 1/28/1911 at 70/10/11 in Orford; cerebral hemorrhage; housewife; widow; b. Orford; Thomas W. Quint (Orford) and Jane Archer (Orford)
Elwyn W., d. 10/5/1903 at 1/2/11 in Orford; cholera infantum; b. Thetford, VT; Oliver C. Mousley (Orford) and Lela E. Sweet (Lyme)
Fred V., d. 12/1/1950 at 50 in Hartford, VT; laborer; single; b. Lyme; Genge Mousley and Julia Dyke
George W., d. 1/15/1905 at 19/9/1 in Orford; single; b. Lyme; George W. Mousley (Lyme) and Julia Dyke (Lyme)
George William, d. 9/15/1928 at 67/0/12 in Orford; farmer; married; b. Lyme; William Mousley (Canada) and Katherine Quint
Julia E., d. 5/19/1948 at 83/10/20 in Orford; housewife; widow; b. Lyme; Volney Dyke (Lyme) and Sarah Hall (Lyme)
Leila E., d. 10/17/1963 at 80 in Thetford, VT; housewife; b. Lyme; John W. Sweet and Alice Lamphere
Max O., d. 8/10/1974 at 74 in Orford; laborer; b. Orford; George W. Mousley and Julia Dyke
Oliver, d. 6/27/1947 at 70/6/8 in Thetford, VT; b. Orford; William E. Mousley (Canada) and Julia Quint (Orford)
Samuel A., d. 5/25/1957 at 67/10/18 in Hanover; laborer; single; b. Norwich, VT; George Mousley and Julia Dyke
William C., d. 3/16/1978 at 71 in Hanover; laborer; b. Orford; George G. Mousley and Julia Dike

MULLIN,
Louise, d. 3/20/1971 at 43 in Orford; housewife; b. Washington, DC; Leonard R. Minster and Dorothy Kuhn

MUNN,
Charles H., d. 1/18/1950 at 80 in Hanover; retired; married; b. Canterbury; Henry Munn and Julia Titus
John E., d. 1/16/1924 at 43 in Hanover; garage owner; single; b. W. Fairlee, VT; Henry Munn (W. Fairlee, VT) and Julia Titus
Kathleen M., d. 3/21/1961 at 86/7/1 in Haverhill; ret. housewife; widow; b. Northfield, MN; George Ordway and Elizabeth Crooks
Reginald, d. 10/10/1974 at 78 in Bradford, VT; retired; b. W. Fairlee, VT; Charles Munn and Kathleen Ordway

NEER,
S. Hollis, d. 10/30/1985 in Orford

NELSON,
Charles W., d. 3/23/1916 at 81/6/16 in Orford; chr. endocarditis; retired; widower; b. Corinth, VT

NEWCOMB,
Asahel W., d. 1/27/1904 at 72/11/19 in Orford; farmer; married; b. Orford; Asahel W. Newcomb (Thetford, VT) and Laura Taylor (Thetford, VT)
Laura T., d. 2/12/1887 at 86/8/27 in Orford; housewife; married; b. Thetford, VT
Nancy J. T., d. 2/3/1896 at 75/2/4 in Fairlee, VT; housewife; married; b. Newbury, VT; Jonas Tucker (Spencer, MA) and Nancy Johnson (Newbury, VT)
Orette A., d. 12/29/1899 at 64/1/2 in Orford; dropsy from heart disease; housewife; married; b. Piermont; Chandler Cass (Hebron) and Dinah Glores (Alexandria)

NEWSOM,
Thomas Reed, d. 10/9/1961 at 42/7/28 in Orford; law editor; single; b. Union Pt., GA; William Newsom and Inda Young

NICHOLS,
Mae A., d. 7/9/1952 at 69/1/22 in Orford; housewife; widow; b. Finley, OH; John Aurand and Annette Stack

NICKERSON,
Daniel Hugh, d. 11/22/1930 at 60/10/5 in Haverhill; laborer; b. NS

NILES,
Benjamin F., d. 10/31/1905 at 81/8/4 in Orford; farmer; married; b. Orford; Benjamin H. Niles (Orford) and Martha D. Savage (Wentworth)

George F., d. 9/13/1938 at 82/7/22 in Enfield; retired; married; b. Enfield; Benjamin F. Niles (Orford) and Mary P. Newell (Orford)

Harriet F., d. 5/25/1923 at 79/5/3 in Manchester; retired; married; b. Orford; Wincoe F. Wright (Dunstable) and Mary Worcester (Plymouth)

Harrison, d. 4/22/1969 at 90 in Orford; Curtis Publish. Co.; b. Brooklyn, NY; Winfred Niles and Ellen Beatty

Howard E., d. 4/11/1917 at 79/8/13 in Orford; none; single; b. Orford; Benjamin H. Niles (Newbury, VT) and Martha Savage (Orford)

Lenore, d. 5/5/1988

Nellie E., d. 1/8/1955 at 80/11/21 in Manchester; housewife; widow; b. Lyme; Edgar Smith and Delinah Worthen

NOLET,
Henry Joseph, d. 2/19/1950 at 63 in Orford; carpenter; b. St. Benedine, PQ; Francois Nolet and Leocadie Pouliet

NORDSTROM,
Sandra L., d. 12/17/1996 in Orford; ----- and Pearl Nordstrom

NORRIS,
Cora R., d. 11/23/1936 at 78/9/7 in Lexington, MA; retired; widow

Elizabeth N., d. 2/10/1903 at 79/0/28 in Orford; cerebral apoplexy; single; b. Dorchester; David Norris (Dorchester) and Sophia Wright (Dunstable)

George S., d. 10/3/1925 at 90/3/9 in Lexington, MA; retired; married; b. Orford; David Norris (Dorchester) and Sophia Wright (Nashua)

John A., d. 2/2/1903 at 76/7/29 in Orford; typhoid fever; laborer; widower; b. Londonderry; Joseph W. Norris (Corinth, VT) and Maria Adams

NORTON,
Maude E., d. 10/16/1966 at 84 in Haverhill; housework; b. Vershire, VT; William Bacon and Ellen Patterson

NOTEMYER,
Priscilla, d. 1/4/1940 at 0/3/29 in Hanover; b. Brattleboro, VT; Chesley Notemyer (Waterville, VT) and Ellen Symonds (Elmore, VT)

NOYES,
Howard, d. 10/4/1992 in Lebanon; George Noyes and Mary Morin
Joan, d. 5/24/2001 in Lebanon; Maurice Baker and Hattie Streeter

NUTTER,
Evelyn, d. 4/21/1971 at 48 in Hanover; housewife; b. Wells River, VT; Arthur Johnson and Minnie Barrett
Kenneth L., d. 10/2/2000 in White River Jct., VT; John Nutter and Flora Cassady
Norman E., d. 6/22/1944 at 20/2/19 at Normandy Beach; US Army; single; b. Waits River, VT; John Nutter and Flora Cassidy; buried 10/17/1948

NUTTING,
Julia Ann, d. 3/28/1941 at 78/1/21 in Plymouth; housewife; widow; b. Orford; George Learned (Reading, VT) and Chastina Hartwell (Piermont)

OLIVER,
Ernistine, d. 9/3/1915 at 11/0/25 in Orford; heart failure from diphtheria; b. Boston, MA; Freeman Oliver (Malden, MA) and Eleanor Oliver (Malden, MA)

ORCUTT,
Mary Jane, d. 11/19/1928 at 86/7/11 in Windsor, VT; housewife; widow; b. Orford; James M. Learned (Weathersfield, VT) and Orrilla Darrocutt (Windsor, VT)

OWSLEY,
John E., d. 7/14/1953 at 71 in Orford; business executive; married; b. Chicago, IL; Heaton Owsley and Carolyn Byrne

Mary M., d. 4/12/1971 at 74 in Hanover; housewife; b. Mankato, MN; Munson Burton and Belle McDonald

PAGE,
son, d. 9/25/1895 at 0/4/1 in Orford; brain fever; b. Orford; Charles W. Page and Emma J. Dike
Addie, d. 7/17/1930 at 73/5/25 in Orford; housewife; married; b. Orford; Charles Baker and Susan Horner
Calista K., d. 6/16/1907 at 77/10/19 in Orford; cerebral hemorrhage; teacher; single; b. Wentworth; Enoch Page and Betsey W. Giles
George Freeman, d. 12/24/1956 at 92/3/24 in Haverhill; retired farmer; widower; b. Orford; Thomas Page and Elizabeth J. Smith
George Raymond, d. 4/7/1934 at 25/5/25 in Haverhill; laborer; single; Freeman G. Page (Orford) and Addie Baker (Orford)
Leon F. G., d. 8/21/1893 at 0/4/1 in Orford; whooping cough; b. Orford; George F. Page (Orford) and Annie M. Baker

PAIGE,
Eva H., d. 12/24/1955 at 80/4/22 in Long Beach, CA; housewife; widow; b. Orford; John E. Hall and Susan P. Brown

PARKER,
Charles, d. 5/5/2003 in Woodsville; Walter Parker and Carrie Kittredge
Freda, d. 12/25/1990 in Orford; Ralph Marsh and Gladys Cutler
Myra, d. 1/3/1892 at 74/0/30 in E. Concord, VT; la grippe; domestic; married
Ralph E., d. 4/9/2001 in Concord; Charles Parker and Freda Marsh

PARKINGTON,
Dorothy M., d. 8/4/2004 in Lebanon; William Crofts and Lenore Gade

PARTRIDGE,
Fred F., d. 12/12/1926 at 72/5/19 in Orford; retired; b. Peacham, VT; Harry Partridge (NH) and Cynthia Merrill (NH)

PASTORFIELD,
John L., d. 11/2/2003 in Hanover; Charles Pastorfield and Victoria Paschal

PATCH,
son, d. 5/30/1888 at 0/0/3 in Orford; b. Orford; William H. Patch (Orford) and Ella M. White (Orford)
Ethel Sarah, d. 8/29/1962 at 80/4/9 in Ashland; housewife; widow; b. Norwich, VT; George W. Mousley and Julia E. Dyke
George M., d. 1/23/1934 at 69/10/13 in Orford; carpenter; married; b. Orford; Daniel Patch (Orford) and Lydia Phelps (Orford)
Henry L., d. 7/9/1957 at 75/1/26 in Hanover; sexton; married; b. Orford; William Patch and Ella White
William H., d. 3/1/1891 at 37/7/9 in Orford; laborer; married; b. Orford; Daniel Patch (Orford) and Lydia Phelps

PATTEN,
stillborn son, d. 4/5/1941 at – in Orford; b. Orford; John W. Patten (Hampden, ME) and Elizabeth M. Butters (Hartland, ME)

PAYNE,
Elsie, d. 2/11/1922 at 30/6/9 in Keene; housewife; married; b. Orford; Alphonso Smith (Manchester) and Clar'a Worthen (Wentworth)

PEARSON,
Irene E., d. 5/4/1996 in Rumney; Carl Lindgren and Emma Anderson

PEASE,
Abbie M., d. 4/15/1949 at 86/4/8 in Seymour, CT; retired; widow; b. Sandwich
Chase M., d. 4/27/1915 at 57/9/22 in Wentworth; meningitis; farmer; b. Ellsworth; Samuel Pease (Barnstead) and Martha Moulton (Ellsworth)
Dorice H., d. 12/13/1971 at 69 in Haverhill; housework; b. Orford; Francis R. Pease and Mabel C. Sherburne
Edwin S., d. 8/18/1948 at 77/5/3 in Warren; merchant; married; b. Wentworth; Samuel Pease (Ellsworth) and Sarah Randall (Ellsworth)
Edythe L., d. 9/10/1906 at 29/4/17 in Orford; housewife; married; b. Lisbon; Darius Quimby (Easton) and Lucy A. Smith (Haverhill)

Florence M., d. 5/1/1952 at 68 in Warren; rug maker; widow; b. Franconia; Edward Edgerly and Stella M. Combs

Francis R., d. 2/5/1925 at 61/10/27 in Orford; farmer; married; b. Ellsworth; Samuel Pease (Ellsworth) and Sarah Randall

Glenn, d. --/--/1989

Henry H., d. 3/16/1920 at 67/5/12 in Orford; farmer; married; b. Ellsworth; Samuel Pease (Ellsworth) and Martha Moulton (Ellsworth)

Howard S., d. 11/25/1912 at 19/8/19 in Orford; gunshot wound; farmer; single; b. Orford; Henry H. Pease (Ellsworth) and Abbie M. Gault (Sandwich)

Mabel C., d. 7/18/1956 at 88/2/1 in Orford; retired housewife; b. Orford; Luther Sherburn and Angelina Clifford

Samuel J., d. 2/13/1907 at 70/5/26 in Orford; cardiac disease; farmer; married; b. Ellsworth; Samuel D. Pease (Ellsworth) and Martha Moulton (Ellsworth)

PEAVEY,

Pearl E., d. 5/23/1977 at 73 in Hanover; housewife; b. Canada; Herbert Greene and Nellie Bragg

PEBBLES,

Almena, d. 11/30/1907 at 70/2/20 in Orford; cerebral hemorrhage; housewife; married; b. Lyme; Jephthah Taylor (Lyme) and Fravilla Hall (Lyme)

Ellen M., d. 11/12/1920 at 75/3/26 in Orford; housewife; widow; b. Plymouth; Asabel Blodgett (Groton) and Prucilla Webster (Plymouth)

Hazen, d. 4/22/1920 at 83/9/3 in Orford; farmer; married; b. Orford; John Pebbles (New Salem, MA) and Dilla H. Weed (Unity)

William F., d. 3/4/1922 at 87/6/23 in Orford; farmer; widower; b. Orford; John Pebbles (New Salem) and Della Weed (Unity)

PENNOCK,

Lizzie D., d. 4/12/1918 at –6 in Lyme; housekeeper; divorced; b. Stratford; William Dennis (Stratford) and Lucelia Curtis (Stratford)

PERKINS,
Clyde L., d. 4/4/1915 at 0/2/3 in Orford; tuberculosis; b. Piermont; Ralph C. Perkins (Hardwick, VT) and Maude Barnett (Walden, VT)

PERRY,
Inez Cora, d. 1/19/1967 at 77 in Orford; housewife; b. Benton; Isaac Lindsey and Jennie Clark
Leighton A., d. 9/6/1997 in Hanover; Charles A. Perry and Inez Lindsey
Lisa Lucille, d. 4/27/1963 at 0/0/1 in Hanover; b. Hanover; Leighton A. Perry and Lucille M. Gilbert
Walter, d. 12/26/1989 in Hanover; Charles Perry and Priscilla Fectueau

PETERS,
Julie A., d. 10/25/2001 in Orford; Martin Eggland and Vivian Eggland

PETERSON,
Peter M., d. 10/31/1891 at 90/6/3 in Orford; widower; b. Denmark

PHELPS,
Adolphus, d. 12/23/1889 at 80/10/8 in Orford; old age; laborer; widower; b. Orford; Nathaniel Phelps
Charlotte, d. 12/21/1911 at 87/8/1 in Orford; senile dementia; housewife; widow; b. Orford; Joseph Hancock (New Braintree, MA) and Lydia Burr
Christine H., d. 9/14/1962 in Salem; medical secretary; b. Somerville, MA; removal from caducous vault 5/18/1964
Edward Grant, d. 12/22/1951 at 83 in Suffolk, MA; retired; single; b. Orford; John Hale Phelps and Charlotte Hancock
Elmer H., d. 2/18/1967 at 72 in Salem, MA; b. Orford; John Phelps and Charlotte Hancock
Fannie F., d. 4/19/1892 at 78 in Cambridge, MA; paralysis
John, d. 5/16/1932 at 72 in Hanover; farmer; single; John H. Phelps (Orford) and Charlotte Hancock (Orford)
John H., d. 1/18/1898 at 77/5/27 in Orford; heart disease; farmer; married; b. Orford; Elihu Phelps (Hollis) and Rebecca Hale (Orford)
Joseph H., d. 9/23/1939 at 75/6/19 in Hanover; farmer; single; b. Orford; John H. Phelps (Orford) and Charlotte Hancock (Orford)

Julius, d. 9/27/1972 at 102 in Haverhill; retired; b. Ayer Jct., MA; Charles S. Phelps and Martha B. Chapin
Marcia, d. 9/20/1946 at 72/0/1 in Boston, MA
Oscar H., d. 6/18/1933 at 80/3/29 in Salem Depot; b. Orford; John H. Phelps (Orford) and Charlotte Hancock (Orford)

PHILBRICK,
Alvin S., d. 6/27/1934 at 84/7/20 in Orford; retired; married; b. Wentworth; Samuel Philbrick (NH) and Mary S. Roberts (NH)
Emma J., d. 2/8/1935 at 63 in Hanover; housewife; widow; b. Thetford, VT; Anson Moulton (Ellsworth) and Emeline Randall (Ellsworth)

PICKNELL,
Nancy, d. 3/30/1973 at 78 in Haverhill; housewife; b. NY; Pardin Jameison and Elaine Purdy

PIERCE,
son, d. 8/4/1946 at – in Hanover; b. Hanover; Chester A. Pierce (Haverhill) and Dorothy M. Pike (Lyme)
Charles E., d. 7/9/1917 at 33/6/8 in Fairlee, VT; widower; buried West Cem.
Charles Gilman, d. 2/2/1909 at 0/0/24 in Fairlee, VT; b. Fairlee, VT; Charles E. Pierce (Orford) and Mabel Hutchinson
Dorothy, d. 1/3/1990 in Orford; Lon Pike and Lucy Jewell
Elsie H., d. 1/14/2000 in Albuquerque, NM; Arthur Pierce and Mary Partridge
Emeline, d. 11/21/1917 at 80/1/4 in Fairlee, VT; widowe; buried West Cem.
Frank A., d. 12/13/1918 at 43 in Cumberland, RI
Harry A., d. 9/18/1921 at 47/10/5 in Plymouth; dentist; married; b. Orford; John R. Pierce (Orford) and Melvina Weld (Orford)
John R., d. 11/1/1895 at 69/5/3 in Orford; abs. of liver; blacksmith; b. Orford; John R. Pierce and Emily Dame
John R., d. 5/20/1946 at 64/1/2 in Boston, MA; b. Orford; Charles R. Pierce (Fairlee, VT) and Angie Eastman (Vershire, VT)
Martha A., d. 6/16/1964 at 96 in Northampton, MA
May, d. 11/5/1983 in Lebanon; Fred Patridge and Harriet Albee

PIERSON,
Ernest, d. 8/27/1961 at 82/0/3 in Haverhill; farmer; widower; b. Topsham, VT; Rufus Pierson and Luella Darling
Evelyn N., d. 6/6/1994 in Lebanon; Alvin B. Weeks and Florence Hardy
Luella Abbie, d. 9/25/1939 at 84/3/22 in Orford; housewife; widow; b. Groton, VT; Peter Darling (Groton, VT) and Mary E. Hooper (Groton, VT)
Martha W., d. 12/13/1896 at 51/4 in Brooklyn, NY
Nettie E., d. 2/18/1932 at 46/3/15 in Orford; housewife; married; b. Topsham, VT; Carlos Wright (Newbury, VT) and Carrie Page (Groton, VT)
Wallace Henry, d. 7/22/1965 at 57 in Hartford, VT; laborer; b. Topsham, VT; Ernest Pierson and Nellie Wright
William, d. 6/3/1984 in Hanover

PIKE,
Earl H., d. 5/14/1968 at 69 in Orford; farmer; b. Lyme; Henry M. Pike and Lizzie A. Tripp
James E., d. 6/7/1975 at 21 in Orford; laborer; b. Woodsville; Weymouth Pike, Sr. and Helen Marsh
Lucy, d. 9/3/1968 at 84 in Haverhill; housewife; b. Canada; Frank Jewell and Eliza Jewell
Myrtle, d. 6/5/1970 at 81 in Concord; housewife; b. Canada

PILLSBURY,
Mary Jane, d. 9/12/1899 at 82/3/10 in Orford; croupous dysentery; housewife; widow; b. Haverhill; David Stanley and Hannah Maxwell (Scotland)
William R., d. 8/7/1899 at 84/6/17 in Orford; old age; married; b. Bridgewater; Calup Pillsbury and Nancy Nelson

PIPER,
Ray, d. 1/15/1890 at 0/4/23 in Orford; brain disease; b. Orford; Charles E. Piper (laborer, Fairlee, VT) and Sarah A. Robertson (Stratford)
Sarah A., d. 1/24/1891 at 62/6/2 in Fairlee, VT; housewife; married; b. Manchester; Elisha Harrington and Mary Bailey
Virginia, d. 12/2/1923 at 6/3/12 in Brattleboro, VT; b. Lyme; Frank A. Piper (Orford) and Vivian French (Orford)

Vivian F., d. 8/10/1980 in Hanover; Walter French and Nellie F. Knight

POMEROY,
Charlotte Harriman, d. 6/1/1965 at 59 in St. Charles, MO; housewife; b. Malden, MA

POOR,
Maria M., d. 4/19/1905 at 78/1/19 in Orford; housewife; married; b. Vershire, VT; Page George and Laura M. Matson
Shirley M., d. 1/24/1999 in Orford; Alva Lyndes and Gladys Blodgett
Stephen B., d. 2/22/1907 at 81/2/24 in Orford; exhaustion; farmer; widower; b. Strafford, VT; William Poor (Andover, MA) and Abigail Frary

PORTER,
Charles F., d. 2/8/1917 at 77/11 in Wolfeboro; widower; buried West Cem.
Louise J., d. 2/6/1917 at 72/2/18 in Wolfeboro; married; buried West Cem.

PORTEOUS,
Thomas C., d. 11/18/1967 at 76 in Orford; salesman; b. Newport, Wales; Thomas Porteous and Emily Carver

PRATT,
John, d. 4/12/1893 at 86/10/4 in Orford; bronchitis; merchant; b. Orford; Joseph Pratt (Salem, MA) and Lydia Mann

PRESCOTT,
Manvers N., d. 9/4/1937 at 58/9/8 in Hanover; merchant; married; b. Washington, VT; Nelson Prescott (Washington, VT) and Lucretia Everett (Lyme)
Ruth S., d. 5/19/1978 at 56 in Hanover; postmaster; b. Fairlee; Manvers Prescott and Josie Everett
William H., d. 12/26/1958 at 81/1/25 in Orford; florist; married; b. Pawtucket, RI; Chauncey Preston (sic) and ----- Newell

PRESCOTT PLANTE,
Gertrude I., d. 1/27/2001 in Orford; Danvers Prescott and Josie Everett

PRESSEY,
Elizabeth, d. 11/10/1946 at 78/0/23 in Hanover; housewife; widow; b. Orange, NJ
Horace, d. 7/10/1925 at 70/6/10 in Hanover; farmer; married; b. Canaan St.; Albert Pressey (NH) and Alvira Thompson (NH)
Mary M., d. 5/7/1910 at 78/3/26 in Orford; housewife; widow
Miranda, d. 6/20/1920 at 84 in Haverhill; housewife; widow; b. Canaan

PRESTON,
Almira, d. 7/27/1987
Harold W., d. 4/16/1943 at 16/7/14 in Hanover; creamery worker; single; b. Thetford, VT; William H. Preston (Pawtucket, RI) and Mabel French (Thetford, VT)
Juanita, d. 2/1/1931 at 3/0/3 in Woodsville; b. Thetford, VT; William Preston (Pawtucket, RI) and Mabel French (Thetford, VT)
Mabel Pearl, d. 2/14/1965 at 69 in Haverhill; housewife; b. Thetford, VT; Arthur French and Mary Squires

PRETTYMAN,
Clara, d. 8/10/1908 at 35/7/15 in Orford; erysipelas; housewife; married; b. Philadelphia, PA; Thomas J. Bains (Philadelphia) and Matilda E. Yates (Wilmington, DE)
Lulu R., d. 1/10/1954 at 80/6/19 in Ft. Lauderdale, FL; retired housewife; married; b. Milford, DE; Frank Reedy and Sally Anderson (1958)
Virgil, d. 10/13/1957 at 83/7/0 in Ft. Lauderdale, FL; retired; widower; b. Townsend, DE; C. W. Prettyman and Emma Gooding (1958)
Virgil, Jr., d. 4/17/1961 at 51 in Ft. Lauderdale, FL; married; Virgil Prettyman and Lulu R. -----

PROPER,
Dora E., d. 10/23/1906 at 0/1 in Orford; b. Orford; Alonzo Proper (Highgate, VT) and Emma J. Gardner (Newbury, VT)

PUSHEE,
James A., d. 2/21/1979 in Orford; Dean Pushee and Vera Movelle
Olyph, d. 9/5/1967 at 58 in Orford; carpenter; b. Lyme; David Pushee and Mary Gilbert

PUTNAM,
Elizabeth G., d. 2/1/1923 at 86/4/27 in Boston, MA
Minnie, d. 1/12/1982 in Orford; Francis Cornwall and Annie Langdon

PUTNEY,
Walter S., d. 11/22/1924 at 66/7/4 in Orford; carpenter; married; b. NH; Charles Putney (NH) and Mary Bean (NH)

QUACKENBUSH,
Frederick O., d. 5/4/1957 at 77 in Springfield, MA; retired; widower; b. Northampton, MA; Joseph Quackenbush and Harriet Allen
Grace E., d. 7/8/1956 at 61/10/9 in Hanover; housewife; married; b. Woonsocket, RI; William O. Hackett and Margaret Ryan

QUINT,
Alvarado B., d. 4/23/1923 at 66/11/9 in Orford; carpenter; married; b. Lyme; Thomas J. Quint (Orford) and Jane Archer (Orford)

RACE,
Harry, d. 2/7/1962 at 65/1/21 in Hanover; farmer; widower; b. Ripton, VT; John Race and Anna Lewis

RADFORD,
William Ernest, d. 4/12/1950 at 78 in Orford; laborer; widower; b. Wentworth

RAMSAY,
Ulric A., d. 9/11/1933 at 69/0/4 in St. Johnsbury, VT; retired; married; b. Piermont; Dean Ramsay (NH) and Mary Griggs (Sutton, PQ)

RAMSEY,
Ruth E., d. 11/14/1925 at 58/3/7 in N. Thetford, VT; domestic; married; b. Orford; Frank Tallman (Orford)
Ruth M., d. 2/11/1904 at 0/0/1 in Orford; b. Orford; Ulric A. Ramsey (Piermont) and Ruth E. Tallman (Orford)

RANDALL,
Rosa C., d. 4/8/1892 at 32/7/10 in Orford; heart disease; domestic; married; b. Orford; Dow Y. Simpson and Martha A. Blodgett

REED,
Clarence Cleveland, d. 5/20/1958 at 75/5/5 in Haverhill; farmer; widower; b. Mr. Kisco, NY; Oscar Reed and Annie Mead
Donald R., d. 5/7/1997 in Lebanon; Clarence Reed and Josephine Allen
Edna, d. 9/18/1987
Mary Agnes, d. 7/5/1956 at 73/1/11 in Orford; own home; married; b. Brooklyn, NY; John O'Flaherty

RENFREW,
Alexander N., d. 2/18/1923 at 96/1/13 in Orford; retired; widower; b. Newbury, VT; James Renfrew (Scotland) and ----- Nelson

RENNEY,
Emeline Hackett, d. 6/16/1900 at 75 in Orford; aortic insufficiency; housewife; widow; b. Alexandria; Justin Hackett and ----- Heath

RHOADES,
Asa S., d. 11/17/1907 at 79/11/23 in Orford; exhaustion; laborer; widower; b. Derby, VT; John Rhoades and ----- Dudley
Lettie I., d. 5/26/1974 at 76 in Port Jarvis, NY; b. Orford; Wilbur Rhoades and Emma Simpson
Mildred M., d. 9/12/1906 at 0/1/3 in Orford; b. Orford; Wilbur Rhoades (Waits River, VT) and Emma S. Simpson (Orford)

RHODES,
Eliza A., d. 10/14/1900 at 67/11/27 in Orford; weakness of heart; housewife; married; b. Rockingham, VT; Charles G. Lovejoy (Claremont) and Melinda Amsden (Grafton, VT)
Emma L., d. 12/6/1921 at 59/4/18 in Orford; housewife; married; b. Orford; John B. Simpson (Franklin Falls) and Mary A. Brown (Rumney)
Francis E., d. 7/4/1935 at 18/4/3 in Newbury, VT; single; George Rhodes (Orford)
George W., d. 4/21/1969 at 84 in Hanover; gardener; b. Orford; Wilbur Rhodes and Emma Simpson
J. F. B., d. 3/31/1889 at 0/1/6 in Orford; congestion lungs; b. Orford; Wilbur Rhodes (Hanover) and Emma Simpson (Orford)
Lettie, d. 9/26/1892 at 0/4 in Orford; cholera infantum; b. Orford; Wilbur Rhodes (Washington, VT) and Emma Simpson (Orford)

Mabel C., d. 10/21/1971 at 92 in Lebanon; housewife; b. Orford; Perley Chapman and Mary E. Willis

Mary, d. 1/25/1941 at 50/7/17 in Haverhill; housewife; married; b. Orford; Wilbur Rhodes (Topsham, VT) and Emma Simpson (Orford)

Wilbur, d. 8/2/1922 at 56/11/24 in Orford; laborer; widower; b. Topsham, VT; Charles Roades (Topsham, VT) and Jane Magoon (Topsham, VT)

RICHARDSON,

Arthur J., d. 4/26/1932 at 69/1/14 in Orford; farmer; married; b. Orford; John Richardson (Lisbon) and Clara P. Johnson (Bradford, VT)

Catherine, d. 7/24/1921 at 82/11/23 in Orford; none; single; b. Orford; Joel Richardson (Craftsbury, VT) and Sarah Bailey (Boscawen)

Clara P., d. 11/3/1888 at 63/3/24 in Orford; widow; b. Bradford, VT; Haines Johnson (Bradford, VT) and Jane Sawyer (Bradford, VT)

Hattie G., d. 2/14/1960 at 92/7/4 in Orford; retired housewife; widow; b. Lyme; James Gardner and Emeline Breck

James B., d. 8/30/1911 at 78/8/21 in Orford; exhaustion from con., vomiting; J. of Sup. Ct. of Mass.; married; b. Orford; Joel Richardson and Sarah Bailey (Dunbarton)

Kyle, d. 9/4/1992 in Lebanon; Neil Washburn and Nancy Washburn

Sarah B., d. 8/15/1889 at 87/6/11 in Orford; softening of brain; housewife; widow; b. Hopkinton; Phineas Bailey and Sarah Bailey

RICHMOND,

Chastina L., d. 11/14/1969 at 66 in Watertown, MA; b. Orford; William E. Learned and Ida M. Bailey

Gould S., d. 3/2/2001 in Exeter

RIDER,

Lucy, d. 8/12/1889 at 71/2/11 in Orford; congestion of brain; b. Kirby, VT; James Rider and Nancy Snow (Leominster, MA)

RILEY,

Charles H., d. 9/5/1910 at 87/5/12 in Orford; farmer; married; b. Boston, MA; George Riley and Sally Storey (Salem, MA)

Elmira G., d. 2/11/1915 at 81/2/10 in Orford; acute bronchitis; housewife; widow; b. Mendon, VT; John Griggs and Charlotte Farnum (Walpole)

Fannie E., d. 3/31/1888 at 27/5 in Ludlow, VT; married

Jennie L. Barnes, d. 3/16/1924 in Boston, MA; received from MA Cremation Society for interment West Cemetery 10/21/1924

Mary Griggs, d. 11/4/1957 at 88/8/10 in Laconia; retired teacher; single; b. Orford; Charles Henry Riley and Almira L. Griggs

Maud S., d. 3/1/1895 at 22/8/3 in Orford; pneumonia; teacher; b. Orford; Charles H. Riley (farmer) and Elmira L. Griggs

Sarah, d. 3/2/1894 at 84/9/23 in Orford; old age; b. Danville, VT; George Riley (Wethersfield, MA) and Sally Story

ROBERTS,
Anna L., d. 11/18/1956 at 82/2/2 in Orford; housewife; widow; b. Fleetwood, PA; Gottlieb Diemand and Amelia Griesmer

Earl H., d. 6/8/1957 at 62/11/11 in Orford; machinist; married; b. Morton, PA; Charles E. Roberts and Annie L. Diemand

Ella M., d. 9/5/1937 at 81/6/17 in Ryegate, VT; widow

Emma, d. 3/6/1915 at 61/3 in Concord; acute inanition; housewife; widow; b. Washington, VT

John, d. 12/28/1890 at 81/5/18 in Orford; old age; farmer; married; b. Orford; Clark Roberts (Linesboro, MA) and Sarah Bennis (Reading, VT)

Leonard M., d. 3/15/1913 at 79/4/9 in Orford; acute bronchitis; farmer; married; b. Orford; John Roberts (Orford) and Nancy Quint (Orford)

Maurice A., d. 5/12/1949 at 33/8/24 in Orford; restaurant owner; married; b. S. Strickley, Canada; Mederic Roberts and Delia Groulx

Nancy Quint, d. 10/27/1896 at 84/9/20 in Orford; housewife; widow; b. Orford; Benjamin Quint

ROBINSON,
George, d. 11/6/1966 at 54 in Hanover; disabled; b. Thetford, VT; Arthur J. Robinson and Abbie Winam

ROLFE,
Gladys, d. 7/7/1988

ROLLINS,
son, d. 10/24/1916 at 0/0/3 in Orford; lack of vitality; b. Orford; Ella M. Rollins (Wentworth)
Alfred Henry, d. 8/14/1929 at 44/0/8 in St. Johnsbury, VT
Amy N., d. 9/4/1900 at 1/11 in Orford; ehcturo coteles; b. Orford; F. E. Rollins and Emma A. Sanders
Esther M., d. 2/11/1916 at 78/7/18 in Orford; chronic endocarditis; retired; widow; b. Rumney; Benjamin Brown and Mary Colby
Frank H., d. 8/8/1893 at 0/1/17 in Orford; pneumonia; b. Orford; Hiram B. Rollins (Rumney) and Addie Hammond
George E., d. 3/20/1908 at 21/2 in Orford; acute endocarditis; laborer; single; b. Orford; Fred E. Rollins (Campton) and Emma A. Saunders (Hanover)
Hiram B., d. 5/28/1919 at 55 in Warren; laborer; married; b. Orford; Moses J. Rollins (Ellsworth) and Esther Brown (Rumney)
John O., d. 5/--/1932 at 71/2/6 in Meredith; laborer; single; b. Orford; Moses Rollins (Ellsworth) and Esther M. ----- (Rumney)
Minnie E., d. 8/28/1903 at 0/1 in Orford; cholera infantum; b. Orford; W. A. Rollins (Orford) and Laura Durant (W. Newbury, VT)

ROOT,
Howard, d. 6/13/1920 at 22/11/9 in Orford; ins. solicitor; single; b. Rutland, VT; Edward L. Root (Norwich, VT) and Leona LeBoeuf (Montpelier, VT)

RUGG,
Amanda P., d. 11/5/1915 at 77/4/18 in Orford; apoplexy; housewife; widow; b. Thetford, VT; Stephen Ellis (Thetford, VT) and Abigail Newcomb (Thetford, VT)
Frank M., d. 11/6/1951 at 63 in Hartford, VT; carpenter; b. Fairlee, VT; Edward Rugg and Eliza Belville
Marshall E., d. 11/4/1927 at 94/6/18 in Orford; farmer; b. Thetford, VT; Edward Rugg and ----- Sawyer

RUSSELL,
Carlie P., d. 12/6/1913 at 26/11/27 in Orford; pulmonary tuberculosis; nurse; single; b. Orford; George N. Russell (Orford) and Eliza A. French (Brunswick)
Florence A., d. 3/6/1959 at 80 in Hanover

George N., d. 11/29/1931 at 77/8/27 in Concord; farmer; married; b. Orford; Nathan Russell (Pelham) and Persis Hancock (Montpelier, VT)

Nathaniel, d. 8/15/1889 at 78/6/13 in Orford; old age; farmer; married; b. Pelham; Nathaniel Russell and Mary Bradford (Pelham, MA)

Persis, d. 11/18/1895 at 81/4/23 in Orford; old age; housekeeper; b. Montpelier, VT; Joseph Hancock and Lidia Peck

RUTLEDGE,
Alfred, d. 12/12/1990 in Orford; Perley Rutledge and Violet Marden
Clarence R., d. 9/19/1896 at 0/3/13 in Orford; b. Orford; Charles W. Rutledge (Amherst, NS) and Mary A. Wilson (Greensboro, VT)

RYAN,
Edward P., d. 4/22/1956 at 75/9/4 in Concord; dentist; married; b. Muncie, IN; Wamper Ryan and Belle Rhea

Mabel C., d. 6/27/1971 at 81 in Fairhope, AL; housewife; b. Paris, TX; William Chapman and Nancy Cloud

SANBORN,
son, d. 5/24/1931 at – in Orford; b. Orford; Harry J. Sanborn (Rumney) and Lulu R. Blake (Plymouth)

Arlene B., d. 9/17/1973 at 71 in Orford; housewife; b. Strafford, VT; John Bacon and Blanche Swift

Asa O., d. 7/29/1931 at 72/5/15 in Haverhill; farmer; widower; b. Hanover; John Sanborn (Canada) and Martha Fitch (Hanover)

Asa Ray, d. 11/16/1934 at 45 in Hanover; salesman; married; b. Orford; Asa O. Sanborn (Etna) and Hattie E. Stone (Orford)

David, d. --/--/1989

Evelyn B., d. 3/8/1967 at 54 in Orford; housewife; b. Plymouth; Harry Blake and Elizabeth Hamilton

Flora Mabel, d. 2/14/1939 at 81/6/17 in Orford; housewife; married; b. Rumney; Unite K. Hutchins (Benton) and Joanna Sanborn

Fred J., d. 7/19/1953 at 73 in Hanover; married; b. Bradford, VT; Charles Sanborn and Abbie Chase

Harry J., d. 8/24/1964 at 79 in Orford; farmer; b. Rumney; Joseph Sanborn and Flora Hutchins

Hattie E., d. 9/30/1927 at 66/9/6 in Orford; housewife; married; b. Orford; Samuel Stone (Orford) and Martha Niles (Orford)

Hattie May, d. 3/23/1898 at 0/0/3 in Orford; hemorrhage of bowels;
 b. Orford; Asa O. Sanborn (Hanover) and Hattie E. Stone
 (Orford)
Helen B., d. 7/11/2001 in Orford; George Baker and Alice Franklin
Joseph, d. 4/4/1985 in Haverhill
Joseph Ovid, d. 4/23/1944 at 83/5/3 in Orford; farmer; widower; b.
 Ellsworth; Samuel Sanborn (Ellsworth)
Lulu R., d. 12/28/1966 at 78 in Orford; housewife; b. Orford; Francis
 Blake and Cora Heath
Robert B., Sr., d. 8/14/1965 at 56 in Haverhill; mill man; b. Bath;
 Harry J. Sanborn and Lulu Blake
Roy Stone, d. 7/7/1956 at 61/10/9 in Naples, FL; single; b. Orford;
 Asa O. Sanborn and Hattie E. Stone
Ruth F., d. 6/6/1934 at 23/0/26 in Orford; housewife; married; b.
 Orford; Arthur L. Franklin (Orford) and Marion Clark (Orford)

SANDERS,
Charles F., d. 9/5/1902 at 1/0/12 in Orford; cholera infantum; b.
 Orford; Harry G. Sanders (Orford) and Mary E. Willis (Piermont)
Nancy S., d. 9/27/1900 at 68/0/30 in Orford; dysentery; housewife;
 married; b. Danbury; John F. Eastman and Betsey Chandler

SANDERSON,
Ainslie, d. 11/26/1975 at 72 in Orford; housewife; b. NS; Arthur
 Smith and Susan Salsbury
Ronald, d. 5/9/1959 at 24 in Hanover

SARGENT,
Amelia W., d. 9/16/1927 at 83/0/22 in Orford; housewife; married; b.
 W. Fairlee, VT; Joseph Worthley (Bradford, VT) and Eliza
 Sanborn (Bradford, VT)
Collins Leavitt, d. 9/17/1950 at 69 in Orford; farmer; married; b.
 Norwich, VT; Hiram M. Sargent and Sarah A. Clark
Josiah Pearson, d. 3/14/1929 at 85/7/5 in Orfordville; farmer;
 widower; b. Candia; Josiah Sargent (NH) and Abigail Pearson
Lucius H., d. 5/22/1927 at 72/9/15 in Haverhill, MA; farmer; married;
 b. Orford; Robert B. Sargent (Orford) and Lydia Tucker
 (Newbury, VT)
Mary Ella, d. 12/12/1944 at 83/1/25 in Haverhill, MA; widow; b.
 Rumney; Joseph Spaulding (Rumney) and Mary Ordway (Turin,
 NY)

Richard R., d. 12/5/1975 at 37 in Burlington, VT; factory worker; b. Enfield; Ralph H. Sargent and Mabel Preston

Robert B., d. 7/9/1892 at 66/5/19 in Orford; abscess of brain; farmer; married; b. Orford; Bailey Sargent and Mary Bradford

Robert Edward, d. 9/6/1961 at 58 in Charlotte, NC; b. Orford; Lucius Sargent and Ella Spaulding

SAUNDERS,

Grace L., d. 3/9/1904 at 0/6/11 in Orford; b. Orford; Harry G. Saunders (Orford) and Nettie L. Mack (Piermont)

Harry G., d. 4/9/1909 at 43/0/2 in Orford; carpenter; married; b. Hanover; Sylvester Saunders (Wentworth) and Nancy Eastman (Danbury)

Sylvester J., d. 6/12/1906 at 78/2/12 in Orford; farmer; widower; b. Wentworth; Henry Saunders

SAVAGE,

Adeliza W., d. 5/8/1927 at 39/9/5 in Francestown; stenographer; single; b. Orford; Thomas Savage (Orford) and Ida Mack (Piermont)

Almira A., d. 1/12/1953 at 93 in Center Harbor; b. Orford; George Savage

Charles T., d. 6/18/1891 at 64/3/18 in Orford; farmer; married; b. Orford; George Savage (New Salem, MA) and Rebecca Adams

Ernest W., d. 6/11/1975 at 78 in Old Saybrook, CT

Ida R., d. 3/5/1944 at 81/8/3 in Henniker; retired; widow; b. Piermont; Ruel Savage and Grace Holmes

Mary H., d. 3/14/1921 at 71/9/14 in Woonsocket, RI; buried in Orford East Cem.

Thomas T., d. 1/2/1903 at 44 in Warren; heart disease; farmer; married; b. Orford; George Savage, 2nd (Orford) and Rosanna M. Merrill (Groton)

SAVERY,

Darrell, d. 8/12/1985 in Fairlee, VT

SAWYER,

Amos B., d. 12/25/1958 at 62/11/10 in Orford; salesman retired; b. Bradford, VT; Amos B. Sawyer and Nancy Avery

Menta, d. 3/27/1987

SCANLON,
Debbie A., d. 5/26/1998 in Haverhill; Lewis Horton and Susan Derosa
Sherwood A., d. 12/4/1998 in Lebanon; Sherwood Scanlon and Lorraine King

SCHANZE,
Emma, d. 6/29/1968 at 92 in Orford; housewife; b. Germany; Johann Steets and Charlotte Wilnet

SCHOELZEL,
Herman Walter, d. 11/8/1959 at 47 in Orford

SCHOFIELD,
Ernest H., d. 4/29/1958 at 66/5/10 in Shelburne, MA; woodcutter; widower; b. Everett, MA; Henry Schofield
Lois Marjorie, d. 5/11/1928 at 0/0/6 in Orford; b. Orford; Ernest Schofield (Everett, MA) and Gladys Johnston (NS)

SCHULTZ,
William, d. 11/18/1986

SCHULZ,
Elizabeth, d. 7/16/1982 in Orford; Bernhard Schanze and Anna -----

SCHWARZ,
Robert C., d. 5/21/2000 in Orford; Thomas Schwarz and Sophie Jhrig
Sophie, d. 11/21/2002 in Bradford, VT; Peter Ihrig and Freida Ihrig
Thomas, d. 11/13/1964 at 63 in Orford; farmer; b. Zurich, Switzerland; Anton Schwarz and Ann Huber

SCOTT,
daughter, d. 6/16/1908 at 0/0/1 in Orford; premature birth; b. Orford; Athol P. Scott (Windham) and Edith M. Heald (Lowell, MA)
Walter, d. 11/2/1896 at 57/6/12 in Orford; traveling salesman; married; b. Fort Ann, NY; Henry N. Scott (Hebron, NY) and Hannah Oatman (Hartford, NY)

SEARS,
Bessie E., d. 6/26/1896 at 16/6/13 in Orford; single; b. Middleton, VT; Dexter C. Sears (Governeur, NY) and Bettie O. Scott (Fort Ann, NY)
E. Charles, d. 9/16/1889 at 22/10/23 in Orford; drowning; laborer; single; b. Sparta, WI; Dexter C. Sears (NY) and Betty O. Scott (Fort Ann, NY)

SHALLOW,
Earle, d. 4/28/1970 at 71 in Haverhill; b. NH; Frank Shallow and Margaret Nadeau

SHATTUCK,
Madelyn, d. 7/5/1979 in Hanover; Sidney G. Judge and Martha Brown

SHAW,
Carl E., d. 9/22/1968 at 61 in Orford; merchant; b. Waterbury, CT; Ancil E. Shaw and Mary C. Hosmer

SHELDON,
Clarendia F., d. 3/23/1923 at 92/2/24 in Orford; none; widow; b. Orford; Isaac Fisk (Hill) and Mary Brown (Orford)
Levi G., d. 3/15/1904 at 68/2/11 in Orford; laborer; married; b. Orford; George A. Sheldon and Sarah N. Avery

SHEPARD,
Frank F., d. 2/1/1952 at 66 in Bradford, VT; carpenter; married; b. Moria, NY; Steve Shepard and Charlotte Wood

SHERBURN,
Harriet E., d. 10/9/1893 at 49/10/2 in Orford; paralysis; housewife; b. Plymouth; Asahel Blodgett (Groton) and Pricilla W. Webster
Luther P., d. 10/29/1911 at 81/5/5 in Orford; apoplexy; farmer; widower; b. Loudon; George W. Sherburn and Martha Yeaton

SHERIDAN,
Thomas P., d. 2/27/1936 at 74/5/7 in Whitefield; retired; widower; b. Lancaster; Thomas Sheridan and Flora Daneau

SHERRY,
Margaret S., d. 1/25/1971 at 74 in Fitchburg, MA
Nicholas J., d. 4/23/1952 at 58 in Hanover; plumber; married; b. Summit, NJ; Timothy Sherry and Anna Mooney

SHONIO,
Lillian Amelia, d. 7/4/1944 at 68 in Orford; housewife; married; b. Moretown, VT; Lorenzo Warren (Middlesex, VT) and Ellen M. Phelps (Swanton, VT)

SHORT,
Earl E., d. 11/27/1929 at 2/1/13 in Warren; b. Warren; George Short (Walpole) and Nellie Wright (Piermont)

SHUMWAY,
Carroll, d. 7/27/1978 at 74 in Hanover; carpenter; b. VT; Carroll Shumway and Mary Kider

SILVER,
Mary, d. 7/19/1889 at 75/9/5 in Orford; abdominal tumor; widow; b. Tuftonboro; Joseph Runnells

SIMONDS,
Roxana, d. 12/30/1904 at 82/11/22 in Orford; housewife; widow; b. Strafford, VT; Noah Roberts (Strafford, VT) and Mary Cam (Strafford, VT)

SIMONS,
Laura W., d. 11/30/1919 at 82/10 in Orford; domestic; widow; b. Orford; William Wilcox (Thetford, VT) and Elvira Downs (Thetford, VT)
Royal W., d. 1/24/1891 at 83/11 in Orford; farmer; married; b. Orford; Reuben Simons (Orford) and Theda Phelps
William W., d. 8/1/1924 at 59/1/10 in Hanover; farmer; single; b. Orford; Albert Simons (Orford) and Laura Wilcox (Orford)

SIMPSON,
Carl M., d. 7/5/1920 at 18/11/15 in Fairlee, VT; single; Herman L. Simpson (Orford) and Ella Hackett (Orford)
Dan Y., d. 11/21/1919 at 82/9/26 in Orford; retired; widower; b. Rumney; George Simpson and Polly Savage

Eliza, d. 12/4/1891 at 84/0/24 in Orford; domestic; widower; b. Hampton; Samuel Lamprey (Hampton) and Anna Johnson

Herman, d. 3/17/1926 at 65/9/11 in Haverhill; laborer; widower; b. Orford; John Simpson (Franklin) and Mary Brown (Rumney)

John B., d. 8/7/1898 at 71/9/21 in Orford; apoplexy; laborer; married; b. Boscawen; George Simpson and Mary Savage (Orford)

Margaret, d. 7/29/1903 at 30/11/23 in Orford; phthisis pulmonalis; housewife; married; b. Inverness, PQ; David McIntyre (PQ) and Agnes Lowe (PQ)

Martha A., d. 12/8/1891 at 53/4/6 in Orford; housewife; married; b. Plymouth; Asahel Blodgett (Plymouth) and Priscilla W. Webster

Mary, d. 10/10/1902 at 71/2/9 in Orford; apoplexy; housewife; widow; b. Rumney; Benjamin Brown and Mary Brown

Minnie I., d. 7/10/1945 at 80/0/15 in Orford; housewife; widow; b. Benton; John Savage (Orford) and Hulda Edmester (MA)

Roscoe Leslie, d. 5/17/1961 at 70/8/27 in Orford; laborer; married; b. Orford; Herman Simpson and Ella Hackett

SKINNER,
Harland C., d. 1/28/2000 in Show Low, AZ; Harris Skinner and Rose Brown

Harris F., d. 1/4/1961 at 76/9/2 in Cheyenne, WY; retired farmer; married; b. Lowell, VT; Galen Skinner and Ellen Cross

SLEEPER,
Mark, d. 6/17/1976 at 19 in Orford; bridge main.; b. NH; Harry Sleeper and Evelyn Rudd

SLIGHT,
M. Thomas, d. 8/24/1959 at 18 in Orford

SMITH,
daughter, d. 6/3/1898 at – in Orford; premature birth; b. Orford; Carl C. Smith (Windsor, VT) and Mary E. Mann (Orford)

Amelia, d. 10/20/1888 at 82/3/26 in Orford; housewife; widow; Richard Brown (England)

Bruce, d. 11/30/1961 at 24/10/26 in Haverhill; single; b. Fairlee, VT; George Smith and Leona Bailey

Carrol, d. 9/7/1955 at 79/0/16 in Waterbury, VT; single; b. Orford; Alphonso Smith and Clarinda Worthen

Chester, d. 1/3/1927 at 87/1/5 in Barre, VT; widower

Clarence E., d. 8/11/1890 at 36/5/27 in Orford; consumption; brick mason; married; b. Orford; Nelson Smith (Hartford, VT) and Eliza Riley (RI)

Clarence S., d. 4/29/1922 at 53/0/5 in Orford; laborer; married; b. Lyme; Alphonso Smith (Manchester) and Clar'a Worthen (Wentworth)

Clarinda F., d. 10/15/1896 at 47/4 in Orford; housewife; married; b. Orford; Ezekiel Worthen (Boscawen) and Rebecca Brown (Orford)

Ellen A., d. 7/13/1908 at 71/2 in Orford; obstruction of bowels; housewife; married; b. Thetford, VT; ----- Currier

Eva Archer, d. 3/14/1961 at 72/10/22 in Fairlee, VT; retired; b. Orford; Josiah H. Archer and Mary R. Hannaford

Geneva, d. 11/10/1966 at 52 in Thetford, VT; housewife

George, Sr., d. 12/19/1976 at 66 in Hanover; b. VT; George Smith and Nellie Patch

George C., d. 8/18/1887 at 1/0/12 in Orford; b. Calais, VT; Walter S. Smith (Calais, VT) and Flora B. Smith (Thetford, VT)

Hazen L., d. 4/6/1973 at 65 in Orford; painter; b. Quechee, VT; Lewis Smith and Eva Archer

Ina Malora, d. 11/9/1896 at 23/8/4 in Orford; domestic; single; b. Pittsfield, VT; John R. Smith (Orford) and Mary J. Perkins (Barnard, VT)

Joel, d. 5/15/1956 at 55/4/12 in Hanover; painter; married; b. Orford; Clarence Smith and Sarah Ann Archer

Juniata D., d. 8/28/1926 at 73/5/8 in Orford; housewife; b. Ellsworth, ME; Addison Dodge (Alden, ME) and Mary E. Garland (Ellsworth, ME)

Leona, d. 2/24/1985 in Bradford, VT

Luthur, d. 11/15/1924 at 85/7/11 in Orford; retired; b. Nashua; John Smith (Nashua) and Amelia Brown

Margaret A., d. 7/7/1903 at 32 in Orford; phthisis pulmonalis; domestic; single; b. Orford; Alphonso Smith (Manchester) and Clarinda Worthen (Wentworth)

Marion, d. 4/10/1960 at 47/2/19 in Barre, VT; housewife; married; b. Barnet, VT; John Nutter and Flora Cassidy

Mary Perkins, d. 5/27/1918 at 76/2/14 in Orford; retired; married; b. Barnard, VT; Gardner Perkins (Barnard, VT) and Mary A. Speare (Barnard, VT)

Mehitable R., d. 11/12/1905 at 97/3/29 in Orford; widow; b. Bath; Ebenezer Ricker and Betsy Hurd

Paul A., d. 11/11/1954 at 1/0/9 in Hanover; b. Woodsville; Guy Smith and Virginia Roberts
R. Mary, d. 10/18/1986
Roland W., d. 10/14/1920 at 35/9/26 in Orford; board sawyer; divorced; William B. Smith
Sarah Harriet, d. 6/4/1950 at 81 in Warren
Siltonia B., d. 1/22/2000 in Zephyrhills, FL; Jesse Shonio and Lillian Warren
Thomas Howard, d. 4/27/1958 at 69/5/14 in Lebanon; laborer; married; b. Canada; Charles Smith and Isabel Walker
Verne F., d. 1/24/1967 at 88 in Chardon, OH
Virginia R., d. 1/19/1994 in Lebanon; Maurice Roberts, Sr. and Clementine Richardson

SPAGNOLA,
Roy, d. 7/13/1990 in Orford; Louis Spagnola and Irene Semon

SPEAR,
Robert, d. 10/15/1983 in Orford; Lewis Spear and Edith Gardner

SPENCER,
Georgia, d. 8/27/1924 at 33 in Hanover; housewife; married; b. Orford; Josiah H. Archer (Orford) and Mary Hannaford (Orford)
Harold C., d. 5/29/1965 at 57 in Orford; st. hwy. dept.; b. Barrington; Harry Spencer and Bessie Chesley
James E., d. 9/24/1947 at 64/9/1 in Claremont; int. decorator; widower; b. Wolfville, NS

SPIESS,
Paul A., d. 5/7/1960 at 61/9/9 in Hanover; farmer; single; b. Buehr, Switzerland; Robert Spiess and Verena Kuang

SPOONER,
Henry S., d. 10/18/1909 at 47/8/4 in Orford; plumber; single; b. Barnard, VT; Sherman C. Spooner (Stockbridge, VT) and Mary J. Perkins (Barnard, VT)

STANLEY,
Hubbard S., d. 3/28/1919 at 82/1/13 in Orford; farmer; widower; b. Piermont; Jonathan Stanley (Amherst) and Azuboh Leonard (Piermont)

STANTON,
Harry E., d. 3/23/1903 at 10/1/15 in Orford; acute tuberculosis; b. Orford; John S. Stanton (Elizabeth, NJ) and Alice M. Gilbert (Burlington, VT)
John S., d. 4/25/1903 at 43 in Orford; pneumonia; laborer; married; b. Elizabeth, NJ

STEARNS,
child, d. 2/26/1963 at 14 hrs. in Hanover; b. Hanover; Eli R. Stearns and Ramona H. Ladeau

STETSON,
son, d. 5/21/1921 at 0/0/0 in Hanover; b. Hanover; Harry W. Stetson (Lyme) and Alice L. Greaves (Mapleville, RI)
Abbie J., d. 5/11/1891 at 28/10/28 in Orford; dressmaker; married; b. Orford; John S. Corliss (Stowe, VT) and Olive E. Cheney
Leroy, d. 1/17/1919 at 64/8/6 in Orford; farmer; married; b. Orford; Daniel Stetson and Mary Hooper
Luella W., d. 12/20/1920 at 73/5/1 in Orford; none; widow; b. Orford; Moses Williams (NH) and Elvira Simonds
Lydia D., d. 2/24/1907 at 78/2/14 in Orford; pneumonia; housewife; married; b. Orford; Adolphus Phelps and Hannah Whitcomb
Otis, d. 7/17/1917 at 81 in Orford; farm laborer; widower; b. Lyme; Amos Stetson and Sabina Wheeler
Rebecka D., d. 2/10/1903 at 61/1/17 in Orford; peritonitis; housewife; married; b. Haverhill; Amos Drown and Olive Crouch
William, d. 9/27/1910 at 71/5/25 in Orford; farmer; widower; b. Orford; William Stetson and Sarah Newell

STEVENS,
Alvah B., d. 7/23/1908 at 72/6 in Orford; chronic Bright's disease; farmer; widower; Charles J. Stevens and Mary Brock
Alvah M., d. 4/13/1943 at 82/8/30 in Newport; lumber dealer; married; b. Orford; Henry Stevens (Orford) and Sarah Dana (Orford)
Angie N., d. 4/6/1933 at 69/6/18 in Concord; housewife; married; b. Orford; John Lamprey (Orford) and Mary Eastman (Vershire, VT)
Bessie R., d. 7/9/1963 at 70 in Norwich, VT; housewife; b. New Fairfield, CT; Arthur Beers and Nellie Boughton

Charles J., d. 3/28/1888 at 81/8/23 in Orford; brick mason; widower; b. Piermont; Parker Stevens and Tabitha Davis

Dana E., d. 3/17/1966 at 75 in Norwich, VT; retired; b. Orford; Alvah Stevens and Angie Lamprey

Faith G., d. 4/8/1893 at 0/0/1 in Orford; marasmus; b. Orford; Alvah M. Stevens (Orford) and Angie N. Lamprey

Frances, d. 7/19/1945 at 51/7/12 in Hanover; housewife; married; b. Boston, MA; Francis Hall (Northfield, VT) and Clara Phelps (Orford)

Frank A., d. 8/12/1962 at 76/3/18 in Concord; farmer; married; b. Orford; Alvah M. Stevens and Angie N. Lamprey

Henry, d. 1/8/1895 at 65/11/2 in Orford; heart disease; farmer; b. Orford; Charles J. Stevens and Mary Brock

Wallace A., d. 12/21/1928 at 0/0/1 in Hanover; b. Hanover; Frank Alvah Stevens (Orford) and Evelyn K. Lufkin (Thetford, VT)

William J., d. 10/14/1958 at 74/7/11 in Hanover; retired eng.; married; b. Wilton Jct., IA; Edward G. Stevens and Josephine V. Nevitt

STICKNEY,
Jedediah, d. 4/7/1892 at 85/11/17 in Orford; apoplexy; farmer; widower; b. Orford; Nathan Stickney and H. Burkley

STILL,
Clara Rachel, d. 9/3/1917 at 53/11/24 in Fairlee, VT; married; buried West Cem.

Eugene L., d. 1/8/1928 at 71/11/17 in Fairlee, VT; retired

STOCKMAN,
Francis, d. 8/22/1978 at 33 in Orford; carpenter; b. Haverhill; Gerald Stockman and Lucille Thomson

STONE,
Leland, d. 9/11/1992 in Orford; George Stone and Hazel Barker

STRECKER,
William Fulton, d. 10/20/1957 at 43/2/8 in Orford; radio repair; married; b. Montreal, Canada; Charles Strecker and Daisy Fulton

STREETER,
Carl M., d. 6/17/1994 in Haverhill; Ray Streeter and Stella Cushing
Peter F., d. 6/5/1960 at 80/11 in Fairlee, VT; patrolman; married; b. Monroe; Wilfred Streeter and Amanda Raymond
Ray N., d. 4/16/1951 at 64 in Orford; carpenter; married; b. Lisbon; Roland Streeter and Hattie Decker
Sarah Anne, d. 7/28/1964 at 86 in Piermont; housewife; b. Orford; Josiah Archer and Mary Hannaford
Stella M., d. 9/17/1973 at 81 in Orford; housewife; b. McIndoes Falls, VT; George Cushing and Dora Proper

STRONG,
Charles, d. 1/23/1932 at 70/6 in Manchester; gate tender; widower; b. Orford; Ephraim B. Strong (Orford) and Amanda J. Page (Wentworth)
Emelia, d. 11/3/1890 at 66/7/15 in Orford; disease of spine; domestic; single; b. Orford; Ebenezer N. Strong (Orford) and Mira Bailey
Emily W., d. 7/14/1937 at 77/7/15 in Milwaukee, WI; ret. teacher; single; b. Orford; Ephram B. Strong (Orford) and Amanda ----- (Wentworth)
Ephraim B., d. 12/14/1894 at 75/3/14 in Orford; cerebral apop.; farmer; b. Orford; Ebenezer N. Strong (Orford) and Myra Biley
Lucinda, d. 3/23/1892 at 63/10/9 in Omaha, NE; heart disease; domestic; widow; b. Orford; Abijah Stone and Mehitable Gage

SUNBURY,
Helen Elizabeth, d. 1/10/1931 at – in Woodsville; b. Woodsville; Arthur Sunbury (Waterford, VT) and Bernice Howe (W. Hopkinton)

SUNDERHAUF,
Mildred C., d. 9/8/1994 in Lebanon; Lewis W. Coburn and Minnie Runnels
Milo, d. 4/1/2004 in Lanham, MD; Gunther Sunderhauf and Mildred Coburn

SWANSON,
Ellen, d. 9/10/1924 at 84/3/10 in Orford; none; widow; b. England; Horatio Snook (England) and Alice Giles (England)

Harry, d. 7/27/1934 at 47 in Hanover; real est. agent; single; b. New York, NY; Alexander Swanson (Scotland) and Ellen ----- (England)

SWETT,
Linda Kinney, d. 3/11/1939 at 91/9/13 in Orford; ret. housewife; widow; b. Plainfield, VT; A. H. Whittlesey (Plainfield, VT) and Nancy Kinney (Plainfield, VT)

TALLMAN,
Almon J., d. 9/9/1908 at 32/11/11 in Orford; diphtheria; laborer; single; b. Orford; James H. Tallman (Orford) and Ann E. Smith (Manchester)
Ann E., d. 12/5/1897 at 52 in Orford; housewife; married; Jonathan Smith
Charles C., d. 3/30/1889 at 49/7/19 in Orford; consumption; farmer; married; b. Orford; William Tallman (Lyme) and Philamelia Culver (Berlin, VT)
Emily J., d. 7/25/1907 at 67/7/15 in Orford; asthemia gravis; housewife; widow; b. Orford; ----- Bickford (Northfield) and Lucina Coburn (Orford)
Forest P., d. 4/30/1947 at 65/6/7 in Thetford, VT; laborer; widower; b. Orford; James H. Tallman (Orford) and Elizabeth Smith (Manchester)
Frank D., d. 4/8/1931 at 14/6/25 in Hanover; b. Orford; Forest P. Tallman (Orford) and Jennie B. Rhodes (Orford)
James H., d. 1/28/1927 at 85/3/23 in Orford; farmer; widower; b. Orford; William Tallman and Hahnah Culver (Lyme)
Jennie R., d. 12/28/1927 at 41/3/19 in Orford; housewife; married; b. Orford; Wilber Rhodes (Strafford, VT) and Emeline Simpson (Orford)
Jerry W., d. 4/18/1973 at 60 in Concord; b. Orford; Forrest P. Tallman and Jennie Rhodes
William C., d. 5/9/1904 at 35/9/12 in Orford; none; single; b. Orford; Charles C. Tallman (Orford) and Emily J. Bickford (Orford)

TARDIFF,
Davila, d. 12/6/1985 in Orford

TATHAM,
Donald A., d. 9/8/1996 in Lebanon; Arthur Tatham and Mary Brown

Virginia, d. 3/26/1986

TATTERSALL,
George E., d. 9/21/1924 at 77/11/21 in Lyme; laborer; married; b. England; Abram Tattersall (England)

TATTERSOLL,
Mary Helen, d. 10/27/1942 at 91/2/7 in Haverhill; widow; b. Plainfield

TAYLOR,
Elmer, d. --/--/1989
Hunter Alan, d. 12/6/2002 in Lebanon; Timothy Taylor and Jennifer Findley

TERRY,
Henry C., d. 5/27/1925 at 76/8/15 in Orford; farmer; married; b. Canada; William Terry (England) and Lucy DeGoosh (Canada)
Sarah P., d. 2/9/1932 at 87/8/23 in Orford; retired; widow; b. W. Fairlee, VT; ----- West

THAYER,
Gilbert M., d. 6/22/1935 at 58/5/4 in Orford; bookkeeper; married; Joseph S. Thayer (Concord, MA) and Jane Brown (NY)

THOMAS,
Daniel W., d. 7/9/1974 at 69 in Nevada City, MT; retired; b. Butte, MT; Daniel W. Thomas and Elizabeth Beck
May, d. 6/7/2004 in Haverhill, MA; Michele Falzone and Nicolina Castiglione

THOMPSON,
son, d. 3/25/1891 at – in Orford; b. Orford; Warner W. Thompson (Chicopee, MA) and Christina Collins
Christian C., d. 2/2/1901 at 38 in Orford; cancer of the brain; housewife; married; James Collins (Ireland)
Warner, d. 6/7/1936 at 44/0/13 in Orford; laborer; married; b. Orford; Warner Thompson (Goshen Mill Village) and Christina Collins (Chicopee, MA)

THOMSON,
Meldrim, Governor, d. 4/19/2001 in Orford; Meldrim Thomson and Marion Booth

TIBBETTS,
John, d. 7/28/1917 at 53/8/28 in Orford; farmer; divorced; b. Canada; George Tibbetts (Canada)

TILLOTSON,
Benjamin M., d. 1/17/1890 at 70/9/27 in White River Jct., VT; heart failure; married
Daniel, d. 9/7/1935 at 85/10/13 in Haverhill; laborer; widower; b. Orford; Daniel F. Tillotson (Orford) and Amanda Tillotson
Daniel F., d. 2/23/1888 at 74/1/3 in Orford; farmer; married; b. Orford; Daniel Tillotson (Orford) and Abigail B. Tillotson (Newbury, VT)
Daniel F., d. 5/26/1953 at 75 in Manchester; married; b. Orford; Daniel Tillotson and Della R. Gardner
Dilla R., d. 11/24/1887 at 38/10/14 in Orford; domestic; married; b. Lyme; Zachariah Gardner (Lyme) and Mary A. Robinson (Springfield)
L. G., d. 5/30/1893 at 63/8/25 in Orford; liver disease; domestic; b. Orford; Eben E. Woodbury and Eliza Seaver
Mary E., d. 11/3/1894 at 34/0/8 in Orford; tuberculosis; dressmaker; b. Orford; Charles H. Tillotson (Orford) and L. G. Woodbury
May, d. 5/10/1916 at 49/1/21 in St. Johnsbury, VT; cancer liver
Sarah Amanda, d. 7/2/1901 at 89 in Orford; old age; housewife; widow

TITUS,
Cora Cynthia C., d. 5/24/1940 at 57/0/12 in Lyme; housewife; married; b. Vershire, VT; George Church (Vershire, VT) and Sarah Aldrich (Vershire, VT)

TOBELMAN,
William T., d. 3/28/2002 in Lebanon; Gustave Tobelman and Helen Close

TOMES,
Vincent, d. 5/14/1985 in Haverhill

TRASK,
Frank, d. 6/12/1937 at 28/6/26 in Orford; laborer; married; b. NS; Oscar Trask (NS) and Dora Stanton (NS)
Leo Ernest, d. 11/3/1948 at 0/11/3 in Nashua; buried in Orford 11/3/1949

TRAVERSE,
Edward L., d. 8/17/1948 at 51 in Orford; laborer; single; b. Tinmouth, VT; John Traverse (Ireland) and Ida Van Gilder (Hartford, VT)

TROTT,
Nellie H., d. 3/11/1923 at 54/8/3 in Malden, MA

TRUSSELL,
infant, d. 1/22/1933 at – in Fairlee, VT; b. Fairlee, VT; Kenneth Trussell (Orford) and Margaret McMillan (W. Fairlee, VT)
Benjamin F., d. 3/5/1916 at 80/5/26 in Fairlee, VT; prostatic disease; carpenter, millwright; married; b. Orford; Benjamin Trussell (Hopkinton) and Aseneth English (Lyme)
Emma Adeline, d. 5/11/1930 at 88/0/22 in Fairlee, VT; housewife; widow; b. Orford; Nathaniel Russell (Pelham) and Persis Hancock (Montpelier, VT)
George F., d. 5/18/1934 at 60/0/1 in Fairlee, VT; mechanic; married; b. Orford; Benjamin F. Trussell (Orford) and Emma A. Russell (Orford)
Grace T., d. 2/2/1946 at 68/3/22 in Fairlee, VT; widow; b. Bristol
Kenneth, d. 9/20/1969 at 62 in Hanover; disabled; b. Orford; George Trussell and Grace Tilton

TUBBS,
Eliza Della, d. 6/29/1940 at 67/2/16 in Hanover; housewife; married; b. W. Newbury, VT; George McIndoe (W. Newbury, VT) and Cedelia E. Griswold (Griswold Mills, NY)

TUSBURY,
Bonnie, d. 12/7/1981 in Hanover; Herbert Wilkie and Lois Chapman

TUTTLE,
Elijah, d. 12/15/1888 at 85/1/2 in Orford; blacksmith; widower
Freeman H., Sr., d. 5/27/1994 in Lebanon

TYLER,
Donald Lewis, d. 6/22/1962 at 46/11/23 in Fairlee, VT; manager; married; b. Haverhill; Leon Tyler and Arlene Dow

ULTSCH,
John B., d. 3/17/1898 at – in Orford; cancer of throat; soap maker; married; b. Germany

VANDERBILT,
Beatrice F., d. 12/24/1974 at 67 in Orford; secretary; b. Staten Island, NY; Cornelius Vanderbilt and Beatrice Barlow

VEYSEY,
Duane, d. 5/29/1982 in Orford; Wilmot H. Veysey and Arlene B. Gould

VEZINA,
Leo, d. 4/4/1954 at 73/9/12 in Hanover; retired; married; b. Quebec City, Canada; Francis Vezina and Josephine Myazau
Mary, d. 10/22/1957 at 81/2/8 in Fairlee, VT; retired housewife; widow; b. Kindsey, Canada; Joseph Parker and Olive Bruce

VIETOR,
Edward W., d. 5/16/1936 at 84/8/10 in Orford; retired physician; widower; b. Newton, NY; Theodore Vietor (Germany) and Emily Fowler (NY)
Kate P., d. 2/10/1930 at 72 in Hanover; housewife; married; b. Orford; John H. Phelps (Orford) and Charlotte Hancock (Orford)

VILLAR,
Paul, d. 7/7/1990 in Hanover; Ralph Villar and Dora Velasque

VOGELMAN,
Clara, d. 5/31/1967 at 97 in Hanover; none; b. Sweden; Olaf Magnuson

VON DETTE,
Archie, d. 7/27/1977 at 87 in Hartford, VT; laborer; b. VT; Adolphas Von Dette and Louise Robideau
Josephine, d. 12/14/1985 in Orford

WADSWORTH,
Burton, d. --/--/1989

WALCOTT,
John T., d. 8/24/1915 at 75/5/18 in Orford; myocarditis; retired

WALDSMITH,
Edward, Jr., d. 6/16/1970 at 55 in Hanover; music arranger; b. MA; Edward Waldsmith, Sr. and Esther -----

WARD,
Henry, d. 1/25/1960 at 74/11 in Benton; retired; married; b. Baltic, CT; James E. Ward and Mary Jane Bacon
Mary A., d. 9/6/1965 at 84 in Haverhill; housewife; b. Bradford, VT; Albion C. Kidder and Martha Worthen

WARREN,
Edward W., d. 9/24/1961 at 83/1/14 in Hanover; retired broker; married; b. Boston, MA; George E. Warren and Anna Dennis
Gertrude V., d. 5/3/1966 at 83 in Haverhill; housewife; b. Hancock, VT; Clarence G. Vinton and Julia Wilson
Herbert E., d. 9/30/1966 at 80 in Hanover; ret. teacher; b. Fairlee, VT; Herbert Warren and Rose Pierce
Herbert P., d. 5/12/1927 at 72/0/29 in Arlington, MA; merchant; married; b. Wolcott, VT; Samuel Warren and Eliza Herrick (Randolph, VT)

WASHBURN,
Abram C., d. 12/1/1927 at 74/3/28 in Lexington, MA; contractor; married; b. Pomfret, VT; George Washburn (Pomfret, VT) and Lucy Hewett (Pomfret, VT)
Bernice H., d. 12/2/1948 at 53/0/7 in Orford; housewife; married; b. Orford; Walter S. Horton (Barnard, VT) and Mary Stone (Orford)
Emma F., d. 11/12/1923 at 66/9/7 in Orford; housewife; married; b. Orford; John Lovejoy (Orford) and Mary A. Lamphrey (Orford)
Frank E., d. 10/5/1926 at 79/3/25 in Orford; farmer; b. Granville, VT; George Washburn (Pomfret, VT) and Lucy Hewett (Pomfret, VT)
Gengia A., d. 8/28/1948 at 92 in Lexington, MA; retired; widow; b. Orford; Royal Beal (Lyme) and Josephine Johnson (Newbury, VT)

George, d. 8/23/1896 at 77/1/2 in Orford; farmer; married; b. Pomfret, VT; Nathan Washburn (Pomfret, VT) and Mary Bruce (Sharon, VT)

Harvey Lovejoy, d. 5/13/1970 at 78 in Hanover; farmer; Frank E. Washburn and Emma Lovejoy

Henry F., d. 1/17/1960 at 71/1/27 in Hanover; retired; single; b. Orfordville; Frank Washburn and Emma Lovejoy

Romanzo N., d. 3/22/1887 at 47/7/18 in Orford; bookkeeper; married; b. Natick, MA; David Washburn (Natick, MA) and Eliza J. Parker (Framingham, MA)

WATSON,
Melzar L., d. 1/11/1953 at 74 in Bellows Falls, VT; farmer; married; b. Franconia; Ai Watson

WEED,
Benjamin M., d. 7/2/1896 at 93/3/11 in Orford; farmer; widower

Benjamin M., d. 12/9/1928 at 90/11/2 in Haverhill; retired; widower; b. Orford; Benjamin M. Weed (Unity) and Mary Eames (Orford)

WEEKS,
Alvin B., d. 4/11/1960 at 74/1/25 in Orford; retired; married; b. Nottingham; George A. Weeks and Angie Turner

Charles A., d. 5/17/1960 at 52/5/20 in Orford; patrolman; married; b. Fairlee, VT; Alvin B. Weeks and Florence Hardy

Forrest W., d. 4/10/2003 in Orford; Alvin Weeks and Florence Hardy

George, d. 1/16/2001 in Floral City, FL; Elvin Weeks and Florence West

George F., d. 8/9/1932 at 44/9/24 in Thetford, VT; married

Nellie J., d. 6/30/1903 at 57/11/1 in Orford; acute peritonitis; housewife; married; b. Nashua; Edwin R. Reed (Westford, MA) and Lucy S. Farr (Gloucester, MA)

WEIBEL,
Eleanor C., d. 12/7/1980 in Hanover; Alyman Davis and Ida Clough

John, d. 5/9/1955 at 68/8/4 in Hanover; retired; married; b. Dracut, MA; Casper Weibel and Catherine Wehinger

WEST,
Edwin B., d. 1/21/1891 at 49/10/5 in Orford; farmer; married; b. Orford; Gilman West (Piermont) and Elmira Osborn

WESTGATE,
Kate, d. 9/22/1889 at 24/10/14 in Orford; heart failure; housewife; married; b. Piermont; Charles Tarbox (Piermont) and Mary Welch (Washington, VT)

WHEELER,
Abbie A., d. 4/24/1927 at 75/6/15 in Orford; housewife; married; b. Wethersfield, VT; Simeon Hastings and Mary Pennyman
Charles, d. 9/15/1896 at 57/6/8 in Orford; sawyer; single; b. Orford; D. P. Wheeler (Fairlee, VT) and Mary Ann Wheeler (Lincoln, MA)
Eliza J., d. 3/15/1896 at 68/0/17 in Orford; housewife; married; b. Hopkinton, MA; Daniel J. Coburn (Orford) and Eliza Knowlton (Hopkinton, MA)
Harriet F., d. 10/26/1900 at 61/10/20 in Orford; Bright's disease; widow
Sarah B., d. 5/3/1897 at 52/1/13 in Orford; domestic; single; b. Plainfield; N. M. Wheeler (RI) and Hannah Bean (Plainfield)
William Henry, d. 11/21/1929 at 88/1/23 in Orford; retired farmer; widower; b. Plainfield; Nathaniel Wheeler

WHITCHER,
John Wesley, d. 11/16/1919 at 21/4/8 in Orford; laborer; single; b. Wentworth; John W. Whitcher (Wentworth) and Agnes Merrill (W. Rumney)

WHITCOMB,
Aurelia, d. 10/21/1908 at 85/0/9 in Orford; bronchial pneumonia; housewife; widow; b. Orford; Horatio Roberts (Orford) and Sophronia Freeman
Jonathan, d. 1/10/1903 at 88/2/28 in Orford; old age; mechanic and carpenter; widower; b. Orford
R. E., d. 4/1/1892 at 73 in Bradford, VT; apoplexy; painter; married; b. Hartford, VT; Rufus Whitcomb and Martha Oliver

WHITE,
Ada L., d. 10/19/1928 at 60/11/27 in Orford; housewife; married; b. Lancaster; Moses Hibbard (Piermont) and Elizabeth Bickford (Orford)
Catriona, d. 6/26/2002 in Farmington, CT

Jeffrey Bryant, d. 2/1/1964 at 3 in Havre, MT; b. Kaiserslatern, Germany; Milton L. White and Barbara A. Huckins

Moses H., d. 12/20/1963 at 70 in Hanover; retired; b. Concord; Theodore H. White and Ada L. Hibbard

Myrtle E., d. 3/11/1899 at 0/0/1 in Orford; marasmus; b. Orford; Theodore H. White (laborer, Portsmouth) and Ada L. Hibbard (Lancaster)

Peter, d. 3/7/1906 at 85/9 in Orford; laborer; widower; b. Canada; Francis White (France) and Catherine Oakes (Canada)

Rebekah P. P., d. 10/26/1892 at 68/5/20 in Orford; strangulated hernia; housewife; married; b. Barnet, VT; Solomon Perce and Phoebe Parker

Theodore H., d. 7/11/1949 at 82/0/0 in Lisbon; carpenter; widower; b. Portsmouth

WHITMAN,

Caleb F., d. 11/6/1902 at 68/6/8 in Orford; valvular disease of heart; farmer; married; b. Orford; David Whitman (Lyme) and Rebecca G. Freeman (Orford)

Grace S., d. 12/11/1903 at 16/7/25 in Orford; general tuberculosis; single; b. Orford; John W. Cooledge (Benton) and Emma L. Whitman (Orford)

WILCOX,

Ada L., d. 8/7/1887 at 31 in Orford; married; b. Haverhill; Warren Mitchell and ----- Anderson

David, d. 2/25/1925 at 76/6/21 in W. Lebanon; retired; widower; b. Orford; William Wilcox (Thetford, VT) and Elvira Downer (Thetford, VT)

Dwight M., d. 6/14/1946 at 66/4/24 in Vancouver, BC; b. Orford; David Wilcox (Orford) and Ada Mitchell (Haverhill)

Eliza H., d. 8/30/1945 at 62/8/9 in Hanover; housewife; married; b. Orford; Walter S. Horton (S. Royalton, VT) and Mary Stone (Orford)

Harry Pratt, d. 1/25/1947 at 70/10/20 in Hanover; widower

Isabel G., d. 8/9/1917 at 66/6/10 in Hanover; housewife; married; b. Chester

Lillian Washburn, d. 9/22/1920 at 42/9/3 in Orford; housewife; married; b. Roxbury, MA; George Washburn (Gr'nvi'le, VT) and Franceria Mann (Orford)

William C., d. 2/25/1889 at 81/0/11 in Orford; old age; farmer; widower; b. Thetford, VT; David Wilcox

WILKIE,
Lois Chapman, d. 5/18/1926 at 31/4/17 in Lunenburg, VT; housewife; b. Orford; Perley Chapman (Tewksbury, MA) and Mary E. Willis (Warren)

WILLARD,
Ellen A., d. 8/28/1932 at 78/1/7 in Conway
Jean, d. 4/23/1951 at 92 in Jamaica Plain, NY
Mary, d. 5/11/1936 at 82/2/28 in Concord; retired; single; b. Brooklyn, NY; John S. Willard (Orford) and Mary Wilcox
Mary W., d. 7/15/1920 at 93/11/16 in Concord; retired; widow; b. Orford; Leonard Wilcox (New Braintree, MA) and Almira Morey (Orford)
Reginald P., d. 8/13/1910 at 1/1/13 in Orford; b. Bradford; George R. Willard (Brooklyn, NY) and Agnes L. Putney (Suncook)

WILLEY,
Charlie Bert, d. 1/1/1951 at 71 in Haverhill
Janet M., d. 10/13/1967 at 24 in Montreal, Canada; housewife; b. Orford; Glenn G. Marsh and Verna Hibbard
Rose I., d. 11/16/1975 at 65 in Lebanon; housewife; b. Orford; Henry G. Baker and Inez Smith
Wilson M., Jr., d. 11/22/2003 in Lebanon; Wilson M. Willey and Rose Baker
Wilson Marshal, d. 5/17/1995 in Hartford, VT; Harry Allen Willey and Amy Esther Morrell

WILLIAMS,
Cornelia, d. 1/19/1900 at 49/10/28 in Orford; pneumonia; housewife; married; b. Lyman; Lorenzo Williams (Bath) and Susan Scales
Elvira P., d. 3/9/1892 at 80/7/9 in Orford; old age; housewife; widow; b. Orford; Nathaniel Simonds
Frank S., d. 10/28/1955 at 84/9/1 in Concord; widower; b. N. Troy, VT; Simon Williams and Phoebe -----
Hezekiah S., d. 1/31/1893 at 77 in Orford; inanition; stonemason; b. Orford

James H., d. 11/18/1899 at 65/4/18 in Orford; bronchial consumption; soap maker; single; b. Orford; Moses Williams (Orford) and Elvira P. Simons

Mary M., d. 3/14/1963 at 90 in Orford; retired nurse; b. Jericho, VT; John McLaughlin and Catherine Leddy

Sarah L., d. 7/19/1942 at 76/3 in Hanover; housewife; married; b. Rockland, ME; Jonathan A. Low and ----- Achorn

WILLIS,

Clarence D., d. 6/11/1994 in Orford; Eugene Willis and Nellie Flanders

Daniel Shaw, d. 3/13/1916 at 83/7/2 in Orford; intest. impaction; farmer; widower; b. Mansfield, MA; Job Willis (MA) and Matilda Noyes (Warren)

Linwood, d. 1/17/1990 in Woodsville; Clarence Willis and May Rogers

Marcia, d. 8/12/1991 in Hanover; Lewis Simmons and Alice Smith

Miranda Hazelton, d. 7/26/1898 at 68/6/21 in Orford; abdominal tumor; housewife; married; b. Orford; James Hazelton (Chester) and Betsy McMurphy (Londonderry)

Nellie A., d. 11/3/1957 at 87/8/28 in Fairlee, VT; retired housewife; widow; b. Warren; Sylvester Flanders and Sarah Willey

Ruth May, d. 3/27/1979 in Orford; Harold H. Ibelle and Blanche Bates

WILSON,

Alfred E., d. 5/31/2004 in White River Jct., VT; George A. Wilson and Marie T. Machacek

Ella P., d. 3/26/1953 at 77 in Haverhill; retired; widow; b. Concord; Frederik E. French and Ella Carr

Florence L., d. 4/12/1957 at 83/5/2 in Lebanon; housewife; widow; b. Orford

George A., d. 12/20/1994 in Lebanon; George A. Wilson and Marie T. Machacek

George Aitken, d. 4/2/1959 at 69 in Orford; housewife; widow; b. Orford; John O. Carr and Mary E. Edwards

John Thomas, d. 3/13/1918 at 77/4/23 in Newport, RI; lawyer; married; b. Boston, MA; Andrew Wilson (Canada) and Sarah White (Watertown, MA)

Marie T., d. 11/22/1982 in Orford; Anton Machacek and Beatrice Kozlik

Mildred, d. 11/21/2001 in White River Jct., VT; Carl Andreason and Agnes Skrasted

Pleasantine C., d. 1/8/1938 at 90/9/21 in Orford; housewife; widow; b. Orford; Hartwell C. Cushman (Landaff) and Mary Ann Earl (Taunton, MA)

William Francis, d. 7/2/1941 at 56/7/16 in Brattleboro, VT; poultry raising; single; b. Winchester, MA; John Thomas Wilson (Cambridge, MA) and Pleasantine Cushman (Orford)

WINN,

Hannah E. Sargent, d. 3/8/1938 at 84/8/23 in Orford; ret. housewife; widow; b. Piermont

WOOD,

Charles Joseph, d. 6/21/1929 at 78/6/4 in Orford; farmer; married; b. Canada; Hazen Wood (Sherbrooke, PQ) and Eliza Porter (Waterloo, PQ)

WOODARD,

Kenneth, d. 9/24/1907 at 0/5/6 in Orford; inanition; b. Orford; Byron Woodard (Enosburg, VT) and Belle Coburn (Berkshire, VT)

WOODBURY,

John E., d. 4/28/1887 at 75/10/5 in Rockingham, VT

Lafayette, d. 7/12/1891 at 63/10/11 in Orford; farmer; widower; b. Orford; Ebenezer Woodbury (Portsmouth) and Eliza Seavey

WOODS,

Patience, d. 1/30/1944 at 101/11/8 in Haverhill; retired; widow; b. Troy, VT; Joseph Boardman (Canada) and Eliza Porter (France)

WOODWARD,

daughter, d. 11/13/1920 at 24 hr. in Hanover; b. Hanover; Norman Woodward (Orford) and Grace Lear (Sunapee)

Belle C., d. 6/27/1963 at 91 in Haverhill; housewife; b. E. Berkshire, VT; David Coburn and Lucy Smith

Byron N., d. 3/31/1942 at 69/9/3 in W. Los Angeles, CA; retired; married; b. Enosburg, VT; Norman Woodward (Highgate, VT) and Lucy Temple (Enosburg, VT)

Elton Carmi, d. 3/20/1971 at 66 in Orford; chauffeur; b. Lyme;
Herbert E. Woodward and Jennie C. Coburn
Emerson S., d. 3/7/1902 at 0/7/21 in Orford; pneumonia; b. Orford;
Byron N. Woodward (Enosburg, VT) and Belle Coburn
(Berkshire, VT)
Evelyn, d. 12/17/1948 at 61 in Allentown, PA; housewife; married; b.
Sharon, VT; George Burgess and Mary A. Bruce
Grace, d. 1/16/1988
Herbert Eugene, d. 11/23/1940 at 81/10/7 in Orford; farmer; married;
b. Montgomery, VT; Horatio Woodward (VT) and Sarah Temple
(VT)
Jennie C., d. 6/9/1945 at 83/6/1 in Orford; housewife; widow; b. E.
Berkshire, VT; David Coburn (E. Berkshire, VT) and Lucy Smith
(E. Berkshire, VT)
Norman C., d. 8/5/1987

WORKMAN,
Samuel Melvill, d. 3/20/1955 at 76/6/15 in Orford; caretaker; married;
b. Canaan, VT; Timothy Workman and Adelaid Thomas

WRIGHT,
Charles, d. 6/17/1920 at 2 ½ hrs. in Orford; b. Orford; Charles Wright
(Piermont) and Mildred Durick (Piermont)
Charles A., d. 1/10/1978 at 80 in Plymouth; mechanic; b. Piermont;
Tilden B. Wright and Mary Page
Clarence Kent, d. 1/1/1942 at 81/6/8 in Denver, CO; retired; married;
b. Orford; Parker Wright (Plymouth) and Susan M. Eaton
(Wentworth)
Cora Ann, d. 11/25/1916 at 51/4/3 in Orford; pul. tuberculosis;
housewife; married; b. Fairlee, VT; Ed. D. Carpent (Fairlee, VT)
and M. Donough (Montpelier, VT)
Frank Ren, d. 4/25/1944 at 83/8/23 in Orford; farmer; married; b.
Newport, VT; Charles Wright (St. Johnsbury, VT) and Harriet
Umpher (Burke, VT)
Louisa J., d. 3/4/1902 at 68/0/6 in Orford; Brights disease;
housewife; widow; b. Wentworth; Jesse Eaton (Wentworth) and
Ellinor Page (Wentworth)
Parker, d. 11/25/1898 at 78/6/19 in Orford; old age; farmer; married;
b. Dorchester; Wincol F. Wright (Nashua) and Lydia Polard
(Plymouth)

Sarah Margaret, d. 11/1/1901 at 1/9/9 in Orford; bronchial pneumonia; b. Orford; Clarence N. Wright (Orford) and Cora A. Carpenter (Fairlee, VT)

WYMAN,
Katherine M., d. 10/27/1911 at 68/7/17 in Orford; apoplexy; housewife; married; b. Orford; Henry Dayton (Orford) and Julia A. Whitcomb (Johnstown, NY)
Mathew Frederick, d. 3/21/1918 at 79 in Harrisburg, PA
Robert, d. 6/3/1997 in Lebanon; Joseph Wyman and Margaret -----

YOUNG,
son, d. 6/18/1952 at 7 ¼ hrs. in Hanover; b. Hanover; Leon F. Young and Winifred Butman
son, d. 2/14/1953 at 13 hrs., 7 mins. in Hanover; b. Hanover; Leon F. Young and Winifred Streeter
Leon F., d. 6/8/2001 in Lebanon; Leon Young and Louise Columbia
Ralph L., d. 8/20/1978 at 34 in Orford; laborer; b. NH; Stanley C. Young and Alice L. Moses
Winifred S., d. 10/11/1998 in Lebanon; ----- and Marion Streeter

PIERMONT BIRTHS

ADAMS,
Lorraine Barbara, b. 10/4/1945 in Haverhill; sixth; Harry Adams (farm laborer, E. Ryegate, VT) and Margaret Douse (Passumpsic, VT)
Merelyn J., b. 6/24/1933 in Piermont; second; Reynold Adams (laborer, Kingfield, ME) and Marie Lamontagne (Piermont, ME)

ALDRICH,
Sharon Marie, b. 4/2/1951 in Haverhill; first; Kenneth N. Aldrich (student, Whitefield) and Henrietta H. Noyes (Piermont)

AMES,
son, b. 12/10/1900 in Piermont; third; Asa E. Ames (farmer, 29, Orford) and Susie E. Robie (30, Piermont)
daughter, b. 9/9/1904 in Piermont; first; Samuel H. Ames (clerk in store, 32, Orford) and Maud E. Day (23, Jay, VT)
son, b. 9/16/1906 in Piermont; fifth; Arthur E. Ames (buttermaker, 35, Orford) and Ludell Underhill (36, Piermont)
Arthur M., b. 11/18/1905 in Piermont; second; Samuel Homer Ames (store clerk, 33, Orford) and Maud E. Day (25, Jay, VT)
Asa E., b. 5/1/1904 in Piermont; fourth; Arthur Ames (buttermaker, 33, Orford) and Ludella Underhill (34, Piermont)
Delma M., b. 1/21/1907 in Piermont; third; Samuel H. Ames (merchant, 35, Orford) and Maud Day (26, Jay, VT)
Eleanor L., b. 8/16/1916 in Piermont; fifth; Samuel H. Ames (post master, Orford) and Maud E. Day (Jay, VT)
Homer D., b. 11/19/1908 in Piermont; fourth; Samuel H. Ames (merchant, Orford) and Maud E. Day (Jay, VT)
Marion E., b. 5/20/1899 in Piermont; third; Arthur Ames (box maker, 30, Orford) and Ludella Underhill (29, Piermont)
Menta, b. 5/3/1895 in Piermont; first; Asa E. Ames (farmer, 24, Orford) and Susie E. Robie (25, Piermont)
Mildred, b. 3/15/1899 in Piermont; second; Asa A. Ames (farmer, 29, Orford) and Susie E. Robie (26, Piermont)

ANDROSS,
daughter, b. 3/25/1892 in Piermont; third; Thomas H. Andross (farmer, 36, Bradford, VT) and Belle Stetson (31, Orford)

ANSLEY,
Jason Pierce, b. 8/9/1965; Rufus Ansley and Rebecca A. Pierce

AREMBURG,
Eric Earl, b. 1/9/1959; Daniel Richard Aremburg and Shirley Louise George
Marie Ellen, b. 8/8/1948 in Haverhill; Earl W. Aremburg (farmer, Gilead, ME) and Bertha E. Frappier (Bradford Ctr., VT)

ARNOLD,
Douglas O., b. 9/5/1927 in Piermont; second; Elwin Arnold (farmer, Haverhill) and Gertrude Owens (Littleton)

ASTBURY,
Janet Edith, b. 8/20/1939 in Piermont; first; Earl Astbury (farm laborer, Vershire, VT) and Della Dunbar (Lyme)

ATKINS,
Lyndal Maurice, Jr., b. 11/22/1935 in Woodsville; first; Lyndal Maurice Atkins (truck driver, Hardwick, VT) and Ethel Wilson (Bradford, VT)

AVERY,
Danny Ray, b. 6/6/1971; Harold Avery and Linda M. Johnson
Ralph, b. 8/3/1908 in Piermont; first; Arthur Avery (laborer, Rumney) and Lottie Rollins (Orford)

BALCH,
Beverly Mae, b. 5/5/1934 in Piermont; first; Mason E. Balch (laborer, Lyme) and Bertha L. Hart (Canaan); residence - Lyme Ctr.

BARBER,
Tina Marie, b. 8/1/1976; Stuart B. Barber and Doris E. Hood

BARNES,
Alice Evangeline, b. 1/1/1967; Erva M. Barnes and Dorothy E. Armstrong
Erva Morgan, b. 12/29/1995; Evva Barnes and Katy Blaine
Medora Whitney, b. 12/14/1976; Charles C. Barnes and Lillian F. Barnes
Paul Erva, b. 2/19/1968; Erva M. Barnes and Dorothy E. Armstrong
Susan Ellen, b. 12/24/1974; Erva M. Barnes and Dorothy E. Armstrong

BARTLE,
Jonathan Robert, b. 5/31/1986; John Duane Bartle and Jenniffer Suzzette Winn

BATCHELDER,
Edith Grace, b. 8/26/1897 in Piermont; Harlow Batchelder (trader, 31, Rumney) and Hettie Lowell (23, Piermont)
Roland Francis, b. 2/20/1935 in Piermont; fifth; Nathaniel M. Batchelder (farmer, Plainfield, VT) and Ruth Vincent (E. Montpelier, VT)

BEAN,
Kathie Louise, b. 10/25/1955 in Haverhill; third; Malcolm C. Bean (farmer, Waltham, MA) and Theresa M. Bardsley (Waltham, MA)

BEARDSLEY,
Nadine A., b. 7/22/1949 in Haverhill; first; Carl E. Beardsley (laborer, Boston, MA) and Barbara A. Hackett (Hanover)

BEDFORD,
Arvilla M., b. 1/13/1909 in Piermont; first; Ernest Bedford (farmer, Wolcott, VT) and Grace L. Perkins (Hardwick, VT)

BEEBE,
Rebecca Suzanne, b. 9/4/1978; Martin S. Beebe and Donna L. Gehman

BEEDE,
Mildred I., b. 5/7/1905 in Piermont; fifth; Albert Beede (farmer, 33, Topsham, VT) and Lillian I. Heath (32, Worcester, NH)

BETZ,
Brandon Willis, b. 1/13/2002; Michael Betz and Jennifer Betz
Devyn Carol, b. 1/18/2003; Michael Betz and Jennifer Betz
Joseph Michael, b. 6/1/2000; Michael Betz and Jennifer Betz
Tori Jean, b. 1/18/2003; Michael Betz and Jennifer Betz

BISHOP,
Anne Marie, b. 7/1/1951 in Haverhill; fourth; Harold R. Bishop (mgr., A&P, Philmont, NY) and Maxine E. Morrill (Haverhill)

Frederick Moses, b. 10/21/1954 in Haverhill; sixth; Harold R. Bishop (A & P mgr., Mellenville, NY) and Maxine E. Morrill (Haverhill)
Janelle Marie, b. 10/20/1964; Ronald A. Bishop and Charlotte L. Bean
John Edward, b. 5/20/1958 in Haverhill; eighth; Harold R. Bishop (store manager, Philmont, NY) and Maxine E. Morrill (Piermont)
Thomas Allen, b. 8/13/1956 in Haverhill; seventh; Harold R. Bishop (chain store mgr., Philmont, NY) and Maxine E. Morrill (Piermont)

BIXBY,
David Vernon, b. 2/24/1946 in Haverhill; sixth; Vernon J. Bixby (farmer, Canada) and Gertrude M. Walls (Woburn, MA)
Grace Carol, b. 10/1/1941 in Piermont; fifth; Vernon J. Bixby (farmer, Alberta, Canada) and Gertrude M. Walls (Woburn, MA)

BLAIR,
son, b. 1/13/1903 in Piermont; first; Oliver Blair (laborer, 32, Larigmal, PQ) and Addie L. Curtis (41, Piermont)
Marie A., b. 8/26/1930 in Piermont; third; Herbert Blair (electrician, Piermont) and Marguerite Judkins (Manchester)
Raymond O., b. 8/7/1929 in Piermont; second; Herbert Blair (electrician, Piermont) and Marguerite Judkins (Manchester)
Richard Paul, b. 2/2/1928 in Piermont; first; Herbert Blair (electrician, Piermont) and Marguerite Judkins (Warren)

BLAISDELL,
Ethel G., b. 12/23/1908 in Piermont; third; Harry E. Blaisdell (farmer, Piermont) and Grace A. Dunkley (Haverhill)
Harold F., b. 2/27/1914 in Piermont; first; Fred D. Blaisdell (farmer, Piermont) and Della T. Clement (Campton)
Olive M., b. 7/22/1906 in Piermont; second; Harry E. Blaisdell (farmer, 33, Piermont) and Grace A. Dunkley (26, E. Haverhill)

BLANCHARD,
son, b. 5/28/1907 in Piermont; first; Raymond Blanchard (farmer, 24, Piermont) and Mabel F. Cushing (18, Newport)
Carol Irene, b. 12/14/1947 in Hanover; third; Ralph L. Blanchard (farmer, Watertown, CT) and Lina Abigail Dibble (Agawam, MA)

Clyde, b. 10/23/1925 in Piermont; sixth; Ray Blanchard (farmer, Piermont) and Mable Cushing (Newport, VT)
Heather Mary, b. 10/11/1998; Brian Wayne Blanchard and Linda Marie Bordelon
Richard Austin, b. 8/6/1946 in Hanover; second; Ralph L. Blanchard (farmer, Watertown, CT) and Lina A. Dibble (Agawam, MA)
William, b. 9/1/1950 in Haverhill; third; Carroll Blanchard, Jr. (farmer, White River Jct., VT) and Dorothy E. Bohn (Springfield, MA)

BOARDMAN,
daughter, b. 8/15/1902 in Piermont; first; George H. Boardman (farmer, 47, Swanton, VT) and Jennie L. Goodwin (27, Canada)

BONETT,
Daniel Raymond, b. 4/4/1919 in Piermont; second; Raymond C. Bonett (farmer, Piermont) and Cora A. Bowker (Piermont)
Elwin K., b. 7/29/1926 in Piermont; first; Raymond E. Bonett (mail carrier, Monroe) and Gladys K. Webster (Piermont)
Richard Delwin, b. 12/7/1962; Elwin K. Bonett and Charlotte M. Clement
Rosemary Kay, b. 6/18/1957 in Haverhill; second; Elwin K. Bonett (mill worker, Piermont) and Charlotte M. Clement (Lyngsboro, MA)

BOUTIN,
Kyle Adam, b. 10/31/1995; Adam Boutin and Dawn Stygles

BOWKER,
Lucy Maria, b. 1/2/1898 in Piermont; third; Francis P. Bowker (farmer, 34, Canada, PQ) and Dora M. Underhill (30, Piermont)

BOWLES,
Eda Lileth, b. 11/27/1899 in Piermont; second; Albert E. Bowles (farm laborer, 44, New Boston) and Vilona B. Aldridge (31, Livingston, MO)

BRADFORD,
Wallace A., b. 12/1/1911 in Piermont; first; Arthur Bradford (farmer, Montpelier, VT) and Gertrude Fales (Lowell, MA)

BRALEY,
daughter, b. 5/8/1897 in Piermont; Charles Lewis Braley (farmer, 22, Paris, France) and Etta Ama Batchelder (21, Stanstead, PQ)
son, b. 9/4/1898 in Piermont; second; Charles Louis Braley (farmer, 23, Paris, France) and Etta Batchelder (23, Canada)

BROOKS,
Harold Benjamin, b. 12/9/1942 in Hanover; eighth; Earl S. Brooks (farmer, Bradford, VT) and Bessie E. Dexter (Topsham, VT)
Marie Ann, b. 10/16/1938 in Haverhill; fifth; Carl S. Brooks (farmer, Bradford, VT) and Bessie Dexter (Topsham, VT)
Priscilla Jean, b. 12/30/1959; Olin Brooks, Jr. and Maxine E. Fulford
Tyler Edward, b. 8/9/1990; Rudolph Brooks, Jr. and Linda Varney

BROWN,
Florence Caroline, b. 3/7/1920 in Piermont; second; Edson Lane Brown (farmer, Ryegate, VT) and Daphana Daisy Smith (Hyde Park, VT); residence - N. Haverhill
Rachael Katherine, b. 4/12/1982; Charles Townsend Brown and Karen Joan Buchanan
Sarah Hutchinson, b. 8/24/1983; Charles Townsend Brown and Karen Joan Buchanan
William Eldridge, b. 5/11/1987; Charles Townsend Brown and Karen Buchanan

BURBANK,
daughter, b. 7/14/1895 in Piermont; first; D. Willard Burbank (farmer, Sandwich) and Minnie E. Stickeny (Lyman)

BUSH,
Matthew Philip, b. 8/11/1977; Philip W. Bush and Lorraine A. Riggs

CAMP,
daughter, b. 7/12/1897 in Piermont; Edward M. Camp (farmer, 32, Morristown, VT) and Martha Bowker (29, Canada)

CARLE,
David Willis, b. 12/25/1948 in Haverhill; first; Franklin G. Carle (farmer, Orford) and Lorraine H. Bates (Chelsea, VT)
Debra Ellen, b. 4/6/1953 in Haverhill; second; Franklin G. Carle (farmer, Orford) and Lorraine H. Bates (Chelsea, VT)

CARLIN,
Ratio J., b. 11/8/1904 in Piermont; third; William Carlin (laborer, 31, Newport, VT) and Hattie M. Gilmore (20, Bristol, RI)

CARMEN,
Helen Mabel, b. 5/21/1923 in Piermont; second; Royal Carmen (farmer, Boston, MA) and Beth Gorham (Lyndonville, VT)

CARTER,
Ashlee Dawn, b. 1/3/1986; Derrol Nathan Carter and Kristie Lane McClellan
Joshua Alan, b. 9/6/1982; Darrol Nathan Carter and Kristie Lane McClellan
Paul W., b. 2/4/1931 in Woodsville; first; Paul W. Carter (clerk, Concord) and Dorothy Howard (S. Barre, VT)

CASILE,
Gerolamo Carmen, b. 6/20/1971; Carmen Casile and Barbara A. Harrington

CASSADY,
Harley William, b. 2/15/1955 in Hanover; first; Henry Cassady (US Army, IN) and Dorothy L. Bixby (Wentworth)

CELLEY,
Eunice, b. 1/6/1899 in Piermont; second; Herbert V. Celley (carpenter, 46, Bridgewater, VT) and Stella L. Vergin (30, Piermont)
Lehman H., b. 6/5/1897 in Piermont; Herbert V. Celley (carpenter, 45, Bridgewater, VT) and Stella L. Virgin (29, Piermont)

CHANDLER,
Grace E., b. 8/16/1916 in Piermont; third; Jay Chandler (farmer, Piermont) and Lilla M. Smith (W. Fairlee, VT)
Kathleen A., b. 12/5/1914 in Piermont; second; Jay E. Chandler (farmer, Piermont) and Zilla M. Smith (W. Fairlee, VT)
Merrill E., b. 2/8/1912 in Piermont; first; Jay E. Chandler (farmer, Piermont) and Zilla M. Smith (W. Fairlee, VT)
Uri G., b. 12/4/1913 in Piermont; first; Lester Chandler (farmer, Piermont) and D. Daisy Tenney (Franklin Falls)

CHASE,
daughter, b. 12/29/1899 in Piermont; third; Walter E. Chase (farmer, 28, Wentworth) and Mary B. Smith (25, Orford)
daughter, b. 12/31/1900 in Piermont; fourth; Walter E. Chase (farmer, Wentworth) and Mary Smith (Orford)

CHAYER,
Clarice M., b. 3/7/1913 in Piermont; third; Lewis A. Chayer (farmer, Cambridge, VT) and Alice Mudgett (Haverhill)

CHENEY,
Cheryl Ann, b. 4/13/1953 in Haverhill; fourth; Irvin P. Cheney (mill laborer, S. Ryegate, VT) and Rita H. Horton (Piermont)
Russell Paul, b. 11/16/1945 in Haverhill; first; Irvin Cheney (farmer, S. Ryegate, VT) and Rita Horton (Piermont)
Wanda Jean, b. 7/14/1970; Wayne E. Cheney and Alta L. Lawn

CHILD[S],
daughter, b. 12/5/1895 in Piermont; second; Harlow N. Child (farmer, 35, W. Fairlee, VT) and Lawna A. Underhill (23, Piermont)
Edith E., b. 12/6/1894; first; Harlow N. Childs (farmer, W. Fairlee) and L. A. Underhill (Piermont)
Palmer H., b. 2/9/1907 in Piermont; fourth; Harlow N. Childs (farmer, 45, W. Fairlee, VT) and Louena A. Underhill (33, Piermont)
Ruth A., b. 6/8/1904 in Piermont; third; Harlow N. Childs (farmer, 43, W. Fairlee, VT) and Lovena A. Underhill (31, Piermont)

CLARK,
Adam Damien, b. 5/4/1985; Brian John Clark and Lisa Dawn French
Amanda Marie, b. 8/12/1988; Brian J. Clark and Lisa D. French

CLEAVES,
Aidan Fremont, b. 8/9/1995; Faunce L. Cleaves and Margaret E. Ritchie
Helen Larrabee, b. 12/23/1992; Faunce Cleaves and Margaret Ritchie
Ina Faunce, b. 8/13/1991; Faunce Cleaves and Margaret Ritchie

CLOUGH,
Duane Paul, b. 9/23/1966; Roy H. Clough and Louise J. Randall

Lisa Jean, b. 11/30/1967; Ray H. Clough and Louise J. Ramsdell

COLBY,
son, b. 3/5/1900 in Piermont; second; Henry G. Colby (farmer, 34, Topsham, VT) and Mertie M. Woods (26, Piermont)
Carol Ann, b. 6/21/1959; Jack Lyman Colby and Esther Rose Witham
Darlene Lois, b. 2/17/1964; Jack L. Colby and Esther R. Witham
Doris Ellen, b. 3/29/1929 in Piermont; second; Jerry Colby (laborer, Sutton, VT) and Daisy Cass (Newark, VT)
Ian Michael, b. 10/12/1974; Allen R. Colby and Jane P. Jesseman
Jack L., b. 4/17/1930 in Piermont; third; Jerry Colby (farmer, Sutton, VT) and Daisy Cass (Newark, VT)
Rachel Mae, b. 9/3/1961; Jack L. Colby and Esther R. Witham
Roger Lee, b. 7/5/1960; Jack L. Colby and Esther R. Witham

COLE,
Daniel James, b. 4/6/2004; James Cole and Stacey Cole

CONERY,
Alma B., b. 9/23/1931 in Piermont; third; Edward Connery (farmer, N. Wilbraham) and Marion E. Smith (Walden, VT)
Boyd Kenneth, b. 3/3/1936 in Piermont; sixth; Edward Conery (laborer, N. Wilbraham, MA) and Marion Smith (Walden, VT)
Edward Henry, b. 9/27/1937 in Piermont; seventh; Edward Conery (laborer, N. Wilbraham, MA) and Marion Smith (Walden, VT)
Edward Henry, Jr., b. 4/29/1946 in Woodsville; first; Edward H. Conery (state hgwy employee, N. Wilbraham, MA) and Carrie M. Smith (Plymouth)
Ewvia G., b. 3/21/1933 in Piermont; fourth; Edward Connery (farmer, N. Wilbraham, MA) and Marion E. Smith (Walden, VT)
James S., b. 4/27/1950 in Haverhill; second; Edward H. Conery (laborer, N. Wilbraham, MA) and Carrie M. Smith (Plymouth)
Leslie Harold, b. 3/6/1928 in Piermont; first; Edward H. Conery (laborer, N. Wilbraham, MA) and Marioro Smith (Walden, VT)
Lloyd E., b. 8/15/1930 in Piermont; second; Edward Conery (farmer, N. Wilbraham, MA) and Marion Smith (Walden, VT)
Marilyn N., b. 11/26/1934 in Piermont; fifth; Edward Conery (laborer, N. Wilbraham, MA) and Marion Smith (Walden, VT)

COOKMAN,
Don E., b. 10/31/1926 in Woodsville; second; Carl Cookman (farmer, Lyme Ridge, Canada) and Nellie Heath (Manchester)

COOKSOM,
George B., b. 5/27/1921 in Piermont; second; Charles Cookson (laborer, Warren) and Rosie M. Ball (Topsham, VT)

CORLISS,
son, b. 2/19/1900 in Piermont; seventh; Carns P. Corliss (farmer, 43, Newbury, VT) and Belle Andross (31, Piermont)
stillborn daughter, b. 9/18/1901 in Piermont; first; Silas J. Corliss (laborer, 33, Newbury, VT) and Agnes Campbell (28, Piermont)
daughter, b. 12/28/1901 in Piermont; eighth; Carns Corliss (butcher, 44) and Bell Andross (32, Piermont)
Jennie M., b. 3/11/1898 in Piermont; sixth; Carnes P. Corliss (butcher, 41, Newbury, VT) and Bell M. Andross (29, Piermont)
Marie Kay, b. 11/1/1967; John E. Corliss and Dorothy M. Wright
Marla Jean, b. 11/1/1967; John E. Corliss and Dorothy M. Wright
Marlene Jo, b. 11/1/1967; John E. Corliss and Dorothy M. Wright
Mona Mae, b. 12/5/1964; John E. Corliss and Dorothy M. Wright

COVERT,
Alyvia Edith, b. 8/11/1994; Harold Covert and Lisa Knapton
Etta Laurel, b. 10/26/1997; Harold Daniel Covert and Lisa Knapton
Joia Lynn, b. 2/19/2001; Harold Covert and Lisa Covert

CRAFT,
stillborn daughter, b. 11/24/1895 in Piermont; first; J. J. Craft (farmer, 29, Lowell, VT) and Mary A. Edwards (26, Lowell, VT)
son, b. 7/4/1899 in Piermont; fourth; Samuel A. Craft (farmer, 38, Lowell, MA) and Emily L. Edwards (37, Bakersfield, VT)

CRAFTS,
son, b. 3/19/1900 in Piermont; third; Warren E. Crafts (farmer, 31, Lowell, VT) and Osee B. Sleeper (29, Des Moines, IA)

CRAWFORD,
son, b. 5/10/1899 in Piermont; seventh; Charles O. Crawford (farmer, 34, Dalton) and Bertha Wilson (29, Chazy, NY)

CROSS,
Ernest C., b. 4/8/1894; ninth; Eugene M. Cross (farmer, Piermont) and Anna M. Howland (NY)

CROWELL,
Bryan Erik, b. 2/21/1974; James N. Crowell and Theresa I. Selepack

CROWLEY,
Timothy Patrick, b. 9/13/1971; William Crowley, Jr. and Patricia L. Richie

CUMMINGS,
Doris Millie, b. 11/3/1941 in Hanover; third; Leon O. R. Cummings (laborer, Thetford, VT) and Millie Y. French (Piermont)
Irene Millie, b. 5/4/1938 in Haverhill; stillborn; first; Leon Cummings (farmer, Thetford, VT) and Millie Y. French (Piermont)
Janet Millie, b. 7/13/1940 in Hanover; second; Leon O. Cummings (laborer, Thetford, VT) and Millie Y. French (Piermont)
Kenne Andrew, b. 11/2/1982; Andrew Scott Cummings and Julia Marie Jagger
Regis Asa, b. 9/19/1984; Andrew Scott Cummings and Julia Marie Jagger
Robert Fred, b. 7/27/1942 in Piermont; second; Bernard F. Cummings (creamery employee, Thetford, VT) and Vivian A. Potter (Whitefield, ME)

CURRY,
Meagan Hailey, b. 5/25/1998; Christopher Todd Curry and Sherry Lynn Ward

CUSHING,
stillborn son, b. 12/7/1898 in Piermont; seventh; George Cushing (farmer, 38, Derby, VT) and Dora Prosser (32, Highgate, VT)
son, b. 10/18/1902 in Piermont; tenth; George Cushing (farmer, 46, Holland, VT) and Dara Prossell (35, Highgate, VT)

CUSHMAN,
Joshua Franklin, b. 6/12/1919 in Piermont; third; George K. Cushman (laborer, Bradford, VT) and Eva May Colby (Lyndonville)

Lurlene V., b. 11/30/1917 in Piermont; second; George K. Cushman (laborer, Bradford, VT) and Eva Colby (Lyndonville, VT)

CUTLER,
son, b. 1/16/1900 in Piermont; second; Judson H. Cutler (farmer, 20, Stowe, VT) and Belle Preston (22, N. Duxbury, VT)
son, b. 8/2/1901 in Piermont; third; Judson H. Cuttler (farmer, 22, Stowe, VT) and Bell Preston (24, Duxbury, VT)

CUTTING,
daughter, b. 4/22/1900 in Piermont; first; Fred D. Cutting (farmer, 26, Benton) and Sadie D. Flanders (21, Warren)
Charles, b. 6/4/1904 in Piermont; second; Fred D. Cutting (farmer, 30, Benton) and Sadie Flanders (25, Warren)
June A., b. 1/11/1913 in Piermont; third; Fred D. Cutting (farmer, Benton) and Sadie Flanders (Warren)

DAHLFRED,
John Ellis, b. 9/15/1944 in Haverhill; first; Vincent R. Dahlfred (Lt., US Army, Concord) and Enid Howard (Piermont)

DALEY,
Marcella Jean, b. 3/9/1995; William V. Daley III and Elizabeth L. Bayne

DALY,
Jeremy Matthew, b. 4/26/1988; Steven F. Daly and Stephanie B. Gordon
Rachel Gia, b. 10/21/1985; Steven Francis Daly and Stephanie Beth Gordon

DARLING,
Claudia Marion, b. 11/20/1948 in Piermont; first; Wayne K. Darling (farmer, Vershire, VT) and Rose M. Callahan (Denver, CO); residence - Vershire, VT
Larry Clifford, b. 2/12/1940 in Hanover; third; Charles B. Darling (trucking, S. Ryegate, VT) and Nettie Mae Welch (Groton, VT)

DAVIDSON,
Cooper Michael, b. 3/12/2000; Christopher Davidson and Lori Davidson

Mark Christopher, b. 12/7/1993; Christopher M. Davidson and Dawn
    E. Sellinger
Scott James, b. 2/9/1973; Harry Davidson and June Godfrey

DAVIS,
Eric Frank, b. 11/14/1919 in Piermont; third; Floyd F. Davis (farmer,
    E. Charleston, VT) and Ida M. Moulton (NY City, NY)
Irene May, b. 1/28/1926 in Piermont; fourth; Floyd F. Davis (farmer,
    Charleston, VT) and Ida M. Moulton (New York City)
Rachel Anne, b. 5/2/1993; Brent G. Davis and Diane C. Hutchins
Wesley Arthur, b. 9/19/1989; David D. Davis and Christa A.
    Blanchard

DAY,
daughter, b. 12/2/1899 in Piermont; first; Ernest D. Day (farmer, 21,
    Troy, VT) and Luna M. Webster (18, Monroe)
daughter, b. 10/15/1902 in Piermont; second; Ernest D. Day (farmer,
    24, Troy, VT) and Luna M. Webster (21, Monroe)
daughter, b. 11/2/1902 in Piermont; first; George H. Day (farmer, 32,
    Topsham, VT) and Addie M. Green (23, Bradford, VT)
son, b. 8/7/1906 in Piermont; second; George H. Day (laborer, 35,
    Topsham, VT) and Addie M. Green (27, Bradford, VT)
George N., b. 7/9/1913 in Piermont; fourth; George H. Day (farmer,
    Topsham, VT) and Addie M. Green (Bradford, VT)
Martha D., b. 5/16/1908 in Piermont; third; George H. Day (laborer,
    Topsham, VT) and Addie M. Green (Bradford, VT)
Martin H., b. 6/24/1910 in Piermont; third; Ernest D. Day (laborer,
    Troy, VT) and Luna M. Webster (Monroe)
Martina, b. 7/4/1934 in Woodsville; first; Martin H. Day (farmer,
    Piermont) and Lurena Leavitt (W. Stewartstown)
Mildred, b. 10/16/1899 in Piermont; first; Oren Day (painter, 23,
    Troy, VT) and Gertrude Woods (20, Monroe)
Nancy, b. 10/6/1936 in Woodsville; second; Martin H. Day (farmer,
    Piermont) and Lurena Leavitt (W. Stewartstown)

DEARBORN,
Carolyn Elaine, b. 7/22/1941 in Woodsville; first; Howard S.
    Dearborn (mill worker, E. Haverhill) and Esther A. Winn
    (Piermont)
Henry Francis, b. 6/29/1940 in Hanover; second; Henry F. Dearborn
    (farmer, Pike) and Helen C. Stevens (Piermont)

Nancy Helen, b. 4/23/1937 in Hanover; first; Henry F. Dearborn (farmer, E. Haverhill) and Helen C. Stevens (Piermont)

DEBELOIS,
Nicholas Stanley, b. 12/21/1999; Richard Debelois and Helen Debelois

DELANEY,
Joshua Chase, b. 8/31/1997; William Delaney and Pamela Stevens

DENNIS,
daughter, b. 2/16/1891 in Piermont; second; George R. Dennis (farmer, Piermont) and Carrie F. Church
son, b. 5/24/1895 in Piermont; second; Byron H. Dennis (farmer, 26, Orford) and Eva May Spencer (21, Stratford)
daughter, b. 11/1/1901 in Piermont; fourth; Byron H. Dennis (farmer, 32, Orford) and Eva May Spencer (28, Stratford)
Menter, b. 5/14/1898 in Piermont; third; Byron H. Dennis (farmer, 29, Orford) and Eva May Spencer (24, Stratford)
Mildred E., b. 2/2/1904 in Piermont; sixth; Byron Dennis (farmer, 34, Orford) and Eva M. Spencer (31, Stratford)

DEPALO,
Marie Danielle, b. 1/27/1981; Joseph P. DePalo and Lorraine Fanelli
Michael Joseph, b. 11/3/1983; Joseph Peter DePalo and Lorraine Fanelli

DERRICK,
son, b. 8/20/1902 in Piermont; first; George Derrick (farmer, 29) and Lulu Rollins (19); residence - E. Piermont

DESSERT,
Cecelia Teresa, b. 8/10/1957 in Haverhill; fifth; Maurice A. Dessert (farm laborer, Lebanon) and Barbara S. Follansbee (Enfield)
Conrad Joseph, b. 4/29/1960; Maurice A. Dessert and Barbara S. Follansbee
Elise Irene, b. 2/7/1964; Maurice A. Dessert and Barbara S. Follansbee

DIGRAZIA,
Shara Lisa Angelica Drew, b. 9/7/1984; Donald Thomas DiGrazia and Wanda Hope Drew

DODGE,
Joseph Allen, b. 1/22/1984; Allen Parker Dodge and Karen Louise Inman

DREW,
Ralph Harris, b. 1/26/1952 in Haverhill; fourth; Ralph P. Drew (farmer, Glover, VT) and Thelma I. Peters (Lisbon)
Wanda Hope, b. 2/8/1949 in Haverhill; third; Ralph P. Drew (farmer, Glover, VT) and Thelma I. Peters (Lisbon)

DUBE,
Douglas Lawrence, b. 1/28/1987; Jeffrey P. Dube and Correna Leigh Underhill
Mark Thomas, b. 2/23/1989; Jeffrey P. Dube and Correna L. Underhill

DUFF,
son, b. 5/16/1910 in Piermont; fourth; Edward T. Duff (farmer, N. Monroe) and Maud M. Hyde (Stanstead, PQ)

DUNBAR,
Betty Ann, b. 7/7/1939 in Piermont; fourth; John R. Dunbar (farm laborer, Lyme) and Edith Billingham (Lyme)
Christopher White, b. 6/22/1981; Randy W. Dunbar and Barbara Jane Putnam
Erin Elizabeth, b. 5/23/1985; Randy White Dunbar and Barbara Jane Putnam

DYKE,
Joshua John, b. 12/7/1990; Tracy Dyke and Tammy Anderson

EASTMAN,
son, b. 6/29/1916 in Piermont; third; David F. Eastman (farmer, Corinth, VT) and Bertha M. Hartley (Bradford, VT)
Virginia May, b. 12/24/1940 in Piermont; third; Earl Eastman (laborer, Bradford, VT) and Irene Clark (Newbury, VT)

EDDY,
Kelly Ann, b. 8/28/1968; William P. Eddy and Jayne M. Welch

ELDER,
Benjamin Gath, b. 6/12/1975; Robert D. Elder and Helen M. Kendall
Mary Ruth Candace, b. 7/1/1972; Robert D. Elder and Helen M. Kendall

ELLSWORTH,
Arthur H., b. 2/17/1908 in Piermont; second; Ernest S. Ellsworth (farmer, Wentworth) and Bertha E. Winn (W. Fairlee, VT)
Ernest David, b. 6/2/1940 in Haverhill; second; Frank J. Ellsworth (farmer, Piermont) and Ethel M. Woodbury (Wells River, VT)
John Carl, b. 11/15/1938 in Haverhill; first; Arthur H. Ellsworth (carpenter, Piermont) and Gladys I. Locke (Lyman)
Leslie Everett, b. 2/22/1943 in Haverhill; third; Frank John Ellsworth (farmer, Piermont) and Ethel M. Woodbury (Wells River, VT)
Mary Ellen, b. 6/20/1938 in Haverhill; first; Frank J. Ellsworth (farmer, Piermont) and Ethel M. Woodbury (Wells River, VT)
Nellie Eda, b. 9/1/1941 in Woodsville; second; Arthur H. Ellsworth (laborer, Piermont) and Gladys I. Locke (Lyman)
Nellie F., b. 7/19/1914 in Piermont; third; Ernest J. Ellsworth (farmer, Wentworth) and Bertha E. Winn (W. Fairlee, VT)
Steven John, b. 6/6/1961; John E. Ellsworth and Ella E. Hurlbert

EMERSON,
Howard E., b. 7/6/1927 in Piermont; first; Frank Emerson (laborer, Bradford, VT) and Edith Blanchard (Orford); residence - Bradford, VT
Ruth May, b. 10/30/1929 in Piermont; second; Frank O. Emerson (laborer, Bradford, VT) and Edith Blanchard (Orford)

EMERY,
Bernice N., b. 10/19/1915 in Piermont; first; Fay S. Emery (farmer, Piermont) and Gladys Chesley (Lyme)
Christie Elizabeth, b. 5/–/1918 in Piermont; third; Fay S. Emery (farmer, Piermont) and Gladys C. Chesley (Lyme)
Erma Alice, b. 4/19/1917 in Lyme; second; Fay S. Emery (farmer, Piermont) and Gladys Chesley (Lyme)
Marjorie Ruth, b. 4/2/1923 in Piermont; fourth; Fay Emery (farmer, Piermont) and Gladys Chesley (Lyme)

Roger M., b. 4/12/1917 in Piermont; second; Frank S. Emery (farmer, Piermont) and Mary Horton (Orford)

Vilma Louise, b. 11/12/1919 in Piermont; fourth; Fay S. Emery (farmer, Piermont) and Gladys C. Chesley (Lyme)

ENO,

Jacob Ross, b. 8/25/1983; Ross William Eno and Rosemary Kay Bonett

EVANS,

son, b. 7/8/1892 in Piermont; sixth; Joseph O. Evans (farmer, 33, Piermont) and Josephene Celley (33, Waterbury, VT)

stillborn daughter, b. 8/15/1923 in Piermont; third; Arthur M. Evans (farmer, Piermont) and Jessie L. Robie (Piermont)

Christina, b. 2/3/1938 in Haverhill; fifth; William Evans (farmer, Manchester) and Elizabeth Carter (Wilmot)

Mark A., b. 3/15/1899 in Piermont; seventh; Joseph O. Evans (farmer, 40, Piermont) and Josephine E. Celley (40, Waterbury, VT)

Richard Freeman, b. 10/14/1921 in Piermont; second; Arthur M. Evans (farmer, Piermont) and Jessie L. Robie (Piermont)

Robert A., b. 4/11/1927 in Piermont; fourth; Arthur M. Evans (farmer, Piermont) and Jessie L. Robie (Piermont)

Ruth Mamie, b. 1/16/1920 in Piermont; first; Arthur M. Evans (creameryman, Piermont) and Jessie L. Robie (Piermont)

FADDEN,

daughter, b. 5/30/1932 in Piermont; second; Stanley Fadden (farmer, N. Thornton) and Edna Keith (Haverhill)

Allen Dural, b. 11/26/1936 in Woodsville; Donald S. Fadden (laborer, W. Thornton) and Frances Hartwell (Piermont)

Althea Mary, b. 5/24/1944 in Haverhill; second; Robert E. Fadden (farmer, Thornton) and Priscilla M. Horton (Piermont)

Beverly L., b. 5/18/1927 in Piermont; ninth; Dana Fadden (farmer, Thornton) and Esther Downing (W. Thornton)

Cicilia Ann, b. 5/25/1976; Ronald B. Fadden and Sharon A. Miller

Deborah Elaine, b. 10/28/1953 in Haverhill; fourth; Donald S. Fadden (grader operator, W. Thornton) and Frances M. Hartwell (Piermont)

Donna Esther, b. 7/11/1947 in Woodsville; third; Donald S. Faddem
    (state hgwy employee, W. Thornton) and Frances M. Hartwell (Piermon
Joyce Linda, b. 3/13/1949 in Haverhill; second; Edward Fadden
    (farmer, W. Thornton) and Lois H. Bean (Orford)
Lawrence Dexter, b. 1/4/1943 in Haverhill; first; Robert E. Fadden
    (farmer, W. Thornton) and Priscilla Mae Horton (Piermont)
Patricia M., b. 8/25/1939 in Haverhill; second; Donald Fadden
    (laborer, Piermont) and Francese Hartwell (Piermont)
Ronald Bruce, b. 5/31/1952 in Haverhill; third; Edward Fadden
    (farmer, W. Thornton) and Louise H. Bean (Orford)
Stanley F., Jr., b. 10/19/1933 in N. Haverhill; third; Stanley F.
    Fadden (farmer, NH) and Edna Marion Keith (NH)
Stanton Wayne, b. 2/25/1946 in Haverhill; first; Edward Fadden
    (farmer, W. Thornton) and Lois H. Bean (Orford)

FAGNANT,
Janet Louise, b. 10/20/1943 in Piermont; fifth; Alcide Fagnant
    (farmer, Montreal, Canada) and Laurette Paquette (St. Brigide,
    Canada)
John Edward, b. 10/26/1946 in Haverhill; sixth; Alcide G. Fagnant
    (farmer, Montreal, Canada) and Laurette Paquette (Ste.
    Brigide, Canada)
Joseph Louis L., b. 4/25/1937 in Ashland; third; Alcide G. Fagnant
    (truck driver, Montreal, PQ) and Laurette A. Paquette (St.
    Brigide, Canada)
Marie Rachel, b. 3/4/1941 in Piermont; fourth; Alcide Fagnant
    (farmer, Montreal, PQ) and Laurette Pauquette (St. Bridgette,
    Canada)

FEARON,
Christina Louise, b. 5/11/1967; Wayne D. Fearon and Roberta A.
    Granger
Glenn David, b. 1/8/1969; Wayne Fearon and Roberta Ann Granger

FELCH,
Loula May, b. 9/12/1918 in Piermont; first; Allen D. Felch (farmer,
    Morgan, VT) and Bertha M. Cookman (S. Durham, ME)

FELLOWS,
daughter, b. 9/9/1899 in Piermont; second; Charles O. Fellows (carpenter, 33, Dorchester) and Ina B. Simpson (33, Piermont)

FENOFF,
Roberta Lee, b. 8/28/1954 in Haverhill; third; Bertram C. Fenoff (farmer, E. Thetford, VT) and Barbara A. Wheeler (E. Ryegate, VT)

FIELDS,
Katherine Lynn, b. 5/27/1990; Dale Fields and Patricia Van Ells

FITZGERALD,
Hazel Martha, b. 4/25/1919 in Piermont; fifth; Ernest E. Fitzgerald (farmer, Derry) and Hazel Marshall (Lyme)

FITZSIMMONS,
Faith, b. 5/22/1934 in Malden, MA; first; John P. Fitzsimmons (minister, Newport, RI) and Maisie M. Manuel (Campbellton, NF)

FLANDERS,
son, b. 10/15/1901 in Piermont; sixth; Rufus E. Flanders (farmer, 35, Warren) and Martha Moody (27, N. Benton)

FOOTE,
Charles Avery, b. 3/30/1948 in Lebanon; first; Claude R. Foote (mill worker, Piermont) and Leona Irene Page (Thetford, VT)
Claude A. R., b. 2/14/1917 in Piermont; first; Everett H. Foote (farmer, Warren) and Edna M. Robie (Piermont); residence - Warren
Everett John, b. 12/23/1921 in Piermont; second; Charles E. Foote (farmer, Webster) and Eunice M. Patten (Webster)
Floyd John, b. 3/8/1919 in Piermont; third; Leslie M. Foote (farmer, Warren) and Effie M. Foote (Orford)
Jeanne Irene, b. 3/4/1951 in Lebanon; second; Claude R. Foote (lumberman, Piermont) and Leona I. Paige (Thetford, VT)

FORD,
Sue Ann, b. 5/23/1960; George M. Ford and Sylvia J. Boardman

FRENCH,
son, b. 12/12/1900 in Piermont; fifth; Herbert H. French (laborer, Warren) and Eva M. Whitman (Canada, PQ)
daughter, b. 9/5/1902 in Piermont; second; Charles B. French (farmer, 30, Warren) and Mabel Molway (25, Piermont)
daughter, b. 8/1/1911 in Piermont; second; Lewis G. French (farmer, Orford) and Josephine M. Everett (Haverhill)
Brenda Susan, b. 8/11/1951 in Haverhill; third; Ancil G. French (merchant, Beverly, MA) and Juanita G. Maxwell (Bradford, VT)
Carmen Lee, b. 4/10/1975; William C. French and Nancy H. Lund
Chester L., b. 8/14/1913 in Piermont; third; Lewis G. French (farmer, Orford) and Josephine Everett (Haverhill)
Constance Alice, b. 10/19/1922 in Piermont; first; Raymond P. French (jeweler, Norwich, CT) and Eunice Dricilla Celley (Piermont)
Edward W., b. 4/21/1916 in Piermont; fourth; Louis G. French (farmer, Orford) and Sophronia M. Everett (Haverhill)
Edward William, Jr., b. 3/22/1940 in Hanover; first; Edward W. French (laborer, Piermont) and Grace Belle Bean (Orford)
James Edward, b. 10/23/1942 in Orford; second; Edward W. French (farm laborer, Piermont) and Grace Belle Bean (Orford)
James Eric, b. 2/27/1964; James E. French and Bonnie L. Colby
Kelly Jean, b. 8/13/1972; Ronald L. French and Jeannine V. Beaupre
Marion Shirley, b. 12/12/1947 in Woodsville; third; Edward W. French (woodsman, Piermont) and Grace Bean (Orford)
Millie Yvonne, b. 6/17/1918 in Piermont; fifth; Lewis G. French (farmer, Orford) and Josie M. Everett (Haverhill)
Ronald Lewis, b. 12/3/1951 in Hanover; fourth; Edward W. French (lumberman, Piermont) and Grace B. Bean (Orford)
Sarah Leigh, b. 3/25/1967; James E. French and Bonnie L. Colby

FULLER,
Jean Marie, b. 2/12/1946 in Lyme; third; William A. Fuller (truck driver, Wheelock, VT) and Martha C. Chase (Hillsboro)

GAMSBY,
Curtis Leon, b. 11/25/1937 in Woodsville; first; Leon Gamsby (farmer, Lenoxville, PQ) and Violet E. Smith (Coaticook, PQ)
Daisy I., b. 5/28/1928 in Piermont; second; Walter Gamsby (laborer, Duddsville, Canada) and Flossie Smith (Coaticook, Canada)

Otis George, b. 1/1/1943 in Haverhill; second; Leon P. Gamsby (farmer, Sherbrooke, PQ) and Violet Estella Smith (Coaticook, PQ)

Shirley A., b. 5/25/1925 in Piermont; first; Walter Gamsby (farmer, Canada) and Flossie A. Smith (Coaticook, PQ)

GARDNER,
Heidi Lea, b. 4/3/1958 in Hanover; eighth; Harold Gardner, Sr. (maintenance man, Orfordville) and Sophrania Emerson (Topsham, VT)

Stephen Allen, b. 12/31/1952 in Warren; seventh; Harold H. Gardner (farmer, NH) and Sophronia Emerson (VT)

GARRIGAN,
John William, b. 6/9/1988; Brian J. Garrigan and Karen A. Salois

GAUDETTE,
Dylan Scott, b. 1/5/1996; Jeffrey S. Gaudette and Katherine I. Outille

Noah Peter, b. 4/12/1998; Jeffrey S. Gaudette and Katherine Irene Dutille

GAULT,
Ula M., b. 2/12/1917 in Piermont; eighth; George F. Gault (farmer, Salmon Falls) and Eva M. Bagley (Sandwich); residence - Sandwich

GAUTHIER,
Jean Marie, b. 9/3/1934 in Piermont; second; Frank Gauthier (mechanic, Lebanon) and Grace Bailey (Claremont)

June Delores, b. 6/4/1933 in Piermont; first; Frank Gauthier (laborer, Lebanon) and Grace Braley (Claremont)

GENOSESE,
Mariorio Sinfosa, b. 2/10/1928 in Piermont; third; Pasquale Genosese (farmer, Italy) and Elizabeth Tarella (Worcester, MA)

GEORGE,
Gerald, b. 8/22/1936 in Piermont; third; Walter George (laborer) and Ruth Wilson (Manchester); residence - Manchester

GERMAIN,
Frederick Jay, Jr., b. 3/25/1965; Frederick Jay Germain, Sr. and
   Virginia A. Thurston

GILBERT,
son, b. 7/26/1902 in Piermont; first; John Gilbert (barber, 42, Rouses
   Point, NY) and Georgianna Hubbard (22, Stratford)

GILSON,
George W., b. 9/17/1912 in Piermont; third; Herbert H. Gilson
   (farmer, Royalston, MA) and Elizabeth L. Johnson (Newbury,
   VT)
Herbert H., b. 5/5/1914 in Piermont; fourth; Bert Hayes (farmer,
   Royalston, MA) and Elizabeth Johnson (Newbury, VT)

GOLFMAN,
Miron, b. 2/6/1993; Michael J. Golfman and Svetlana Grabovskaya

GOODRICH,
Russel L., b. 9/12/1938 in Haverhill; first; Clarence Goodrich (farmer,
   Bath) and Lillian Harris (Ctr. Haverhill)

GOODWIN,
son, b. –/–/1895 in Piermont; first; Lulu Goodwin
son, b. 4/18/1899 in Piermont; third; John M. Goodwin (butter
   maker, 41, Boston, MA) and Cora A. Abbott (35, Newbury, VT)
Mary E., b. 7/1/1894; tenth; John W. Goodwin (farmer, Warren) and
   Lizzie Hutton (Bath)

GOULD,
daughter, b. 12/25/1899 in Piermont; fifth; Amons Gould (farmer, 42,
   NB) and Charity Stevens (27, NB)
Alison Elizabeth, b. 3/7/1973; H. Russell Gould and Shirley Litchfield
Althea J., b. 10/21/1912 in Piermont; first; Leon R. Gould (farmer,
   Colebrook) and Clara R. Buzzell (Stewartstown)
Gabrielle Rae, b. 12/18/1987; Harry Russell Gould, Jr. and Linda
   Bonnett
Gordon M., b. 3/4/1910 in Piermont; third; William W. Gould (farmer,
   Colebrook) and Carrie Kenney (Canada)
Harry R., Jr., b. 10/19/1931 in Hanover; fourth; Harry R. Gould
   (merchant, Piermont) and Florence E. Craig (Middletown, CT)

Harry Russell, IV, b. 5/2/1957 in Hanover; first; Harry R. Gould, III (store partnership, Hanover) and Shirley Litchfield (Farmington, ME)

Helen Rena, b. 10/10/1920 in Piermont; second; Harry R. Gould (farmer, Piermont) and Eva Thomas Craig (Middletown, CT)

Hildegarde, b. 5/3/1917 in Piermont; second; Leon R. Gould (farmer, Colebrook) and Clara R. Buzzell (Crossbury, PQ)

Leslie Lynn, b. 8/27/1958 in Hanover; second; Harry R. Gould (merchant, Hanover) and Shirley E. Litchfield (Farmington, ME)

Marion F., b. 6/29/1925 in Piermont; third; Harry Gould (merchant, Piermont) and Florence Craig (Middletown, CT)

Stella May, b. 8/12/1919 in Piermont; third; Walter H. Gould (lumberman, Colebrook) and Sarah Chamberlain (Stewartstown)

GOVETOWN,

Paul Allen, b. 11/30/1919 in Piermont; stillborn; first; Hooper R. Govetown (clergyman, Marblehead, MA) and Elsie Rosco (Beaver Harbor)

GRAY,

Adreana Carmel, b. 7/11/1988; Daren H. Gray and Joanne P. Hardy

Gabrielle Jasmin, b. 1/18/1993; Daren H. Gray and Joanne P. Hardy

Michaela Anne, b. 1/5/1945 in Hanover; third; Douglas Gray (pulp cutter, Danville, VT) and Noreen Young (Arlington, MA)

GREEN,

James Howard, b. 10/25/1947 in Woodsville; fourth; Erving H. Green (laborer, Randolph, VT) and Myrtle H. Cushman (Woodsville)

GREGG,

son, b. 10/28/1946 in Piermont; thirteenth; Hazel Irene Chase (Penacook)

GUNETTE,

Mary Pauline, b. 6/16/1937 in Piermont; first; Joseph H. Gunette (lumberman, Troy, VT) and Mary D. Robillard (Troy, VT)

HACKETT,

son, b. 9/8/1909 in Piermont; second; Harley C. Hackett (laborer, Orford) and Jeanne Everson (Melrose, MA)

Arlene Elaine, b. 5/15/1945 in Haverhill; second; Warren Hackett (US Army, Piermont) and Harriet Carter (Danville, VT)
Barbara A., b. 5/24/1930 in Hanover; thirteenth; Harley Hackett (farmer, Orford) and Joanne Everson (Melrose, MA)
Charles Donald, b. 1/3/1922 in Piermont; ninth; Harley C. Hackett (laborer, Orford) and Jeanie ----- (Melrose, MA)
Clarence, b. 2/19/1913 in Piermont; fourth; Harley C. Hackett (farmer, Orfordville) and Jeanne Everson (Melrose, MA)
David H., b. 2/21/1911 in Piermont; third; Harley C. Hackett (farmer, Orfordville) and Jennie E. Everson (Melrose, MA)
Dorothy L., b. 5/17/1914 in Piermont; fifth; Harley C. Hackett (laborer, Orford) and Jeanne E. Everson (Melrose, MA)
Earlwin Theodore, b. 8/6/1942 in Piermont; first; Warren T. Hackett (farm laborer, Piermont) and Harriet E. Carter (Danville, VT)
Evelyn, b. 5/5/1933 in Hanover; fourteenth; Harley Hackett (road agent, Orford) and Jeanne Emerson (Melrose, MA)
Harry H., b. 5/23/1920 in Haverhill; eighth; Harley Hackett (laborer, Orford) and Etta J. Everson (Melrose, MA)
Helen J., b. 4/29/1915 in Piermont; sixth; Harley C. Hackett (laborer, Orford) and Jeanne E. Everson (Melrose, MA)
Loraine, b. 2/19/1950 in Haverhill; third; Warren T. Hackett (farmer, Piermont) and Harriet E. Carter (Danville, VT)
Richard Jilson, b. 9/23/1918 in Piermont; seventh; Harley C. Hackett (laborer, Orford) and Jennie Etta Everson (Melrose, MA)
Warren T., b. 8/10/1923 in Piermont; tenth; Harley Hackett (laborer, Orfordville) and Jeanne Everson (Melrose, MA)
Winfield, b. 7/12/1925 in Piermont; eleventh; Harley Hackett (laborer, Orfordville) and Jeanne Emerson (Melrose, MA)

HALL,
Andrew David, b. 9/21/1983; Michael Howard Hall and Betsey Emily Eaton
Thomas Michael, b. 12/1/1980; Michael H. Hall and Betsy E. Eaton

HAMILTON,
Babett Hazel, b. 11/2/1946 in Piermont; eighth; James L. Hamilton (planer oper., Craftsbury, VT) and Mary H. Brooks (Littleton)

HANKS,
daughter, b. 4/2/1900 in Piermont; fourth; John M. Hanks (farmer, 36, Canada, PQ) and Lillian Hanks (26, Jay, VT)

Ethel M., b. 10/8/1903 in Piermont; sixth; John M. Hanks (farmer, 39, Canada) and Lillian A. Huntley (30, Jay, VT)
Vivian, b. 7/1/1896 in Piermont; J. M. Hanks (laborer, 32, Sutton, PQ) and Lillian Huntley (22, Groton, VT)

HANNIFORD,
Pauline M., b. 9/22/1902 in Piermont; first; Samuel G. Hanniford (surveyor, 25, Stewartstown) and Julia M. Dodge (25, Piermont)

HARRIS,
Heidi, b. 7/8/1981; Sumner P. Harris and Joyce C. Freese
Mary-Jane, b. 8/22/1975; Sumner P. Harris and Joyce C. Freese

HARTLEY,
Dana Ernest, b. 3/4/1988; Ernest W. Hartley, Jr. and Pamela Jean Hatch
Diane Margaret, b. 3/14/1952 in Haverhill; third; Ernest D. Hartley (elec. contr., Bradford, VT) and Mildred A. Hill (Pike)
Ernest Wallace, b. 6/13/1941 in Woodsville; first; Ernest D. Hartley (electrician, Bradford, VT) and Mildred Alice Hall (Haverhill)
Ronald Edward, b. 8/11/1959; Ernest D. Hartley and Mildred Alice Hill
Wendell Frederick, b. 5/17/1945 in Haverhill; second; Ernest Hartley (electrician, Bradford, VT) and Mildred Hill (Pike)

HARTWELL,
Barbara A., b. 10/14/1934 in Bradford, VT; fourth; George Hartwell (farmer, Haverhill) and Ida Robie (Piermont)
Francis May, b. 4/27/1919 in Piermont; first; George J. Hartwell (farm laborer, Haverhill) and Ida G. Robie (Piermont)
Harold Wesley, b. 3/22/1920 in Piermont; second; George J. Hartwell (farmer, Haverhill) and Ida G. Robie (Piermont)
Virginia, b. 2/9/1925 in Piermont; third; George Hartwell (laborer, Haverhill) and Ida Robie (Piermont)

HATCH,
daughter, b. 4/24/1894; third; Fred N. Hatch (farmer, Jericho, VT) and Cornelia G. Thomas (N. Fayston)
Vernon Clark, b. 6/6/1920 in Piermont; first; Harry Wilder Hatch (farmer, Boston, MA) and Ivie Jennie Lindsey (Haverhill)

HAZEN,
Amy Lynn, b. 12/21/1970; Bruce A. Hazen and Lois M. Adams
David Ray, b. 7/1/1965; George R. Hazen and Charlene H. Thurston
John Henry, b. 9/5/1955 in Lebanon; fourth; William S. Hazen (mgr. lumber co., Norwich, VT) and Hazel Anderson (S. Londonderry, VT)

HEATH,
son, b. 12/10/1891 in Piermont; first; Joshua M. Heath (farmer, 22, Warren) and Ada M. Chase (20, Wentworth)
daughter, b. 9/16/1894; second; Joshua A. Heath (farmer, Warren) and Ida M. Chase (Wentworth)

HENRY,
Carmen Lynn, b. 7/3/1983; Bruce Philip Henry and Leslie Lynn Gould
Morgan Evelyn, b. 9/23/1990; Bruce Henry and Leslie Gould
Tiffany Ann, b. 5/4/1993; Bruce P. Henry and Leslie L. Gould

HERSEY,
Robert Maurice, b. 2/10/1925 in Piermont; second; Everett Hersey (farmer, Quincy, MA) and Margery E. Turner (Thetford, VT)

HIBBARD,
Lloyd Clarence, b. 4/30/1919 in Piermont; fourth; Clarence G. Hibbard (farmer, Orford) and Maude E. McClaskey (Wentworth)
Madeline E., b. 7/9/1916 in Piermont; second; C. G. Hibbard (creameryman, Orford) and Maud McClosky (Wentworth)
Sibyl Clare, b. 8/10/1917 in Piermont; third; Clarence G. Hibbard (laborer, Orford) and Maud McClauskey (Wentworth)
Thelma N., b. 10/2/1921 in Piermont; fifth; Clarence G. Hibbard (farmer, Orford) and Maude McCloskey (Wentworth)

HILL,
daughter, b. 5/22/1912 in Piermont; fourth; Orlando B. Hill (laborer, Piermont) and Lola Howland (Piermont)
Arnold M., b. 1/8/1918 in Piermont; eighth; Orlando B. Hill (farmer, Piermont) and Lola L. Howland (Piermont)
Caroline M., b. 8/30/1914 in Piermont; sixth; Orlando B. Hill (laborer, Piermont) and Lola L. Howland (Piermont)

Ervill, b. 7/6/1916 in Piermont; seventh; O. B. Hill (farmer, Piermont) and Lula L. Howland (Piermont)
Eva Barbara, b. 8/28/1919 in Piermont; fourth; Clarence F. Hill (farmer, Norton, VT) and Eva J. Morse (Mansonville, PQ)
Florence E., b. 4/9/1906 in Piermont; first; Orlando B. Hill (farmer, 23, Piermont) and Lulu Howland (17, Piermont)
Lillian M., b. 11/4/1904 in Piermont; second; George T. Hill (laborer, 24, Piermont) and Flora L. Davis (20, Barnet, VT)
Marion, b. 4/17/1905 in Piermont; first; Lewis M. Hill (laborer, 27, Piermont) and Bertha Jane Hood (17, Topsham, VT)
Moses Joseph, b. 8/30/1914 in Piermont; fifth; Orlando B. Hill (laborer, Piermont) and Lola L. Howland (Piermont)
Oscar B., b. 6/2/1907 in Piermont; second; Orlando B. Hill (farmer, 23, Piermont) and Lula Howland (19, Piermont)
Trillium Skylar Castleberry, b. 5/16/1986; Craig Barclay Hill and Mardi Roberts
Vendett Virginia, b. 1/26/1918 in Piermont; third; Clarence F. Hill (laborer, Norton, VT) and Eva J. Morse (Potton, PQ)

HODSDON,
stillborn son, b. 10/17/1927 in Piermont; third; Harrison Hodsdon (farmer, Piermont) and Edith E. Childs (Piermont)
Agnes Edith, b. 9/22/1928 in Piermont; fourth; Harrison Hodsdon (farmer, Piermont) and Edith E. Childs (Piermont)
Albert Edgar, b. 6/18/1935 in Piermont; fourth; Harrison Hodsdon (farmer, Piermont) and Edith Childs (Piermont)
Bertha, b. 6/28/1924 in Piermont; first; Harrison Hodsdon (farmer, Piermont) and Edith R. Childs (Piermont)
Jean E., b. 1/18/1926 in Piermont; second; Harrison Hodsdon (farmer, Piermont) and Edith E. Childs (Piermont)

HOLLAND,
Luke Tatsuo, b. 5/24/2003; Raymond Holland and Andrea Holland

HOLLSTEIN,
Danielle Lee, b. 5/30/1988; Karl A. Hollstein and Nina M. Gleason

HOOD,
son, b. 9/4/1912 in Piermont; first; Herbert H. Hood (farmer, FL) and Elsie Morrill (Bradford, VT)

Donald Everett, b. 1/6/1947 in Woodsville; sixth; Harold R. Hood (farmer, Piermont) and Willimena Sawyer (Piermont)
Doris Eleanor, b. 2/23/1945 in Haverhill; fifth; Harold Hood (farmer, Topsham, VT) and Wilhelimine Sawyer (Piermont)
Russell S., b. 5/16/1924 in Piermont; third; Perley M. Hood (laborer, Topsham, VT) and Margie Stevens (Corinth, VT)

HORTON,
stillborn son, b. 6/18/1894; eleventh; William H. Horton (farmer, Barnet, VT) and Mary Chesley (Compton, PQ)
daughter, b. 1/24/1897 in Piermont; William H. Horton (farmer, 55, Barnard, VT) and Mary Chesley (45, Compton, PQ)
Bernard, b. 12/26/1904 in Piermont; first; William Horton (farmer, 21, Orford) and Hattie E. Webster (21, Monroe)
Clara L., b. 4/2/1891 in Piermont; ninth; William H. Horton (farmer, 50, Barnard, VT) and Mary J. Chesley (39, Campton, ON)
John Edward, b. 2/21/1951 in Haverhill; ninth; Bernard G. Horton (creamery mgr., Piermont) and Eva M. Lewis (Wilder, VT)
Kenneth Russell, b. 6/10/1970; John E. Horton and Arlene W. Wyman
Louis William, b. 3/4/1939 in Piermont; sixth; Bernard Horton (laborer, Piermont) and Eva Louis (Wilder, VT)
Marcella J., b. 2/3/1931 in Piermont; fourth; Bernard Horton (truck driver, Piermont) and Eva Lewis (Orford)
Marion A., b. 3/13/1927 in Piermont; second; Bernard Horton (laborer, Piermont) and Eva Lewis (Wilder, VT)
Mary L., b. 9/2/1932 in Piermont; fifth; Bernard Horton (laborer, Piermont) and Eva Lewis (Wilder, VT)
Priscilla, b. 12/24/1924 in Piermont; first; Bernard Horton (laborer, Piermont) and Eva Louis
Ralph Henry, b. 1/29/1948 in Haverhill; eighth; Bernard G. Horton (creamery mgr., Piermont) and Eva M. Lewis (Wilder, VT)
Richard Paul, b. 2/24/1946 in Piermont; seventh; Bernard G. Horton (creamery mgr., Piermont) and Eva M. Lewis (Wilder, VT)
Rita Helen, b. 4/5/1929 in Piermont; third; Bernard Horton (laborer, Piermont) and Eva Lewis (Norwich, VT)

HOUSE,
Erika Avens, b. 11/24/1987; William David House and Andra Avens

HOWARD,
son, b. 2/15/1892 in Piermont; fourth; William A. Howard (physician, 36, Near Aurora, NY) and Ella A. Howard (33, Hudson); residence - Chicago, IL
Ellis Woodruff, b. 1/4/1923 in Piermont; second; Ray W. Howard (merchant, E. Haven, VT) and Nita A. Palmer (Mystic, PQ)
Enid, b. 3/21/1921 in Piermont; first; Ray W. Howard (merchant, E. Haven, VT) and Nita A. Palmer (Mystic, PQ)
Joseph F., b. 12/8/1894; fifth; William A. Howard (physician) and ---- (Hudson)
Margaret A., b. 8/3/1927 in Piermont; third; Earl V. Howard (merchant, E. Haven, VT) and Amy M. Saunders (E. Montpelier, VT)

HOWE,
Oliver Milo, b. 4/17/1918 in Piermont; second; Oliver E. Howe (boxmaker, Benton) and Mildred V. Sawyer (Piermont); residence - Haverhill
Richard W., b. 2/16/1921 in Piermont; first; Oscar Glenn Howe (farmer, Londonderry, VT) and Bertha M. Wilson (Newfane, VT); residence - Brookline, VT

HOWLAND,
son, b. 7/31/1892 in Piermont; second; Nathaniel H. Howland (farmer, 36, Landaff) and E. M. Little (33, Lisbon)
Iola M., b. 2/26/1917 in Piermont; third; William L. Howland (farmer, Orford) and Florence M. Peavitt (Cliftondale, MA)

HOYT,
Anthony Young, b. 11/19/1968; Manson Y. Hoyt, Jr. and Susan I. Parent

HUNTINGTON,
Kolin Joshua, b. 5/29/1997; Jeffrey L. Huntington and Laureen E. Merrill
Kyle Jeffrey, b. 7/25/1994; Jeffrey Huntington and Laureen Merrill

HUSE,
Carl Frank, b. 6/19/1969; Michael Huse and Cornelia Emerson
Michael David, Jr., b. 11/22/1967; Michael D. Huse and Cornelia E. Emerson

HUTCHINS,
Michael John, b. 9/8/2000; Joshua Hutchins and Jennifer Hutchins
Nicholas Ryan, b. 12/13/1979; Roger P. Hutchins and Teresa A. Rodimon
Rowen Scott, b. 4/13/2004; Nicholas Hutchins and Megan Hutchins

HUTCHINSON,
Margaret L., b. 4/29/1917 in Piermont; second; Theodore Hutchinson (farmer, Stannard, VT) and Ruth M. Corliss (Charlestown)

HYBELS,
Kevin Robert, b. 10/14/1997; Ralph C. Hybels and Catherine L. Smith

JACKSON,
Michael Paul, b. 3/30/1978; Lee E. Jackson and Cindy L. Elliott

JAMES,
Bradley Arthur, Jr., b. 5/21/1978; Bradley A. James and Sandra L. Gilson
Christopher, b. 8/4/1999; Nelson James and Deborah Cloud

JASMIN,
Arthur Chester, b. 10/12/1953 in Haverhill; third; Paul G. Jasmin (farmer, Peabody, MA) and Olive M. Virgin (Livermore Falls, ME)

JEROME,
Katherine G., b. 9/8/1934 in Woodsville; first; Carroll Jerome (laborer, Greensboro, VT) and Lucy Boardman (E. Haverhill)

JESSEMAN,
Cindy Lee, b. 12/12/1957 in Haverhill; third; Everett A. Jesseman (gas sta. attendant, Haverhill) and Doris E. Shover (W. Topsham, VT)
Debra Jo, b. 4/8/1954 in Haverhill; second; Roger W. Jesseman (auto salesman, Piermont) and Stella M. Lee (Grantsboro, NC)
Doreen Ann, b. 12/25/1954 in Haverhill; second; Everett A. Jesseman (ser. sta. op., Woodsville) and Doris E. Shover (W. Topsham, VT)

Everett A., b. 1/10/1927 in Woodsville; second; Arthur F. Jesseman (laborer, Campton) and Gladys I. Field (Piermont)

Gloria Lee, b. 1/24/1949 in Haverhill; second; Roger W. Jesseman (auto salesman, Piermont) and Stella M. Lee (Grantsboro, NC)

Jane Paulette, b. 10/12/1953 in Haverhill; first; Everett A. Jesseman (service station op., Woodsville) and Doris E. Shover (W. Topsham, VT)

Linda Kay, b. 4/1/1947 in Woodsville; first; Roger W. Jesseman (timekeeper, Topsham, VT) and Stella M. Lee (Grantsboro, NC)

Paula, b. 10/12/1950 in Haverhill; third; Roger W. Jesseman (salesman, Piermont) and Stella M. Lee (Grantsboro, NC)

Roger Wilfred, b. 1/16/1922 in Piermont; first; Arthur F. Jesseman (wounded soldier, Campton) and Gladys Field (Pike)

JETTE,

Charles William, b. 2/23/1949 in Hanover; fourth; Ovila P. Jette (farm laborer, Lebanon) and Ruth A. Charbono (Canaan)

JEWELL,

Neel Wayne, b. 11/15/1949 in Hanover; first; Mansil C. Jewell (logger) and Hazel K. Landry (Concord, VT)

JOHNSON,

Cecilia Elizabeth, b. 6/1/1953 in Haverhill; first; Arby N. Johnson, Jr. (farmer, Woodsville) and Lois F. Webler (Washington, DC)

JONES,

stillborn son, b. 4/14/1930 in Piermont; fifth; Fredrick Jones (farmer, Danville, CT) and Lucy Sawyer (Piermont)

Celia M., b. 1/4/1925 in Piermont; third; Frederick Jones (farmer, Danville, CT) and Lucy A. Sawyer (Piermont)

Dorothy A., b. 6/22/1931 in Piermont; sixth; Frederick Jones (laborer, Danville, CT) and Lucy A. Sawyer (Piermont)

Frederick M., b. 10/10/1926 in Piermont; fourth; Frederick Jones (laborer, Danville, CT) and Lucy Sawyer (Piermont)

Hazel Doris, b. 4/5/1933 in Piermont; sixth; Frederick Jones (laborer, Danville, CT) and Lucy Sawyer (Piermont)

Kris Anne, b. 7/20/1973; Leonard Jones and Karlette Hendriks

Lara Judi, b. 6/20/2001; Harold Jones and Jayne Jones

JORDAN,
Marion L., b. 6/31/1907 (sic) in Piermont; fourth; Herman Jordan (laborer, 32, Canada, PQ) and Jennie Smith (32, Guildhall, VT)
Sylvester R., b. 3/12/1915 in Piermont; fourth; Sylvester P. Jordan (farmer, Stewartstown) and Mabel V. Sulham (Marshfield, VT)

JULIEN,
Steven Raymond, b. 3/27/1961; Raymond A. Julien and Bertha J. Szuch

KEITH,
Madelyn P., b. 2/18/1931 in N. Haverhill; first; Stanley F. Fadden (farmer, W. Thornton) and Edna Keith (N. Haverhill)

KENISTON,
Rosenna Diane, b. 5/14/1953 in Haverhill; first; Hugh L. Keniston (US Army, Bath) and Mary L. Horton (Piermont)

KENNEDY,
Kathryn Ann, b. 1/18/1956 in Haverhill; sixth; Kevin B. Kennedy (asst. co. agent, Bruno, Saskatchewan) and Joan B. Hendry (Hamilton, ON)

KENNEY,
Edward T., b. 7/28/1930 in Piermont; first; Dorothy Kenney

KENNY,
Thomas Alan, b. 1/28/1965; John F. Kenny and Mary I. Murphy

KEOUGH,
Philip Arnold, b. 2/23/1943 in Haverhill; ninth; Harold M. Keough (farm laborer, Concord) and Myrtle B. McGuire (Landaff)

KIDDER,
Melissa Meagan, b. 4/26/1985; Ricky Allen Kidder and Alice Jane Robinson

KING,
Bernard F., b. 12/1/1932 in Piermont; first; Richard King (laborer, Lunenburg, VT) and Lillian Bresse (Newport, VT)

KINGHORN,
Guy Burton, b. 12/6/1936 in Woodsville; third; Clement T. Kinghorn (plumber, Hardwick, VT) and Meda Stanley (Piermont)
Thomas Brenden, b. 9/30/1959; Guy Burton Kinghorn and Lana Lee Davis

KNAPP,
daughter, b. 1/19/1891 in Piermont; fourth; Fred Knapp (farmer, 35, Piermont) and Ella Harris (30, Warren)
daughter, b. 4/10/1895 in Piermont; sixth; Fred Knapp (farmer, 39, Piermont) and Ella Harris (34, Warren)
son, b. 11/26/1903 in Piermont; seventh; Fred Knapp (farmer, 48, Piermont) and Ella S. Harris (43, Warren)
Ray A., b. 2/16/1891 in Piermont; fourth; Albert A. Knapp (farmer, 43, Haverhill) and Irene D. Pike (33, Newbury, VT)

KOCH,
Amber Lynn, b. 6/18/1997; Peter J. Koch and Lisa M. Eastman
Felicity Rose, b. 8/12/2000; Peter Koch and Lisa Koch

KORTSCH,
Dieter Illes, b. 9/2/1965; Dieter E. Kortsch and Erika M. Yeles

LADEAU,
child, b. 3/12/1892 in Piermont; first; Frank E. Ladeau (farmer, 23, Eden, VT) and Hattie Mann (22, Waldron, VT)
daughter, b. 2/20/1906 in Piermont; fifth; Eugene Ladeau (farmer, 32, Wolcott, VT) and Bernice Skinner (31, Williamstown, VT)
Caroline E., b. 6/19/1907 in Piermont; first; Albert C. Ladeau (laborer, 20, Orford) and Abbie Cushing (17, McIndoes, VT)
W. McKinley, b. 7/12/1896 in Piermont; F. E. Ladeau (laborer, 27, Eden, VT) and Hattie M. Mann (27, Walden, VT)

LANG,
Alexis Meda, b. 6/27/2000; Timothy Lang and Tanya Lang
Jonathan Warren, b. 9/3/1985; Robert John Lang and Shirley Ann Lincoln
Timothy Michael, b. 5/6/1978; Robert J. Lang and Shirley A. Lincoln

LANGLEY,
Michael Todd, b. 1/11/1994; Todd Langley and Cynthia Slayton

LECLAIR,
Paul Edwin, b. 2/21/1956 in Littleton; third; Edwin B. LeClair (salesman, Littleton) and Frances A. Goode (Littleton)

LEMAY,
daughter, b. 6/29/1905 in Piermont; ninth; Sim LeMay (farmer, 34, Three Rivers, MS) and Ida Stone (32, Newbury, VT)

LEONARD,
son, b. 9/6/1895 in Piermont; second; John N. Leonard (farmer, Bath) and Agnes Wilson (MI)
son, b. 7/23/1897 in Piermont; John N. Leonard (farmer, 28, Bath) and Agnes S. Wilson (26, Grindstone City, MI)
Henry M., b. 11/16/1903 in Piermont; fourth; John N. Leonard (farmer, 34, Bath) and Agnes S. Wilson (32, Grindstone City, MI)
Rita J., b. 4/16/1915 in Piermont; fifth; John N. Leonard (farmer, Bath) and Agnes S. Wilson (Grindstone City, MI)

LIBBE,
Ernest W., b. 8/8/1927 in Piermont; first; Wilfred J. Libbe (farmer, Canada) and Wilma G. ------ (Russia)

LOUGEE,
son, b. 3/18/1891 in Piermont; fourth; Sylvester J. Lougee (laborer, 39, Gilmanton) and Orlany D. Kemp (40, Stanstead, PQ)

LUCE,
son, b. 3/21/1899 in Piermont; third; Lester F. Luce (farmer, 30, Tunbridge, VT) and Rena Hubbard (22, Canada, PQ)

LUNNIE,
son, b. 4/28/1908 in Piermont; first; William Lunnie (farmer, Canada) and Mary J. Young (Bristol, RI)

LYNDE,
Charles A., b. 5/28/1927 in Piermont; third; Albert W. Lynde (farmer, Landaff) and Leona I. Delage (Franconia)

MARSH,
Vernon A., b. 10/14/1916 in Piermont; first; Fred E. Marsh (steam r. eng., Orford) and Beulah O. Cutting (Piermont); residence - Woodsville

MARTIN,
Richard Warren, b. 11/6/1954 in Haverhill; third; Barry Warren Martin (plumber, Hanover) and Margaret E. Clifford (Albany, NY)
Wesley, b. 7/27/1950 in Haverhill; second; Wilfred C. Martin (farmer, Bristol, CT) and Joan G. Gallagher (Brooklyn, NY)

MASON,
Gyle E., b. 12/30/1914 in Piermont; first; Leon E. Mason (farmer, Topsham, VT) and Annie R. Powers (Topsham, VT)

MAXFIELD,
Dale W., b. 8/17/1930 in Woodsville; second; Albert Maxfield (farmer, Wolcott, VT) and E. Irene Smith (Stanford, CT)
Elaine, b. 12/13/1939 in Hanover; first; Howard Maxfield (truck driver, N. Thetford, VT) and Hester West (Hanover)
Richard, b. 4/27/1928 in Woodsville; first; Albert Maxfield (farmer, Wolcott, VT) and Ethelyn Smith (Stamford, CT)

MAZZILLI,
Anthony Paul, b. 2/22/1991; Peter Mazzilli and Lisa M. Fontaine
Joseph Adam, b. 1/23/1994; Peter Mazzilli, Jr. and Lisa Marie Fontaine

McAULEY,
son, b. 12/21/1898 in Piermont; first; Auley McAuley (stone cutter, 31, Millville, NS) and Ida May Smith (19, Piermont)

McCLELLAN,
Sarah Lynn, b. 10/18/1977; Owen C. McClellan and Debra Jesseman

McCONNELL,
Beatrice M., b. 9/7/1931 in Piermont; ninth; Forest McConnell (farmer, Whitefield) and Rosetta Northrop (Danbury, CT)

McKEAGE,
Elaine Gladys, b. 4/27/1921 in Piermont; fourth; Ray McKeage
  (farmer, Pittsburg) and June Mae Gould (Colebrook)
Lyman Ray, b. 6/18/1922 in Piermont; fifth; Ray A. McKeage
  (farmer, Pittsburg) and Junie M. Gould (Colebrook)
Muriel A., b. 7/5/1913 in Piermont; first; Ray A. McKeag (farmer,
  Pittsburg) and Jennie M. Gould (Stewartstown)

McLURE,
Paul Wayne, II, b. 12/6/1974; Paul W. McLure and Shirley Sayers

McQUIRRIE,
May E., b. 12/2/1896 in Piermont; William S. McQuirrie (stone cutter,
  27, NB) and Emma E. Knights (19, S. Paris, ME)

MEDLICOTT,
Allethiere Anne, b. 7/6/1982; Alexander Guild Medlicott, 3rd and Kristi
  Lee Medill
Emilia Lee, b. 5/27/1985; Alexander Guild Medlicott III and Kristi Lee
  Medill

MELLO,
Heidi Leigh, b. 3/11/1967; Frank R. Mello, Jr. and Marilyn Hight

METCALF,
daughter, b. 9/10/1894; first; John P. Metcalf (farmer, Piermont) and
  Carrie R. Grimes (Orford)
daughter, b. 10/7/1903 in Piermont; third; John P. Metcalf (farmer,
  32, Piermont) and Caroline R. Grimes (30, Orford)
Abigail, b. 4/28/1972; John E. Metcalf and Abby M. Johnson
Ai Burgess, b. 7/25/1970; John E. Metcalf and Abby M. Johnson
Asa Norman, b. 5/24/1973; John Metcalf and Abby Johnson
Daniel M., b. 4/3/1901 in Piermont; second; John Metcalf (farmer,
  30, Piermont) and Caroline R. Grimes (28, Orford)
Harold Wayne, b. 9/30/1947 in Piermont; seventh; Earl L. Metcalf
  (farmer, Underhill, VT) and Carrie E. Paronto (Lowell, VT);
  residence - Orange, VT
Harry Burgess, b. 3/14/1909 in Piermont; fourth; John P. Metcalf
  (farmer, Piermont) and Carrie R. Grimes (Orford)
John Edward, b. 12/9/1943 in Haverhill; first; Harry B. Metcalf
  (farmer, Piermont) and Shirley Mary Smith (Walden, VT)

Marianne, b. 11/21/1946 in Haverhill; second; H. Burgess Metcalf (farmer, Piermont) and Shirley M. Smith (Walden, VT)

MICHENFELDER,
Jacob Adam, b. 1/4/1985; Robert Richard Michenfelder and Barbara Ann Walsh

MILLER,
daughter, b. 8/2/1949 in Haverhill; second; Ernest Glen Miller (mill worker, Waterville, VT) and Ona D. Corrow (Hardwick, VT)
Cynthia Nina, b. 8/2/1949 in Haverhill; first; Ernest Glen Miller (mill worker, Waterville, VT) and Ona D. Corrow (Hardwick, VT)
Dorothy Ann, b. 9/14/1953 in Piermont; fourth; Ernest G. Miller (farm laborer, Waterville, VT) and Ona D. Corrow (Hardwick, VT)
Rita May, b. 4/22/1955 in Piermont; fourth; Ernest G. Miller (farm laborer, Waterville, VT) and Ona D. Corrow (Hardwick, VT)

MISURACA,
Cody Alexander Disco, b. 7/5/1990; James Misuraca and Annmarie Disco

MITCHELL,
Diane, b. 7/19/1950 in Haverhill; first; Robert L. Mitchell (farm laborer, Ryegate, VT) and Irene E. McDonald (Groton, VT)

MONAGHAN,
Eve Carling, b. 6/27/1998; John Monaghan and Susan Mary Knapp
Matthew Liam, b. 3/19/2002; John Monaghan and Susan Monaghan

MONTGOMERY,
Ruth A., b. 11/15/1927 in Woodsville; fifth; True W. Montgomery (carpenter, Kirby, VT) and Alice May Luce (Piermont)
W. T., b. 10/6/1924 in St. Johnsbury, VT; foirth; True Montgomery (farmer, Kirby, VT) and Alice May Luce (Piermont)

MOORE,
Irene Lillian, b. 4/21/1935 in Hanover; first; John William Moore (truck driver, Concord, VT) and Dorothy L. Hackett (Piermont)
Janet Delores, b. 12/1/1942 in Hanover; second; John Moore (farm laborer) and Dorothy Hackett (Piermont)

Raymond Lee, b. 8/13/1945 in Hanover; third; Thomas Moore (laborer, Hingham, MA) and Ellen Walker (Franklin); residence - Nantasket Beach, MA

MORRILL,
Charles Roderic, b. 3/31/1918 in Piermont; third; Frederic Morrill (farmer, White Rock, RI) and Beulah H. Brown (Haverhill)
Garry Allen, b. 9/18/1946 in Haverhill; first; Philip C. Morrill (farmer, Piermont) and Elizabeth A. Cowan (Colebrook)
Mark Phillip, b. 2/8/1953 in Haverhill; second; Phillip C. Morrill (bulldozer operator, Piermont) and Elizabeth Alice Cowan (Claremont)
Marshall B., b. 6/10/1914 in Piermont; first; Frederick Morrill (mail carrier, White Rock, RI) and Beulah Brown (Haverhill)
Mattie F., b. 4/2/1891 in Piermont; fifth; Charles F. Morrill (farmer, 38, Ryegate, VT) and Carrie L. Pratt (32, Boston, MA)
Maxine Elizabeth, b. 1/1/1920 in Piermont; fourth; Frederick Morrill (farmer, White Rock, RJ) and Beulah Brown (Haverhill)
Philip Conrad, b. 1/25/1923 in Piermont; fifth; Frederick Morrill (farmer, White Rock, RI) and Beullah H. Brown (Haverhill)
Phyllis A., b. 11/11/1916 in Piermont; second; Frederick Morrill (RFD car., White Rock, PQ) and Beulah H. Brown (Haverhill)

MORRISON,
Christie E., b. 12/27/1891 in Piermont; first; Horace E. Morrison (mechanic, 24, Haverhill) and Ida M. Robie (23, Corinth, VT)

MORSE,
Bernard O., b. 9/20/1909 in Piermont; second; George O. Morse (farmer, Jay, VT) and Lura E. Hatch (Jericho, VT)
Grace E., b. 2/16/1916 in Piermont; first; F. G. Morse (farmer, Sutton, PQ) and Susie M. Winn (Haverhill)
Martin, b. 3/15/1919 in Piermont; stillborn; second; Franklin A. Morse (farmer, Sutton, PQ) and Susie M. Winn (Haverhill)

MORTON,
Tammy Lynn, b. 12/28/1967; Wallace E. Morton, Sr. and Althea M. Fadden
Wallace Edward, Jr., b. 5/2/1966; Wallace E. Morton and Althea M. Fadden

MOSES,
Ramona, b. 10/14/1939 in Haverhill; first; Otis Moses (laborer, Haverhill) and Pearl Spink (Warsaw, NY)

MOULTON,
Ardell L., b. 6/17/1938 in Piermont; seventh; Rockwood Moulton (laborer, Landaff) and Bernice Blandin (Fairlee, VT)
Leon Roy, Jr., b. 3/2/1958 in Haverhill; first; Leon R. Moulton (truck driver, Woodsville) and Ellen G. Dugdale (Hanover)

MUGFORD,
stillborn daughter, b. 5/5/1922 in Piermont; seventh; Fred Stephen Mugford (farmer, Boston, MA) and Lucy F. Tarbox (Orford)
Clendon Edwin, b. 5/5/1922 in Piermont; sixth; Fred Stephen Mugford (farmer, Boston, MA) and Lucy F. Tarbox (Orford)
Mildred Lucy, b. 5/1/1923 in Piermont; eighth; Fred Mugford (laborer, PEI) and Lucy Tarbox (Orford)

MURPHY,
John Richard, b. 5/11/1940 in Hanover; first; Robert B. Murphy (carpenter, Machias, ME) and Doris R. Goodwin (Plymouth)
Kenneth John, b. 1/25/1949 in Hanover; fourth; William B. Murphy (storehouse supt., NH) and Genevieve H. Leary (Charleston, MA)
Roberta Dale, b. 8/20/1941 in Hanover; second; Robert B. Murphy (p. shovel op'r, Machias, ME) and Doris R. Goodwin (Plymouth)

MUSTY,
Ann, b. 6/9/1923 in Piermont; third; Alfred Musty (farmer, Canada) and Marion Gorham (Lyndonville, VT)
Bill, b. 3/13/1951 in Haverhill; second; Robert G. Musty (carpenter, Lyndonville, VT) and Alberta P. Mitchell (San Francisco, CA)
Jacob Joseph Piro, b. 6/15/1979; Samuel A. Musty and Cynthia J. Piro
Jane Ellen, b. 9/28/1946 in Hanover; first; Edgar H. Musty (farmer, Lyndonville, VT) and Katherine P. Walter (Bedford, PA)
Jim, b. 1/8/1953 in Haverhill; third; Robert G. Musty (carpenter, Lyndonville, VT) and Alberta P. Mitchell (San Francisco, CA)
Matthew Robert, b. 12/27/1987; Jim Musty and Mary Beth Ritchie
Michael James, b. 12/12/1985; Jim Musty and Mary Beth Ritchie

Peter Edgar, b. 6/3/1954 in Haverhill; fourth; Edgar H. Musty
    (farmer, Lyndonville, VT) and Katherine P. Walter (Cessna, PA)
Rose M., b. 2/22/1950 in Haverhill; first; Robert G. Musty (carpenter,
    Lyndonville, VT) and Alberta P. Mitchell (San Francisco, CA)
Samuel Alfred, b. 12/16/1948 in Haverhill; second; Edgar H. Musty
    (farmer, Lyndonville, VT) and Katherine P. Walter (Cessna, PA)
Susan Paula, b. 6/15/1951 in Haverhill; third; Edgar H. Musty
    (farmer, Lyndonville, VT) and Katherine P. Walter (Ceasna, PA)

NEAL,
Greyson Donald, b. 11/17/2000; Ronald Neal and Jennifer Neal

NELSON,
Adam David, b. 3/12/1998; Daniel James Nelson and Deborah Lynn
    Cloud
Alice M., b. 4/16/1910 in Piermont; second; Ernest H. Nelson
    (laborer, Fayston, PQ) and Mabel LaPlant (Haverhill)
Jamie Lee, b. 2/14/2002; Daniel Nelson and Deborah Nelson
Samantha Elizabeth, b. 9/11/1995; Daniel J. Nelson and Deborah L.
    Cloud

NEWTON,
Kenneth Ray, b. 10/1/1973; Willard Newton and Edna Sanborn

NORCROSS,
daughter, b. 1/21/1895 in Piermont; first; Frank Norcross (laborer,
    22, Bradford, VT) and Amelia Stone (17, Piermont)

NOYES,
Gail Marie, b. 8/13/1957 in Haverhill; fourth; George H. Noyes, Jr.
    (laborer, Piermont) and Bette A. Chase (Woodsville)
George Henry, III, b. 9/28/1958 in Haverhill; fifth; George Henry
    Noyes, II (laborer, Piermont) and Bette A. Chase (Haverhill)
George Henry, Jr., b. 8/14/1934 in Piermont; fourth; George Henry
    Noyes (farmer, Haverhill) and Mary S. Morris (Haverhill)
Henrietta A., b. 12/2/1931 in Piermont; third; George H. Noyes, Jr.
    (farmer, Haverhill) and Mary S. Morris (N. Haverhill)
Howard, b. 7/24/1939 in Piermont; fifth; George H. Noyes, Jr.
    (farmer, Haverhill) and Mary S. Moran (Haverhill)
Howard Roger, Jr., b. 9/7/1962; Howard Roger Noyes, Sr. and Joan
    S. Baker

Kathy Ann, b. 8/12/1956 in Haverhill; third; George H. Noyes, Jr. (farmer, Piermont) and Bette A. Chase (Woodsville)
Pamela Susan, b. 1/8/1958 in Haverhill; first; Woodrow Noyes, Jr. (truck driver, Haverhill) and Joan M. Jewell (E. Corinth, VT)
Patricia Ann, b. 12/25/1960; Howard Roger Noyes and Joan S. Baker
Veronica Lee, b. 10/13/1953 in Haverhill; first; George H. Noyes (laborer, Piermont) and Bette A. Chase (Woodsville)

NUTTING,
Joan E., b. 4/3/1932 in Lisbon; second; Edward Nutting (farmer, N. Haverhill) and Katherine Varney (Lisbon)

NYSTROM,
Alden Edmund, b. 3/4/1956 in Haverhill; fourth; Robert E. Nystrom (trackman RR, Cambridge, MA) and Marcella J. Horton (Piermont)
Carl Edwin, b. 3/10/1955 in Haverhill; third; Herbert Nystrom (RR trackman, Cambridge, MA) and Marcella J. Horton (Piermont)
Linda Jean, b. 6/25/1949 in Haverhill; first; Robert E. Nystrom (trackman RR, Cambridge, MA) and Marcella J. Horton (Piermont)

OAKES,
Alex Austin, b. 9/9/1993; Daniel A. Oakes and Michelle A. Morrissette
Amanda Erin, b. 5/18/1983; Dale Allen Oakes and Kathleen Mae Martin
Brenda Lee, b. 12/6/1962; Wendell G. Oakes and Virginia M. Rogers
Dale Allen, b. 6/9/1957 in Hanover; first; Wendall G. Oakes (farmer, Bath) and Virginia Rogers (W. Fairlee, VT)
Daniel Albert, b. 5/27/1960; Wendell G. Oakes and Virginia M. Rogers
Jesse Alexander Goudiase, b. 7/26/1991; Daniel A. Oakes and Michelle A. Morrissette
Jessica Caitlin, b. 3/1/1986; Dale Allen Oakes and Kathleen Mae Martin
Jonathan Ryan, b. 4/12/1989; Dale A. Oakes and Kathleen M. Martin

Neil Rodney, b. 8/8/1946 in Haverhill; sixth; Glen W. Oakes (farmer, Colebrook) and Lottie M. Gates (Monroe)

Rodney Glen, b. 7/15/1959; Wendell George Oakes and Virginia Mae Rogers

Susan Viola, b. 11/6/1952 in Haverhill; first; Wayne G. Oakes (farmer, Barnet, VT) and Edith A. Magoon (W. Fairlee, VT)

Winfield Bruce, b. 2/14/1944 in Haverhill; fifth; Glen Oakes (farmer, Columbia) and Lottie Gates (Monroe)

OULTON,

Anne Marie, b. 12/9/1934 in Woodsville; second; John Oulton (farmer, Barnston, PQ) and Bessie Winn (Piermont)

Beth Joan, b. 4/29/1940 in Haverhill; third; John Oulton (farm laborer, Barnston, PQ) and Bessie Mae Winn (Piermont)

Faith Mae, b. 10/7/1942 in Haverhill; fourth; John David Oulton (farm laborer, Barnston, Canada) and Bessie Maw Winn (Piermont)

PAGE,

Jacob Luther, b. 1/11/1993; Jeffrey P. Page and Kathryn A. Streeter

Justin Jeffrey, b. 7/18/1990; Jeffrey Page and Kathryn Streeter

PARONTO,

Fayette Chester, b. 3/7/1928 in Piermont; first; Clyde S. Paronto (truckman, RR co., Montgomery, VT) and Violet M. French (Piermont); residence - Newport, VT

PARTRIDGE,

Rebecca Vileta, b. 12/10/1951 in Haverhill; first; Lawrence I. Partridge (farmer, Livermore Falls, ME) and Priscilla M. Brown (Brockton, MA)

PATRIDGE,

Warren F., b. 12/4/1912 in Piermont; first; Salan A. Patridge (farmer, Haverhill) and Jessie G. Easton (Springfield, NS)

PATTERSON,

Jocelyn Anne, b. 9/29/2003; Ronald Patterson and Merriel Patterson

PERKINS,

Bruce Edgar, b. 9/23/1959; Glen Elwin Perkins and Agnes Edith Hodsdon

Clyde L., b. 1/31/1915 in Piermont; second; Ralph C. Perkins (farmer, Hardwick, VT) and Maud L. Barnett (Hardwick, VT)
David Ernest, b. 4/28/1961; Glen E. Perkins and Agnes E. Hodsdon
Gerry Edwin, b. 5/26/1968; Glen E. Perkins and Agnes E. Hodsdon
Glen Elwin, b. 6/20/1918 in Piermont; third; Ralph Clyde Perkins (laborer, Hardwick, VT) and Maud L. Barnet (Hardwick, VT)
Irene Ethel, b. 1/4/1922 in Piermont; first; Clarence H. Perkins (farmer, Haverhill) and Florence E. Wright (Charleston, VT)
Pauline, b. 4/13/1924 in Piermont; second; Clarence H. Perkins (farmer, Haverhill) and Florence Wright (Charleston, VT)
Valerie Ann, b. 12/27/1985; David Ernest Perkins and Debra Jean Fox

PERRY,
Richard Walter, b. 7/7/1941 in Woodsville; first; Walter Harold Perry (laborer, Saranac, NY) and Beatrice B. Fillian (Wentworth)
Robert Phelon, b. 10/12/1918 in Piermont; third; Phelon O. Perry (farmer, Warren) and Maud A. Jewett (Lisbon)

PETERS,
Claribel, b. 6/11/1914 in Piermont; second; Walter E. Peters (farmer, Brandon, NY) and Bertha M. Hill (Lynn, MA)

PEYTON,
Shamus Gardner, b. 4/26/1997; James J. Peyton and Heidi L. Gardner

PICKERING,
Emma E., b. 1/23/1891 in Piermont; second; George Pickering (farmer, 40, Rome, Italy) and Emma J. Blanchard (23, Piermont)

PIKE,
Louise May, b. 8/30/1932 in Piermont; second; Archie W. Pike (woodsman, Halifax, VT) and Hazel E. Starkey (Dover, VT)
Ruberta E., b. 9/3/1932 in Piermont; third; Laurence H. Pike (elec. worker, Warren) and Rose A. Stalbard (Warren)

PIPER,
Timothy Scott, b. 2/23/1991; Scott R. Piper and Lisa M. Farnham

PLANTE,
Joseph Allen, b. 11/15/1984; Gregoire Joseph Plante and Theresa Marie Nutting

POLLOCK,
Amber Marie, b. 3/24/1994; Scott Pollock and Nicole Dow

POMBAR,
Joshua David, b. 2/22/1974; Thomas A. Pombar and Carol A. Yankee

PREST,
Alyssa Skye, b. 5/3/2000; Cameron Prest and Heather Prest
Emily Sierra, b. 5/7/2003; Cameron Prest and Heather Prest

PRIOR,
Danielle Christene, b. 10/4/1991; Trevor Prior and Heather Schmid
Eric David, b. 6/27/1994; Trevor Prior and Heather Schmid

PUSHEE,
Geoffrey Michael, b. 5/14/1986; David Jeffers Pushee and Michelle Marie Smith
Jason Paul, b. 12/28/1979; Paul R. Pushee and Inez L. Bailey

PUTNAM,
Barbara Jane, b. 5/4/1954 in Hanover; first; Jasper E. Putnam (farmer, Hanover) and Jean C. Davis (Woodsville)
Carrie Marie, b. 10/15/1983; William Norman Putnam and Cynthia Louise Reardon
Daniel Bradbury, b. 5/7/1990; William Putnam and Cynthia Reardon
Edward John, b. 8/27/1958 in Hanover; fourth; Jasper E. Putnam (farmer, Hanover) and Jean C. Davis (Woodsville)
Evan Paul, b. 6/19/1986; James Edward Putnam and Ellen Marie Ackerman
Faith Davis Robb, b. 1/9/1990; James Putnam and Ellen Ackerman
Glen Emery, b. 2/27/1984; James Edward Putnam and Ellen Marie Ackerman
James Edward, b. 11/27/1956 in Hanover; third; Jasper E. Putnam (dairy farmer, Hanover) and Jean C. Davis (Woodsville)

Jasper E., b. 11/18/1926 in Hanover Hosp.; first; George W. Putnam, Jr. (farmer, Newbury, VT) and Marion Corliss (Bradford, VT)

Lois C., b. 11/11/1931 in Hanover; third; George W. Putnam (farmer, W. Newbury, VT) and Marion Corliss (Bradford, VT)

Timothy William, b. 12/21/1981; William N. Putnam and Cynthia L. Reardon

William Norman, b. 5/5/1955 in Hanover; second; Jasper E. Putnam (farmer, Hanover) and Jean C. Davis (Woodsville)

RAMSEY,
son, b. 5/26/1904 in Piermont; fourth; Alex H. Ramsey (quarryman, 38, PEI) and Josephine Newcomb (38, PEI)

daughter, b. 6/21/1906 in Piermont; fifth; Alex Ramsey (stonecutter, 39, PEI) and Josephine Newcomb (39, PEI)

RATEL,
Jonathan Robert, b. 1/1/1996; Robert J. Ratel and Bernadette M. Moran

Keith Richard, b. 3/20/1990; Robert Ratel and Bernadette Moran

REED,
Patricia Ann, b. 3/28/1961; Richard A. Reed and Beverly J. Spencer

RENEAU,
son, b. 2/8/1895 in Piermont; fifth; Joseph Reneau (laborer, 34, Canada) and Clara Stone (29, Holland, VT)

RICH,
Alec Robert, b. 4/27/1988; Blair R. Rich and Annette I. McKean

Kevin Francis, b. 11/8/1967; Peter M. Rich and Beverly J. LeBrun

RISLEY,
daughter, b. 6/26/1892 in Piermont; fourth; Robert L. Risley (merchant, 40, Hanover) and Sarah J. Ames (33, Holderness)

RITCHIE,
David Fremont, b. 1/29/1957 in Haverhill; fourth; George F. Ritchie (farmer, Newbury, VT) and Helen L. Proshek (Toledo, OH)

Margaret Elaine, b. 1/21/1955 in Haverhill; third; George F. Ritchie (farmer, Newbury, VT) and Helen L. Proshek (Toledo, OH)

Mary Beth, b. 5/17/1953 in Haverhill; second; George F. Ritchie (farmer, Newbury, VT) and Helen L. Proshek (Toledo, OH)
Robert Andrew, b. 3/7/1952 in Haverhill; first; George F. Ritchie (farmer, Newbury, VT) and Helen L. Proshek (Toledo, OH)

RIVERA,
Christine Anne, b. 5/21/1962; Valentine Rivera and Rose L. Strout
James Burt, b. 8/31/1960; Ismael Rivera and Josephine E. Wheeler
Joyce Mae, b. 3/30/1962; Ismael R. Rivera and Josephine E. Wheeler
Julie Ann, b. 11/13/1959; Ismael Rivera and Josephine Ethel Wheeler

ROBIE,
daughter, b. 2/1/1895 in Piermont; fourth; Freeman A. Robie (farmer, 32, Corinth, VT) and Mary H. Grimes (28, Orford)
daughter, b. 10/28/1897 in Piermont; Freeman A. Robie (farmer, 34, Corinth, VT) and Mary H. Grimes (30, Orford)
son, b. 11/12/1900 in Piermont; seventh; Freeman A. Robie (farmer, 38, Corinth, VT) and Mary H. Grimes (34, Orford)
Alan Timothy, b. 3/18/1974; Terry Robie and Maurice Harbison
Christopher Freeman, b. 8/22/1972; Lyman E. Robie and Betty Sue Wright
Edna, b. 2/3/1896 in Piermont; Freeman A. Robie (farmer, 33, Corinth, VT) and Mary H. Grimes (29, Orford)
Eileen Louise, b. 5/13/1947 in Lebanon; first; Keith M. Robie (creamery foreman, Piermont) and Verna E. Tucker (Orange, VT)
Freeman E., b. 1/13/1925 in Piermont; third; Lyman Robie (farmer, Piermont) and Diana G. Shumway (Bradford, VT)
Keith Melwin, b. 8/9/1920 in Piermont; first; Lyman E. Robie (farmer, Piermont) and Gwendolyn D. Shumway (Bradford, VT)
Lyman Emerson, b. 11/29/1948 in Haverhill; second; Freeman E. Robie (farmer, Piermont) and Winona J. Emerson (W. Newbury, VT)
Neil Patrick, b. 3/26/1975; Lyman E. Robie and Betty Sue Wright
Paul Lyman, b. 6/6/1929 in Piermont; fourth; Lyman C. Robie (farmer, Piermont) and Gwendolyn Shumway (Bradford, VT)
Surlene Mamie, b. 3/16/1922 in Piermont; second; Lyman E. Robie (farmer, Piermont) and Gwendolyn Shumway (Bradford, VT)

Timothy Alan, b. 10/20/1951 in Haverhill; third; Freeman E. Robie (farmer, Piermont) and Winona J. Emerson (W. Newbury, VT)
Todd Wayne, b. 6/14/1954 in Haverhill; fourth; Freeman E. Robie (farmer, Piermont) and Winona J. Emerson (W. Newbury, VT)
Valerie Ann, b. 8/18/1955 in Lebanon; first; Paul L. Robie (asst RR agent, Piermont) and Barbara A. Sargent (Thetford, VT)

ROBINS,
Britta Lynn, b. 11/23/1985; Ross Kildow Robins and Jennifer Lynn Way
Melanie Diane, b. 6/17/1987; Ross Kildow Robins and Jennifer Lynn Way

ROBINSON,
Frederick T., b. 9/23/1912 in Piermont; first; Frederick C. Robinson (mail carrier, Piermont) and Effie M. Humphrey (Haverhill)
Kasey Nicole, b. 7/6/1998; James Arther Robinson and Lisa Lynn Swasey
Parker James, b. 4/26/1995; James A. Robinson and Lisa L. Swasey
Philip S., b. 5/4/1914 in Piermont; second; Frederick C. Robinson (farmer, Piermont) and Effie M. Humphrey (Haverhill)

ROBY,
Francis E., b. 4/15/1927 in Piermont; first; Hial G. Roby (farmer, Pittsburg) and Mabel G. Davis (Stratford)

RODIMON,
Alice L., b. 7/2/1913 in Piermont; fourth; Amos L. Rodimon (farmer, Piermont) and Grace Hood (Randolph, VT)
Amos Glenn, b. 5/12/1915 in Piermont; fifth; Amos T. Rodimon (farmer, Piermont) and Grace Hood (Randolph, VT)
Charles E., b. 6/4/1896 in Piermont; Charles H. Rodimon (farmer, 41, Piermont) and Gertrude Ladeau (24, Craftsbury, VT)
Christopher Michael, b. 4/18/1982; Frank William Rodimon, Jr. and Carol Sue Moody
Evelyn G., b. 4/29/1905 in Piermont; first; Amos T. Rodimon (farmer, 19, Piermont) and Grace E. Hood (19, Randolph, VT)
Fletcher D., b. 2/24/1908 in Piermont; second; Amos L. Rodimon (farmer, Piermont) and Grace E. Hood (Randolph, VT)

Kenneth P., b. 9/22/1909 in Piermont; third; Amos L. Rodimon (laborer, Piermont) and Grace E. Hood (Randolph, VT)

Teresa Ann, b. 11/16/1955 in Haverhill; first; Frank W. Rodimon (truck driver, Haverhill) and Louise M. Hood (Haverhill)

Vernon W., b. 8/28/1901 in Piermont; fourth; Charles H. Rodimon (farmer, 46, Piermont) and Gertrude Ladeau (29, Craftsbury, VT)

Walter Edward, b. 6/23/1934 in Woodsville; third; Charles E. Rodimon (farmer, Piermont) and Annie Farrell (Bellows Falls, VT)

Walter J., b. 9/9/1899 in Piermont; third; Charles H. Rodimon (farmer, 44, Piermont) and Gertrude H. Ladeau (27, Craftsbury, VT)

ROGERS,

Edward A., b. 5/11/1897 in Piermont; Edward S. Rogers (farmer, 28, Piermont) and Bessie Maude Evans (21, Worcester, MA)

Kassidee Fay, b. 1/29/1999; Shawn Rogers and Karlyce Brown

Kaylee Nicole, b. 4/27/1996; Shawn Rogers and Karlyce A. Brown

Matthew Lincoln, b. 1/12/1968; Clyde E. Rogers, Jr. and Joyce E. Cole

ROLLINS,

son, b. 7/8/1909 in Piermont; seventh; Hiram B. Rollins (farmer, Rumney) and Ada Patch (Carroll)

daughter, b. 8/21/1909 in Piermont; fifth; William Rollins (farmer, Orford) and Laura Durant (W. Topsham, VT)

Wesley W., b. 7/28/1914 in Piermont; sixth; Willis A. Rollins (farmer, Orford) and Laura E. Durant (W. Topsham)

ROSE,

Stella Euphemia, b. 9/11/2004; Brian Rose and Alison Rose

ROY,

stillborn daughter, b. 12/6/1895 in Piermont; first; Will Roy (laborer, 22, Canada) and Lillian P. Lamontagne (18, Piermont)

Hazel Etta, b. 6/28/1897 in Piermont; William Roy (laborer, 24, Lampton, PQ) and Effie M. Page (29, Hooksett)

ROYSTON,
Della M., b. 4/26/1915 in Piermont; third; Byron Royston (laborer, N. Troy, VT) and Nellie M. Davis (Hyde Park, VT)

SALADINO,
Peter Joseph, IV, b. 5/15/1985; Peter Joseph Saladino III and Kathryn Ann Page

SARGENT,
Chet Allan, b. 10/6/1962; Robert C. Sargent and Susan Jo Johnson
Peggy Sue, b. 11/3/1965; Robert C. Sargent and Susan J. Johnson

SAWYER,
daughter, b. 9/7/1899 in Piermont; third; Milo B. Sawyer (farmer, 27, Piermont) and Alice B. Rodimon (20, Piermont)
Barbara M., b. 2/23/1931 in Piermont; first; Wilhelmine Sawyer (Piermont)
Beatrice M., b. 10/30/1939 in Haverhill; third; Maynard Sawyer (farmer, Piermont) and Margaret Smith (Haverhill)
Betty Anne, b. 12/7/1946 in Haverhill; fourth; Maynard E. Sawyer (farmer, Piermont) and Margaret Smith (Haverhill)
Clyde Baily, b. 1/27/1898 in Piermont; second; Milo B. Sawyer (farmer, 26, E. Topsham, VT) and Alice B. Rodimon (19, Piermont)
Janice Ellen, b. 3/14/1938 in Haverhill; second; Maynard Sawyer (farmer, Piermont) and Margaret Smith (Haverhill)
Max E., b. 1/11/1912 in Piermont; seventh; Milo B. Sawyer (farmer, Topsham, VT) and Alice B. Rodimon (Piermont)
Milo W., b. 2/12/1909 in Piermont; sixth; Milo B. Sawyer (farmer, E. Topsham, VT) and Alice Rodimon (Piermont)
Virginia, b. 10/16/1896 in Piermont; Milo B. Sawyer (farmer, 25, Topsham, VT) and Alice B. Rodimon (18, Piermont)
Wilhelmine, b. 3/4/1907 in Piermont; fifth; Milo B. Sawyer (farmer, 35, E. Topsham, VT) and Alice B. Rodimon (28, Piermont)

SAYERS,
Cynthia Jane, b. 7/12/1958 in Haverhill; first; Scott L. Sayers (farmer, Groton, VT) and Martha J. Nelson (Woodsville)
John Henry, b. 5/18/1951 in Haverhill; second; Raymond E. Sayers (laborer, Barre, VT) and Evelyn M. Wheelock (E. Thetford, VT)
Larry Scott, b. 9/27/1959; Scott Leo Sayers and Martha Jane Nelson

SEPESSY,
Douglas Alan, b. 4/25/1962; Henry L. Sepessy and Priscilla Mae Shafer
Henry Lewis, III, b. 10/23/1960; Henry L. Sepessy, Jr. and Priscilla M. Shafer
William Anthony, b. 3/23/1959; Henry Lewis Sepessy, Sr. and Thelma Mabel Anthony

SHEPARD,
Annette, b. 5/21/1950 in Haverhill; second; Stanley L. Shepard (laborer, W. Lebanon) and Theresa M. Cassady (Woodsville)
Henrietta Rose, b. 3/22/1949 in St. Johnsbury, VT; first; Stanley L. Shepard (farmer, W. Lebanon) and Theresa M. Cassady (Haverhill)
Michael Don, b. 12/3/1948 in Haverhill; first; Don N. Shepard (farmer, Canaan) and Princetta J. Bailey (Groton, VT)
Vivian Edna, b. 1/19/1949 in Haverhill; first; Ray R. Shepard (laborer, Hanover) and Lorraine E. Peck (Woodsville)

SHINNERS,
Corey Michael, b. 1/29/1986; Peter Hayes Shinners and Kathleen Denise Snider
Jacob Matthew, b. 9/27/1988; Peter H. Shinners and Kathleen D. Snider

SHIPMAN,
Emily Gerard, b. 5/27/1981; Frederick W. Shipman and Gail W. Thornton
Jeremiah Piper, b. 3/26/1985; Philip Walter Shipman and Emilie Allison Piper
Luke Morse, b. 11/29/1981; Philip W. Shipman and Emilie A. Piper
Nathan William, b. 12/27/1977; Frederick W. Shipman and Gail W. Thornton

SIBLEY,
Jennie, b. 6/21/1907 in Piermont; third; Fay W. Sibley (farmer, 30, Milton, VT) and Stella Bourne (29, Canada, PQ)

SIMMONS,
Marcia A., b. 8/12/1911 in Piermont; first; Lewis A. Simmons (farmer, Wentworth) and Alice G. Smith (Piermont)

SIMPSON,
son, b. 2/1/1895 in Piermont; first; John F. Simpson (carpenter, 22, Piermont) and Lillian Marden (20, Haverhill)
daughter, b. 5/26/1898 in Piermont; second; John F. Simpson (carpenter, 26, Piermont) and Lillian M. Marden (23, Haverhill)
Harold B., b. 6/28/1915 in Piermont; second; John B. Simpson (farmer, Orford) and Carrie L. Molway (Piermont)
Harry J., b. 2/3/1914 in Piermont; first; John B. Simpson (farmer, Orford) and Carrie Molway (Piermont)
Heather Elaine, b. 2/25/1976; John B. Simpson and Jennifer L. Simpson
John Bradley, b. 4/29/1944 in Haverhill; second; John B. Simpson (farmer, Orford) and Dorothy Robinson (Woodsville)
Judith Ann, b. 2/19/1940 in Haverhill; first; John B. Simpson (farmer, Orford) and Dorothy Robinson (Woodsville)
Julie Lee, b. 5/18/1969; John B. Simpson and Jennifer L. Tanzi
Julie Mitchell, b. 12/5/1954 in Littleton; second; William M. Simpson (farmer, Woodsville) and Ellen L. Morse (Medford, MA)

SMITH,
son, b. 3/25/1897 in Piermont; Harvey W. Smith (farmer, 52, Haverhill) and Eliza Corliss (42, Piermont)
son, b. 12/2/1911 in Piermont; first; Loren G. Smith (farmer, Piermont) and Emma Ryalls (Manchester)
Albion LaForest, b. 8/25/1923 in Piermont; second; Albion L. Smith (farmer, W. Fairlee, VT) and Addie White (Haverhill)
Anson Aully, Jr., b. 8/5/1919 in Piermont; fourth; Anson A. Smith (farmer, Piermont) and Viola N. Scott (FL)
Beverly Nan, b. 10/26/1939 in Hanover; fifth; Vernus L. Smith (laborer, Haynesville, ME) and Angeline Brown (Presque Isle, ME)
Brittney Rose, b. 12/23/1999; Dennis Smith and Darcy Taylor
Carl Henry, b. 8/30/1927 in Haverhill; sixth; Edwin Smith (farmer, McIndoes, VT) and Beatrice Eastman (Landaff)
Evelyn F., b. 5/20/1914 in Piermont; second; Loren G. Smith (farmer, Piermont) and Emma M. Ryals (Manchester)
Everett G., b. 2/8/1929 in Hanover; ninth; George F. Smith (farmer, Stannard, VT) and Bertha Paronto (Montgomery, VT)
Gerald Leon, b. 9/1/1923 in Hanover; sixth; George F. Smith (farmer, Stannard, VT) and Bertha C. Paronto (Montgomery, VT)

Gordon W., b. 12/2/1927 in Piermont; seventh; George F. Smith (farmer, Stannard, VT) and Bertha Paronto (Montgomery, VT)
Gregory Alan, b. 1/3/1990; Dennis Smith and Michelle Ayala
James A., b. 3/20/1926 in Piermont; fifth; Edwin H. Smith (farmer, McIndoe, VT) and Beatrice Eastman (Landaff)
Judith Rena, b. 9/11/1939 in Haverhill; first; Harold W. Smith (teacher, Percy) and Josephine Stebbins (Piermont)
Katelyn Pauze, b. 9/16/1998; Ralph Douglas Smith and Nicole Cecile Pauze
Kenneth George, b. 10/21/1941 in Piermont; second; Floyd Smith (truck driver, Walden, VT) and Pearl Webster (Piermont)
Lloyd, b. 12/6/1931 in Piermont; third; Joel Smith (farmer, Orford) and Elizabeth Howe (Cornish Flat)
Madeline M., b. 7/12/1914 in Piermont; first; Ansen A. Smith (farmer, Piermont) and Viola N. Scott (Florida, MA)
Mildred A., b. 8/12/1917 in Piermont; third; Anson A. Smith (farmer, Piermont) and Viola N. Scott (FL)
Sylvia Ila, b. 6/14/1934 in Hanover; tenth; George F. Smith (laborer, Stannard, VT) and Bertha C. Paronto (Montgomery, VT)
Viola E., b. 12/29/1915 in Piermont; second; Anson H. Smith (farmer, Piermont) and Viola H. Scott (FL)
Winifred, b. 1/30/1918 in Piermont; first; Albion L. Smith (laborer, W. Fairlee, VT) and Ivalon M. Towle (Bradford, VT)
Winifred Lorraine, b. 8/22/1938 in Piermont; first; Floyd Smith (truck driver, Walden, VT) and Pearl Webster (Piermont)
Zachary Michael, b. 5/13/1992; Dennis Smith and Michelle Ayala

SOUTHWICK,
son, b. 7/2/1898 in Piermont; fourth; Fred E. Southwick (carpenter, 33, Concord) and Emma V. Ford (21, Orford)

STAFFORD,
David Benjamin, b. 10/9/1980; D. Neal Stafford and Janet M. McQuaid

STANFORD,
Robert E., b. 7/22/1926 in Piermont; fifth; Charles C. Stanford (electrician, Henniker) and Beatrice Page (Concord)

STANLEY,
Guy B., b. 3/18/1895 in Piermont; first; Orlo B. Stanley (farmer, 26, Piermont) and Althea M. Wilson (21, Groton, VT)
Meda L., b. 11/30/1904 in Piermont; second; Orlo B. Stanley (farmer, 38, Piermont) and Althea M. Wilson (31, Groton, VT)

STEBBINS,
Frank Morris, b. 8/2/1916 in Piermont; second; Harry E. Stebbins (farmer, Newbury) and Daisey P. Stevens (Franklin)
Geraldine Mae, b. 12/13/1922 in Piermont; third; Clarence B. Stebbins (clerk in store, Newbury, VT) and Nina M. Saunders (Gardiner, ME)
Henry Ellsworth, b. 8/27/1918 in Piermont; second; Harry E. Stebbins (farmer, Newbury, VT) and Daisy P. Stevens (Franklin)
Josephine Effie, b. 11/11/1919 in Piermont; second; Clarence B. Stebbins (tel. lineman, Newbury, VT) and Nina M. Saunders (Gardner, ME)
Madeline E., b. 1/5/1918 in Piermont; first; Clarence B. Stebbins (t. lineman, Newbury, VT) and Nina Saunders (Gardiner, ME)

STETSON,
son, b. 7/2/1899 in Piermont; second; George E. Stetson (laborer, 29, Lyme) and Linnie B. Gould (29, Piermont)
Alice Ann, b. 1/28/1941 in Woodsville; first; Elton Good and Lillian M. Stetson (Piermont)
Bernice E., b. 8/11/1894; first; George Stetson (laborer, Piermont) and Lizzie Hutton (Piermont)
Evelyn B., b. 5/21/1928 in Piermont; sixth; Clinton W. Stetson (farmer, Piermont) and Edna M. Robie (Piermont)
Lillian Maude, b. 5/14/1923 in Piermont; third; Clinton W. G. Stetson (laborer, Piermont) and Edna M. Robie (Piermont)
Mamie L., b. 1/19/1925 in Piermont; fourth; Clinton Stetson (farmer, Piermont) and Edna Robie (Piermont)
Wesley Freeman, b. 4/24/1922 in Piermont; second; Clinton W. G. Stetson (farmer, Piermont) and Edna M. Robie (Piermont)

STEVENS,
son, b. 2/1/1892 in Piermont; first; Leverett E. Stevens (farmer, 52, Piermont) and Clara A. Barnet (41, Newbury, VT)

daughter, b. 5/23/1892 in Piermont; fifth; Frank S. Stevens (farmer, 39, Piermont) and Laura J. Day (24, Haverhill)
stillborn son, b. 6/5/1906 in Piermont; first; Ernest Stevens (farmer, 30, Piermont) and Carrie Taylor (29)
Arlene Elizabeth, b. 7/22/1929 in Piermont; sixth; William R. Stevens (chauffeur, Corinth, VT) and Myrtle Robie (Piermont)
Bryce Alfred, b. 5/29/1954 in Haverhill; second; Donald E. Stevens (creamery wkr., Piermont) and Barbara A. Weaver (Ashland, MA)
Donald E., b. 2/18/1927 in Piermont; fifth; William R. Stevens (laborer, Corinth, VT) and Myrtie R. Stevens (Piermont)
Edith, b. 11/2/1909 in Piermont; second; Ernest L. Stevens (farmer, Piermont) and Caroline Taylor (Bethlehem)
Elizabeth, b. 6/5/1906 in Piermont; first; Fred I. Stevens (gas fitter, 37, Piermont) and Mary M. Morton (22, Plymouth)
Helen C., b. 9/14/1913 in Piermont; third; Ernest L. Stevens (farmer, Piermont) and Caroline J. Taylor (Bethlehem)
Kenneth, b. 12/18/1924 in Piermont; third; Maurise Stevens (farmer, Orford) and Ardella Lines (Wilder, VT)
Laura M., b. 3/24/1910 in Piermont; third; Fred T. Stevens (plumber, Piermont) and Mary Morton (Plymouth)
Lillian H., b. 7/12/1911 in Piermont; first; Harry M. Stevens (farmer, Piermont) and Helen L. Anell (E. Barnet, VT)
Madeline G., b. 9/29/1916 in Piermont; first; William R. Stevens (farmer, E. Corinth, VT) and Myrtie May Robie (Piermont)
Martha E., b. 7/9/1912 in Piermont; fourth; Fred T. Stevens (farmer, Piermont) and Mary Morton (Plymouth)
Melvin Robie, b. 8/11/1922 in Piermont; fourth; William R. Stevens (laborer, Corinth, VT) and Myrtie M. Robie (Piermont)
Michelle Ann, b. 7/6/1969; Thomas Stevens and Kathleen Merrill
Pamela Lynn, b. 1/26/1973; Thomas Stevens and Kathleen Merrill
Samuel Edward, b. 4/18/1918 in Piermont; second; William R. Stevens (farmer, E. Corinth, VT) and Myrtie M. Robie (Piermont)
William Alfred, b. 5/29/1920 in Piermont; third; William R. Stevens (laborer, E. Corinth, VT) and Myrtie M. Robie (Piermont)

STEVENS-METCALF,
Helen Mae, b. 11/16/1995; Ai Metcalf and Michelle A. Stevens
Kathleen Margaret, b. 12/29/1996; Ai Metcalf and Michelle Stevens

STOCKWELL,
son, b. 5/29/1895 in Piermont; Charles E. Stockwell (laborer, 35, Stanbridge, PQ) and Emma Morse (22, Canada)

STONE,
stillborn son, b. 5/29/1898 in Piermont; first; Thomas Stone (farmer, 36, Waterville, ME) and Rosa Laflam (26, Fitzwilliam)
son, b. 7/20/1900 in Piermont; first; Fred Stone (laborer, 29, Newbury, VT) and Mary Bowse (39, England)
Joseph H., b. 2/20/1900 in Piermont; fifth; Thomas Stone (farmer, 38, Waterville, PQ) and Rose Laflam (28, Fitzwilliam)
Vanessa L., b. 1/4/1930 in Piermont; third; Elwin Stone (farmer, Sheffield, VT) and Alice Drew (Glover, VT)

STREETER,
Hattie M., b. 8/4/1909 in Piermont; first; Ray N. Streeter (laborer, Lisbon) and Stella M. Cushing (McIndoes, VT)

SUNDNAS,
David John, b. 5/5/1981; John E. Sundnas and Janis D. Vincent
Erika Lynn, b. 7/16/1978; John E. Sundnas and Janice D. Vincent

SWEENEY,
Cecilia Mackenzie, b. 4/12/2004; Christopher Sweeney and Christine Sweeney
Fiona Gail, b. 4/17/2001; Christopher Sweeney and Christine Sweeney

TARBOX,
Carleton Ornal, b. 8/7/1921 in Piermont; third; Walter H. Tarbox (creameryman, Orford) and Muriel House (Troy, VT)
Franklin Charles, b. 3/26/1920 in Piermont; second; Charles A. Tarbox (farmer, Piermont) and Eunice Belle Glover (New York City)
James E., b. 7/30/1924 in Piermont; first; Earl Tarbox (chef, Piermont) and Florence Metcalf (Hardwick, VT)
Mabel T., b. 2/2/1894; first; Charles A. Tarbox (farmer, Orford) and Martha S. Horton (Orford)
Mary Glover, b. 1/11/1922 in Piermont; third; Charles A. Tarbox (farmer, Orford) and Eunice B. Glover (New York, NY)

Milton Walter, b. 4/29/1919 in Piermont; second; Walter H. Tarbox (farmer, Orford) and Muriel L. House (Troy, VT)

TAYLOR,
Bernice L., b. 12/5/1932 in Piermont; fourth; Theodore Taylor (laborer, Chelsea, VT) and Dorothy Deck (Danbury, CT)

TEBBETTS,
stillborn son, b. 8/12/1895 in Piermont; second; John Tebbetts (laborer, 34, Canada) and Rosa Stone (Lyman)

THAYER,
Dalton Tyler, b. 12/15/1994; Peter Thayer and Michelle Fagnant

THOMSON,
Matthew David, b. 10/23/1996; Dean K. Thomson and Gayle E. Balcom
Nicholas Dean, b. 4/6/1994; Dean Thomson and Gayle Balcom
Riley Elizabeth, b. 1/6/2000; Dean Thomson and Gayle Thomson

TIBAULT,
Rosa, b. 5/24/1894; first; John Tibault (farmer, Canada) and Rosa B. Stone (Derby Line, VT)

TIBBETTS,
Laurie Lee, b. 1/29/1962; John D. Tibbetts and Thelma O. Boudreau

TIRRELL,
Sarah Beth, b. 11/21/1981; Stanford W. Tirrell and Carol M. Cassady

TOWLE,
son, b. 12/–/1895 in Piermont; first; Ora Towle (Piermont)

TRAPP,
Tucker John Peterbuilt, b. 3/6/1998; Peter Norman Trapp and Erika Marie Leavey

TRUSSELL,
Elizabeth Ann, b. 7/19/1968; Paul F. Trussell and Lois C. Bishop
James Edward, b. 1/29/1973; Paul Trussell and Lois Bishop

Peter George, b. 12/11/1970; Paul F. Trussell and Lois C. Bishop

UNDERHILL,
daughter, b. 8/19/1892 in Piermont; first; Leon H. Underhill (farmer, 22, Piermont) and Jennie A. Norris (20. Corinth, VT)
son, b. 12/5/1906 in Piermont; fourth; Ernest Underhill (farmer, 36, Piermont) and Elizabeth H. Convers (33, Stewartstown)
Barton D., b. 1/14/1912 in Piermont; fourth; Leon H. Underhill (farmer, Piermont) and Jennie C. Norris (Corinth, VT)
Calvin Lawrence, b. 4/26/1970; Lawrence F. Underhill and Nancy J. Minshull
Cathleen Jane, b. 1/23/1967; Lawrence F. Underhill and Nancy J. Minshull
Christopher Lawrence, b. 5/28/1998; Calvin L. Underhill and Jean K. C. Carter
Correna Leigh, b. 3/11/1963; Lawrence F. Underhill and Nancy J. Minshull
Cynthia Lenore, b. 6/23/1965; Lawrence F. Underhill and Nancy J. Minshull
Douglas Henry, b. 12/8/1940 in Haverhill; third; Henry W. Underhill (carpenter, Piermont) and Selina M. Comford (Brighton, England)
Ernest S., b. 7/28/1934 in Woodsville; second; Stephen Underhill (farmer, Piermont) and Helen Manchester (Bath)
Henry W., b. 8/17/1897 in Piermont; Ernest S. Underhill (farmer, 27, Piermont) and Elizabeth H. Converse (23, Stewartstown)
Horace, b. 11/27/1902 in Piermont; second; Ernest Underhill (farmer, 32, Piermont) and Elizabeth Converse (29, Stewartstown)
Hugh Thomas, b. 5/13/1945 in Haverhill; fifth; Stephen Underhill (farmer, Piermont) and Helen Manchester (Bath)
Janet May, b. 11/6/1928 in Woodsville; second; Henry W. Underhill (farmer, Piermont) and Selina Maude Canfield (Brighton, England)
John H., b. 6/12/1930 in Woodsville; first; Stephen Underhill (farmer, Piermont) and Helen Manchester (Barnet, VT)
Joyce, b. 9/25/1925 in Woodsville; first; Henry Underhill (farmer, Piermont) and Maude Comford (Brighton, England)
Kimberly Anne, b. 9/2/2003; Calvin Underhill and Jean Underhill
Lawrence F., b. 2/15/1940 in Haverhill; third; Stephen L. Underhill (farmer, Piermont) and Helen G. Manchester (Orford)

Mary T., b. 4/1/1904 in Piermont; third; Ernest Underhill (farmer, 33, Piermont) and Elizabeth Converse (30, Stewartstown)
Miriam Louise, b. 11/10/1943 in Haverhill; fourth; Stephen L. Underhill (farmer, Piermont) and Helen G. Manchester (Bath)
Wyatt John, b. 5/21/2004; Jeffrey Underhill and Abigal Underhill

VAUGHAN,
son, b. 5/21/1895 in Piermont; first; William H. Vaughan (laborer, 25, S. Wales) and Mary Breason (20, E. Burke, VT)

VEGHTE,
Elizabeth C., b. 12/3/1969; Lewis Veghte, Jr. and Barbara Hess
William Lewis, b. 6/13/1967; Lewis Veghte, Jr. and Barbara Hess

VEILLETTE,
Kara Marie, b. 11/4/1992; Theresa Veillette

VERRILL,
James Thomas, b. 7/15/1949 in Haverhill; first; Thomas A. Verrill (US Army, Gorham, ME) and Dorothy A. Jones (Piermont)

VEZINA,
Louis, b. 9/3/1909 in Piermont; fifth; Leon Vezina (laborer, Quebec, PQ) and Mary Parker (Kinsey, PQ)

WAGSTAFF,
Morgan Ashley, b. 5/3/2003; Erik Wagstaff and Rebecca Wagstaff

WAKEFIELD,
Janis Wilma, b. 11/15/1947 in Woodsville; first; Howard O. Wakefield (merchant, Westfield, VT) and Rosalie Eaton (Bradford, VT)

WATERMAN,
Michael Richard, b. 10/11/1954 in Haverhill; second; Richard D. Waterman (mechanic, Lebanon) and Irma Alice Tullar (Corinth, VT)
Molly Kay, b. 6/24/1956 in Haverhill; third; Richard D. Waterman (mechanic, Lebanon) and Irma A. Tullar (Corinth, VT)

WEBSTER,
daughter, b. 8/21/1898 in Piermont; first; Freeman H. Webster (laborer, 24, Haverhill) and Mabel A. Mann (20, Orford)
son, b. 1/31/1912 in Piermont; fourth; Walter C. Webster (laborer, Piermont) and Lizzie Howland (Piermont)
Charles E., b. 9/19/1910 in Piermont; third; Walter Webster (laborer, Piermont) and Lizzie Howland (Piermont)
Clara B., b. 11/19/1908 in Piermont; second; Walter C. Webster (laborer, Piermont) and Lizzie Howland (Piermont)
Daniel Walter, b. 10/8/1923 in Piermont; eighth; Walter Webster (laborer, Piermont) and Lizzie Howland (Piermont)
Evelyn L., b. 8/9/1931 in Piermont; eleventh; Walter Webster (mill hand, Piermont) and Lizzie Howland (Piermont)
Floyd W., b. 4/5/1917 in Piermont; sixth; Walter C. Webster (board sawyer, Piermont) and Lizzie Howland (Piermont)
Harry L., b. 9/23/1907 in Piermont; first; Walter C. Webster (laborer, 21, Piermont) and Lizzie Howland (17, Piermont)
Howard W., b. 2/10/1921 in Piermont; seventh; Walter C. Webster (board sawyer, Piermont) and Lizzie Howland (Piermont)
Madeline B., b. 7/30/1914 in Piermont; fourth; Freman H. Webster (farmer, Haverhill) and Mabel A. Mann (Orford)
Marjorie A., b. 10/5/1916 in Piermont; third; Ralph A. Webster (mill man, Piermont) and Hattie D. Molnay (Piermont)
Nelson K., b. 3/31/1911 in Piermont; third; Freeman H. Webster (farmer, Haverhill) and Mabel Mann (Orford)
Vera G., b. 3/20/1926 in Piermont; ninth; Walter Webster (laborer, Piermont) and Lizzie Howland (Piermont)
Verna E., b. 2/19/1914 in Piermont; fifth; Walter C. Webster (bd. sawyer, Piermont) and Lizzie Howland (Piermont)
Walter Charles, b. 10/7/1928 in Piermont; tenth; Walter Webster (laborer, Piermont) and Lizzie Howland (Piermont)

WELCH,
Hilda R., b. 1/11/1950 in Haverhill; third; Walter F. Welch (farmer, Groton, VT) and Alberta L. Shepard (Hartford, VT)
Nancy Ann, b. 6/16/1943 in Haverhill; third; Robert O. Welch (farm laborer, Newbury, VT) and Myrle F. Gilman (Laconia)
Ronald Stewart, b. 4/17/1947 in Woodsville; second; Walter F. Welch (farmer, Groton, VT) and Alberta L. Shepard (Hartford, VT)

WENTWORTH,
Myrrhanda Kay, b. 4/22/1992; Cynthia Wentworth

WESTERLUND,
Kimberly Cash, b. 1/1/1991; William N. Westerlund III and Karrie K. Daniels
Kristine Carter, b. 7/11/1992; William Westerlund III and Kerrie Daniels

WHEELER,
Gordon, b. 10/11/1925 in Piermont; second; Fred K. Wheeler (farmer, Newbury, VT) and Leona M. Sawyer (Piermont)
Kenneth, b. 7/28/1924 in Piermont; first; Fred K. Wheeler (laborer, Newbury, VT) and Leona M. Sawyer (Piermont)

WHITAKER,
Lydia Rose, b. 2/9/1999; Leonard Whitaker and Deborah Garlitz
Seth Noah, b. 10/27/1996; Leonard Whitaker and Deborah A. Garlitz
Zachary Bob, b. 8/15/1993; Leonard Whitaker and Deborah A. Garlitz

WHITE,
son, b. 7/25/1910 in Piermont; first; Edwin G. White (teleph. insp., Orangeburg, NY) and Edith Ford (Warren); residence - Concord
Brenna Leigh, b. 1/28/1996; Randy D. White and Jennifer Z. Van Karssen
Bryon Alexander, b. 3/19/1998; Randy Dean White and Jennifer Zena Vankarssen
Chelsea Danielle, b. 11/16/1993; Donald A. White III and Kathleen M. Partington
Chester J., b. 5/27/1898 in Piermont; fourth; William M. White (stone cutter, 28, E. Haven, VT) and Nellie Horne (23, Ryegate, VT)
Lena B., b. 6/4/1911 in Piermont; first; James White (laborer, NS) and Katherine M. Gildine (Barnard, VT)
Michael John, b. 4/25/1997; Timothy G. White and Terri F. Dematt
Rian Richard, b. 10/4/2004; Donald White and Kathleen White
Thomas Robert, b. 3/3/1992; Donald White III and Kathleen Partington
Tiffany Elizabeth, b. 11/14/1976; Paul S. White and Barbara L. Hemingway

Timothy Stuart, b. 12/27/1978; Paul S. White and Barbara L. Hemingway

WHITNEY,
Isabelle B., b. 4/29/1905 in Piermont; first; George R. Whitney (farmer, 20, Stowe, ME) and Grace E. Ladeau (19, Fitzwilliam)

WILKINS,
Maggie Beth, b. 9/9/1980; Ricky A. Kidder and Diane V. Wilkins
Taylor Lee, b. 12/31/1995; Timothy M. Wilkins and Charity L. Nowell

WILLIAMS,
Beth Frances, b. 9/3/1973; Kenneth Williams and Lorraine Adams
Steven Michael, b. 4/28/1971; Kenneth Williams and Lorraine B. Adams

WILSON,
Carolyn Ann, b. 3/31/1951 in Haverhill; third; Henry I. Wilson (laborer, Piermont) and Phyllis M. Keith (N. Haverhill)
George Hazen, b. 9/9/1921 in Piermont; sixth; Hazen Wilson (teamster, Groton, VT) and Nellie Fairbrother (Barnet, England)
Henry Isaac, b. 3/23/1918 in Piermont; fifth; Hazen G. Wilson (laborer, Groton, VT) and Nellie Fairbrather (Canada, PQ)
Henry Stanley, b. 1/3/1938 in Haverhill; first; Henry I. Wilson (laborer, Piermont) and Phyllis Mae Keith (Haverhill)
Jimmie, b. 10/24/1937 in Piermont; first; Dorothy Wilson (Lexington, MA)
Norman Edward, b. 11/29/1936 in Woodsville; third; Clayton B. Wilson (laborer, Quincy, MA) and Doris Brouin (Manchester)

WINN,
son, b. 9/11/1897 in Piermont; Frank P. Winn (farmer, 45, Piermont) and Nellie Putnam (44, Haverhill)
Bessie M., b. 4/2/1910 in Piermont; first; Frank J. Winn (farmer, W. Fairlee, VT) and Rosette Underhill (Piermont)
Donald Jennings, b. 6/27/1940 in Piermont; fifth; Frank Haines Winn (farmer, Piermont) and Verne Jennings (W. Fairlee, VT)
Esther A., b. 10/10/1914 in Piermont; second; Frank J. Winn (farmer, W. Fairlee, VT) and Rosetta M. Underhill (Piermont)
Frank H., b. 3/25/1910 in Piermont; first; Hiram Winn (farmer, Piermont) and Hope Morse (Haverhill)

George P., b. 11/2/1927 in Piermont; first; Parker C. Winn (farmer, Piermont) and Esther B. Hood (Topsham, VT)
Gerald Haines, b. 11/27/1937 in Haverhill; third; F. Haines Winn (farmer, Piermont) and Verne Jennings (W. Fairlee, VT)
Janet Lea, b. 12/28/1954 in Haverhill; second; William H. Winn (farmer, Piermont) and Christine A. Wheeler (Lisbon)
Jason Robert, b. 5/7/1980; Joanne Winn
Jo Ann, b. 12/28/1954 in Haverhill; first; William H. Winn (farmer, Piermont) and Christine A. Wheeler (Lisbon)
John Ellis, b. 12/5/1938 in Haverhill; fourth; F. Haines Winn (farmer, Piermont) and Verne Jennings (W. Fairlee, VT)
Laura Belle, b. 5/5/1940 in Haverhill; third; Parker Cole Winn (farmer, Piermont) and Esther Hood (Topsham, VT)
Marion K., b. 12/1/1911 in Piermont; second; Hiram P. Winn (farmer, Piermont) and Hope A. Morse (Haverhill)
Ronald Hiram, b. 7/12/1936 in Woodsville; second; Frank H. Winn (farmer, Piermont) and Verne Jennings (W. Fairlee, VT)
Velma Rose, b. 2/16/1942 in Haverhill; sixth; Frank Haines Winn (farmer, Piermont) and Verne Jennings (W. Fairlee, VT)
Violet May, b. 8/16/1935 in Woodsville; first; Frank Haines Winn (farmer, Piermont) and Verne Jennings (W. Fairlee, VT)
William H., b. 4/6/1924 in Piermont; third; Frank J. Winn (farmer, W. Fairlee, VT) and Rosette Underhill (Piermont)

WINNBERRY,
Caleb John, b. 1/22/1998; Mark Steven Winberry and Cynthia Mary Merchant
Ethan Luke, b. 5/27/1999; Mark Winnberry and Cynthia Merchant

WISWELL,
daughter, b. 3/12/1895 in Piermont; second; Guy A. Wiswell (merchant, 27, Clarksville) and Mary C. Burbeck (30, Brunswick, VT)

WOODARD,
Pauline Sue, b. 1/16/1961; Russell W. Woodard and Marie S. Landry

WOODWARD,
Jacob John, b. 12/27/1991; Robert J. Woodward and Kathleen A. Hurlburt

Robert Edward, b. 11/22/1989; Robert J. Woodward and Kathleen A. Hurlburt

WORTHLEY,
stillborn son, b. 1/2/1911 in Piermont; fifth; George W. Worthley (farmer, Corinth, VT) and Lydia Brainerd (Putney, VT)

WRIGHT,
son, b. 1/28/1897 in Piermont; Tilden B. Wright (farmer, Warren) and Mary E. Page (Lincoln, VT)
daughter, b. 12/23/1898 in Piermont; third; Tilden B. Wright (farmer, 28, Warren) and Mary E. Page (27, Lincoln, VT)
son, b. 12/28/1902 in Piermont; third; Fred L. Wright (teamster, 28, Wentworth) and Lizzie M. Kenerson (25, Concord, VT)
daughter, b. 5/8/1912 in Piermont; second; Arthur G. Wright (farmer, Piermont) and Nancy Flanders (Warren)
Alan G., b. 5/13/1968; Ralph A. Wright and Marylin R. Goss
Floyd E., b. 3/24/1921 in Piermont; fourth; Frank R. Wright (farmer, Newport, VT) and Lila Wilson (Charleston, VT)
Gilbert M., b. 5/7/1906 in Piermont; fifth; Fred L. Wright (farmer, 31, Wentworth) and Lizzie Kenerson (28, Concord, VT)
Harold Arthur, b. 10/25/1933 in Piermont; first; Forrest E. Wright (farmer, Piermont) and Althea M. Dow (Wentworth)
John A., b. 9/15/1969; Ralph Wright and Marylin Gass
Kevin F., b. 6/20/1965; Ralph A. Wright and Marylin R. Goss
Wesley N., b. 9/14/1925 in Piermont; first; Malcolm Wright (laborer, Bradford, VT) and Delia Merritt (Topsham, VT)

YOUNG,
Chasity Lynn, b. 3/8/1982; Alton Rollo Young and Mellisa Belle Young
Rufus B., b. 11/17/1927 in Piermont; second; Rufus B. Young (laborer, Waterford, VT) and Electa Bailey (Contoocook); residence - Littleton

YOUNGMAN,
Lyndsey Morgan, b. 8/2/2001; Kurt Youngman and Jamie Youngman

[UNKNOWN],
   son, b. 11/20/1922 in Piermont; second; Pasquale ----- (farmer, Italy) and Elizabeth Zarella (Worcester, MA)

PIERMONT MARRIAGES

ABBOTT,
Edward J. of Bradford, VT m. Margaret M. **Bateson** of Bradford, VT 11/23/1904 in Piermont; H - 25, laborer, b. Thetford, VT, s/o E. M. C. Abbott (Bradford, VT, blacksmith); W - 28, housework, 2nd, b. St. Johns, d/o ----- White (Roxbury, MA, deceased)

ACKERMAN,
Larry D. of Piermont m. Lisa M. **Hall** of Pike 5/18/1985

ADAMS,
Reynold E. of Portland, ME m. Marie **LaMontagne** of Piermont 7/19/1929 in Piermont; H - 22, laborer, b. Kingfield, ME, s/o Eleary Adams (Strong, ME, fireman) and Edna R. Jordan (Portland, ME, domestic); W - 19, domestic, b. Piermont, d/o Clarence LaMontagne (Piermont, laborer) and Susie O. Gould (Colebrook, housewife)

ALDRICH,
Henry S. of Bath m. Dorothy S. **Howard** of Piermont 7/19/1941 in Hanover; H - 36, ins. adjuster, b. Bath, s/o Hiram F. Aldrich (Bath, laborer) and Agnes F. Southard (Lisbon, housewife); W - 30, secretary, 2nd, divorced, b. S. Barre, VT, d/o Earl Vail Howard (E. Haven, VT, merchant) and Amy M. Sanders (Montpelier, VT, post mistress)
Kenneth N. of Dalton m. Henrietta Helen **Noyes** of Piermont 12/30/1950 in Piermont; H - 21, student, b. Whitefield, s/o William S. Aldrich (Dalton) and Nila Smith (Dalton); W - 19, student, b. Piermont, d/o G. Henry Noyes (Pike) and Mary Morin (Woodsville)

ALFREDS,
Gary S. of Stafford Springs, CT m. Lee A. **Clark** of Stoughton, MA 3/2/1984

ALLEN,
Ethan C. of Piermont m. Nina **Newell** of Piermont 5/16/1909 in Wentworth; H - 31, farmer, b. Coventry, VT, s/o Harrison Allen (Coventry, VT, farmer); W - 31, housework, 2nd, b. Barnard, VT, d/o Charles Newell (Barnard, VT, blacksmith)

AMES,

Arthur E. of Piermont m. Alice L. **Underhill** of Piermont 10/14/1891 in Piermont; H - 20, laborer, b. Orford, s/o Asa Ames (Orford, farmer) and Mary W. Runnels (Piermont); W - 21, teacher, b. Piermont, d/o Edward Underhill (Piermont, farmer) and Emily Libby (Newbury)

Asa E. of Piermont m. Susie Ella **Robie** of Piermont 11/15/1892 in Piermont; H - 21, laborer, b. Orford, s/o Asa A. Ames (Orford) and Mary Runnells (Piermont); W - 20, domestic, b. Piermont, d/o Lyman M. Robie (Corinth, VT) and Eunice A. Coffman (Piermont)

Asa Edward of Piermont m. Esther G. **Brown** of Manchester 11/15/1924 in Manchester; H - 20, student, b. Piermont, s/o Arthur E. Ames (Orford, creamery); W - 20, student, b. Manchester, d/o Frank Brown (Manchester, mill owner)

ANDERSON,

Albert Solomon of W. Quincy, MA m. May Thelma **Brock** of Piermont 8/7/1928 in Piermont; H - 26, minister, b. Groton, VT, s/o Solomon Anderson (Sweden, stone cutter) and Etta Mae Clark (Groton, VT, housewife); W - 22, student, b. S. Newbury, VT, d/o Ernest F. Brock (Newbury, VT, farmer) and Olive E. Knight (Newbury, VT, housewife)

ANDROSS,

Clarence E. of Piermont m. Rosana C. **Marston** of Topsham, VT 3/7/1891 in Corinth, VT; H - 26, laborer, b. Piermont, s/o E. P. Andross (Bradford, VT, blacksmith) and Sarah A. Whitcomb (Troy, VT); W - 22, domestic, b. Orange, VT, d/o Josiah B. Marston (Orford, farmer) and Chastina C. Beach (Corinth, VT)

ANTHONY,

George S. of Westfield, NJ m. Wanda H. **Drew** of Piermont 5/29/1971

ATKINS,

Lyndal of Haverhill m. Ethel **Wilson** of Piermont 6/6/1935 in Haverhill; H - 20, laborer, b. Hardwick, VT, s/o Harland Atkins (Wolcott, VT, janitor) and Ada Richardson (Wolcott, VT, housewife); W - 22, clerk, b. Bradford, VT, d/o Hazen Wilson

(Corinth, VT, deceased) and Nellie Fairbrother (England, domestic)

AUSTIN,
Ernest H. of Piermont m. Josie M. **French** of Orford 10/1/1932 in Orford; H - 58, laborer, b. W. Fairlee, VT, s/o George A. Austin (Worcester, MA, deceased) and Nellie DeGoosh (deceased); W - 41, domestic, 2nd, divorced, b. Swiftwater, d/o Edward Everett (Lyman, deceased) and Mary Elliott (Benton, deceased)

BAGLEY,
J. F. of Corinth, VT m. Jane A. **Bagley** of Corinth, VT 6/4/1898 in Piermont; H - 53, farmer, 2nd, b. Corinth, VT, s/o Jonathan Bagley (Corinth, VT, farmer); W - 45, domestic, 2nd, b. Fairlee, VT, d/o Henry H. Clark (Bradford, VT, farmer)
Lynford G. of Topsham, VT m. Mary E. **Austin** of Island Pond, VT 5/29/1938 in Piermont; H - 23, finisher in bobbin mill, b. W. Topsham, VT, s/o Fred C. Bagley (W. Topsham, VT, mink farmer) and Lena Keyes (Orange, VT, housewife); W - 23, school teacher, b. Richmond, PQ, d/o Harry Austin (Ellsworth Falls, ME, RR disp'r) and Daphne Hall (Island Pond, VT, inn keeper)

BAILEY,
Henry J. of Piermont m. Margaret **Wilmot** of Lyme 8/7/1932 in Bradford, VT; H - 26, laborer, b. Bradford, VT, s/o Charles Bailey (Albany, NY, deceased) and Della Bathrow (Orford, housewife); W - 18, domestic, b. Lyme, d/o Elber Wilmot (farmer) and Myrtle Cummings (Lyme, housewife)
Martin J. of Corinth, VT m. Lillie A. **Gamsby** of Bradford, VT 9/22/1903 in Piermont; H - 35, laborer, 2nd, b. Corinth, VT, s/o Joel Bailey (Corinth, VT, farmer); W - 17, housework, b. Canada, PQ, d/o Rufus A. Gamsby (Canada, PQ, laborer)

BAKER,
Bradley H. of Orford m. Clara B. **Webster** of Piermont 11/4/1926 in Orford; H - 24, laborer, b. Orford, s/o Henry G. Baker (Orford, blacksmith) and Inez Smith (Orford, housewife); W - 17, domestic, b. Piermont, d/o Walter Webster (Piermont, laborer)
Robert D. of Concord m. Winifred Loraine **Smith** of Concord 8/15/1959

Samuel M., Jr. of Marblehead, MA m. Carol (Nichols) **Smith** of Marblehead, MA 6/4/1988

BALCH,
Mason of Lyme m. Bertha **Hart** of Piermont 2/10/1934 in Orford; H - 19, laborer, b. Lyme, s/o Harvey Balch (Taftsville, VT, laborer) and Lillian Morrill (Taftsville, VT, housewife); W - 17, at home, b. Canaan, d/o Frank Hart (Lyme, laborer) and Julia Buckley (Ireland, housewife)

Roy of Piermont m. Olive W. **Blanchard** of Piermont 1/6/1930 in Piermont; H - 24, farmer, b. Hartford, VT, s/o Harvey Balch (laborer) and Josephine Morrill (Taftsville, VT, housewife); W - 18, housewife, b. Orford, d/o Ray Blanchard (laborer) and Mabel Cushing (Newport, VT, housewife)

BAND,
Richard A. of Candia m. Jean C. **Bishop** of Piermont 6/17/1970

BARBER,
Stuart B. of Benton m. Doris E. **Hood** of Piermont 6/4/1972

BARNATAS,
Adam Joseph of Piermont m. Donna Drew **Huntington** of Piermont 6/25/1994

BARNES,
Charles C. of Piermont m. Lillian F. **Barnes** of Piermont 10/15/1976

BARTLE,
John D. of Piermont m. Jenniffer S. **Winn** of Piermont 12/31/1983

BATCHELDER,
Melvin J. of Piermont m. Nettie B. **Austin** of Piermont 6/25/1892 in Wentworth; H - 33, farmer, 2nd, b. Warren, s/o Reuben Batchelder (Warren) and Laura O---- (Warren); W - 23, domestic, b. Haverhill, d/o George A. Austin (Worcester, MA) and Nellie Degoosh (Orange, VT)

Robert P. of Piermont m. Annie V. **Eaton** of Bradford, VT 7/4/1942 in Bradford, VT; H - 22, machinist, b. Plainfield, VT, s/o Natt. M. Batchelder (Plainfield, VT, farmer) and Ruth C. Vincent (E. Montpelier, VT, housewife); W - 17, none, b. Bradford, VT, d/o

John F. Eaton (W. Fairlee, VT, carpenter) and Wilma H. Butterfield (Haverhill, housewife)

BEACH,
James F. of Laconia m. Diane G. **Mitchell** of Piermont 11/3/1971

BEAMIS,
Lee Weeks of Haverhill m. Virginia E. **Hartwell** of Piermont 1/11/1942 in Haverhill; H - 23, clerk, b. Worcester, MA, s/o Frank John Beamis (Haverhill, mail messenger) and Louise Pierce (Haverhill, housewife); W - 16, student, b. Piermont, d/o George J. Hartwell (Haverhill, mill worker) and Ida M. Robie (Piermont, housewife)

BEAN,
Bertram P. of Piermont m. Agnes **Guilmette** of Manchester 6/3/1937 in Lyme; H - 25, truck driver, b. Orford, s/o Philip Bean (Orford, farmer) and Blanche Burnham (Dorchester, deceased); W - 22, domestic, b. St. Johnsbury, VT, d/o Philip Guilmette (Canada, laborer) and Charlotte Hartshorn (St. Johnsbury, VT, deceased)

Merton of Bradford, VT m. Evelyn **Webster** of Piermont 3/24/1951 in Bradford, VT; H - 18, laborer, b. Corinth, VT, s/o Richard Bean (Woodsville) and Beatrice Huntington (Corinth, VT); W - 19, presser, b. Plymouth, d/o Walter Webster (Piermont) and Elizabeth Howland (Piermont)

Richard of Orford m. Beatrice **Huntington** of Corinth, VT 2/13/1935 in Piermont; H - 22, farmer, b. Haverhill, s/o Carroll J. Bean (Orford, none) and Lutheria M. Heath (Barnet, VT, housewife); W - 21, at home, b. Corinth, VT, d/o Dana Huntington (Corinth, VT, farmer) and Eva Hooker (Corinth, VT, housewife)

Wallace B. of Orford m. Josie M. **Fadden** of Piermont 6/19/1929 in Piermont; H - 25, chauffeur, b. Orford, s/o Charles L. Bean (Sandwich, farmer) and Carrie E. Gardner (Lyme, housewife); W - 24, school teacher, b. Thornton, d/o Dana Fadden (Thornton, farmer) and Esther Downing (Thornton, housewife)

BEARDSLEY,
Carl of Piermont m. Barbara **Hackett** of Piermont 12/12/1948 in Piermont; H - 23, laborer, b. Boston, MA, s/o George Beardsley (Boston, MA, supt. of bldgs.) and Bessie Chandler (NS,

housewife); W - 18, waitress, b. Hanover, d/o Harley C. Hackett (Haverhill, retired) and Jeannie Everson (Melrose, MA, housewife)

BEAULIEU,
Donald Norman of Piermont m. Tracy Lynn **Nolan** of Piermont 7/12/1997

BEEDE,
Robert R. of Hardwick, VT m. Edith **Darling** of Walden, VT 3/15/1930 in Woodsville; H - 28, truckman, 2nd, b. Albany, VT, s/o William H. Beede (Albany, VT, farmer) and Gertrude Rowell (Albany, VT, housewife); W - 20, domestic, b. Groton, VT, d/o Marshall Darling (Groton, VT, farmer) and Lottie Keniston (Groton, VT, housewife)

BELL,
Charles A. of Los Angeles, CA m. Lovena L. **Pershing** of Los Angeles, CA 2/2/1985

BERGERON,
Richard, Jr. of Orford m. Laura Lee **Fowler** of Piermont 6/12/1993

BERRY,
Bruce Orlin of W. Newbury, VT m. Joan Arlene **Hammod** of W. Newbury, VT 10/15/1994

BETZ,
Lorin John of Whitefield m. Edith M. **Stevens** of Piermont 11/16/1935 in Piermont; H - 28, at home, b. Berlin, s/o John Betz (Germany, inn keeper) and Lina Martin (Germany, housewife); W - 26, teacher, b. Piermont, d/o Ernest L. Stevens (Piermont, farmer) and Carolina Taylor (Bethlehem, housewife)

BICKFORD,
Fred H. of Bradford, VT m. Luella B. **Ford** of Piermont 9/16/1891 in Piermont; H - 22, buttermaker, b. Lebanon, s/o James H. Bickford (Glover, VT, buttermaker) and Emma Hadlock (Newbury, VT); W - 22, lady, b. Orford, d/o Edward Ford (Orford, drover) and Harriet Gould (Piermont)

BIGELOW,
Carl A. of Montpelier, VT m. Olive F. **Daudlin** of Montpelier, VT
5/24/1937 in Lyme; H - 22, mechanic, b. Crown Point, NY, s/o
Glenn A. Bigelow (Bridport, VT, farmer) and Dianthia Putnam
(Ticonderoga, NY, deceased); W - 19, housework, b. Westfield,
VT, d/o Napoleon Daudlin (Granby, PQ, laborer) and Eva Barrie
(St. Paul, PQ, housewife)

Paul W. of Waterbury, VT m. Ruth E. **Dewey** of Stowe, VT 3/5/1960

BILLINGTON,
John E. of Boise, ID m. Patricia L. (Duncan) **Hennessey** of Boise, ID
8/9/1987

BISHOP,
John E. of Piermont m. Nancy J. **Henry** of Keene 8/28/1982

BIXBY,
Daniel A. of Vershire, VT m. Joanne **Cummings** of Vershire, VT
7/15/1989

David V. of Piermont m. Barbara A. **Knapp** of Piermont 11/30/1963

Reginald W. of Piermont m. Jeanette M. **Haines** of Warren
11/2/1957 in Barrington; H - 22, carpenter, b. Wentworth, s/o
Vernon J. Bixby (Alberta, Canada) and Gertrude Walls
(Woburn, MA); W - 18, stenographer, b. Warren, d/o Wilbur N.
Haines (Newmarket) and Cora A. Morrison (Warren)

BLAIR,
Herbert P. of Piermont m. Marguerite B. **Judkins** of Orford
7/23/1927 in Woodsville; H - 24, electrician, b. Piermont, s/o
Oliver J. Blair (Ottawa, Canada, clerk) and Addie L. Center
(Piermont, housewife); W - 19, domestic, b. Warren, d/o Amos
Judkins (laborer) and Minnie Kelley (Bangor, ME, housewife)

Oliver of Piermont m. Addie L. **Curtis** of Piermont 12/26/1901 in
Piermont; H - 30, laborer, b. L'Orijinal, Canada, s/o Oliver Blair
(L'Orijinal, Canada, carpenter); W - 40, dressmaker, b.
Piermont, d/o Charles Curtis (Piermont, farmer)

BLAISDELL,
Fred D. of Piermont m. Della J. **Clement** of Bradford, VT 2/13/1913
in Lisbon; H - 39, farmer, b. Piermont, s/o John E. Blaisdell

(Piermont, farmer); W - 22, housework, b. Campton, d/o Harry E. Clement (Warren, laborer)

Rupert of Piermont m. Dorothy **Keyes** of Haverhill 7/21/1928 in Haverhill; H - 24, stenographer, b. Groton, VT, s/o Harry Blaisdell (Piermont, farmer) and Grace Dunkley (Haverhill, housewife); W - 22, clerk, b. Hollis, ME, d/o William Keyes (Haverhill, farmer) and Anna Cotton (Concord, housewife)

BLAKEBROUGH,

James of Piermont m. Anna **Hubbard** of Woodsville 9/12/1931 in Woodsville; H - 28, laborer, b. Brookfield, VT, s/o James Blakebrough (Bridgeport, CT, deceased) and Olive Batchelder (Brookfield, VT, housewife); W - 28, domestic, d/o Irving Hubbard (Dalton, painter) and Elvah Powers (Lunenburg, VT, housewife)

BLANCHARD,

Albert of Bradford, VT m. Loraine **Oakes** of Piermont 2/5/1950 in Bradford, VT; H - 18, US Army, b. Bridgewater, VT, s/o Frank Blanchard (Bridgewater, VT) and Mildred Furman (Bridgewater, VT); W - 18, none, b. Barnet, VT, d/o Glenn Oakes (Colebrook) and Lottie Gates (Monroe)

Raymond of Piermont m. Mabel E. **Cushing** of Orford 5/30/1906 in Piermont; H - 23, laborer, b. Piermont, s/o E. W. Dennis (Stratford, VT, farmer); W - 17, housework, b. Newport, VT, d/o George Cushing (Derby Line, laborer)

BLODGETT,

Joseph Andre of Corinth, VT m. Bonnie Lynn **Hayward** of E. Corinth, VT 7/14/1990

Lenn. B. of Stratford m. Katherine S. **Webster** of Haverhill 12/31/1899 in Piermont; H - 25, merchant, 2nd, b. Stratford, s/o Loyal B. Blodgett (Stratford, merchant); W - 22, housework, b. Piermont, d/o Charles S. Webster (Boscawen, farmer)

BOARDMAN,

George of Piermont m. Jennie **Goodwin** of Piermont 6/24/1901 in Orfordville; H - 46, farmer, 2nd, b. Swanton, VT, s/o Joseph Boardman (England, merchant); W - 26, housework, b. Canada, d/o John Gardner (farmer)

BONETT,
Elwin K. of Piermont m. Charlotte M. **Clement** of Pike 12/13/1952 in Piermont; H - 26, truck driver, b. Piermont,. s/o Raymond Bonett (Monroe) and Gladys K. Webster (Piermont); W - 18, student, b. Tyngsboro, MA, d/o Edward P. Clement (Lowell, MA) and Vivian Adams (Lowell, MA)

Ray E. of Piermont m. Cora **Bowker** of Piermont 12/5/1910 in Piermont; H - 19, laborer, b. Monroe, s/o Daniel P. Bonett (Kirby, VT, deceased); W - 20, housework, b. Piermont, d/o Francis P. Bowker (Canada, PQ, farmer)

Ray E. of Piermont m. Gladys K. **Webster** of Piermont 2/6/1926 in Orford; H - 34, mail carrier, 2nd, divorced, b. Monroe, s/o Daniel Bonett (Kirby, VT, deceased) and Edna Turner (Monroe, deceased); W - 27, clerk, b. Piermont, d/o Freeman Webster (Haverhill, farmer) and Mabel Mann (Orford, housewife)

BOUTIN,
Adam Lee of Haverhill m. Dawn Marie **Stygles** of Piermont 6/10/1995

BOWES,
Arthur of Piermont m. Eva **Merchant** of Bradford, VT 11/26/1901 in Haverhill; H - 21, laborer, b. Chateaugay, NY, s/o George Bowes (England, mechanic); W - 18, housework, b. Newbury, VT, d/o Joseph Merchant (Stratford, laborer)

BOYNTON,
Fred A. of Lyme m. Minnie E. **Lewis** of Piermont 5/21/1934 in Orford; H - 66, retired, 3rd, b. Ballston Spa, NY, s/o John F. Boynton (Mercier, ME, iron worker) and Sarah J. Coombs (Utica, NY, deceased); W - 52, housekeeper, 3rd, b. Vershire, VT, d/o George A. Church (Vershire, VT, board sawyer) and Sarah F. Aldrich (Corinth, VT, deceased)

BRACKETT,
James S. of Orford m. Vonda S. **Cummings** of Piermont 5/29/1982

BREED,
Tracy S. of Unity m. Millicent B. **Howland** of Piermont 4/22/1919 in Piermont; H - 26, farmer, b. Unity, s/o Schuyler G. Breed (Unity,

farmer); W - 24, teacher, b. Piermont, d/o Nathaniel Howland (Landaff, farmer)

BRICK,
Keith M. of Piermont m. Laurie Ann **Fay** of Piermont 5/30/1998

BRIER,
Stephen E. of Newbury, VT m. Roxanne J. **Carter** of Newbury, VT 10/14/1989

BRIGGS,
Robert H. of Lincoln m. Elizabeth E. **Jackson** of Piermont 11/5/1977

BROCHU,
John of Piermont m. Pamela J. **Demick** of S. Ryegate, VT 8/18/2001

BROCK,
Carl Fenton of Piermont m. Mildred **Melendy** of Newbury, VT 10/8/1927 at Lake Placid Club, NY; H - 26, farmer, b. Newbury, VT, s/o Ernest F. Brock (Newbury, VT, farmer) and Olive Knight (Newbury, VT, housewife); W - 30, domestic, b. Boston, MA, d/o Lester L. Melendy (S. Fairlee, VT, deceased) and Grace Aldrich (Vershire, VT, housewife)

BROOKS,
Fred E. of Bradford, VT m. Myrtie E. **Scales** of Bradford, VT 4/29/1911 in Piermont; H - 19, farmer, b. Bradford, VT, s/o W. E. Brooks (Lyme, farmer); W - 21, housework, b. Bradford, VT, d/o Steven Scales (Bradford, VT, carpenter)
Olin C., Jr. of Piermont m. Maxine E. **Fulford** of Piermont 3/7/1959

BROWN,
Bert of Piermont m. Mamie **Hubbard** of Piermont 8/26/1909 in Haverhill; H - 52, farmer, b. Barton, VT, s/o John Brown (deceased); W - 57, housework, 2nd, b. Canada
Nowell S. of Piermont m. Janice M. **Boyce** of Woodsville 2/3/1973

BRYAR,
Kenneth B. of Piermont m. Eva L. **Tucker** of Newbury, VT 6/24/1920 in Bradford, VT; H - 22, farmer, b. Boston, MA, s/o George B.

Bryar (N. Groton); W - 20, b. Newbury, VT, d/o Jonas Tucker (Newbury, VT)

BURBECK,
Perry J. of Woodsville m. Christie **Ritchie** of Piermont 9/20/1953 in Newbury, VT; H - 66, retired, 2nd, b. Haverhill, s/o William O. Burbeck (Haverhill) and Carrie Blanchard (Cumberland Ctr., ME); W - 61, music teacher, 3rd, b. Piermont, d/o H. E. Morrison (Haverhill) and Ida M. Robie (Corinth, VT)

BURNAKA,
John Robert of Shelton, CT m. Deborah Lynn **Hessberger** of Shelton, CT 5/26/2001

BURNELL,
Marc of Northfield, VT m. Kathryn **Davis** of Northfield, VT 11/12/2004

BURROUGHS,
Robert Orser of Newbury, VT m. Amy Blanche **Downing** of Orford 5/30/1927 in Orford; H - 21, farmer, b. Newbury, VT, s/o Ralph E. Burroughs (Newbury, VT, farmer) and Jessie L. Orser (Carlisle, NS, housewife); W - 21, domestic, b. Thornton, d/o Daniel Downing (W. Thornton, farmer) and Kate E. Ward (W. Thornton, housewife)

BURTON,
John F. of W. Somerville m. Sadie Iva **Hill** of Piermont 3/2/1898 in Piermont; H - 42, painter, b. Hillsboro, s/o Henry S. Burton (New York City, farmer); W - 32, book keeper, b. Piermont, d/o Joseph Hill (Barnston, PQ, tub maker)

CALANDRELLI,
Emilio R. of Stamford, CT m. Deanne J. **Correa** of Stamford, CT 11/27/1980

CALLENDER,
Wilbur of Bath m. Marion F. **Goued** of Piermont 8/14/1947 in Piermont; H - 22, student, b. Littleton, s/o Robert S. Collender (Northfield, MA, farmer) and Ada M. Welles (Franconia, housewife); W - 21, teacher, b. Piermont, d/o Harry R. Goued

(Piermont, merchant) and Eva F. Craig (Middletown, CT, housewife)

CARR,
William O. of Piermont m. Gertie N. **Stanley** of Piermont 4/26/1892 in Piermont; H - 24, blacksmith, b. Washington, VT, s/o Robert Carr (Corinth, VT) and Ella Lawrence (Fairlee, VT); W - 20, domestic, b. Piermont, d/o Hubbard S. Stanley (Piermont) and Lucy ----- (Barnston, PQ)

CELLEY,
Herbert V. of Piermont m. Stella L. **Virgin** of Piermont 9/7/1892 in Haverhill; H - 35, mechanic, 2nd, b. Bridgewater, VT, s/o Richard V. Celley and Eunice Barrett; W - 26, domestic, b. Piermont, d/o Reed S. Virgin and Kate Edwards

CHADDOCK,
Craig C. of Lennoxville, PQ m. Jane Kate **Musty** of Lennoxville, PQ 9/1/1927 in Piermont; H - 46, retail grocer, b. Randboro, PQ, s/o Charles Chaddock (Eaton, PQ, deceased) and Malinda Eastman (Whitefield, deceased); W - 27, clerk, b. Lennoxville, PQ, d/o George Musty (England, deceased) and Ellen O. Boyle (Ireland, domestic)

CHAMBERLAIN,
Conant Harvey of Piermont m. Esther Beryl **Heron** of Piermont 9/21/1949 in Warren; H - 21, mechanic, b. Enosburg Falls, VT, s/o Clarence Chamberlain (Enosburg Falls, VT) and Glenna Cassavant (Sheldon, VT); W - 26, domestic, b. Burton Heron (Rutland, VT) and Flora M. Ray (Broome, Quebec)

CHARPENTIER,
Keith L. of Piermont m. Catherine J. **Fleming** of Piermont 7/29/1989

CHASE,
Lewis R. of Piermont m. Marina A. **Gonchar** of Piermont 7/24/2003

CHENEY,
Irvin of Bradford, VT m. Rita **Horton** of Piermont 4/15/1945 in Bradford, VT; H - 22, laborer, 2nd, b. Ryegate, VT, s/o Alfred Cheney (Barnet, VT) and Emma Farnsworth (Irving, MA); W -

16, domestic, b. Piermont, d/o Bernard Horton (Piermont) and Eva Lewis (Wilder, VT)

CHICOINE,
Roger L. of Bradford, VT m. Monica L. **Hodge** of Bradford, VT 9/6/1985
Ronald L. of Bradford, VT m. Marlene J. **Corliss** of Bradford, VT 8/11/1989

CHILD,
William of Piermont m. Rosina A. **Plaisted** of Piermont 7/13/1901 in Piermont; H - 67, farmer, 3rd, b. Bath, s/o Dwight P. Child (Bath, farmer); W - 47, domestic, 2nd, b. Jackson, d/o George Hackett (Jackson, farmer)

CHURCHILL,
Winston of Barre, VT m. Frances R. **Colombo** of Barre, VT 12/22/1948 in Piermont; H - 27, student, b. Graniteville, VT, s/o William M. Churchill (Morrisville, VT, deceased) and Agnes Pratt (Barre, VT, deceased); W - 25, tel. opr., b. Barre, VT, d/o Frank Colombo (Italy, deceased) and Mary Carminati (Italy, housewife)

CLARK,
Harry E. of Stannard, VT m. Alice M. **Skinner** of Lowell, VT 12/31/1907 in Piermont; H - 29, hay dealer, b. Stannard, VT, s/o Joseph Clark (Stannard, VT, farmer); W - 28, teacher, b. Lowell, VT, d/o Charles Skinner (Lowell, VT, deceased)
Herbert A. of Piermont m. Marcia L. **Gay** of Melrose, MA 10/25/1899 in Wentworth; H - 36, farming, 2nd, b. Piermont, s/o Amos H. Clark (Piermont, farmer); W - 34, typesetter, b. Augusta, ME, d/o Benjamin G. Gay (Salem, ME, farmer)
Paul W. of Littleton m. Patricia J. **Provost** of Piermont 1/31/1970
Russell J. of Piermont m. Darlene H. **Potter** of Piermont 10/31/2003

CLAYBURN,
Joseph of Piermont m. Eda P. **Fellows** of Piermont 3/9/1921 in White River Jct., VT; H - 41, boxmaker, b. England, s/o Harry Clayburn (England, farmer); W - 21, tel. oper., b. Piermont, d/o Charles O. Fellows (Dorchester, carpenter)

William Albert of Piermont m. Vira May **Noyes** of Haverhill 11/10/1928 in Woodsville; H - 38, box maker, b. Atheston, PQ, s/o Harry Clayburn (Manchester, England, deceased) and Catherine Bellington (Shersbury, Wales, deceased); W - 21, domestic, b. Haverhill, d/o George Henry Noyes (Haverhill, farmer) and Lepha Anne Danfort (Haverhill, deceased)

CLEAVES,
Faunce Leslie of Piermont m. Margaret Elaine **Ritchie** of Piermont 4/16/1988

CLOGSTON,
Donald P. of Bradford, VT m. Joanne **Parker** of Piermont 11/18/1984

CLOUGH,
George L. of Piermont m. Martha B. **Reoneau** of Piermont 7/26/1913 in Concord; H - 48, farmer, 4th, divorced, b. Piermont, s/o Horace Clough (Washington, VT, farmer); W - 45, domestic, 2nd, divorced, b. Piermont, d/o Aaron Barton (Piermont, farmer)

COLBY,
Allen R. of Fairlee, VT m. Jane P. **Jesseman** of Piermont 6/3/1972
Jack of Piermont m. Esther Rose **Witham** of Bradford, VT 11/5/1958 in Piermont; H - 28, laborer, b. Piermont, s/o Jerry Colby (Sutton, VT) and Daisy Cass (E. Newark, VT); W - 28, dish washer, b. E. Barre, VT, d/o Wilbur Witham (Worcester, VT) and Bessie Ainsworth (Hardwick, VT)

COLCORD,
Daniel of Piermont m. Mable P. **Bartlett** of Goffstown 3/27/1921 in Goffstown; H - 41, farmer, b. Springfield, s/o Moses C. Colcord (Plaistow, farmer); W - 31, stenographer, b. Goffstown, d/o Lucian Bartlett (Groton, farmer)

COLE,
David W. of Piermont m. Elva L. **Parker** of Piermont 6/5/1976
David W. of Piermont m. Nancy A. **Monahan** of Piermont 12/24/1983

David Wayne of Piermont m. Mabel Louise **Fowler** of Lyme 7/23/1966

James Mark, Jr. of Wells River, VT m. Julie Lee **Simpson** of Wells River, VT 6/26/1993

James Mark, Sr. of Piermont m. Stacey Lynn **Cramer** of Piermont 6/1/2002

COLOMBO,

Americo of Barre, VT m. Mary **Roberts** of E. Barre, VT 7/1/1936 in Piermont; H - 25, office manager, b. Quincy, MA, s/o Roberto Colombo (Italy, deceased) and Lucio Calabrese (Italy, housekeeper); W - 23, domestic, b. Swanton, VT, d/o Lyman Roberts (Swanton, VT, quarryman) and Edith Lentz (Canada, housewife)

CONERY,

Edward H. of Piermont m. Carrie May **Smith** of N. Woodstock 2/4/1943 in Rumney; H - 38, US Army, 2nd, b. Springfield, MA, s/o Bernard Conery (Boston, MA, deceased) and Mary A. Bishop (N. Wilbraham, MA, deceased); W - 28, school teacher, b. Plymouth, d/o Ransom F. Smith (N. Woodstock, deceased) and Carrie Stone (Brimfield, MA, deceased)

Edward Henry of Walden, VT m. Marion Estella **Smith** of Piermont 6/15/1927 in Piermont; H - 21, farmer, b. N. Wilbraham, MA, s/o Bernard Conery (Boston, MA, laborer) and Mary A. Bishop (N. Wilbraham, MA); W - 19, domestic, b. Walden, VT, d/o George F. Smith (Stannard, VT, farmer) and Bertha C. Paronto (Montgomery, VT, housewife)

Lloyd E. of Piermont m. Dorothy L. **Nelson** of Wolfeboro 3/30/1952 in Wolfeboro; H - 21, Armed Forces, b. Piermont, s/o Edward H. Conery (MA) and Marion Smith (VT); W - 21, ins. rater, b. MA, d/o Louis P. Nelson (MA) and Lillian V. Chamberlain (NH)

CONVISOR,

Lionel of Piermont m. Joanne **Hertel** of Piermont 7/19/1948 in Warren; H - 26, musician, b. New York, NY, s/o Elias Convisor (Russia, musician) and Fannie Klikaff (Russia, housewife); W - 25, musician, b. Sheboygan, WI, d/o Andrew Hertel (Chilton, WI, clothier) and Sabina Altenbach (Sheboygan, WI, housewife)

COOK,
Edward J. of Barre, VT m. Hittie M. **Hurst** of Corinth, VT 12/2/1902 in Piermont; H - 21, machinist, b. Easton, s/o Charles E. Cook (Hyde Park, VT, farmer); W - 26, housework, 2nd, b. Corinth, VT, d/o Henry L. Mead (Corinth)

COOKSON,
Charles of Piermont m. Rosie M. **Ball** of Piermont 5/31/1921 in Piermont; H - 50, laborer, 2nd, widower, b. Warren, s/o Abram Cookson (ME, farmer); W - 36, domestic, b. Topsham, VT, d/o Edwin F. Ball (Topsham, VT, farmer)

CORLISS,
John E. of Bradford, VT m. Dorothy M. **Wright** of Bradford, VT 12/15/1962
Silas J. of Piermont m. Myrtie J. **Goodell** of Penacook 11/28/1916 in Charlestown; H - 48, carpenter, divorced, b. Newbury, VT, s/o Rinaldo Corliss (Newbury, VT, farmer); W - 36, domestic, widow, b. Thetford, VT, d/o James B. Whitcomb (Straford, VT, farmer)

CORREN,
Ray Edward of Hudson, MA m. Catherine Anne **Szuch** of Piermont 6/4/1955 in Woodsville; H - 25, student, b. John Corren (Portugal) and Marie DeCarmo (Portugal); W - 20, secretary, b. Bellows Falls, VT, d/o Alec Szuch (Hungary) and Mary Daniels (Benson, VT)

CORTHELL,
Michael A. of Abington, MA m. Mary E. **Dyer** of Abington, MA 10/31/1991

COVERT,
Harold Daniel of Piermont m. Lisa **Knapton** of Piermont 12/4/1993

CRAM,
Charles D. of Piermont m. Theodora M. **Bourgeois** of Buzzard Bay, MA 12/31/1954 in Hudson; H - 30, adv. business, b. IL, s/o Kenneth B. Cram (IL) and Helen Donnelly (IL); W - 27, housewife, 2nd, b. Germany, d/o Joseph Seidl (Germany) and Maria Kisslinger (Germany)

CRANE,
Louis L., Jr. of Piermont m. Isabel D. **Hollman** of Hanover 2/25/1933 in Hanover; H - 24, author, b. Butte, MT, s/o Louis L. Crane (Lexington, MA, broker) and Ruth Houghton (Concord, MA, housewife); W - 27, secretary, 2nd, b. Meadville, PA, d/o Frank C. Doan (Nelsonville, OH, minister) and Isabel Wilson (Winchester, MA, housewife)

CREPS,
Dean R. of Plymouth m. Ann M. **Bishop** of Piermont 9/30/1971

CROWE,
Donald P. of Bristol, CT m. Virginia J. (Smith) **Stetson** of Bristol, CT 1/4/1986

CUMMINGS,
Andrew S. of Piermont m. Julia A. **Jagger** of Piermont 5/29/1982
Henry J. of Orford m. Lena **Vizina** of Thetford, VT 6/30/1921 in Piermont; H - 45, farmer, 2nd, divorced, b. Thetford, VT, s/o James Cummings (Thetford, VT, farmer); W - 19, domestic, b. Canada, d/o Leon Vizina (Canada, farmer)
Leon O. of Bradford, VT m. Millie Y. **French** of Piermont 9/25/1935 in Woodsville; H - 23, farmer, b. Thetford, VT, s/o Asa Cummings (Thetford, VT, farmer) and Nellie Randall (Wentworth, deceased); W - 17, domestic, b. Piermont, d/o Louis French (Orford, deceased) and Josie Everett (Swiftwater, housewife)

CUNNINGHAM,
Forest D. of Bradford, VT m. Pearl May **Knapp** of Piermont 12/29/1915 in Piermont; H - 36, carpenter, 2nd, divorced, b. Harrington, ME, s/o Michael Cunningham (Cherryfield, ME, soldier); W - 22, millinery, b. Piermont, d/o Albert A. Knapp (Haverhill, farmer)

CUTTING,
Fred D. of Piermont m. Lula **Rollins** of Haverhill 2/10/1921 in Piermont; H - 48, farmer, 2nd, divorced, b. Benton, s/o Charles Cutting (Haverhill, farmer); W - 46, housework, 3rd, divorced, b. Benton, d/o Parker Bancroft
Paul Allen of Piermont m. Cheryl Ann **Page** of Piermont 5/25/2002

DARGIE,
John Cox of Haverhill m. Susan Petre **Bishop** of Piermont 1/9/1965
Philip E. of Haverhill m. Doris **St. Cyr** of Haverhill 6/1/1928 in
 Woodsville; H - 24, farmer, b. Haverhill, s/o Peter Dargie
 (Canada, farmer) and Rosana Beauhen (Canada, housewife);
 W - 17, at home, b. Pittsburg, d/o Fred St. Cyr (Northern Mills,
 VT, farmer) and A. Mallin (Canada, housewife)

DARLING,
Herbert A. of Piermont m. Marion A. **Corliss** of Piermont 8/30/1926
 in Piermont; H - 55, harness maker, 2nd, widower, b. Keene, s/o
 William Darling (Chesterfield, deceased) and Eleanor Hill
 (Chesterfield, deceased); W - 61, domestic, 2nd, widow, b.
 Pembroke, ME, d/o George E. Williams (England, deceased)
 and Hannah McLaughlin (Eastport, ME, deceased)

DAVIDSON,
George H. of Cheshire, CT m. Laura **Bradley** of Piermont 8/13/1983

DAVIS,
Ellis C. of Piermont m. Lucia S. **Batchelder** of Bradford, VT
 8/12/1938 in Bradford, VT; H - 23, radio operator, b. E.
 Charleston, VT, s/o Floyd F. Davis (E. Charleston, VT, farmer)
 and Ida May Moulton (New York, NY, housewife); W - 22, book-
 keeper, b. Bradford, VT, d/o Ernest A. Batchelder (Bradford,
 VT, deceased) and Lucia B. Whitten (Plymouth, MA,
 housewife)
Ronald B. of Nashua m. Joyce L. **Wilson** of Piermont 12/10/1966
William A. of Bradford m. Evaline A. **Blake** of Sutton 5/18/1906 in
 Piermont; H - 36, farmer, b. Newbury, VT, s/o Alfred Davis
 (Bradford, VT, deceased); W - 19, housework, b. Sutton, VT,
 d/o Irvin Blake (Stark, engineer)

DAY,
Ernest D. of Piermont m. Lena M. **Webster** of Piermont 5/7/1899 in
 Piermont; H - 20, farmer, b. Troy, VT, s/o Martin Day (Wolcott,
 VT, farmer); W - 18, housework, b. Monroe, d/o Henry D.
 Webster (Monroe, carpenter)
Frank L. of Piermont m. Maud E. **Austin** of Piermont 11/25/1903 in
 Piermont; H - 29, farmer, b. Wolcott, VT, s/o Martin Day

(Wolcott, VT, farmer); W - 26, housework, b. W. Fairlee, VT, d/o George Austin (Worcester, MA, farmer)

George H. of Piermont m. Addie **Green** of Piermont 8/14/1901 in Piermont; H - 31, farming, b. W. Topsham, s/o Martin Day (Wolcott, VT, farmer); W - 22, housework, b. Bradford, VT, d/o George Green (Topsham, VT, deceased)

Martin H. of Piermont m. Lurena **Leavitt** of Colebrook 8/31/1932 in Colebrook; H - 22, farmer, b. Piermont, s/o Ernest D. Day (Jay, VT, farmer) and Luna M. Webster (Monroe, housewife); W - 29, teacher, b. Stewartstown, d/o Claude Leavitt (Colebrook, deceased) and Stella Lord (Newport, PQ, housewife)

DEANE,

John E. of Piermont m. Helen T. **Acres** of Piermont 9/22/1945 in Bradford, VT; H - 64, farmer, b. Lowell, MA, s/o Henry W. Deane (Haverhill) and Hattie Chamberlain (Haverhill); W - 56, housekeeper, 2nd, b. Boston, MA, d/o Frederick Spaulding (Pittston, ME) and Victoria Williams (Pittston, ME)

DEARBORN,

Earl G. of Piermont m. Hazel P. **Meaney** of Piermont 4/30/1935 in Canaan; H - 25, farmer, b. E. Haverhill, s/o Guy L. Dearborn (E. Haverhill, deceased) and Julia Sherman (Cookshire, Canada, waitress); W - 27, domestic, 2nd, divorced, b. Franklin, d/o Israel S. Braley (Northfield, retired) and Mabel A. Badney (Claremont, housewife)

Henry F. of E. Haverhill m. Helen C. **Stevens** of Piermont 3/25/1936 in N. Haverhill; H - 26, laborer, b. E. Haverhill, s/o Henry F. Dearborn (E. Haverhill, farmer) and Grace L. Silver (Haverhill, housewife); W - 22, at home, b. Piermont, d/o Ernest L. Stevens (Piermont, farmer) and Caroline J. Taylor (Bethlehem, housewife)

Howard S. of E. Haverhill m. Esther A. **Winn** of Piermont 7/18/1936 in N. Haverhill; H - 25, farmer, b. E. Haverhill, s/o Henry F. Dearborn (E. Haverhill, farmer) and Grace L. Silver (Haverhill, housewife); W - 21, at home, b. Piermont, d/o Frank J. Winn (W. Fairlee, VT, farmer) and Rosetta Underhill (Piermont, housewife)

DEGOOSH,
Richard of E. Thetford, VT m. Doris S. **Colton** of E. Thetford, VT 7/31/1982

DEL POZZO,
Sven A. of Piermont m. Nicole **Harvalik** of Kingston 6/26/1999

DEMETRULES,
William J. of Bradford, VT m. Shirley C. **Long** of E. Corinth, VT 12/27/1968

DENCHFIELD,
William of Denver, CO m. Mildred E. **Underhill** of Piermont 9/4/1895 in Piermont; H - 29, printer, b. Chillicothe, IL, s/o John Denchfield and Henrietta Pierce (Oswego, NY); W - 25, teacher, b. Piermont, d/o John H. Underhill (Piermont) and Emma C. Bagley (Hopkinton, MA)

DENNIS,
Dwight of Piermont m. Lillian V. **McCoy** of Irasburg, VT 3/12/1898 in Piermont; H - 25, farmer, b. Orford, s/o Emore Dennis (Stratford, farmer); W - 18, house work, b. Irasburg, VT, d/o ---- McCoy

Frank A. of Piermont m . Ellen A. **Foster** of Wentworth 10/26/1901 in Piermont; H - 43, engineer, 2nd, b. Stratford, s/o William Dennis (Stratford, farmer); W - 42, housework, 2nd, b. Wentworth, d/o Uriah Calbain (Wentworth, farmer)

Harry E. of Piermont m. Bertha **Hibbard** of Piermont 4/18/1900 in Haverhill; H - 27, farmer, b. Orford, s/o Elmore Dennis (Stratford, farmer); W - 27, housework, b. Piermont, d/o Benjamin Hibbard (Piermont)

DEROSIA,
Thomas K. of Haverhill m. Ann M. **Woodward** of Piermont 8/14/1971

DIERHOI,
William H. of Highland Springs, VA m. Mildred **Tyler** of Piermont 7/3/1923 in Piermont; H - 33, school prin., b. Richmond, MN, s/o Hans Dierhoi (Elstrup, Denmark, retired); W - 25, teacher, b. W. Medford, MN, d/o Leslie G. Tyler (Benton, farmer)

DIETER,
Paul Matthew of Piermont m. Joan Elaine **Robie** of Piermont 4/21/1988

DIETRICH,
Hastings L. of Piermont m. Dorothy M. **Bonniwell** of Richmond, VA 10/25/1975

DIMICK,
Ernest H. of Hardwick, VT m. Ruth **Cochran** of Hardwick, VT 2/17/1914 in Piermont; H - 22, farmer, b. Hardwick, VT, s/o Albert G. Dimick (Wolcott, VT, farmer); W - 18, housework, b. Cabot, VT, d/o Thomas Cochran (Craftsbury, VT, farmer)

DODGE,
Charles L. of Piermont m. Maud E. **George** of Fairlee, VT 6/14/1911 in Lyme; H - 21, com. traveler, b. Piermont, s/o Charles Dodge (Corinth, VT, com. trav.); W - 22, teacher, b. Brattleboro, d/o Austin W. George (Norwich, VT, carpenter)

Forrest E. of Topsham, VT m. Marion A. **Horton** of Piermont 5/11/1946 in Piermont; H - 27, machinist, 2nd, b. Calais, VT, s/o Elmer A. Dodge (E. Montpelier, VT, retired) and Maude E. Lane (Hardwick, VT, housewife); W - 19, domestic, b. Piermont, d/o Bernard G. Horton (Orford, creamery mgr.) and Eva M. Lewis (Wilder, VT, housewife)

DOE,
Harry F. of S. Newbury, VT m. Mabel E. **Stilwell** of Bradford, VT 10/28/1913 in Piermont; H - 29, musician, 2nd, divorced, b. S. Newbury, VT, s/o Edson Doe (S. Newbury, retired); W - 22, housework, b. Princeton, NJ, d/o John Stilwell (Princeton, NJ, printer)

Harry F. of Piermont m. Mabel S. **Doe** of Piermont 8/13/1938 in N. Haverhill; H - 54, musician, 3rd, divorced, b. S. Newbury, VT, s/o Edson Doe (S. Newbury, VT, deceased) and Esther Howland (Newbury, VT, deceased); W - 47, housewife, 2nd, divorced, b. Princeton, NJ, d/o John H. Stillwell (Princeton, NJ, deceased) and Belle Emerson (Newbury, VT, retired)

DREW,
Dennis W. of Piermont m. Marie F. **Campbell** of Piermont 4/12/1969

DUBE,
Jeffery P. of Piermont m. Correna L. **Underhill** of Piermont 3/20/1982
Steven Allen of Woodsville m. Rebecca Ruth **Kohanski** of Bradford, VT 8/3/2002
Victor R., Jr. of Woodsville m. Kimberly E. **Williams** of Piermont 8/9/1986

DUGAL,
Drew L. of Piermont m. Rose M. **Musty** of Piermont 9/23/1973

DUGUID,
Elwin J. of Barre, VT m. Avis G. **Hill** of Barre, VT 6/13/1936 in Piermont; H - 24, clerk, b. Barre, VT, s/o John H. Duguid (Scotland, stonecutter) and Mary Lillie (Barre, VT, housewife); W - 22, domestic, b. Barre, VT, d/o Irman Hill (Fayston, VT, carpenter) and Goldie Clark (Orange, VT, housewife)

DUNBAR,
Randy W. of Piermont m. Barbara J. **Putnam** of Piermont 6/4/1977

DUNNELLS,
Leslie J., Jr. of Bradford, VT m. Deborah A. **Louthier** of Bradford, VT 9/29/1984

DUPUIS,
Cleo F. of Northumberland m. Sitelka J. **Smith** of Piermont 6/9/1947 in Haverhill; H - 29, hotel bus., b. Berlin, s/o Emile F. DuPuis (Norton Mills, VT, hotel business) and Mabel Gayne (Berlin, housewife); W - 24, school teacher, b. Columbia, d/o Arthur L. Smith (S. Columbia, painter) and Rosina Grapes (Columbia, deceased)

DWINELL,
Stanley F. of Bradford, VT m. Constance A. **Bray** of Springfield, MA 12/18/1943 in Piermont; H - 23, medical student, b. Haverhill, s/o Franklin P. Dwinell (E. Calais, VT, physician) and Elizabeth D. Smith (Portland, CT, tel. operator); W - 21, college student, b. Springfield, MA, d/o Milton F. Bray (Fitchburg, VT, mgr. tire co.) and Mildred Corliss (Piermont, housewife)

DYKE,
Jason Roger of Piermont m. April Clarissa **Screton** of Piermont 7/7/2001

EASTER,
Richard C. of Corinth, VT m. Amanda **Buck** of Corinth, VT 8/30/1910 in Piermont; H - 25, farmer, 2nd, b. England, s/o Charles F. Easter (England, farmer); W - 25, housework, 2nd, b. Chicago, IL, d/o Ernest Buck (Germany, deceased)

EATON,
Ronald H. of Bradford, VT m. Carolyn A. **Wilson** of Piermont 11/16/1974

EDDY,
William P. of Piermont m. Jayne M. **Welch** of Piermont 2/4/1968

EISLER,
Everett B. of Piermont m. Ann **Musty** of Piermont 10/19/1947 in Piermont; H - 28, carpenter, 2nd, divorced, b. Yonkers, NY, s/o Warren V. Eisler (Yonkers, NY, retired) and Jeannette Treulieb (Mt. Vernon, NY, housewife); W - 24, lab. tech., b. Piermont, d/o Alfred Musty (Lennoxville, PQ, bus driver) and Marion J. Gorham (Lyndonville, VT, housewife)

ELLIOTT,
Basil of Lisbon m. Bernice E. **Stetson** of Piermont 1/1/1918 in Lisbon; H - 22, farmer, b. Lisbon, s/o James G. F. Elliott (Lisbon, farmer); W - 22, nurse, b. Piermont, d/o George Stetson (Orford, expressman)

ELLSWORTH,
Arthur H. of Piermont m. Gladys I. **Locke** of Haverhill 8/28/1932 in Henniker; H - 24, laborer, b. Piermont, s/o Ernest Ellsworth (Wentworth, farmer) and Bertha Winn (Fairlee, VT, housework); W - 18, at home, b. Lyman, d/o Earl S. Locke (Lyman, farmer) and Helen Burbank (Landaff, housework)
Ernest J. of Piermont m. Bertha E. **Winn** of Piermont 1/12/1905 in Piermont; H - 26, farmer, b. Wentworth, s/o John Ellsworth (Wentworth, farmer); W - 22, housework, b. W. Fairlee, d/o Frank P. Winn (Piermont, farmer)

Frank J. of Piermont m. Ethel M. **Woodbury** of Woodsville 9/15/1934 in Woodsville; H - 28, farmer, b. Piermont, s/o Ernest Ellsworth (Wentworth, farmer) and Bertha Winn (W. Fairlee, VT, housewife); W - 25, clerk, b. Wells River, VT, d/o Frank Woodbury (deceased) and Mae Titus (Woodstock, housewife)

John of Piermont m. Ella **Hurlburt** of Piermont 6/15/1957 in Bradford, VT; H - 18, farmer, b. Woodsville, s/o Arthur Ellsworth (Piermont) and Gladys Locke (Lyman); W - 16, housework, b. Stewartstown, d/o Burnham Hurlburt (Clarksville) and Gertrude Nason (Island Pond, VT)

EMERSON,

Claude D. of Newbury m. Gladys E. **Barrett** of Piermont 2/28/1906 in Piermont; H - 21, laborer, b. Newbury, VT, s/o Daniel Emerson (Newbury, VT, farmer); W - 17, housework, b. Chelsea, VT, d/o Charles Barrett (Woodbury, VT)

Frank R. of Bradford, VT m. Rosenna D. **Keniston** of Piermont 11/27/1971

Ulysses of Newbury, VT m. Gladys **Hill** of Piermont 10/22/1933 in W. Newbury, VT; H - 20, laborer, b. Newbury, VT, s/o Claude Emerson (Newbury, VT, farmer) and Gladys Barrett (Chelsea, VT, housewife); W - 15, domestic, b. Haverhill, d/o Harold Hill (Newport, VT, deceased) and Lucy Sawyer (Piermont, housewife)

EMERY,

Fay S. of Piermont m. Gladys C. **Chesley** of Lyme 7/24/1915 in Lyme Ctr.; H - 27, farmer, b. Piermont, s/o George S. Emery (Suncook, farmer); W - 18, school teacher, b. Lyme, d/o Frank A. Chesley (W. Fairlee, VT, farmer)

Frank S. of Piermont m. Mamie J. **Horton** of Piermont 4/27/1904 in Haverhill; H - 22, farmer, b. Piermont, s/o George Emery (Piermont, farmer); W - 18, housework, b. Orford, d/o William H. Horton (E. Barnard, VT, farmer)

William S. of Piermont m. Maud E. **Robie** of Piermont 4/30/1902 in Tilton; H - 26, clergy, b. Newcastle, s/o Jothan Emery (Bidaford, ME, ship fitter); W - 18, milliner, b. Bradford, VT, d/o Freeman A. Robie (Piermont, farmer)

ENNIS,
Arthur of NY m. Florence **Buxton** of Manchester 8/3/1930 in Haverhill; H - 33, chauffeur, 2nd, b. Ireland, s/o Michael Ennis (Ireland, deceased) and Margaret Henney (Ireland, deceased); W - 23, waitress, b. Providence, RI, d/o Charles Buxton (Providence, RI, electrician) and Florence Shippe (Providence, RI, housewife)

EVANS,
Arthur M. of Piermont m. Jessie **Robie** of Piermont 6/–/1919 in Piermont; H - 26, creamery, b. Piermont, s/o Joseph O. Evans (Piermont, farmer); W - 24, tel. oper., b. Piermont, d/o Freeman A. Robie (E. Corinth, farmer)

FABRIZIO,
John P. of Bristol, CT m. Donna L. **Dolce** of Bristol, CT 10/31/1981

FADDEN,
Donald S. of Piermont m. Francese **Hartwell** of Piermont 6/26/1936 in Orford; H - 18, farmer, b. W. Thornton, s/o Dana Fadden (W. Thornton, farmer) and Esther Downing (W. Thornton, housewife); W - 18, domestic, b. Piermont, d/o George J. Hartwell (Haverhill, farmer) and Ida Robie (Piermont, housewife)

Edward of Piermont m. Lois Henrietta **Bean** of Orford 2/28/1942 in Haverhill; H - 27, farmer, b. W. Thornton, s/o Dana Fadden (W. Thornton, farmer) and Esther Downing (W. Thornton, housewife); W - 17, student, b. Piermont, d/o Bernard Horton (Piermont, creamery man) and Ava Lewis (Wilder, VT, housewife)

Lawrence D. of Piermont m. Ernestine D. **Greenwood** of Haverhill 12/31/1971

Lawrence D. of Piermont m. Lenora A. **Prue** of Piermont 8/18/1979

Lawrence D. of Piermont m. Ernestine D. **Beck** of Piermont 3/31/1991

Ronald B. of Piermont m. Sharon A. **Miller** of Pike 10/5/1974

Stanley F. of Piermont m. Edna **Keith** of Haverhill 2/19/1931 in N. Haverhill; H - 21, laborer, b. W. Thornton, s/o Dana Fadden (Thornton, farmer) and Esther Downing (Thornton, housewife); W - 18, domestic, b. Haverhill, d/o Michael Keith (Canada, deceased) and Lilla White (housewife)

FAGNANT,
Alcide G. of Piermont m. Martha **Fortier** of Woodsville 10/7/1961
Fernand R. of Piermont m. Nancy M. **Ball** of Warren 11/16/1957 in Woodsville; H - 22, truck driver, b. Troy, VT, s/o Alcide Fagnant (Canada) and Laurette Paquette (Canada); W - 17, unemployed, b. Benton, d/o Reginald H. Ball (Landaff) and Charlotte Griffin (Tilton)
Leon of Piermont m. Jo Ann Shirley **Jones** of Woodsville 8/16/1958 in Woodsville; H - 21, const. equip. operator, b. Ashland, s/o Alcide Fagnant (Canada) and Laurette Paquette (Canada); W - 19, secretary, b. Thornton, d/o George Jones (Thornton) and Violet Vintner (Bury, PQ)
Richard A. of Piermont m. Annabelle M. **Smith** of Haverhill 5/19/1956 in Haverhill; H - 21, student, b. VT, s/o Alcide Fagnant (Canada) and Laurette Paquette (Canada); W - 19, secretary, b. NH, d/o William C. Smith (VT) and Mildred Perkins (NH)
Robert E. of Piermont m. Cynthia M. **Fournier** of Woodsville 5/22/1976

FAIRBROTHER,
Ernest H. of Corinth, VT m. Julia F. **Ward** of Vershire, VT 6/27/1911 in Piermont; H - 26, farmer, b. England, s/o Henry Fairbrother (England, harnessmaker); W - 19, housework, b. Vershire, VT, d/o Edwin Ward (Vershire, VT, farmer)

FARNHAM,
Homer W. of Topsham, VT m. Abbie **Farnham** of Topsham, VT 12/2/1891 in Piermont; H - 43, farmer, b. Westminster, MA, s/o Smith Farnham (Topsham, VT, farmer) and Julia Wilder (MA); W - 36, domestic, 2nd, b. Washington, VT, d/o Benjamin Hoyt (Washington, VT, farmer) and Sarah Pilch (Wales)

FELCH,
Allen D. of Piermont m. Bertha M. **Cookman** of Piermont 5/24/1915 in Haverhill; H - 63, farmer, 3rd, widower, b. Morgan, VT, s/o George C. Felch (Lyman, carpenter); W - 34, housekeeper, 2nd, divorced, b. Bethel, PQ, d/o Darwin Stanhope (St. Johnsbury, VT, farmer)
Emory A. of Natick, MA m. Ethel G. **Blaisdell** of Piermont 10/14/1931 in Piermont; H - 24, civil engineer, b. Natick, MA,

s/o Albert A. Felch (Natick, MA, deceased) and Jessie S. Keep (Cochituate, MA, housework); W - 22, domestic, b. Piermont, d/o Harry E. Blaisdell (Piermont, farmer) and Grace A. Dunkley (Haverhill, housewife)

FELLOWS,
Charles O. of Dorchester m. Ina B. **Simpson** of Piermont 12/15/1894; H - 27, carpenter, b. Dorchester, s/o Leonard S. Fellows (Dorchester, farmer) and Sarah B. Fellows (Augusta, ME, housewife); W - 29, teacher, b. Piermont, d/o William C. Simpson (Orford, carpenter) and Anna Stickney (Bolton, housewife)

FENOFF,
Avery A. of Piermont m. Margaret **Barette** of Piermont 5/23/1928 in Haverhill; H - 20, painter, b. Barnet, VT, s/o Joseph Fenoff (Barnet, VT, farmer) and Mabel Amell (Barnet, VT, domestic); W - 18, domestic, b. St. Johnsbury, VT, d/o Clarence Barette (Lexington, MA, drover) and Josephine Ferris (Danville, VT, domestic)

FERNALD,
Robert D. of Piermont m. Amy L. **Bertalott** of Wayne, PA 7/31/1971

FIARTLING,
Eric Scott of Newburyport, MA m. Nancy Ellen **Black** of Newburyport, MA 12/15/1996

FIELDS,
Sean Michael of Piermont m. Jennifer Lee **Woods** of Piermont 11/7/1998

FISCHER,
Jeffrey William of Piermont m. Chrismas Mary **Converse-Fischer** of Piermont 4/20/1985

FISHMAN,
Richard of Piermont m. Ann Marie **Disco** of Piermont 7/9/1994

FOOTE,

Claude R. of Piermont m. Leona Irene **Paige** of Thetford Ctr., VT 6/14/1946 in Orford; H - 29, laborer, b. Piermont, s/o Everett Foote (Warren, laborer) and Edna M. Robie (Piermont, housewife); W - 18, student, b. Thetford Ctr., VT, d/o Harry A. Paige (S. Royalton, VT, laborer) and Helen M. Savery (Rutland, VT, housewife)

Everett H. of Orford m. Edna M. **Robie** of Piermont 11/4/1917 in Piermont; H - 20, farmer, b. Warren, s/o Bert L. Foote (Warren, farmer); W - 21, housework, b. Piermont, d/o Freeman A. Robie (Corinth, VT, farmer)

FORD,

Edward G. of Piermont m. Eva E. **Towle** of Piermont 11/21/1900 in Somerville, MA; H - 23, farmer, b. Orford, s/o Edward Ford (Piermont, drover); W - 26, housework, b. Piermont, d/o Frank B. Towle (Piermont, farmer)

FRENCH,

Chester L. of Piermont m. Caroline **Batchelder** of N. Haverhill 9/23/1938 in N. Haverhill; H - 25, laborer, b. Piermont, s/o Lewis French (Piermont, deceased) and Josie Everett (Haverhill, housewife); W - 18, domestic, b. N. Haverhill, d/o William Batchelder (Nashua, laborer) and Martha Clifford (Haverhill, housewife)

Edward W. of Piermont m. Grace Belle **Bean** of Orford 6/3/1939 in Woodsville; H - 23, laborer, b. Piermont, s/o Louis French (Orford, deceased) and Josie Everett (Swiftwater, housewife); W - 21, domestic, b. Orford, d/o Joseph Bean (Sharon, VT, deceased) and Mabel Davis (Mansonville, PQ, housewife)

Edward W. of Piermont m. Nancy C. **Mason** of Piermont 12/18/2002

Ernest G. of Piermont m. Shirley E. **Dunbar** of Piermont 10/23/1971

Ernest G. of Piermont m. Jeanette L. **Whitney** of Piermont 10/13/1979

George A. of Piermont m. Marion J. **Sanderson** of Piermont 4/18/1911 in Piermont; H - 32, laborer, b. Warren, s/o Caleb O. French (Warren, laborer); W - 34, housework, 3rd, b. England, d/o John Cooke (England, sailor)

Harry W. of Piermont m. Delia B. **Tetreau** of Piermont 7/31/1910 in Piermont; H - 28, farmer, b. Piermont, s/o William French

(Canada, farmer); W - 25, housework, 2nd, b. Sherbrook, PQ, d/o Joseph Tetreau (Canada, night watchman)
James E. of Piermont m. Bonnie Lee **Colby** of Fairlee, VT 2/20/1960
James E. of Piermont m. Kimberly A. **Winot** of Piermont 6/16/1985
Leslie A. of Piermont m. Bessie M. **Perkins** of Orford 12/25/1909 in Orford; H - 20, tel. work, b. Nashua, s/o Herbert H. French (Wentworth); W - 21, housework, b. Hardwick, d/o Edgar E. Perkins (Walden, VT)
Louis C. of Piermont m. Josie **Everett** of Swiftwater 7/13/1907 in Piermont; H - 19, farmer, b. Piermont, s/o W. H. French (farmer); W - 16, housework, b. Swiftwater, d/o Edward Everett (Lyman, farmer)
Michael E. of Ballston Spa, NY m. Charlene R. **Vachon** of Ballston Spa, NY 10/30/1983
Ronald L. of Piermont m. Jeannine V. **Beaupre** of Bradford, VT 10/30/1971
William C. of Piermont m. Nancy H. **Lund** of Newbury, VT 10/26/1974

FROST,
Gregory R. of E. Corinth, VT m. Ann F. **Carrier** of E. Corinth, VT 9/22/1990

FROTHINGHAM,
William P. of Boston, MA m. Georgiana **Sanderson** of Piermont 9/30/1906 in Piermont; H - 57, conveyancer, b. Boston, MA, s/o Albert Frothingham (Boston, MA, deceased); W - 62, housework, 3rd, b. Natick, MA, d/o Sherborn Seavey (Boston, MA, deceased)

FULFORD,
Howard A., Jr. of Piermont m. Victoria U. **Spooner** of Topsham, VT 8/3/1968

FUMAGALLI,
Frank of Buffalo, NY m. Filomena **Sabbatino** of Buffalo, NY 7/16/1933 in Piermont; H - 39, photographer, b. Italy, s/o Flavio Fumagalli (Italy, deceased) and Filomena Prega (Italy, deceased); W - 30, domestic, b. Buffalo, NY, d/o Nicholas Sabbatino (Italy, none) and Carmen Pedana (Italy, deceased)

GABOREE,
Leo E. of Northfield, VT m. Marion B. **Buska** of Northfield, VT 5/16/1959

GADWAH,
Claude of Piermont m. Cyrene **Jolin** of Woodsville 7/11/1932 in Piermont; H - 20, laborer, b. Columbia, s/o Leslie Gadwah (Colebrook, laborer) and Ellen Belenger (W. Stewartstown, housewife); W - 18, domestic, b. Haverhill, d/o William Jolin (Whitefield, mechanic) and Flora Wilson (Haverhill, housewife)

GALE,
Frederick H. of White River Jct., VT m. Shirley F. **Raymond** of Lebanon 11/27/1965

GAMSBY,
Leon of Piermont m. Violet E. **Smith** of Piermont 11/6/1931 in Orford; H - 27, laborer, b. Sherbrooke, Canada, s/o Charles Gamsby (Quebec, game warden) and Hattie Muzzy (Bradford, VT, housewife); W - 21, domestic, b. Coaticooke, PQ, d/o George N. Smith (PQ, farmer) and Jennie Orr (Quebec, deceased)

Walter of Piermont m. Flossie A. **Smith** of Piermont 12/3/1924 in Orford; H - 35, farmer, b. Dudwell, PQ, s/o Rufas A. Gamsby (Dudwell, PQ, farmer); W - 23, dressmaker, b. Coaticook, PQ, d/o George N. Smith (Dudwell, PQ, farmer)

GARDNER,
Harold H. of Piermont m. Sophronia E. **Long** of Bradford, VT 5/31/1952 in Piermont; H - 38, laborer, 2nd, b. Orford, s/o Ned Gardner (Orford) and Hattie Coolidge (Orford); W - 36, waitress, 2nd, b. Topsham, VT, d/o Ralph Emerson (Topsham, VT) and Luvia Evans (Topsham, VT)

Harold H., Jr. of Piermont m. Sylvette **White** of Corinth, VT 12/27/1952 in Corinth, VT; H - 19, USAF, b. Bradford, VT, s/o Harold H. Gardner (Orford) and Phyllis Scruton (Woodsville); W - 18, book keeper, b. Laconia, d/o Worthy D. White (Corinth, VT) and Olive Hastings (Corinth, VT)

Stephen A. of Piermont m. Rebecca **Hyde** of Bradford, VT 6/5/1971

GEORGE,
Daniel S. of Woodsville m. Leslie A. **Harrington** of Piermont 1/23/1981

GILBERT,
Franklin of Williston, VT m. Louise **Doe** of Williston, VT 5/21/1976

GILLINGHAM,
Kenneth C. of White River Jct., VT m. Lois Carrie **Putnam** of Piermont 9/6/1953 in Piermont; H - 28, car insp. B&M RR, 2nd, b. White River Jct., VT, s/o Chester Gillingham (Newport) and Alice Newell (Claremont); W - 21, secretary, b. Hanover, d/o William Putnam (W. Newbury, VT) and Marion Corliss (Bradford, VT)

GILMAN,
Harold H. of Rochester, NY m. Gladys G. **Rodimon** of Piermont 12/30/1912 in Haverhill; H - 20, Kodak mkr., b. Stoneham, MA, s/o Samuel W. Gilman (Bangor, ME, farmer); W - 19, teacher, b. Piermont, d/o Charles H. Rodimon (Piermont, farmer)

GILSON,
William E. of Piermont m. Stella A. **Cressey** of Piermont 1/29/1902 in Piermont; H - 35, farmer, 2nd, b. Fitzwilliam, s/o Henry N. Gilson (Fitzwilliam); W - 21, housework, b. Cumberlin, ME, d/o Lorenzo E. Cressey (Falmouth, ME)

GLADSTONE,
Arthur of Piermont m. Barbara S. **Gardiner** of Port Credit, ON 8/25/1971

GOODRICH,
Clarence E. of Piermont m. Lillian J. **Harris** of Haverhill 9/10/1938 in Piermont; H - 25, farm laborer, b. Bath, s/o Arthur Goodrich (Canada) and Florence Riely (Washington, VT, housekeeper); W - 18, domestic, b. Haverhill, d/o William Harris (Haverhill) and Lillian Hutchins (Boston, MA, housekeeper)
Cyrus A. of Hillsboro m. Carrie L. **Bowles** of Piermont 1/4/1894; H - 22, carpenter, b. NY, s/o Randolph Goodrich (Constable, NY, farmer) and Christina Smith (Hillsborough, housewife); W - 28,

domestic, b. Suncook, d/o Benson Bowles and Sabrina Brown (Lyme, housewife)

GOODWIN,
Albion J. of Cape Neddick, ME m. Doris E. **Howard** of Piermont 6/24/1930 in Piermont; H - 22, teacher, b. Cape Neddick, ME, s/o Albion Goodwin (Cape Neddick, ME, postman) and Anna F. Norton (Cape Neddick, ME, housewife); W - 24, teacher, b. E. Burke, VT, d/o Earl V. Howard (E. Haven, VT, merchant) and Amy M. Sanders (Montpelier, VT, housewife)

J. Ralph of Plymouth m. Christie **Morrison** of Piermont 10/10/1912 in Piermont; H - 23, clerk, b. Warren, s/o Charles B. Goodwin (Warren, farmer); W - 20, teacher, b. Piermont, d/o H. Eugene Morrison (Haverhill, manufacturer)

John Floyd of Piermont m. Ruth Elizabeth **Jewell** of Piermont 9/21/1940 in Piermont; H - 24, shovel operator, b. Plymouth, s/o John R. Goodwin (Warren, deceased) and Christie E. Morrison (Piermont, music super.); W - 22, school teacher, b. Woodsville, d/o Charles W. Jewell, Jr. (Corinth, VT, state patrolman) and Carrie Jane Wilson (Groton, VT, housewife)

GOTTLIEB,
Sidney M. of Piermont m. Lynn **Walchli** of Piermont 12/11/1973

GOULD,
Harry R. of Piermont m. Eva F. **Craig** of Pike 11/9/1912 in Piermont; H - 22, clerk, b. Piermont, s/o Nelson M. Gould (Piermont, teaming); W - 20, housework, b. Middletown, CT, d/o John Craig (England, mill foreman)

Harry R. of Piermont m. Shirley E. **Litchfield** of Orford 7/15/1956 in Orford; H - 24, merchant, b. Hanover, s/o Harry R. Gould (Piermont) and Florence Craig (Middletown, CT); W - 19, clerk, b. Farmington, ME, d/o Wilson G. Litchfield (Martha's Vineyard, MA) and Arlene A. Blanchard (Farmington, ME)

Leon R. of Piermont m. Clara R. **Buzzell** of Colebrook 3/6/1912 in Warren; H - 20, farmer, b. Stewartstown, s/o Charles A. Gould (Colebrook, farmer); W - 18, housework, b. Stewartstown, d/o Andrew B. Buzzell (Conticook, PQ, farmer)

GRAY,
Harley of Piermont m. Hattie **Pike** of Piermont 10/11/1916 in Piermont; H - 21, laborer, b. Lyme, s/o Jack Gray (Sheffield, VT, engineer); W - 16, housewife, b. Lyme, d/o Henry M. Pike (Lyme, laborer)

GRIFFIN,
George F. of Chelsea, VT m. Anna M. **Russell** of Chelsea, VT 3/31/1909 in Piermont; H - 23, farming, b. Chelsea, VT, s/o Joseph H. Griffin (Boston, MA, farmer); W - 20, housekeeper, b. Rapid City, Dak., d/o Joseph Russell (SD, farmer)

GRIFFITHS,
Charles W. of Wolcott, VT m. Irene Alice **Hill** of Hardwick, VT 9/15/1938 in Piermont; H - 20, laborer, b. Franklin, MA, s/o John W. Griffiths (Wolcott, VT, chief police) and Nancy Fletcher (Albany, VT, deceased); W - 18, waitress, b. Hardwick, VT, d/o Arthur Hill (Stanstead, PQ, merchant) and Alma Bedard (Stanstead, PQ, housewife)

GRISWOLD,
Jeffrey Scott of Piermont m. Brenda Dorothy **Clark** of Piermont 10/26/2002

HACKETT,
Harley C. of Piermont m. Julia **Everson** of Melrose, MA 8/18/1906 in Piermont; H - 18, laborer, b. Orford, s/o David D. Hackett (Haverhill, farmer); W - 19, housework, d/o ----- (deceased)
Harry D. of Piermont m. Maud E. **Smith** of Manchester 7/4/1912 in Manchester; H - 24, laborer, b. Orford, s/o David D. Hackett (Haverhill, farmer); W - 20, teacher, b. Manchester, d/o Herbert M. Smith (Rochester, VT, farmer)
Richard T. of Piermont m. Ruth A. **Morey** of Claremont 6/1/1946 in Orford; H - 27, laborer, 2nd, b. Piermont, s/o Harley C. Hackett (Orford, salesman) and Jeannie Everson (Melrose, MA, housewife); W - 24, nurse maid, b. Haverhill, d/o Wesley E. Morey (Orford, mill worker) and Emily Hill (Newport, VT, housewife)
Warren T. of Piermont m. Harriet E. **Carter** of Piermont 2/15/1942 in Piermont; H - 18, laborer, b. Piermont, s/o Harley C. Hackett (Orfordville, laborer) and Jeannie Emerson (Melrose, MA,

housewife); W - 16, domestic, b. Danville, VT, d/o Fred Ernest Carter (Craftsbury, VT, farmer) and Hattie Marden (Stoneham, MA, housekeeper)

HALL,
David of Littleton m. Mary Lettia **Clayburn** of Piermont 6/12/1915 in Littleton; H - 39, laborer, 2nd, b. Biddeford, ME, s/o King Hall (Canada, PQ, laborer); W - 28, housework, b. Canada, PQ, d/o Harry Clayburn (Canada, PQ, laborer)

HANCHETT,
Merlyn Ivan of Lyme m. Doris E. **Bartlett** of Tilton 10/13/1930 in Piermont; H - 27, farmer, b. Lyme, s/o Ivan D. Hanchett (Plainfield, deceased) and Florence Clark (Orange, domestic); W - 21, clerk, b. Tilton, d/o Charles C. Bartlett (Bath, weaver) and Maude M. Haywood (Northfield, housewife)

HANLEY,
Scott Robert, Jr. of Piermont m. Delores Vesta **Harrington** of Piermont 6/1/1996

HANNAFORD,
Samuel of Piermont m. Julia M. **Dodge** of Piermont 6/26/1901 in Piermont; H - 24, surveyor, b. Stewartstown, s/o Fordyce Hannaford (Tilton, farmer); W - 24, millinery, b. Piermont, d/o Charles Dodge (Piermont, salesman)

HARTLEY,
Ernest of Bradford, VT m. Mildred **Hill** of Piermont 8/24/1939 in Bradford, VT; H - 22, electrician, b. Bradford, VT, s/o Wallace Hartley (Bradford, VT, veneer maker) and Alice Morey (Bradford, VT, housewife); W - 19, b. Piermont, d/o Harold Hill (Newport, VT) and Lucy Sawyer (Piermont, housewife)
Ernest W., Jr. of Piermont m. Pamela J. **Hatch** of Bradford, VT 6/2/1984
Wendell of Piermont m. Junt **Norcross** of Bradford, VT 10/19/1963

HAYWARD,
Norman E. of Bradford, VT m. Josephine **Little** of Bradford, VT 8/7/1909 in Piermont; H - 21, machinist, b. Groton, VT, s/o

Francis E. Hayward (ME, deceased); W - 20, dressmaker, b. Newbury, VT, d/o John Little (deceased)

HAZEN,
Allen R. of Piermont m. Betsy **Birchard** of Piermont 8/29/1959
Bruce A. of Piermont m. Lois M. **Adams** of Orford 7/4/1970
George R. of Piermont m. Joyce **Lahaye** of Lebanon 12/24/1954 in Enfield; H - 23, truck driver, 2nd, b. Norwich, VT, s/o Ray S. Hazen (Norwich, VT) and Frances Burner (Beaver Meadow, VT); W - 20, waitress, b. Lebanon, d/o Daniel Lahaye (Lebanon) and Thresa LaBrun (Lebanon)

HEATH,
Theodore M. of Newbury, VT m. Alice Mae **French** of Piermont 7/19/1941 in Bradford, VT; H - 33, truck driver, b. Groton, VT, s/o Hazen C. Heath (Groton, VT) and Lillian Carter (Groton, VT); W - 38, personal maid, b. Piermont, d/o Bert C. French (Warren) and Mabel Molway (Piermont)

HEATON,
Ray G. of Reading, MA m. Dorothy L. **Souvaine** of Reading, MA 6/23/1973

HEMENWAY,
Ronald L. of Piermont m. Marie F. **Drew** of Piermont 11/20/1976

HENRY,
Bruce P. of Piermont m. Leslie L. **Gould** of Piermont 7/25/1981

HERRICK,
Frederick R. of E. Westmoreland m. Marjorie Jean **Mellin** of Piermont 10/23/1955 in Piermont; H - 24, professional horseman, b. Brattleboro, VT, s/o Louis D. Herrick (Chesterfield) and Maverette Randall (Chesterfield); W - 28, author, 2nd, b. Stamford, CT, d/o Kenneth B. Mellin (New York, NY) and Marjorie Bates (Stamford, CT)
Homer M. of Piermont m. Mae Louise **Perkins** of Piermont 1/10/1942 in Piermont; H - 60, tourist home, 2nd, b. Willimantic, CT, s/o Frank E. Herrick (Willimantic, CT, deceased) and Helen Martin (Willimantic, CT, deceased); W - 29, domestic, b.

Orford, d/o Ralph C. Perkins (Hardwick, VT, mill owner) and Maude Barnet (Walden, VT)

HERRING,
William L. of Montpelier, VT m. Jean E. **White** of Montpelier, VT 8/28/1965

HIBBARD,
C. G. of Piermont m. M. M. **Curtis** of Piermont 8/12/1913 in Lebanon; H - 18, store clerk, b. Orford, s/o George A. Hibbard (Lancaster, farmer); W - 23, housework, b. Wentworth, d/o George McCloskey (Laconia, miner)

HIGGINS,
Michael Gilbert of Piermont m. Beth Frances **Williams** of Piermont 5/29/1993

HILL,
Craig B. of Piermont m. Mardi **McGregor** of Piermont 12/1/1985
Harold F. of Piermont m. Lucy A. **Sawyer** of Piermont 2/20/1918 in Piermont; H - 19, farmer, b. Norton, VT, s/o John Hill (Newport, VT, farmer); W - 18, housework, b. Piermont, d/o Milo B. Sawyer (Topsham, VT, farmer)
Louis M. of Piermont m. Bertha J. **Hood** of Waits River, VT 1/6/1904 in Pike Sta.; H - 25, carpenter, b. Piermont, s/o Moses C. Hill (Canada, PQ, farmer); W - 17, housework, b. Waits River, d/o Henry E. Hood (Lyme, farmer)
Orlando B. of Piermont m. Lola L. **Howland** of Piermont 1/7/1905 in Piermont; H - 20, farmer, b. Piermont, s/o Moses C. Hill (Barnston, PQ, farmer); W - 16, housework, b. Piermont, d/o Lee Howland (Easton, farmer)

HITCHNER,
Alan L. of Wakefield, RI m. Peggy **DeGoosh** of Wakefield, RI 9/11/1982

HODGE,
Fred Orrin of Corinth, VT m. Annie P. **Bowles** of Piermont 6/20/1917 in Piermont; H - 24, farmer, b. Corinth, VT, s/o Orinn Hodge (Corinth, VT, farmer); W - 25, housework, b. Deering, d/o Albert E. Bowles (New Boston, farmer)

Herbert J. of Fairlee, VT m. Beverly **Fadden** of Piermont 8/4/1951 in Piermont; H - 23, farmer, b. Hanover, s/o Avery Hodge (Fairlee, VT) and Mary A. McIndus (Fairlee, VT); W - 24, secretary, b. Piermont, d/o Dana Fadden (W. Thornton) and Esther B. Downing (W. Thornton)

HODSDON,

Harrison of Piermont m. Bertha D. **Bennett** of Piermont 5/2/1917 in Piermont; H - 43, farmer, b. Piermont, s/o Aaron G. Hodsdon (Piermont, farmer); W - 34, housekeeper, 2nd, b. Brookbury, PQ, d/o Isaac B. Downes (Brookbury, PQ, farmer)

Harrison of Piermont m. Edith Emilie **Childs** of Piermont 5/1/1922 in Haverhill; H - 48, farmer, 2nd, widower, b. Piermont, s/o Aaron Hodsdon (Piermont, farmer); W - 27, governess, b. Piermont, d/o Harlow Childs (W. Fairlee, VT, farmer)

HOGAN,

Austin William of Piermont m. Sarah Ann (Gillord) **Western** of Piermont 11/15/1995

Michael R. of Piermont m. Kristen M. **Stitt** of Laconia 9/6/1997

HOLDEN,

James M. of Paris, ME m. Florence B. **Rollins** of Piermont 10/20/1915 in Piermont; H - 28, laborer, b. Woodstock, ME, s/o James M. Holden (Paris, ME, deceased); W - 18, housework, b. Campton, d/o Henry H. Rollins (Orford, laborer)

Willard Edwin of Graniteville, VT m. Delores Anne **Budrow** of Barre, VT 10/16/1954 in Piermont; H - 30, carpenter, b. Barre, VT, s/o Wilman Holden (Colebrook) and Mildred Thompson (Barre, VT); W - 19, domestic, b. Barre, VT, d/o Leroy Budrow (Barre, VT) and Olive Laso (Plattsburgh, NY)

HOLLAND,

David of Sugar Hill m. Darolyn **Meder** of Sugar Hill 1/10/1998

HOLMES,

George B. of Hartford, CT m. Judith A. **Bernier** of Middletown, CT 2/11/1967

HOOD,

Donald E. of Piermont m. Sally **McAllen** of Bradford, VT 12/31/1966

Harold R. of Piermont m. Wilhelmene **Sawyer** of Piermont 10/13/1932 in E. Haverhill; H - 24, farmer, b. Newbury, VT, s/o Maurice Hood (Topsham, VT, deceased) and Ida Smith (Topsham, VT, deceased); W - 25, housework, b. Piermont, d/o Milo B. Sawyer (Topsham, VT, farmer) and Alice Rodimon (Piermont, housewife)

Merle of Bradford, VT m. Bertha **Arnold** of Piermont 4/22/1933 in Bradford, VT; H - 29, meat cutter, b. Corinth, VT, s/o Henry Hood (Vershire, VT, laborer) and Minnie Flanders (Corinth, VT, housewife); W - 20, at home, b. Haverhill, d/o Walter Arnold (Haverhill, farmer) and Blanche Hardy (Haverhill, housewife)

HORTON,

Bernard G. of Piermont m. Eva May **Lewis** of Piermont 5/20/1924 in Piermont; H - 19, laborer, b. Piermont, s/o William L. Horton (Orford, laborer); W - 17, waitress, b. Wilder, VT, d/o George F. Lewis (Binghamton, NY, deceased)

Henry A. of Piermont m. Emma A. **Foote** of Orford 8/15/1917 in Claremont; H - 25, carpenter, b. Piermont, s/o William H. Horton (Barnard, VT, farmer); W - 22, housework, b. Warren, d/o Bert S. Foote (Warren, farmer)

John E. of Piermont m. Arlene W. **Wyman** of Pike 12/21/1969

Ralph of Piermont m. Mary A. **Metcalf** of Piermont 8/27/1927 in Haverhill; H - 20, accountant, b. Orford, s/o William L. Horton (Orford, truck driver) and Hattie E. Webster (Monroe, housework); W - 23, clerk, b. Piermont, d/o John P. Metcalf (Piermont, farmer) and Carrie R. Grimes (Orford, housewife)

Richard Paul of Plympton, MA m. Sandra Lee **Gunter** of Plympton, MA 5/17/1997

William L. of Piermont m. Hattie E. **Webster** of Orford 7/7/1903 in Piermont; H - 20, laborer, b. Orford, s/o William H. Horton (Barnard, VT, farmer); W - 19, housework, b. Monroe, d/o Henry D. Webster (Monroe)

HOWARD,

Earl S. of Piermont m. Audrey B. **Clark** of Tilton 1/16/1953 in Belmont; H - 21, truck driver, b. Woodsville, s/o Paul W. Carter (Concord) and Dorothy S. Howard (S. Barre, VT); W - 22, office worker, b. Warren, d/o Wilbur A. Clark (Meredith) and Dorothy M. Sweet (Sheffield)

Stephen E. of Haverhill m. Elsie M. **Brill** of Swiftwater 10/14/1931 in Piermont; H - 24, elec. contractor, b. Haverhill, s/o John A. Howard (Haverhill, farmer) and Elma A. Lupren (Newbury, VT, teacher); W - 25, waitress, b. Landaff, d/o George Brill (Eden, VT, farmer) and Martha Sargent (Eden, VT, housewife)

Zedock of Orford m. Mabel A. **Rice** of Piermont 5/20/1934 in Orford; H - 41, teamster, 2nd, b. Orford, s/o Anderson Howard (Lyme, deceased) and Julia Cutting (Contoocook, PQ, deceased); W - 45, domestic, 3rd, b. Claremont, d/o Israel Vadney (Canada, deceased) and Clara Austin (Lowell, MA, deceased)

HOWE,

Oliver E. of Piermont m. Mildred V. **Sawyer** of Piermont 5/5/1915 in Haverhill; H - 22, farmer, b. Benton, s/o Samuel Howe (Benton, farmer); W - 18, housework, b. Piermont, d/o Milo B. Sawyer (Topsham, VT, farmer)

HOWLAND,

Moses N. of Piermont m. May A. **Randall** of Piermont 2/18/1892 in Piermont; H - 72, farmer, 2nd, b. Easton, s/o Daniel Howland (Lisbon) and Betsy Stevens (Lisbon); W - 32, domestic, b. London, England, d/o Edward Randall and Annie -----

William L. of Piermont m. Florence P. **Aldridge** of E. Lyme, CT 11/30/1904 in Piermont; H - 20, laborer, b. Orford, s/o Lee Howland; W - 25, housework, b. Cambridge, MO, d/o William H. Aldridge

HUBBARD,

Willie E. of Piermont m. Ida B. **Hall** of Orford 4/13/1905 in Haverhill; H - 22, board sawyer, b. Canaan, VT, s/o Charles Hubbard (Palmyra, ME, deceased); W - 18, housework, b. Orford, d/o William B. Hall (Orford, farmer)

HUMPHREY,

Maurice T. of Bradford, VT m. Mabel A. **Zwicker** of Bradford, VT 4/18/1936 in Auburn; H - 27, poultry dealer, b. Bradford, VT, s/o Ernest R. Humphrey (Newbury, VT, meat cutter) and Sadie Tenney (Boston, MA, housewife); W - 21, librarian, b. E. Corinth, VT, d/o George W. Zwicker (Liverpool, NS, carpenter) and Anna Divoll (E. Corinth, VT, housewife)

Wilbert of Orford m. Flossie A. **Gamsby** of Piermont 11/9/1936 in Bradford, VT; H - 37, farmer, 2nd, widower, b. Albert Mines, PQ, s/o William Humphrey (Albert Pines, PQ) and Elizabeth Cahoon (Albert Pines, PQ); W - 33, domestic, 2nd, widow, b. Coaticook, PQ, d/o George Smith (Dudswell, PQ) and Jennie Orr (Dudswell, PQ)

HUNT,
Jesse M. of E. Corinth, VT m. Hazel E. **Newton** of Starksboro, VT 8/21/1926 in Orford; H - 26, butter maker, b. Chelsea, VT, s/o Charles Hunt (Tunbridge, VT, deceased) and Martha Flanders (Sharon, VT, domestic); W - 20, waitress, b. Peru, VT, d/o Timothy Newton (Starksboro, VT, farmer) and Annie Flint (Starksboro, VT, housewife)

HUNTINGTON,
George E. of Bradford, VT m. Donna L. **Drew** of Piermont 9/19/1963

HURLBERT,
Scott L. of Haverhill m. Yvonne **Ayala** of Haverhill 9/1/1984

HUTCHINS,
Nicholas Ryan of Piermont m. Megan Marie **Stocking** of Fairlee, VT 7/21/1999
Roger P. of Haverhill m. Teresa A. **Rodimon** of Piermont 6/22/1974
Roger P. of Piermont m. Beth J. **Cushing** of Piermont 7/17/2004

IGNACIO,
Kent of Piermont m. Jeanne **Engley** of Piermont 2/9/2003

INGALLS,
Carroll H. of N. Haverhill m. Dorothy Irene **Day** of Piermont 9/5/1925 in Piermont; H - 23, clerk, b. N. Haverhill, s/o Willis H. Ingalls (Stanstead, PQ, farmer) and Julia May Bartlett (Brownington, VT, housewife); W - 25, P.O. clerk, b. Piermont, d/o Ernest D. Day (Troy, VT, farmer) and Luna M. Webster (Monroe, housewife)

INGERSON,
James Douglas of Haverhill m. Paula Lee **Estes** of Haverhill 3/15/1997

JACKSON,
Lee E. of Piermont m. Cindy L. **Elliot** of Piermont 10/4/1975

JACOBS,
Abe of Pittfield, VT m. Rose **Streeter** of Corinth, VT 1/15/1895 in Piermont; H - 22, salesman, b. Germany, s/o Moses Jacobs (Germany) and Belna Jacobs (Germany); W - 19, domestic, b. Corinth, VT, d/o G. Streeter

JAMES,
Bradley, Jr. of Piermont m. Jessica **Schroeder** of CA 10/3/2004
Bradley A. of Piermont m. Sandra L. **Gilson** of E. Haverhill 4/9/1976
Delbert of Piermont m. Laura **Picknell** of Bradford, VT 5/2/1964

JESSEMAN,
Everett A. of Piermont m. Doris E. **Jesseman** of Piermont 6/21/1952 in Piermont; H - 25, fill sta. att., b. Haverhill, s/o Arthur Jesseman (Campton) and Gladys Fields (Pike); W - 21, domestic, b. Topsham, VT, d/o Urban Shover (Topsham, VT) and Emma M. King (Topsham, VT)
William of Piermont m. Nellie F. **Wilson** of Piermont 10/3/1937 in Piermont; H - 59, laborer, 2nd, widower, b. Dorchester, s/o Harrison Jesseman (Dorchester, deceased) and Mariah Walden (Dorchester); W - 48, housekeeper, 2nd, widow, b. High Barnet, England, d/o Henry Fairbrother (England)

JOHNSON,
Bert E., Jr. of Topsham, VT m. Gertrude Irene **Bijolle** of Piermont 4/10/1959
Charles W. of Piermont m. Lizitte C. **Blake** of Piermont 5/2/1917 in Piermont; H - 41, farmer, b. Newbury, VT, s/o George A. Johnson (Newbury, VT, farmer); W - 32, housekeeper, 2nd, b. Kanosa, PQ, d/o George Glover (Winnipeg, MB, farmer)
Henry L. of Bradford, VT m. Janet **McLerran** of Piermont 2/27/1999
James of Newbury, VT m. Caroline **Gaffield** of Bradford, VT 7/26/1910 in Piermont; H - 69, farming, 2nd, b. Scotland, s/o William Johnston (sic) (Scotland, laborer); W - 69, housewife, 2nd, b. Bradford, VT, d/o John Wilson (Corinth, VT, farmer)

JOHNSTON,
Bradford G. of Piermont m. Leni **Magaziner** of Piermont 5/31/1976

JONES,
Frederick of Piermont m. Lucy **Hill** of Piermont 2/23/1924 in Haverhill; H - 23, laborer, b. Daneville, CT, s/o William Jones (Wales, England, deceased); W - 24, domestic, 2nd, b. Piermont, d/o Milo Sawyer (Topsham, VT, farmer)

KELLEY,
Brian A. of Piermont m. Madeline E. **Fulford** of Piermont 2/28/1970

KELSEA,
Kenneth A. of Warren, NY m. Irene F. **Strapponi** of Warren, NY 6/24/1950 in Piermont; H - 32, shovel opr., 2nd, b. Colebrook, s/o James I. Kelsea (Colebrook) and Louise Long (NS); W - 30, factory worker, 2nd, b. Littleton, d/o Basil Elliot (Littleton) and Bernice Stetson (Piermont)

KENISTON,
Bertrand E., Jr. of Piermont m. Doris Elizabeth **Grimes** of Haverhill 7/6/1963
Hugh L. of Piermont m. Mary L. **Horton** of Piermont 12/29/1951 in Piermont; H - 22, Cpl. in US Army, b. Bath, s/o Bertrand E. Keniston (Kittery, ME) and Mary S. Morin (Woodsville); W - 19, waitress, b. Piermont, d/o Bernard G. Horton (Piermont) and Eva M. Lewis (Piermont)

KENT,
Chester O. of Piermont m. Myrtie E. **Underhill** of Piermont 6/26/1895 in Piermont; H - 24, mechanic, b. Randolph, s/o Horace E. Kent (Roxbury, VT) and Lucy C. Snow (Brookfield, VT); W - 29, milliner, b. Piermont, d/o Edward Underhill (Piermont) and Emily Libby (Newbury, VT)

KEYSAR,
Craig S. of Piermont m. Rebekah **Page** of Piermont 8/14/2004

KIMBALL,
Harold F. of Haverhill m. Mamie L. **Stetson** of Piermont 12/11/1943 in Orford; H - 24, farmer, b. N. Haverhill, s/o Harland G. Kimball (Haverhill, farmer) and Bertha Shallow (Haverhill, housewife); W - 18, unemployed, b. Piermont, d/o Clinton Stetson (Piermont, lumberman) and Edna Robie (Piermont, housewife)

KINCAID,
Arthur E. of Bradford, VT m. Katherine **Davis** of Bradford, VT 3/11/1934 in Piermont; H - 20, laborer, b. Sutton, VT, s/o Leon Kincaid (Sutton, VT, laborer) and Lillian Stanhope (Sutton, PQ, housewife); W - 20, at home, b. Bradford, VT, d/o William Davis (Bradford, VT, deceased) and Evelyn Blake (Sutton, VT, housewife)

KINGHORN,
Clement T. of Bradford, VT m. Medy L. **Stanley** of Piermont 8/23/1926 in Piermont; H - 21, plumber, b. Hardwick, VT, s/o Lyman J. Kinghorn (Granby, VT, plumber) and Carrie Crowley (Barton, VT, housewife); W - 21, teacher, b. Piermont, d/o Orlo B. Stanley (Piermont, farmer) and Althea Wilson (Groton, VT, deceased)

Guy B. of Piermont m. Lana Lee **Davis** of Fairlee, VT 9/13/1958 in Fairlee, VT; H - 21, merchant, b. Haverhill, s/o Clement Kinghorn (Hardwick, VT) and Meda L. Stanley (Piermont); W - 18, bookkeeper, b. Englewood, NJ, d/o Reginald Davis (Nyack, NY) and Gertrude Schaub (Jersey City, NJ)

S. Robert of Piermont m. Barbara A. **Taylor** of Bradford, VT 12/26/1952 in Piermont; H - 19, USAF, b. Haverhill, s/o Clement T. Kinghorn (Hardwick, VT) and Meda L. Stanley (Piermont); W - 19, lab. tech., b. St. Johnsbury, VT, d/o Leo F. Taylor (Newport) and Thelma Dunham (Corinth, VT)

KINGSBURY,
Allan L. of Bradford, VT m. Kathleen A. **Goodell** of Piermont 11/18/1978

KNAPP,
Dale H. of Piermont m. Jean M. **Pushee** of Lyme 6/16/1971

David K. of Concord m. Rosemary J. **Woodard** of Piermont 9/29/1975

Dexter A. of Piermont m. Susan J. **Pushee** of Piermont 7/1/1967

Ray A. of Piermont m. Julia B. W. **Tewksbury** of Haverhill 2/17/1916 in Haverhill; H - 25, farmer, b. Piermont, s/o Albert A. Knapp (Piermont, farmer); W - 22, P.O. clerk, b. Newbury, VT, d/o Stratton W. Tewksbury (Newbury, VT, farmer)

KOCH,
Michael S. of Piermont m. Lori Lyn **Armstrong** of Springfield, VT 9/11/1989

Peter Jeffrey of Piermont m. Lisa Marie **Eastman** of Dover 5/22/1993

KOLOSEIKE,
Walter F. of Rochester, NY m. Mary F. **Underhill** of Piermont 8/22/1935 in Piermont; H - 40, teacher, b. Rochester, NY, s/o Frank L. Koloseike (Germany, farmer) and Emilie C. Taraschke (Germany, housewife); W - 31, teacher, b. Ernest S. Underhill (Piermont, farmer) and Elizabeth Converse (Stewartstown, home maker)

KOMOROWSKI,
James P. of Piermont m. Heidi L. **Meagher** of Piermont 5/26/1984

KROELL,
Rolf of Germany m. Alexandra **Ibenthal** of Germany 7/5/2002

LABOUNTY,
Peter Nelson of Piermont m. Nancy Ellen **Sandell** of Piermont 6/24/1994

LADEAU,
Albert C. of Piermont m. Abbie P. **Cushing** of Piermont 6/16/1906 in Piermont; H - 20, laborer, b. Orfordville, s/o Charles Ladeau (Colchester, VT, laborer); W - 16, housework, b. McIndoe, VT, d/o George Cushing (Derby Line, VT, laborer)

Frank E. of Piermont m. Hattie M. **Mann** of Fairlee, VT 2/21/1891 in Bradford, VT; H - 22, laborer, b. Eden, VT, s/o Joseph Ladeau (Colchester, VT, farmer) and Elizabeth Ladeau; W - 21, domestic, b. Waldon, VT, d/o George C. Mann (Woodbury, VT, mechanic) and Edna Shurtleff

Herbert J. of Piermont m. May E. **Warwick** of Piermont 9/9/1911 in Haverhill; H - 27, farmer, 2nd, b. Fitzwilliam, s/o Joseph Ladeau (Colchester, VT, chairmaker); W - 33, housework, 2nd, b. Grindstone, MI, d/o John Wilson (Vianna, PQ, carpenter)

Joseph of Baldwinsville, MA m. Hattie S. **Smith** of Piermont 9/9/1914 in Pike; H - 67, chauffeur, 2nd, b. Colchester, VT, s/o

Francis Ladeau (Canada, laborer); W - 47, housework, 2nd, b. Vershire, VT, d/o Lyman Titus (Vershire, VT, farmer)

Joseph W. of Piermont m. Lucena A. **Clifford** of Piermont 4/1/1899 in Orford; H - 31, farmer, b. Eden, VT, s/o Joseph Ladeau (Colchester, VT, farmer); W - 17, housework, 2nd, b. Jay, VT, d/o P. S. Hadlock (Troy, VT, farmer)

LAFOE,

Howard E. of Piermont m. Elizabeth R. **Collins** of Piermont 11/2/1932 in Piermont; H - 20, farmer, b. Newport, VT, s/o Albert LaFoe (W. Derby, VT, farmer) and Edith Blake (W. Derby, VT, housewife); W - 18, domestic, b. Merrimac, d/o Ralph Collins (Sanbornton, laborer) and Lulu Ballan (housework)

LALOND,

Harold F. of Exeter m. Muriel E. **Burns** of Piermont 12/30/1967

LAMARRE,

Bruce L. of Bath m. Julie M. **Simpson** of Piermont 6/15/1974

LAMB,

Nelson F. of Bradford, VT m. Hazel M. **Andross** of Piermont 10/12/1909 in Piermont; H - 21, station agent, 2nd, b. E. Orange, VT, s/o Frank Lamb (S. Ryegate, veterinary); W - 17, housework, b. Piermont, d/o Thomas H. Andross (Piermont, farmer)

LAMONTAGNE,

Archiel of Piermont m. Dale G. **Abbott** of Bradford, VT 12/24/1902 in Piermont; H - 21, harnessmaker, b. Piermont, s/o Jed'ie Lamontagne (farmer); W - 18, housework, b. Haverhill, d/o E. M. C. Abbott (blacksmith)

C. G. of Piermont m. Susie O. **Aldrich** of Piermont 10/11/1905 in Piermont; H - 26, farmer, b. Bartlett, s/o Gideon Lamontagne (Canada, farmer); W - 28, housework, 2nd, b. Colebrook, d/o Harry Gould (don't know, deceased)

Jeddie of Piermont m. Ella M. **Holden** of Abington, CT 9/25/1895 in Piermont; H - 36, farmer, 2nd, b. Quebec, s/o Henry Lamontagne (PQ) and Eliza Cross (PQ); W - 27, housewife,

2nd, b. Woodstock, CT, d/o Benjamin Kimball (Woodstock, CT) and Narcissa H. Perham (Bethel, ME)

LANG,
Timothy m. of Piermont m. Tanya R. **Mercado** of Springfield 2/12/2000

LAPORT,
Reg. W. of Piermont m. Grace M. **Preston** of Orford 7/13/1931 in Woodsville; H - 22, mechanic, 2nd, b. Brandon, VT, s/o Alex LaPort (Chazee, NY, deceased) and Margaret LaVoice (NY, deceased); W - 18, domestic, b. Pawtucket, RI, d/o William Preston (laborer) and Mabel French (Thetford, VT, housewife)

LARKHAM,
Glen H. of Bradford, VT m. Wendy L. **Kimball** of Bradford, VT 10/12/1985

LEARD,
Alder C. of Piermont m. Claire **Asselin** of Piermont 8/4/1937 in St. Johnsbury, VT; H - 39, inn keeper, 2nd, divorced, b. PEI, s/o Joseph B. Leard (PEI) and Mary E. Mutlast (PEI); W - 36, b. ME, d/o John Asselin (Canada) and Ruth Whitcher (Warren)

LEAZER,
Herbert S. of Piermont m. Ethel F. **Adkin** of Lakeport 8/26/1914 in Lakeport; H - 28, school teacher, b. Piermont, s/o Stephen C. Leazer (Boston, MA, farmer); W - 22, teacher, b. Lakeport, d/o Thomas Adkin (England, deceased)

LEBARRON,
William G. of Piermont m. Ida T. **Bliss** of Fairlee, VT 11/17/1902 in Lyme; H - 41, farmer, b. Northfield, VT, s/o James S. LeBarron (New Bedford, MA, mechanic); W - 38, housework, b. Bradford, VT, d/o William C. Bliss (Bradford, VT, farmer)

LEBEAUX,
Edward S. of Piermont m. E. Pearl **Dexter** of Haverhill 6/22/1920 in Haverhill; H - 26, farmer, b. Rutland, MA, s/o John E. Lebeaux (Canada, farmer); W - 21, teacher, b. E. Haverhill, d/o Henry Dexter (Franconia, farmer)

LEE,
Ray Stevens of Fairlee, VT m. Bulah Olive **Cutting** of Piermont 4/30/1924 in Bradford, VT; H - 23, fireman, b. Little Rock, KY, s/o Robert M. Lee (Brookfield, KY); W - 24, domestic, 2nd, b. Piermont, d/o Fred D. Cutting (Piermont, farmer)

LEETE,
Alan Grant of Piermont m. Nancy **Larson** of Fairlee, VT 6/4/1988

LEONARD,
John N. of Piermont m. Aggie S. **Wilson** of Piermont 12/30/1891 in Haverhill; H - 22, farmer, b. Bath, s/o George E. Leonard (Ryegate, VT, farmer) and Abbie A. Childs (Bath); W - 20, lady, b. MI, d/o John Wilson (Canada, mechanic) and Agnes O'Neil (Canada)

John R. of Haverhill m. Marion E. **Ames** of Piermont 9/28/1921 in Piermont; H - 24, mechanic, b. Piermont, s/o John N. Leonard (Bath, farmer); W - 22, teacher, b. Piermont, d/o Arthur E. Ames (Orford, creamery man)

LEWIS,
George F. of Hanover m. Minnie E. **Tasey** of Piermont 1/2/1911 in Piermont; H - 49, carpenter, 2nd, b. Binghamton, NY, s/o Charles F. Lewis (Plainfield, gunsmith); W - 31, housework, 2nd, b. Vershire, VT, d/o George H. Church (Vershire, VT, millman)

LITTLE,
Charles E. of Strafford, VT m. Lillian **Martin** of Chelsea, VT 5/29/1930 in Piermont; H - 70, fireman, 3rd, b. Lyman, s/o George Little (Lyman, deceased) and Elizabeth Cram (Lyman, deceased); W - 56, nurse, 3rd, b. Calais, VT, d/o Nathan Bailey (Greensboro, VT, deceased) and Susan Luce (Elmore, VT, deceased)

LOCKE,
Kenneth E. of Warner m. Cindy L. **Jesseman** of Piermont 6/21/1975

LOCKWOOD,
Harold S. of Piermont m. Linda L. **Fowler** of Piermont 5/25/1985

LOTMAN,
Peter Silvester of Piermont m. Michelle Marie (Daigle) **Furno** of Piermont 10/11/1997

LOUGEE,
Walter E. of Piermont m. Martha **McDonald** of Lyme 7/14/1909 in Haverhill; H - 29, farmer, b. Bradford, VT, s/o Sylvester Lougee (Laconia, farmer); W - 28, housework, 3rd, b. Patton, PQ, d/o George Dunbar (Guildhall, VT, farmer)

LOVEJOY,
Albert G. of Orford m. Mary A. **Howe** of Piermont 12/22/1891 in Piermont; H - 40, farmer, b. Orford, s/o Clark Lovejoy (Orford, farmer) and Sabrina Brown (Orford); W - 28, teacher, b. Hanover, d/o Jonathan H. Howe (Underhill, VT, mill man) and Eunice A. Worth (Hanover)

LOVERIN,
Stanley M. of Laingsburg, MI m. Dorothy G. **Masher** of Montpelier, VT 7/8/1957 in Piermont; H - 25, USAF, b. Eden, VT, s/o Mark Loverin (Eden, VT) and Theda Paranto (Lowell, VT); W - 24, factory wrk., b. E. Montpelier, VT, d/o Guy W. Masher (Newport, VT) and Ruth Dobey (Montpelier, VT)

LUCE,
Perley G. of Piermont m. Evelyn **Durgee** of St. Johnsbury, VT 5/27/1928 in E. Haverhill; H - 25, laborer, b. Orford, s/o Leslie Luce (Chelsea, VT, farmer) and Rose Hubbard (Canada, housewife); W - 18, domestic, b. St. Johnsbury, VT, d/o Herbert Durgee (NB, laborer) and Emma Briggs (St. Johnsbury, VT, housewife)

LYONS,
Dennis H. of Barre City, VT m. Cheryl D. **Spooner** of Barre City, VT 7/27/1998

LYSTER,
Edward T. of Piermont m. Regenna **Schauer** of Lyme Ctr. 6/30/1972

MARCOTT,
Robert E. of Bradford, VT m. Joann L. **Pushee** of Bradford, VT 7/12/1980

MARDIN,
Clement of Piermont m. Edith **Hill** of Piermont 10/21/1917 in Piermont; H - 33, farmer, b. Lisbon, s/o Willard Mardin (Lisbon, carpenter); W - 17, housework, b. Newport, VT, d/o John Hill (Newport, VT, farmer)

MARTIN,
Wilfred C. of Piermont m. Joan G. **Martin** of Piermont 9/11/1952 in Haverhill; H - 25, farmer, 2nd, b. Bristol, CT, s/o Wesley A. Martin (New Britain, CT) and Hazel M. Martin (Houlton, ME); W - 20, housewife, 3rd, b. Brooklyn, NY, d/o Archibald Gallagher (Brooklyn, NY) and Lydia Wells (Brooklyn, NY)

MASON,
Donald C. of Gainesville, FL m. Anna S. **Mason** of Piermont 6/16/1972

Ralph of Topsham, VT m. Dorothy L. **Ralston** of Ryegate, VT 11/13/1933 in Orford; H - 28, farmer, b. Topsham, VT, s/o Almon F. Mason (Moretown, VT, deceased) and Mary A. Page (Corinth, VT, deceased); W - 18, domestic, b. Ryegate, VT, d/o Robert Ralston (Inverness, Canada, farmer) and Gertrude Merin (PA, housewife)

MASSA,
John A. of Winthrop, MA m. Frances Sybil **Hazen** of Piermont 9/7/1958 in Winthrop, MA; H - 27, b. Somerville, MA, s/o Ralph Massa and Anna Massa; W - 22, hairdresser, b. Canaan, d/o Roy Hazen (W. Hartford, VT) and Frances Burnor (Pittsfield, VT)

MASURE,
Basil C. of N. Thetford, VT m. Marguerite **Blodgett** of Piermont 7/8/1944 in Piermont; H - 17, laborer, b. Lyndon, VT, s/o Louis H. Masure (Sutton, VT, laborer) and Valentine E. Aldrich (Pompanoosic, VT, housewife); W - 19, domestic, b. Wheelock, VT, d/o Earl F. Blodgett (Washington, IN, lathe operator) and Agnes A. Sherburne (Wheelock, VT, housewife)

MAXFIELD,
Albert D. of Piermont m. Laura M. **Merrill** of Salisbury 1/23/1915 in Franklin; H - 20, farmer, b. Wolcott, VT, s/o Daniel Maxfield (Wolcott, VT, farmer); W - 19, housework, b. Salisbury, d/o Benjamin Merrill (New London, mason)
Albert D. of Piermont m. Ethelyn I. **Smith** of Piermont 6/23/1921 in Piermont; H - 26, farmer, 2nd, widower, b. Wolcott, VT, s/o Dan S. Maxfield (Wolcott, VT, farmer); W - 18, domestic, b. Stamford, CT, d/o James H. Smith (Stamford, CT, farmer)
Andrew C. of Piermont m. Ella M. **Bowker** of Bradford, VT 6/1/1913 in Piermont; H - 20, laborer, b. Wolcott, VT, s/o Daniel Maxfield (Wolcott, VT, farmer); W - 17, housework, b. Piermont, d/o Francis P. Bowker (Warden, PQ, farmer)

MAYOTTE,
James E. of Piermont m. Robin F. **Berkowitz** of Piermont 8/6/1986

McAULEY,
Auley of Piermont m. Ida M. **Smith** of Piermont 1/3/1898 in Piermont; H - 30, stone cutter, b. Piermont, s/o Murdock McAuley (Scotland, farmer); W - 18, house work, b. Piermont, d/o Harvey Smith (Haverhill, farmer)

McCLELLAN,
Owen C. of Bradford, VT m. Debra J. **Jesseman** of Piermont 6/24/1972

McDONALD,
Finley R. of Piermont m. Emma V. **Koley** of Piermont 10/5/1963
Floyd E. of Piermont m. Martha L. **Goldsmith** of Piermont 9/11/1980

McKEAGE,
Ray of Piermont m. Junie **Wright** of Piermont 11/28/1912 in Piermont; H - 20, farming, b. Pittsburg, s/o Robert McKeage (store clerk); W - 23, housework, 2nd, b. Colebrook, d/o Charles Gould (Colebrook, deceased)

McLAM,
Norman G. of Topsham, VT m. Lurline M. **Robie** of Piermont 10/6/1946 in Piermont; H - 28, merchant, b. Piermont, s/o Norman W. McLam (Topsham, VT, lathe operator) and Myrtle

S. Blood (Keene, housewife); W - 24, reg. nurse, b. Topsham, VT, d/o Lyman Robie (Piermont, farmer) and Gwendolyn Shumway (Bradford, VT, housewife)

McTAGUE,
William D. of Piermont m. Katherine M. **Piper** of Lyme 10/16/1965

MEAGHER,
Patrick C. of Hartford, VT m. Heidi L. **Gardner** of Piermont 10/1/1977

MERRITT,
Robert E. of W. Fairlee, VT m. Mary R. **Wilson** of W. Fairlee, VT 8/15/1987

METCALF,
Ai of Piermont m. Michelle **Stevens** of Piermont 9/17/1994
Asa M. of Piermont m. Heidi J. **Osgood** of Piermont 5/3/2003
Asa Norman of Piermont m. Melissa Susan **Burmaster** of Piermont 10/14/2000
H. Burgess of Piermont m. Emily G. **Morrill** of E. Haverhill 8/13/1973
Harry B. of Piermont m. Shirley Mary **Smith** of Piermont 6/21/1942 in Lincoln; H - 33, farmer, b. Piermont, s/o John P. Metcalf (Piermont, farmer) and Ava Lewis (Orford, housekeeper); W - 26, school teacher, b. Walden, VT, d/o George F. Smith (Stannard, VT, truck driver) and Bertha Paronto (Montgomery, VT, housewife)
John E. of Piermont m. Abby M. **Johnson** of Northwood 1/31/1970
John P. of Piermont m. Carrie R. **Grimes** of Piermont 6/17/1891 in Piermont; H - 21, farmer, b. Piermont, s/o Burgess C. Metcalf (Piermont, farmer) and Mary N. Messer (Piermont); W - 19, clerk, b. Orford, d/o Edward E. Grimes (Orford, merchant) and Amanda T. Davis (Benton)

MILLER,
George H. of W. Newbury m. Ellen R. **Johnson** of Piermont 1/1/1906 in Piermont; H - 24, farmer, b. Ryegate, VT, s/o James Miller (Reygate, VT, deceased); W - 23, housework, b. Piermont, d/o George A. Johnson (Newbury, VT, farmer)

MITCHELL,
Scott A. of Middlesex, MA m. Stephanie Ann **Young** of Cambridge, MA 5/29/1982

MONAGHAN,
John III of Piermont m. Susan Mary **Kapp** of Piermont 5/14/1995

MONTGOMERY,
True of Piermont m. Alice **Luce** of Piermont 4/17/1915 in Haverhill; H - 21, carpenter, b. Kirby, VT, s/o Frank Montgomery (St. Johnsbury, VT, laborer); W - 19, housework, b. Piermont, d/o Lester Luce (Tunbridge, VT, teamster)

MOODY,
David J. of Pike m. Doreen A. **Jesseman** of Piermont 9/14/1974
Ronald P. of Pike m. Marie L. **Rodimon** of Piermont 6/17/1973

MOORE,
Donald Clesson of Haverhill m. Amy Margaret **Winot** of Haverhill 9/18/1999
John W. of Littleton m. Dorothy L. **Hackett** of Piermont 10/20/1934 in Piermont; H - 26, farmer, b. Concord, s/o William J. Moore (Canada, farmer) and Edith Williams (Littleton, deceased); W - 20, domestic, b. Piermont, d/o Harley Hackett (Orford, road agent) and Jeanie Emerson (Melrose, MA, housewife)

MOREY,
Wesley Earl of Piermont m. Emma **Hill** of Piermont 5/31/1919 in Piermont; H - 21, farming, b. Orford, s/o Irving Morey (Orford, laborer); W - 20, housework, b. Newport, d/o John Hill (Morgan, VT, farmer)

MORGAN,
William J. of Plainville, CT m. Penny J. **Stetson** of Plainville, CT 7/21/1979

MORRILL,
Charles R. of Piermont m. Evelyn E. **Schmukler** of Piermont 7/16/1967
Philip C. of Piermont m. Elizabeth **Cowan** of N. Haverhill 11/23/1945 in N. Haverhill; H - 22, farmer, b. Piermont, s/o Frederick Morrill

(White Rock, RI, deceased) and Beulah Brown (Haverhill, housewife); W - 18, nurse maid, b. Claremont, d/o Andrew Cowan and Bessie Stacey (housekeeper)

MORRIS,
Edward J. of Piermont m. Daisy **Stevens** of Piermont 9/14/1898 in Haverhill; H - 34, farmer, b. E. Fairfield, s/o Thomas Morris (Ireland, farmer); W - 22, house work, b. Plymouth, d/o Charles Stevens (Plymouth, farmer)

MORSE,
Clarence E. of Hyde Park, MA m. Delia E. **Sleeper** of Hyde Park, MA 6/8/1904 in Piermont; H - 21, farmer, b. Hyde Park, MA, s/o Moses Morse (Middlesex, VT, machinist); W - 19, housework, b. Hyde Park, MA, d/o George Sleeper (Washington, blacksmith)
Franklin A. of Piermont m. Susie M. **Winn** of Piermont 8/8/1911 in Piermont; H - 36, farmer, b. Sutton, PQ, s/o Romaine Morse (Canada, farmer); W - 20, housework, b. Piermont, d/o Frank P. Winn (Piermont, farmer)
George O. of Piermont m. Lura E. **Hatch** of Piermont 12/21/1904 in Piermont; H - 27, carpenter, b. Jay, VT, s/o Bominer Morse (Sutton, Canada, farmer); W - 17, housework, b. Jericho, VT, d/o Fred N. Hatch (Jericho, VT, farmer)

MOUROUSAS,
Theodore of Cambridge, MA m. Grace L. **Perry** of Cambridge, MA 8/20/1966

MUCHMORE,
Daniel C. of Piermont m. Jennie M. **Ward** of Piermont 8/18/1915 in Piermont; H - 47, farmer, b. Orford, s/o Henry S. Muchmore (Concord, farmer); W - 32, housework, 3rd, divorced, b. E. Orange, VT, d/o Henry Morse (Cabot, VT, retired)
Daniel C. of Piermont m. Josephine **French** of Piermont 9/7/1930 in Haverhill; H - 62, farmer, 2nd, b. Orford, s/o Henry Muchmore (Concord, deceased) and Sally Chase (Warren, deceased); W - 39, housework, 2nd, b. Swiftwater, d/o Edward Everett (Lyman, deceased) and Mary Elliott (Benton, deceased)

MUNROE,
James A. of Dover m. Nellie E. **Ellsworth** of Piermont 10/19/1968

MURDOCK,
Harry S. of Piermont m. Marie Jeanne **Labbe** of Laconia 9/26/1942 in Haverhill; H - 33, monu. business, b. Piermont, s/o Jesse F. Murdock (Portland, ME, deceased) and Mary Merchant (Alexandria, housekeeper); W - 37, waitress, b. St. Henedine, Canada, d/o Joseph Labbe (Ste. Henedine, Canada, retired) and Marie LaCasse (Ste. Marguerite, Canada, housewife)

MURPHY,
Jeremiah C. of Bradford, VT m. Thelma **Hawkins** of St. Johnsbury, VT 9/5/1927 in Piermont; H - 24, papermaker, b. Bradford, VT, s/o Jeremiah M. Murphy (County Cork, Ireland, railroad man) and Mary Mayer (Canada, housewife); W - 25, teacher, b. Barton, VT, d/o Azro A. Hawkins (St. Johnsbury, VT, farmer) and Lottie Parker (St. Johnsbury, VT, housewife)

Robert B. of Piermont m. Doris R. **Goodwin** of Piermont 2/12/1938 in Piermont; H - 22, painter, b. Machias, ME, s/o John H. Murphy (Machias, ME, Coast Guard) and Geneva Huntley (Machias Port, ME, housewife); W - 23, recreational advisor, b. Plymouth, d/o John R. Goodwin (Weirs, P.O. clerk) and Christie Morrison (Piermont, music sup'r)

MUSTY,
Edgar H. of Piermont m. Katherine P. **Walter** of Waterville, OH 5/18/1944 in Piermont; H - 25, in US Army, b. Lyndonville, VT, s/o Alfred Musty (Johnville, PQ, farmer) and Marion J. Gorham (Lyndon, VT); W - 24, stenographer, b. Bedford, PA, d/o Samuel Walter (Cessna, PA, farmer) and Fannie M. Lenard (housewife)

Jim of Piermont m. Mary B. **Ritchie** of Piermont 9/27/1980

Samuel A. of Piermont m. Cynthia J. **Piro** of Barre, VT 3/11/1972

MYSTROM,
Robert E. of Bradford, VT m. Marcella J. **Horton** of Piermont 7/3/1948 in Bradford, VT; H - 21, trucking, b. Cambridge, MA, s/o Carl E. Mystrom (Sweden) and Lillian Swanson (Cambridge, MA); W - 17, domestic, b. Piermont, d/o Bernard

G. Horton (Piermont, creamery mgr.) and Eva Lewis (Wilder, VT, housewife)

NELSON,
Daniel James of Pike m. Deborah Lynn **Cloud** of Piermont 2/4/1995

NICHOLS,
Larry E. of Ashland m. Sharon H. **Long** of Piermont 7/3/1970

NOBLE,
Joseph S. of Haverhill m. Freda **Greenland** of Haverhill 8/6/1941 in Piermont; H - 24, clerk, b. Toronto, Canada, s/o Hyman Noble (Austria, retired) and Rose Roth (Austria, housewife); W - 23, sales girl, b. Cincinnati, OH, d/o Jacob Greenland (Russia, farmer) and Bessie Fridkin (Russia, housewife)

NORCROSS,
Frank B. of Piermont m. Amelia **Stone** of Corinth, VT 12/18/1894; H - 22, laborer, b. Bradford, VT, s/o Moses Norcross (Bradford, VT, farmer) and Sarah Norcross (Haverhill, housewife); W - 18, domestic, b. Piermont, d/o Frank Stone (Canada, farmer) and Sophrona Stone (Canada)
Frank B. of Haverhill m. Abbie **Bunker** of Haverhill 4/8/1905 in Piermont; H - 31, farmer, 2nd, b. Bradford, VT, s/o Moses Norcross (Albany, VT, deceased); W - 17, housework, b. Haverhill, d/o Frank Bunker (don't know, deceased)

NORTON,
Richard Norman of Piermont m. Miriam Louise **Underhill** of Piermont 9/11/1965

NOYES,
George H. of Piermont m. Bette A. **Chase** of Haverhill 8/8/1953 in Piermont; H - 18, farm laborer, b. Piermont, s/o G. Henry Noyes (Haverhill) and Mary Morin (Woodsville); W - 18, waitress, b. Woodsville, d/o Forrest Chase (Tilton) and Georgia LaFrance (S. Newbury, VT)
Mark F. of Piermont m. Marion **Clark** of Thetford Ctr., VT 8/14/1937 in E. Haverhill; H - 26, farmer, b. Haverhill, s/o George H. Noyes (Haverhill, farmer) and Leapha A. Danforth (Haverhill, deceased); W - 29, domestic, b. Thetford Ctr., VT, d/o Briton

Clark (Thetford Ctr., VT, farmer) and Alice N. Barron (Boston, MA, housewife)

Roger H. of Piermont m. Joan S. **Baker** of Orfordville 10/18/1958 in Orford; H - 19, farmer, b. E. Haverhill, s/o G. Henry Noyes (E. Haverhill) and Mary Morin (Woodsville); W - 20, mill worker, b. Woodsville, d/o Maurice S. Baker (Orford) and Hattie Streeter (Piermont)

O'DONNELL,

Cris A. of Bradford, VT m. Annette J. **Hartley** of Bradford, VT 7/11/1987

Dana L. of Bradford, VT m. Stephanie L. **Merrill** of Piermont 2/8/1975

OAKES,

Dale A. of Piermont m. Kathleen M. **Martin** of Bradford, VT 6/21/1980

Daniel Albert of Piermont m. Michelle A. **Morrissette** of Piermont 8/6/1988

Neil R. of Piermont m. Dorothy F. **Hutchins** of Piermont 9/14/1984

Rodney G. of Piermont m. Gina M. **Giudici** of Piermont 8/1/1990

Wayne G. of Piermont m. Edith Anna **Magoon** of W. Fairlee, VT 11/26/1949 in Piermont; H - 19, farmer, b. McIndoes Falls, VT, s/o Glen W. Oakes (Colebrook) and Lottie M. Gates (Monroe); W - 18, domestic, b. W. Fairlee, VT, d/o George C. Magoon (Washington, VT) and Violet A. George (Derry)

Wendell of Piermont m. Virginia **Rogers** of Vershire, VT 8/3/1956 in Vershire, VT; H - 20, farmer, b. Piermont, s/o Glen Oakes (Columbia) and Lottie Gates (Monroe); W - 20, none, b. Vershire, VT, d/o Allen Rogers (Tunbridge, VT) and Madeline Magoon (Washington, VT)

Winston L. of Piermont m. Jane E. **Stoddard** of N. Haverhill 2/22/1969

ODIORNE,

Christopher G. of Piermont m. Sheila A. **Salomaa** of Bradford, VT 7/22/1989

ONEIDO,

Mark of Bradford, VT m. Beatrice **Pike** of Piermont 10/25/1959

ORDWAY,
Eugene E. of Fairlee, VT m. Karen E. **Merrill** of Piermont 6/23/1972

ORMSBY,
David E. of Piermont m. Marion F. **Clark** of Haverhill 6/16/1934 in Woodsville; H - 28, mechanic, b. Cambridge, MA, s/o William H. Ormsby (Troy, NY, farmer) and Georgiana Andrews (Granville, NY, housewife); W - 22, domestic, b. Westminster, VT, d/o Willis A. Clark (Andover, VT, farmer) and Gladys M. Bell (Wentworth, housewife)

ORTOWSKI,
Thomas F. of Piermont m. Judy E. **Kinney** of Claremont 8/21/1999

OSGOOD,
Christopher Karl of E. Barre, VT m. Marie A. **McLam** of E. Barre, VT 9/3/1988

Dean W. of Bradford, VT m. Joan A. **Mellin** of Piermont 9/9/1956 in Piermont; H - 20, student, b. Haverhill, s/o C. Walton Osgood (Glover, VT) and Alzoda Allen (Walden, VT); W - 21, office clerk, b. Stamford, CT, d/o Kenneth B. Mellin (NY) and Marjorie Bates (Stamford, CT)

OULTON,
John D. of Piermont m. Bessie Mae **Winn** of Piermont 5/21/1932 in Lyme; H - 29, farmer, b. Barnston, PQ, s/o William Oulton (St. John, NB, deceased) and Lucy Taylor (PQ, deceased); W - 22, domestic, b. Piermont, d/o Frank J. Winn (W. Fairlee, VT, farmer) and Rosette Underhill (Piermont, housewife)

PALMER,
Vernon of E. Thetford, VT m. Eunice F. **Preston** of Piermont 8/14/1937 in Orford; H - 23, mechanic, b. Thetford, VT, s/o Ernest Palmer (Chateaugay, NY, farmer) and Grace Wilbur (Chateaugay, NY, housewife); W - 19, domestic, b. Thetford, VT, d/o William Preston (Pawtucket, RI, laborer) and Mabel French (Thetford, VT, housewife)

PARKER,
Ralph E. of Bradford, VT m. Joanne **Winn** of Piermont 6/27/1975

PARKHURST,
Joseph O. of Fulton, NY m. Lisa L. (Clemons) **Congdon** of Fulton, NY 10/5/1996

PARONTO,
Clyde G. of Danville, VT m. Violet M. **French** of Piermont 5/29/1926 in Piermont; H - 24, truck driver, b. Montgomery, VT, s/o Levi Paronto (Enosburg, VT, farmer) and E. Stella Duso (Danville, VT, housewife); W - 17, domestic, b. Piermont, d/o Louis French (Orford, laborer) and Josie Everett (Swiftwater, deceased)

PARSONS,
Lawrence T. of Piermont m. Ruth E. **Stone** of Piermont 9/7/1917 in Piermont; H - 21, teamster, b. Forest Hill, NS, s/o George E. Parsons (Boston, MA, ice dealer); W - 21, housework, b. Boston, MA, d/o ----- Stone (Halifax, NS, laborer)

PEARL,
Christopher Glen of Barnet, VT m. Gail Michel **Lamarre** of Piermont 7/6/2002

PEAVEY,
Robert E. of Piermont m. Millie E. **Knapp** of Piermont 6/19/1901 in Piermont; H - 23, cheesemaker, b. Randolph, VT, s/o Charles L. Peavey (Randolph, VT, tailor); W - 23, housework, b. Piermont, d/o Albert Knapp (Piermont, farmer)

PERKINS,
Bruce E. of Piermont m. Sally J. **Fox** of Lebanon 4/27/1979
Clarence H. of Haverhill m. Florence **Wright** of Piermont 1/29/1921 in Haverhill; H - 21, farmer, b. Haverhill, s/o Charles C. Perkins (Haverhill, farmer); W - 19, tel. oper., b. Charleston, VT, d/o Frank Wright (Newport, VT, farmer)
Glen E. of Piermont m. Agnes E. **Hodsdon** of Piermont 8/24/1958 in Piermont; H - 40, carpenter, b. Piermont, s/o Ralph Perkins (Hardwick, VT) and Maude Barnet (Walden, VT); W - 29, florist, b. Piermont, d/o Harrison Hodsdon (Piermont) and Edith Childs (Piermont)
Ralph C. of Piermont m. Florence G. **Wright** of Bradford, VT 9/20/1923 in Haverhill; H - 33, farmer, 2nd, b. Hardwick, VT, s/o

Edgar C. Perkins (Hardwick, VT, farmer); W - 29, domestic n., b. Topsham, VT, d/o Carlos M. Wright (Newbury, VT, farmer)

PETERSON,
Robert H. of Massapequa, NY m. Veronica H. **Hart** of Massapequa, NY 8/21/1976

PEYTON,
James Joseph, Jr. of Piermont m. Heidie Lea **Gardner** of Piermont 11/5/1994

PFEIFER,
Keith Machold of Piermont m. Jane Elizabeth **Slayton** of Piermont 10/16/1993

PIERCE,
Frank E. of Piermont m. Susie **Clampet** of Newbury, VT 9/14/1898 in Haverhill; H - 46, carpenter, 2nd, b. S. Royalton, s/o Ebenezer Pierce (Canada, farmer); W - 42, house work, 2nd, b. Canada, d/o ----- Lawrence (Canada, farmer)

PIPER,
Eric D. of Lebanon m. Theresa L. **Stygles** of Lebanon 8/3/1979

PIRIE,
James C. of Durham m. Roberta L. **Mitchell** of Piermont 1/9/1982

PONTE,
Robert Francis of Brighton, MA m. Sheila Diane **Winn** of Brighton, MA 8/25/1990

PORFIDO,
Alphonse F. of Littleton m. Marjorie A. **Webster** of Piermont 2/14/1942 in Littleton; H - 21, clerk, b. Littleton, s/o Emilio Porfido (Italy, merchant) and Carmela Potito (Italy, housewife); W - 23, at home, b. Piermont, d/o Ralph A. Webster (Haverhill, deceased) and Hattie R. Molway (Haverhill, housewife)

PREGENT,
Randy S. of Morrisville, VT m. Susan E. **Wescott** of Morrisville, VT 7/20/1991

PRESCOTT,
George C. of Bradford, VT m. Esther M. **Rollins** of Piermont 6/25/1910 in Haverhill; H - 20, painter, b. Bradford, VT, s/o John G. Prescott (Hartley, PQ, deceased); W - 16, housework, b. Compton, d/o Hiram Rollins (Rumney, farmer)

PREST,
Cameron Scott of Piermont m. Heather Faye **Clark** of Fairlee, VT 8/5/1995

PRIOR,
Trevor David of Bulawayo, Zimbabwe m. Heather Christene **Schmid** of Piermont 5/7/1992

PROVOST,
Norman R. of Piermont m. Dorothy M. **Humphrey** of Fairlee, VT 11/15/1969

PUSHEE,
Olyph of Lyme m. Doris **Johnson** of Piermont 12/11/1934 in Lebanon; H - 24, farmer, b. Lyme, s/o David Pushee (Lyme, farmer) and Minnie Gilbert (Passumpsic, VT, housewife); W - 18, domestic, b. Thetford, VT, d/o Edwin Johnson (carpenter) and Mildred Silloway (W. Fairlee, VT, housewife)
Paul R. of Piermont m. Inez L. **Coburn** of Piermont 7/9/1977

PUTNAM,
G. W., Jr. of Piermont m. Marion G. **Corliss** of Manchester, CT 12/31/1921 in Manchester, CT; H - 25, farmer, b. Newbury, VT, s/o George W. Putnam (farmer); W - 26, b. Bradford, VT, d/o Windsor Corliss
James E. of Piermont m. Ellen M. **Ackerman** of Piermont 5/26/1979
Jasper Edgar of Piermont m. Jean Collins **Davis** of Hanover 5/23/1953 in Hanover; H - 26, farmer, b. Hanover, s/o William Putnam (W. Newbury, VT) and Marion Corliss (Bradford, VT); W - 27, nurse, b. Woodsville, d/o Norman Davis (Moultonboro) and Marjorie Tyler (W. Newbury, MA)
William of Piermont m. Gladys C. **Emery** of Piermont 2/3/1966
William N. of Piermont m. Cynthia L. **Reardon** of Somersworth 11/12/1977

RALSTON,
Robert H. of Ryegate, VT m. Alice G. **Stowell** of Ryegate, VT 5/25/1936 in Piermont; H - 53, farmer, 2nd, divorced, b. Canada, s/o Henry Ralston (Canada, farmer) and Agnes Wright (Canada, housewife); W - 42, housewife, 2nd, divorced, b. Bath, d/o Joseph Shanty (Monroe, railroad man) and Eliza Tome (England, housewife)

RAMSEY,
Earl Edwin of Piermont m. Edith May **Belyea** of Warren 11/28/1917 in Haverhill; H - 24, engineer, b. Haverhill, s/o Alex Ramsey (PEI, farmer); W - 18, housemaid, b. Warren, d/o James Belyea (NB, farmer)

RAPER,
James of Piermont m. Dorothy N. **Harris** of Piermont 12/24/2002

RATEL,
Robert James of Piermont m. Bernadette Mary **Moran** of Piermont 9/17/1988

RATTAZZI,
Peter W. of Barre, VT m. Marion **Kiser** of Barre, VT 7/3/1933 in Piermont; H - 28, musician, b. Groton, VT, s/o Peter W. Rattazzi (Senivia, Italy, stone cutter) and Lucoa Puccini (Alanzen, Italy, housewife); W - 18, domestic, b. Plainfield, VT, d/o Carl Kiser (Plainfield, VT, farmer) and Hattie Wheelock (Calais, VT, housewife)

REARDON,
Bradbury Maurice of E. Kingston m. Linda B. **Trickey** of E. Kingston 3/20/1994

REED,
Marshall J. o f Strafford, VT m. Anna E. **Cummings** of Strafford, VT 1/19/1937 in Canaan; H - 29, laborer, b. Pittsford, VT, s/o Edwin A. Reed (farmer) and Catherine LaVoice (retired); W - 18, b. Randolph, VT, d/o Henry B. Cummings (Strafford, VT, farmer) and Elizabeth Bean (housewife)

RENEAU,
Charles A. of Piermont m. Marguerite F. **Lang** of Haverhill 10/7/1944 in Woodsville; H - 51, bookkeeper, 2nd, b. Piermont, s/o George Reneau (N. Adams, MA, deceased) and Martha Barton (Piermont, housewife); W - 40, store clerk, b. Bath, d/o Albert J. Lang (Bath, deceased) and Cora S. Buck (Bath, housewife)

REXFORD,
Guy L. of Piermont m. Vera **King** of Bradford, VT 11/10/1933 in Bradford, VT; H - 26, farmer, b. E. Burke, VT, s/o Wilbur Rexford (Canada) and Sarah Goodwin (Canada); W - 22, domestic, b. Lunenburg, VT, d/o Louis C. King and Nettie M. Parks (Whitefield)

RICHARDSON,
Erwin N. of Bradford, VT m. Virginia A. **Fortier** of Bradford, VT 1/24/1937 in Claremont; H - 28, salesman, 2nd, divorced, b. Topsham, VT, s/o Center Richardson (Topsham, VT, retired) and Annabelle Fowler (Newbury, VT, housewife); W - 21, waitress, b. E. Haverhill, d/o Cyrelle Fortier (Notre Dame, PQ, laborer) and Adella Derosia (Benton, housewife)

RITCHIE,
Robert A. of Piermont m. Kathleen P. **Leary** of Newbury, VT 12/28/2003

Tait M. of Piermont m. Christie E. **Goodwin** of Piermont 7/31/1950 in Fitzwilliam; H - 64, farmer, 2nd, b. New York, NY, s/o David McKerrocher (Scotland) and Jane Tait (Scotland); W - 58, music teacher, 2nd, b. Piermont, d/o Horace E. Morrison (Haverhill) and Ida M. Rabie (Corinth, VT)

RIVERA,
Valentin of Piermont m. Rose L. **Strout** of Lyme 12/16/1961

ROBERTSON,
Neil B. of Piermont m. Aloha J. **Mason** of Lyndon Ctr., VT 11/8/1952 in Lyndon Ctr., VT; H - 20, truck driver, b. St. Johnsbury, VT, s/o Paul H. Robertson (Danville, VT) and Ada Bates (Enfield, MA); W - 19, waitress, b. Lyndon Ctr., VT, d/o Harold F. Mason (Stratford) and Eunice Chandler (Cabot, VT)

William J. of Piermont m. Deborah A. **Bickford** of Plymouth 4/9/1971

ROBIE,
Freeman E. of Piermont m. Winona J. **Emerson** of Newbury, VT 6/30/1945 in Wells River, VT; H - 20, farming, b. Piermont, s/o Lyman Robie (Piermont, farmer) and Gwendolyn Shumway (Bradford, VT, housewife); W - 16, at home, b. Newbury, VT, d/o Clinton Emerson (Newbury, VT, laborer) and Lena Crosby (Derby, VT, housewife)
Keith Melvin of Piermont m. Verna E. **Tucker** of Fairlee, VT 5/10/1946 in Orford; H - 25, creamery laborer, b. Piermont, s/o Lyman Robie (Piermont, farmer) and Gwendolyn Shumway (Bradford, VT, housewife); W - 22, stenographer, b. Orange, VT, d/o Wyness E. Tucker (Brookfield, VT, farmer) and Alice R. Morse (Royalton, VT, housewife)
Lyman Edward of Piermont m. G. D. **Shumway** of Bradford, VT 2/18/1920 in Lebanon; H - 19, baker, b. Piermont, s/o Freeman Robie (Corinth, VT, farmer); W - 16, in school, b. Bradford, VT, d/o Ellis B. Shumway (Bradford, VT, farmer)
Lyman M. of Piermont m. Mittie **Morse** of Plymouth 11/14/1911 in Plymouth; H - 74, farmer, 3rd, b. Corinth, VT, s/o Jonathan Robie (Candia, farmer); W - 63, housework, 2nd, d/o Winthrop Elliott (Benton, farmer)
Paul L. of Piermont m. Barbara A. **Sargent** of Fairlee, VT 12/27/1954 in Lyme; H - 25, RR agent, b. Piermont, s/o Lyman E. Robie (Piermont) and Gwendolyn Shumway (Bradford, VT); W - 18, domestic, b. Thetford, VT, d/o Murray L. Sargent (Thetford, VT) and Edna Hill (Canada)
Terry E. of Piermont m. Cheryl R. **Prest** of Piermont 9/16/1978
Todd W. of Hartford, VT m. Debra Ann (Lund) **Harlow** of Hartford, VT 6/27/1987

ROBINSON,
Fred C. of Piermont m. Effie M. **Humphrey** of Piermont 6/21/1911 in Piermont; H - 28, R. L. carrier, b. Piermont, s/o Charles Robinson (Piermont, farmer); W - 19, housework, b. Haverhill, d/o Edward Humphrey (Piermont, farmer)

RODIMON,
Frank of Piermont m. Louise M. **Hood** of Piermont 10/2/1953 in Piermont; H - 28, trucking, b. Haverhill, s/o Charles Rodimon (Piermont) and Annie Farrell (Pike); W - 19, domestic, b. Haverhill, d/o Harold R. Hood (Topsham, VT) and Wilhelmine Sawyer (Piermont)
Frank W. of Piermont m. Dorothy L. **Cassady** of Concord 11/15/1980
Frank W. of Piermont m. Laura A. **Nickles** of Piermont 9/11/1999
Frank W., Jr. of Piermont m. Carol S. **Moody** of Piermont 9/26/1981
Michael E. of Piermont m. Brenda L. **Ste. Marie** of N. Haverhill 3/22/1980
Walter E. of Piermont m. Jacqueline A. **Cote** of N. Haverhill 6/30/1956 in Haverhill; H - 21, USAF, b. Haverhill, s/o Charles E. Rodiman (Piermont) and Annie Farrell (Pike); W - 19, student, b. St. Johnsbury, VT, d/o Wilfred R. Cole (Littleton) and Theda L. Page (Newbury, VT)

ROGERS,
Edward S. of Piermont m. Bessie M. **Evans** of Piermont 6/20/1894; H - 25, farmer, b. Piermont, s/o Albert Rogers (Piermont, farming) and Anna Underhill (housewife); W - 18, lady, b. Worcester, d/o R. A. Evans (Piermont, granite dealer) and Abbie Matterson (Honsdale, PQ, lady)
Shawn Richard of Piermont m. Karlyce Ann **Brown** of Piermont 11/2/1996

ROSE,
Brian Keith Matthew of Fairlee, VT m. Alison Elizabeth **Gould** of Fairlee, VT 8/12/2000

ROY,
Wendall P. of E. Barnet, VT m. Alice M. **Blaisdell** of Piermont 12/28/1937 in Northfield, MA; H - 30, toy mfr., b. Barnet, VT, s/o John G. Roy and Ellen Paddleford; W - 29, stenographer, b. Piermont, d/o Harry C. Blaisdell (Piermont, farmer) and Grace Dunkley (Haverhill, housewife)

RUTHERFORD,
Gary of Lyndonville, VT m. Shirley A. **Estrella** of Lyndonville, VT 6/10/1972

John R. of N. Haverhill m. Gretchen A. **Hyden** of W. Seattle, WA 12/27/2003

RYAN,
Paul Charles of Piermont m. Deanna (Correa) **Calandrelli** of Piermont 8/7/1988

SALADINO,
Peter J. of Piermont m. Marylyn H. (Morris) **Inglesby** of Haverhill 6/28/1986
Peter J., Jr. of Piermont m. Mary F. **Boardman** of St. Johnsbury, VT 8/28/1968
Peter J., III of Piermont m. Kathryn A. **Page** of Woodsville 11/17/1984

SALLEY,
H. Homer of Orlando, FL m. Marion G. **Musty** of Piermont 7/1/1960

SAMPSON,
George L. of Dorchester, MA m. Ethel J. **Messer** of Cambridge, MA 4/18/1934 in Piermont; H - 28, sales manager, b. Plymouth, MA, s/o Ira L. Sampson (Plymouth, MA, mason) and Mary A. Barnes (Boston, MA, none); W - 30, at home, 3rd, b. Dorchester, MA, d/o William Johnson (Belmont, MA, retired) and Jessie Sutherland (Canada, deceased)

SANDERS,
Karl Walton of Brunswick, GA m. Juanita Debbie **Saladino** of Jacksonville Beach, FL 2/7/1998

SARGENT,
Christopher L. of Morrisville, VT m. Jennifer J. **Colby** of Morrisville, VT 7/6/1991
Paul A. of Fairlee, VT m. Joan M. **Tyler** of Fairlee, VT 9/9/1984

SAUNDERS,
Frank E. of Piermont m. Ella **Rollins** of Piermont 3/1/1909 in Piermont; H - 37, laborer, 2nd, b. Orford, s/o Sylvester Saunders (Wentworth, farmer); W - 34, housekeeper, 2nd, b. W. Topsham, VT, d/o Erastus Huntley (New York, NY, farmer)

SAWYER,

Clyde B. of Piermont m. Lily **Ward** of Monroe 6/30/1920 in N. Haverhill; H - 22, laborer, b. Piermont, s/o Milo B. Sawyer (Topsham, VT, farmer); W - 23, teacher, b. Monroe, d/o Robert Ward (England, farmer)

Maynard of Piermont m. Margaret **Smith** of Haverhill 10/26/1934 in Haverhill; H - 22, farmer, b. Piermont, s/o Milo D. Sawyer (Topsham, VT, farmer) and Alice Rodimon (Piermont, housewife); W - 20, domestic, b. Haverhill, d/o Edwin Smith (Lisbon, laborer) and Beatrice Eastman (Lyme, housewife)

Milo B. of Piermont m. Alice B. **Rodimon** of Piermont 12/27/1895 in Piermont; H - 23, farmer, b. Topsham, VT, s/o Elva Sawyer (Topsham, VT) and Eliza Hood (Topsham, VT); W - 18, housekeeper, b. Piermont, d/o Charles Rodimon (Piermont) and Hattie Willey

SCHMID,

John G. of Portland, ME m. Linda **Sawyer** of Portland, ME 5/27/1994

SCHWARZ,

Thomas R. of Piermont m. Jenniffer S. (Winn) **Bartle** of Piermont 1/4/1997

SCRUTON,

Sansford E. of Bradford, VT m. Lois Edna **Stetson** of Piermont 6/23/1946 in Piermont; H - 21, creamery worker, b. Bradford, VT, s/o Walter I. Scruton (Topsham, VT, retired) and Iva Humphrey (Piermont, housewife); W - 19, waitress, b. Piermont, d/o Clinton W. Stetson (Piermont, lumber dlr.) and Edna M. Robie (Piermont, housewife)

SEARER,

Mark J. of Piermont m. Ruth C. **Farr** of Somerville, MA 6/6/1931 in Raymond; H - 26, student, b. Fayston, VT, s/o Frank J. Searer (Waitsfield, VT, lumberman) and Mary Egan (Waitsfield, VT, deceased); W - 24, stenographer, b. Melrose, MA, d/o Alton Farr (Moretown, VT, electrician) and Mary Rose (Newfoundland, matron)

SEPESSY,
Henry L., Jr. of Piermont m. Priscilla Mae **Shafer** of Orford 6/22/1958 in Orford; H - 20, mechanic, b. Newark, NJ, s/o Henry L. Sepesay (Long Island, NY) and Thelma Anthony (Newark, NJ); W - 18, student, b. Burlington, VT, d/o Philip Bean (Orford) and Ida Prebar (Burlington, VT)
Henry L., Jr. of Piermont m. Bertha J. **Julien** of Piermont 7/18/1965

SHELDON,
Ernest R. of Proctorsville, VT m. Alice (Stetson) **Landry** of Proctorsville, VT 9/3/1988

SHEPARD,
Don Nelson of Piermont m. Princetta L. **Bailey** of Groton, VT 2/28/1948 in Piermont; H - 23, farmer, b. Canaan, s/o Frank Shepard (Morie, NY, farmer) and Rose Bombard (Bangor, NY, housewife); W - 24, nurse, b. Groton, VT, d/o Ralph Bailey (W. Topsham, VT, farmer) and Goldie Darling (Groton, VT, housewife)
Stanley L. of Piermont m. Theresa M. **Cassady** of Groton, VT 8/14/1948 in Piermont; H - 27, farmer, b. Lebanon, s/o Frank Shepard (Morie, NY, farmer) and Rose Bombard (Bangor, NY, housewife); W - 20, student, b. Haverhill, d/o Henry W. Cassady (Kinsey Falls, PQ, farmer) and Meroa Emery (Groton, VT, housewife)

SHERWOOD,
Walter D. of Ridgefield Park, NJ m. Irene **White** of Plymouth 8/29/1930 in Piermont; H - 23, teacher, b. Spring Valley, NY, s/o Walter T. Sherwood (Spring Valley, NY, broker) and Edith E. Gowdy (New York City, housewife); W - 23, teacher, b. Plymouth, d/o Alfred White (Warrensburg, NY, manager) and Mamie C. Edgerly (Lakeport, housewife)

SHIELDS,
Peter E. of Kansas City, MO m. Mary M. **Moran** of Kansas City, MO 1/1/1983

SHILDS,
Samuel A. of Piermont m. Marion S. **Robbins** of Piermont 11/1/1952 in Piermont; H - 22, farmer, b. Springfield, MA, s/o

Samuel Shilds (Ireland) and Janet Jevons (England); W - 21, student, b. Piermont, d/o Eugene B. Robbins (Vicksburg, MS) and Florence Smith (Rangoon, Burma)

SHOREY,
F. Langdon of Rochester m. Florence M. **Evans** of Rochester 8/13/1922 in Piermont; H - 54, photographer, 2nd, widower, b. Rochester, s/o Ezra Shorey (Rochester); W - 34, housekeeper, 2nd, divorced, b. Sanford, ME, d/o George Evans (Rochester, printer)

SIMPSON,
J. Ralph of Piermont m. Elsie D. **Mitchell** of Clifton, NJ 11/27/1920 in Haverhill; H - 25, RFD carrier, b. Piermont, s/o John F. Simpson (Piermont, carpenter); W - 31, clerk, b. Haverhill, MA, d/o James P. Mitchell (Sedgwick, ME, farmer)

John B. of Piermont m. Carrie **Malway** of Piermont 12/24/1912 in Haverhill; H - 19, farmer, b. Orford, s/o Herman L. Simpson (Rumney, farmer); W - 20, housework, b. Haverhill, d/o Levi Malway (Canada, laborer)

John B. of Piermont m. Dorothy E. **Robinson** of Piermont 4/19/1933 in Bradford, VT; H - 38, farmer, 2nd, b. Orford, s/o Herman Simpson (Orford) and Ella Hackett (Orford); W - 19, at home, b. Haverhill, d/o Charles Robinson (England) and Eliza Lee (England)

John Bradley of Piermont m. Jennifer Lee **Harrington** of Claremont 3/13/1965

John Bradley of Piermont m. Mary E. (Lombardi) **Meder** of Piermont 2/21/1987

John F. of Piermont m. Lillian M. **Marden** of Haverhill 7/27/1894; H - 22, carpenter, b. Piermont, s/o William Simpson (Orford, carpenter) and Anna Stickney (Bolton, PQ, housewife); W - 19, teacher, b. Haverhill, d/o Lyman Marden, Jr. (Haverhill, farmer) and Emma Day (Haverhill, housewife)

Roscoe L. of Piermont m. Nina L. **Wright** of Wentworth 7/22/1912 in Wentworth; H - 18, farmer, b. Orfordville, s/o Herman L. Simpson (Rumney, farmer); W - 22, housework, b. Wentworth, d/o Tilden Wright (Warren, farmer)

SIMS,
Robert G. of Piermont m. Jean S. **Gadwah** of Piermont 5/19/1973

SLACK,
Bert E. of Corinth, VT m. Emma **Wilson** of Corinth, VT 5/29/1891 in Piermont; H - 24, blacksmith, b. Corinth, VT, s/o C. J. Slack (farmer) and May E. Chapman; W - 18, domestic, b. Corinth, VT, d/o Lyman Wilson and Emma Hastings

SMITH,
Albion L. of Piermont m. Addie Elsie **White** of N. Haverhill 12/9/1919 in Piermont; H - 26, farmer, b. W. Fairlee, s/o LaForrest Smith (Chelsea, VT, farmer); W - 21, housework, b. N. Haverhill, d/o Allen White (Cambridge, VT, miner)

Altan of Piermont m. Elizabeth **Clogston** of Bradford, VT 9/11/1956 in Bradford, VT; H - 30, laborer, 2nd, b. Corinth, VT, s/o Ned Smith (W. Fairlee, VT) and Emma Lunna (Manchester); W - 29, housekeeper, 2nd, b. Worcester, MA, d/o William Jascelyn (Worcester, MA) and Florence White (Worcester, MA)

Alton R. of Piermont m. Evelyn **Gray** of Piermont 11/28/1948 in Dover; H - 22, laborer, b. Corinth, VT, s/o Edward O. Smith (W. Fairlee, VT, fireman) and Emma Parker (Manchester, housewife); W - 21, domestic, b. Goffstown, d/o Arthur Gray (New Boston, taxi driver) and Bertha Coburn (Fitzwilliam, housewife)

Anson A. of Piermont m. Viola **Scott** of N. Haverhill 11/22/1913 in Haverhill; H - 17, farmer, b. Piermont, s/o Harry Smith (Haverhill, farmer); W - 18, housework, b. FL, d/o Ernest V. Scott (Greensboro, VT, store)

Arnold Chase of Piermont m. Belinda Flo **Schnitzler** of Piermont 6/28/1997

Edward O. of Piermont m. Ruth K. **Ramsdell** of Bradford, VT 6/20/1955 in Bradford, VT; H - 69, retired, 2nd, b. W. Fairlee, VT, s/o Oscar W. Smith (Vershire, VT) and Louise Alexander (Harpswell, ME); W - 49, bookkeeper, 2nd, b. Bradford, VT, d/o Charles Kenyon (Bradford, VT) and Alice Andruss (Bradford, VT)

Floyd L. of Piermont m. Pearl D. **Webster** of Bradford, VT 8/14/1932 in Bradford, VT; H - 22, chauffeur, b. Walden, VT, s/o George F. Smith (Stannard, VT, workman) and Bertha C. Paronto (Montgomery, VT, housewife); W - 21, at home, b. Piermont, d/o George L. Webster (Monroe, laborer) and Gladys E. Risley (Piermont, housewife)

Jerry E. of Haverhill m. Michaelle R. **Paquette** of Piermont 3/18/1972

Kenneth G. of Piermont m. Charlotte K. **Chase** of Bradford, VT 9/9/1961

Laurence of Haverhill m. Eola **Jewell** of Piermont 8/1/1935 in Piermont; H - 26, truck operator, b. Haverhill, s/o Everett Smith (Haverhill, farmer) and Mamie Elliott (Haverhill, housewife); W - 21, nurse, b. E. Corinth, VT, d/o Charles W. Jewell (Corinth, VT, patrolman) and Carrie Wilson (Corinth, VT, housewife)

Leroy B. of S. Jacksonville, FL m. Nora K. **Womble** of S. Jacksonville, FL 12/9/1945 in S. Jacksonville, FL; H - 27, teacher, s/o George F. Smith (Stowe, VT, truck driver) and Bertha Paronto (Walden, VT, deceased); W - 20, d/o James Womble (bus driver) and Rega Mae (housewife)

Loren G. of Piermont m. Emma M. **Ryalls** of Piermont 5/1/1911 in Piermont; H - 53, farmer, b. Piermont, s/o George H. Smith (Peacham, VT, farmer); W - 26, cheese foiling, b. Manchester, d/o Edwin Ryalls (England, engineer)

Norman M. of Newport, VT m. Audra **Blodgett** of Thetford, VT 4/25/1931 in N. Stratford; H - 28, trackman, b. Holland, VT, s/o Francis Smith (Stanstead, PQ, lumberman) and Ida G. Tarbee (Cassville, PQ, housewife); W - 26, teacher, b. Ocala, FL, d/o Joseph T. Blodgett (Hebron, deceased) and Alice B. Johnson (Columbus, TX, housewife)

Robert H. of Piermont m. Helen M. **Grimes** of Haverhill 10/3/1948 in Haverhill; H - 17, clerk, b. Haverhill, s/o Margaret Smith (Bath, housewife); W - 17, unem., b. Haverhill, d/o Gerald W. Grimes (N. Troy, VT, mechanic) and Mildred Jones (Hyde Park, VT, housewife)

Stanley R. of Piermont m. Doris E. **Nutter** of Piermont 5/27/1989

Theodore D. of Georgetown, MA m. Nelda V. **Coulter** of Piermont 5/25/1991

Wilfred L. of Piermont m. Eleanor L. **Cooley** of Easton 4/10/1960

William C. H. of Piermont m. Mildred E. **Parker** of Haverhill 9/25/1919 in Haverhill; H - 20, farmer, b. Sheldon, VT, s/o Byron E. Smith (Waterville, VT, farmer); W - 18, housework, b. Haverhill, d/o Ernest N. Perkins (Haverhill, farmer)

SOUCY,

David S. of Hamilton, NY m. Wendy J. **Osgood** of Hamilton, NY 7/1/1989

SOULE,
Charles Nelson, IV of Piermont m. Heather Anne **Hawes** of Piermont 7/7/2001

SOUZA,
Everett J. of Piermont m. Lottie A. **Miranowicy** of Piermont 6/23/1958 in Woodsville; H - 52, chef, 2nd, b. Fall River, MA, s/o Manuel C. Souza (Azores, Portugal) and Elizabeth Augustus (Fall River, MA); W - 42, waitress, b. Fall River, MA, d/o Charles Miranowicz (Poland) and Dorothy Walaszek (Poland)

SPAULDING,
Harry G. of Piermont m. Kate **Molway** of Piermont 6/5/1899 in Piermont; H - 21, farmer, s/o Orvil Noyes (Lunenburg, VT, laborer); W - 18, housework, b. Haverhill, d/o Levi Molway (Canada, PQ, laborer)

SPENCER,
Hugh E. of Orford m. Evelyn B. **Stetson** of Piermont 6/10/1947 in Claremont; H - 30, trackman, b. Orford, s/o James E. Spencer (Wolfville, NS, int. dec.) and Georgia Archer (Orford, deceased); W - 19, mill worker, b. Piermont, d/o Clinton W. Stetson (Piermont, lumberman) and Edna Robie (Piermont, housewife)

SPIRES,
Franklin of S. Portland, ME m. Isabel **LaPan** of Portland, ME 11/6/1954 in Piermont; H - 31, quarryman, 2nd, b. Canada, s/o John Spires (England) and Ethel Bird (England); W - 29, housewife, 2nd, b. Burlington, VT, d/o John Buska (NY) and Ella Santamore (NY)

STANLEY,
Orlo B. of Piermont m. Altha M. **Wilson** of Corinth, VT 8/2/1894; H - 26, farmer, b. Piermont, s/o Hubbard Stanley (Piermont, farmer) and Lucy Stanley (Barnstead, PQ, housewife); W - 21, domestic, b. Groton, VT, d/o Isaac M. Wilson (farmer) and Caroline Heath (housewife)

STEBBINS,

Harry E. of Piermont m. Daisy P. **Morris** of Piermont 11/15/1913 in Haverhill; H - 52, farmer, 2nd, widower, b. Newbury, VT, s/o Tyler C. Stebbins (Newbury, VT, farmer); W - 37, housekeeper, 2nd, widow, b. Franklin

STETSON,

Clinton W. of Piermont m. Edna M. **Foote** of Piermont 8/25/1921 in Lyme; H - 22, farmer, b. Piermont, s/o George Stetson (Dorchester, MA); W - 25, tel. operator, 2nd, divorced, b. Piermont, d/o Freeman Robie (Corinth, VT, farmer)

Louis O. of Piermont m. Bessie M. **Drury** of Orford 5/6/1902 in Piermont; H - 24, butcher, b. Piermont, s/o Henry F. Stetson (Orford, butcher); W - 18, domestic, b. Worcester, MA, d/o S. C. Drury (Holden, MA, moulder)

Wesley Freeman of Piermont m. Virginia Jane **Smith** of New Britain, CT 11/5/1955 in Orford; H - 33, stock clerk, 2nd, b. Piermont, s/o Clinton W. Stetson (Piermont) and Edna R. Robie (Piermont); W - 19, seamstress, b. Orford, d/o Hazen L. Smith (Quechee, VT) and Lizzie B. King (E. Montpelier, VT)

STEVENS,

Ernest L. of Piermont m. Caroline J. **Taylor** of Piermont 6/13/1905 in Piermont; H - 29, farmer, b. Piermont, s/o Leveret E. Stevens (Piermont, farmer); W - 28, dressmaker, b. Bethlehem, d/o O. S. Taylor (Lisbon, deceased)

George of Piermont m. Florence **Mathers** of E. Corinth, VT 10/21/1916 in Piermont; H - 19, farmer, b. E. Corinth, VT, s/o Lenie R. Stevens (Corinth, VT, farmer); W - 18, housewife, b. York State, d/o George Mathers (NY, farmer)

George H. of Piermont m. Emma A. **Plummer** of Laconia 5/8/1895 in Laconia; H - 51, farmer, 2nd, b. Piermont, s/o George W. Stevens (Piermont) and Maria Emerson (Piermont); W - 29, dressmaker, 2nd, b. Campton, d/o George W. Plummer (Campton) and Marcia Ham (Thornton)

George L. of Piermont m. Flossie Ida **French** of Piermont 11/3/1919 in Piermont; H - 22, laborer, b. Corinth, VT, s/o Lennie R. Stevens (Corinth, VT, farmer); W - 19, domestic, b. Piermont, d/o William H. French (Landaff, farmer)

Harry N. of Piermont m. Helen **Anell** of Piermont 10/31/1910 in Haverhill; H - 36, gas fitter, b. Piermont, s/o Munroe Stevens

(Piermont, stone cutter); W - 18, housework, b. N. Thetford, d/o Albert Anell (E. Corinth, sect. boss)
Lennie R. of Piermont m. Georgiana **Warner** of Piermont 12/28/1915 in Haverhill; H - 48, farmer, 2nd, widower, b. Corinth, VT, s/o Samuel C. Stevens (Corinth, VT, farmer); W - 34, housekeeper, 2nd, divorced, b. Bradford, VT, d/o James Clark (Bradford, VT, farmer)
Thomas E. of Piermont m. Kathleen A. **Merrill** of Piermont 12/28/1968
Thomas E. of Piermont m. Barbara A. **Eastman** of Springfield, VT 7/26/2002
William R. of Piermont m. Myrtie M. **Robie** of Piermont 6/14/1916 in Piermont; H - 20, farmer, b. E. Corinth, VT, s/o Lenie R. Stevens (Topsham, VT, farmer); W - 23, tel. operator, b. Piermont, d/o Freman A. Robie (Corinth, VT, farmer)
William R. of Piermont m. Gladys K. **Bonett** of Piermont 1/5/1946 in Lyme; H - 50, farmer, widower, b. Corinth, VT, s/o Lennie P. Stevens (Corinth, VT, deceased) and Geneva Bishop (Topsham, VT, deceased); W - 47, housewife, 2nd, widow, b. Piermont, d/o Freeman Webster (Haverhill, deceased) and Mabel Mann (Orford, housewife)
William R. of Piermont m. Mary S. **Noyes** of Piermont 5/22/1967

STEVER,
Bruce H. of Bradford, VT m. Martina **Day** of Piermont 7/8/1956 in Piermont; H - 22, stock clerk, b. Brattleboro, VT, s/o Harold C. Stever (Enfield, MA) and Beatrice Prescott (Brattleboro, VT); W - 21, school teach., b. Haverhill, d/o Martin H. Day (Piermont) and Lurena Leavitt (W. Stewartstown)

STEWART,
John D. of Cambridge, MA m. Jane E. **Musty** of Piermont 6/7/1969

STIMPSON,
Homer C. of Bradford, VT m. Barbara K. **Bixby** of Piermont 6/14/1975

STOCKMAN,
Anthony of Bradford, VT m. Karen E. **Locke** of Bradford, VT 12/21/1982

STONE,
George H. of Piermont m. Sada M. **Morey** of Piermont 1/21/1905 in Piermont; H - 22, laborer, b. Haverhill, s/o Frank Stone (Canada, farmer); W - 18, housework, b. Orford, d/o Irwin Morey (don't know, deceased)

STOUT,
Arthur Elkins of Piermont m. Barbara B. **Sargent** of N. Ferrisburg, VT 10/26/1996

STROHM,
Jeffrey Dale of Salt Lake City, UT m. Jade Courtney **Huntington** of Ft. Collins, CO 9/23/1999

STYGLES,
Henry Ralph of Piermont m. Dora **Blanchard** of Piermont 2/25/1935 in Piermont; H - 28, laborer, b. Belvedere, VT, s/o Elias Stygles (Johnson, VT, deceased) and Myrtle Burns (Waterville, VT, housewife); W - 19, domestic, b. Orford, d/o Ray Blanchard (Piermont, laborer) and Mabel Cushing (Newport, VT, housewife)
Michael L. of Piermont m. Lean J. **Weeks** of Orford 12/13/1980
Michael L. of Piermont m. Wendy **Hodge** of Piermont 3/10/1991
Ray A. of Piermont m. Vera M. **Leach** of N. Haverhill 10/10/1950 in Piermont; H - 22, laborer, b. Waterville, VT, s/o George C. Stygles (Waterville, VT) and Flossie Miller (Canada); W - 18, domestic, b. Hartland, VT, d/o Lloyd Leach (Colebrook) and Bessie Shute (Colebrook)

SWAIN,
Earl C. of Piermont m. Lillian M. **Smith** of Orford 8/30/1922 in Orford; H - 21, farmer, b. Warren, s/o Harry W. Swain (Ellsworth, farmer); W - 23, teacher, b. Orford, d/o Clarence Smith (Lyme)

SYLVESTER,
Peter A. of Bradford, VT m. Marie K. **Corliss** of Bradford, VT 6/21/1986

SYMES,
Richard J. of Natick, MA m. Maude E. **Huse** of White River Jct., VT 6/25/1921 in Piermont; H - 28, farmer, b. Natick, MA, s/o Andrew Symes (Natick, MA, shoemaker); W - 37, cook, 3rd, widow, b. Bradford, VT, d/o Frank Ford (laborer)

TAISEY,
William J. of Newbury, VT m. Louise F. **Wheeler** of Newbury, VT 9/6/1915 in Lebanon; H - 24, laborer, b. Newbury, VT, s/o Daniel D. Taisey (Groton, VT, deceased); W - 55, housekeeper, 2nd, divorced, b. New York, NY, d/o Edward Johnson (Newbury, VT, deceased)

TAPLIN,
Kenneth P. of Barre, VT m. Nancy **Day** of Piermont 11/18/1956 in Piermont; H - 22, US Navy, b. Montpelier, VT, s/o Paul L. Taplin (Chelsea, VT) and Elinore Allen (Chelsea, VT); W - 20, secretary, b. Haverhill, d/o Martin H. Day (Piermont) and Lurena Leavitt (W. Stewartstown)

TARBOX,
Charles A. of Piermont m. Eunice Belle **Glover** of Fairfield Ave., CT 4/2/1918 in Bridgeport, CT; H - 50, farmer, 2nd, b. Orford, s/o Charles Tarbox (Piermont, deceased); W - 24, none, b. NY City, d/o James A. Glover (farmer)
Earl of Piermont m. Florence L. **Metcalf** of Piermont 7/1/1916 in Piermont; H - 21, laborer, b. Piermont; W - 21, school teacher, b. Piermont, d/o John P. Metcalf (Piermont, farmer)

TAYLOR,
John R. of Montpelier, VT m. Carolyn K. **Lupien** of Montpelier, VT 9/3/1968

TETZLOFF,
Donald H. of Barre, VT m. Harriet E. **Ranney** of Springfield, VT 6/25/1938 in Piermont; H - 24, credit mgr., b. Burlington, VT, s/o Charles Tetzloff (Providence, RI, machinist) and Susanna Brown (Chatham, housewife); W - 22, student, b. Springfield, VT, d/o Clarence Ranney (Montpelier, VT, drafting eng.) and Susanna Hinkley (Burlington, VT, housewife)

THAYER,
Clarence E. of Haverhill m. Marion A. **Wright** of Piermont 6/2/1967
Peter Paul of N. Haverhill m. Michele Lynn **Fagnant** of Piermont 9/9/1989

THIBODEAU,
Richard Paul of Piermont m. Nancy Ann Marie **Overton** of Piermont 5/18/2002

THOMPSON,
Charles S. of Bradford, VT m. Marion S. **French** of Piermont 8/19/1967
Paul R. of Bradford, VT m. Joyce E. **Smead** of Bradford, VT 8/18/1984
Theodore of Piermont m. Ann **Crory** of Piermont 7/14/2001
Wayne of Piermont m. Elizabeth **Wescott** of Piermont 8/11/2001
William C., Jr. of Manchester m. Marianne **Metcalf** of Piermont 8/16/1969

THURSTON,
Judgson C. of San Mateo, CA m. Veronica L. **Dobbins** of San Mateo, CA 6/3/1989

TILLEY,
Andrew C. of Wilbraham, MA m. Eleanor G. **Valiquette** of Springfield, MA 11/25/1950 in Piermont; H - 31, salesman, 2nd, b. Longmeadow, MA, s/o Harvy W. Tilley (W. Springfield, MA) and Harriet Willis (Dana, MA); W - 30, sewer, 2nd, b. Springfield, MA, d/o Fred. Quackenbush (N. Hampton, MA) and Grace Hackett (Woonsocket, RI)

TIRRELL,
Stanford W. of Piermont m. Carol M. **Broillard** of Piermont 8/17/1981

TITUS,
Howard O. of Newbury, VT m. Claire R. **Leard** of Newbury, VT 6/14/1947 in Piermont; H - 34, truck driver, 2nd, divorced, b. Bethel, VT, s/o Charles W. Titus (Strafford, VT, farmer) and Marcia Godfrey (Strafford, VT, housewife); W - 39, housekeeper, 2nd, widow, b. Bath, ME, d/o John B. Asselin

(Drummondville, Canada, deceased) and Ruth A. Whicher (Warren, deceased)

TOWNE,
John P. of Bradford, VT m. Kitty A. **Dickinson** of Bradford, VT 2/3/1984

TREVITHICK,
K. W. of Post Mills, VT m. Eleanor R. **Davis** of Piermont 12/13/1947 in Piermont; H - 30, electrician, 2nd, divorced, b. Vershire, VT, s/o John C. Trevithick (Butte, MT, deceased) and Nina M. McClare (Nashville, TN, retired); W - 29, secretary, b. E. Charleston, VT, d/o Floyd F. Davis (E. Charleston, VT, retired) and Ida M. Moulton (New York, NY, housewife)
Thomas N. of Piermont m. Rebecca L. **Paquette** of Piermont 9/1/1984

TRISCHMAN,
Keith B. of Bradford, VT m. Karen E. (Locke) **Stockman** of Bradford, VT 3/20/1987

TROMBLY,
George Alex of Piermont m. Esther M. **Williams** of Piermont 9/5/1914 in Piermont; H - 22, farming, b. Sciota, NY, s/o George Trombly, Jr. (Sciota, NY, farmer); W - 20, housework, b. Topsham, VT, d/o Loren Williams (Topsham, VT, farmer)

TROTTIER,
Theodore A. of Wilder, VT m. Josephine G. **Braley** of Wilder, VT 9/18/1941 in Orford; H - 28, store owner, b. Wilder, VT, s/o Anatale J. Trottier (Canada, storekeeper) and Jennie Radigan (Governeur, NY, housewife); W - 21, waitress, b. Grafton, d/o Gilbert W. Braley (Danbury, bridge carp.) and Edna W. Sturtevant (Orange, housewife)

TRUSSELL,
James E. of Piermont m. Ann M. **Winslow** of Piermont 6/7/2004

TRYBULSKI,
Walter A. of Sunapee m. Brenda M. **Trombley** of Piermont 7/7/1990

TYLER,
Wildern C. of Piermont m. Bessie I. **Knighton** of Bath 5/16/1922 in Bath; H - 24, laborer, b. Benton, s/o Byron M. Tyler (Benton, farmer); W - 19, domestic, b. Victory, VT, d/o Leroy S. Knighton (Bulliver, Canada, factory sup.)

UNDERHILL,
Bernard L. of S. Manchester, CT m. Hazel Ida **Manchester** of Piermont 1/18/1929 in Lyme; H - 32, mechanic, b. Orford, s/o Leon Underhill (Piermont, farmer) and Jennie Norris (Corinth, VT, housewife); W - 29, school teacher, b. Barnet, VT, d/o Frank F. Manchester (Barnet, VT, deceased) and Ida M. Stewart (Lunenburg, VT, housewife)
Berton of Piermont m. Mabelle R. **Carle** of Orford 10/22/1935 in W. Newbury, VT; H - 23, farmer, b. Piermont, s/o Leon H. Underhill (Piermont) and Jennie A. Norris (Corinth, VT); W - 17, at home, b. Malden, NY, d/o Vernon Carle (Woodstock, NY) and Mae Bryer (Lancaster)
Calvin Lawrence of Piermont m. Jean Keniston **Carter** of Lyme 10/1/1994
Eric K. of Piermont m. Theresa E. **Marran** of Piermont 6/1/1985
Eric K. of Piermont m. Georgette D. **Thibeault** of Piermont 10/9/1999
Ernest S. of Piermont m. Elizabeth H. **Converse** of Piermont 9/26/1895 in Piermont; H - 24, farmer, b. Piermont, s/o Horace P. Underhill (Piermont) and Lucy Palmer (Orford); W - 22, teacher, b. Stewartstown, d/o W. A. C. Converse (Lyme) and Mary Tibbets (Stewartstown)
Henry W. of Piermont m. Selina Maudie **Cornford** of Piermont 12/25/1923 in Piermont; H - 26, farmer, b. Piermont, s/o Ernest S. Underhill (Piermont, farmer); W - 22, domestic, b. Brighton, England, d/o William G. Cornford (Sussex Co., England, salesman)
Hugh L. of Piermont m. Kathleen L. **Shope** of Gardeau, PA 7/27/1968
Hugh T. of Piermont m. Patricia A. **Reardon** of Somersworth 4/7/1978
Jeffrey S. of Piermont m. Abigail **Metcalf** of Piermont 11/22/1996
John H. of Piermont m. Florence P. **Rogers** of Dover 10/6/1956 in Orford; H - 26, student, b. NH, s/o Stephen Underhill (NH) and

Helen Manchester (NH); W - 33, inspector, 2nd, b. Canada, d/o George Beairsto (Canada) and Mildred Barstow (ME)

Lawrence F. of Piermont m. Nancy J. **Minshull** of Fairlee, VT 8/7/1960

Stephen L. of Piermont m. Helen G. **Manchester** of Piermont 8/20/1929 in Piermont; H - 22, farmer, b. Piermont, s/o Ernest S. Underhill (Piermont, farmer) and Elizabeth Converse (Stewartstown, housewife); W - 21, school teacher, b. Bath, d/o Frank F. Manchester (Barnet, VT, deceased) and Ida M. Stewart (Lunenburg, VT, housewife)

UPHAM,
Brad L. of Nashua m. Jenny E. **Johnson** of Piermont 12/31/1983

VIGEANT,
Leon L. of Manchester m. Mary E. **Saunders** of Manchester 6/13/1932 in Canaan; H - 36, salesman, 2nd, divorced, b. Morrisville, VT, s/o Wallace Vigeant (VT, deceased) and Inez E. Newton (VT, none); W - 34, office work, 2nd, widow, b. Manchester, d/o Mohre Patrick (Ireland, deceased) and Mary Lyons (Ireland, deceased)

VOGT,
William P. of Pittsfield, MA m. Carolyn E. **Dearborn** of Lenox, MA 10/8/1966

WAKEFIELD,
H. O. of Piermont m. Rosalee **Eaton** of Bradford, VT 5/8/1947 in Piermont; H - 41, merchant, 2nd, divorced, b. Westfield, VT, s/o Dexter A. Wakefield (Montgomery Ctr., VT, deceased) and Katherine Gilbeaut (Potten, PQ, housewife); W - 21, office nurse, b. Bradford, VT, d/o John Eaton (W. Fairlee, VT, millwright) and Wilma Butterfield (Haverhill, housewife)

WALLING,
Nelson W. of Bloomfield, VT m. Sarah L. **Piper** of Bradford, VT 1/22/1907 in Piermont; H - 33, farmer, b. Bloomfield, VT, s/o George W. Walling (Bloomfield, VT, farmer); W - 23, housework, b. Bradford, VT, d/o Adna Piper (Bradford, VT, farmer)

WALTERS,
Allen V. of Piermont m. Donmna M. **Calgan** of Piermont 5/18/1974

WARD,
Steven F. of Fairlee, VT m. Terry L. **Ellsworth** of Piermont 6/3/1978

WARREN,
Eber F. of Grantsboro, NC m. Linda K. **Jesseman** of Piermont 12/30/1971

WATROUS,
George H. of Piermont m. Cynthia J. **Sayers** of Piermont 5/19/1979

WATSON,
Leroy of Bradford, VT m. Olive **Hawes** of Waterbury, VT 7/11/1938 in N. Haverhill; H - 20, filling station operator, b. Bradford, VT, s/o James Watson (Websterville, VT, candy dist.) and Frances Simpson (Bradford, VT, candy dist.)

WEAVER,
DuVernette R. of Piermont m. Patricia M. **Ochs** of Piermont 1/28/1961

WEBSTER,
Allen D. of Piermont m. Ruth A. **Forbes** of Nashua 2/2/1944 in Colebrook; H - 36, in US Army, b. Piermont, s/o Ralph Webster (Piermont, deceased) and Hattie O. Molway (Haverhill, housewife); W - 34, secretary, b. Colebrook, d/o Fred E. Forbes (Groveton, farmer) and Annie K. Johnson (Canada, housewife)

Floyd W. of Piermont m. Olive L. **Duplease** of Winchendon, MA 11/28/1942 in Winchendon, MA; H - 25, soldier, b. Piermont, s/o Walter Webster (Piermont, bd. sawyer) and Lizzie Howland (Piermont, housewife); W - 21, fore-lady, b. Bridgeport, CT, d/o Charles E. Duplease and Rose A. Jamelin

Frank J. of Bradford, VT m. Carrie **Chase** of Bradford, VT 9/23/1917 in Piermont; H - 33, farmer, b. Frankfort, ME, s/o George F. Webster (ME, farmer); W - 40, housework, 2nd, b. NH, d/o ----- French (Canaan, engineer)

Freeman H. of Piermont m. Mabel **Mann** of Orford 6/20/1898 in Piermont; H - 24, farmer, b. Haverhill, s/o Charles Webster

(Boscawen, farmer); W - 20, house work, b. Orford, d/o Zerah Mann (Orford, farmer)

Henry M. of Piermont m. Willow **Jenkins** of Thetford, VT 3/6/1926 in Orford; H - 25, laborer, b. Orford, s/o Freeman Webster (Haverhill, farmer) and Mabel Mann (Orford, housewife); W - 18, domestic, b. NY, d/o Will Jenkins (NY, laborer) and Leta Hill (NY, housewife)

Herbert E. of Hill m. Catherine E. **Day** of Hill 3/1/1921 in Piermont; H - 21, laborer, b. Thetford, VT, s/o John Webster (Lyme); W - 32, housework, 2nd, divorced, b. E. Corinth, VT, d/o Jasper Day (Orange, VT)

Howard W. of Piermont m. Margaret Irene **Rees** of Winchendon, MA 7/4/1940 in Winchendon, MA; H - 19, lumber worker, b. Piermont, s/o Walter C. Webster and Lizzie Howland; W - 25, seamstress, b. Amherst, NS, d/o William H. Rees and Effie M. Chapman

Ralph A. of Piermont m. Hattie **Molway** of Piermont 3/28/1914 in Piermont; H - 31, board sawyer, b. Piermont, s/o Charles Webster (Boscawen, farmer); W - 27, domestic, b. Piermont, d/o Levi Molway (Canada, PQ, laborer)

Walter C. of Piermont m. Lizzie **Howland** of Piermont 5/29/1907 in Piermont; H - 21, laborer, b. Piermont, s/o Charles Webster (Boscawen, farmer); W - 17, housework, b. Piermont, d/o Lee Howland (Easton, farmer)

Walter Charles of Piermont m. Shirley E. **Ackerman** of Fairlee, VT 1/17/1950 in Piermont; H - 21, US Army, b. Piermont, s/o Walter Webster (Piermont) and Elizabeth Howland (Piermont); W - 21, chambermaid, b. Hanover, d/o Louis Ackerman (St. Albans, VT) and Esther Sanborn (Fairlee, VT)

WEEKS,

George E. of Orford m. Ruth **Evans** of Piermont 12/21/1905 in Piermont; H - 25, farmer, b. Orford, s/o John S. Weeks (Piermont, farmer); W - 20, school teacher, b. Piermont, d/o Joseph O. Evans (Piermont, farmer)

George W. of Piermont m. Verna B. **Lynes** of Miami, FL 5/4/1973

James K. of Marlboro, MA m. Paula S. **Jesseman** of Piermont 6/16/1973

WESCOTT,
David Terrett of Piermont m. Jody Ann **Short** of Montpelier, VT 1/6/1996

WEST,
Fred of Piermont m. Priscilla **Peterson** of Piermont 3/20/1915 in Warren; H - 29, teamster, b. Bennington, s/o William West (Bennington, VT, farmer); W - 38, housework, 2nd, divorced, b. Stowe, VT, d/o Lewis Shernenan (Johnson, VT, farmer)

WHEELER,
Kenneth of Haverhill m. Leona **Sawyer** of Piermont 1/26/1924 in Haverhill; H - 21, farmer, b. Newbury, VT, s/o Warren Wheeler (Canada, farmer); W - 20, domestic, b. Piermont, d/o Milo Sawyer (Topsham, VT, farmer)

WHITCOMB,
Charles S. of Contoocook m. Ada C. **Abbott** of Piermont 2/6/1907 in Piermont; H - 42, physician, 2nd, b. Henniker, s/o Arthur Whitcomb (Henniker, deceased); W - 35, saleslady, 2nd, b. Warren, d/o John Goodwin (Moultonboro, deceased)
John Edward of Lancaster m. Judith A. **Simpson** of Piermont 8/5/1961
Robert S. of Bradford, VT m. Shonda A. **Montgomery** of Bradford, VT 6/30/1989

WHITE,
Donald Austin III of Piermont m. Kathleen Marion **Partington** of Bradford, VT 6/17/1989
Vincent G. of Bradford, VT m. Ethel H. **Aldrich** of St. Johnsbury, VT 9/5/1936 in Piermont; H - 23, clerk, b. Pike, s/o Melvin E. White (Canada, farmer) and Stella B. Heath (Barton, VT, housekeeper); W - 27, nurse, b. Bury, Canada, d/o Thomas Harrison (Canada, farmer) and Mabel Bennett (Canterbury, Canada, deceased)

WHITNEY,
George R. of Piermont m. Grace E. **Ladeau** of Piermont 12/24/1904 in Piermont; H - 19, farmer, b. Stowe, ME, s/o David E. Whitney (Boston, MA, farmer); W - 18, housework, b. Fitzwilliam, d/o Joseph Ladeau (Colchester, VT, farmer)

WILKINS,
Timothy Matthew of Orford m. Charity Lyn **Nowell** of Orford 6/10/1995

WILLIAMS,
Steven Michael of Piermont m. Tiffany Beth **Cole** of Lyme 10/3/1992
Wade Allen of Piermont m. Tina Marie **Benjamin** of Bradford, VT 11/18/1988

WILMOTT,
David L. of Washington, VT m. Anna **Rios** of Piermont 12/31/1966

WILSON,
Charles H. of Piermont m. Minnie E. **Nutting** of N. Haverhill 4/11/1912 in Plymouth; H - 30, lunch wagon, b. Grindstone, MI, s/o John Wilson (Vienna, ON, carpenter); W - 20, housework, b. N. Haverhill, d/o Charles Nutting (Ashland, section boss)
Chester A. of Piermont m. F. M. **Humphreys** of Pike 8/3/1913 in Haverhill; H - 29, machinist, b. Grindstone, MC, s/o John Wilson (Vienna, Canada, carpenter); W - 24, housework, b. Windsor, VT, d/o John M. Humphrey (Keene, laborer)
Edward of Piermont m. Jessie M. **Stevens** of Haverhill 12/31/1899 in Haverhill; H - 24, laborer, b. Grindstone, MI, s/o John Wilson (Vienna, Canada, carpenter); W - 21, housework, b. Piermont, d/o George H. Stevens (Piermont, hotel keeper) (see following entry)
Edward of Haverhill m. Jessie M. **Stevens** of Haverhill 1/1/1900 in Haverhill; H - 24, laborer, b. Grindstone City, MI, s/o John Wilson (Vienna, Canada, carpenter); W - 21, housework, b. Piermont, d/o George H. Stevens (Piermont, hotel keeper) (see preceding entry)
George of Piermont m. Bertha **Cross** of Haverhill 1/14/1902 in Piermont; H - 21, farmer, b. Somerville, MA, s/o G. M. J. Wilson (Southampton, farmer); W - 17, housework, b. Piermont, d/o Eugene Cross (Piermont, carpenter)
George H. of Piermont m. Annie A. **Guay** of Haverhill 11/8/1945 in Newbury, VT; H - 24, laborer, b. Piermont, s/o Hazen A. Wilson (Groton, VT, deceased) and Nellie Fairbrother (Barnet, London, England, housewife); W - 18, bookkeeper, b. Boltonville, VT, d/o Harold Guay (Canada, fireman) and Alice M. Paul (W. Stewartstown, housewife)

Hazen A. of Corinth, VT m. Nellie **Fairbrother** of Piermont 4/24/1909 in Piermont; H - 26, farmer, 2nd, b. Groton, VT, s/o Isaac M. Wilson (Groton, VT, farmer); W - 20, housework, b. Barnet, England, d/o Henry Fairbrother (Wadhurst, England, harnessmaker)

Henry Isaac of Piermont m. Phyllis Irene **Keith** of Bradford, VT 7/10/1937 in Orford; H - 20, laborer, b. Piermont, s/o Hazen Wilson (Groton, VT, deceased) and Nellie Fairbrother (Brandon, England, housekeeper); W - 19, domestic, b. Haverhill, d/o Joseph E. Keith (Stamford, CT, deceased) and Mary F. Currier (Haverhill, housewife)

Henry Stanley of Piermont m. Linda Jean **Bagley** of Bradford, VT 9/9/1962

James L. of Haverhill m. Charlotte E. **Gould** of Piermont 5/3/1943 in Piermont; H - 36, US Army, 2nd, b. Haverhill, s/o James W. Wilson (Bad Axe, MI, carpenter) and Mary Cady (deceased); W - 24, school teacher, b. Haverhill, d/o Harry R. Gould (Piermont, merchant) and Eva Florence Craig (Middletown, CT, housewife)

Robert B. of Piermont m. Emma L. **Thurston** of Corinth, VT 11/25/1905 in Piermont; H - 26, farmer, b. Groton, VT, s/o Isaac M. Wilson (Groton, VT, farmer); W - 47, school teacher, 2nd, b. Corinth, VT, d/o Malon Humphrey (Vershire, VT, farmer)

William A. of Newport, VT m. Myrtie E. **Holden** of Piermont 11/28/1899 in Piermont; H - 26, farmer, b. Watertown, NY, s/o William E. Wilson (London, England, mechanic); W - 17, housework, b. S. Paris, ME, d/o Cyrus Holden (Paris, ME, machine agt.)

WINN,

Frank H. of Piermont m. Verne **Jennings** of W. Fairlee, VT 9/23/1934 in Piermont; H - 24, farmer, b. Piermont, s/o Hiram P. Winn (Piermont, deceased) and Hope A. Morse (Haverhill, retired); W - 20, laundress, b. W. Fairlee, VT, d/o Alonzo Jennings (Walpole, farmer) and Daisy Mae Geyer (Scottdale, PA, housewife)

Frank J. of Piermont m. Rosetta **Underhill** of Piermont 1/24/1908 in Piermont; H - 29, farmer, b. W. Fairlee, VT, s/o Frank P. Winn (Piermont, farmer); W - 27, housework, b. Piermont, d/o Horace Underhill (Piermont, farmer)

Frank P. of Piermont m. Hannah C. **Emery** of Piermont 1/17/1925 in Piermont; H - 73, farmer, 2nd, widower, b. Piermont, s/o John Winn (Danville, VT, farmer) and Phoebe Van Dusen (Peru, NY, housewife); W - 70, housekeeper, 2nd, widow, b. Wentworth, d/o Samuel Sargent (Bow, farmer) and Mary J. Davis (housewife)

Hiram P. of Piermont m. Hope A. **Morse** of Piermont 4/14/1909 in Piermont; H - 32, farmer, b. Piermont, s/o Frank Winn (Piermont, farmer); W - 21, housework, b. Haverhill, d/o Caleb Morse (Haverhill, farmer)

Parker C. of Piermont m. Esther B. **Hood** of Piermont 6/30/1926 in Haverhill; H - 28, farmer, b. Piermont, s/o Frank Winn (Piermont, deceased) and Nellie M. Putnam (Haverhill, deceased); W - 24, waitress, b. Newbury, VT, d/o Morris Hood (Newbury, VT, deceased) and Ida May Smith (Topsham, VT, domestic)

Robert E. of Piermont m. Rose Mae **Higbee** of Norfolk, VA 4/29/1985

William H. of Piermont m. Christine A. **Wheeler** of Haverhill 7/29/1950 in Fitzwilliam; H - 26, farmer, b. Piermont, s/o Frank J. Winn (W. Fairlee, VT) and Rosette Underhill (Piermont); W - 24, clerk in store, b. Lisbon, d/o Clinton J. Wheeler (Bulver, Canada) and Gertrude Taylor (Orford)

WOLF,

Benno of Piermont m. Mildred **Herzberg** of Piermont 9/16/1948 in Piermont; H - 40, steward, b. Schnaittach, Germany, s/o Mayer Wolf (Scnaittach, Germany, deceased) and Frieda Buchanan (Germany, deceased); W - 32, cashier, b. Vilna, Poland, d/o Isaac Herzberg (Vilna, Poland, merchant) and Sara Bergman (Vilna, Poland, housewife)

WOOD,

Daniel R. of Bristol, CT m. Tracy A. **Halpin** of Rockville, CT 8/28/1987

Edward J. of Plainville, CT m. Geraldine A. **Blackler** of New Britain, CT 8/4/1984

WOODARD,

F. J., Jr. of E. Corinth, VT m. Mary E. **Newton** of E. Corinth, VT 9/12/1938 in Woodsville; H - 26, truck driver, b. Somerset, MA,

s/o Frank J. Woodard (Barresville, MA, retired) and Harriet
Simpson (Bradford, VT, housewife); W - 22, domestic, b.
Starksboro, VT, d/o Timothy Winters (Ripton, VT, farmer) and
Hattie Flint (Hancock, VT, housewife)

WOODBURY,
Gilman T. of Woodsville m. Marion K. **Winn** of Piermont 3/31/1933
in Woodsville; H - 27, mechanic, b. Woodsville, s/o Frank H.
Woodbury (Woodstock, plumber) and Mae Titus (Woodstock,
housewife); W - 21, domestic, b. Piermont, d/o Hiram Winn
(Piermont, farmer) and Hope Morse (Haverhill, none)

WOODMAN,
B. W. of Washburn, ME m. Margaret **Howard** of Piermont 6/21/1947
in Piermont; H - 21, farmer, b. Washburn, ME, s/o Wallace
Woodman (Washburn, ME, farmer) and Bertha Crouse
(Washburn, ME, housewife); W - 19, student, b. Piermont, d/o
Earl V. Howard (E. Haven, VT, merchant) and Amy M. Sanders
(Montpelier, VT, housewife)

WORTHEN,
Fayette F. of Piermont m. Eva May **Miller** of Cambridge, MA
6/30/1921 in Somerville, MA; H - 29, farmer, b. Melrose, MA,
s/o Frank Worthen (farmer); W - 29, teacher, b. Danvers, MA,
d/o Albert Miller

WORWICK,
Percy J. of Putney, VT m. May E. **Wilson** of Piermont 11/30/1899 in
Haverhill; H - 21, mechanic, b. Putney, VT, s/o George
Worwick (Birmingham, England, farmer); W - 21, paperfinisher,
b. Grindstone, MI, d/o John W. Wilson (Vienna, Canada,
carpenter)

WRIGHT,
Archibald M. of Piermont m. Delia Alice **Merritt** of Piermont
6/27/1925 in Piermont; H - 22, laborer, b. Bradford, VT, s/o
Archibald M. Wright (VT, painter) and Dora ----- (Canada,
housewife); W - 19, domestic, b. E. Topsham, VT, d/o Oscar H.
Merritt (E. Corinth, VT, farmer) and May Hunter (Groton, VT,
housewife)

Arthur C. of Piermont m. Ada M. **Dunklin** of Rumney 7/15/1907 in Rumney; H - 23, farmer, b. Piermont, s/o Ximenus P. Wright (Croton, MA, farmer); W - 17, housework, b. Orange, VT, d/o Henry Dunklin (London, England, farmer)

Arthur G. of Piermont m. Nancy D. **Flanders** of Warren 3/28/1910 in Wentworth; H - 26, farmer, 2nd, b. Piermont, s/o H. P. Wright (Lowell, MA, farmer); W - 19, housework, b. Warren, d/o Rufus Flanders (Warren, farmer)

Edward of Piermont m. Nettie L. **Pike** of Haverhill 10/12/1902 in E. Haverhill; H - 26, laborer, b. Warren, s/o Irwin B. Wright (Lowell, MA, farmer); W - 19, housework, b. Haverhill, d/o Burns Pike (Haverhill, farmer)

Harry E. of Piermont m. Editha C. **Ranno** of Woodsville 7/1/1915 in Wentworth; H - 29, laborer, b. Piermont, s/o Ximenus Wright (Groton, MA, farmer); W - 16, student, b. Woodsville, d/o Horace Ranno (Salisbury, VT, laborer)

Tilden B. of Piermont m. Mary E. **Paige** of Shapleigh, ME 6/6/1894; H - 23, farmer, b. Warren, s/o J. Wright (Lowell, MA, farming) and Lizzie M. Wright (Canterbury, housewife); W - 22, dressmaker, b. Lincoln, d/o Fenno B. Paige (Lincoln, VT, salesman) and Lavina S. Paige (Lincoln, VT)

WYKES,

Howard F. of Barre, VT m. Lillian M. **Naughton** of Barre, VT 5/16/1937 in Orford; H - 26, mechanic, b. Mineville, NY, s/o Harry B. Wykes (Mariah Ctr., NY, farmer) and Mary D. Twillzer (Mineville, NY, housewife); W - 25, stenographer, b. Barre, VT, d/o William Naughton (Scotland, stonecutter) and Margaret Craigmyle (Scotland, housewife)

YOUNG,

Alton R. of Corinth, VT m. Melissa B. **Stygles** of Piermont 12/11/1979

Dwight Richard of Piermont m. Jean Marie **Osgood** of Piermont 6/6/1998

Robert E. of Bradford, VT m. Jean M. **Putnam** of Piermont 7/30/1950 in Piermont; H - 22, jr. accountant, b. Barre, VT, s/o William A. Young (Ely, VT) and Marjorie Thompson (Holyoke, MA); W - 20, cashier, b. Hanover, d/o William Putnam (W. Newbury, VT) and Marion Corliss (Bradford, VT)

YOUNGMAN,
Kurt Michael of Piermont m. Jaime **Defosses** of Woodsville 8/30/1997

YUSAVAGE,
Charles W. of Piermont m. Irene Ardell **Smith** of Pike 8/16/1941 in N. Haverhill; H - 20, laborer, b. Forest City, PA, s/o William Yusavage (Forest City, PA, deceased) and Mary Babarice (Forest City, PA, housewife); W - 19, domestic, b. Benton, d/o William Smith (Piermont, laborer) and Mildred Perkins (Pike, housewife)

Abbott, Ada C. (Goodwin) - Whitcomb, Charles S.
Abbott, Dale G. - Lamontagne, Archiel
Ackerman, Ellen M. - Putnam, James E.
Ackerman, Shirley E. - Webster, Walter Charles
Acres, Helen T. (Spaulding) - Deane, John E.
Adams, Lois M. - Hazen, Bruce A.
Adkin, Ethel F. - Leazer, Herbert S.
Aldrich, Ethel H. (Harrison) - White, Vincent G.
Aldrich, Susie O. (Gould) - Lamontagne, C. G.
Aldridge, Florence P. - Howland, William L.
Ames, Marion E. - Leonard, John R.
Andross, Hazel M. - Lamb, Nelson F.
Anell, Helen - Stevens, Harry N.
Armstrong, Lori Lyn - Koch, Michael S.
Arnold, Bertha - Hood, Merle
Asselin, Claire - Leard, Alder C.
Austin, Mary E. - Bagley, Lynford G.
Austin, Maud E. - Day, Frank L.
Austin, Nettie B. - Batchelder, Melvin J.
Ayala, Yvonne - Hurlbert, Scott L.

Bagley, Jane A. (Clark) - Bagley, J. F.
Bagley, Linda Jean - Wilson, Henry Stanley
Bailey, Princetta L. - Shepard, Don Nelson
Baker, Joan S. - Noyes, Roger H.
Ball, Nancy M. - Fagnant, Fernand R.
Ball, Rosie M. - Cookson, Charles
Barette, Margaret - Fenoff, Avery A.
Barnes, Lillian F. - Barnes, Charles C.
Barrett, Gladys E. - Emerson, Claude D.
Bartle, Jenniffer S. (Winn) - Schwarz, Thomas R.
Bartlett, Doris E. - Hanchett, Merlyn Ivan
Bartlett, Mable P. - Colcord, Daniel
Batchelder, Caroline - French, Chester L.
Batchelder, Lucia S. - Davis, Ellis C.
Bateson, Margaret M. (White) - Abbott, Edward J.
Bean, Grace Belle - French, Edward W.
Bean, Lois Henrietta - Fadden, Edward
Beaupre, Jeannine V. - French, Ronald L.
Beck, Ernestine D. - Fadden, Lawrence D.
Belyea, Edith May - Ramsey, Earl Edwin

Benjamin, Tina Marie - Williams, Wade Allen
Bennett, Bertha D. (Downes) - Hodsdon, Harrison
Berkowitz, Robin F. - Mayotte, James E.
Bernier, Judith A. - Holmes, George B.
Bertalott, Amy L. - Fernald, Robert D.
Bickford, Deborah A. - Robertson, William J.
Bijolle, Gertrude Irene - Johnson, Bert E., Jr.
Birchard, Betsy - Hazen, Allen R.
Bishop, Ann M. - Creps, Dean R.
Bishop, Jean C. - Band, Richard A.
Bishop, Susan Petre - Dargie, John Cox
Bixby, Barbara K. - Stimpson, Homer C.
Black, Nancy Ellen - Fiartling, Eric Scott
Blackler, Geraldine A. - Wood, Edward J.
Blaisdell, Alice M. - Roy, Wendall P.
Blaisdell, Ethel G. - Felch, Emory A.
Blake, Evaline A. - Davis, William A.
Blake, Lizitte C. (Glover) - Johnson, Charles W.
Blanchard, Dora - Stygles, Henry Ralph
Blanchard, Olive W. - Balch, Roy
Bliss, Ida T. - LeBarron, William
Blodgett, Audra - Smith, Norman M.
Blodgett, Marguerite - Masure, Basil C.
Boardman, Mary F. - Saladino, Peter J., Jr.
Bonett, Gladys K. (Webster) - Stevens, William R.
Bonniwell, Dorothy M. - Dietrich, Hastings L.
Bourgeois, Theodora M. (Seidl) - Cram, Charles D.
Bowker, Cora - Bonett, Ray E.
Bowker, Ella M. - Maxfield, Andrew C.
Bowles, Annie P. - Hodge, Fred Orinn
Bowles, Carrie L. - Goodrich, Cyrus A.
Boyce, Janice M. - Brown, Nowell S.
Bradley, Laura - Davidson, George H.
Braley, Josephine G. - Trottier, Theodore A.
Bray, Constance A. - Dwinell, Stanley F.
Brill, Elsie M. - Howard, Stephen E.
Brock, May Thelma - Anderson, Albert Solomon
Broillard, Carol M. - Tirrell, Stanford W.
Brown, Esther G. - Ames, Asa Edward
Brown, Karlyce Ann - Rogers, Shawn Richard
Buck, Amanda - Easter, Richard C.

Budrow, Delores Anne - Holden, Willard Edwin
Bunker, Abbie - Norcross, Frank B.
Burmaster, Melissa Susan - Metcalf, Asa Norman
Burns, Muriel E. - LaLond, Harold F.
Buska, Marion B. - Gaboree, Leo E.
Buxton, Florence - Ennis, Arthur
Buzzell, Clara R. - Gould, Leon R.

Calandrelli, Deanna (Correa) - Ryan, Paul Charles
Calgan, Donna M. - Walters, Allen V.
Campbell, Marie F. - Drew, Dennis W.
Carle, Mabelle R. - Underhill, Berton
Carrier, Ann F. - Frost, Gregory R.
Carter, Harriet E. - Hackett, Warren T.
Carter, Jean Keniston - Underhill, Calvin Lawrence
Carter, Roxanne J. - Brier, Stephen E.
Cassady, Dorothy L. - Rodimon, Frank W.
Cassady, Theresa M. - Shepard, Stanley L.
Chase, Bette A. - Noyes, George H.
Chase, Carrie (French) - Webster, Frank J.
Chase, Charlotte K. - Smith, Kenneth G.
Chesley, Gladys C. - Emery, Fay S.
Childs, Edith Emilie - Hodsdon, Harrison
Clampet, Susie (Lawrence) - Pierce, Frank E.
Clark, Audrey B. - Howard, Earl S.
Clark, Brenda Dorothy - Griswold, Jeffrey Scott
Clark, Heather Faye - Prest, Cameron Scott
Clark, Lee A. - Alfreds, Gary S.
Clark, Marion - Noyes, Mark F.
Clark, Marion F. - Ormsby, David E.
Clayburn, Mary Lettia - Hall, David
Clement, Charlotte M. - Bonett, Elwin K.
Clement, Delia J. - Blaisdell, Fred D.
Clifford, Lucena A. (Hadlock) - Ladeau, Joseph W.
Clogston, Elizabeth (Jascelyn) - Smith, Altan
Cloud, Deborah Lynn - Nelson, Daniel James
Coburn, Inez L. - Pushee, Paul R.
Cochran, Ruth - Dimick, Ernest H.
Colby, Bonnie Lee - French, James E.
Colby, Jennifer J. - Sargent, Christopher L.
Cole, Tiffany Beth - Williams, Steven Michael

Collins, Elizabeth R. - LaFoe, Howard E.
Colombo, Frances R. - Churchill, Winston
Colton, Doris S. - DeGoosh, Richard
Congdon, Lisa L. (Clemons) - Parkhurst, Joseph O.
Converse, Chrismas Mary - Fischer, Jeffrey William
Converse, Elizabeth H. - Underhill, Ernest S.
Cookman, Bertha M. (Stanhope) - Felch, Allen D.
Cooley, Eleanor L. - Smith, Wilfred L.
Corliss, Marie K. - Sylvester, Peter A.
Corliss, Marion A. (Williams) - Darling, Herbert A.
Corliss, Marion G. - Putnam, G. W., Jr.
Corliss, Marlene J. - Chicoine, Ronald L.
Cornford, Selina Maudie - Underhill, Henry W.
Correa, Deanna J. - Calandrelli, Emilio R.
Cote, Jacqueline A. - Rodimon, Walter E.
Coulter, Nelda V. - Smith, Theodore D.
Cowan, Elizabeth - Morrill, Philip C.
Craig, Eva F. - Gould, Harry R.
Cramer, Stacey Lynn - Cole, James Mark, Sr.
Cressey, Stella A. - Gilson, William E.
Crory, Ann - Thompson, Theodore
Cross, Bertha - Wilson, George
Cummings, Anna E. - Reed, Marshall J.
Cummings, Joanne - Bixby, Daniel A.
Cummings, Vonda S. - Brackett, James S.
Curtis, Addie L. - Blair, Oliver
Curtis, M. M. (McCloskey) - Hibbard, C. G.
Cushing, Abbie P. - Ladeau, Albert C.
Cushing, Beth J. - Hutchins, Roger P.
Cushing, Mabel E. - Blanchard, Raymond
Cutting, Bulah Olive - Lee, Ray Stevens

Darling, Edith - Beede, Robert R.
Daudlin, Olive F. - Bigelow, Carl A.
Davis, Eleanor R. - Trevithick, K. W.
Davis, Jean Collins - Putnam, Jasper Edgar
Davis, Katherine - Kincaid, Arthur E.
Davis, Kathryn - Burnell, Marc
Davis, Lana Lee - Kinghorn, Guy B.
Day, Catherine E. - Webster, Herbert E.
Day, Dorothy Irene - Ingalls, Carroll H.

Day, Martina - Stever, Bruce H.
Day, Nancy - Taplin, Kenneth P.
Dearborn, Carolyn E. - Vogt, William P.
Defosses, Jaime - Youngman, Kurt Michael
DeGoosh, Peggy - Hitchner, Alan L.
Demick, Pamela J. - Brochu, John
Dewey, Ruth E. - Bigelow, Paul W.
Dexter, E. Pearl - Lebeaux, Edward S.
Dickinson, Kitty A. - Towne, John P.
Disco, Ann Marie - Fishman, Richard
Dobbins, Veronica L. - Thurston, Judson C.
Dodge, Julia M. - Hannaford, Samuel
Doe, Louise - Gilbert, Franklin
Doe, Mabel S. (Stillwell) - Doe, Harry F.
Dolce, Donna L. - Fabrizio, John P.
Downing, Amy Blanche - Burroughs, Robert Orser
Drew, Donna L. - Huntington, George E.
Drew, Marie F. - Hemenway, Ronald L.
Drew, Wanda H. - Anthony, George S.
Drury, Bessie M. - Stetson, Louis O.
Dunbar, Shirley E. - French, Ernest G.
Dunklin, Ada M. - Wright, Arthur C.
Duplease, Olive L. - Webster, Floyd W.
Durgee, Evelyn - Luce, Perley G.
Dyer, Mary E. - Corthell, Michael A.

Eastman, Barbara A. - Stevens, Thomas E.
Eastman, Lisa Marie - Koch, Peter Jeffrey
Eaton, Annie V. - Batchelder, Robert P.
Eaton, Rosalee - Wakefield, H. O.
Elliot, Cindy L. - Jackson, Lee E.
Ellsworth, Nellie E. - Munroe, James A.
Ellsworth, Terry L. - Ward, Steven F.
Emerson, Winona J. - Robie, Freeman E.
Emery, Gladys C. - Putnam, William
Emery, Hannah C. (Sargent) - Winn, Frank P.
Engley, Jeanne - Ignacio, Kent
Estes, Paula Lee - Ingerson, James Douglas
Estrella, Shirley A. - Rutherford, Gary
Evans, Bessie M. - Rogers, Edward S.
Evans, Florence M. - Shorey, F. Langdon

Evans, Ruth - Weeks, George E.
Everett, Josie - French, Louis C.
Everson, Julia - Hackett, Harley C.

Fadden, Beverly - Hodge, Herbert J.
Fadden, Josie M. - Bean, Wallace B.
Fagnant, Michele Lynn - Thayer, Peter Paul
Fairbrother, Nellie - Wilson, Hazen A.
Farnham, Abbie (Hoyt) - Farnham, Homer W.
Farr, Ruth C. - Searer, Mark J.
Fay, Laurie Ann - Brick, Keith M.
Fellows, Eda P. - Clayburn, Joseph
Flanders, Nancy D. - Wright, Arthur G.
Fleming, Catherine J. - Charpentier, Keith L.
Foote, Edna M. (Robie) - Stetson, Clinton W.
Foote, Emma A. - Horton, Henry A.
Forbes, Ruth A. - Webster, Allen D.
Ford, Luella B. - Bickford, Fred H.
Fortier, Martha - Fagnant, Alice G.
Fortier, Virginia A. - Richardson, Erwin N.
Foster, Ellen A. (Calbain) - Dennis, Frank A.
Fournier, Cynthia M. - Fagnant, Robert E.
Fowler, Laura Lee - Bergeron, Richard, Jr.
Fowler, Linda L. - Lockwood, Harold S.
Fowler, Mabel Louise - Cole, David Wayne
Fox, Sally J. - Perkins, Bruce E.
French, Alice Mae - Heath, Theodore M.
French, Flossie Ida - Stevens, George L.
French, Josephine (Everett) - Muchmore, Daniel C.
French, Josie M. (Everett) - Austin, Ernest H.
French, Marion S. - Thompson, Charles S.
French, Millie Y. - Cummings, Leon O.
French, Violet M. - Paronto, Clyde G.
Fulford, Madeline E. - Kelley, Brian A.
Fulford, Maxine E. - Brooks, Olin C., Jr.
Furno, Michelle Marie (Daigle) - Lotman, Peter Silvester

Gadwah, Jean S. - Sims, Robert G.
Gaffield, Caroline (Wilson) - Johnson, James
Gamsby, Flossie A. (Smith) - Humphrey, Wilbert
Gamsby, Lillie A. - Bailey, Martin J.

Gardiner, Barbara S. - Gladstone, Arthur
Gardner, Heidi L. - Meagher, Patrick C.
Gardner, Heidie Lea - Peyton, James Joseph, Jr.
Gay, Marcia L. - Clark, Herbert A.
George, Maud E. - Dodge, Charles L.
Gilson, Sandra L. - James, Bradley A.
Giudici, Gina M. - Oakes, Rodney G.
Glover, Eunice Belle - Tarbox, Charles A.
Goldsmith, Martha L. - McDonald, Floyd E.
Gonchar, Marina A. - Chase, Lewis R.
Goodell, Kathleen A. - Kingsbury, Allan L.
Goodell, Myrtie J. (Whitcomb) - Corliss, Silas J.
Goodwin, Christie E. (Morrison) - Ritchie, Tait M.
Goodwin, Jennie - Boardman, George
Goodwin, Doris R. - Murphy, Robert B.
Goued, Marion F. - Callender, Wilbur
Gould, Alison Elizabeth - Rose, Brian Keith Matthew
Gould, Charlotte H. - Wilson, James L.
Gould, Leslie L. - Henry, Bruce P.
Gray, Evelyn - Smith, Alton R.
Green, Addie - Day, George H.
Greenland, Freda - Noble, Joseph S.
Greenwood, Ernestine D. - Fadden, Lawrence D.
Grimes, Carrie R. - Metcalf, John P.
Grimes, Doris Elizabeth - Keniston, Bertrand E., Jr.
Grimes, Helen M. - Smith, Robert H.
Guay, Annie A. - Wilson, George H.
Guilmette, Agnes - Bean, Bertram P.
Gunter, Sandra Lee - Horton, Richard Paul

Hackett, Barbara - Beardsley, Carl
Hackett, Dorothy L. - Moore, John W.
Haines, Jeanette M. - Bixby, Reginald W.
Hall, Ida B. - Hubbard, Willie E.
Hall, Lisa M. - Ackerman, Larry D.
Halpin, Tracy A. - Wood, Daniel R.
Hammod, Joan Arlene - Berry, Bruce Orlin
Harlow, Debra Ann (Lund) - Robie, Todd W.
Harrington, Delores Vesta - Hanley, Scott Robert, Jr.
Harrington, Jennifer Lee - Simpson, John Bradley
Harrington, Leslie A. - George, Daniel S.

Harris, Dorothy N. - Raper, James
Harris, Lillian J. - Goodrich, Clarence E.
Hart, Bertha - Balch, Mason
Hart, Veronica H. - Peterson, Robert H.
Hartley, Annette J. - O'Donnell, Cris A.
Hartwell, Francese - Fadden, Donald S.
Hartwell, Virginia E. - Beamis, Lee Weeks
Harvalik, Nicole - Del Pozzo, Sven A.
Hatch, Lura E. - Morse, George O.
Hatch, Pamela J. - Hartley, Ernest W., Jr.
Hawes, Heather Anne - Soule, Charles Nelson, IV
Hawes, Olive - Watson, Leroy
Hawkins, Thelma - Murphy, Jeremiah C.
Hayward, Bonnie Lynn - Blodgett, Joseph Andre
Hazen, Frances Sybil - Massa, John A.
Hennessey, Patricia L. (Duncan) - Billington, John E.
Henry, Nancy J. - Bishop, John E.
Heron, Esther Beryl - Chamberlain, Conant Harvey
Hertel, Joanne - Convisor, Lionel
Herzberg, Mildred - Wolf, Benno
Hessberger, Deborah Lynn - Burnaka, John Robert
Hibbard, Bertha - Dennis, Harry E.
Higbee, Rose Mae - Winn, Robert E.
Hill, Avis G. - Duguid, Elwin J.
Hill, Edith - Mardin, Clement
Hill, Emma - Morey, Wesley Earl
Hill, Gladys - Emerson, Ulysses
Hill, Irene Alice - Griffiths, Charles W.
Hill, Lucy (Sawyer) - Jones, Frederick
Hill, Mildred - Hartley, Ernest
Hill, Sadie Iva - Burton, John F.
Hodge, Monica L. - Chicoine, Roger L.
Hodge, Wendy - Stygles, Michael L.
Hodsdon, Agnes E. - Perkins, Glen E.
Holden, Ella M. (Kimball) - Lamontagne, Jeddie
Holden, Myrtie E. - Wilson, William A.
Hollman, Isabel D. (Doan) - Crane, Louis L., Jr.
Hood, Bertha J. - Hill, Louis M.
Hood, Doris E. - Barber, Stuart B.
Hood, Esther B. - Winn, Parker C.
Hood, Louise M. - Rodimon, Frank

Horton, Marcella J. - Mystrom, Robert E.
Horton, Mamie J. - Emery, Frank S.
Horton, Marion A. - Dodge, Forrest E.
Horton, Mary L. - Keniston, Hugh L.
Horton, Priscilla Mae - Fadden, Robert E.
Horton, Rita - Cheney, Irvin
Howard, Doris E. - Goodwin, Albion J.
Howard, Dorothy S. - Aldrich, Henry S.
Howard, Margaret - Woodman, B. W.
Howe, Mary A. - Lovejoy, Albert G.
Howland, Lizzie - Webster, Walter C.
Howland, Lola L. - Hill, Orlando B.
Howland, Millicent B. - Breed, Tracy S.
Hubbard, Anna - Blakebrough, James
Hubbard, Mamie - Brown, Bert
Humphrey, Dorothy M. - Provost, Norman R.
Humphrey, Effie M. - Robinson, Fred C.
Humphreys, F. M. - Wilson, Chester A.
Huntington, Beatrice - Bean, Richard
Huntington, Donna Drew - Barnatas, Adam Joseph
Huntington, Jade Courtney - Strohm, Jeffrey Dale
Hurlburt, Ella - Ellsworth, John
Hurst, Hittie M. (Mead) - Cook, Edward J.
Huse, Maude E. (Ford) - Symes, Richard J.
Hutchins, Dorothy F. - Oakes, Neil R.
Hyde, Rebecca - Gardner, Stephen A.
Hyden, Gretchen A. - Rutherford, John R.

Ibenthal, Alexandra - Kroell, Rolf
Inglesby, Marylyn H. (Morris) - Saladino, Peter J.

Jackson, Elizabeth E. - Briggs, Robert H.
Jagger, Julia A. - Cummings, Andrew S.
Jenkins, Willow - Webster, Henry M.
Jennings, Verne - Winn, Frank H.
Jesseman, Cindy L. - Locke, Kenneth E.
Jesseman, Debra J. - McClellan, Owen C.
Jesseman, Doreen A. - Moody, David J.
Jesseman, Jane P. - Colby, Allen R.
Jesseman, Linda K. - Warren, Eber F.
Jesseman, Paula S. - Weeks, James K.

Jewell, Eola - Smith, Laurence
Jewell, Ruth Elizabeth - Goodwin, John Floyd
Johnson, Abby M. - Metcalf, John E.
Johnson, Doris - Pushee, Olyph
Johnson, Ellen R. - Miller, George H.
Johnson, Jenny E. - Upham, Brad L.
Jolin, Cyrene - Gadwah, Claude
Jones, Jo Ann Shirley - Fagnant, Leon
Judkins, Marguerite B. - Blair, Herbert P.
Julien, Bertha J. - Sepessy, Henry L., Jr.

Kapp, Susan Mary - Monaghan, John, III
Keith, Edna - Fadden, Stanley F.
Keith, Phyllis Irene - Wilson, Henry Isaac
Keniston, Rosenna D. - Emerson, Frank R.
Keyes, Dorothy - Blaisdell, Rupert
Kimball, Wendy L. - Larkham, Glen H.
King, Vera - Rexford, Guy L.
Kinney, Judy E. - Ortowski, Thomas F.
Kiser, Marion - Rattazzi, Peter W.
Knapp, Barbara A. - Bixby, David V.
Knapp, Millie E. - Peavey, Robert E.
Knapp, Pearl May - Cunningham, Forest D.
Knapton, Lisa - Covert, Harold Daniel
Knighton, Bessie I. - Tyler, Wildern C.
Kohanski, Rebecca Ruth - Dube, Steven Allen
Koley, Emma V. - McDonald, Finley R.

Labbe, Marie Jeanne - Murdock, Harry S.
Ladeau, Grace E. - Whitney, George R.
Lahaye, Joyce - Hazen, George R.
Lamarre, Gail Michel - Pearl, Christopher Glen
LaMontagne, Marie - Adams, Reynold E.
Landry, Alice (Stetson) - Sheldon, Ernest R.
Lang, Marguerite F. - Reneau, Charles A.
LaPan, Isabel (Buska) - Spires, Franklin
Larson, Nancy - Leete, Alan Grant
Leach, Vera M. - Stygles, Ray A.
Leard, Claire R. (Asselin) - Titus, Howard O.
Leary, Kathleen P. - Ritchie, Robert A.
Leavitt, Lurena - Day, Martin H.

Lewis, Eva May - Horton, Bernard G.
Lewis, Minnie E. (Church) - Boynton, Fred A.
Litchfield, Shirley E. - Gould, Harry R.
Little, Josephine - Hayward, Norman E.
Locke, Gladys I. - Ellsworth, Arthur H.
Locke, Karen E. - Stockman, Anthony
Long, Sharon H. - Nichols, Larry E.
Long, Shirley C. - Demetrules, William J.
Long, Sophronia E. (Emerson) - Gardner, Harold H.
Louther, Deborah A. - Dunnells, Leslie J., Jr.
Luce, Alice - Montgomery, True
Lund, Nancy H. - French, William C.
Lupien, Carolyn K. - Taylor, John R.
Lynes, Verna B. - Weeks, George W.

Magaziner, Leni - Johnston, Bradford G.
Magoon, Edith Anna - Oakes, Wayne Glen
Malway, Carrie - Simpson, John B.
Manchester, Hazel Ida - Underhill, Bernard L.
Manchester, Helen G. - Underhill, Stephen L.
Mann, Hattie M. - Ladeau, Frank E.
Mann, Mabel - Webster, Freeman H.
Marden, Lillian M. - Simpson, John F.
Marran, Theresa E. - Underhill, Eric K.
Marston, Rosana C. - Andross, Clarence E.
Martin, Joan G. (Gallagher) - Martin, Wilfred C.
Martin, Kathleen M. - Oakes, Dale A.
Martin, Lillian (Bailey) - Little, Charles E.
Masher, Dorothy G. - Loverin, Stanley M.
Mason, Aloha J. - Robertson, Neil B.
Mason, Anna S. - Mason, Donald C.
Mason, Nancy C. - French, Edward W.
Mathers, Florence - Stevens, George
McAllen, Sally - Hood, Donald E.
McCoy, Lillian V. - Dennis, Dwight
McDonald, Martha (Dunbar) - Lougee, Walter E.
McGregor, Mardi - Hill, Craig B.
McLam, Marie A. - Osgood, Christopher Karl
McLerran, Janet - Johnson, Henry L.
Meagher, Heidi L. - Komorowski, James P.
Meaney, Hazel P. (Braley) - Dearborn, Earl G.

Meder, Darolyn - Holland, David
Meder, Mary E. (Lombardi) - Simpson, John Bradley
Melendy, Mildred - Brock, Carl Fenton
Mellin, Joan A. - Osgood, Dana W.
Mellin, Marjorie Jean - Herrick, Frederick R.
Mercado, Tanya R. - Lang, Timothy M.
Merchant, Eva - Bowes, Arthur
Merrill, Karen E. - Ordway, Eugene E.
Merrill, Kathleen A. - Stevens, Thomas E.
Merrill, Laura M. - Maxfield, Albert D.
Merrill, Stephanie L. - O'Donnell, Dana L.
Merritt, Delia Alice - Wright, Archibald M.
Messer, Ethel J. (Johnson) - Sampson, George L.
Metcalf, Abigail - Underhill, Jeffrey S.
Metcalf, Florence L. - Tarbox, Earl
Metcalf, Marianne - Thompson, William C., Jr.
Metcalf, Mary A. - Horton, Ralph
Miller, Eva May - Worthen, Fayette F.
Miller, Sharon A. - Fadden, Ronald B.
Minshull, Nancy J. - Underhill, Lawrence F.
Miranowicy, Lottie A. - Souza, Everett J.
Mitchell, Diane G. - Beach, James F.
Mitchell, Elsie D. - Simpson, J. Ralph
Mitchell, Roberta L. - Pirie, James C.
Molway, Hattie - Webster, Ralph A.
Molway, Kate - Spaulding, Harry G.
Monahan, Nancy A. - Cole, David W.
Montgomery, Shonda A. - Whitcomb, Robert S.
Moody, Carol S. - Rodimon, Frank W., Jr.
Moran, Bernadette Mary - Ratel, Robert James
Moran, Mary M. - Shields, Peter E.
Morey, Ruth A. - Hackett, Richard T.
Morey, Sada M. - Stone, George H.
Morrill, Emily G. - Metcalf, H. Burgess
Morris, Daisy P. - Stebbins, Harry E.
Morrison, Christie - Goodwin, J. Ralph
Morrissette, Michelle A. - Oakes, Daniel Albert
Morse, Hope A. - Winn, Hiram P.
Morse, Mittie (Elliott) - Robie, Lyman M.
Musty, Ann - Eisler, Everett B.
Musty, Jane E. - Stewart, John D.

Musty, Jane Kate - Chaddock, Craig C.
Musty, Marion G. - Salley, H. Homer
Musty, Rose M. - Dugal, Drew L.

Naughton, Lillian M. - Wykes, Howard F.
Nelson, Dorothy L. - Conery, Lloyd E.
Newell, Nina - Allen, Ethan C.
Newton, Hazel E. - Hunt, Jesse M.
Newton, Mary E. - Woodard, F. J., Jr.
Nickles, Laura A. - Rodimon, Frank W.
Nolan, Tracy Lynn - Beaulieu, Donald Norman
Norcross, Junt - Hartley, Wendell
Nowell, Charity Lyn - Wilkins, Timothy Matthew
Noyes, Henrietta Helen - Aldrich, Kenneth N.
Noyes, Mary S. - Stevens, William R.
Noyes, Vira May - Clayburn, William Albert
Nutter, Doris E. - Smith, Stanley R.
Nutting, Minnie E. - Wilson, Charles H.

Oakes, Loraine - Blanchard, Albert
Ochs, Patricia M. - Weaver, DuVernette R.
Osgood, Heidi J. - Metcalf, Asa M.
Osgood, Jean Marie - Young, Dwight Richard
Osgood, Wendy J. - Soucy, David S.
Overton, Nancy Ann Marie - Thibodeau, Richard Paul

Page, Cheryl Ann - Cutting, Paul Allen
Page, Kathryn A. - Saladino, Peter J., III
Page, Rebekah - Keysar, Craig S.
Paige, Leona Irene - Foote, Claude R.
Paige, Mary E. - Wright, Tilden B.
Paquette, Michaelle R. - Smith, Jerry E.
Paquette, Rebecca L. - Trevithick, Thomas N.
Parker, Elva L. - Cole, David W.
Parker, Joanne - Clogston, Donald P.
Parker, Mildred E. - Smith, William C. H.
Partington, Kathleen Marion - White, Donald Austin, III
Perkins, Bessie M. - French, Leslie A.
Perkins, Mae Louise - Herrick, Homer M.
Perry, Grace L. - Mourousas, Theodore
Pershing, Lovena L. - Bell, Charles A.

Peterson, Priscilla (Shernenan) - West, Fred
Picknell, Laura - James, Delbert
Pike, Beatrice - Oneido, Mark
Pike, Hattie - Gray, Harley
Pike, Nettie L. - Wright, Edward
Piper, Katherine M. - McTague, William D.
Piper, Sarah L. - Walling, Nelson W.
Piro, Cynthia J. - Musty, Samuel A.
Plaisted, Rosina A. (Hackett) - Child, William
Plummer, Emma A. - Stevens, George H.
Potter, Darlene H. - Clark, Russell J.
Prest, Cheryl R. - Robie, Terry E.
Preston, Eunice F. - Palmer, Vernon
Preston, Grace M. - LaPort, Reg. W.
Provost, Patricia J. - Clark, Paul W.
Prue, Lenora A. - Fadden, Lawrence D.
Pushee, Jean M. - Knapp, Dale H.
Pushee, Joann L. - Marcott, Robert E.
Pushee, Susan J. - Knapp, Dexter A.
Putnam, Barbara J. - Dunbar, Randy W.
Putnam, Jean M. - Young, Robert E.
Putnam, Lois Carrie - Gillingham, Kenneth C.

Ralston, Dorothy I. - Mason, Ralph
Ramsdell, Ruth K. (Kenyon) - Smith, Edward O.
Randall, May A. - Howland, Moses N.
Ranney, Harriet E. - Tetzloff, Donald H.
Ranno, Editha C. - Wright, Harry E.
Raymond, Shirley F. - Gale, Frederick H.
Reardon, Cynthia L. - Putnam, William N.
Reardon, Patricia A. - Underhill, Hugh T.
Rees, Margaret Irene - Webster, Howard W.
Reonough, Martha B. (Barton) - Clough, George L.
Rice, Mabel A. (Vadney) - Howard, Zedock
Rios, Anna - Wilmott, David L.
Ritchie, Christie (Morrison) - Burbeck, Perry J.
Ritchie, Margaret Elaine - Cleaves, Faunce Leslie
Ritchie, Mary B. - Musty, Jim
Robbins, Marion S. - Shilds, Samuel A.
Roberts, Mary - Colombo, Americo
Robie, Edna M. - Foote, Everett H.

Robie, Jessie - Evans, Arthur M.
Robie, Joan Elaine - Dieter, Paul Matthew
Robie, Lurline M. - McLam, Norman G.
Robie, Maud E. - Emery, William S.
Robie, Myrtie M. - Stevens, William R.
Robie, Susie Ella - Ames, Asa E.
Rodimon, Alice B. - Sawyer, Milo B.
Robinson, Dorothy E. - Simpson, John B.
Rodimon, Gladys G. - Gilman, Harold H.
Rodimon, Marie L. - Moody, Ronald P.
Rodimon, Teresa A. - Hutchins, Roger P.
Rogers, Florence P. (Beairsto) - Underhill, John H.
Rogers, Virginia - Oakes, Wendell
Rollins, Ella (Huntley) - Saunders, Frank E.
Rollins, Esther M. - Prescott, George C.
Rollins, Florence B. - Holden, James M.
Rollins, Lula (Bancroft) - Cutting, Fred D.
Russell, Anna M. - Griffin, George F.
Ryalls, Emma M. - Smith, Loren G.

St. Cyr, Doris - Dargie, Philip E.
Ste. Marie, Brenda L. - Rodimon, Michael E.
Sabbatino, Filomena - Fumagalli, Frank
Saladino, Juanita Debbie - Sanders, Karl Walton
Salomaa, Sheila A. - Odiorne, Christopher G.
Sandell, Nancy Ellen - Labounty, Peter Nelson
Sanderson, Georgiana (Seavey) - Frothingham, William P.
Sanderson, Marion J. (Cooke) - French, George A.
Sargent, Barbara A. - Robie, Paul L.
Sargent, Barbara B. - Stout, Arthur Elkins
Saunders, Mary E. (Patrick) - Vigeant, Leon L.
Sawyer, Leona - Wheeler, Kenneth
Sawyer, Linda - Schmid, John G.
Sawyer, Lucy A. - Hill, Harold F.
Sawyer, Mildred V. - Howe, Oliver E.
Sawyer, Wilhelmene - Hood, Harold R.
Sayers, Cynthia J. - Watrous, George H.
Scales, Myrtie E. - Brooks, Fred E.
Schauer, Regenna - Lyster, Edward T.
Schmid, Heather Christene - Prior, Trevor David
Schmukler, Evelyn E. - Morrill, Charles R.

Schnitzler, Belinda Flo - Smith, Arnold Chase
Schroeder, Jessica - James, Bradley, Jr.
Scott, Viola - Smith, Anson A.
Screton, April Clarissa - Dyke, Jason Roger
Shafer, Priscilla Mae - Sepessy, Henry L., Jr.
Shope, Kathleen L. - Underhill, Hugh L.
Short, Jody Ann - Wescott, David Terrett
Shover, Doris E. - Jesseman, Everett A.
Shumway, G. D. - Robie, Lyman Edward
Simpson, Ina B. - Fellows, Charles O.
Simpson, Judith A. - Whitcomb, John Edward
Simpson, Julie Lee - Cole, James Mark, Jr.
Simpson, Julie M. - Lamarre, Bruce L.
Skinner, Alice M. - Clark, Harry E.
Slayton, Jane Elizabeth - Pfeifer, Keith Machold
Sleeper, Delia E. - Morse, Clarence E.
Smead, Joyce E. - Thompson, Paul R.
Smith, Annabelle M. - Fagnant, Richard A.
Smith, Carol (Nichols) - Baker, Samuel M., Jr.
Smith, Carrie May - Conery, Edward H.
Smith, Ethelyn I. - Maxfield, Albert D.
Smith, Flossie A. - Gamsby, Walter A.
Smith, Hattie S. (Titus) - Ladeau, Joseph
Smith, Ida M. - McAuley, Auley
Smith, Irene Ardell - Yusavage, Charles W.
Smith, Lillian M. - Swain, Earl C.
Smith, Margaret - Sawyer, Maynard
Smith, Marion Estella - Conery, Edward Henry
Smith, Maud E. - Hackett, Harry D.
Smith, Shirley Mary - Metcalf, Harry B.
Smith, Sitelka J. - DuPuis, Cleo F.
Smith, Violet E. - Gamsby, Leon
Smith, Virginia Jane - Stetson, Wesley Freeman
Smith, Winifred Loraine - Baker, Robert D.
Souvaine, Dorothy L. - Heaton, Ray G.
Spooner, Cheryl D. - Lyons, Dennis H.
Spooner, Victoria U. - Fulford, Howard A., Jr.
Stanley, Gertie N. - Carr, William O.
Stanley, Medy L. - Kinghorn, Clement T.
Stetson, Bernice E. - Elliott, Basil
Stetson, Evelyn B. - Spencer, Hugh E.

Stetson, Lois Edna - Scruton, Sansford E.
Stetson, Mamie L. - Kimball, Harold F.
Stetson, Penny J. - Morgan, William J.
Stetson, Virginia J. (Smith) - Crowe, Donald P.
Stevens, Daisy - Morris, Edward J.
Stevens, Edith M. - Betz, Lorin John
Stevens, Helen C. - Dearborn, Henry F.
Stevens, Jessie M. - Wilson, Edward
Stevens, Michelle - Metcalf, Ai
Stilwell, Mabel E. - Doe, Harry F.
Stitt, Kristen M. - Hogan, Michael R.
Stocking, Megan Marie - Hutchins, Nicholas Ryan
Stockman, Karen E. (Locke) - Trischman, Keith B.
Stoddard, Jane E. - Oakes, Winston L.
Stone, Amelia - Norcross, Frank B.
Stone, Ruth E. - Parsons, Lawrence T.
Stowell, Alice G. (Shanty) - Ralston, Robert H.
Strapponi, Irene (Elliot) - Kelsea, Kenneth A.
Streeter, Rose - Jacobs, Abe
Strout, Rose L. - Rivera, Valentin
Stygles, Dawn Marie - Boutin, Adam Lee
Stygles, Melissa B. - Young, Alton R.
Stygles, Theresa L. - Piper, Eric D.
Szuch, Catherine Anne - Corren, Ray Edward

Tasey, Minnie E. (Church) - Lewis, George F.
Taylor, Barbara A. - Kinghorn, S. Robert
Taylor, Caroline J. - Stevens, Ernest L.
Tetreau, Delia B. - French, Harry W.
Tewksbury, Julia B. W. - Knapp, Ray A.
Thibeault, Georgette D. - Underhill, Eric K.
Thurston, Emma L. - Wilson, Robert B.
Towle, Eva E. - Ford, Edward G.
Trickey, Linda B. - Reardon, Bradbury Maurice
Trombley, Brenda M. - Trybulski, Walter A.
Tucker, Eva L. - Bryar, Kenneth B.
Tucker, Verna E. - Robie, Keith Melvin
Tyler, Joan M. - Sargent, Paul A.
Tyler, Mildred - Dierhoi, William H.

Underhill, Alice L. - Ames, Arthur E.

Underhill, Correna L. - Dube, Jeffery P.
Underhill, Mary E. - Koloseike, Walter F.
Underhill, Mildred E. - Denchfield, William S.
Underhill, Miriam Louise - Norton, Richard Norman
Underhill, Myrtie E. - Kent, Chester O.
Underhill, Rosetta - Winn, Frank J.

Vachon, Charlene R. - French, Michael E.
Valiquette, Eleanor G. (Quackenbush) - Tilley, Andrew C.
Virgin, Stella L. - Celley, Herbert V.
Vizina, Lena - Cummings, Henry J.

Walchli, Lynn - Gottlieb, Sidney M.
Walter, Katherine P. - Musty, Edgar H.
Ward, Jennie M. (Morse) - Muchmore, Daniel C.
Ward, Julia F. - Fairbrother, Ernest F.
Ward, Lily - Sawyer, Clyde B.
Warner, Georgiana (Clark) - Stevens, Lennie R.
Warwick, May E. (Wilson) - Ladeau, Herbert J.
Webster, Clara B. - Baker, Bradley H.
Webster, Evelyn - Bean, Merton
Webster, Gladys K. - Bonett, Ray E.
Webster, Hattie E. - Horton, William L.
Webster, Katherine S. - Blodgett, Lenn B.
Webster, Lena M. - Day, Ernest D.
Webster, Marjorie A. - Porfido, Alphonse F.
Webster, Pearl D. - Smith, Floyd L.
Weeks, Lean J. - Stygles, Michael L.
Welch, Jayne M. - Eddy, William P.
Wescott, Elizabeth - Thompson, Wayne
Wescott, Susan E. - Pregent, Randy S.
Western, Sarah Ann (Gillord) - Hogan, Austin William
Wheeler, Christine A. - Winn, William H.
Wheeler, Louise F. (Johnson) - Taisey, William J.
White, Addie Elsie - Smith, Albion L.
White, Irene - Sherwood, Walter D.
White, Jean E. - Herring, William L.
White, Sylvette - Gardner, Harold H., Jr.
Whitney, Jeanette L. - French, Ernest G.
Williams, Beth Frances - Higgins, Michael Gilbert
Williams, Esther M. - Trombly, George Alex

Williams, Kimberly E. - Dube, Victor R., Jr.
Wilmot, Margaret - Bailey, Henry J.
Wilson, Aggie S. - Leonard, John N.
Wilson, Altha M. - Stanley, Orlo B.
Wilson, Carolyn A. - Eaton, Ronald H.
Wilson, Emma - Slack, Bert E.
Wilson, Ethel - Atkins, Lyndal
Wilson, Joyce L. - Davis, Ronald B.
Wilson, Mary R. - Merritt, Robert E.
Wilson, May E. - Worwick, Percy J.
Wilson, Nellie F. (Fairbrother) - Jesseman, William
Winn, Bertha E. - Ellsworth, Ernest J.
Winn, Bessie Mae - Oulton, John D.
Winn, Esther A. - Dearborn, Howard S.
Winn, Jenniffer S. - Battle, John D.
Winn, Joanne - Parker, Ralph E.
Winn, Marion K. - Woodbury, Gilman T.
Winn, Sheila Diane - Ponte, Robert Francis
Winn, Susie M. - Morse, Franklin A.
Winot, Amy Margaret - Moore, Donald Clesson
Winot, Kimberly A. - French, James E.
Winslow, Ann M. - Trussell, James E.
Witham, Esther Rose - Colby, Jack
Womble, Nora K. - Smith, Leroy B.
Woodard, Rosemarie J. - Knapp, David K.
Woodbury, Ethel M. - Ellsworth, Frank J.
Woods, Jennifer Lee - Fields, Sean Michael
Woodward, Ann M. - DeRosia, Thomas K.
Wright, Dorothy M. - Corliss, John E.
Wright, Florence - Perkins, Charles H.
Wright, Florence G. - Perkins, Ralph C.
Wright, Junie (Gould) - McKeage, Ray
Wright, Marion A. - Thayer, Clarence E.
Wright, Nina L. - Simpson, Roscoe L.
Wyman, Arlene W. - Horton, John E.

Young, Stephanie Ann - Mitchell, Scott A.
Zwicker, Mabel A. - Humphrey, Maurice T.

PIERMONT DEATHS

ABBOTT,
Fred A., d. 2/20/1921 at 78 in Londonderry; farmer; single; John T. G. Abbott
Sarah Elizabeth, d. 1/1/1906 at 71/10/20 in Piermont; housekeeper; single; b. Piermont; John P. G. Abbott (Piermont) and Sally F. Stevens (Piermont)

ADAMS,
Jon H., d. 7/27/2000 in Woodsville
Robert H., d. 5/1/1985 in Westfield, MA

ADLER,
Ann M., d. 12/14/1977 in Berlin, VT

ALDERMAN,
Lillian M., d. 10/1/1986 in Keene

ALDRICH,
Dorothy Sybil, d. 10/27/2003 in Plymouth
Henry S., d. 6/25/1978 in Barre, VT
Lorenzo Dow, d. 4/9/1925 at 2/4/4 in Piermont; retired (?); single; b. Canada; Louis Aldrich (Canada) and Judith Case (Canada)

ALESSANDRINI,
Mura, d. 6/10/1956 at 48 in Hanover; housewife; married; b. Westbrook, ME; Jesse H. Dorsett and Margaret Chick

ALEXANDER,
Kathleen Brown, d. 9/19/1998 in Piermont

ALLAN,
Sylvia, d. 12/6/2004 in Piermont

ALLEN,
Miriam B., d. 1/24/1936 at 89/9/19 in N. Brookfield, MA
Mrs. Walter D., d. 9/18/1935 at 50/5/16 in Piermont; housewife; married; b. Stoneham, MA; Alfred J. Mardin (Canada) and Hattie T. Dunn (Greensboro, VT)

AMES,
Alice Ludelle, d. 12/27/1951 at 81 in Allston, MA; housewife; married; b. Piermont; Edward Underhill and Emily Libbey
Arthur E., d. 8/29/1958 at 86 in Cambridge, MA; retired; widower; b. Orford; Asa Ames and Mary Runnals
Isabel M., d. 9/8/1970 in Worcester, MA
Mary, d. 11/30/1910 at 69/6/6 in Lyme; nurse; widow; b. Piermont; Arthur Runnels (Haverhill) and Luella Hall (Hanover)
Maude E., d. 10/23/1970 in Worcester, MA
Mildred M., d. 6/25/1904 at 5/3/10 in Piermont; b. Piermont; Asa Ames (Orford) and Susie E. Robie (Piermont)
Roland E., d. 1/18/1976 in Piermont
Samuel H., d. 4/1/1954 at 81 in Worcester, MA; store-keeper; married; b. Orford; Asa Ames and Mary Runnells

ANDROSS,
Eleazer P., d. 12/16/1904 at 79 in Concord; blacksmith; widower; b. VT; ----- Andross and Mary Andross
Jennie Clay, d. 5/11/1949 at 88/1/2 in Bradford, VT; retired sch. tch.; single; b. Piermont; Eleazer Andross and Sarah Whitcomb

ANSLEY,
Rhoda M., d. 5/23/1988 in Piermont
Rufus, d. 1/5/1961 at 60 in Hanover

ARPIN,
Francis L., d. 12/27/1996 in Haverhill

ATWOOD,
Mary E., d. 9/27/1931 at 60/11/8 in Piermont; housewife; married; b. Orford; Charles R. Tarbox (Piermont) and Mary A. Welch (Hyde Park, VT)

AUSTIN,
Ernest, d. 3/30/1954 at 74 in Haverhill; laborer; married; b. W. Fairlee, VT; George Austin and Nellie DeGoosh
George A., d. 10/8/1914 at 76/10/20 in Piermont; neuralgia of the heart; farmer; widower; Ann Butterfield
Ivan, d. 3/3/1978 in Haverhill
Josephine, d. 2/17/1977 in Haverhill

Nellie L., d. 6/5/1909 at 63/6/15 in Piermont; housewife; married; Moses DeGoosh (Barnet, VT) and Ann Jones (England)

AVERILL,
Elva M., d. 5/26/1937 at 88/9/23 in E. Montpelier, VT; retired; widow
Henry L., d. 3/21/1910 at 64/5/26 in Piermont; box maker; married; b. Orange, VT; Leonard D. Averill and Ann E. Lamphire
Leonard B., d. 4/7/1895 at 81/6/23 in Piermont; la grippe, heart failure; cooper; widower; b. Mt. Vernon, VT; Daniel Averill and Dolly French

AVERY,
George, d. 7/6/1928 at 47/2/22 in Piermont; laborer; single; b. Corinth, VT; Charles M. Avery (Boston, MA) and Isobel Magoon (Corinth, VT)

BABBITT,
Mary Tarbox, d. 3/13/1963 at 89 in Haverhill

BAILEY,
Henry A., d. 4/21/1967 in Hanover

BALL,
Amos B., d. 3/3/1923 at 92/7/22 in Piermont; retired; single; b. Sutton, VT; Arad Ball and Sylvia Beck (Sutton, VT)

BARBER,
Doris E., d. 9/21/1987 in Hanover
Harry, d. 11/20/1964 at 96 in Piermont

BARKER,
Gladys M., d. 9/26/1978 in Piermont
William G., d. 3/16/1981 in Haverhill

BARNES,
Erva Morgan, d. 10/28/1996 in Lebanon

BARTON,
Aaron, d. 1/27/1894 at 85/5/2; heart failure; farmer; married; b. Croydon; Amos Barton

Aaron, d. 9/16/1921 at 77/10/15 in Piermont; farmer; married; b.
   Piermont; Aaron Barton (Croydon) and Melana Rogers
Albert, d. 3/6/1908 at 69/0/1 in Piermont; farmer; single; b. Croydon;
   Aaron Barton (Croydon) and Melena Barton (Lemington, VT)
Melana, d. 2/6/1905 at 92/3/12 in Piermont; widow; b. Lemington,
   VT; Thaddeus Rogers and Philana Putnam
Sophronia, d. 1/11/1924 at 78/10/17 in Piermont; housewife; widow;
   b. Bow; Moses Colby (NH) and Elizabeth Clement (NH)

BATCHELDER,
Edith G., d. 9/5/1897 at 0/0/11 in Piermont; cyanosis; b. Piermont;
   Harlow Batchelder (Rumney) and Hettie Lowell (Piermont)
Martha C., d. 11/30/1980 in Laconia
Melvin J., d. 4/4/1930 at 77/8/8 in Concord; farmer; married; b.
   Warren; Reuben Batchelder (Orford) and Laura Osborn
   (Warren)
Nattie Merle, d. 1/2/1944 at 49/7/23 in Piermont; cattle dealer;
   married; b. Plainfield, VT; Aldro Batchelder (Plainfield, VT) and
   Addie Wheeler (Marshfield, VT)
Nettie (Mrs.), d. 12/27/1938 at 69/6/16 in Haverhill; rug maker;
   widow; b. E. Haverhill; George Austin and Nettie DeGoosh
   (Bradford, VT)
Vienna, d. 2/23/1892 at 82 in Piermont; old age; housewife; married;
   b. Warren; Richard Whiteman and Phebe Willoughby
William C., d. 10/21/1964 at 68 in Laconia

BEACH,
Diane G., d. 7/12/1986 in Piermont

BEAN,
Eliza A., d. 1/12/1933 at 81/3/13 in Williamstown, MA; retired;
   widow; Hosea Bickford
Lutheria, d. 3/14/1981 in Woodsville
Sarah E., d. 4/4/1926 at 85 in Cambridge, MA; retired; widow; b.
   Piermont

BEDFORD,
Arvilla, d. 5/17/1994 in Haverhill
Benjamin, d. 9/27/1915 at 73/9 in Piermont; farmer; married; b.
   England
Ernest B., d. 7/16/1960 at 77 in Hanover

Grace Lillian, d. 12/25/1953 at 68 in Piermont; housewife; married; b. Hardwick, VT; Edgar Perkins and Bertha Stone

BEEDE,
Melessa, d. 2/3/1904 at 61/5/29 in Piermont; housework; widow; b. Springfield; Luther Thompson (Hartford, VT) and Amy Russell (Springfield, VT)

BELMONT,
Anita, d. 7/15/1942 at 60 in Piermont; nursing; widow; b. England; Arthur Joyel

BERG,
Welman M., d. 6/5/1898 at 34/2 in Bloomingdale; epilepsy; single; b. NY

BICKFORD,
Daniel C., d. 1/2/1902 at 70 in Concord; farmer; single; b. Piermont
Elizabeth, d. 10/3/1902 at 71/1/8 in Norridgewock; widow
Levi C., d. 11/30/1897 at 67/8/8 in Piermont; fatty degen. of heart; laborer; widower; b. Piermont; Isaac Bickford (Northwood) and Lucinda Coburn (Orford)
Phillips G., d. 11/16/1926 at 62/3/24 in Rockland, MA
Sarah J. L., d. 8/24/1891 at 51/7/21 in Piermont; dressmaker; married; b. Coventry, VT; James Frazier (Lyndon, VT) and Emily Bean (Concord, VT)

BILL,
Bert, d. 10/7/1895 at 1/1/10 in Piermont; cerebro-spinal meningitis; b. Whitefield; Carl Bill (VT) and Mary Adams (Montpelier, VT)

BISHOP,
Harold Richard, d. 6/14/1985 in Crown Point, NY
Maxine Elizabeth, d. 5/3/1993 in Bath

BIXBY,
Charles M., d. 10/23/1921 at 58/10/11 in St. Johnsbury, VT; retired; married; b. Piermont; Daniel Bixby and Mary Lamb
Daniel, d. 4/16/1897 at 60/5/15 in Piermont; duodenal ulcers; carpenter; married; b. Piermont; John M. Bixby (Piermont) and Elizabeth Fifield (Hampton Falls)

Elizabeth, d. 10/13/1892 at 80/4/18 in Piermont; old age; housewife; widow; b. Hampton Falls; Richard Fifield (Northfield) and Esther Phelps (Sanbornton)

Gertrude M., d. 5/8/1988 in Piermont

Grace Carol, d. 12/24/1951 at 10 in Hanover; b. Piermont; Vernon Bixby and Gertrude Walls

John, d. 8/30/1905 at 73/2 in Piermont; farmer; widower; b. Piermont; John Minot Bixby and Elizabeth Fifield

Mary, d. 12/5/1922 at 82/0/27 in Newport, VT; none; widow; b. Haverhill; Joseph Lamb (Fairlee, VT) and Mary Woodbury (Haverhill)

Vernon J., d. 11/25/1997 in Plymouth

Willard, d. 12/24/1951 at 14 in Thetford, VT; b. Piermont; Vernon Bixby and Gertrude Walls

BLAIR,

Addie B., d. 12/26/1957 at 85 in Haverhill; housekeeper; widow; b. Hartford, VT; Charles Bedell and Helen Clough

Adelaide L., d. 10/11/1929 at 68/0/16 in Piermont; housewife; married; b. Piermont; Charles Curtis (Piermont) and Elizabeth Hill (Barnston, PQ)

Herbert P., d. 3/8/1976 in Plymouth

Oliver, d. 2/26/1959 at 86 in Hanover

BLAISDELL,

Anna K., d. 3/16/1932 at 78/4 in Piermont; retired; widow; b. Newbury, VT; John D. Martin (Newbury, VT) and Martha Johnson (Newbury, VT)

Emma, d. 4/7/1924 at 84/1/18 in Piermont; retired; widow; b. New York City; William B. Farr (Biddeford, England) and Harriet Beare (Biddeford, England)

Harriet, d. 7/29/1960 at 80 in Bradford, VT

Harry E., d. 9/26/1948 at 74/10/17 in Piermont; farmer; married; b. Piermont; John Blaisdell (Piermont) and Emma Facy (Vineland, NY)

John E., d. 12/22/1908 at 72/1/30 in Piermont; farmer; married; b. Piermont; J. Blaisdell (Plainfield) and Mary DeMary (Hanover)

William, d. 2/14/1939 at 68/2/16 in Hanover; farmer; single; b. Piermont; John E. Blaisdell (Piermont) and Emma G. Facey (New York City)

BLAKE,
Annie W., d. 11/22/1922 at 68/1/9 in Gardner, MA; housekeeper; single; b. Melrose, MA; John Blake (Auburn, ME) and Ann Hoyt (Wilton, ME)
Manfred W., d. 2/14/1905 at 57 in Brighton, VT; widower; John Blake

BLANCHARD,
Herman L., d. 3/20/1977 in Hartford, VT
Mabel C., d. 9/17/1972 in Haverhill
Raymond, d. 12/19/1952 at – in Hanover; retired; married; b. Piermont; ----- Blanchard and Sarah -----

BLODGETT,
Catherine S., d. 3/25/1903 at 25/9/11 in Stratford; domestic; married; b. Haverhill; Charles Webster (Piermont) and Belle Knapp (Piermont)
Cora A., d. 1/22/1899 at 25/9 in Piermont; housewife; married; b. Sandwich; George E. Webster and Nancy Pettengill
Edith C., d. 5/11/1958 at 57 in Brookline, MA; domestic; single; b. N. Stratford; Leonard B. Blodgett and Katherine S. Webster

BOARDMAN,
Jennie, d. 4/23/1904 at 30/11/23 in Piermont; housewife; married; b. Canada; John Goodwin (Warren) and Melessia Hutton (Haverhill)

BONETT,
Charlotte, d. 6/4/2000 in Plainfield
Edna M., d. 7/4/1917 at 57/4/21 in Piermont; housekeeper; widow; b. NH; Loren Turner and Luella Hastings (NH)
Elwin K., d. 6/29/1993 in Piermont
Raymond E., d. 3/8/1936 at 44/5/11 in Woodsville; mail messenger; married; b. Monroe; Daniel P. Bonett (Kirby, VT) and Edna Turner (Monroe)
Richard, d. 6/3/1968 in Hanover

BONNETT,
Daniel, d. 4/25/1945 at 26 in Italy; US Army; single; b. Piermont; Ray Bonnett and Cora Bowker

Daniel P., d. 3/11/1895 at 42 in Piermont; pneumonia; farmer; married; b. Kirby, VT; M. H. Bonnett (VT) and Julia A. Page (VT)

BOOTH,
Isabella B., d. 9/6/1958 at 72 in Piermont; retired; widow; b. Glasgow, Scotland; Thomas Blann and Isabella Petrie

BOWEN,
Henry W., d. 12/23/1890 at 33/11 in NJ; laborer; single; b. Warren; Augustus H. Bowen (Grafton) and Sybil Biffins (Assonnett, MA)

BOWKER,
Elvira, d. 6/29/1896 at 70/10/28 in Piermont; dis. of brain; married
Francis, d. 4/30/1942 at 77/11/24 in Waterbury, VT; retired; married; b. Canada; Stephen C. Bowker (Parishville, NY) and Maria P. Brown (Derby Line, VT)
Medora M., d. 9/16/1929 at 61/11/16 in Bradford, VT; housewife; married; b. Piermont; Horace Underhill (Piermont) and Lucy A. Palmer (Orford)

BOWLES,
Albert E., d. 4/8/1931 at 75/10/18 in Piermont; farmer; married; b. New Boston; Benson Bowles (Sugar Hill) and Sabrina Bowen (Sugar Hill)
Vilona, d. 2/20/1943 at 74/4/15 in Haverhill; retired; widow; b. Farmersville, MO; William H. Aldrich and Mary E. Hathaway

BOYNTON,
Fred Aaron, d. 10/22/1941 at 74/6/2 in Piermont; retired guide; married; b. Waterville, ME; John Boynton and Mary -----
Minnie Elizabeth, d. 4/7/1947 at 66/9/4 in Haverhill; retired; widow; b. Vershire, VT; George Church

BRALEY,
Abbie May, d. 6/1/1897 at 0/0/24 in Piermont; premature birth; b. Piermont; Charles L. Braley (Paris, France) and Etta A. Batchelder (Stanstead, PQ)
Arthur E., d. 3/4/1899 at 0/6 in Piermont; b. Piermont; Charles T. Braley (Alexandria) and Etta Batchelder (Canada)

Charles, d. 3/2/1939 at 47/7/21 in Haverhill; laborer; widower; b. Lyme; Charles Braley (NS) and Flora Dunbar (Canada)

BRAMAN,
James, d. 12/2/2001 in Piermont
Lawrence, d. 2/24/1987 in Hanover

BRAYNARD,
Edward D., d. 6/29/1932 at 78/9/29 in Piermont; farmer; widower; b. Haverhill; Lyrander Braynard (Haverhill) and Rachel A. Foster (Wentworth)
Mary Ella M., d. 4/8/1926 at 73/3/13 in Piermont; housewife; married; b. Haverhill; Coolidge Marston (Haverhill) and Lucy Frary (Benton)

BREED,
Tracy S., d. 12/23/1920 at 28/2/1 in Piermont; farmer; married; b. Unity; Schuyler Breed (Unity) and Ella Straw (Unity)

BREWER,
Alice Agusta, d. 11/30/1986 in Haverhill
James T., d. 10/11/1987 in Piermont

BROOKE,
Zillah M., d. 2/25/1972 in Thetford, VT

BROOKS,
Arthur, d. 6/26/1953 at 65 in Waterbury, VT
Bertha, d. 4/20/1973 in Hanover

BROWN,
Benjamin F., d. 6/18/1925 at 9/2/18 in Piermont; school boy; b. Lyndonville, VT; William Brown (Montgomery, VT) and Mable Farmer (Lowell, VT)
Hazel P., d. 9/5/1901 at 0/0/24 in Piermont; C. E. Brown
Lizzie T., d. 1/25/1958 at 86 in Piermont; housewife; widow; b. Haverhill; Wooster B. Titus and Ardell French
William B., d. 12/17/1938 at 58/4/15 in Piermont; farmer; married; b. Montgomery, VT; Charles Brown (Montgomery, VT) and Edna Contubar (VT)

BURBANK,
Georgianna, d. 9/25/1900 at 12/3/26 in Piermont; b. Piermont; Arthur Burbank (Sandwich) and Anna I. Leonard (Bath)
John C., d. 12/23/1902 at 82/4/8 in Piermont; retired; widower; b. Haverhill; Charles Burbank

BURBECK,
Christie G., d. 10/10/1977 in Meredith
Perry J., d. 6/19/1958 at 71 in Piermont; teacher; married; b. Haverhill; William Burbeck and Carrie Blanchard

BURLEY,
Joanne R., d. 8/28/1960 at 16 in Piermont

BURNS,
Lester, d. 2/22/1970 in Hanover

BUSHAW,
Belle A., d. 7/23/1934 at 74/3/12 in Lisbon; housewife; married; b. Orford; Daniel N. Stetson (Orford) and Mary J. Hooker (Orford)

BUTSON,
Ethel May, d. 5/29/1917 at 24 in St. Johnsbury, VT; t. nurse; single; b. VT; James Butson (VT) and Louise Matthews (England)

BYRON,
Bernard H., d. 8/21/1975 in White River Jct., VT
Mabel E., d. 2/24/1988 in N. Haverhill

CALDWELL,
Robert, d. 6/15/1971 in Haverhill
Samuel J., d. 10/12/1969 in Piermont

CAMP,
daughter, d. 7/13/1897 at 0/0/1 in Piermont; feebleness; b. Piermont; Edward M. Camp (Morristown, VT) and Martha Bowker (Canada, PQ)
Emily M., d. 11/29/1908 at 81/5/18 in Lawrence, MA; widow; b. Stoddard; Jonathan Knights (Westmoreland) and Dorothy Joslyn (Stoddard)

Martha L., d. 9/5/1925 at 57/5/14 in Rumford, ME; housemaid; single; b. Canada; Stephen Bowker (Canada)

CARLE,
David Willis, d. 12/27/1948 at 0/0/2 in Haverhill; b. Haverhill; Franklin Carle (Orford) and Lorraine H. Bates (Chelsea, VT)
Franklin G., d. 4/21/1979 in Haverhill
Lorraine Hazel, d. 4/6/1996 in Haverhill

CARLIN,
William R., d. 11/12/1904 at 0/0/5 in Piermont; b. Piermont; William Carlin and Hattie M. Gilmore

CARMAN,
Beth G., d. 2/22/1980 in Bellows Falls, VT
Fred G., d. 3/28/2002 in Keene
Hewlett S., d. 7/1/1922 at 68/6/7 in Piermont; retired; married; b. Marysville, NB; Stephen Carman (Maugersville, NB) and Nann Tilton (Musquash, NB)
Laura Maude, d. 5/10/1939 at 75/4/21 in Bellows Falls, VT; retired; widow; b. Yarmouth, NS; John Kinney (NS)
Royal, d. 8/15/1956 at 62 in Alstead; mechanic; married; b. Boston, MA; Hewlett Carman and Laura Kinney

CARR,
Gertie M., d. 1/29/1928 at 55/5/20 in Los Angeles, CA; housewife; married; b. Piermont; Hubbard Stanley (Piermont) and Lucy Hill (Benson, PQ)
William O., d. 8/2/1934 at 66 in Anderson, IN; blacksmith; married; b. Orange, VT; Robert Carr (Orange, VT) and Louise Lawrence

CARTER,
George C., d. 4/2/1904 at 73 in St. Johnsbury, VT; laborer; single; b. Piermont; Benjamin Carter

CELLEY,
Edwin R., d. 2/16/1928 at 91/9/1 in Piermont; retired; widower; b. Bridgewater, VT; Richard Celley (Bridgewater, VT) and Eunice Bassett (Bridgewater, VT)

Eliza J., d. 9/23/1929 at 84/3/3 in Rumney; retired; married; b. Fayston, VT; Wilder Thomas (Chesterfield, VT) and Rachel Johnson (Fayston, VT)

Herbert V., d. 11/27/1921 at 70/8/9 in Piermont; farmer; married; b. Bridgewater, VT; Richard Celley (VT) and Eunice Bassett

Ida Felch, d. 5/4/1924 at 81/8/3 in Piermont; housekeeper; married; b. Piermont; Parker Felch (Candia) and Hannah Gould (NH)

Nelson, d. 4/15/1933 at 89/9/22 in Haverhill; carpenter; widower; b. Bridgewater, VT; Richard Celley and Eunice Bassett (Goffstown)

Stella Virgin, d. 8/7/1938 at 70/2/8 in Haverhill; housewife; widow; b. Piermont; Reid Virgin (Franklin) and Caroline Avery (Newbury, VT)

CHALMERS,
George, d. 4/17/1946 at 64/2/25 in Piermont; carpenter; married; b. Topsham, VT; William Chalmers (Newbury, VT) and ----- Olmstead (Newbury, VT)

CHANDLER,
Emma C., d. 5/28/1900 at 44/2/13 in Piermont; housework; married; b. Piermont; Josiah Merrill (Orford) and Philander Towle (Piermont)

Frank, d. 12/23/1928 at 79/6/19 in Vershire, VT; retired; widower; b. Piermont; Uri Chandler (Piermont) and Lois Rogers (Lemington, VT)

George W., d. 1/29/1926 at 87/10/2 in Los Angeles, CA; retired; widower; b. Piermont; Hill Chandler and Mary Filley

Gilman, d. 3/2/1914 at 77/11/22 in Piermont; softening of brain senility; farmer; widower; b. Piermont; Uri Chandler (Piermont) and Mary A. Rogers (Piermont)

Jay E., d. 7/19/1918 at 34/0/12 in St. Johnsbury, VT; farmer; married; b. Piermont; Frank Chandler (Piermont) and Emma Merrill (Piermont)

Lucy A., d. 12/2/1891 at 36/1/5 in Piermont; housewife; married; b. Canada; Stephen C. Bowker (NY) and Maria P. Brown (Derby Line, VT)

CHASE,
Amos L., d. 3/25/1951 at 84 in Warren; farmer; married; b. Piermont; Henry Chase and Zilpah Wright

Florence, d. 6/11/1960 at 73 in Haverhill
Henry, d. 1/18/1926 at 85/7/6 in Wentworth; farmer; married; b. Piermont; Daniel Chase (Meredith) and Lavina Clement (Warren)
Mabel M., Mrs., d. 11/7/1935 at 55/9/6 in Piermont; housekeeper; divorced; b. Enfield; Charles Johnson and Anne Hastings (Plainfield)
Viola, d. 9/17/1900 at 0/3/19 in Piermont; b. Piermont; Walter Chase (Wentworth) and Hannah B. Smith (Orford)
Zilpha A., d. 9/12/1928 at 84/2/29 in Wentworth; retired; widow

CHENEY,
Donald Wayne, d. 12/29/1993 in Haverhill

CHILDS,
Elsie, d. 12/20/1962 at 67 in Concord
Harlow N., d. 3/13/1920 at 59/9/11 in Piermont; farmer; married; b. W. Fairlee, VT; Charles Childs (W. Fairlee, VT) and Harriet Humphrey (Corinth, VT)
Lowena Adelaide, d. 1/23/1938 at 65/4 in Piermont; housewife; widow; b. Piermont; Horace P. Underhill (Piermont) and Lucy Palmer (Orford)
Ruth A., d. 2/13/1995 in Rutland, VT

CLARK,
A'geno E., d. 1/14/1896 at 47 in Piermont; pneumonia; farmer; married; Daniel Clark and Lucy Brown
Clarence E., d. 8/12/1991 in Piermont
Ella E., d. 12/8/1896 at 37/9 in Piermont; apoplexy; married; b. Norwich, VT; John Follansby
Ellen, d. 6/4/1934 at 81/9/20 in Haverhill; retired
Fred Ivan, d. 6/10/1992 in Piermont
George A., d. 5/15/1905 at 49/0/8 in Piermont; farmer; married; b. Piermont; Amos H. Clark (Piermont) and Ann E. Piper (Andover)
Herbert Amos, d. 2/28/1937 at 73/8/25 in Piermont; farmer; widower; b. Piermont; Amos H. Clark and Ann Piper
Homer D., d. 3/24/1922 at 43/5/16 in Pike; laborer; single; b. Chelsea, VT; Algeno E. Clark (Vershire, VT) and Ellen M. Luce (Lunbridge, VT)

Leander D. H., d. 1/25/1921 at 70/1/1 in Piermont; farmer; married;
    b. Vershire, VT; Daniel Clark (Berlin, ME) and Lucy Brown
    (Enosburg, VT)
Louise M., d. 2/12/1937 at 71/9/17 in Piermont; housewife; married;
    b. Augusta, ME; Benjamin G. Gay (Wells, ME) and Margaret E.
    Gay (Charlestown, MA)
Martha, d. 9/6/1963 at 88 in Williamstown, MA
Mildred L., d. 11/5/1982 in Piermont
Minnie, d. 10/1/1933 at 72/4/9 in Piermont; retired; widow; b.
    Chelsea, VT; Frank Columbia (Canada) and Sophia Clough
    (VT)

CLAYBURN,
Catherine C., d. 8/15/1927 at 71/11/20 in Piermont; retired; widow;
    b. England; Thomas Bebbington (Wales) and Hannah Winnill
    (England)
George, d. 2/24/1919 at 26/5/17 in France; PVT, AEF; single; b. NY;
    Harry Clayburn (England) and Charlotte Bevington (England)
Harry, d. 5/13/1925 at 70/8/5 in Piermont; retired; married; b.
    Manchester, England; Harry Clayborn (Yorkshire, England) and
    Mary Garside (England)
Joseph, d. 12/20/1970 in Haverhill
Thomas H., d. 3/8/1931 at 53/11/29 in N. Haverhill; box maker;
    single; b. England; Harry T. Clayburn (England) and Catherine
    Bebbington (Wales)
Vira N., d. 5/1/1993 in Haverhill
William A., d. 7/26/1961 at 71 in Piermont

CLEVELAND,
Alton Bud, d. 1/16/2002 in Haverhill

CLOUGH,
Anna Sargent, d. 12/16/1917 at 77/3/17 in Piermont; housewife;
    married; b. Bow; Samuel Sargent (NH) and Mary Davis
George L., d. 6/24/1920 at 55/5/26 in Haverhill; blacksmith; married;
    b. Piermont; Horace Clough (Washington, VT) and Anna
    Sargent (Bow)
Martha B., d. 6/5/1952 at 85 in Piermont; retired; widower; b.
    Piermont; Aaron Barton and Sophronia Colby

Sarah A., d. 5/19/1903 at 76/5/21 in Piermont; housework; widow; b. Piermont; Benjamin Towle (Portsmouth) and Sarah Kinney (Portsmouth)

COCHRAN,
Mark, d. 7/27/1894 at 84/7/21; paralysis; farmer; married; b. Allenstown; John Cochran (Pembroke) and Mary McDaniels (Pembroke)
Willis, d. 3/21/1894 at 85/7/20; old age; carpenter; married; b. Goffstown; John Cochran

COFFRAN,
Elvira, d. 9/10/1922 at 81/0/3 in Piermont; none; single; b. Piermont; Mary Coffran (Pembroke) and Susan Cilley (Piermont)

COLBY,
Clarence E., d. 8/9/1952 at 19 in Laconia; laborer; single; b. VT; Jerry Colby and Daisy Cass
Daisy Mae, d. 3/12/1963 at 57 in Piermont
Doris E., d. 10/25/1957 at 28 in Piermont; housework; divorced; b. Piermont; Jerry Colby and Daisy Cash
Elizabeth E., d. 7/19/1915 at 90/7/3 in Goffstown; housewife; widow; b. Bow; John Hammond (Bow) and Hannah Hammond (Bow)
Jack L., d. 11/28/1975 in St. Johnsbury, VT
Maretta, d. 5/12/1922 at 70/7/23 in Goffstown; housekeeper; single; b. Piermont; Moses Colby (Bow) and Elizabeth Colby (Bow)

COLE,
infant, d. 12/24/1967 in Bell, Texas
Archie, d. 9/17/1994 in Hartford, VT

COLLINS,
John, d. 2/12/1901 at 88/10/7 in Piermont; farmer; widower; b. Warren; John Collins (Warren) and Polly Colby (Warren)

CONERY,
Marion Smith, d. 9/27/1937 at 29/7/21 in Piermont; housewife; married; b. Walden, VT; George Smith (Stannard, VT) and Bertha Paronto (Montgomery, VT)

CONVERSE,
Sarah W. S., d. 8/1/1935 at 97/0/27 in Piermont; housekeeper; widow; b. Lyme; Reuben Waite (Lyme) and Pamelia Gelbert (Lyme)

CORLISS,
daughter, d. 9/18/1901 at – in Piermont; b. Piermont; S. J. Corliss (Newbury, VT) and Agnes Campbel (Piermont)
Catherine, d. 8/6/1954 at 58 in Springfield, MA; school teacher; single; b. Haverhill; Carnes P. Corliss and Isabel Andross
Ellis B., d. 12/15/1962 at 70 in Belmont, MA
Erna H. A., d. 11/3/1992 in Farmington, ME
George B., d. 3/24/1946 at 67/11/12 in Haverhill; farmer; married; b. Newbury, VT; Edson Corliss (Newbury, VT) and Eva Buchanan (Newbury, VT)
Helen M., d. 9/28/1907 at 74/5/23 in Orford; nurse; widow; b. Bradford, VT; Jonathan Martin and Martin Barnes
Isabelle A., d. 11/21/1941 at 73/4/26 in Springfield, MA; re. housekeeper; widow; b. Piermont; Eleazer P. Andross (VT) and Sarah A. Whitcomb (Troy, VT)
Jonathan M., d. 9/1/1914 at 63/9/16 in Haverhill; cerebral hemorrhage; widower; Rinalds Corliss (Newbury, VT) and Helen Martin
Luella, d. 7/11/1962 at 84 in Haverhill
Marla Jane, d. 11/3/1967 in Barre, VT
Paul, d. 4/24/1896 at 0/9 in Piermont; humor fr. birth; b. Haverhill; Carns P. Corliss and Belle W. Andrews
Rinaldo, d. 4/26/1894 at 74/11/24; uraemia; farmer; married; b. Newbury, VT; Jonathan Corliss (Newbury) and ----- (Germany)
Silas Joseph, d. 1/1/1944 at 75/8/6 in Haverhill; carpenter; single; b. Newbury, VT; Rhinaldo Corliss (Newbury, VT) and Helen Martin (Bradford, VT)

COSGROVE,
Dennis James, d. –/–/1998 in Boston, MA

COSTELLO,
Dulcie R., d. 10/21/1982 in Hanover

COTNOIR,
Olive C., d. 7/14/1957 at 85 in Piermont; housewife; widow; b. Canada; Alec Cote and Sophia Springer

COULTER,
Donald, Jr., d. 11/19/1978 in Piermont

CRAFT,
daughter, d. 11/24/1895 at – in Piermont; premature birth; b. Piermont; J. J. Craft (Lowell, VT) and Mary H. Edwards (Lowell, VT)
Mary A., d. 11/25/1895 at 26/10/9 in Piermont; convulsions; housewife; married; b. Lowell, VT; J. Edwards (Lowell, VT) and Mary Tillotson

CRAM,
Helen B., d. 5/29/1962 at 63 in Piermont
Kenneth B., d. 7/24/1960 at 63 in Piermont

CRAWFORD,
George Delmer, d. 9/29/1899 at 0/4/19 in Piermont; b. Piermont; Charles O. Crawford and Bertha Wilson

CREIGHTON,
Arthur F., Sr., d. 11/3/1980 in Lebanon

CROCHETIERE,
Alice L., d. 10/14/1995 in Lebanon

CROSS,
Lucy A., d. 4/4/1902 at 67/2/5 in Concord; widow; b. Piermont; Jonathan Stanley (Amherst) and Azubah ----- (Hanover)

CRUZ,
Heriberto R., d. 7/24/1961 at 29 in Piermont

CUMMINGS,
Clyde, d. 8/28/2004 in Piermont
Doris Millie, d. 11/28/1941 at 0/0/24 in Piermont; b. Hanover; Leon O. R. Cummings (Thetford, VT) and Millie French (Piermont)

Irene M., d. 5/4/1938 at 0/0/0 in Haverhill; b. Haverhill; Leon
   Cummings (Thetford, VT) and Millie Y. French (Piermont)
Leon O. R., d. 8/6/1973 in Hanover
Millie Yvonne, d. 9/18/1988 in Lebanon

CURRIE,
Ellen E., d. 12/13/1895 at 39/1/13 in Piermont; puerjuval septicemia;
   housewife; married; b. Bethlehem; Nathan B. Dexter
   (Bethlehem) and E. A. Young (Lisbon)
Muriel R., d. 2/1/1971 in Lebanon

CURRIER,
George W., d. 9/22/1972 in Hanover

CURRY,
Sarah G., d. 12/30/1970 in Piermont

CURTIS,
Charles, d. 3/20/1907 at 79/11/26 in Piermont; married; b. Piermont;
   Milton Curtis (Tunbridge, VT) and Sarah Curtis (Tunbridge, VT)
Elizabeth, d. 1/21/1908 at 73/8/10 in Piermont; retired; widow; b.
   Barnston, PQ; Thomas Hill (Canada) and Phoebe Copp
   (Moultonboro)

CUSHING,
son, d. 12/7/1898 at – in Piermont; stillborn; b. Piermont; George
   Cushing (farmer, Derby, VT) and Dora Prosser (Highgate, VT)

CUTTING,
David C., d. 6/20/1923 at 90/10/15 in Belmont; farmer; single; b.
   Piermont; Langdon Cutting (Orford) and Anthis Kendrick
   (Orford)
Fred D., d. 6/27/1927 at 53/11/11 in Piermont; farmer; divorced; b.
   Benton; Charles W. Cutting (Haverhill) and Ella A. Welch
   (Benton)

DALEY,
William V., Jr., d. 6/10/1978 in Hanover

DARLING,
Herbert A., d. 11/1/1931 at 62/0/23 in Piermont; mail carrier; married; b. NH
Marion A., d. 3/4/1943 at 83/1/8 in Waltham, MA; retired; widow; b. Pembroke, ME; George E. Williams (Manchester, England) and Hannah M. Langlin (Eastport, ME)

DAVIS,
Floyd F., d. 7/2/1975 in Hanover
Georgia L., d. 3/20/1971 in Union, NJ
Ida M., d. 2/24/1986 in Hanover
Marjorie D., d. 10/26/1996 in Bradford, VT
Norman, d. 5/16/1988 in N. Haverhill
Sarah A., d. 4/15/1905 at 81/1/10 in Piermont; widow; b. Piermont; Winthrop G. Torsey and Theodosia Tyler (Piermont)
William, d. 2/3/1899 at 79/0/24 in Piermont; farmer; married; b. Northfield, VT; Jonathan Davis and ----- Bartlett
William, d. 5/14/1901 at 48 in Piermont; farmer; married; Augustine Davis (VA) and Lann Davis (VA)
Winifred, d. 7/6/1928 at 22/2/6 in Piermont; laborer; single; b. Strafford, VT; Randall J. Davis (Canada) and Ella Moses (Strafford, VT)

DAY,
Ernest D., d. 1/24/1962 at 83 in Hanover
Frank, d. 1/28/1948 at 72 in Plymouth; farmer; widower; b. Wolcott, VT; Martin Day (Wolcott, VT) and Susan Dillingham (Williamstown, VT)
George H., d. 3/5/1950 at 79 in Barnet, VT; farmer (ret.); single; b. W. Topsham, VT; Martin Day and S. M. Dillingham
Luna M., d. 7/27/1977 in Haverhill
Lurena L., d. 4/2/1973 in Hanover
Margaret E., d. 3/2/1917 at 14/4/15 in Piermont; student or housemaid; single; b. Piermont; Ernest D. Day (Troy, VT) and Luna M. Webster (Monroe)
Martin, d. 1/29/1910 at 69/6/4 in Piermont; postmaster; married; b. VT; Lucius Day (VT) and Elmira Frost (VT)
Martin H., d. 5/9/1987 in Bradford, VT
Maude L., d. 10/2/1942 at 65/7/14 in Haverhill; housewife; married; b. W. Fairlee, VT; George Austin (Worcester, MA) and Nellie DeGoosh (Orange, VT)

Susan M., d. 12/30/1914 at 70/8/28 in Piermont; chronic nephritis; housewife; widow; b. Wolcott, VT; Hallen Dillingham and Roxana Bailey

DEAL,
Eleanor D., d. 11/23/1973 in Piermont
Harry R., d. 10/26/1966 at 85 in Piermont
Mary Emma, d. 10/10/1914 at 56/7/2 in Piermont; cerebral apoplexy; housewife; married; b. Piermont; Charles Rogers (Piermont) and Charlotte Underhill (Piermont)
William B., d. 2/5/1923 at 69/8/14 in Piermont; saddler; widower; b. Highgate, VT; Adam Deal and Anna Burchill (England)

DEAN,
Hattie C., d. 6/19/1934 at 80/7/9 in Piermont; dom. nurse; widow; b. Pike; L. Chamberlain (Mansfield, MA) and Jane Burbank (Haverhill)

DEARBORN,
Esther Adelaide Winn, d. 12/28/1947 at 33/2/18 in Piermont; housewife; married; b. Piermont; Frank Winn and Rosette Underhill (Piermont)
Helen, d. 2/1/2004 in Hartford, VT
Henry, d. 3/2/1997 in Bradford, VT
Howard, d. 7/9/2001
Nancy, d. 10/14/2004 in Hartford, VT
Scott L., d. 4/25/1998

DEEB,
Joseph, d. 7/25/1918 at 20/1/26 in Piermont; chef; single

DEETER,
Roberta, d. 5/19/2004 in Lebanon

DELABAR,
Domenick, d. 7/29/1963 at 69 in New York, NY

DENNIS,
Byron, d. 9/28/1920 at 51/1/27 in Hanover; farmer; married; Emory Dennis (NH) and Olive Cross (VT)

Edward W., d. 1/25/1917 at 60/7/6 in Piermont; farmer; widower; b. Stratford; William R. Dennis (Stratford) and Luceba Curtice (Stratford)

Harry E., d. 6/2/1905 at 32/4/6 in Piermont; farmer; married; b. Orford; Emore Dennis (Stratford) and Olive M. Cross (Troy, VT)

Minta, d. 5/–/1899 at 0/2/8 in Piermont; b. Piermont; Byron A. Dennis (Orford) and Eva M. Spencer (Stratford)

Mrs. Edwin, d. 5/16/1895 at 32 in Piermont; septicemia; housewife; married; b. Haverhill; Horace Blanchard (Haverhill) and Eliza Stevens (Piermont)

DEVENDORF,
Elizabeth C., d. 10/30/1936 at 88/9/20 in Piermont; retired; widow; b. Albany, NY; James Osborn (New Haven, CT) and C. Van Rensselaer (Albany, NY)

DIVAN,
Carroll, d. 10/16/2001 in N. Haverhill

DODGE,
Anna, d. 3/16/1914 at 63/8/21 in Piermont; chronic nephritis; none; widow; b. Piermont; Peasley Messer (Bow) and Hanna Ford (Bradford, VT)

Betty, d. 2/1/1924 at 84/10/5 in Belmont; retired; widow; b. Piermont; Langdon Cutting (Orford) and Anthia Kendrick

Charles, d. 10/4/1912 at 63/2/5 in Piermont; tr. salesman; married; b. Corinth, VT; Croydon Dodge (Newport) and Lydia Hamblet (Lunenburg)

Olive A., d. 3/15/1941 at 84/4/13 in Concord; school teacher; single; b. Lisbon; Hamilton Dodge (Newport) and Mahitable Hamblett (Piermont)

DOWNING,
Henry J., d. 5/7/1950 at 53 in Piermont; laborer; divorced; b. Pike; Henry Downing and Agnes Patnaude

DREW,
Fannie Mildred, d. 3/14/1967 in Piermont

Harris Joseph, d. 4/11/1949 at 57/0/22 in Piermont; mill laborer; married; b. Glover, VT; Noah H. Drew and Mamie Smith

Ralph H., d. 8/31/1971 in Hanover

Ralph Percy, d. 9/10/1995 in Denver, CO
Thelma P., d. 1/19/1974 in Hanover

DROWN,
Charles A., d. 10/3/1901 at 17/8/19 in Boston, MA; b. Piermont; Stephen Drown (Piermont) and Melissa Drown (Piermont)
Mary, d. 5/–/1899 at 49 in Piermont; domestic; widow
Melissa B., d. 2/8/1908 at 61/4/9 in Boston, MA; married; b. Piermont; Amos B. Rodimon (Piermont) and Lucy A. Ladd (Salem, MA)

DRURY,
Abbie C., d. 6/26/1938 at 74/10/20 in Piermont; housewife; widow; b. Piermont; Robert Evans (Piermont) and Abbie Matteson
Admon C., d. 5/27/1927 at 69/7/23 in Piermont; retired; married; b. Holden, MA; William H. Drury (Holden, MA)

DUBE,
Jeffrey Philip, Jr., d. 12/9/1996 in Haverhill

DUMOND,
Hamilton, d. 8/8/1934 at 84/6/5 in Haverhill; retired; single; b. NY; Jacob Dumond and Harriet Kiff

DUNKLEY,
Daniel Winn, d. 10/27/1942 at 82/0/21 in Piermont; RR foreman; widower; b. E. Haverhill; Daniel W. Dunkley and Sarah -----

DUNKLIN,
Ada M., d. 12/27/1907 at 18/3/20 in Piermont; housewife; married; b. Orange, VT; Henry Dunklin (London, England) and Alice B. Linton (Danville, VT)

DURANT,
Joseph Albert, d. 1/8/1919 at 35/3/22 in Piermont; farm lab.; single; b. Topsham, VT; Frederick Durant (Carlisle, MA) and Lois Gilson (Lowell, MA)

DURFEY,
Lillie, d. 6/20/1963 at 82 in Haverhill

EASTMAN,
son, d. 6/26/1916 at 0/0/17 in Piermont; b. Piermont; David Eastman (Corinth, VT) and Bertha M. Hart (Bradford, VT)

EATON,
George, d. 10/29/1955 at 82 in Concord; retired farmer; married; b. Landaff; Henry Eaton
Lizzie, d. 5/29/1962 at 95 in Piermont
Ray P., d. 7/19/1970 in Hanover

EDDY,
James H., d. 6/9/1971 in Bradford, VT

EGGLESTON,
Cora, d. 4/5/1979 in Berlin, VT

EISLER,
Jeanette M., d. 11/30/1990 in Buffalo, WY
Warren V., d. 5/13/1979 in Haverhill

ELLSWORTH,
Bertha Ellen, d. 10/18/1964 at 81 in Piermont
Ernest John, d. 11/17/1949 at 71 in Piermont; farmer; married; b. Wentworth; J. Belle Ellsworth and Flora Hutchins

EMERSON,
Harold, d. 8/7/1995 in Albuquerque, NM

EMERY,
Christie, d. 3/22/1932 at 13/9/28 in Haverhill; single; b. Piermont; Fay S. Emery (Piermont) and Gladys C. Chesley (Lyme)
Fay E., d. 4/12/1954 at 65 in Haverhill; farmer; married; b. Piermont; George Emery and Hannah Sargent
Frank S., d. 12/6/1958 at 77 in Bradford, VT; widower; George Emery and Hannah Sargent
George S., d. 4/29/1911 at 63/4/24 in Piermont; farmer; married; b. Suncook; Jacob Emery (Pembroke) and Mary Emery (Candia)
Mary Jane, d. 1/24/1945 at 59/2/24 in Hanover; housewife; married; b. Orford; William Horton (Barnard, VT) and Mary Chesley (Compton, PQ)

Mrs. Mary, d. 6/11/1892 at 76/5/4 in Piermont; chronic inflammation of liver; domestic; widow; b. Candia; Elijah Smith (Candia) and Sally Smith (Candia)

Roger M., d. 5/7/1978 in Hartford, VT

ERWIN,

Amande, d. 9/9/1931 at – in DeRuyter, NY

Lemuel S., d. 3/3/1915 at 66/6/13 in Bradford, VT; carpenter; married; b. Woodsville; Percival Erwin and Louisa Pike (Haverhill)

EUSTACE,

William, d. 7/9/1958 at 63 in Piermont; shoemaker; widower; b. Bromley, England; William J. Eustace and Emily Jones

EVANS,

daughter, d. 8/15/1923 at 0/0/0 in Piermont; b. Piermont; Arthur M. Evans (Piermont) and Jessie L. Robie (Piermont)

Ada, d. 11/20/1906 at 19/6/23 in Hanover; telephone girl; single; b. Piermont; Joseph O. Evans (Piermont) and Josephine Celley (Waterbury, VT)

Alvin A., d. 6/4/1998 in N. Haverhill

Arthur M., d. 12/29/1968 in Haverhill

Dan, d. 10/15/1918 at 37/0/16 in Dodge, GA; soldier; single; b. Piermont; Joseph O. Evans (Piermont) and Josephine Celley (Waterbury, VT)

Ella M., d. 12/7/1897 at 39 in CO; consumption; housewife; married; b. Piermont; Roswell Hunt (Piermont) and Mary Mead

Ellen M., d. 9/14/1899 at 54 in Cleveland, OH; music teacher; single; b. Piermont; Joseph O. Evans (Piermont) and Hannah Grant (Pembrook)

Guy R., d. 10/14/1918 at 29/3/13 in Piermont; farmer; single; b. Piermont; Joseph O. Evans (Piermont) and Josephine Celley (Waterbury, VT)

Helen, d. 11/15/1967 in Tewksbury, MA (see following entry)

Helen, d. 11/18/1967 in Tewksbury, MA (see preceding entry)

Jessie R., d. 11/13/1976 in Haverhill

Joseph Orn, d. 2/23/1928 at 69/6/6 in Piermont; farmer; married; b. Piermont; Joseph O. Evans (Piermont) and Hannah Grant

Josephine, d. 3/2/1939 at 79/9/15 in Piermont; housewife; widow; b. Duxbury, VT; Richard Celley (Bridgewater, VT) and Julia Thomas (Fayston, VT)

Mark A., d. 9/7/1915 at 16/5/23 in Piermont; student; single; b. Piermont; Joseph O. Evans (Piermont) and Josephine C. Celley (Waterbury, VT)

Richard F., d. 3/6/1923 at 1/4/20 in Piermont; b. Piermont; Arthur M. Evans (Piermont) and Jessie L. Robie (Piermont)

Robert A., d. 6/9/1921 at 80/10/10 in Piermont; retired; married; b. Piermont; Robert Evans

Robert Arthur, d. 11/21/1988 in N. Haverhill

EVERETT,
Edward N., d. 10/16/1919 at 64/1/2 in Piermont; widower; b. Lyman; Nathaniel Everett (Hanover) and Mary Stearns (Littleton)

FACEY,
Harriet, d. 2/25/1895 at 83/1 in Piermont; pneumonia; lady; widow; b. Biddeford, England; William Beare (Biddeford, England) and Alice Ferlfard (Biddeford, England)

FACY,
Edwin John, d. 1/15/1925 at 76/8/13 in Piermont; retired; single; b. Cleveland, OH; William Facy (England) and Harriet Beare (England)

FADDEN,
daughter, d. 5/30/1932 at 0/0/1 in Piermont; b. Piermont; Stanley Fadden (W. Thornton) and Edna Keith (Haverhill)
Dana S., d. 2/12/1971 in Haverhill
Edward, d. 5/2/1972 in Thetford, VT
Esther B., d. 4/7/1981 in Piermont
Francese M., d. 12/11/1980 in New London

FAGNANT,
Alcide G., d. 12/20/1976 in Hanover
Laurette, d. 4/3/1959 at 46 in Hanover
Martha Ellen, d. 10/21/1999 in N. Haverhill

FAIRBROTHER,
Ellen, d. 2/1/1935 at 77/2/21 in Piermont; retired; widow; b. Ashdown, England
Henry, d. 4/8/1927 at 69/5/29 in W. Fairlee, VT; harness maker; married; b. England; Horace Fairbrother (England) and Harriot ----- (England)
Percy, d. 6/28/1969 in Turners Falls, MA

FELCH,
Charles E., d. 2/2/1919 at 68/6/13 in San Francisco, CA; painter; married; b. Piermont; Parker Felch (Sandwich) and Hannah Gould (Canaan)
Hannah, d. 2/21/1892 at 85/11 in Piermont; old age; housewife; married; b. Canaan; Amos Gould (Boxford, MA) and Rebekah Gould (Derry)
Henry H., d. 10/7/1907 at 62/11/14 in San Diego, CA; poultry business; married; b. Orford; Parker Felch (Sandwich) and Hannah Gould (Canaan)
Parker, d. 6/23/1894 at 86/1/21; pneumonia; farmer; widower; b. Sandwich; Lewis Felch
Sarah F., d. 9/22/1923 at 81/9/4 in San Diego, CA; retired; widow; b. Piermont; Moses Learned (Piermont) and Hannah Jewett (Wentworth)

FELLOWS,
Charles O., d. 8/11/1949 at 82 in Brattleboro, VT; retired; widower; b. Dorchester; Leonard Fellows and Sarah Bowden
Ina B., d. 7/22/1924 at 58/10/2 in Piermont; housewife; married; b. Piermont; William Simpson (Orford) and Anna Stickney (Orford)
Myrtle Victoria, d. 5/8/1989 in Brattleboro, VT
Oscar Simpson, d. 3/16/1992 in E. Windsor, CT

FERINE,
Isabel M., d. 6/11/1975 in Hanover
Walter John, d. 3/2/1997 in Haverhill

FIELD,
Omer W., d. 5/25/1897 at 28 in Pike Station; suffocation in sand pit; laborer; single; b. Derby, VT; Horace Field (Newport, VT) and Hannah H. Black (Derby, VT)

FIELDS,
Lela E. Lowell, d. 8/31/1937 at 66/2/10 in Piermont; retired; widow;
b. Piermont; Josiah F. Lowell (Piermont) and Martha McAllister (Piermont)

FIFIELD,
Lucinda, d. 1/9/1891 at 90 in Haverhill; widow; b. Piermont

FILMER,
Bessie, d. 10/17/1971 in Hanover
Thomas C., d. 4/10/1976 in Haverhill

FLAGG,
Joseph M., d. 10/28/1950 at 79 in Piermont; retired; married; b. Auburn, ME; John Flagg and Almeda Small

FLANDERS,
Phillie, d. 10/7/1902 at 7/0/3 in Piermont; b. Warren; Rufus Flanders (Warren) and Lulu Bancroft (Barton)

FLETCHER,
Harriet C., d. 7/6/1912 at 77/1/9 in Piermont; widow; b. Vershire, VT; Perley Humphrey and Mahitable Heath

FLINT,
Burton Murray, d. 6/8/1947 at 74/10/22 in Piermont; veterinary; married; b. Lyme; Wesley Flint (Lyme) and Olivia Cook (Dorchester)
Ella L., d. 6/9/1950 at 71 in Haverhill; housewife; widow; b. Piermont; William Horton and Mary Chesley
Ralph M., d. 11/3/1967 in Lyme (see following entry)
Ralph M., d. 11/15/1967 in Lyme (see preceding entry)

FOOTE,
Emily Agnes, d. 8/7/1945 at 41/9/21 in Piermont; housewife; married; b. Putney, VT; George Warwick (England) and Mae Wilson (Piermont)

FORBES,
Hattie Elizabeth C., d. 10/13/1943 at 78/2/20 in Piermont; housekeeper; married; b. Pittsford, VT; Charles Cooley (Pittsford, VT) and Mary Whitcomb (Stockbridge, VT)

FORD,
Abram D., d. 10/20/1900 at 70/9/10 in Piermont; farmer; married; b. Piermont; Aldin Ford and Sally Phelps (Orford)
Dora, d. 3/29/1894 at 41/8/1; housewife; married; b. Easton; Samuel Howland (Lisbon) and Lucinda Bowles (Lisbon)
Edward, d. 8/27/1907 at 72/10/1 in Bradford, VT; married; b. Orford; Alden Ford and Sally Phelps (Orford)
Eliza E., d. 1/20/1908 at 71/8/23 in Piermont; retired; widow; b. Boston, MA; William Barrows (England) and Sarah Barlow (England)
Emma C., d. 2/25/1939 at 89 in St. Petersburg, FL; retired; widow; John Bagley
Eva, d. 5/20/1935 at 61/4/4 in Barton, VT; housewife; married; b. Piermont; Frank B. Towle (Piermont)
Nettie T., d. 11/11/1932 at 69/7/7 in Piermont; retired; widower; b. Cambridge, MA; ----- Adams and Georgia Serey
Sally D., d. 12/25/1895 at 89/0/17 in Piermont; old age; widow; b. Orford; Joel Phelps
William E., d. 8/1/1932 at 71/2/13 in Piermont; janitor; married; b. Boston, MA; Alden Ford (Orford)

FOSTER,
David, d. 5/8/1906 at 68/3/18 in Piermont; farmer; widower; b. Haverhill; David Foster (Pelham) and Laura Thurston (Hartford, VT)
Lavina L., d. 2/2/1903 at 63/7/16 in Piermont; housekeeper; married; b. Thetford; Jabez Hall

FRENCH,
Alfred, d. 4/30/1918 at 27/6/9 in Piermont; farmer; single; b. Piermont; William H. French (Landaff) and Alice Drown (N. Haverhill)
Alice M., d. 1/24/1944 at 88/4/13 in Concord; retired; widow; Richard Drown (Piermont)

Charles Bertram, d. 12/30/1936 at 65/9/7 in Piermont; blacksmith; married; b. Warren; Caleb O. French (Boscawen) and Caroline Clement (Warren)
Chester L., d. 5/15/1985 in Hanover
Edward M., Sr., d. 1/26/1988 in Piermont
Gladys B., d. 9/3/1907 at 11/1/6 in Piermont; b. Piermont; Willie A. French (Landaff) and Alice M. Drown (Haverhill)
Grace, d. 12/31/2000 in Hanover
Harold A., d. 6/19/1898 at 1/1/1 in Piermont; cerebral meningitis; b. Warren; Herbert French (carpenter, Warren) and Eva M. Whiteman (Canada)
Harry W., d. 6/30/1956 at 73 in Concord; retired; widower; b. Piermont; William H. French and Alice M. Drown
Herbert, d. 2/9/1999 in Lebanon
Louis G., d. 3/22/1926 at 37/9/7 in Piermont; laborer; married; b. Orford; William French (NH) and Marlie Drown (NH)
Mabel, d. 2/7/1970 in Haverhill
Marietta, d. 7/26/1904 at 62/1/21 in Piermont; housewife; married; b. Suncook; Jacob Emery and Mary Smith
Mary, d. 4/19/1987 in Haverhill
Maud, d. 4/22/1987 in Bradford, VT
Maurice, d. 9/26/1977 in Haverhill
Nellie M., d. 3/2/1896 at 10/10/9 in Piermont; pneumonia; b. Piermont; William H. French and Alice M. Drown
Ruth Aileen, d. 2/22/1995 in Windsor, VT

FROTHINGHAM,
Georgiana, d. 3/1/1920 at 84/1/18 in Piermont; retired; married; b. Natick, MA; Gilman Seavey (MA) and Mary Walker (MA)
William P., d. 4/10/1924 at 74/9/25 in Piermont; retired; widower; b. Boston, MA; Abner Frothingham (Boston, MA) and Elizabeth W. Beal (Boston, MA)

FULFORD,
Barbara E., d. 1/14/2003 in Lebanon
Howard A., d. 7/6/1983 in Piermont

FULLER,
Dan Burton, d. 4/10/1995 in Haverhill

GAFFIELD,
George D., d. 3/30/1974 in Haverhill
Ruth L., d. 7/18/1992 in N. Haverhill

GAMSBY,
Flora Belle, d. 11/28/1946 at 73/8/14 in Corinth, VT; housewife; married
Laura Ann, d. 11/23/1936 at 75/4/19 in Piermont; housewife; married; b. Dudswell, Canada; Alfred Lathrop (Canada) and Clorendo Andrews (Canada)
Leon, d. 10/8/1968 in Concord
Rufus Alexander, d. 7/11/1941 at 89/5/16 in Hanover; retired; farmer; widower; b. Canada; Royal Gamsby (Canada) and Betsy Hall (Canada)
Walter A., d. 3/21/1931 at 42/11/17 in Piermont; farmer; married; b. Dudsville, PQ; Rufus Gamsby (Canada) and Laura Lothrop (Canada)
Warren, d. 5/10/1964 at 79 in Barre, VT

GANNETT,
William H., d. 5/20/1895 at 56/9/16 in Piermont; pneumonia; farmer; married; b. Haverhill; William Gannett (Springfield, VT) and Charlotte W. Cross (Piermont)

GARDNER,
Edmond James, d. 3/16/1942 at 5/10/3 in Piermont; b. Hanover; Harold Gardner (Orford) and Phylis Scruton (Bradford, VT)
Harold, d. 6/25/1999 in Haverhill

GARVEN,
Sarah, d.1/8/1913 at 71/8/28 in Piermont; senile dementia; none; widow; b. Berlin, VT; Elisha Silloway (Berlin, VT, butcher) and Rhoda Hill

GENOVESE,
Elizabeth G., d. 8/17/1972 in Piermont
Pasquale, d. 2/1/1959 at 69 in St. Johnsbury, VT

GEORGE,
John E., d. 12/9/1968 in Piermont

GILBERT,
Ernest E., d. 5/27/1996 in Concord
Helen, d. 6/27/2004 in Concord
Jessie G., d. 6/27/1982 in Haverhill
Lulu Grace, d. 2/26/1899 at 14/7/19 in Piermont; housework; single;
  b. Orford; John Gilbert (Rouses Point, NY) and Lydia J. Grant
  (Vershire, VT)

GILLEN,
James J., d. 3/13/1989 in Haverhill

GILMAN,
H. Margharita, d. 5/9/1930 at – in Brattleboro, VT; single
Helen Frances, d. 11/17/1922 at 76/11/17 in Piermont; none; single;
  b. Bangor, ME; Jonathan Gilman (ME) and Lydia Brown (ME)
Helen Marie, d. 4/24/1943 at 46/7/1 in Springfield, VT; housewife
Ruth, d. 4/3/1964 at 56 in Concord

GLOVER,
James, d. 11/19/1933 at 65 in Hanover; married
Julia Belle, d. 11/4/1941 at 75/8/17 in Georgia, VT; retired; widow

GOLDFIELD,
Cady, d. 8/18/1952 at 64 in Piermont; housewife; married; b. Russia;
  ----- and ----- Grant
Joseph, d. 8/18/1952 at 65 in Piermont; retired; married; b. Russia

GOLDSMITH,
Edna, d. 3/20/1976 in Hanover
Vincent J., d. 5/18/1978 in Haverhill

GOODFLEISCH,
Shirley Theresa, d. 4/24/1998 in Lebanon
Theodore J., d. 10/24/2000 in Piermont

GOODWIN,
Elizabeth, d. 6/11/1898 at 66/11 in Piermont; disease of heart;
  domestic; married; b. Newbury, VT; Moses Clark (Newbury,
  VT) and Anna Kincade (Newbury, VT)
John F., d. 4/1/2003

John Ralph, d. 2/1/1918 at 29/3/7 in FL; soldier; married; b. Warren; Charles B. Goodwin (Warren) and Nellie E. Marcy (Elyria, OH)

GORHAM,
Cathie L., d. 10/25/1947 at 78/11/14 in Haverhill; retired; widow; b. Lyndon, VT; Reuben Pierce (E. Burke, VT) and Celia Church

GOULD,
Alfred R., d. 1/15/1913 at 85/0/1 in Piermont; gangrene of foot; farmer; widower; b. Piermont; Theodore A. Gould (Hanover, farmer) and Sibil Lund (Warren)
Carrie Kenney, d. 12/6/1927 at 57/7/23 in N. Haverhill; housewife; married; b. Dudswell, PQ; Major Kenny and ----- (England)
Charlotte Alice, d. 7/21/1940 at 79/11/2 in Piermont; none; widow; b. Piermont; Reed Virgin (Franklin) and Sarah Emerson (Piermont)
Edna S., d. 7/10/1904 at 67/7/18 in Piermont; housewife; married; b. Newport; John Wilmoth
Florence C., d. 12/1/1972 in Haverhill
Gordon, d. 11/18/1920 at 10/8/14 in Piermont; school boy; b. Piermont; William W. Gould (Colebrook) and Carrie Kenney (Dudwell, PQ)
Harry R., d. 10/25/1950 at 61 in Hanover; merchant; married; b. Piermont; Nelson Gould and Charlotte Virgin
Nelson Martin, d. 3/10/1919 at 57/3/28 in Piermont; farmer; married; b. Piermont; Alfred R. Gould (Piermont) and Edna S. Welmoth (Vershire, VT)
Stella May, d. 8/12/1919 at 0/0/0 in Piermont; b. Piermont; Walter H. Gould (Colebrook) and Sarah Chamberlin (Stewartstown)
William H., d. 11/13/1928 at 69/9/15 in Haverhill; farmer; widower; b. Colebrook

GRAW,
Florence S., d. 6/23/1958 at 73 in Piermont; housewife; married; b. N. Stratford; Charles Martin and Effie Page

GRIMES,
Amanda T., d. 8/24/1929 at 83/11/24 in Piermont; retired; widow; b. Benton; William Davis (Benton) and Sarah Torsby (Piermont)
Edward E., d. 11/3/1908 at 67/4/6 in Piermont; retired; married; b. Orford; Nathan Grimes (Orford) and Mary Howland (Lisbon)

Mary Howland, d. 12/15/1899 at 88/5 in Piermont; domestic; widow; b. Lisbon; Stephen Howland (England) and ----- Parker (Lisbon)

HACKETT,
Charles Donald, d. 1/4/1922 at 4 hrs. in Piermont; b. Piermont; Harley C. Hackett (Orford) and Jeanie Everson (Melrose, MA)
David D., d. 11/22/1927 at 70/0/0 in Piermont; farmer; widower; b. Haverhill; Moses Hackett (VT) and Elvira Dickerson (VT)
Harley Clarence, d. 1/8/1953 at 63 in Piermont; laborer; married; b. Orfordville; David D. Hackett and Edna Marsh
Harry D., d. 10/6/1918 at 30/11/16 in Piermont; farmer; single; b. Piermont; David Hackett (Haverhill) and Edna Marsh (W. Fairlee, VT)
Jeanne E., d. 3/18/1976 in Unity
Ralph, d. 3/23/1925 at 15 in Hanover; school boy; single; b. Piermont; Harley Hackett (Orford) and Jeanne Everson (MA)

HADLOCK,
Fred H., d. 1/23/1955 at 80 in Piermont; ret. school prin.; married; b. Jay, VT; Sylvester Hadlock and Luella Day

HALE,
Mary K., d. 1/28/1973 in Piermont

HALL,
Eleazer M., d. 10/11/1909 at 90/11/16 in Warren; none; widower
Mira P., d. 6/29/1910 at 88/6/23 in Warren; widow; b. Piermont; Charles Rogers

HALLECK,
daughter, d. 5/13/1965 at – in Springfield, MA

HANNAFORD,
Fordyce H., d. 9/18/1932 at 80/9/28 in Piermont; retired merchant; married; b. Sanbornton; Samuel Hannaford (Northfield, VT) and Lucy M. Hannaford (Boscawen)
Julia M., d. 6/12/1966 at 88 in Haverhill
Kate D., d. 7/7/1933 at 77/10/5 in Piermont; retired; widow; b. Bloomfield, VT; Rollin W. Holbrook (Bloomfield, VT) and Orpha J. French (Bloomfield, VT)

Samuel G., d. 2/20/1952 at 74 in Haverhill; retired; married; b. Stewartstown; Fordyce Hannaford and Kate D. Holbrook

HANNET,
Henry, d. 11/12/1912 at 64/8/12 in Piermont; laborer; married; b. St. Johnsbury; John Hannet (St. Johnsbury)

HARDY,
Ann D., d. 12/18/1915 at 81/10/1 in Piermont; dressmaker; widow; b. Alexandria; John Bailey (Berwick, ME) and Ann D. Ladd (Boston, MA)
Josiah, d. 3/3/1912 at 80/7/15 in Piermont; retired; married; b. Haverhill; Joseph Hardy (Haverhill, MA) and Lucy Jeffers (Haverhill)

HARE,
Margaret M., d. 7/29/1991 in Vero Beach, FL

HARLOW,
Bonnie M., d. 6/24/2002 in Piermont

HARRIS,
Abigail H., d. 9/12/1914 at 93/4/25 in Piermont; infirmities incident to age; none; widow; b. Wentworth; Job S. Eaton (Lowell, MA) and Sally Brown (Lowell, MA)

HART,
Franklin, d. 4/11/1962 at 74 in Hanover

HARTWELL,
George J., d. 2/8/1983 in Hanover
Harold W., d. 3/22/1920 at 0/0/1-3 in Piermont; b. Piermont; George J. Hartwell (Haverhill) and Ida G. Robie (Piermont)
Jennie S. Scott Sleeper, d. 12/2/1905 at 57/4/22 in Piermont; married; b. Stowe, VT; Horace A. Scott (Hartland, CT) and Josephine Knapp (England)

HASELTON,
Frank W., d. 10/7/1934 at 76/2/2 in Piermont; retired; single; b. Charleston, IL; Joel Hazelton (Orford) and Sarah Messier (Piermont)

HATFIELD,
Ellen Duval, d. 1/25/1961 at 83 in Haverhill

HAWARD,
David E., d. 10/11/1977 in Richmond, VA

HAZEN,
Bruce A., d. 11/3/1982 in Piermont
John Henry, d. 12/25/1955 at 0/3 in Piermont; b. Lebanon; William Hazen and Hazel Anderson
William S., d. 9/15/1987 in Piermont

HEATH,
Alice, d. 6/22/1986 in Piermont
Theodore M., d. 7/20/1978 in Hanover

HIBBARD,
Benjamin, d. 12/11/1898 at 76/11/16 in Piermont; senility; farmer; widower; b. Piermont; George Hibbard (Bath) and Mira Runnells (Haverhill)
Bertha R., d. 5/12/1950 at 77 in Bradford, VT; retired; widow; b. Piermont; B. Hibbard and Hannah Hibbard
Clarence G., d. 4/12/1962 at 67 in Plymouth
Emma A., d. 1/21/1955 at 82 in Orford; retired; widow; b. Concord; John Witham and Dolly Stales
Ernest E., d. 12/31/1930 at 34/3/3 in Concord; laborer; single; b. Orford; George Hibbard (Lancaster) and Emily Whittan (Epping)
Fanny, d. 3/20/1938 at 71/10/19 in Piermont; typesetter; single; b. Piermont; Benjamin Hibbard (Piermont) and Hannah Spaulding (Plainfield)
George, d. 10/3/1924 at 65/1/5 in Concord; farmer; married; b. Piermont; Moses Hibbard (Piermont) and Elizabeth Bickford (Piermont)
Hazel Irene, d. 6/20/1967 in Haverhill
John, d. 6/8/2001 in Claremont
Julia E., d. 2/19/1941 at 77/3/8 in Haverhill; housekeeper; single; b. Piermont; Benjamin Hibbard (Piermont) and Hannah C. Spaulding (Plainfield)

Kate T., d. 9/22/1916 at 62/11/4 in Piermont; housekeeper; single; b.
    Piermont; Ben. Hibbard (Piermont) and Hannah Spalding
    (Plainfield, VT)
Lillian, d. 7/19/1998 in Hudson, FL
Lloyd Clarence, d. 8/10/1986 in Hartford, VT
Madeline Effie, d. 4/4/1919 at 2/8/21 in Piermont; b. Piermont;
    Clarence Hibbard (Orford) and Maude McCloskey (Wentworth)
Maude M., d. 6/9/1979 in Haverhill

HILL,
Carlos L., d. 4/27/1905 at 64/7/29 in Bradford, VT; laborer; widower;
    b. Canada; Samuel Hill (Canada) and Mary Heath (Canada)
Ervill Russell, d. 9/3/1991 in Woodsville
George Thomas, d. 2/19/1947 at 66/5/1 in Haverhill; carpenter;
    divorced; b. Piermont; Moses Hill (Canada) and Mary Thomas
    (Manchester)
Jennie, d. 10/2/1902 at 51/5/20 in Haverhill; married
Joseph, d. 10/24/1935 at 93/2/13 in Boston, MA; laborer; widower; b.
    Canada; Thomas Hill (Barnston, PQ) and Phoebe Copp
    (Moultonboro)
Lola L., d. 12/29/1918 at 30/5/16 in Piermont; housewife; married; b.
    Piermont; Lee Howland (NH) and Clara Nichols (USA)
Lulu B., d. 8/7/1944 at 69/4/9 in Littleton; housewife; married; b.
    Benton; Parker Bancroft and Nancy Plumer
Mary T., d. 2/8/1931 at 79/9/25 in Montpelier, VT; retired; widow; b.
    Lyme; William Thomas (England) and Nancy Cook
Moses C., d. 4/10/1908 at 67/6/1 in Piermont; farmer; married; b.
    Quebec; Thomas Hill (Barnston, PQ) and Phoebe Copp
    (Moultonboro)
Orlando B., d. 6/1/1962 at 77 in Abington, MA
Oscar, d. 10/12/1987 in N. Haverhill
Polly J., d. 6/19/1917 at 73/10/8 in Piermont; housewife; married; b.
    Piermont; Benjamin Towle (NH) and Sarah Kenney (NH)
Weston W., d. 2/17/1903 at 66 in W. Brookfield, MA; laborer;
    married; b. Piermont; Thomas Hill (Canada) and Febe Copp

HOAG,
Roeina C., d. 2/21/1917 at 89/7/10 in Piermont; housekeeper;
    widow; b. Starksboro, VT; George Wright (Starksboro, VT) and
    Rachel Rhodes (Starksboro, VT)

HOBBS,
Eunice V., d. 7/20/2003 in Lebanon
Josiah, d. 8/26/1918 at 20/1/26 in Piermont; laborer; single; b. Tamworth; Herbert Hobbs (Tamworth)

HODGE,
Annie, d. 7/20/1927 at 36/8/0 in Haverhill; housewife; married; b. Deering; Albert Bowles (New Boston) and Vilona Belle Aldridge (Livingston C., MO)
Fred O., d. 5/3/1979 in Berlin, VT

HODGES,
Albert, d. 9/30/1936 at 54/3/15 in Piermont; b. Archogue, NB; Ha'genson Hodges and Rachel Wilbur
Jamie, d. 1/29/1976 in Piermont

HODSDEN,
Aaron G., d. 4/4/1917 at 70/5 in Piermont; farmer; married; b. Piermont; Cyrus K. Hodsden (Kennebunk, ME) and Belinda Skinner (Sandwich)

HODSDON,
son, d. 10/17/1927 at 0/0/0 in Piermont; b. Piermont; Harrison Hodsdon (Piermont) and Edith E. Childs (Piermont)
Albert S., d. 10/7/1918 at 39/1/27 in Piermont; farmer; single; b. Piermont; Aaron G. Hodsdon (Piermont) and Emma Eastman (Vershire, VT)
Augustus L., d. 9/10/1910 at 50/0/23 in Boston, MA; single; b. Piermont; Cyrus K. Hodsdon (Kennebunk, ME) and Belinda Skinner (Sandwich)
Belinda, d. 9/14/1902 at 85/4/8 in Piermont; widow; b. Sandwich; Jedediah Skinner (Sandwich) and Annie Quimby (Sandwich)
Belinda, d. 7/14/1907 at 56/10/1 in Piermont; at home; single; b. Piermont; Cyrus K. Hodsdon (Kennebunk, ME) and Belinda W. Skinner (Sandwich)
Bertha D., d. 12/14/1919 at 36/8/14 in Piermont; housewife; married; b. Brookbury, PQ; Isaac B. Downes (Bookbury) and Emily M. Clark (Brookbury)
Emma S., d. 4/21/1928 at 78/9 in Piermont; housewife; widow; b. Vershire, VT; Charles Eastman (Vershire, VT) and Angeline Gove (Strafford, VT)

Esther, d. 6/10/1981 in Haverhill
Harrison, d. 3/14/1956 at 82 in Piermont; farmer; married; b. Piermont; Aaron Hodsdon and Emma Eastman
Jean, d. 3/11/1996 in Colebrook
William E., d. 5/5/1898 at 23/2/8 in Piermont; abscess of liver; laborer; single; b. Piermont; Aaron G. Hodsdon (Piermont) and Emma Eastman (Vershire, VT)

HOGAN,
Sarah A., d. 10/26/1999 in Piermont

HOLDEN,
Bertha M., d. 10/2/1895 at 2/6/2 in Piermont; gastric fever; b. Abington, CT; J. M. Holden (Paris, ME) and Etta M. Kimball (Woodstock, ME)

HOLLINGSWORTH,
Mable, d. 8/5/1925 at 21/10/28 in Piermont; camp counselor; single; b. Ardmore, PA; Lof. Hollingsworth (Scotch Plains, NJ) and Gertrude Rinehart (Hope, NJ)

HOLLOS,
Fred, d. 2/27/1981 in Piermont

HOLOWAY,
Percie U., d. 4/21/1987 in New Port Richie, FL

HOOD,
Harold, d. 7/24/2000 in Pittsfield, MA
Harold R., d. 7/12/1969 in Piermont
Marianne, d. 8/20/1987 in N. Haverhill
Sally, d. 8/19/1982 in Hanover
Wilhelmine S., d. 12/20/1976 in Haverhill

HORTON,
Bernard G., d. 3/1/1973 in Piermont
Clara L., d. 10/2/1891 at 0/6 in Piermont; b. Piermont; William H. Horton (Barnard, VT) and Mary Chesley (Campton, PQ)
Edith Smith, d. 10/8/1959 at 74 in Portland, ME
Eva Mae, d. 9/10/1999 in Bradford, VT

Fred A., d. 10/30/1951 at 82 in Hanover; retired farmer; married; b. Orford, William H. Horton and Lydia Wilder
Hattie W., d. 5/5/1974 in Lebanon
Louise A., d. 5/28/1975 in Lebanon
Mary Jane, d. 6/28/1922 at 70/7/20 in Piermont; retired; widow; b. Compton, PQ; John E. Chesley (NH) and Hannah Moody (NH)
Nora M., d. 10/30/1902 at 5/2/25 in Piermont; single; b. Woodsville; Charles Horton and Hattie T. Horton
Osborne A., d. 12/24/1934 at 47/10/1 in Portland, ME; manager; married; b. Orford; William H. Horton (Barnard, VT) and Mary Chesley (Compton, PQ)
William H., d. 2/13/1915 at 74/10/7 in Piermont; farmer; married; b. Barnard, VT; Allen Horton (Rehoboth, MA) and Lucinda Smith (Westmoreland)
William L., d. 2/10/1946 at 62/6/9 in Piermont; laborer; married; b. Orford; William H. Horton (Barnard, VT) and Mary Jane Chesley (Compton, PQ)

HOSFORD,
Lavina, d. 3/16/1902 at 71/8/4 in Piermont; teacher; single; b. Lyme; Joel Hosford and Alice Kendrick (Lyme)

HOWARD,
Amy S., d. 6/29/1961 at 75 in Haverhill
Earl V., d. 1/25/1959 at 82 in Haverhill
Nita P., d. 8/11/1970 in Boscawen
Ray W., d. 11/23/1970 in Boscawen

HOWE,
Eunice A., d. 3/23/1895 at 66/11/28 in Piermont; cancer; housewife; married; b. Hanover; Nathaniel Worth (Canaan) and Patty Chandler (Hanover)
Ira H., d. 4/20/1892 at 77/4 in Piermont; blood poison; laborer; widower; b. Guildhall, VT; Samuel Howe (Marlborough, MA) and Lois Rosebrook (Guildhall, VT)

HOWLAND,
Carl E., d. 12/23/1960 at 68 in Haverhill
Clara L., d. 9/7/1907 at 52/6/10 in Piermont; housewife; married; William Nichols (Concord) and Adaline Wolcott (Charlestown, VT)

Elva Little, d. 5/29/1924 at 64/10/25 in Piermont; housewife; married;
b. Lisbon; William Little (Lyman) and Betsy Noyes

Frank, d. 12/22/1947 at 61/5/9 in Piermont; laborer; single; b.
Piermont; Lee Howland (Easton) and Clara Nichols (Lancaster)

Lee, d. 8/7/1937 at 83/2/1 in Piermont; retired farmer; widower; b.
Landaff; Samuel Howland (Landaff)

Moses N., d. 4/23/1901 at 83/1/14 in Piermont; farmer; married; b.
Landaff; Daniel Howland (Lisbon) and Betsy Stone (Lisbon)

Nathaniel H., d. 3/1/1933 at 76/7/19 in Piermont; farmer; widower; b.
Landaff; M. N. Howland (Landaff) and Phoebe Howe (Benton)

Phebe, d. 6/27/1891 at 77/4/23 in Piermont; housewife; married; b.
Benton; Peter Howe and Mary Powers

Roger, d. 3/3/1994 in N. Haverhill

William S., d. 10/6/1918 at 34/2/8 in Piermont; concretor; married; b.
Orford; Lee Howland (NH) and Clara Nichols (WSA)

HUBBARD,
Mary, d. 5/31/1928 at 78/11/16 in Concord; housewife; widow; b.
Coaticook, PQ; Joseph Pardo (Canada) and Julia ----- (Canada)

HUMPHREY,
Edmond B., d. 3/1/1916 at 57/9/8 in Piermont; farmer; married; b.
Piermont; Noah Humphrey (Croydon) and Adeline Dow (Croydon)

HUNT,
Mary R., d. 11/18/1913 at 82/2/2 in Piermont; softening of brain;
none; widow; b. Benton; Moses Mead (VT, farmer) and Mary Mathews (VT)

Roswell, d. 4/13/1901 at 72/5/5 in Piermont; farmer; married; b.
Piermont; Samuel Hunt (Charlestown) and Matilda Lull (Hartland, VT)

HURLBURT,
Clara M., d. 11/16/1956 at 99 in Piermont; retired; widow; b.
Concord; ----- Davis and ----- Mead

IZZO,
Sydney Ann, d. 2/4/2002 in Piermont

JACKSON,
Ellen M. Austin, d. 1/3/1992 in N. Haverhill
Paul W., d. 1/30/1985 in St. Albans, VT

JACOBS,
Samuel, d. 7/30/1953 at 85 in Hanover; retired; widower; b. Hungary

JENNINGS,
Daisy, d. 1/26/1974 in Hanover
Melvin, d. 7/25/1999 in Lebanon

JESSEMAN,
Arthur F., d. 3/5/1964 at 70 in Piermont
Gladys F., d. 12/2/1974 in Haverhill
Nellie, d. 10/2/1963 at 74 in Haverhill
Roger W., d. 7/18/1976 in Hanover
Stella, d. 6/11/2000 in Piermont
William A., d. 6/20/1953 at 75 in Woodsville; retired; married; b. Dorchester; Harrison Jesseman and Maria Waldron

JEWELL,
Carrie W., d. 1/8/1969 in Haverhill
Charles W., d. 3/20/1951 at 60 in Piermont; hgy. patrolman; married; b. Corinth, VT; Charles W. Jewell and Flora Page

JOHNDRO,
Ella Elvira, d. 4/25/1892 at 14/8/5 in Piermont; epileptic convulsions; student; single; b. Holland, VT; Alexander Johndro (Derby, VT) and Delia H. Elliot (Underhill, VT)

JOHNSON,
Isabella B., d. 2/24/1916 at 72/3/1 in Piermont; housekeeper; married; b. Ryegate, VT; Walter Buchanan (Scotland) and Mary Buchanan (Scotland)
Lizzie A., d. 5/30/1891 at 17/2/5 in Piermont; single; b. Newbury, VT; George Johnson (Newbury, VT) and Isabell Buchanan (Ryegate, VT)
Rob, d. 7/11/1894 at 25; found dead; laborer; single

JONES,
Frederick, d. 9/11/1959 at 57 in Hanover

Kate, d. 3/2/1900 at 41/5/2 in Piermont; housework; single; b. Springfield, VT; George Jones (Whitefield) and Loenza Ward (Springfield, VT)
Lucy, d. 10/27/1971 in Haverhill

KANIUKA,
child, d. 11/30/1960 at 22 hrs. in PA

KEELER,
Thelma B., d. 2/20/1976 in Vernon, CT

KENISTON,
Doris, d. 6/17/2004 in Woodsville
Hugh Louis, d. 12/4/1985 in Hartford, VT

KENNESON,
Pearl, d. 3/26/1972 in Hanover
Walter E., d. 1/23/1968 in Piermont

KENNEY,
Helen M., d. 1/25/1979 in Concord

KENT,
Chester A., d. 9/10/1931 at 61/0/15 in Lisbon; expressman; married; b. Randolph, VT; Horace Kent (Randolph, VT) and Lucy Snow
Eda E., d. 1/23/1896 at 46/3/29 in Piermont; pneumonia; housewife; married; b. Piermont; J. A. Emerson and Elizabeth P. Bean
Myrta E., d. 9/10/1960 at 94 in Lisbon

KENYON,
Jeanne Clara, d. 3/28/1992 in Berkeley, CA

KEYES,
Barbara A., d. 9/17/1930 at 0/0/3 in Watertown, MA; George Keyes and Pauline Hannaford (Piermont)
George E., d. 3/28/1950 at 47 in Woburn, MA; auto inv. service; married; b. Quincy, MA; Frank Keyes and Clara Hildreth

KIMBALL,
Catherine, d. 11/15/1921 at 87/10/15 in Pontiac, MI; retired; widow
Paul R., d. 5/11/1965 at 43 in Piermont

William E., d. 7/21/1926 at 60/1/11 in Haverhill; carpenter; widower; b. Lunenburg, VT; Daniel Kimball (Lunenburg, VT) and Martha Hutton (England)

KING,
Grace, d. 11/18/1975 in Northampton, MA
Lillie, d. 4/27/1951 at 64 in Hartford, CT

KINGHORN,
Clement T., d. 4/25/1946 at 41/1/16 in Piermont; plumber; married; b. Hardwick, VT; Lyman J. Kinghorn (Granby, VT) and Carrie Crowley (Barton, VT)
Meda, d. 3/16/1997 in Newbury, VT

KLEINLEIN,
Edith G., d. 7/22/1960 at 80 in Piermont

KNAPP,
Albert A., d. 7/3/1932 at 84/6/3 in Piermont; none; widower; b. Haverhill; Henry Knapp (Haverhill) and Sarah Burbank (Haverhill)
Harold P., d. 5/8/1910 at 6/5/12 in Piermont; b. Piermont; Fred Knapp (Piermont) and Ella Harris (Warren)
Irene E., d. 9/30/1922 at 63/11/25 in Haverhill; housewife; married; b. Newbury, VT; John D. Pike (Newbury, VT) and Jane Poor (Goffstown)
Ray A., d. 2/9/1954 at 62 in Concord; farmer; married; b. Piermont; Albert A. Knapp and Irene Pike

LABARRON,
Ella H., d. 10/23/1899 at 35/1/28 in Piermont; housewife; married; b. Colebrook; Harry Gould (Sharon, VT) and Melvina Fisk (Columbia)

LABELLE,
Rita Helen, d. 4/30/2002 in Laconia

LAMKIN,
Willis, d. 9/8/1895 at 25/1/6 in Piermont; typhoid fever; railroad man; married; b. Waterville, PQ; Dow Lamkin (Stratford) and Sarah A. Bass (Lancaster)

LAMONTAGNE,
  Clarence G., d. 3/6/1973 in St. Johnsbury, VT
  Etta, d. 12/27/1935 at 67 in Hanover; housewife; married; b.
    Woodstock, ME; Benjamin Kimball (Milan) and Narcissus
    Perkins (Bethel, ME)
  Gideon, d. 6/28/1943 at 90/9/24 in Haverhill; retired; widower; b.
    LaPoint, PQ; Henry LaMontagne (France) and Philamon
    LaCrosse (France)
  Jay, d. 1/24/1973 in Haverhill
  Lionel R., d. 1/5/1979 in Tamarac, FL
  Lucy, d. 5/7/1894 at 33/3/28; consumption; housewife; married; b.
    Lunenburg; Daniel Kimball (Lunenburgh) and Martha Hutton
    (England)
  Regina, d. 11/27/1993 in Ft. Lauderdale, FL
  Susie G., d. 5/20/1956 at 82 in Haverhill; housewife; married; b.
    Colebrook; Oscar Gould and Melvina Hicks

LAMPREY,
  Daniel, d. 2/24/1928 at 78/6 in Piermont; retired; single; ----- and
    Mary M. Coffin (Newburyport, MA)
  Mary M., d. 10/17/1909 at 87/7/15 in Piermont; housework; widow; b.
    Newburyport, MA; ----- Coffin and Mary Moody

LANDRY,
  Mary Metcalf, d. 11/24/1989 in Piermont

LANG,
  Cora B., d. 7/19/1953 at 89 in Piermont; retired; widow; b. Bath;
    Timothy Buck and Alice Lang

LAPIERRE,
  Almonsor, d. 3/5/1960 at 66 in Piermont

LAROCK,
  Annie M., d. 10/15/1898 at 38/5/5 in Piermont; pulmonary
    tuberculosis; domestic; married; b. Holyoke, MA; Benjamin T.
    Grover (Portsmouth) and Celia A. Todd (Jittgey Pond)

LATHE,
  William A., d. 3/11/1938 at 81/9/25 in Piermont; farmer; widower; b.
    Newport, VT

LATONA,
Frank, d. 6/21/2004 in Lebanon

LAWRENCE,
Chester Fred, d. 10/11/1943 at 70/10/18 in Piermont; laborer; single;
   b. Fairfield, VT; Charles Lawrence (Canada) and Harriet Lawrence (Sheldon, VT)
Ellen, d. 4/8/1926 at 86/10/29 in Piermont; retired; widow; b. Piermont; Uri Chandler (Piermont) and Mary A. Rogers (Lemington, VT)
Joseph, d. 1/31/1923 at 81/10/26 in Piermont; farmer; married; b. Fairlee, VT; ----- and ----- Pierce

LEARD,
Alder C., d. 6/16/1946 at 78/3/23 in Haverhill; retired; married; b. Canada; Joseph Leard (Canada) and Mary Matard (Canada)

LEARNED,
Harley William, d. 4/5/1992 in White River Jct., VT

LEAZER,
Herbert S., d. 9/26/1968 in Hanover
Sophia, d. 9/17/1904 at 98 in Piermont; widow; b. Canada
Stephen C., d. 4/25/1931 at 83/11/19 in Piermont; retired; married; b. Boston, MA; Joseph Leazer (Canada) and Sophia Clement (Canada)

LEBAR[R]ON,
Ida Bliss, d. 7/25/1925 at 70/1/27 in Piermont; domestic; widow; b. Fairlee, VT; William Bliss (Bradford, VT) and Esther Hood (Thetford, VT)
James S., d. 6/4/1901 at 71/9/4 in White River Jct., VT
William, d. 9/29/1912 at 51/6/2 in Piermont; farmer; married; b. Whitefield; James LeBaron (Cambridgeport) and ----- (Northfield, VT)

LEE,
Dorothy C., d. 7/15/1963 at 53 in Hanover
Ellen F., d. 9/29/1962 at 81 in Concord
Fred C., d. 9/8/1975 in Burlington, VT
Fred C., Jr., d. 5/15/1967 in Littleton

John C., d. 4/11/1936 at 80/1/24 in Haverhill; retired; widower; b.
　　Benton; James C. Lee (England)
Lillian Ona, d. 4/9/1926 at 69/4 in Haverhill; housewife; married; b.
　　Strafford; Wallace Johnson (NH) and Jane Curtis (NH)
Phyllis Alice, d. 8/21/2000 in S. Burlington, VT
Ruth Gertrude, d. 6/21/1985 in Haverhill

LEMAY,
son, d. 8/7/1895 at 1 in Piermont; disease of bowels; Simon Lemay
　　and Ida Stone

LEONARD,
Agnes, d. 11/15/1961 at 90 in Haverhill
George E., d. 6/8/1914 at 71/6/28 in Piermont; hypertrophy of
　　prostate botharny, operation; farmer; married; b. Ryegate, VT;
　　John Leonard (Ryegate, VT) and Rachel Nelson (Newbury, VT)
George Ernest, d. 7/6/1928 at 19/11/2 in Piermont; laborer; single; b.
　　Orford; William Leonard (Wentworth) and Ida Bailey
　　(Wakefield, MA)
George W., d. 8/8/1967 in Pt. Washington, NY
Marion Ames, d. 2/17/1999 in Alexandria, VA

LIBBEY,
Erving J., d. 11/14/1934 at 84/4/12 in Bradford, VT; retired; married;
　　b. Piermont; John A. Libbey (Warren) and Angeline Prescott
　　(Deerfield, MA)

LIBBIE,
Angeline, d. 2/14/1916 at 91/4/17 in Lisbon; retired; widow; b. White
　　Hall, NY; Joseph Prescott (Deerfield) and Rachel Abbott
　　(Deerfield)

LINTON,
George Fenton, d. 3/2/1940 at 21/10/21 in Piermont; laborer; single;
　　b. Corinth, VT; George Henry Linton (Corinth, VT) and Florence
　　B. Miles (Topsham, VT)

LITTLE,
Nellie L., d. 7/10/1928 at 63/8 in Bellows Falls, VT; housewife;
　　married; b. Piermont; Abram D. Ford (Piermont) and Eliza E.
　　Barrons (Boston, MA)

LOOMIS,
Alonzo, d. 2/14/1917 at 66/11/23 in Piermont; lumberman; single; b. Skowhegan, ME; George Loomis (Manchester) and Randella -- --- (Manchester)

LORETTE,
Bertha S., d. 11/14/1953 at 74 in Haverhill; retired; widow; b. Orford; Serah Mann and Jane Hicks

LOTHROP,
Katherine S., d. 5/10/1993 in Lebanon

LOUGEE,
Jessie M., d. 9/9/1909 at 0/1/7 in Piermont; b. Piermont
John F., d. 12/4/1906 at 85/3/4 in Piermont; laborer; widower; b. Gilmanton; John Lougee (Gilmanton) and Hoffie Gilman
Lydia A., d. 12/9/1895 at 74/1/16 in Piermont; pneumonia; housewife; married; b. Gilmanton; James Hull
O. E., d. 8/28/1896 at 45/6/18 in Piermont; consumption; housewife; married; b. Stanstead, PQ; Joseph Kemp

LOWELL,
Josiah F., d. 1/6/1929 at 90/9/21 in Piermont; ret. farmer; widower; b. Piermont; Richard Lowell (England) and Mahitable Flanders (Piermont)
Martha Grace, d. 6/6/1920 at 84/5/0 in Piermont; housewife; married; b. Piermont; Joseph McAllister (Plymouth) and Mary Muchmore (Orford)

LUCE,
son, d. 10/17/1928 at 0/0/0 in Haverhill; b. Haverhill
child, d. 6/29/1931 at – in Haverhill; b. Haverhill; Theodore Luce
Evelyn Ada, d. 11/15/1997 in Newburyport, MA
Leslie, d. 3/16/1937 at 68/7 in Haverhill; laborer; widower; b. Tunbridge, VT; Jabez Luce and Mary Clark
Rose E., d. 1/28/1931 at 54/6/8 in Haverhill; housework; married; Charles H. Hubbard and Mary Pario (Canada)

LUDMANN,
Jennie Miller, d. 10/26/1991 in Lebanon

LUKER,
Effie, d. 8/30/1932 at – at Lake Tarleton Club; chambermaid; married

LUTZ,
Dorothy A., d. 8/18/2003 in Wilder, VT
Robert, Jr., d. 5/1/2003 in Manhattan, NY
Robert Lurin, d. 4/13/1995 in Bradford, VT

LYNES,
Madeline Rose, d. 7/13/2003 in Inverness, FL

MACALLAN,
Ivis S., d. 3/4/1980 in Haverhill

MACFARLANE,
Thomas L., d. 1/17/1957 at 71 in Piermont; oil dealer; married; b. Victoria, TX; James MacFarlane and Margaret Fisher

MACK,
Delbert W., d. 4/19/1991 in Hanover

MACRI,
Frank R., d. 2/25/1994 in Piermont

MADDEN,
Leon I., d. 9/19/1959 at 76 in Piermont

MANCHESTER,
Ida Stewart, d. 9/7/1940 at 73/5 in Piermont; housewife; widow; b. Lunenburg, VT; Charles Stewart (Lunenburg, VT) and Seruah Thomas (Lunenburg, VT)
Lemuel S., d. 3/8/1946 at 49/10/11 in W. Hartford, CT; clerk; married; Frank Manchester and Ida Stewart (Lunenburg, VT)

MANNING,
Robert Douglas, d. 1/15/1991 in Hanover

MANSON,
Adella L., d. 5/3/1953 at 81 in San Francisco, CA; single

Charles, d. 8/23/1902 at 58/3/13 in Epping; turnkey; widower; b. Bradford, VT; George Manson (Corinth, VT) and Rebecca Wheaton (Hanover)

MARCHINO,
Nancy, d. 1/–/1998 in Portland, ME

MARDEN,
Amelia D., d. 8/9/1905 at 69 in Lansdale, PA; widow; b. PA; Isiah Erdmann (PA)

MARSH,
Bessie, d. 2/5/1936 at 4/4/9 in Haverhill; b. Orford; Arthur Marsh and Irene Goddard (St. Johnsbury, VT)

MARTIN,
Doris V., d. 11/20/1991 in N. Haverhill
Effie G., d. 3/8/1965 at 94 in Piermont
Erlene A., d. 11/24/1994 in Bradford, VT
Harold F., d. 8/29/1995 in Haverhill
Herbert Rufus, d. 8/27/1991 in Hartford, VT
John D., d. 1/9/1910 at 80/0/16 in Haverhill; farmer; married
Lucy A., d. 7/3/1914 at 80/9/26 in Manchester; old age; widow; b. Henniker; Elijah R. Smith (Henniker) and Lucy Woods (Henniker)
Matilda, d. 12/17/1919 at 88/8/18 in Haverhill; domestic; widow

MASON,
Wayne, d. 11/21/1971 in Haverhill

MATTOON,
Grace M., d. 1/23/1950 at 74 in Barre, VT; housewife; widow; b. Piermont; Harvey Gannett

MAXFIELD,
Albert D., d. 3/14/1963 at 68 in Hanover
Dale W., d. 8/23/1930 at 0/0/6 in Woodsville; b. Woodsville; Albert Maxfield (Wolcott, VT) and E. Irene Smith (Stanford, CT)
Laura M., d. 10/8/1918 at 23/4/29 in Woodsville; housewife; married; b. Salisbury; Frank B. Merrill (Ireland) and Mary A. Lillie (Ireland)

Pauline Isabel, d. 10/3/1918 at 2/3/4 in Piermont; b. Woodsville;
   Albert A. Maxfield (Wolcott, VT) and Laura M. Merrill (Salisbury)
Richard, d. 5/4/1928 at 0/0/7 in Woodsville; b. Woodsville; Albert
   Maxfield (Wolcott, VT) and Ethlyn Smith (Stamford, CT)

MAXWELL,
Darrell J., d. 7/25/1998 in Newport, VT

MAY,
Eliza, d. 3/29/1891 at 78/3/16 in Piermont; housewife; widow; b.
   Orford; William Muchmore (Pembroke) and Mehitable Nelson
   (Allentown)

MAYNARD,
Martha, d. 6/17/1912 at 63/7/4 in Piermont; housekeeper; widow; b.
   NY; ----- Smead and Abigail Richardson

McCANN,
Grace Elizabeth, d. 5/21/1988 in Piermont

McDONALD,
Alice, d. 10/19/1974 in Hanover
Eben M., d. 4/29/1966 at 69 in Haverhill
Winifred, d. 9/13/1963 at 28 in Hanover

McLAM,
Norman Gordon, d. 7/20/1988 in Brevard, FL

McNEIL,
John, d. 9/16/1968 in Woodsville

McTAGUE,
Robert J., d. 1/6/1966 at 79 in Hanover

McTAQUE,
Elizabeth, d. 6/4/1994 in Warwick, RI

MEAD,
Horace Y., d. 2/1/1909 at 69/9/29 in Piermont; laborer; single; b.
   Piermont; Moses Mead (VT) and Mary Matthews (VT)

MEADE,
Julia A., d. 2/22/1920 at 95/0/20 in Bradford, VT; widow

MELLIN,
Kenneth B., d. 7/8/1969 in Hanover
Marjorie Bates, d. 9/23/1988 in Bradford, VT

MESSER,
Dan Y., Jr., d. 5/13/1899 at 44/4 in Salem City, MO; commercial agent; single; b. Piermont; Dan Y. Messer (Piermont) and Eliza Bean (Piermont)

METCALF,
Burgess C., d. 3/22/1914 at 75/7/17 in Piermont; cerebral meningitis; farmer; widower; b. Piermont; John Metcalf (Piermont) and Jerusha Bliss (VT)
Caroline, d. 8/16/1948 at 76/2/20 in Hanover; housewife; widow; b. Orford; Edward Grimes (Orford) and Amanda Davis (Benton)
Eva J., d. 12/10/1949 at 82 in Haverhill; retired; single; b. Piermont; Burgess Metcalf and Mary Messer
John Peasley, d. 5/13/1936 at 66/0/1 in Piermont; farmer; married; b. Piermont; Burgess Metcalf (Piermont) and Mary Messer (Piermont)
Mary, d. 7/25/1900 at 57/3/22 in Piermont; domestic; married; b. Piermont; Peasley Messer (Bow) and Hannah Ford (Bradford, VT)
Shirley S., d. 10/16/1967 in Haverhill

MICHENFELDER,
Barbara Anne, d. 8/12/2002 in Woodsville
Hazel, d. 2/17/2004 in Piermont
Jacob Adam, d. 6/15/2002 in Piermont
Robert, d. 5/12/2004 in Piermont

MILES,
Dale M., d. 10/28/1996 in Winsted, CT
Flora, d. 8/29/1969 in Haverhill

MILLER,
daughter, d. 8/2/1949 at – in Haverhill; b. Haverhill; Ernest Miller and Dora Corrow

MITCHELL,
Helen R., d. 5/8/1973 in Hanover

MOLWAY,
Belle, d. 10/30/1933 at 75/5/5 in Piermont; retired; widow; b. Fairlee, VT; William Bliss (VT) and Esther Reed (VT)

MOORE,
Cary Jerome, d. 11/2/1946 at 16/2/7 in Bradford, VT; student; single; b. Woodsville; Joseph Moore (S. Hadley, MA) and Elizabeth Robertson (Hoboken, NJ)
Elizabeth R., d. 4/9/1980 in Haverhill
Enos W., d. 11/5/1956 at 81 in Malden, MA; dentist; married; b. Bolton, CT; William E. B. Moore and Marion D. Witter
Joseph H., d. 2/13/1966 at 81 in Haverhill
Olin C., d. 5/13/1931 at 73/0/24 in Laconia; RR accountant; widower; b. Brooklyn, NY; Daniel G. Moore
Sarah May, d. 12/27/1925 at 70/11/26 in Laconia; housewife; married; b. Bradford, VT; Eleazer P. Andross (Bradford, VT) and Sarah Whitcomb (Troy, VT)

MOREY,
Ruth M., d. 4/13/1960 at 71 in Bristol, CT

MORGAN,
Jackson, d. 1/19/1960 at 53 in Brockton, MA

MORRILL,
Beulah B., d. 1/18/1980 in Haverhill
Charles R., d. 5/20/1986 in Piermont
Frederick, d. 11/28/1936 at 45/5/4 in Piermont; farmer; married; b. White Rock, RI; Eben Morrill (Durham, PQ) and Nancy Holt (Millbury, MA)
Janette, d. 1/14/1939 at 74/2/28 in Piermont; teacher; single; b. Beaver Dam, WI; Alfred Morrill (Danville, VT) and Lucia Wheeler (Barnston, PQ)
Marshall B., d. 6/29/1914 at 0/0/19 in Piermont; spina bifida; b. Piermont; Frederick Morrill (White Rock, RI) and Beulah Brown (Haverhill)
Phillip Conrad, d. 3/25/1985 in New London

MORRIS,
Edna A., d. 1/15/1923 at 12/7/4 in Piermont; student; b. Haverhill; Edward J. Morris (E. Fairfield, VT) and Daisy Stevens (Franklin)

MORRISON,
Horace Eugene, d. 4/22/1937 at 70/0/2 in Piermont; contractor; married; b. Haverhill; Horace H. Morrison (Roxbury, MA) and Dorcas Huckins (Warren)
Ida M., d. 6/16/1950 at 82 in Piermont; housewife; widow; b. Corinth, VT; Lyman M. Rabie and Eunice Coffran

MORSE,
Anna O., d. 4/22/1907 at 62/7/10 in Piermont; housewife; married; b. New York, NY; Abram Coons (Quacken Kill, NY) and Mary M. Baisam (Quacken Kill)
Elizabeth L., d. 6/11/1892 at 66/11/3 in Piermont; found dead in chair; lady; single; b. Piermont; Antony Morse (Hanover) and Electa Russell Morse (Hanover)
Franklin, d. 5/23/1926 at 51/0/14 in Piermont; farmer; married; b. Sutton, PQ; Rommer Morse (Sutton, PQ) and Annie D. Coons (Franklin, VT)
Martin, d. 3/15/1919 at 0/0/0 in Piermont; b. Piermont; Franklin A. Morse (Sutton, PQ) and Susie M. Winn (Haverhill)
Romina, d. 5/31/1914 at 69/11/25 in Piermont; apoplexy; farmer; widower; b. Sillen, Canada; Nehemiah Morse (Canada) and Sarah Hadlock (Canada)

MOULTON,
Elmore, d. 3/7/1930 at 69 in Hanover; single

MUCHMORE,
Daniel C., d. 10/26/1951 at 83 in Piermont; farmer; widower; b. Orford; Henry Muchmore
Elvira R., d. 11/26/1905 at 70 in Bradford, VT; dressmaker; single; b. Orford; Jeremiah Muchmore and ----- Goodwin
Henry S., d. 4/26/1919 at 83/6/22 in Piermont; farmer; married; b. Concord; James Muchmore (Orford) and Sarah J. Buntin (Dunbarton)
Jennie Mae, d. 7/13/1924 at 41/6/18 in Piermont; housewife; married; b. E. Orange, VT; Henry Morse (Peacham, VT) and Mary Eastman (E. Orange, VT)

Sally M., d. 4/22/1926 at 88/4/13 in Piermont; retired; widow; b. Warren; Daniel Chase (Meredith) and Lavina Clement (Warren)

MUDGETT,
Emily A., d. 1/1/1911 at 54/5/24 in Piermont; housewife; married; b. Haverhill; Daniel W. Day (Parsonsfield, ME) and Hanna B. Gould (Cape Breton)

MUELLER,
Myron M., d. 6/28/1995 in Piermont

MUGFORD,
Fred S., d. 11/21/1951 at 61 in Norwich, VT; married
Lucy, d. 6/17/1950 at 58 in Barre, VT; housewife; married; b. CT; Will F. Tarbox and Castaria Fuller

MURPHY,
Robert B., d. 7/29/1994 in Sebring, FL

MUSTY,
Alberta P., d. 1/18/1991 in Piermont
Alfred, d. 2/17/1959 at 67 in Haverhill
Edgar, d. 11/28/2004 in Piermont
Robert G., d. 2/8/1987 in Piermont

MYATT,
Mary, d. 3/18/1895 at 60 in Piermont; found dead in bed; widow; b. Canada; ----- Cook

NELSON,
Nels Martin, d. 7/4/1947 at 72/2/19 in Piermont; laborer; divorced; b. Providence, RI; Ola Nelson (Oslo, Norway) and Henrietta Olson (Oslo, Norway)

NICHOLS,
Charles E., d. 9/13/1898 at 20/5/16 in Orford; ac. pul. tuberculosis; single; b. Haverhill; William A. Nichols (Hopkinton) and Jannett R. Wolcott (Charlestown)
William A., d. 9/29/1895 at 63/6/11 in Bradford, VT; pneumonia; wheelwright

NOYES,

George Henry, d. 1/10/1964 at 59 in Piermont
George Henry, Sr., d. 7/16/1940 at 69/10/11 in Piermont; farmer; widower; b. Haverhill; Benjamin Noyes (Pembroke) and Mary Wheeler (Haverhill)
Hannah, d. 2/11/1895 at 78/8 in Piermont; old age; single; Isaac Noyes
Keith A., d. 8/24/1963 at 2 in Claremont
Woodrow, Jr., d. 2/18/2004 in Claremont
Woodrow W., d. 9/12/1974 in Haverhill

NUTT,

Elizabeth, d. 4/19/1909 at 66/1/26 in Piermont; housekeeper; single; b. Topsham, VT; Nathaniel Nutt (Topsham, VT) and Mary Orr
Henry H., d. 3/2/1932 at 73/10/15 in Piermont; farmer; single; b. Newbury, VT; Elizabeth Nutt

O'CONNOR,

James W., d. 3/12/1987 in Piermont

OAKES,

Glen W., d. 5/24/1975 in Haverhill
Virginia, d. 1/27/2004 in Piermont

ORR,

Clinton, d. 2/5/1936 at 51/1/5 in Piermont; laborer; widower; b. Dixville, PQ; Thomas Orr (Dixville, PQ)

OWEN,

Robert L., Jr., d. 12/20/1992 in St. Johnsbury, VT
Winifred R., d. 4/1/1991 in Haverhill

PALMER,

Chestina A., d. 2/29/1928 at 76/6/6 in Boston, MA; artist; single; b. Orford; Henry H. Palmer (Orford) and Rosette Quint (Orford)
Richard S., d. 5/23/1927 at 0/6/0 in Haverhill; b. Woodsville; Wenlock Palmer (Haverhill) and Martha Day (Piermont)
Sabria B., d. 7/15/1898 at 67/9/17 in Piermont; cancer of pancreas; domestic; married; Samuel Brown (Lyme) and Ruth Snow (Lyme)

PARKER,
Eunice L., d. 10/5/1969 in Haverhill

PEABODY,
Frank, d. 5/30/1909 at 46/2/7 in Piermont; laborer; single; b. Concord, ME; Lemuel Peabody

PEETS,
Charles Edmunt, d. 6/28/1962 at 67 in Hanover

PENNOCK,
Joel, d. 6/8/1910 at 81/7 in Haverhill; farmer; widower; b. Haverhill; Nathaniel Pennock and Betsey Clark

PERCY,
Sarah M. J., d. 4/6/1968 in Haverhill

PERKINS,
Bertha May, d. 5/18/1940 at 73/9/15 in Piermont; housewife; married; b. Greensboro, VT; Hiram Stone (Claremont) and Susan Lowell (Hatley, PQ)
Edgar Evans, d. 12/9/1942 at 77/7/5 in Piermont; ret. farmer; widower; b. Walden, VT; Charles Perkins (Stannard, VT) and Ruth Jackson (Wheelock, VT)
Glen, d. 7/22/2002 in Rutland City, VT
Ralph C., d. 7/2/1963 at 73 in Haverhill

PETERS,
Alice, d. 9/11/1962 at 88 in Lyme

PETTINGALE,
infant, d. 12/17/1919 at 0/0/0 in Hanover; b. Hanover Hospital; F. J. Petingale and ----- Bowker (Piermont)
Franz J., d. 4/22/1971 in Los Angeles, CA
Lucy B., d. 4/21/1956 at 57 in Wayland, MA; married; b. Piermont; Francis P. Bowker and Dora Underhill

PHELPS,
Eliza, d. 6/10/1903 at 82/3/9 in Wentworth; housekeeper; widow; b. Paris, ME; Tilden Badett and Elizabeth Buell

James, d. 1/4/1901 at 71/9/14 in Wentworth; farmer; married; b. Piermont; ----- (NH)

Sidney W., d. 2/20/1925 at 62 in Boston, MA; laborer; single; b. Piermont; Merrill Phelps (Piermont) and Emma Fisher (Haverhill)

PIERCE,
Helen Dennis, d. 9/19/1927 at 77/11/26 in Norwich, VT; retired; widow; b. Stratford; William Dennis (Stratford) and Lucebee Curtis (Stratford)

PIERSON,
Amos F., d. 3/18/2000 in Woodsville
Ernest, d. 8/27/1961 at 82 in Haverhill
Lawrence, d. 2/18/1988 in Bradford, VT
Nettie R., d. 2/18/1932 at 46/3/15 in Orford; married

PIKE,
John D., d. 1/16/1903 at 80/11/2 in Piermont; farmer; married; b. Haverhill; Isaac Pike and Irene Dole
Kenneth E., d. 7/4/1969 in Piermont

PILLSBURY,
David B., d. 12/11/1914 at 76 in Chattanooga, TN; angina pectoris; none; widower; b. Piermont; David T. Pillsbury (Candia) and Sally Bean (Piermont)
Edward, d. 7/21/1932 at 73/10 in Haverhill; none; single; b. Piermont; William Pillsbury and Mary A. Stanley (Haverhill)

PLANT,
Herbert M., d. 1/8/1955 at 32 in Haverhill; laborer - saw mill; married; b. Haverhill; Herbert L. Plant and Violet Coffin

PLATT,
James, d. 5/10/1901 at 75/6/6 in Piermont; widower; b. England; Harry Platt (Birmingham, England) and Mary Harnwell (Birmingham, England)

POLAND,
Lavina Anna, d. 4/20/1945 at 72/9/15 in Charlestown; housewife; widow; b. Liverpool, England

POOLER,
Chester E., d. 1/10/1958 at 76 in Lyme; laborer; divorced; b.
   Highgate, VT; John Pooler and Ann Rood
Harry, d. 7/26/1972 in Haverhill
Truman, d. 3/19/1963 at 75 in Barre, VT

PORFIDO,
Marjorie A., d. 6/29/2003 in Lebanon

PORTER,
A. B., d. 1/1/1937 at 70 in Haverhill; stone mason

PRATT,
Betsey B., d. 1/12/1898 at 70/9/12 in Piermont; bronchial
   pneumonia; domestic; married; Simon Underhill and Mary G.
   Bagley

PROSHEK,
Emil, d. 11/14/1987 in Bradford, VT
Emma Klein, d. 3/3/1983 in Piermont

PROSL,
Charles, d. 6/23/1944 at 65/2/2 in Piermont; poultry farmer; married;
   b. Tulo, Austria; Hillorymey Prosl (Austria) and Francisco
   Purflinger (Austria)

PROVOST,
Dorothy Anna, d. 10/31/1996 in Woodsville
Norman Rene, d. 9/2/1998 in Haverhill

PUSHEE,
Richard Wells, d. 2/22/1996 in Ryegate, VT

PUTNAM,
Carrie Carleton, d. 6/12/1942 at 80/4/18 in Piermont; retired; widow;
   b. Newbury, VT; George W. Carleton (Newbury, VT) and
   Deborah Huckins (Strafford)
G. William, d. 1/10/1983 in Piermont
George W., d. 11/15/1937 at 75/9/23 in Piermont; retired farmer;
   married; b. W. Newbury, VT; William K. Putnam (W. Newbury,
   VT) and Lucinda Fleming (Newbury, VT)

Gladys Chesley Emery, d. 1/27/1983 in Piermont
Jasper E., d. 6/1/1998 in Haverhill
Marion C., d. 2/15/1962 at 66 in Hanover

QUINT,
Hosea, d. 1/17/1899 at 82/10/24 in Piermont; farmer; married; b. Orford; Samuel Quint and Rosana Stebbins
Prudence R., d. 2/8/1909 at 77/5/5 in Piermont; none; widow; b. Henniker; Elijah R. Smith (Henniker) and Lucy Woods (Henniker)

RAMSEY,
Alexander, d. 1/8/1934 at 66/5/7 in Piermont; stone cutter; married; b. PEI; Neal Ramsey (PEI) and Sarah Ann Wallace (Scotland)
George, d. 4/24/1925 at 74/1/24 in Bradford, VT; farmer; single; b. Piermont; Daniel Ramsey (Piermont) and Mary Culver (Hill)
Harold, d. 3/2/1930 at 25/10/4 in Woodsville; mill foreman; single; b. Piermont; Alexander Ramsey (Canada) and Josephine Neucrumb (Canada)

RAND,
Ella, d. 11/7/1897 at 32/8/17 in Piermont; phleg. erysipelas; housekeeper; widow; b. Royalton, VT; Edward G. Davis and Alma A. Green

RANNEY,
Elsie E., d. 2/11/1932 at 80/0/30 in Fitchburg, MA; widow
Frank, d. 12/24/1936 at 75/3/23 in Fitchburg, MA
Orlana, d. 6/28/1950 at 64 in Fitchburg, MA; school teacher; single

RAPER,
Leona R., d. 1/19/2001 in Woodsville

RATLIFF,
Juanita C., d. 6/5/1993 in Hartford, VT

REARDON,
Herbert A., d. 9/23/1998 in Piermont

RENEAU,
Charles, d. 11/1/1980 in Haverhill

George Henry, d. 2/26/1935 at 82/8/25 in Piermont; cab. maker; divorced; b. Adams, MA; Charles Alfred Reneau (PQ) and Matilda Parker (Campton, PQ)

RISLEY,
Lewis E., d. 2/7/1901 at 76/7/26 in Piermont; stone cutter; widower; b. Hanover; Asa Risley (Hanover) and Severah Kendrick (Thetford, VT)
Robert L., d. 6/16/1935 at 83/10/19 in Piermont; retired; widower; b. Hanover; Lewis E. Risley (Hanover) and Emily Evans (Piermont)
Sadie A., d. 7/2/1931 at 72/8/10 in Bradford, VT; retired; married

RITCHIE,
George, d. 4/27/2003 in N. Haverhill
Helen, d. 1/22/2004 in Lebanon
Joseph B., d. 3/30/1944 at 71/2/27 in Haverhill; laborer; single; b. Derby, VT; William H. Ritchie (Scotland) and Melissa Moon
Nellie M., d. 11/18/1944 at 60/11/10 in Hanover; housewife; married; b. Ryegate, VT; George P. Sanderson (Peacham, VT) and Alice M. Lowe (Ryegate, VT)
Robert Duncan, d. 9/21/1941 at 16/4/18 in Piermont; student; single; b. Bradford, VT; Tait Ritchie (New York City) and Nellie M. Sanderson (Ryegate, VT)
Tait M., d. 9/15/1950 at 64 in Piermont; farmer; married; b. New York, NY; D. McKerrocher and Jeannie Tait

RIVERS,
Frank, d. 8/17/1953 at 91 in Piermont; retired; widower; b. London, England; William Rivers and Jane Cummings

RIX,
Jesse L., d. 10/20/1938 at 76/0/7 in Piermont; farmer; widower; b. Canada; William P. Rix (VT) and Victoria Sorrell (Canada)

ROBBINS,
Eugene B., d. 8/31/1979 in Haverhill
Florence Smith, d. 12/28/1999 in Haverhill

ROBERTSON,
James Walter, d. 9/4/1990 in Piermont

Paul H., d. 11/27/2000 in N. Haverhill

ROBIE,
Eunice A., d. 12/24/1910 at 67/2/6 in Piermont; housewife; married; b. Piermont; Mark Coffren and Susan J. Cilley (Nottingham)
Freeman A., d. 3/20/1933 at 70/3/27 in Piermont; farmer; widower; b. Corinth, VT; Lyman M. Robie (Corinth, VT) and Marinda Avery (Corinth, VT)
Gwendolyn D., d. 9/30/1957 at 53 in Bradford, VT; housewife; married; b. Bradford, VT; Ellis Shumway and Adella -----
Lyman Edward, d. 12/5/1957 at 57 in Bradford, VT; farmer; widower; b. Piermont; Freeman Robie and Mary Grimes
Lyman M., d. 7/11/1915 at 78/1/22 in Fairlee, VT; farmer; married; b. Corinth, VT; Jonathan Robie (Candia) and Eleanor Wilson (Methuen, MA)
Mary H., d. 2/3/1925 at 57/10/25 in Piermont; housewife; married; b. Orford; Edward E. Grimet (Orford) and Amanda F. Davis (Benton)
Timothy A., d. 7/17/1971 in Hanover
Verna T., d. 6/12/2003 in Lebanon

ROBINSON,
Charles, d. 9/20/1914 at 79/2/8 in Piermont; valvular disease of heart; farmer; married; b. Piermont; James E. Robinson and Cynthia Crook
Charles A., d. 2/10/1968 in Concord
Effie M. H., d. 2/8/1916 at 23/10/16 in Hanover; housewife; married; b. Haverhill; Edmond B. Humphrey (Piermont) and Mattie M. Clark (Vershire, VT)
Eliza Anne, d. 3/14/1954 at 76 in Piermont; housewife; married; b. London, England; John R. Lee and Eliza Herbert
Ellen F., d. 11/22/1941 at 92/8/5 in Piermont; re. housekeeper; widow; b. Orford; Frederick Clough (Washington, VT) and Arabelle Sanborn (Washington, VT)
Frederick Charles, d. 8/10/1966 at 83 in Laconia
Iva A., d. 2/24/1978 in Franklin
James, d. 1/22/1903 at 69/9/10 in Hospital; farmer; single; b. Piermont; James Robinson
Philip G., d. 4/16/1971 in Haverhill

RODIMON,
Alice L., d. 7/31/1914 at 1/1 in Piermont; typhoid pneumonia; b. Piermont; Amos L. Rodimon (Piermont) and Grace Hood (Randolph, VT)
Amos, d. 1/26/1937 at 50/8/14 in Plymouth; farmer; married; b. Piermont; Charles H. Rodiman (Piermont) and Hattie Willey
Amos B., d. 10/10/1892 at 70/7 in Piermont; marasmus; farmer; married; b. Piermont; Amos Rodimon (Piermont) and Sarah Hamlet (Newbury, VT)
Annie F., d. 11/14/1973 in Woodsville
Charles E., d. 8/9/1972 in Piermont
Charles H., d. 7/28/1928 at 73/2 in Piermont; farmer; widower; b. Piermont; Amos B. Rodimon (Piermont) and Lucy A. Ladd (Goffstown)
Fletcher, d. 3/22/1908 at 0/0/27 in Piermont; b. Piermont; Amos L. Rodimon (Piermont) and Grace Hood (Randolph, VT)
Frank W., Sr., d. 10/22/1996 in Lebanon
Gertrude H., d. 10/16/1906 at 34/6 in Piermont; housewife; married; b. Craftsbury, VT; Joseph Ladeau (Colchester, VT) and Elizabeth Ladeau
Grace E., d. 7/7/1969 in Franklin
Inez F., d. 2/27/1962 at 76 in Chicago, IL
Kenneth P., d. 11/10/1923 at 14/1/18 in Wentworth; student; b. Piermont; Amos L. Rodiman (Piermont) and Grace E. Hood (Randolph, VT)
Lucy A., d. 1/2/1908 at 85/3/27 in Wentworth; retired; widow; b. Salem, MA; Timothy Ladd and Mary Lane
Mary E., d. 9/6/1896 at 38/6/4 in Bradford, VT; consumption; housewife; married; b. Somerville, MA; Abram Ford and Eliza Burrows
Rodney M., d. 3/10/1931 at 82/7/10 in Bradford, VT; retired; widower; b. Piermont; Amos Rodimon (Piermont) and Lucy A. Ladd (Salem, MA)
Walter J., d. 1/5/1901 at 1/6 in Piermont; b. Piermont; Charles Rodimon (Piermont) and Gertrude Ladeau (Craftsbury, VT)

ROGERS,
Albert, d. 5/18/1902 at 67/1/18 in Los Angeles; farmer; married; b. Piermont; Elisha Rogers (Piermont) and Matilda Barrows (Piermont)

Albert E., d. 1/20/1951 at 83 in Hanover; retired; married; b.
    Piermont; Albert Rogers and Anna Underhill
Anna C., d. 11/24/1934 at 91/2/25 in Haverhill; retired; widow; b.
    Piermont; Stephen Underhill (Piermont) and Sarah Ann
    Stevens (Piermont)
Lillian M., d. 4/22/1927 at 57/9/10 in Newport; housewife; married; b.
    W. Rutland, VT; Robert A. Evans (Piermont) and Abbie
    Mattison (Honesdale, PA)
Moses C., d. 1/20/1905 at 91/5/4 in Piermont; farmer; widower; b.
    Newbury, VT; Charles Rogers (Orange, VT) and Betsy Cooper
    (Orange, VT)
Paul K., d. 7/27/1984 in Haverhill
Sarah T., d. 3/16/1903 at 93/1/25 in Piermont; housekeeper; single;
    b. Newbury, VT; Charles Rogers (Orange, VT) and Betsey
    Cooper (Orange, VT)

ROLLINS,
Emma, d. 4/6/1906 at 0/3/20 in Piermont; b. Orford; William Rollins
    (Orford) and Emma Durant (Topsham, VT)

ROOT,
Cynthia, d. 7/5/1895 at 81 in Peacham, VT; apoplexy

ROTHMANSKY,
Maud A., d. 12/16/1985 in Laconia

ROY,
daughter, d. 12/6/1895 at – in Piermont; premature birth; b.
    Piermont; Will Roy (Canada) and Lillian Lamontagne (Dalton)
Lillian P., d. 12/7/1895 at 19/0/13 in Piermont; angina pectoris;
    housewife; married; b. Dalton; Jeddie Lamontagne (Canada)
    and Lucy Kimball

RUNNELLS,
Arthur, d. 3/22/1894 at 87/3/24; old age; farmer; widower; b.
    Haverhill; Nathaniel Runnells (Lisbon) and Polly Merrill
    (Haverhill, MA)

RUSH,
Charles, d. 1/12/1899 at 86/9/3 in Enfield; farmer; widower; b.
    England; John Rush (England)

Herbert, d. 1/26/1937 at 57/10/11 in Haverhill; laborer; married; b. Orford; John Rush

RUTLEDGE,
Jasper C., d. 6/2/1964 at 71 in Piermont

SACHS,
Manuel S., d. 7/12/1941 at 39/4/5 in Piermont; lawyer; single; b. New Haven, CT; Max G. Sachs (Russia) and Janie Bishna (Russia)

SALADINO,
Mary, d. 9/30/1973 in Piermont
Peter, d. 4/19/2004 in Hartford, VT

SANDERS,
Minnie, d. 11/16/1933 at 67/4/7 in Piermont; retired; widow; b. Worcester, VT; Albert Crone (Worcester, VT) and Pamelia Smith (VT)

SANDERSON,
Frank P., d. 11/26/1909 at 33/8/18 in Piermont; machinist; married; b. Cambridgeport, MA; Simeon Sanderson (Brighton, MA) and Georgiana Seavey (Natick, MA)

SANTANOCITA,
Catherine, d. 4/3/1996 in Haverhill

SANTOS,
Antonio, d. 6/25/1972 in Piermont

SARGENT,
Frances H., d. 8/30/1947 at 83 in Spokane, WA; retired
Mary A., d. 10/11/1911 at 80 in Grand Jct., CO; retired; widow; b. Piermont; Stephen Bean and Polly Brickett

SAWYER,
Alice B., d. 2/14/1970 in Haverhill
Elizabeth, d. 4/30/1915 at 82 in Cambridge, IN; teacher; single; b. Piermont; Joseph Sawyer and Mary Dale Sawyer (Canaan)
Maynard E., d. 11/17/1955 at 43 in Piermont; farm laborer; married; b. Piermont; Milo Sawyer and Alice Rodimon

Milo, d. 2/21/1948 at 75/11/27 in Haverhill; farmer; married; b. E. Topsham, VT; Alvah Sawyer (England) and Eliza Hood (Topsham, VT)
Wesley Milo, d. 1/13/1986 in Haverhill

SAYERS,
John Henry, d. 5/23/1951 at 0/0/5 in Haverhill; b. Haverhill; Raymond Sayers and Evelyn Wheelock

SCANLON,
Debbie Ann, d. 5/26/1998 in Haverhill

SCHMID,
John, d. 2/4/1994 in Lebanon
Louise, d. –/–/1998

SCRUTON,
Lois E., d. 3/30/1965 at 38 in Haverhill

SEARCH,
Florence, d. 3/7/2002 in Lebanon

SEPESSY,
Antonie, d. 9/18/1967 in Hanover
Henry F., d. 9/3/1952 at 68 in Hanover; retired; married; b. New York City; John Sepessy and Anna -----
Henry L., d. 12/7/1970 in Piermont

SHELDON,
Charles Harold, d. 3/26/1989 in Piermont
Elizabeth H., d. 1/3/1974 in Haverhill

SHEPARDSON,
George W., d. 11/22/1925 at 71/4/10 in Piermont; retired; married; b. Warwick, MA; Peter Shepardson (MA)

SHULT,
Carrie M., d. 3/8/1965 at 76 in Piermont

SIMONS,
Albert, d. 6/3/1900 at 58/0/4 in Piermont; farmer; married; b. Orford; Royal Simons (Piermont) and Theta Eggleston (Burke, VT)
Augustus M., d. 9/24/1946 at 79/9/3 in Piermont; wood worker; married; b. Orford; Albert Simons (Orford) and Laura Wilcox (Orford)
Etta B., d. 9/24/1949 at 69/6/15 in Piermont; housewife; widow; b. Laconia; Stephen Bartlett and Alma
Laura Wilcox, d. 11/30/1919 at 82/10 in Orford; domestic; widow; b. Orford; William Wilcox (Thetford) and Elvira Downs (Thetford)
William W., d. 8/1/1924 at 59 in Hanover; farmer; single; b. Orford; Albert Simons (Orford) and Laura Wilcox (Orford)

SIMPSON,
Ama Stickney, d. 4/28/1918 at 81/1/18 in Piermont; retired; widow; b. Millington, PQ; Jedediah Stickney (Millington, PQ) and Nancy Randall (Millington, PQ)
Carrie M., d. 11/29/1974 in Haverhill
Elsie, d. 4/4/1979 in Berlin, VT
George T., d. 12/23/1906 at 75/7/10 in Piermont; farmer; single; b. Orford; Joseph S. Simpson (Orford) and Mary Hobbs (Warren)
John B., d. 6/3/1972 in Haverhill
John Frank, d. 7/9/1942 at 70/1/4 in Haverhill; carpenter; married; b. Piermont; William C. Simpson (Orford) and Anna Stickney (Orford)
John Ralph, d. 11/11/1957 at 62 in Piermont; RFD carrier; married; b. Piermont; John F. Simpson and Lillian Marden
Lillian Marden, d. 7/5/1949 at 74/7/2 in Haverhill; housewife; widow; b. Haverhill; Lyman Marden and Emma Day
Lois Pearl, d. 4/1/1915 at 16/10/5 in Piermont; student; single; b. Piermont; John F. Simpson (Piermont) and Lillian M. Marden (Haverhill)
Maude B., d. 5/19/1965 at 74 in St. Johnsbury, VT
William C., d. 6/9/1901 at 75/7/26 in Piermont; carpenter; married; b. Orford; Joseph Simpson (Orford) and Mary Habbs (Warren)

SINCLAIR,
Avice M., d. 10/25/1966 at 80 in Piermont

SMITH,
son, d. 12/2/1911 at – in Piermont; b. Piermont; Loren G. Smith (Piermont) and Emma Ryalls (Manchester)
Addie E., d. 3/31/1986 in Danvers, MA
Albion L., Sr., d. 2/7/1964 at 70 in Danvers, MA
Anson Aulay, Jr., d. 12/17/1919 at 0/4/12 in Piermont; b. Piermont; Anson A. Smith (Piermont) and Viola N. Scott (FL)
Arvilla H., d. 1/2/1914 at 84/10/11 in Bradford, VT; chronic bronchitis; none; widow; b. Barnston, PQ; Samuel Hill (Portsmouth) and Mary Heath
Bertha, d. 8/5/1943 at 52/10/3 in Piermont; housewife; married; b. Montgomery, VT; Levi Paronto (Enosburg, VT) and Estella Deuso (Montgomery, VT)
Edward O., d. 8/5/1974 in Haverhill
Edward H., d. 9/16/1951 at 66 in Piermont; laborer; widower; b. McIndoes, VT; William Smith and Katherine Wright
Emma E., d. 12/2/1950 at 73 in Piermont; housewife; married; b. Trout Brook, Canada; William Lunnie and Margaret Ricker
Everett George, d. 4/15/1929 at 0/3 in Piermont; b. Hanover; George F. Smith (Stannard, VT) and Bertha C. Paronto (Montgomery, VT)
Floyd L., d. 9/5/1983 in Hanover
George F., d. 2/9/1959 at 75 in Jacksonville, FL
George H., d. 1/21/1902 at 78/4/9 in Piermont; farmer; married; b. Peacham, VT; Ezekiel Smith and Hannah Ingalls
George N., d. 1/9/1934 at 68/2/5 in Piermont; laborer; widower; b. PQ; James Smith (England) and Mary Priest (Coventry, VT)
Gordon Winston, d. 12/7/1927 at 0/0/5 in Piermont; b. Piermont; George F. Smith (Stannard, VT) and Bertha Paronto (Montgomery, VT)
Harvey W., d. 2/26/1919 at 76/1/10 in Piermont; farmer; married; b. Haverhill; Anson A. Smith (Weathersfield, VT) and Mary Rice (Weathersfield, VT)
Ida E., d. 12/4/1933 at 66 in Lunenburg, VT; housewife; married
Jennie M., d. 7/31/1929 at 56/1/11 in Piermont; housewife; married; b. Duddsville, PQ; Thomas C. Orr (PQ) and Stella V. Underwood (VT)
Kenneth W., d. 1/2/1930 at 18/3/13 in Piermont; farmer; single; b. Walden, VT; George F. Smith (Stannard, VT) and Bertha Laronto (Montgomery, VT)

Mahala, d. 3/11/1896 at 78/6/17 in Piermont; la grippe; married; b.
    Warren; Daniel Patch and Betsy Hall
Pearl W., d. 12/6/2002 in Haverhill

SPALDING,
John, d. 3/19/1919 at 86/6/9 in Weirs; retired; married; b. Plainfield;
    Josiah Spalding (Plainfield) and Hannah Cole (Plainfield)

SPAULDING,
Jane, d. 6/6/1910 at 77/2/4 in Weirs; housewife; married; b. Orford;
    Parker Felch (Sandwich) and Hannah Gould (Canaan)

SPENCER,
Hugh Edward, d. 10/19/1984 in Hartford, VT
Nehimiah, d. 5/31/1901 at 60/7/2 in Piermont; mason; married; b.
    Piermont; Nehimiah Spencer (NY) and Ruth Carr

SPRAGUE,
John R., d. 6/17/1972 in Haverhill

STANLEY,
Abbie C., d. 1/25/1912 at 76/0/10 in Piermont; none; widow; b.
    Lyme; Joel Hosford and Alice Kendrick
Althea M., d. 1/5/1918 at 44/0/2 in Piermont; housewife; married; b.
    Groton, VT; Isaac Wilson (Groton, VT) and Caroline E. Heath
    (Groton, VT)
Elizabeth B., d. 6/28/1916 at 92/9/23 in Piermont; housewife; widow;
    b. Troy, VT; John Flint and Elizabeth Balch
George W., d. 10/15/1905 at 67/3/17 in Piermont; laborer; married;
    b. Piermont; Jonathan Stanley (Amherst) and Azubah Leonard
Guy B., d. 7/9/1912 at 17/3/21 in Piermont; laborer; single; b.
    Piermont; Orlo B. Stanley (Piermont) and Althea Wilson
    (Groton, VT)
Hubbard Spencer, d. 3/28/1919 at 82/1/13 in Orford; farmer;
    widower; b. Piermont; Jonathan Stanley (Amherst) and Azuboh
    Leonard (Piermont)
Jonathan, d. 3/3/1892 at 80/2/19 in Piermont; old age; farmer;
    married; b. Amherst; David Stanley and Hannah Maxwell
Orlo B., d. 10/13/1948 at 80/11/2 in Piermont; town clerk; widower;
    b. Piermont; Hubbard Stanley (Piermont) and Lucy A. Hill
    (Barnstead, PQ)

STARK,
Hope, d. 10/24/1982 in Piermont

STETSON,
Bessie, d. 12/20/1982 in VT
Clinton W., d. 3/8/1975 in Hanover
Edna Robie, d. 8/27/1986 in Haverhill
Gordon D., d. 6/1/1920 at 0/2/20 in Boston, MA; b. Milton; Louis O. Stetson (Piermont) and Bessie Drury (Worcester, MA)
Henry Francis, d. 2/6/1943 at 95/7/2 in E. Andover; retired; widower; b. Orford; Daniel N. Stetson (Orford)
Jennie A., d. 2/16/1929 at 76/9/9 in Newport; retired; married; b. Warren; John Goodwin (Warren) and Hannah Sherwell
Linnie B., d. 7/5/1951 at 82 in N. Haverhill; housewife; widow; b. Piermont; Russell Gould and Edna Wilmouth
Louis O., d. 11/18/1963 at 85 in Haverhill
Patricia C., d. 4/1/1998
Wesley, d. 6/17/1985 in New Britain, CT

STEVENS,
son, d. 6/5/1906 at – in Piermont; b. Piermont; Ernest Stevens (Piermont) and Carrie Taylor
Alden, d. 9/30/1896 at 85/11 in Bradford, VT; old age; farmer; widower; b. Piermont; John Stevens and Betsy Fuller
Alden A., d. 5/20/1908 at 66/5/4 in Haverhill; painter; widower; b. Piermont; Henry Stevens (Piermont) and Sophie Rodes (Groton, VT)
Arlene E., d. 5/31/1957 at 27 in Laconia; none; single; b. Piermont; William R. Stevens and Myrtie M. Robie
Betsey A., d. 10/15/1909 at 73/2 in Boscawen; housework; single; b. Piermont; Isaac Stevens and Sally Morrill
Caroline T., d. 8/22/1960 at 83 in Piermont
Clara B., d. 9/28/1899 at 49/2/28 in Piermont; domestic; married; b. Newbury, VT; Gilman Barnett
Daisy, d. 10/4/1967 in Barre, VT
David, d. 4/25/1952 at 2 in Hanover; b. Hanover; Kenneth Stevens and Daisy Gamsby
Doris Anne, d. 6/2/1950 at 26 hrs. in Lebanon; b. Lebanon; Kenneth Stevens and Daisy Gamsby
Ernest L., d. 10/30/1958 at 83 in Piermont; farmer; married; b. Piermont; Leaveritt Stevens and Lizzie Dutton

George H., d. 11/19/1905 at 61/10 in Haverhill; exp. agt. hotel; widower; b. Piermont; George W. Stevens (Piermont) and Mariah Emerson (Piermont)

Kathleen A., d. 11/22/2000 in Lebanon

Kenneth W., d. 12/6/1974 in Burlington, VT

Lennie Reuben, d. 4/2/1944 at 76/8/22 in Piermont; farmer; married; b. E. Corinth, VT; Samuel Stevens (Corinth, VT) and Nancy Emerson

Leverett E., d. 4/4/1915 at 76/0/25 in Piermont; farmer; widower; b. Piermont; George W. Stevens (Piermont) and Maria Emerson (Piermont)

Madeline G., d. 11/24/1916 at 0/1/26 in Piermont; b. Piermont; William Stevens (VT) and Myrtie Robie (Piermont)

Mary A., d. 4/3/1894 at 49/4; heart failure; housewife; married; b. England; Richard Rolf (England) and Elizabeth Reeve (England)

Mary Noyes, d. 5/8/1997 in Lyndonville, VT

Myrtie R., d. 8/2/1945 at 52/5/12 in Piermont; housewife; married; b. Piermont; Freeman Robie (Corinth, VT) and Mamie Grimes (Orford)

Nathan P., d. 10/27/1909 at 34/8/29 in Woodsville; laborer; single; b. Piermont; George H. Stevens (Piermont) and Mary A. Rolfe (Jefferson)

Octavia M., d. 10/17/1911 at 66/2/7 in Haverhill; housework; single; b. Piermont; George W. Stevens (Piermont) and Maria Emerson (Piermont)

Phoebe A., d. 8/12/1908 at 83 in Piermont; housewife; married; b. Kennebunk, ME; Isaac Emery

Sandie P., d. 3/27/1967 in Piermont

William R., d. 4/7/1976 in Haverhill

STICKNEY,
Emma V., d. 4/26/1930 at 78 in Danvers, MA; widow

John G., d. 8/5/1925 at 76 in Hanover; farmer; married; b. Orford; Jedediah Stickney (Orford) and Nancy Randall (Canada)

STONE,
son, d. 5/29/1898 at 0/0/1 in Piermont; premature birth; b. Piermont; Thomas Stone (farmer, Waterville, Canada) and Rosa Laflam (Fitzwilliam)

Frank, d. 3/15/1909 at 69/6/6 in Piermont; farmer; married; b. Waterville, PQ
Fred, d. 2/7/1953 at 81 in Haverhill; retired; widower; b. Newbury, VT; Frank Stone
Mary, d. 9/17/1952 at 91 in Haverhill; housewife; married; b. Manchester, England; Harry Clayburn and Mary Jaiside

STRECKER,
William Fulton, d. 10/20/1957 at 43 in Orford; radio repairman; married; b. Montreal, Canada; Charles Strecker and Daisy Fulton

STREETER,
Sarah Anna, d. 7/28/1964 at 86 in Piermont

STYGLES,
Bruce Henry, d. 9/9/1997 in Haverhill

SWAIN,
Earl C., d. 2/17/1966 at 64 in Hanover
Harry W., d. 12/30/1952 at 79 in Piermont; farmer; married; b. Warren; William Swain and Sarah Caswell
Lillian, d. 9/12/1972 in Bradford, VT
Mattie L., d. 10/11/1961 at 89 in Piermont

SWAN,
Herbert R., d. 3/5/1977 in Hanover

SWETT,
Frank Wellington, d. 3/6/1935 at 80/11/27 in St. Johnsbury, VT
Lydia Kinney, d. 3/11/1939 at 91/9/13 in Orford; retired; widow; b. Plainfield, VT; A. H. Whittlesey (Plainfield, VT) and Nancy Kinney (Plainfield, VT)

SZUCH,
Alec M., d. 10/4/1995 in Haverhill
Mary E., d. 9/7/1984 in Haverhill

TAPLIN,
Anna P., d. 6/16/1930 at 88/6/17 in E. Corinth, VT; widow; b. Groton, VT

TARBOX,
Castara, d. 11/1/1934 at 67 in Miami, FL; retired; widow
Charles A., d. 4/27/1926 at 58/0/30 in Bradford, VT; farmer; married; b. Orford; Charles Tarbox (Piermont) and Mary A. Welch (Hyde Park, VT)
Charles R., d. 4/4/1909 at 77/6/22 in Piermont; none; widower; b. Piermont; Abner Tarbox (Piermont) and Harriet Runnels (Piermont)
Florence M., d. 1/27/1936 at 41/4/19 in Piermont; housewife; married; b. Piermont; John P. Metcalf (Piermont) and Carrie Grimes (Orford)
Freddie, d. 1/28/1883 at 10/11 in Orford; single; "Removed to Burial Lot No. 1, Range 5, Div., East Village Cemetery, Piermont" (1902)
Harriett R., d. 2/27/1904 at 63 in Bradford, VT; housework; single; Abner Tarbox and Harriett Runnells (Haverhill)
Isabelle C., d. 4/6/1926 at 62/9/2 in Bradford, VT; housewife; married
James, d. 12/4/1896 at 0/2/24 in Piermont; pneumonia; b. Piermont; William Tarbox and Castara M. Fuller
James H., d. 2/16/1955 at 88 in Fairfax, VT; widower; b. Piermont; Charles Tarbox and Mary Welch
Lucy A., d. 3/27/1911 at 57 in Sandown; housework; single; b. Piermont; Rodney Tarbox and Salina Cox
Mabel R., d. 4/17/1926 at 32/2/14 in Bradford, VT; domestic; single; Charles Tarbox (Orford) and Martha L. Horton (Orford)
Martha S., d. 2/8/1917 at 45/9/22 in Piermont; housewife; married; b. Orford; William H. Horton (VT) and Lydia A. Wilder (NH)
Mary A., d. 11/30/1901 at 66/1/15 in Piermont; domestic; married; b. Hyde Park, VT; ----- Welch
Rena Regers, d. 6/19/1930 at 69/9/29 in Bradford, VT; married
S. S., d. 9/16/1896 at 77 in W. Fairlee; acute dysentery; b. Vershire, VT; William Cox
William A., d. 10/25/1932 at 70/0/7 in Piermont; janitor; married; b. Piermont; Charles Tarbox (Piermont) and Mary Welch (Hyde Park, VT)
William Allen, d. 1/13/1925 at 0/4/15 in Bradford, VT; b. Bradford, VT; Charles Tarbox (Orford) and Eunice B. Glover (NY)

TAYLOR,
Amanda P., d. 6/7/1900 at 52/3/13 in Piermont; housework; married;
  b. Bethlehem; Moses Philipps (Bethlehem) and J. Philipps
  (Bethlehem)
Olin S., d. 1/18/1901 at 53/4/23 in Piermont; farmer; widower; b.
  Lisbon; John Taylor (Lisbon) and Casstine Stevens (Lisbon)

THAYER,
James M., d. 1/14/1928 at 74/11 in Haverhill; farmer; married; b.
  Franconia; Levi Thayer (Franconia) and Pricilla Spooner
  (Franconia)
Mary, d. 2/23/1928 at 77/6/5 in Haverhill; housewife; widow; b.
  Ottawa, Canada; ----- Brown (Canada)

THURSTON,
Ethan D., d. 6/15/2002 in Piermont

TIBBETS,
son, d. 8/12/1895 at – in Piermont; premature birth; b. Piermont;
  John Tibbets (Canada) and Rosa Stone (Piermont)

TOWLE,
son, d. 12/–/1895 at 0/0/2 in Piermont; b. Piermont; Ora Towle
  (Piermont)
Ella, d. 10/28/1898 at 0/8/7 in Piermont; cholera infantum; b.
  Piermont; Wilmer Towle (Piermont) and Lizzie Wilson (MA)
Ella L., d. 3/26/1896 at 45/4 in Hanover; housewife; married; Simon
  Howard
Frank B., d. 4/16/1917 at 76/3/27 in Bradford, VT; farmer; widower;
  b. Piermont; Benjamin Towle (NH) and Sarah Kenney (NH)
Mary Elizabeth W., d. 6/28/1937 at 60/9/3 in Bradford, VT;
  housewife; married; b. Somerville, MA; George M. Wilson
  (Southampton, MA) and Mary E. Furlong (Gardiner, ME)
Wilmer F., d. 11/16/1937 at 61/2/28 in Bradford, VT; retired farmer;
  widower; b. Piermont; Frank B. Towle (Piermont) and Ella L.
  Howard

TREVITHICK,
Kenneth W., d. 6/13/1992 in Piermont

TULLAR,
Kathleen, d. 8/27/1965 at 50 in Hanover
Rendell C., d. 4/4/1979 in Hanover

UNDERHILL,
Bernard Leon, d. 3/1/1936 at 39/1/22 in Arlington, MA; farmer; married; b. Orford; Leon H. Underhill (Piermont) and Jennie Norris (Corinth, VT)
Bernice L., d. 3/19/1976 in Largo, FL
Cathleen J., d. 6/14/1969 in Hanover
Edward, d. 12/22/1917 at 80/2/0 in Piermont; carpenter; widower; b. Piermont; Stephen Underhill (Piermont) and Sarah N. Stevens (Piermont)
Elizabeth, d. 10/15/1962 at 89 in Haverhill
Ernest S., d. 8/14/1943 at 72/10/16 in Piermont; retired farmer; married; b. Piermont; Horace P. Underhill (Piermont) and Lucy Palmer (Orford)
Hazel Manchester, d. 1/30/1983 in Hanover
Helen M., d. 3/1/1996 in Bradford, VT
Henry W., d. 10/4/1969 in Concord
Horace, d. 2/2/1903 at 0/26 in Piermont; b. Piermont; Ernest Underhill (Piermont) and Elizabeth Converse (Stewartstown)
Horace, d. 12/30/1917 at 81/10/27 in Piermont; farmer; widower; b. Piermont; Stephen Underhill (Piermont) and Sarah N. Stevens (Piermont)
Jennie, d. 5/31/1939 at 67/2/27 in Haverhill; housewife; married; b. Corinth, VT; John Morris (Derry) and ----- Walker
Leon, d. 12/7/1953 at 84 in Haverhill; retired; widower; b. Piermont; Horace Underhill and Lucy Palmer
Maria M., d. 2/13/1904 at 81 in Bradford, VT; housework; widow; ---- Muchmore
Rosette, d. 6/23/1952 at 72 in Piermont; housewife; married; b. Piermont; Horace Underhill and Lucy Palmer
Samuel, d. 9/21/1902 at 81/7/27 in Bradford, VT
Sarah Ann, d. 2/25/1938 at 59/5/11 in Piermont; housework; single; b. Piermont; Horace Underhill (Piermont) and Lucy Palmer (Orford)
Selina Maude, d. 12/15/1973 in Woodsville
Sophrona, d. 10/18/1899 at 82 in Haverhill
Stephen L., d. 1/15/1971 in Haverhill

VAUGHAN,
son, d. 5/21/1895 at 0/0/1 in Piermont; premature birth; b. Piermont; William H. Vaughan (S. Wales) and Mary Breason (Burke, VT)

VEGHTE,
Lewis, Jr., d. 5/5/1981 in Piermont

VIRGIN,
Caroline K., d. 1/24/1906 at 71/6/14 in Newbury, VT; nursing; widow; b. Newbury, VT; George W. Avery (CT) and Vasti Virgin (CT)

WAKEFIELD,
William H., d. 6/20/1977 in Hanover

WALKER,
Jane B., d. 4/26/1911 at 71/8/7 in Piermont; housewife; married; b. W. Barnet, VT; Walter Buchanon (Scotland) and Mary Buchanon (Scotland)

WARDROP,
John H., d. 6/28/1995 in Lebanon

WARREN,
Leon A., d. 8/13/1941 at 50/11/25 in Piermont; postmaster; married; b. Groveton; Frank Warren (Groveton) and Flora Wilkinson (Milan)
Michael, d. 11/29/1981 in Hanover

WATERS,
Annabelle, d. 9/15/1935 at 48/8/19 in Piermont; housework; single; b. Haverhill; Charles W. Waters (Lisbon) and Fannie -----
Walter, d. 2/12/1973 in Haverhill

WEAVER,
Vera M., d. 3/23/1975 in Haverhill
William R., d. 9/12/1978 in Los Gatos, CA

WEBSTER,
Belle Knapp, d. 7/3/1933 at 80/10/15 in Piermont; retired; widow; Henry Knapp (NH)
Charles, d. 5/19/1973 in Piermont

Charles S., d. 6/8/1907 at 67/6/5 in Piermont; glove cutter; married; b. Boscawen; Walter Webster (Boscawen) and Catherine Stevens (Plymouth)
Daniel W., d. 5/15/1995 in Haverhill
Dorothy M., d. 9/22/1992 in Lebanon
Earl N., d. 10/28/1933 at 65/5/19 in St. Johnsbury, VT; married; b. Piermont; Israel Webster (Manchester) and Ellen C. Libbey (Piermont)
Ellen Caroline, d. 8/30/1927 at 79/9/21 in Bradford, VT; retired; widow; b. Bradford, VT; John A. Libby (Warren) and Angeline Prescott (Deerfield)
Freeman Henry, d. 5/6/1945 at 69/11/8 in Haverhill; farmer; married; b. Haverhill; Charles Webster (Boscawen) and Belle Knapp (Piermont)
George L., d. 1/14/1967 in Piermont
Gladys E., d. 5/26/1983 in Haverhill
Hattie M., d. 7/20/1976 in Haverhill
Henry L., d. 6/17/1916 at 0/0/0 in Piermont; b. Piermont; George L. Webster (Monroe) and Gladys E. Risley (Piermont)
Henry M., d. 7/30/1967 in Haverhill
Israel B., d. 4/6/1909 at 71/6/9 in Lisbon; farmer; married; b. Manchester; Joshua Webster and Betsey Underhill
Lena May, d. 10/4/1943 at 68/10/17 in St. Johnsbury, VT; retired; widow
Lizzie H., d. 12/21/1965 at 75 in Haverhill
Mabel M., d. 2/12/1956 at 78 in Haverhill; housekeeper; widow; b. Orford, d/o Zerah Mann and Jane Hicks
Madeline B., d. 9/18/1914 at 0/1/20 in Piermont; pneumonia; b. Piermont; Freman H. Webster (Haverhill) and Mabel Mann (Orford)
Nelson K., d. 8/17/1980 in Miami, FL
Ralph A., d. 1/10/1923 at 39/9/22 in Piermont; lumber dealer; married; b. Piermont; Charles Webster (Boscawen) and Belle Knapp (Haverhill)
Ralph A., d. 11/5/1991 in Piermont
Walter, d. 7/17/1902 at 87/10 in Piermont; farmer; widower; b. Hill; Ebenezer Webster and ----- Wells (Hill)
Walter C., d. 2/6/1956 at 70 in Piermont; retired; married; b. Piermont; Charles Webster and Belle Knapp

WEEKS,
George, d. 10/23/1963 at 83 in Suffern, NY
George W., d. 1/16/2001 in Lecanto, FL
Gladys P., d. 8/6/1970 in Haverhill
Ruth E., d. 3/14/1971 in Ramapo, NY
Vena B., d. 9/16/1985 in Inverness, FL

WESCOTT,
Walter F., d. 10/12/1983 in Hanover

WEST,
George O., d. 1/21/1891 at 27/8 in Piermont; laborer; single; b. W. Fairlee, VT; Oliver West (W. Fairlee, VT) and Maud E. Badger (W. Fairlee, VT)

WESTFALL,
Marion Musty, d. 4/9/1987 in Hanover

WESTGATE,
Elzi W., d. 10/7/1897 at 76/7/23 in Piermont; cancer on face; farmer; widower; b. Cornish, VT; Joseph Westgate and Abigail Lewis
Kate S., d. 9/22/1881 at 16/11/14 in Orford; single; "Removed to Burial Lot No. 1, Range 5, Div., East Village Cemetery, Piermont" (1902)
Kendall, d. 10/8/1923 at 68/1/25 in Piermont; farmer; single; b. Cornish; Elzi W. Westgate (Corinish) and Lydia Pease (Ellsworth)

WHITE,
Charles Henry, d. 2/10/1923 at 80/4/24 in Piermont; retired; widower; b. Lyndon, VT; Charles White and ----- Fisher (VT)
J. O., d. 8/7/1923 at 21 in Piermont; laborer; single; black; b. Royal, NC; Charles White (Royal, NC)
James, d. 3/12/1946 at 79/10/29 in Haverhill; retired; married; b. Canada; Stephen White (NS) and Martha Bainski (NS)
Martha C., d. 3/8/1923 at 92/3/25 in Piermont; retired; widow; b. Brewster, MA; Joseph Crocher
Roxana J., d. 12/4/1911 at 88/2/13 in Manchester; widow; b. Lebanon; Leonard Woodbury (Woodstock, CT) and Betsey Barton (Roylston, MA)
Timothy S., d. 12/30/1978 in Hanover

WHITLOCK,
Betty, d. 7/4/1985 in Tulsa, OK

WHITTAKER,
Ruth, d. 2/23/1896 at 89/1/11 in Piermont; fall; widow; b. Lyme; John Kendrick and Kesia Preble

WHITTIER,
Georgina, d. 9/3/1962 at 82 in Somerville, MA
Walter Leslie, d. 8/1/1948 at 56/2/25; b. Everett, MA

WILKINS,
Donald, d. 2/12/1978 in Hanover
Timothy Matthew, d. 10/1/1996 in Lebanon

WILLEY,
Horace L., d. 5/8/1926 at 78/4/2 in Piermont; retired; widower; b. Topsham, VT; Horace Willey (Sheffield, VT) and Susan Frencg (Newbury, VT)

WILLIAMS,
Abigail A., d. 9/13/1911 at 82/2/16 in Swampscott, MA; housework; married; b. Piermont; Milton Curtis (Norwich, VT) and Sarah Curtis (Tunbridge, VT)
Warren J., Jr., d. 5/29/1989 in Piermont

WILSON,
Beatrice, d. 10/8/1981 in Hanover
Caroline, d. 8/3/1920 at 69/11/28 in Piermont; retired; widow; b. Groton, VT; Robert Heath (Groton, VT) and Lydia Brown (Bradford, VT)
Charles Edwin, d. 10/25/2001 in Woodsville
Charlotte, d. 2/19/2004 in Haverhill
Ellen C., d. 6/12/1914 at 4/7/4 in Piermont; acute pulmonary tuberculosis; b. Corinth, VT; Hazen A. Wilson (Groton, VT) and Nellie Fairbrother (England)
Etta M., d. 8/5/1961 at 88 in Piermont
George H., d. 7/20/1980 in Plymouth
George M. J., d. 1/13/1929 at 77/11/27 in Bradford, VT; bookkeeper; widower; b. Southampton, MA; Thomas B. Wilson (Newburyport, MA) and Sarah Page (Solon, ME)

George Munroe, d. 6/14/1937 at 57/1/19 in Bradford, VT; meat cutter; married; b. Somerville, MA; George M. J. Wilson (Southampton, MA) and Mary E. Furlong (Gardiner, ME)
George Ronald, d. 4/12/1999 in Exeter
Hazen A., d. 4/9/1923 at 39/11/13 in Piermont; laborer; married; b. Groton, VT; Isaac M. Wilson (Groton, VT) and Caroline E. Heath (Groton, VT)
Henry I., d. 9/30/1978 in Hanover
James L., d. 3/3/1988 in Hanover
John W., d. 1/27/1918 at 75/7/8 in Piermont; farmer; married; b. Canada, PQ; James Wilson (NS) and Sophia Griffin (PQ)
Mary E., d. 9/19/1921 at 70/10/23 in St. Johnsbury, VT; housewife; married
Melvin E., d. 7/10/1912 at 45/4/5 in Newbury, VT; farmer; married; b. Grindstone City, MI; John Wilson (Vienna, ON) and Agnes J. Wilson (Whitley, PQ)
Phyllis Keith, d. 2/17/1998 in Westmoreland
Thomas A., d. 10/20/1904 at 21/7/25 in Piermont; laborer; single; b. Somerville, MA; George M. J. Wilson (S. Hampton) and Mary E. Furlong (Gardner, MA)

WING,
Dorothy Elizabeth, d. 11/8/1942 at 68/0/8 in Hartford, CT; housewife; married; b. Piermont; Joseph Hill (Canada) and Polly Towle (Piermont)
Esther, d. 3/10/1957 at 73 in Hanover; retired sch. teacher; married; b. Woodstock, CT; Abiel Fox and Mary Chandler
Harry, d. 3/8/1964 at 87 in Haverhill

WINN,
Don F., d. 11/26/1953 at 64 in Lisbon; married; b. Barre, VT; Daniel Winn and Hattie Minard
Ellen May, d. 9/22/1995 in Haverhill
Frank H., d. 3/9/2001 in Manchester
Frank P., d. 11/13/1925 at 74/7/7 in Piermont; farmer; married; b. Piermont; John Winn (NH) and Phebe Van Dausin (NJ)
Hannah E., d. 3/10/1938 at 84/8/23 in Orford; ret. housewife; widow; b. Wentworth; Samuel Sargent and Mary Davis
Hiram P., d. 9/24/1932 at 56/0/24 in Piermont; farmer; married; b. Piermont; Franklin P. Winn (Piermont) and Nellie Putnam (Haverhill)

Laura Belle, d. 8/2/1969 in Hanover
Lona A., d. 3/3/1979 in Morrisville, VT
Nellie M., d. 5/19/1922 at 68/6/17 in Piermont; housewife; married; b. Haverhill; A. W. Putnam (Derry) and Hannah Cole (Plainfield)
Parker, d. 11/27/1971 in Haverhill
Robert, d. 10/25/1999 in Newbury, VT
William, d. 4/30/1967 in Hanover

WISWELL,
Mary A., d. 3/23/1895 at 3-/3/1 in Piermont; heart failure in child bed; housewife; married; b. Brunswick, VT; George Burbeck and Cylina Wright

WORKMAN,
Florence S., d. 11/30/1965 at 88 in Lyndonville, VT
Samuel M., d. 3/20/1955 at 76 in Orford; retired; married; b. Canaan, VT; Timothy Workman and Adelaide Thomas

WORTHEN,
Alvah, d. 6/29/1894 at 60/10/29; consumption; farmer; married; b. Orford; Ephraim Worthen
Frank F., d. 5/4/1912 at 56/10/21 in Piermont; farmer; married; b. St. Johnsbury; John A. Worthen (Bradford, VT) and Lucy Crafts (Walden, VT)
John A., d. 11/3/1905 at 73/9/13 in Piermont; farmer; widower; b. Bradford, VT; John A. Worthen (Bradford, VT) and Mary A. Runnels (Piermont)
Lucy A., d. 12/3/1902 at 66/3/7 in Piermont; domestic; married; b. Walden, VT; Samuel J. Craft (Westford, MA) and Rebecca Stearns (Deering)

WORTHLEY,
child, d. 1/2/1911 at – in Piermont; b. Piermont; George W. Worthley (Corinth, VT) and Lydia E. Brainard (Putney, VT)

WRIGHT,
Carlos M., d. 6/9/1935 at 76/11/26 in Piermont; retired; widower; b. Newbury, VT; Walter Wright (Hebron) and Elvira Avery (Topsham, VT)
Elwood, d. 4/7/1950 at 69 in Lisbon; farmer; married; James Wright and Susan Kentfield

Florence M., d. 6/20/1980 in Haverhill
Floyd E., d. 3/25/1921 at 0/0/1 in Piermont; b. Piermont; Frank R. Wright (Newport, VT) and Lila M. Wilson (Charleston, VT)
Irwin B., d. 12/28/1908 at 62/2/28 in Wentworth; farmer; married; b. Lowell, MA; Joel Wright (Westford, MA) and Martha B. Wright (Paris, ME)

YOUNG,
D. Albert, d. 10/–/2001 in Burlington, VT
Herbert, d. 9/6/1955 at 62 in Piermont; librarian; widower; b. Canada; John Young and Etta Martin

ZEAMAN,
George R., d. 2/21/1992 in Lebanon

www.ingramcontent.com/pod-product-compliance
Lightning Source LLC
Chambersburg PA
CBHW070003010526
44117CB00011B/1415